Professionals' Perspectives of Corporate Social Responsibility

Samuel O. Idowu · Walter Leal Filho
Editors

Professionals' Perspectives of Corporate Social Responsibility

 Springer

Editors
Samuel O. Idowu
London Metropolitan University
London Metropolitan Business School
84 Moorgate
London
United Kingdom EC2M 6SQ
s.idowu@londonmet.ac.uk

Prof. Walter Leal Filho
Hochschule für Angewandte
Wissenschaften Hamburg
Forschungs- und
Transferzentrum
Lohbruegger Kirchstr. 65
21033 Hamburg
Germany
walter.leal@haw-hamburg.de

ISBN 978-3-642-02629-4   e-ISBN 978-3-642-02630-0
DOI 10.1007/978-3-642-02630-0
Springer Heidelberg Dordrecht London New York

Library of Congress Control Number: 2009934599

Cover design: WMXDesign GmbH

Printed on acid-free paper

Springer is part of Springer Science+Business Media (www.springer.com)

This book is dedicated to all professionals who are genuinely striving to be socially responsible wherever they are on planet Earth.

Foreword

Corporate Social Responsibility (CSR) is a matter of great concern and relevance in today's world. Especially now, when the world is experiencing a difficult economic crisis which is unprecedented since the 1930s, the vision of promoting business accountability to the various stakeholders engaged in a given sector has never been more important.

But CSR is not only about satisfying stakeholders. In order to succeed, it needs to holistically take into account aspects relating to environmental protection, sustainability and good governance in ways not seen before. At Hamburg University of Applied Sciences, we are aware of the relevance of and the need for CSR approaches to be inculcated into all our activities. In our faculties (Sciences, Engineering and Computer Science, Design, Media and Information, Business and Social Sciences), we see CSR as a multi-disciplinary issue. With the creation of our new Competence Centre on Renewable Energy and Energy Efficiency (CC4E), a considerable emphasis is given to both the technological as well as the social aspects of energy efficiency and the use of renewable energy.

This book 'Professionals' Perspectives of Corporate Social Responsibility', edited by one of my colleagues, Prof. Walter Leal Filho (who directs the Research and Transfer Centre 'Applications of Life Sciences' in our Faculty of Life Sciences) and Samuel O Idowu, from London Metropolitan University Business School is a timely publication. It is timely in the sense that it conceptualizes CSR from various professions, sectors and countries, hence demonstrating that, even in times of economic hardship more and more businesses are embracing the principles and ethos of CSR. Much can be gained by recognising the contribution that a diversity of perspectives is able to provide towards the generation of new ideas and innovative approaches to performing business activities in a transparent and ethical way. Many of the excellent papers in this book document examples of good practice with some recommendations of practical character which researchers, practitioners and other stakeholders would find most appropriate in their professional callings. Some of the papers also highlight future research directions, showing some potential research needs that would have to be addressed in the future.

I hope that this book will influence both today's and tomorrow's professionals in following CSR strategies which would enable companies, universities, international organizations, NGOs and others across the world to make our society a more socially responsible place for us all to conduct our day to day activities.

Hamburg, Germany   Michael Stawicki

Preface

Corporate social responsibility (CSR) is a field that impacts on all aspects of human existence. Professions and professionals in both advanced and emerging economies have a lot to consider in the quest to ensure that their activities do not adversely affect society or if they do; how they can best reduce the adverse impact should be of paramount importance to them in our world today. It was realized that there is a pronounced absence in the market of a book that explores how various professions and those that represent these professions in organizations have absorbed CSR's requirements in what they do.

Being socially responsible on the part of corporate entities; some scholars and practitioners have argued is one of the sine qua non of success in modern markets. If this is so, then it is in the best interest of these entities to source out what actions they need to take in order to act responsibly. Responsibility is demonstrated by actions and deeds; not by words or information inserted in some glossy magazines or corporate websites.

It is believed that a book on how different professions and those practicing these professions have interpreted the field of CSR would not only provide some useful insights into how the requirements of CSR are being met by corporate entities but it would also provide a framework for a better understanding of how the field is shaping out as it continues to evolve since its general acceptance worldwide. The world today is radically different from what it used to be several decades ago or even some 12 months ago. As the effect of the unprecedented current global financial crisis continues to affect everyone, it becomes even more important that corporate entities demonstrate the highest order of responsibility in their dealings. Corporate entities function through individuals which therefore makes it imperative for these individuals to fully understand what is expected of them in order to be socially responsible.

This book has been fortunate in its ability to have attracted interests from scholars of both traditional and modern professions. It is therefore hoped that the information it contains will be useful to our readers from any sector of society for example education, industry and commerce, practitioners, international organizations, governments, non-governmental organizations and those who are concerned about the adverse impacts of corporate activities on mankind, the environment and also the future of our planet.

London, UK   Samuel O Idowu
Hamburg, Germany   Walter Leal Filho
Summer 2009

Acknowledgements

Publishing an edited book by several contributors is a team effort of several committed individuals; this book is no exception to that general belief and understanding. Our first 'thank you' therefore goes to all our fantastic contributors who are spread around the world; without whose commendable efforts; there would have been no edited book to publish on how 20 or so professionals have seen their roles in propagating and inculcating the ideas of CSR into their day to day operations! The two Editors appreciate these individuals' hard work and would remain indebted to them all for a very long time if not for ever for making the publication of this book a reality.

There are also some individuals we both want to thank either individually or together.

Samuel O Idowu would like to thank the following friends and colleagues who have assisted him either directly or indirectly to ensure the publication of this second book in the series, Danny O'Brien, Brendan O'Dwyer, Denis Haffner, Andrea J Dunhill, Carol Tilt, Royston Gustavson, Richard Vardy, Timothy J Cleary, Caroline J Evans, Charlotte Housden, Pat Wood, Michael Soda and Samson Nejo. His thanks are due to his brother and sister; Michael A Idowu and Elizabeth A A Lawal, the same are also due to members of his direct clan who have been his confidants and 'impregnable rock of Gibraltar' during the entire process of this volume and who have once again shared with him both the pleasures and travails of the whole exercise: Olufunmilola O Idowu, Rachael T Idowu, Mary T Idowu, Abigail O Idowu and Olaniyi J Idowu. You are all dearly loved and appreciated.

Samuel O Idowu is indebted to some senior and middle level managers at London Metropolitan University for their kind support and encouragements in his publishing venture, the Vice Chancellor, Brian Roper, the Dean of London Metropolitan Business School; Bob Morgan, Tony Curson – LMBS's Associate Deputy Director – Research, Noreen Dawes, Subject Group Leader Accounting and Business Law, John Sedgwick, Photis Lysandrou and all those colleagues who attended the launch of the *Global Practices of CSR*, especially colleagues from the African Business Forum – in particular Jonathan Emanuwa and Adebisi Adewole.

Walter Leal Filho wants to thank Prof. Michael Stawicki, Rector of the Hamburg Universities of Applied Sciences (HAW Hamburg), the Dean of Life Sciences,

Prof. Claus-Dieter Wacker and his team at the Research and Transfer 'Applications of Life Sciences' at HAW Hamburg, for the support provided.

Both Samuel O Idowu and Walter Leal Filho want to thank the following individuals: Tarja Ketola, Paul Phillips, Thomas Coskeran, Sergei Zenchenko and their former Publishing Editor; Dr Niels P Thomas, his PA Barbara Karg and their new Publishing Editor Christian Rauscher.

Contents

Contributors

Marin Amina Industrial Engineering Department, University of Sonora, Sonora, Mexico

Zavala Andrea Industrial Engineering Department, University of Sonora, Sonora, Mexico

Konstantinos G. Aravosis Section of Industrial Management and Operational Research, Faculty of Mechanical Engineering, National Technical University of Athens, Zografos, Athens, Greece

Jean Bowcott Novotel and Mercure Hotels, Central and Greater London Accor Hospitality, London, UK

Timothy T. Campbell Hull Business School, Hull, UK

José-Rodrigo Córdoba Royal Holloway, University of London, London, UK

Sallyanne Decker London Metropolitan University Business School, London, UK

Konstantinos I. Evangelinos Department of Environment, University of the Aegean, Mytilene, Greece

Walter Leal Filho Hamburg University of Applied Sciences, Hamburg, Germany

Ananda Das Gupta Indian Institute of Plantation Management, Bangalore, India

Royston Gustavson The Australian National University, Canberra, Australia

Ralph Hamann University of Cape Town, Cape Town, South Africa

Elizabeth Hogan David Gardiner & Associates, LLC, Washington, DC, USA

Samuel O. Idowu London Metropolitan University Business School, London, UK

Esquer Javier Industrial Engineering Department, University of Sonora, Sonora, Mexico

Zerrin Toprak Karaman University of Dokuz Eylül, Izmir, Turkey

Berna Kirkulak Dokuz Eylul University, Izmir, Turkey

Adam Lindgreen University of Hull Business School, Hull, UK

Céline Louche Vlerick Leuven Gent Management School, Gent, Belgium

Diana Luck London Metropolitan University, London, UK

Velázquez Luis Industrial Engineering Department, University of Sonora, Sonora, Mexico

François Maon Université Catholique de Louvain, Louvain-la-Neuve, Belgium

Ioannis E. Nikolaou Department of Environmental Engineering, Democritus University of Thrace, Xanthi, Greece

Munguía Nora Industrial Engineering Department, University of Sonora, Sonora, Mexico

Olatoye Ojo Obafemi Awolowo University, Ile Ife, Nigeria

Nikolaos A. Panayiotou Section of Industrial Management and Operational Research, Facu, Athens, Greece

Patricia Park Southampton Solent University, Southampton, UK

Liisa Rohweder Haaga-Helia University of Applied Science, Helsinki, Finland

Dyann Ross Edith Cowan University, Perth, Australia

Christopher Sale London Metropolitan University Business School, London, UK

Konstantinos Saridakis National Technical University of Athens, Zografos, Athens, Greece

Antonis Skouloudis Department of Environment, University of the Aegean, Mytilene, Greece

Valérie Swaen Université Catholique de Louvain and IESEG School of Management, Louvain-la-Neuve, Belgium

Carol A. Tilt Flinders Business School, Flinders University, Adelaide, Australia

Anne Virtanen Hamwk University of Applied Sciences, Helsinki, Finland

Karolina Windell University of Uppsala, Uppsala, Sweden

Professionals' Perspectives of CSR: An Introduction

Samuel O. Idowu

We live in an era where corporate entities and those at the helm of managing their affairs – managers are not judged only by their financial performance anymore but also by their positive actions towards their stakeholders and the natural environment; in other words, how socially responsible they are. Reckless and irresponsible actions on the part of corporate leaders are no longer tolerated by citizens. Sadly, there is still a very small minority of people who are either indifference to the adverse impacts of some corporate actions on humanity and the environment or are totally oblivious to the impending catastrophe which these actions or inactions might bring on the natural environment if we fail to change our behaviours or take corrective actions to reduce the adverse impact.

Societies around the world are gradually coming to terms with the understanding that we all have to behave responsibly and change our behaviours in dealing with certain issues which affect mankind regardless of whether we live in an advanced or the less advanced part of the world. Some of the consequences of past corporate actions are gradually unfolding and being felt either with similar or the same level of intensity by us all in terms of climate change or global warming, food crisis; (even in the first world which was thought unthinkable a few years back; talk less of the third world, this is now almost a reality in both parts of the world!), even though the reverse should actually be case (because of the advancements in modern technology in the science of agriculture), drinkable water is also posing some problems, some of man's natural resources endowed by nature are gradually becoming extinct. Scientists are suggesting that things would have to change not just for the sake of the present generation but most importantly for the sake of future generations. Man's natural resources are exhaustible; therefore we can no longer afford; any more to use these resources irresponsibly or behave recklessly with them either as individuals or corporate entities.

S.O. Idowu (✉)
London Metropolitan University Business, London, UK

S.O. Idowu, W.L. Filho (eds.), *Professionals' Perspectives of Corporate Social Responsibility*, DOI 10.1007/978-3-642-02630-0_1,
© Springer-Verlag Berlin Heidelberg 2009

Over the last few years, corporate entities around the world have identified the value creation ability of CSR and have started to weave the so called triple bottom line idea - economic, social and environmental (ESE) considerations in to their strategy. Of course, what constitute CSR actions we argue in the *Global Practices of CSR* (the first book in a series of books on CSR, Sustainability (S), Sustainable Development (SD) and Corporate Governance (CG) depend on a series of factors and circumstances. Interestingly, several scholars and authors have identified – different issues that fall within the domain of CSR for instance, Kotler and Lee (2005) have categorized the following initiatives as issues falling within CSR activities:

- Issues that contribute to community health
- Issues that encourage safety
- Issues that enhance education
- Issues that improve employability
- Issues that enhance the quality of life in the natural environment
- Issues that enhance community and economic developments
- Issues that facilitate the provision of basic human needs and desires

These aforementioned issues fall either under internal or external CSR, needless to say internal CSR, relates to actions taken by an entity to address CSR related issues of its internal stakeholders whilst external CSR are issues relating to an entity's external stakeholders. Corporate entities of today have realized that both classes of stakeholders have enormous power to affect their success or failure in both the marketplace and community; they therefore no longer take issues which affect these stakeholders lightly.

The current economic turmoil and financial meltdown around the world in the form of credit crunch and high commodity prices which has led to several painful strategic decisions being taken on the part different corporate entities have affected every aspect of our lives. We were made to understand through the media that nothing of this scale had been seen worldwide since the 1930s. It is hoped that corporate entities would not take the current climate as an excuse to either cut back or abandon their CSR projects. It is a general belief that during a period of hardship in an individual's life, decisions are made about those things they could survive without; insurances are cancelled or allowed to lapse and not renewed, cutbacks are made in leisure activities and so on. The individual just exists to survive. Corporate entities are not individuals! This is in fact a period when CSR should be seen as a vehicle for social opportunities which provide the impetus for innovation and placing an entity at a competitive advantaged position over its rivals in its line of business or industry by its actions on CSR related issues.

The argument that society and business are interwoven has been used on countless occasions by scholars and advocates of CSR. Business cannot operate without society and conversely society will find it difficult, if not totally impossible to function effectively without business. That the two are interdependent may appear too simplistic an argument, but that is the truth. It therefore follows that what is needed in order for the two to co-exist in harmony is really not confrontation or any form of coercing by NGOs or some activist groups; but an atmosphere that creates the opportunity for a deep understanding between the two. Of course some may argue that the laws of economics may make what is being suggested here difficult. They may argue further that the more business provides in order to satisfy society's social, economic and environmental (SEE) concerns, the more society will demand from business, they are probably right but this editor does not concur with this weak argument. Society owns corporate entities, whether or not they want to accept it, albeit, this ownership may not be direct in the same sense as stakeholders such as shareholders, employees or creditors. It is therefore in society's best interest for business to continue to thrive and prosper; it is through this that prosperity pervades the community. The general acceptance of CSR globally has taken the debate on the interrelationship between the two beyond the level of whether or not society has a say in what is going on inside the walls of a corporate entity in terms of how the entity deals with or interacts with its surrounding community. If one agrees with this argument, then the argument that the more is provided by business the more is demanded no longer holds. The mutual understanding between the two has gone beyond this level.

This book, the *Professionals' Perspectives of Corporate Social Responsibility* provides an insight into how professionals are attempting to absorb the ethos of corporate social responsibility into their daily professional activities. Society now demands that we should all behave responsibly by demonstrating that those issues that are at the core of CSR are as equally important to us in the same way as those traditional issues that professionals are trained to practice in the community. The book has been fortunate in the sense that its contributors, who are professionals in different fields around the world, have each provided an account of how CSR has either changed or redirected thoughts in their professions.

The book has been divided into five parts, each part focusing on professions which we have been grouped together for convenience. Part I – Business and Management – encompasses seven professions in eight chapters, Part II – Engineering – looks at Industrial Engineering in two chapters, Part III – Investment and the Built Environment – considers CSR from the perspectives of Socially Responsible Investment and the Built Environment in three chapters, Part IV – Not-for-Profit Organisations and Leisure – focuses on NGOs, Social Work, Local Authority and the Hotel & Leisure industry in four chapters and Part V – Education, Research and Human Resource Management – completes the book with four chapters from Academia, Consultancy and Human Resource Management dimensions of CSR.

In the first chapter entitled '*Corporate Responsibility, Accounting and Accountants*' Carol A. Tilt argues that traditionally, financial accountability had been the main focus of accountants but for a number of years Accounting academics have been at the forefront of research activities in Social & Environmental Accounting. More recently, accounting practitioners and their professional bodies around the world have also taken a significant interest in the area. The chapter argues that accountants' interest in CSR is wide ranging; inculcating issues such as improving social justice, providing assistance to corporate entities on aspects which help them to address and report on how they have reduced the adverse impact of their activities in their local communities.

In Chap. 2 on *Perspectives of Lawyers in Practice on CSR*, Patricia Park argues that even though CSR is developed within a legal framework but providing advice to corporate entities is dominated by non-lawyers. The chapter focuses on issues relating to international legal imperatives of CSR from its human rights dimension especially as it affects employment and environmental obligations. The chapter also explores the UK's new Companies Act 2006 and its provisions on Directors duties with regard to CSR. The chapter discusses some legal risks in relation to CSR Reports and why lawyers must be actively involved in preparing these reports. It analyses a CSR survey carried out by some international law firms and the findings from the survey.

In Chap. 3 by Samuel O. Idowu entitled *Corporate Social Responsibility from the Perspective of Corporate Secretaries*, notes that members of some chartered professional bodies in the UK who are statutorily eligible to hold office as corporate secretaries have had to absorb all the challenges and opportunities that the field of CSR has thrown at them, albeit in collaboration with their other senior colleagues in organisations. The chapter also argues that modern stakeholders look on corporate entities to meet all their economic, social, ethical, legal and philanthropic responsibilities whilst remaining virtuous, even though meeting these responsibilities may at first sight appear contradictory and impossible. The chapter notes that business and society are interwoven rather than distinct entities. It provides the findings from a UK study carried out in order to identify how corporate secretaries are embedding the ethos of CSR in what they do.

François Maon, Valérie Swaen and Adam Lindgreen in Chap. 4 on *Mainstreaming Corporate Social Responsibility: A Triadic Challenge from a General Management Perspective*, conducted a study of some 75 companies in an attempt to decipher how CSR programmes are designed, implemented and monitored. The chapter identifies three interconnected challenges required to be embedded by senior managers in their organizational processes. These contributors note that mainstreaming CSR as an objective by an entity can be achieved through the development of understanding, on-going dialogue and engagement between the entity and its stakeholders.

In Chap. 5 by Royston Gustavson entitled *The Company Director's Perspective on CSR* argues that the role of a company director as a member of the board is to create value for their organization through performance and conformance. These necessitate him/her working in collaboration with other directors to set mission, values and the strategic direction of the organization in a socially responsible manner and set internal policy and procedures whilst reporting to the company's stakeholders in a transparent way. The author also argues that because directors have access to a wide range of information and resources on CSR, they are able to use this information in a positive way.

Timothy T. Campbell and José-Rodrigo Córdoba in Chap. 6 entitled *The Need to Reconsider Societal Marketing* argue that despite the commendable contributions Marketing and Marketers have made in raising the standards of living around the globe, Marketers are often criticized for being too driven by a philosophy which advocates satisfying customer needs solely for profit. The chapter argues that Marketing has a far greater awareness and sensitivity to social and environmental issues. It notes that Societal Marketing Concept (SMC) – (a concept which extends Marketing beyond the traditional boundaries of company profits and consumer wants) has been used in the marketplace for well over 40 years. These contributors explore how SMC could further extend Marketers contributions to the field of CSR.

In Chap. 7 entitled *An analysis of CSR, Trust and Reputation in the Banking Profession* Sally-Anne Decker and Christopher Sale argue that professionals in the financial services industry are important contributors in determining the financial fortunes, stability and sustainability of modern economies. The chapter using a variety of sociological perspectives suggests that trust, reputational and regulatory risks are of particular concerns in Bankers efforts to embed the ethos of CSR into their activities. The chapter argues that albeit Bankers are perceived to have made some advancement in embedding some of the principles of CSR in their professional callings, but there is still room for the profession to improve on its current standing in the CSR 'league table' in society.

Walter Leal Filho et al. in Chap. 8 examine how the Banking sector in Greece has amalgamated environmental and social concerns into the decision making process. The chapter also analyses the various reporting strategies employed by Banks in Greece whilst simultaneously assessing the sector's sustainability reporting using the Global Reporting Initiative (GRI) scoring systems and Deloitte Touché Tohmatsu reporting scorecard.

In the 9th chapter of the book, entitled *Industrial Engineering's Perspective of CSR*, Luis Velázquez et al. argue that albeit industrial engineering seeks to improve society's quality of life but the production processes and activities required to meet this objective often result in unanticipated adverse impacts on human's health and ecological degradation. The chapter puts forward a case for a new order in the curriculum required for training future engineers; including industrial engineers. This should enable these engineers to be interdisciplinary in their focus and in dealing with issues that alleviate the adverse impact of their profession on the environment.

In Chap. 10; a second chapter on industrial engineering entitled *An Exploratory Study of the CSR Practices in the Greek Manufacturing Sector*, Panayiotou et al. describe the level of CSR practices in the Greek manufacturing sector. The chapter argues that there is a pronounced absence in literature on studies which analyse the level of CSR practices in the Greek manufacturing sector. In order to address this anomaly, the chapter uses an empirical study to identify CSR practices in the most active companies in the Greek industrial sector using an eight category framework based around three issues – economy, environment and society.

In Chap. 11 by Céline Louche entitled *Corporate Social Responsibility: The Investor's Perspective* on Socially Responsible Investment argues that both individual and institutional investors are realizing that firms which adopt a proactive approach in managing their social and environmental risks stand to derive immeasurable benefits in terms of financial and sustainable value creation. The chapter provides information of SRI from three dimensions namely; a general background to SRI, current practices on SRI and issues that are likely to shape the future of the industry.

The twelfth chapter by Olatoye Ojo entitled *Corporate Social Responsibility: The Estate Surveyors and Valuers' Perspective* notes that in the Estate Surveying and Valuation sector, ethics, the environment, sustainable development, infrastructure, capacity building and manpower development and good governance are the CSR issues that are presently of concern. The chapter also argues that strategic and altruistic CSR are glaringly noticeable in the sector. It suggests that educators in the sector need to review the curriculum of real estate education in order to adequately prepare new entrants into the profession to cope with the challenges which the field of CSR would throw at them.

Berna Kirkulak in Chap. 13 entitled *Corporate Social Responsibility and Ethics in Real Estate: Evidence from Turkey* argues that the current global economic crisis could perhaps be traced back to unethical appraisal practices (worldwide) and a limited base of real estate industry skills in Turkey; the author's country of focus.

The chapter argues that the economy of any country which relies too heavily on its Banking sector exposes itself to too much systematic vulnerability which was the case in Turkey and was probably the reason why Turkey's economic meltdown started in 2001 well before the current global meltdown. The chapter discusses the roles of real estate agents and appraisers in Turkey highlighting the serious consequences of fraudulent practices in real estate appraisal in the country.

In Chap. 14, Elizabeth Hogan takes on the issue of CSR in the Non-Governmental Organisations (NGOs) sector with a chapter she titles *Does 'Corporate' Responsibility Apply to Not-for-Profit Organizations?* The chapter explores differences in approach to CSR by multinational corporations (MNCs) and non-governmental organisations (NGOs). It notes that despite some similarities in the resources available to large NGOs and MNCs, the expectations of these NGOs are not well defined. The chapter focusing mainly on three large international NGOs examines the incentives behind their CSR initiatives and considers whether their goals are best met by current practices. The author argues that by integrating socially responsible initiatives into their day to day operations these NGOs greatly enhance the chances of successfully attaining the objectives of their core activities.

Diana Luck and Jean Bowcott in Chap. 15 on *A Hotelier's Perspective of CSR* argue that hoteliers' like their counterparts in other industries have embraced the concept of CSR in their activities. The extent to which the concept have been embraced and engaged with by companies in the industry has varied. The chapter discusses how a key employee of a particular hotel chain sees it absorbs the concept of CSR into its activities both in the UK and internationally. The chapter does not profess to represent CSR practices in the hotel industry but merely an individual's view of how one company has inculcated CSR into its activities.

In Chap. 16 on *Emphasizing the 'Social' in Corporate Social Responsibility: A Social Perspective*, Dyann Ross argues that social work is a profession that seeks social justice and human rights protection for all. Focusing on the lessons derived from a study funded by a multinational mining company in Western Australia to resolve the conflict between the company and its impacted neighbouring community, the chapter notes that through dialogue, mutual respect and respect for social justice; CSR has all the ingredients needed to effect fairness. The field of CSR the chapter argues can facilitate the finding of common ground and ways through dialoguing in order to create the right atmosphere for business and society to coexist in harmony with little or no conflict.

In Chap. 17 entitled *Democratic Gains in Public Administration at Local Level in Terms of CSR: Theory and Practice Based Approaches at Izmir Metropolitan Council, Turkey* Zeriin Toprak Karaman takes on the issue of corporate social responsibility in a local government as seen by Izmir Metropolitan Council in Turkey. Zerrin argues that in an urban structuring, the existence of a diverse cultural group is paramount in ensuring the pervasiveness of social peace thus enabling the democrats in the municipal council to meet part of their CSR requirements. The chapter also notes that; to develop and sustain the ability of a given society to make decisions and collectively implement related CSR strategies; with the help of ongoing learning tools in order to facilitate the development of democratic gains; which are important ingredients that could lead to an ideal social form, several pertinent CSR related questions must be answered.

In the 18th chapter entitled *An Academic's Perspective of the Role of Academics in Corporate Responsibility* Ralph Hamann argues from two standpoints he describes as disconcertingly questionable: that business can contribute positively to sustainable development and that those in academia are in privileged position to assist towards attaining this end regardless of where they are in the world. Having said this, the chapter goes on to argue that there are significant constraints to realizing the academic ideal of open and informed debate about the issue. These constraints the chapter notes stem from the social and cultural context under which academics work and in respect of the limited resources often at the disposal of academics who work in the industry.

Karolina Windell in Chap. 19 entitled *The Proliferation of CSR from two Professional Perspectives: Academic Researchers and Consultants* which aims to contribute a theoretical discussion on the role of those who believe that corporate entities need to change their behaviours towards their stakeholders and the natural environment. The chapter basically explores how academic researchers contribute to the popularization of CSR and how they have used the field to create opportunities for themselves and others.

In the penultimate chapter on *An analysis of the Competence of Business School Teachers in Promoting Sustainable Development in Finland* Liisa Rohweder and Anne Virtanen argue that the last few years have witnessed an extensive coverage of issues relating to business promoting sustainable development (SD). This has happened as a result of the increasing awareness of both the problems and future problems of climate change. That business school teachers are charged with the responsibility to educate tomorrow's business leaders puts them in a privileged position to start the process of change in attitude towards issues relating to sustainable development, these authors argue. The study notes that Finnish business school teachers have a positive attitude and are well versed on sustainable development issues but competence is still lacking on issues relating to them choosing between pedagogical and didactical methods.

In the final chapter on *Corporate Social Responsibility and Human Resource Management: A Strategic-Balanced Model*, Ananda Das Gupta argues that corporate social responsibility and responsible capitalism pose a number of challenges for HRM and corporate leaders. HRM paradigm; the chapter notes is based on a rational strategic management framework which is consistent with rational economic analysis. However, the paradigm is limited in circumstances where corporate entities seek to behave responsibly with regard to a range of internal and external stakeholders and at the same time seek to take a longer term view of CSR issues. The chapter notes that the field of responsible business strategy and practice poses unenviable challenges to corporate entities but these challenges must be addressed in order to shape the future of our world.

A careful read through of the issues highlighted in this introductory chapter to each of the 21 chapters featured in this book should hopefully reveal that these chapters have one common theme and message; that CSR is an important interdisciplinary field to all corporate professionals. Modern corporate entities have come to realize that long term economic growth and success would be far too difficult to achieve if they were perceived by all and sundry to be socially irresponsible. Success is no longer measured only in terms of the bottom line results or share prices on the stock market; in any case a company that is perceived to be socially irresponsible would have a poor bottom line result and lower share prices at the stock exchange. It is now no longer a case (as was previously believed) that it's only society which benefits from corporate CSR actions but the entity actually helps itself to operate sustainably and consequently do well because of its triple bottom line actions Elkington (1997).

Kelly and Littman (2001) argue that 'today, companies seem to have an almost insatiable thirst for knowledge, expertise, methodologies and work practices around innovation'. In my view; which of course; is a general belief, an entity that fails to innovate in its line of business puts itself at a competitive disadvantage amongst its rivals. Kelly and Littman (2001) also note that 'Out there is in some garage an entrepreneur who's forging a bullet with your company's name on it. You've got one option now – to shoot first. You've got to out-innovate the innovators'. If we all agree that innovation is a key to longer term economic success for business, then it is relevant to ask the question – 'how are modern corporate entities dealing with the issue of innovation in the field of corporate social responsibility?' The answer to this and other pertinent issues will be found in the next book in the series on *Innovative Corporate Social Responsibility*.

References

Elkington, J. (1997), Cannibals with Forks: The Triple Bottom Line of 21st Century Business, Capstone, Oxford.

Idowu, S. O. (2005), Corporate social responsibility: What's it really about? *Accountancy Ireland*, 37(4), pp. 86–88.

Idowu, S. O. and Leal Filch, W. (2009), Global Practices of Corporate Social Responsibility, Springer, Berlin.

Kelley, T. and Littman, J. (2001), The Art of Innovation, Harper Collins, London.

Kotler, P. and Lee, N. (2005), Corporate Social Responsibility, John Wiley, Hoboken, New Jersey

Part I
Business and Management

Chapter 1
Corporate Responsibility, Accounting and Accountants

Carol A. Tilt

> *In terms of power and influence you can forget about the church,*
> *forget politics. There is no more powerful institution in society*
> *than business... The business of business should not be about*
> *money, it should be about responsibility. It should be about*
> *public good, not private greed*

> Anita Roddick, *Business as Unusual* (2000)

Abstract Accountants have an important contribution to make to the debate surrounding Corporate Social Responsibility (CSR). While traditionally it has been financial accountability that is the remit of accountants, for many years now, accounting academics have been at the forefront of research and theory on social and environmental accounting and, more recently, practitioners, professional associations and others have taken an interest in the topic. This chapter demonstrates that accountants' interest in CSR is much more wide ranging than simply an interest in the financial impacts on society. Some writers envision a role for accountants in improving social justice and contributing to social and environmental benefits on a global level. The chapter concentrates initially on research about how firms report on social and environmental issues. It then provides a review of some of the research undertaken on the extent of that reporting and on accountants' perspectives on CSR and sustainability more generally. Finally, it outlines the involvement of the profession of accounting in adoption and promotion of corporate social and environmental responsibility.

1.1 Introduction

Accountants have an important contribution to make to the debate surrounding Corporate Social Responsibility (CSR). The major element of accountants' contribution that they have the ability to provide a mechanism for holding corporations

C.A. Tilt (✉)
Flinders Business School, Flinders University, Adelaide, Australia

S.O. Idowu, W.L. Filho (eds.), *Professionals' Perspectives of Corporate Social Responsibility*, DOI 10.1007/978-3-642-02630-0_2,
© Springer-Verlag Berlin Heidelberg 2009

accountable for what they do – holding entities accountable is, after all, what accountants do as a matter of course. While traditionally it has been financial accountability that is the remit of accountants, for many years now, accounting academics have been at the forefront of research and theory on social and environmental accounting and, more recently, practitioners, professional associations and others have taken an interest in the topic. This body of work attempts to 'broaden our thinking about the role of accounting' (Lehman, 2007, p. 35).

The term CSR encompasses a variety of issues revolving around companies' interactions with society. The sorts of issues covered include ethics, governance, social activities such as philanthropy and community involvement, product safety, equal opportunities, human rights and environmental activities. When considering CSR from the perspective of the accounting profession, such consideration is necessarily and inextricably linked with social (and environmental) reporting or accounting. Social accounting was itself a product, in part, of the early social responsibility movement of the 1960s (see Drucker, 1965), but also appeared around the same time the environmental movement emerged (Gray and Guthrie, 2007). Interestingly, while social issues were the initial research focus of accounting academics, these were to some extent overwhelmed by the emphasis on environmental issues that came later, and this emphasis is reflected in the reviews that follow.

This chapter concentrates initially on research about reporting on social and environmental issues (variously called Corporate Social Reporting (CSR – hence it is often confused with Corporate Social Responsibility), Social and Environmental Accounting (SEA) or Corporate Social Disclosure (CSD); more recently the terms 'sustainability reporting' or 'sustainability accounting' have become common). The chapter provides a review of some of the research undertaken on the extent of reporting itself, and on accountants' perspectives on CSR and sustainability. It also reviews the involvement of the profession of accounting in adoption and promotion of corporate social and environmental responsibility, and more recently its involvement in audit, assurance or verification of social and environmental reports.

The accountant's role can traditionally be classified into three areas: the financial accountant, the management accountant and the auditor. In terms of social and environmental accounting, the financial accountant could be said to be primarily interested in social and environmental aspects of assets and liabilities and to report on them in some standard way. The management accountant is concerned with costs and benefits associated with these issues, and the auditor in providing verification or assurance of the social account produced (Medley, 1997; Igalens, 2006). The next sections, however, indicate that the interest of accountants in CSR is in fact much more wide ranging. Some see a role for accountants in improving social justice and contributing to social and environmental benefits for society (Reynolds, 2007).

1.2 Social and Environmental Accounting

There have already been a number of extensive reviews of the social and environmental accounting (SEA) literature (see Thomson, 2007 for a recent and novel approach), notably (Gray et al. 1995a) and (Mathews 1997). Mathews (1997) reviews 25 years of academic work in the area from the early 1970s, classifying it into empirical, normative, philosophical, and various other forms of research. Mathews (1997) provides an excellent history of the early work undertaken on SEA, noting that in these early stages, SEA research predominantly reported 'fairly unsophisticated empirical studies, which attempted to measure the amount of new information being produced and published by a limited number of enterprises' (Mathews, 1997, p. 484). Gray et al. (1995a) show that over the period 1979–1991 social and environmental reporting steadily increased, both in terms of the number of companies choosing to report, and the amount they reported. However, they point out that the level of social reporting was still relatively low compared with other forms of discretionary disclosure, concluding that 'social and environmental performance is still a relatively low priority for companies' (Gray et al., 1995a, p. 68). This chapter will not revisit this early research as it has been well reviewed in other papers, but rather will focus on more recent developments. However, one important element of the earlier work was its explication of the concept of SEA, leading to the definitions still used today.

Gray et al. (1987, p. ix) provide the most useful and commonly used definition of what we mean by SEA. They describe it as:

Communicating the social and environmental effects of organizations' economic actions to particular interest groups within society and to society at large. As such it involves extending the accountability of organizations (particularly companies), beyond the traditional role of providing a financial account to the owners of capital, in particular, shareholders.

O'Dwyer (2006, p. 233) describes social accounting scholars as a group of individuals with 'commitment to stakeholder accountability and democracy'. The work of these scholars views accounting as 'a mechanism aimed at enhancing corporate accountability and transparency to a wide range of external stakeholders, addressing the social, environmental and ethical concerns and values of individuals upon whom a business has a non-economic impact' (O'Dwyer, 2006, p. 220), hence social accounting is a major element of corporate social responsibility, linking it with corporate social responsiveness. More recent analysis of the type and extent of social accounting indicates the variety of reporting mechanisms, including assurance statements, environmental, social and economic performance reports (also called Triple P (people, planet, profit) or Triple Bottom Line reports) and reporting within annual reports and financial statements. Also noted is the variety in the extent and nature of the reporting, particularly across industry sectors and between countries (Labelle et al., 2006). These differences have been shown, however, to be unrelated to profitability, but associated with entity size and the regulatory environment (Stanwick and Stanwick, 2006).

As social accounting in its various forms increases, so too do the frameworks and guidelines devised to assist firms in producing social and environmental information. The Accountability 1,000 framework, created in 1999, is a set of standards that focus on performance indicators, targets and reporting systems. It also has stakeholder engagement as a fundamental principle (Stanwick and Stanwick, 2006). The Global Reporting Initiative (GRI) was established to provide global guidelines for the reporting of social and environmental information, and to ensure consistent reporting. In Australia, a guide to triple bottom line reporting to complement the GRI was developed in 2003 by Environment Australia (Adams and Frost, 2007).

The GRI states[1] its vision as being 'that reporting on economic, environmental, and social performance by all organizations is as routine and comparable as financial reporting'. They provide a *Sustainability Reporting Framework* 'of which the *Sustainability Reporting Guidelines* are the cornerstone' and 'provides guidance for organizations to use as the basis for disclosure about their sustainability performance, and also provides stakeholders a universally-applicable, comparable framework in which to understand disclosed information'. There are 11 reporting principles, encompassing similar attributes to those espoused for financial accounting, such as, auditability, completeness, relevance, accuracy, neutrality, comparability, and timeliness; and also includes transparency, inclusiveness, clarity and context (Stanwick and Stanwick, 2006).

Reporting under the GRI does have 'levels of application' however, so just because a company reports using the GRI framework, it does not mean it will report at the same level as another organisation using the GRI. Part of the GRI requirements is that a company must disclose what level of reporting it is using. Level A is the most comprehensive. A-level companies must respond to every core indicator, either reporting on it, or explaining why it is not material to their business. At level B, companies are asked to report on at least 20 indicators, taking at least one from each area. At the lowest level, C, companies must report on just ten indicators. Unlike the higher levels, C-level companies do not have to disclose their management approach to sustainability. Neither must they comply with some of the guidelines' principles, including 'accuracy', or commit to producing a balanced report.

The GRI is probably the most successful attempt to date, at standardising the reporting of social and environmental information globally (Adams and Frost, 2007). It does not however, come without its critics. Criticisms range from it being labelled as too complex, particularly when first introduced, to being in danger of watering down its own commitment to promoting transparent reporting, since making changes recently. It has also been criticized for having flawed assumptions and weak science when applied to some technical issues. The guidelines are also said to read as if a different group wrote each of the sections (economic, environmental, and social), which is in fact how it was first developed. Notwithstanding the criticisms however, over 3,000 environment and sustainability reports were released using GRI indicators in the 10 years to 2006 (Stanwick and Stanwick, 2006). Adams and Frost (2007, p. 10) however, note that in Australia, reporting on 'social and environmental performance by ... companies is very low and significantly lower than for equivalent British companies'.

While externally reporting on social and environmental issues is generally the remit of the financial accountant, as mentioned earlier, management accountants are involved in internal measurement and identification of social and environmental

---

[1] www.globalreporting.org

costs and benefits. This area of accounting has been most often called 'full cost accounting' (Bebbington et al., 2001, p. 8) who define it as a 'system which allows current accounting and economic numbers to incorporate all potential/actual costs and benefits into the equation including environmental (and perhaps) social externalities to get the prices right'. This then makes those social costs more visible and thus able to be considered in decision making, flows to reporting, and potentially makes the firm more accountable (Antheaume, 2007). For some examples of full cost accounting experiments, see Baxter et al. (2002), Bent (2005) and Taplin et al. (2006).

1.3 Theoretical Research on Accounting and CSR

1.3.1 Motivation to Account for Responsibility

Theoretical work on CSR accounting has produced a number of theories as to the motivation of firms to report or disclose information on their CSR activities, most deriving from the broad theory called Political Economy Theory which is defined as 'the social, political and economic framework within which human life takes place' (Gray et al., 1996, p. 47). Legitimacy theory is one such theory and suggests that reporting is used as a communication mechanism to inform and/or manipulate the perceptions of the firm's actions. Suchman (1995, p. 574) defines legitimacy as:

> ...a generalized perception or assumption that the actions of an entity are desirable, proper, or appropriate within some socially constructed system of norms, values, beliefs, and definitions.

Most research considering CSR focuses on firms that are 'defending' their legitimacy due to a real or perceived threat. Such threats most commonly include bad publicity from the media surrounding a particular event, such as the *Exxon Valdez* oil spill (Patten, 1992; Deegan et al., 2000), or are measured by proxies for public or political 'visibility' such as size or industry (Patten, 1991; Hackston and Milne, 1996; Adams et al., 1998). Other research chooses to focus on particular industries that are more likely to attract attention due to their activities in environmentally or socially sensitive areas (Milne and Patten, 2002; Campbell, 2003). The majority of studies have found evidence to support the notion that firms use communication or accounting to defend or maintain legitimacy in the eyes of society and/or their stakeholders.

The research on firms' use of communication practices to defend their legitimacy has drawn on Lindblom (1994) and (Dowling and Pfeffer, 1975) and identify four communication strategies that a company may use to defend its legitimacy:

1. To inform and educate the relevant publics about changes within the organisation.
2. To change the perceptions of the relevant publics, but does not change its own behaviour.

3. To deflect attention from issues of concern to other issues.
4. To misrepresent activities of concern to the relevant publics.

Stakeholder theory extends legitimacy arguments to consider not only society as a whole but particular stakeholder groups (Deegan, 2002), hence the two theories are said to be 'overlapping perspectives of the issue (of reporting behaviour)' (Gray et al., 1995a, p. 52). These stakeholders demand different information and firms will respond to their demands in a variety of ways (Deegan, 2006). Competing demands from stakeholders has led researchers to consider 'stakeholder management' as a driver of CSR activity and reporting (Gray et al., 1996). This is known as the positive or managerial branch of stakeholder theory, where more powerful stakeholders, that is, those with more control over resources, are more likely to receive attention from the firm (Ullmann, 1985).

Another branch is known as the ethical (moral) or normative branch (Deegan, 2006). The Ethical branch of Stakeholder Theory suggests that all stakeholders have the right to be treated fairly by an organisation. Issues of stakeholder power are not directly relevant and it assumes that management should manage the organisation for the benefit of all stakeholders. Under ethical stakeholder theory, the firm is a vehicle for coordinating stakeholder interests and management have a fiduciary relationship to all stakeholders: where interests conflict, business is managed to attain optimal balance among them (Hasnas, 1998). Each group merits consideration in its own right and also has a right to be provided with information, whether or not that information is used (Deegan, 2006).

There have been many definitions of stakeholders (see Mitchell et al., 1997 for a review of definitions used). A commonly used definition is:

> Any identifiable group or individual who can affect the achievement of an organisation's objectives, or is affected by the achievement of an organisation's objectives (Freeman and Reed, 1983, p. 91).

The major stakeholders of a company therefore include shareholders, employees, creditors, suppliers, customers, banks, government, community, public interest groups and the general public (Ogan and Ziebart, 1991; Tilt, 1997, 2007). Most of this research has focussed on economic or *primary* stakeholders – 'without whose continuing participation the corporation cannot survive as a going concern' (Clarkson, 1995, p. 106), such as shareholders. Studies on non-economic or *secondary* stakeholders, that is 'those who influence or affect, or are influenced or affected by, the corporation, but ...are not engaged in transactions with the corporation and are not essential for its survival' (Clarkson, 1995, p. 107), has been more limited. The research undertaken shows that while a variety of stakeholder groups have an interest in the CSR activities of businesses, most consider their voluntarily produced reports to lack credibility and are generally skeptical of firms' social responsibility reporting (Tilt, 1994). The firms themselves confirm the view that some stakeholders are particularly important (such as shareholders, investors, creditors) but others less so (NGOs, the media, suppliers). For a review of stakeholder influence on CSD, see Tilt (2007).

1.3.2 Forcing or Influencing Responsibility

While research has focused on measuring the level of voluntary SEA, and the motivations for firms to account for CSR issues, there are also debates around whether CSR should be part of the business agenda. Many academics favour mandatory standards or legislated reporting requirements, and various arguments are presented, predominantly focused on the protection of stakeholders' interests (Owen et al., 2001). Unerman and (O'Dwyer 2007, p. 334) on the other hand, provide a case that increased regulation can also 'enhance corporate economic performance and shareholder value' by 'reducing actual and perceived risks inherent in many business activities'. Frost (2007, p. 201) provides evidence that mandatory reporting requirements do increase the level of reporting, showing that the introduction of s. 299(1) (f) into the Australian *Corporations Law* which requires companies to report on their environmental performance with respect to any 'particular and significant environmental regulation'. He found that its introduction 'resulted in a significant increase in the recognition of environmental regulation within the statutory sections, with a subsequent decline of disclosure in the voluntary section'.

Other authors suggest that voluntary information is provided as part of the *social contract*, which for 'business organisations, is based on a political "social contract" between those "empowered" (government) and those who grant them power' (Tozer and Hamilton, 2007, p. 108). Information provided under the social contract includes financial information for shareholders, but has been argued to include information of relevance to a wider range of stakeholders. Under company law, corporations have been 'granted a unique role in society – to create wealth for their shareholders while limiting their liability – without the "normal" social or ethical dimensions of citizenship'. Their success in pursuing their goals of wealth maximisation however, is one of the factors that have led to calls for corporations to be more responsible (Tozer and Hamilton, 2007, p. 110). In addition, examples of socially irresponsible behaviour by companies (such as Enron in the US, and James Hardie Industries in Australia) have fuelled society's demands for firms to be more responsible, transparent and accountable for their actions.

> If we only have great companies, we will merely have a prosperous society, not a great one. Economic growth and power are the means, not the definition, of a great nation. Jim Collins, Business Author and Theorist[2]

Adams (2002, p. 224) describes how most of the theories about SEA have not referred to internal corporate variables, such as 'the process by which companies report and the attitudes of the key players'. While external factors such as size and industry have been extensively investigated, her study concentrated on internal variables that could influence reporting of CSR information including governance structures and procedures, company chair, committees, stakeholder involvement and accountant involvement. She found that these variables do have an influence, but that it varies 'across countries, industries and countries' (Adams, 2002, p. 246). In

---

[2]http://www.woopidoo.com/business_quotes/authors/jim-collins/index.htm

particular, she identified that accountants are rarely involved in data collection for reports produced, particularly for non-financial data.

Much of the research on CSR and related areas by accounting academics to date, has been about how we account for social and environmental activities of organisations, however, the question might be raised as to whether such 'accounting' leads to any change in the behaviour of organisations, in terms of becoming more sustainable. Bebbington (2007, pp. 235–236) suggests that while this is a difficult question to answer, there is 'evidence of change in organizational routines and responsibilities; in use of accounting tools and techniques; and in the types of accounts that organizations produce of their performance'. She goes on to state however, that deeper levels of change, to attitudes and rationales have not occurred and organizations have not embraced the sustainability agenda. The challenge therefore remains, for accountants, business people and society in general, to continue to strive for attitudinal change about CSR if we are indeed going to have an effect on global social and environment issues. The next section therefore reviews the work being undertaken by accounting practitioners and professional associations in this area.

1.4 The Accounting Profession and CSR

Professional accountants are by far one of the most often researched participants in the literature on SEA, as indicated in Thomson's (2007, p. 32) Fig. 1.1. More recently there have been calls for SEA researchers to engage with practice if they are to hope to transform it, something which they have not done to any great extent in the past (Bebbington,1997). Such engagement is not without its critics however.

General Comments
Judges noted that there have been some significant areas of improvement for the 2007 entries. More companies are disclosing information on their approach to public policy and lobbying and the materiality processes in place to identify key issues on which to report. Defining report scope, outlining the major commercial activities and disclosures on governance structures and levels of board involvement in managing sustainability are also elements that more reporters are covering. Judges also noted that companies were doing a better job (but still had some way to go) in putting sustainable development into context by explaining how it relates to the business and its operations/products.

The areas that need to improve in many reports are the detailed disclosures on business strategy and a credible articulation of sustainable development in terms of what it means for the business – as well as a description of the organisation within the wider social and environmental systems in which it operates. Accounting for social and environmental externalities is another area that the majority of companies do not adequately address. Judges also noted that although reports rightly respond to key events and risks, it is essential also to demonstrate a steady, determined integration of sustainable development into operations and processes.

Fig. 1.1 ACCA reporting awards Excerpt
Source: ACCA Report of the Judges (2007, p. 18)

Bebbington (1997, p. 367) describes one of the main sources of criticism as the potential capture of the researcher's agenda by the 'powerful interests with which they engage'. She also notes, that in a study by Gray et al. (1995b), there is evidence of some capture, there is also evidence that at 'an individual and person level'people in organisations recognise that environmental issues require societal change if they are to be addressed (Bebbington, 1997, p. 369). With or without input from academic accountants therefore, the profession continues to be involved in CSR, and social and environmental accounting, in various ways.

1.4.1 Accounting Standards and Frameworks

Many countries have some form of conceptual framework that underpins their accounting standards. A conceptual framework is defined as 'a coherent system of interrelated objectives and fundamentals that is expected to lead to consistent standards' that 'prescribes the nature, function and limits of financial accounting and reporting' (Deegan, 2006). The Australian conceptual framework for accounting has been based on decision-usefulness and accountability objectives for financial reporting, providing a broad definition of users of financial information including the general public (ASRB, 1990). The objective of general purpose financial reports is described as being 'to provide relevant and reliable information to assist users to make and evaluate decisions about the allocation of scarce resources and to allow management and governing bodies to discharge their accountability' (ASRB, 1990), hence a broad interpretation could be that this could include non-financial information such as on social or environmental impacts.

The introduction of International Financial Reporting Standards (IFRS) in many countries (including Australia) has meant the adoption of *Framework for the Preparation and Presentation of Financial Statements* (the Framework). In this Framework, the principal classes of users of financial statements are: 'present and potential investors, employees, lenders, suppliers and other trade creditors, customers, governments and their agencies and the general public' [F.9]. The Framework describes the objective of financial statements as 'the provision of information about the financial position, performance and changes in financial position of an enterprise that is useful to a wide range of users in making economic decisions' [F.12–14]. Hence, again a broad interpretation could include aspects of social and environmental performance. In an exposure draft recently released by the IASB (2008) in conjunction with FASB, however, changes to the Framework have been recommended. The changes would result in a narrower definition of users to only 'capital providers' [S2], but the section on stewardship discusses management's responsibilities which 'include, to the extent possible, protecting the entity's economic resources from unfavourable effects of economic factors such as price changes and technological and social changes' [OB12] thus explicitly recognising the existence of a social dimension to business practice.

While the objectives of accounting found in accounting standards do not explicitly designate a role for accountants in CSR reporting, the profession has shown that it does see a role for itself, demonstrated by the preparation of various discussion papers and projects. For example, the International Federation of Accountants (IFAC)'s Professional Accountants in Business (PAIB) Committee prepared an information paper entitled *Sustainability – the Role of the Professional Accountant in Business* (IFAC, 2006b) that identifies 'mechanisms for enhancing sustainability ...that are directly relevant to the role of professionally qualified accountants'. These include: transparency, standards, stakeholder engagement, codes of conduct, benchmarking, regulation, reporting and assurance.

In addition, the PAIB Committee commissioned a series of telephone interviews, predominantly with professional accountants operating in business throughout the world, to seek their views on the topic. The resulting publication is entitled *Professional Accountants in Business – At the Heart of Sustainability?* (IFAC, 2006a), and concludes that:

> Good ethical practices are here to stay. For professional accountants in business, being answerable for behaviour on the issue of sustainability is vital to improving public perceptions and to winning stakeholders' trust. All professional accountants in business now need the knowledge to handle the responsibility that comes with their expanding roles as it is clear sustainability can no longer be an optional add-on for business (IFAC, 2006a, p. 12)

There have been suggestions that accountants should perhaps not be involved in accounting for social responsibility or environmental issues (Milne, 2007) and that the involvement of the accounting profession is 'antithetical to any long run solutions to such crises' (Maunders, 1996, p. 1). Notwithstanding these observations, the view coming from the accounting profession is a strong suggestion that 'the issue of sustainability needs to move rapidly up the priorities for professional accountants in business'(IFAC, 2006a, p.5), and also shows that business professionals, including accountants, are engaging in innovative and radical approaches to sustainability and corporate social responsibility.

1.4.2 Country Specific Initiatives

In the US and Australia, there does not appear to be the emphasis on CSR and sustainability that is found in the UK and European professional accounting bodies (see below). The American Institute of Certified Public Accountants (AICPA) has little on its website to advertise or promote CSR or accountants' roles in sustainability or social responsibility reporting. Work undertaken in Australia has long been said to simply follow initiatives taken in other countries, such as Canada, the USA and the UK (Medley, 1997).

More recently The Commonwealth Parliamentary Joint Committee on Corporations and Financial Services (PJCCFS) in Australia conducted an inquiry on the social responsibility of corporations, to determine whether the Corporations Act should include a requirement for some organisations 'to report on the social and environmental impact of their activities' (PJCCFS, 2006). Among the recommendations of this report were:

- That companies should inform investors of their top five sustainability risks.
- That companies should be encouraged to include longer-term corporate responsibility performance measures in remuneration packages.
- That the Australian Government should attempt to quantify the benefits of corporate responsibility reporting.

Submissions to this inquiry were sought from relevant stakeholders, including the accounting profession. Unsurprisingly, mandatory reporting was supported by some stakeholder groups, such as the Australian Conservation Foundation, and the St. James Ethics Centre.

The Australian professional body with the largest membership, CPA Australia describes has little about social responsibility on the homepage of their website, choosing to focus on 'triple bottom line' and sustainability. They describe the challenge for accounting: 'The notion of sustainable development raises the contentious issue of whether measurement of outcome is the domain of larger economic and public policy, remote from the commercial activities of business organisations'. It goes on to suggest that 'these definitions challenge the role of accounting in terms of its capacity to provide information that underpins both sustainable development initiatives and commercial activities which have a significant environmental impact'.[3] In their submission to the PJCCFS inquiry however, CPA Australia suggested that organisations do not currently have adequate systems in place to support mandatory reporting. Similarly, the Business Council of Australia opposed any proposal to legislate corporate social responsibility (Adams and Frost, 2007).

The other professional accounting body, the Institute of Chartered Accountants in Australia (ICAA) similarly has little on its homepage about CSR and the profession in general in Australia does not support any moves to make social and environmental reporting mandatory (Adams and Frost, 2007).

The Institute of Chartered Accountants in England & Wales (ICAEW) is the largest professional accountancy body in Europe with over 128,000 members. They state that Accountants have a 'key role to play in measuring and assuring Corporate Responsibility reports and supporting the measurements on which good quality information depends'.[4] Their paper 'Sustainability: the Role of Accountants' (ICAEW, 2004), describes ways in which information supports mechanisms used to promote sustainable development and the challenges and opportunities for accountants that these present. These include benchmarking, tradable permits, reporting and assurance. In an article about the Institute, they are quoted as expounding the role of accountants in promoting corporate social responsibility:

> any CR [corporate responsibility] system would depend on the availability of accurate and reliable information, and on the systems, processes, policies and strategies that support them

---

[3]CPA Australia website: https://www.cpaaustralia.com.au/cps/rde/xchg/SID-3F57FECA-8B03C462/cpa/hs.xsl/14131_8141_ENA_HTML.htm

[4]http://www.icaew.com/index.cfm?route=127637

... CR is, therefore, very much the domain of the accountant; we believe that it is our natural territory (Spencer, 2005).

Globally, the Association of Chartered Certified Accountants (ACCA) holds internationally recognised awards for sustainability reporting, and draws upon the GRI guidelines in their analysis.[5] The aims of the ACCA UK Awards for Sustainability Reporting Awards are:

- to give recognition to those organisations which report and disclose environmental, social or full sustainability information
- to encourage the uptake of environmental, social and sustainability reporting, and
- to raise awareness of corporate transparency issues.

In 2007, the overall winner of the best Sustainability Report was BT Group Pty Ltd. The 2007 Report of the Judges outlines the strengths and weaknesses in the reports of seven winning organisations across different categories. Figure 1.1 provides an excerpt from the report summarising the overall applications and results.

1.4.3 Practitioner Response to CSR

In addition to professional accounting associations, the large accounting (Big 4) firms all state their commitment to CSR and sustainability. An inspection of their websites identifies that they see it important to both state their own commitment to CSR, and to advertise their services to others in helping businesses to develop responsible strategies and prepare reports. Most also offer some form of assurance services in this area.

KPMG for example, on their international website say that they are committed to CSR, categorizing it into four major areas – people, clients, communities and efficiency. Figure 1.2 demonstrates their conception of CSR. They are also signatories to the United Nations Global Compact, stating that the principles are aligned with KPMG's Values. KPMG specifically offer services in this area, and have a trademarked 'Global Sustainability Services',[6] which defines CSR as 'incorporating environmental, social, ethical, and economic issues in the strategy development process'. They consider this to be 'essential if companies are to achieve sustained business performance and maintain stakeholder confidence. Business leaders cannot afford to ignore the impacts of global warming, expanding populations, poor labour conditions, anti-competitive trade practices, political corruption, resource depletion, or increasing pressure for transparency'.

Ernst and Young (Australia) provide dedicated Environment & Sustainability Services, providing 'solutions to contemporary environmental and social business

---

[5]http://www.accaglobal.com/uk/publicinterest/sustainability
[6]http://www.kpmg.com/nr/exeres/1a058b00-3ac6-49cb-bb29-9419d390f657.htm

Corporate Social Responsibility

All organizations have responsibilities to their people, their clients and
society. We believe a real commitment to corporate social responsibility
(CSR) unites an organization, strengthens its reputation and creates vital links
with the communities in which it operates.

People

With many graduates and qualified employees citing CSR as a priority, our
commitments are helping us to attract, develop and unite great people. CSR
projects enable our employees to learn from challenging experiences; gain
fresh perspectives; enhance their skills; and work with a broad range of people
- including senior colleagues.

Clients

Clients actively involved in CSR often prefer to work with like-minded
organizations. Our commitment to transparency and integrity and our strong
desire to make a positive difference to the world reflect the beliefs and actions
of many of our clients.

Communities

There is a strong moral case for CSR, and we believe it is right to support
selected individuals and groups in need - both as an organization and as
individuals.

Efficiency

We are very conscious of our responsibility to make the best use of resources.
We are significantly reducing costs by introducing more efficient approaches
to resources such as paper and energy, and to business travel.

Fig. 1.2 KPMG's conception of CSR
Source: http://www.kpmg.com/About/CSR/

issues'.[7] PriceWaterhouseCoopers (PwC) focuses on what they term 'responsible
leadership'.[8] Both PWC and Ernst and Young provide a variety of services to
clients, including environmental services such as emissions trading services and
environmental risk management; stakeholder engagement processes; development
of metrics and KPIs; sustainability reporting (including TBL/CSR); and verification.

PwC carry out many surveys of businesses and practitioners about the issue of
CSR. In 2003 they asked whether anyone 'beyond a small group of activists, care if
the board is taking into account wider social issues' (PwC, 2003 cited in Dellaportas
et al., 2005, p. 213). They concluded that the general public does care, and hence the
increase in interest in ethical investments. In their submission to the 2006 PJCCFS
inquiry however, PwC, opposed the mandatory inclusion of social information in
annual reports, suggesting it would be of little value (Adams and Frost, 2007).

Deloitte Touché Tohmatsu also offer similar services, but devote a section of their
website to discussion of their approach to corporate responsibility and how they
ensure improvement in this area. Figure 1.3 provides an excerpt from the Deloitte
website.

---

[7]http://www.ey.com/global/Content.nsf/Australia/AABS_-_Sustainable_Development
[8]http://www.pwc.com/extweb/challenges.nsf/docid/58e92287890b5314852570980064acc2

Corporate Responsibility

Deloitte member firms' approach to corporate responsibility is shaped by the
recognition that, because they are a professional services organization, their
impact on society comes in large part from the way they serve clients.
Accordingly, they seek to achieve excellence and continuous improvement in
three ways:

Conduct—responsible business practices in how the member firms are run
and how they serve clients.

People—investing in the talent and diversity of the member firms' current and
future workforce.

Communities—commitment to local communities and shared global
challenges.

To sustain trust and best serve member firm clients, integrity and quality are
the foundation that defines the approach to the operation of member firm
business and the delivery of multidisciplinary professional services to clients.
Each of the nearly 135,000 people of the Deloitte member firms are also
committed to the Deloitte Shared Values, which create a culture of trust across
all of the member firms.

Fig. 1.3 Deloitte Touché Tohmatsu approach to CSR
Source: http://www.deloitte.com/dtt/section_node/0,1042,sid%253D73238,00.html

1.4.4 Assurance Practices

As discussed in the introductory sections, an important role of the accounting profession in CSR is to prepare audit or assurance statements to CSR or sustainability
reports. Owen (2007, p. 168) reports a 'discernable increase in the number of reports
accompanied by some form of externally prepared assurance statement'. The ACCA
and CorporateRegister.com[9] provide a database of reports (Owen, 2007) and Owen
(2007) notes that nearly 40% of them included an assurance statement in 2004, more
than double that found 10 years earlier. Similarly, KPMG's (2005) *International
Survey of Corporate Responsibility Reporting* indicates growth in this area although
the rate of growth is slowing and the nature of the assurance is 'patchy' and is
dominated by the major accounting firms (Owen, 2007, p. 169).

Notwithstanding the growth in this area, there is evidence of much variability in
the practice of CSR and sustainability assurance (O'Dwyer and Owen, 2005; Owen,
2007). CPA Australia's (2004) study of worldwide assurance statements refers to the
variability of assurance statements, noting in particular the name use for the statement, differing objectives and scope, and a tendency not to disclose reporting criteria
or standards used. O'Dwyer and Owen (2005) similarly find variability and incon-
sistencies, although they do point to some improvement in particular practices over
time, particularly in validating data. Pava and Krausz (2006) note that the inconsis-
tencies have already impacted on the credibility of the profession in this area with
stakeholders.

[9]http://www.corporateregister.com

A number of organisations and accountancy bodies have issued guidance in this area, including Accountability who, with the International Register of Certified Auditors, offers a professional qualification in sustainability assurance practice[10] (Owen, 2007). Built on the AA1000 platform, the program is aimed at both internal and external practitioners. Similarly, the accounting body of the Netherlands, NIRVA, drafted a Standard for Assurance Engagements Relating to Sustainability Reports (ED 3410) in 2004. Few countries however, have adopted regulated or mandated standards in this area (Owen, 2007), although IFAC's International Auditing and Assurance Standards Board (IAASB) issues ISAE 3000 *Assurance Engagements Other Than Audits or Reviews of Historical Financial Information* (IAASB, 2004b) and an *International Framework for Assurance Engagements,* (IAASB, 2004a) which have been used to guide assurance of corporate responsibility and sustainability reports (Owen, 2007).

1.5 Industry Specific Involvement

As mentioned earlier, the industry to which a firm belongs has been shown to be significant in determining the level of social and environmental reporting undertaken, along with other firm characteristics such a size and visibility. Some industries in particular have been the focus of research, particularly in studies on environmental accounting where industries that are seen to have a detrimental effect on the physical environment are targeted for research. These studies include analysis of the mining (Guthrie and Parker, 1989; Tilt and Symes, 1999; Peck and Sinding, 2003) and chemical (Adams and Kuasirikun, 2000; Richards et al., 2004) industries for environmental reporting, and the tobacco (Tilling, 2004; Moerman and Van Der Laan, 2005) and financial services (Tsang, 1998; Do et al., 2007) industry for social reporting.

Most studies of the mining industry have found higher than average levels of reporting on environmental issues, higher quality reporting (Peck and Sinding, 2003), and more use of guidelines to inform reporting as such environmentally sensitive industries' impacts are also much more visible (Wilmshurst and Frost, 2000). Peck and Sinding's (2003) analysis of 30 global mining companies found that Australian companies were leaders in environmental reporting compared to Canada and the US. In Australia, this could be attributed to a number of industry initiatives that have been undertaken, such as the Minerals Council of Australia's (MCA) 'code of environmental management' (MCA, 2001) and their 'Enduring Value' framework (MCA, 2004). The council also holds annual conferences on sustainable development. Other initiatives include the Mining Certification Evaluation Project, a project involving WWF, mining companies, the CSIRO (Commonwealth Scientific and Industrial Research Organisation) and the MCA, to evaluate the use of

---

[10]http://www.irca.org/certification/certification_11.html

third party certification of mine sites; and the Greenhouse Challenge Program,[11] a cooperative partnership between industry and the Australian Government to: reduce greenhouse gas emissions, accelerate the uptake of energy efficiency, integrate greenhouse issues into business decision-making, and to provide more consistent reporting of greenhouse gas emissions levels. Tilt and Symes (1999) review the complex taxation legislation around mining companies in Australia and the special provisions that apply to these companies, in particular the deductibility of mine site rehabilitation. Tilt and Symes (1999) suggest that much of the early research on environmental reporting by mining companies may have been misleading as much of the 'voluntary' disclosure was likely driven by taxation advantages, rather than CSR.

There are other international initiatives of the mining industry, including the Global Mining Initiative, a 1999 commitment from nine global mining companies to engage and research sustainable development strategies. Yongavanich and Guthrie (2004) analysed reporting by the top 100 Australian companies from the energy and materials sector, and while they found that mining companies report more than other companies, they presented evidence that the mining industry performed poorly in terms of 'social indicator' reporting. Jenkins and Yakovleva (2006) analysed ten large global mining companies and found that disclosure had generally increased and become more sophisticated over time. They note however, that not all companies were alike, with definite leaders appearing, and also noted the increase of web-based communication media.

Mining companies report on social, as well as environmental, responsibility, increasingly in separate social and environmental reports. Much of their social disclosure relates to the local communities in which they operate. A research report from the Cardiff University centre for Business Relationships, Accountability, Sustainability, Society (BRASS) found however, that the 'decision of [mining] companies to develop community strategies does not stem from a moral choice; it is as a strategic response to social challenges that constantly shift the background of constraints in which the organisation must operate' (Jenkins and Yakovleva, 2007).

1.6 Non Accountant Involvement in Accounting

Not only accountants are involved with, or comment on, accounting for CSR issues. Many NGOs play an important role (Tilt, 2007), for example, WWF produced an analysis of environmental reporting by mining companies in 1999 and 2000 producing a *Mining Company Environmental Report Scorecard* for Australian mining companies that were signatories to the *Australian Minerals Industry Code for Environmental Management* (WWF, 1999). The Scorecard rates each company's environmental report according to a set of criteria. Deegan and Blomquist (2005)

---

[11] http://www.greenhouse.gov.au/challenge/index.html

found that production of the Scorecard resulted in changes to reporting by individual companies, and revisions being made to the Code.

The Age newspaper in Australia also produces a scorecard, called the *Company Reputation Index (CRI)*, which rates the top 100 Australian companies on their environmental, social and ethical performance (Age, 2000). The criteria used to produce the measures are developed by representatives from social and environmental community groups who rate each company. Similar reputation indexes exist in the USA, such as the FORTUNE/Roper Corporate Reputation Index which classifies companies into, among other things, 'winners', 'losers', 'irrelevant' and 'falling stars' (PR Influences, 2005).

Most NGOs have been found to be skeptical of corporation's motives for social disclosure, and studies have suggested that their reports lack credibility, and are on the whole insufficient in information (Tilt, 1994; Gadenne and Danastas, 2004; Tilt, 2004). These Australian NGOs have also stated preference for quantified information although at the time most reporting was simply narrative, and the use of separate social reports (as opposed to providing this information in annual reports) (Tilt, 1994). That even go so far as to say they do not consider companies to be honest about their social and environmental impacts (Tilt, 2004).

In Ireland, O'Dwyer et al. (2005), found that there is a demand for social disclosure information by NGOs, motivated primarily by a desire for accountability, but that, like in Australia, current CSD practice in Ireland is viewed with scepticism and there is an antagonistic relationship between corporations and NGOs (O'Dwyer et al., 2005).

1.7 Conclusion

This chapter has reviewed the academic and professional literature on the contribution of accounting and accountants to the debate and practice of corporate social responsibility. The accountant is perhaps not the first person to spring to mind when discussing issues of sustainability, social responsibility and social justice. The accounting profession however, is implicated more than ever when we consider the role of business in ensuring a better future for our society and our planet.

Some of the examples provided in this chapter indicate a broadening of the scope of corporate accountability to encompass issues and concepts found an increasingly complex business environment. These changes could be argued to be the result of 'a more expansive and justifiable interpretation of our basic and long-held view of corporate accountability' (Pava and Krausz, 2007, p. 148) and that the accountant should therefore be at the 'forefront of the changes' (Pava and Krausz, 2007, p. 149). 'Accounting is a powerful tool ... which has conventionally been used in optimizing the economic performance of organizations' (Unerman et al., 2007, p. 3) and as such, there is no reason that the same tools cannot be used to enhance their social and environmental performance. It is important to note however, that conventional accounting tools and reporting mechanisms are not able to capture completely the social and environmental impacts of business (O'Dwyer, 2006). Thus, CSR scholars' focus has been on the 'emergence of new accountings' (Gray, 2002) such as full cost accounting (Bebbington et al., 2001), sustainable cost calculations (Bebbington and Gray, 2001) and shadow accounting (Dey, 2007).

Accounting has always been the language of business, so it is not unexpected that it plays an important role as that language evolves to include information and responsibility beyond the purely financial. Business leaders, corporate executives and the wealth-holders in our society are being asked to take the lead in improving the lives of the people. In turn they are being called to account for their actions in making (or not making) this contribution. Accountants provide the mechanisms to provide that account.

> Too many leaders act as if the sheep... their people... are there for the benefit of the shepherd, not that the shepherd has responsibility for the sheep. Ken Blanchard, Author, Speaker and Consultant[12]

References

ACCA (2007), Report of the Judges - ACCA UK Awards for Sustainability reporting 2007, ACCA, London.

Adams, C.A. (2002), "Internal Organisational Factors Influencing Corporate Social and Ethical Reporting: Beyond Current Theorising", *Accounting, Auditing and Accountability Journal*, Vol. 15, No. 2, pp. 223–250.

Adams, C.A., and Frost, G.R. (2007), "Managing Social and Environmental Performance: Do Companies Have Adequate Information?" *Australian Accounting Review*, Vol. 17, No. 3, pp. 2–11.

Adams, C.A., Hill, W.Y., and Roberts, C.B. (1998), "Corporate Social Reporting Practices in Western Europe: Legitimating Corporate Behavior?" *British Accounting Review*, Vol. 30, No. 1, pp. 1–21.

Adams, C.A., and Kuasirikun, N. (2000), "A Comparative Analysis of Corporate Reporting on Ethical Issues by UK and German Chemical and Pharmaceutical Companies", *European Accounting Review*, Vol. 9, No. 1, pp. 53–80.

Age, The (2000), "Company Reputation Index. Methodology", *The Age*, 26 October, (Electronic), www.theage.com.au/news/20001030/A8982-2000Oct26.html [Accessed: 26 March 2001].

Antheaume, N. (2007), "Full Cost Accounting. Adam Smith Meets Rachel Carson?" In Unerman, J., Bebbington, J. and O'Dwyer, B. (Eds.), *Sustainability Accounting and Accountability*, Routledge, London.

ASRB (1990), *"Objectives of General Purpose Financial Reporting"*, Statement of Accounting Concepts (SAC) 2, Victoria, Australia, Accounting Standards Review Board.

Baxter, T., Bebbington, J., and Cutteridge, D. (2002), *Spe 73968: The Sustainability Assessment Model (Sam)*, Society of Petroleum Engineers Inc.

Bebbingon, J. (2007), "Changing Organizational Attitudes and Culture through Sustainability Accounting", In Unerman, J., Bebbington, J., and O'Dwyer, B. (Eds.), *Sustainability Accounting and Accountability*, Routledge, Abingdon.

Bebbington, J. (1997), "Engagement, Education and Sustainability: A Review Essay on Environmental Accounting", *Accounting, Auditing and Accountability*, Vol. 10, No. 3, pp. 365–381.

---

[12]http://www.woopidoo.com/business_quotes/authors/ken-blanchard-quotes.htm

Bebbington, J., and Gray, R. (2001), "An Account of Sustainability: Failure, Success and a Reconceptualization", *Critical Perspectives On Accounting*, Vol. 12, No. 5, pp. 557–588.

Bebbington, J., Gray, R., Hibbit, C., and Kirk, E. (2001), *Full Cost Accounting: An Agenda for Action*, ACCA, London.

Bent, D. (2005), *Towards a Monetised Triple Bottom Line for an Alcohol Producer, Using Stakeholder Dialogue to Negotiate a 'Licence to Operate' by Constructing an Account of Social Performance*, Forum for the Future, London.

Campbell, D. (2003), "Intra- and Intersectoral Effects in Environmental Disclosures: Evidence for Legitimacy Theory?" *Business Strategy and the Environment*, Vol. 12, No. 6, pp. 357–371.

Clarkson, M.B.E. (1995), "A Stakeholder Framework for Analyzing and Evaluating Corporate Social Performance", *Academy of Management Review*, Vol. 20, No. 1, pp. 92–117.

CPA Australia (2004), *Triple Bottom Line: A Study of Assurance Statements Worldwide*, CPA Australia, Melbourne.

Deegan, C. (2002), "The Legitimising Effect of Social and Environmental Disclosures – A Theoretical Foundation", *Accounting, Auditing and Accountability Journal*, Vol. 15, No. 3, pp. 282–311.

Deegan, C. (2006), *Financial Accounting Theory*, McGraw-Hill Australia, Sydney.

Deegan, C., and Blomquist, C. (2005), "Stakeholder Influence on Corporate Reporting: An Exploration of the Interaction between the World Wide Fund for Nature and the Australian Minerals Industry", *Accounting, Organizations and Society*, Vol. 31, No. 4–5, pp. 343–372.

Deegan, C., Rankin, M., and Voght, P. (2000), "Firms' Disclosure Reactions to Major Social Incidents: Australian Evidence", *Accounting Forum*, Vol. 24, No. 1, pp. 101–130.

Dellaportas, S., Gibson, K., Alagiah, R., Hutchinson, M., Leung, P., and Van Homrigh, D. (2005), *Ethics, Governance & Accountability, a Professional Perspective*, John Wiley & Sons Australia Ltd, Milton, Qld.

Dey, C. (2007), "Developing Silent and Shadow Accounts", In Unerman, J., Bebbingon, J., and O'Dwyer, B. (Eds.), *Sustainability Accounting and Accountability*, Routledge, Abingdon.

Do, H., Tilt, C.A., and Tilling, M.V. (2007), "Social and Environmental Reporting by Westpac Bank", Paper presented at the *Asia Pacific Interdisciplinary Research in Accounting Conference*, Auckland, July.

Dowling, J., and Pfeffer, J. (1975), "Organizational Legitimacy: Social Values and Organizational Behavior", *Pacific Sociological Review*, Vol. 18, No. 1, pp. 122–136.

Drucker, P. (1965), "Is Business Letting Young People Down?" *Harvard Business Review*, Vol. 43 Nov/Dec, p. 54.

Freeman, R., and Reed, D. (1983), "Stockholders and Stakeholders: A New Perspective on Corporate Governance", *California Management Review*, Vol. 25, No. 2, pp. 88–106.

Frost, G. (2007), "The Introduction of Mandatory Environmental Reporting Guidelines: Australian Evidence", *Abacus*, Vol. 43, No. 2, pp. 190–216.

Gadenne, D., and Danastas, L. (2004), "A Study of External Pressure Group Influence on Corporate Social Disclosure", Paper presented at the *Corporate Governance and Ethics Conference*, Sydney, June 28–30.

Gray, R. (2002), "The Social Accounting Project and Accounting Organizations and Society: Privileging Engagement, Imagination, New Accountings and Pragmatism over Critique?" *Accounting, Organizations and Society*, Vol. 27, No. 7, pp. 687–708.

Gray, R., and Guthrie, J. (2007), "Social Accounting and the Academic Community: Of Foundations, Jubilees, and Consistency", In Gray, R. and Guthrie, J. (Eds.), *Social Accounting, Mega Accounting and Beyond: A Festschrift in Honour of M. R. Mathews*, The Centre for Social and Environmental Accounting Research, St. Andrews.

Gray, R., Kouhy, R., and Lavers, S. (1995a), "Corporate Social and Environmental Reporting: A Review of the Literature and a Longitudinal Study of UK Disclosure", *Accounting, Auditing and Accountability*, Vol. 8, No. 2, pp. 47–77.

Gray, R., Owen, D., and Adams, C.A. (1996), *Accounting and Accountability: Changes and Challenges in Corporate Social and Environmental Reporting*, Prentice-Hall, London.

Gray, R., Owen, D., and Maunders, K. (1987), *Corporate Social Reporting – Accounting & Accountability*, Prentice-Hall, UK.

Gray, R., Walters, D., Bebbington, J., and Thomson, I. (1995b), "The Greening of Enterprise: An Exploration of the (Non) Role of Environmental Accounting and Environmental Accountants in Organisational Change", *Critical Perspectives On Accounting*, Vol. 6, No. 3, pp. 211–239.

Guthrie, J., and Parker, L.D. (1989), "Corporate Social Reporting: A Rebuttal of Legitimacy Theory", *Accounting and Business Research*, Vol. 19, No. 76, pp. 343–352.

Hackston, D., and Milne, M.J. (1996), "Some Determinants of Social and Environmental Disclosures in New Zealand Companies", *Accounting, Auditing and Accountability*, Vol. 9, No. 1, pp. 77–108.

Hasnas, J. (1998), "The Normative Theories of Business Ethics: A Guide for the Perplexed", *Business Ethics Quarterly*, Vol. 8, No. 1, pp. 19–42.

IAASB (2004a), *International Framework for Assurance Engagements*, New York, International Auditing and Assurance Standards Board, International Federation of Accountants Committee.

IAASB(2004b), *ISAE 3000 Assurance Engagements Other Than Audits or Reviews of Historical Financial Information*, New York, International Auditing and Assurance Standards Board, International Federation of Accountants Committee.

IASB(2008), *Exposure Draft – Conceptual Framework for Financial Reporting*, International Accounting Standards Board.

ICAEW(2004), *Sustainability: The Role of Accountants*, The Institute of Chartered Accountants in England & Wales.

IFAC(2006a), *Professional Accountants in Business – At the Heart of Sustainability?* Professional Accountants in Business Committee, International Federation of Accountants.

IFAC(2006b), *Sustainability – The Role of the Professional Accountant in Business*, Professional Accountants in Business Committee, International Federation of Accountants.

Igalens, J. (2006), "Institutional Acceptance of Corporate Social Responsibility", In Allouche, J. (Ed.), *Corporate Social Responsibility Volume 1: Concepts, Accountability and Reporting* (pp. 317–332), Palgrave Macmillan, New York.

Jenkins, H., and Yakovleva, N. (2007), "Social, Ethical and Environmental Disclosure (SEED) in the Global Mining Industry", *Centre for Business Relationships, Accountability, Sustainability, Society, Cardiff University* (Electronic), http://www.brass.cf.ac.uk/projects/Socio-Environmental_Impacts_of_Business–CSR_and_Mining.html, Accessed 21 December 2007.

Jenkins, H.M., and Yakovleva, N. (2006), "Corporate Social Responsibility in the Mining Industry: Exploring Trends in Social and Environmental Disclosure", *Journal of Cleaner Production*, Vol. 14, No. 3–4, pp. 271–284.

KPMG(2005), *International Survey of Corporate Responsibility Reporting*, KPMG, Amsterdam.

Labelle, R., Schatt, A., and Sinclair-Desgagné, B. (2006), "Corporate Sustainability Reporting", In Allouche, J. (Ed.), *Corporate Social Responsibility Volume 1: Concepts, Accountability and Reporting*, Palgrave Macmillan, New York.

Lehman, G. (2007), "Ethics, Communitarianism and Social Accounting", In Gray, R. and Guthrie, J. (Eds.), *Social Accounting, Mega Accounting and Beyond: A Festschrift in Honour of M. R. Mathews*, The Centre for Social and Environmental Accounting Research, St. Andrews.

Lindblom, C.K. (1994), "The Implications of Organizational Legitimacy for Corporate Social Performance and Disclosure", Paper presented at the *Critical Perspectives On Accounting*, New York.

Mathews, M.R. (1997), "Twenty-Five Years of Social and Environmental Accounting Research", *Accounting, Auditing and Accountability*, Vol. 10, No. 4, pp. 481–531.

Maunders, K. (1996), "'Environmental Accounting' – Is It Necessarily an Oxymoron?" Paper presented at the *Environmental Accountability Symposium*, Canberra International Hotel, ACT, 16–17 February.

MCA(2001), *Australian Minerals Industry Code for Environmental Management*, Minerals Council of Australia, Canberra.

MCA (2004), *Enduring Value: The Australian Minerals Industry Framework for Sustainable Development*, Minerals Council of Australia, Canberra.

Medley, P. (1997), "Environmental Accounting – What Does It Mean to Professional Accountants?" *Accounting, Auditing and Accountability,* Vol. 10, No. 4, pp. 594–600.

Milne, M.J. (2007), "Downsizing Reg (Me and You)! Addressing the 'Real' Sustainability Agenda at Work and Home", In Gray, R. and Guthrie, J. (Eds.), *Social Accounting, Mega Accounting and Beyond: A Festschrift in Honour of M. R. Mathews,* The Centre for Social and Environmental Accounting Research, St. Andrews.

Milne, M.J., and Patten, D.M. (2002), "Securing Organizational Legitimacy: An Experimental Decision Case Examining the Impact of Environmental Disclosures", *Accounting, Auditing and Accountability,* Vol. 15, No. 3, pp. 372–405.

Mitchell, R.K., Agle, B.R., and Wood, D.J. (1997), "Toward a Theory of Stakeholder Identification and Salience: Defining the Principle of Who and What Really Counts", *The Academy of Management Review,* Vol. 22, No. 4, pp. 853–886.

Moerman, L., and Van Der Laan, S. (2005), "Social Reporting in the Tobacco Industry: All Smoke and Mirrors?" *Accounting, Auditing and Accountability Journal,* Vol. 18, No. 3, pp. 374–389.

O'Dwyer, B. (2006), "Theoretical and Practical Contributions of Social Accounting to Corporate Social Responsibility", In Allouche, J. (Ed.), *Corporate Social Responsibility Volume 1: Concepts, Accountability and Reporting,* Palgrave Macmillan, New York.

O'Dwyer, B., and Owen, D.L. (2005), "Assurance Statement Practice in Environmental, Social and Sustainability Reporting", *British Accounting Review,* Vol. 37, No. 2, pp. 205–229.

O'Dwyer, B., Unerman, J., and Bradley, J. (2005), "Perceptions on the Emergence and Future Development of Corporate Social Disclosure in Ireland: Engaging the Voices of Non-Governmental Organisations", *Accounting, Auditing and Accountability Journal,* Vol. 18, No. 1, pp. 14–43.

Ogan, P., and Ziebart, D.A. (1991), "Corporate Reporting and the Accounting Profession: An Interpretive Paradigm", *Journal of Accounting, Auditing & Finance,* Vol. 6, No. 3, pp. 387–406.

Owen, D. (2007), "Assurance Practice in Sustainability Reporting", In Unerman, J., Bebbington, J., and O'Dwyer, B. (Eds.), *Sustainability Accounting and Accountability,* Routledge, Abingdon.

Owen, D.L., Swift, T., and Hunt, K. (2001), "Questioning the Role of Stakeholder Engagement in Social and Ethical Accounting, Auditing and Reporting", *Accounting Forum,* Vol. 25, No. 3, pp. 264–282.

Patten, D.M. (1991), "Exposure, Legitimacy, and Social Disclosure", *Journal of Accounting and Public Policy,* Vol. 10, pp. 297–308.

Patten, D.M. (1992), "Intra-Industry Disclosure in Response to the Alaskan Oil Spill: A Note on Legitimacy Theory", *Accounting, Organizations and Society,* Vol. 17, No. 5, pp. 471–475.

Pava, M.L., and Krausz, J. (2006), "The Broadening Scope of Corporate Accountability: Some Unanswered Questions", In Allouche, J. (Ed.), *Corporate Social Responsibility,* Palgrave Macmillan, New York.

Pava, M.L., and Krausz, J. (2007), "The Broadening Scope of Corporate Accountability: Some Unanswered Questions", In Allouche, J. (Ed.), *Corporate Social Responsibility,* Palgrave Macmillan, New York.

Peck, P., and Sinding, K. (2003), "Environmental and Social Disclosure and Data Richness in the Mining Industry", *Business Strategy and the Environment,* Vol. 12, No. 3, pp. 131–146.

PJCCFS (2006), *Corporate Responsibility: Managing Risk and Creating Value,* Commonwealth of Australia, Parliament House, Canberra.

PR Influences (2005), "US Reputation Survey Tells How It Is" (Electronic), www.compad.com.au/cms/prinfluences/articles/225 [Accessed: 16 January 2006].

Reynolds, M. (2007), "Accounting, Communication, Social Responsibility and Justice – A Short Essay on Complexity", In Gray, R. and Guthrie, J. (Eds.), *Social Accounting, Mega Accounting and Beyond: A Festschrift in Honour of M. R. Mathews,* The Centre for Social and Environmental Accounting Research, St. Andrews.

Richards, J.P., Glegg, G.A., and Cullinane, S. (2004), "Implementing Chemicals Policy: Leaders or Laggards?" *Business Strategy and the Environment,* Vol. 13, No. 6, pp. 388–402.

Roddick, A. (2000), *Business as Unusual,* Harper Collins Publishers, London.

Spencer, R. (2005), "Corporate Responsibility: New Opportunities for Chartered Accountants?" *London Accountant, ICAEW* (Electronic), http://www.icaew.com/index.cfm?route=142194 [Accessed: 21 December 2007].

Stanwick, P.A., and Stanwick, S.D. (2006), "Environment and Sustainability Disclosures: A Global Perspective on Financial Performance", In Allouche, J. (Ed.), *Corporate Social Responsibility Volume 2: Performances and Stakeholders*, Palgrave Macmillan, New York.

Suchman, M.C. (1995), "Managing Legitimacy: Strategic and Institutional Approaches", *Academy of Management Review,* Vol. 20, No. 3, pp. 571–610.

Taplin, J., Bent, D., and Aeron-Thomas, D. (2006), *Developing a Sustainability Accounting Framework to Inform Strategic Business Decisions: A Case Study from the Chemicals Industry*, Forum for the Future, London.

Thomson, I. (2007), "Mapping Sustainability Accounting", In Unerman, J., Bebbington, J., and O'Dwyer, B. (Eds.), *Sustainability Accounting and Accountability*, Routledge, Abingdon.

Tilling, M. (2004), "Communication at the Edge: Voluntary Social and Environmental Reporting in the Annual Report of a Legitimacy Threatened Corporation", Paper presented at the *APIRA Conference 2004*, Singapore, 4–6 July.

Tilt, C.A. (1994), "The Influence of External Pressure Groups on Corporate Social Disclosure Some Empirical Evidence", *Accounting, Auditing and Accountability,* Vol. 7, No. 4, pp. 47–72.

Tilt, C.A. (1997), "Environmental Policies of Major Companies: Australian Evidence", *British Accounting Review,* Vol. 29, No. 4, pp. 367–394.

Tilt, C.A. (2004), "Influences on Corporate Social Disclosure: A Look at Lobby Groups Ten Years On", *School of Commerce Research Paper Series, Flinders University,* No. 01-01 (Electronic), www.ssn.flinders.edu.au/commerce/researchpapers/#04 [Accessed: 28 July 2005].

Tilt, C.A. (2007), "External Stakeholders' Perspectives on Sustainability Reporting", In Unerman, J., Bebbington, J., and O'Dwyer, B. (Eds.), *Sustainability Accounting and Accountability*, Routledge, New York.

Tilt, C.A., and Symes, C.F. (1999), "Environmental Disclosure by Australian Mining Companies: Environmental Conscience or Commercial Reality?" *Accounting Forum,* Vol. 23, No. 2, pp. 137–154.

Tozer, L., and Hamilton, F. (2007), "Re-Energising the Social Contract in Accounting: The Case of James Hardie Industries", In Grah, R. and Guthrie, J. (Eds.), *Social Accounting, Mega Accounting and Beyond: A Festschrift in Honour of M. R. Mathews*, The Centre for Social and Environmental Accounting Research, St. Andrews.

Tsang, E.T.W. (1998), "A Longitudinal Study of Corporate Social Reporting in Singapore: The Case of the Banking, Food and Beverage and Hotel Industries", *Accounting, Auditing and Accountability,* Vol. 11, No. 5, pp. 624–635.

Ullmann, A. (1985), "Data in Search of a Theory: A Critical Examination of the Relationships Among Social Performance, Social Disclosure and Economic Performance of US Firms", *Academy of Management Review,* Vol. 10, No. 3, pp. 540–557.

Unerman, J., Bebbington, J., and O'Dwyer, B. (2007), "Introduction to Sustainability and Accountability", In Unerman, J., Bebbington, J., and O'Dwyer, B. (Eds.), *Sustainability Accounting and Accountability*, Routledge, Abingdon.

Unerman, J., and O'Dwyer, B. (2007), "The Business Case for Regulation of Corporate Social Responsibility and Accountability", *Accounting Forum,* Vol. 31, No. 4, pp. 332–353.

Wilmshurst, T.D., and Frost, G.R. (2000), "Corporate Environmental Reporting: A Test of Legitimacy Theory", *Accounting, Auditing and Accountability,* Vol. 13, No. 1, pp. 10–26.

WWF (1999), *Mining Environmental Reports: Ore or Overburden?* World Wide Fund for Nature Australia, Melbourne.

Yongavanich, K., and Guthrie, J. (2004), "Extended Performance Reporting: An Examination of the Australian Mining Industry", Paper presented at the *Asia Pacific Interdisciplinary Research in Accounting Conference*, Singapore, 4–6 July.

Chapter 2
Perspectives of Lawyers in Practice on CSR

Patricia Park

> *Lose money for the firm, I will be very understanding; lose a*
> *shred of reputation for the firm, I will be ruthless*
>   Warren Buffett, inaugural address as Chairman of Solomon
> Brothers (1991).

Abstract Although Corporate Social Responsibility (CSR) is developed within a legal framework this area of legal advice is mainly dominated by non-lawyers. This chapter discusses the development of CSR, the international legal imperatives with regard to human rights, particularly in employment, environmental obligations, and the new UK Companies Act, which provides for more specific duties of directors with regard to CSR. These legal imperatives are discussed within the context of the triple bottom line of people, planet, and profit. An argument is put forward for the need for either in-house lawyers or independent law firms to be involved in the decision making process at Board level in particular during discussions on CSR. The chapter also discusses the legal risks with regard to CSR Reports and the need for legal advice across the whole area of CSR. An analysis of a survey of international law firms and CSR is discussed, with examples of the wide range of projects undertaken by the firms and the impact the projects have. The outcome of a survey of regional law firms on the perceptions of lawyers and CSR is also discussed.

2.1 Introduction

Corporate Social Responsibility (CSR), that is an understanding of the social, ethical and environmental impact of the activities of a business, is becoming an increasingly important preoccupation of business managers. This is often thought of primarily as a response to moral or ethical imperatives. However, many of the most significant social obligations are imposed on business as a direct result of the application of environmental and public international law principles. In fact CSR is part of an

P. Park (✉)
Southampton Solent University, Southampton, UK

S.O. Idowu, W.L. Filho (eds.), *Professionals' Perspectives of Corporate Social Responsibility*, DOI 10.1007/978-3-642-02630-0_3,
© Springer-Verlag Berlin Heidelberg 2009

international drive towards transparency and accountability of business activities and a way of monitoring how businesses perform against environmental, ethical and social indices.

Responsibility for advising business on CSR has not automatically fallen to lawyers, however, CSR is developed within a legal framework and no other professional, than the in-house lawyer, has such ready access to Boardrooms and also enjoys legal privilege, resulting in CSR issues being discussed on a frequent basis. Given that a number of companies take on CSR on a voluntary basis by introducing codes of conduct, these can shape the standard of care which is legally expected of a company. Lawyers from independent law firms can help companies manage their legal risks, safeguard corporate reputations, and turn the challenges of globalisation into a competitive advantage, by taking a third party view.

All lawyers, whether in-house or from an independent law firm, can help companies identify risks and understand the implications of a wide range of international guidelines and standards. The law reflects the morals and values of society, and as these values change, so the interpretation of the law changes to mirror that shift. Lawyers, accordingly, take on the responsibility of not only advising on 'black letter law', but of the changing interpretation of legal instruments.

2.2 Background

The concept of CSR is not new, its origins can be traced back to ancient Mesopotamia when King Hammurabi (circa 1700 BC) introduced a code in which builders, innkeepers or farmers were put to death if their negligence caused the deaths of others, or major inconvenience to local citizens. In 1622 disgruntled shareholders in the Dutch East India Company started to issue pamphlets complaining about management secrecy and self-enrichment. (BRASS) Since the nineteenth century there have been shining examples of businesses such as The Rowntree Corporation, investing in model housing, healthcare and education for workers and their families. But the more modern vision of CSR is a more systematic and integrated programme to assess the environmental and social impact of the business and to manage it in a strategic manner.

The globalisation of business has heightened the necessity for companies to improve their awareness of the effects of their increasingly complex and diverse operations in a wide variety of geographical regions, some of them unfamiliar to management until recently. The growth of market liberalisation in many parts of the world has increased the importance of a company's ability to make a satisfactory account of its activities in the field of CSR. Most importantly, the increasing regulatory supervision in both the environmental and particularly the health and safety fields is felt most keenly. Stringent requirements are imposed in relation to money laundering and the financial dealings of suspected terrorists. Many of these requirements impose positive duties upon the business of documentation and information, together with the requirements for monitoring and reporting systems.

2.3 What has the Law to do with CSR?

Business activities are described, facilitated and confined by the law. There is little business activity which is not a legal matter and therefore has a legal impact of some kind. The very fundamental of a sound CSR policy is legal compliance with international minimum standards for environmental and labour protection. The understanding of the nature and impact of legal obligations on the business is a basic precondition to designing a workable CSR policy. Not only in the various jurisdictions in which the company operates but also in respect of public international law, which may impose more onerous standards than do local laws. In almost all areas of CSR, it is the international law obligations that set the agenda for business activities rather than the (frequently lower) local standards.

The understanding of legal concepts, rules and processes are essential to business and CSR, with limited liability, lender responsibility, shareholder rights and responsibilities of the parent company for subsidiaries all central to understanding a company's responsibilities and liabilities.

2.4 International and Governmental Developments in the Field of CSR

The Organisation for Economic Co-Operation and development (OECD) adopted a set of guidelines for multinational companies in September 2000. These guidelines commit businesses to contribute to economic, social and environmental progress with a view to achieving sustainable development and respect for human rights. This very broad statement goes on to identify the areas in which businesses are called upon to engage in capacity-building in the countries in which they operate and not seek exemptions from local environmental, health and safety, labour or tax laws, even when they are offered to them. Nor should they engage in any 'improper involvement' in local political activities. Given that this is a voluntary code there is little enforcement or sanctions against those who do not comply. However, compliance would go to due diligence and may create a defence in any litigation.

There are two main areas in which international law sets down obligations with respect to CSR the first being the major environmental treaties including the Convention on Biological Diversity; the Climate Change Convention and the Kyoto Protocol; and the specific wildlife treaties including the Convention on Migratory Species and the RAMSAR Convention on Wetlands. The second are the principal human rights treaties such as the Universal Declaration on Human Rights; the International Covenants on Economic, Social and Cultural Rights and on Civil and Political Rights (ICESCR and ICCPR); the UN Conventions on Racial and Sexual Discrimination; the UN Convention on the Rights of the Child, and the 'core conventions' of the International Labour Organisation.

Additionally the UN Sub-Commission on the Promotion and Protection of Human Rights has produced a paper *Norms on the responsibilities of trans-national corporations and other business enterprises with regard to human rights* (UN 2002). Essentially the provisions urge trans-national corporations to comply with the obligations already set out in the national and international human rights law, but the following are worthy of note.

- The extent of human rights which are protected by the Norms go beyond the widely ratified texts of the international conventions and include the Optional Protocols to the ICCPR. These provide for individual petition to the Commission and abolition of the death penalty. They also include the controversial 'right to development'.
- Equal opportunity provisions under the Norms refer to 'affirmative action' measures to overcome historic discrimination.
- The obligation to provide a living wage requires consideration of the needs of the worker for adequate living conditions with a view towards progressive improvement.
- Not only is there an obligation to respect national laws but this is extended to certain policy instruments, including the notoriously undefined 'public interest' and development objectives.
- Included is an obligation to ensure that goods and services provided are not used to subvert human rights.
- An ill-defined obligation not to deal in materials which are harmful or potentially harmful to consumers is also included.
- Environmental obligations require observance of the precautionary principle, 'bioethics' and compliance with the 'wider goal of sustainable development'. This again extends beyond the international law provisions, which require the state to observe these principles.
- The Norms require states to set up legal and administrative structures to ensure that the Norms are implemented but the nature and extent of those structures remain within the discretion of the state.
- More precisely, the Norms envisage 'reparation' being made to those whose human rights have been adversely affected by trans-national corporations.

The International Chamber of Commerce claim that companies perceive these Norms, as currently drafted, as essentially offering little assistance to corporations in identifying their human rights obligations other than listing the international conventions. The difficulties that corporations indentify include the need to limit the scope of positive duties imposed on corporate entities, the determination of adequate remuneration and the extensive obligation to pay reparation. They also perceive a problem with the general nature of the Norms which leads to a broad interpretation, which creates a difficulty for companies to find insurance against the potential costs of failing to comply with the Norms. Nevertheless, some of the Norms enjoy a consensus in the international community, such as the prohibition on forced labour and the provisions involving international criminal law.

The Report for the UN produced by Professor John Ruggie (2008) emphasises that it is the States who should promote a corporate culture of respect for human rights and regulate parent companies which are registered within their jurisdictions, even if the activities in question are managed through foreign subsidiaries. Professor Ruggie also believes that there is a governance gap which should be filled, at least in part, in this way. Companies should manage human rights risks with the same management tools used in relation to other risks, such as health and safety, and undertake due diligence in relation to human rights in all aspects of their operations.

The UK Companies Act 2006 introduced many reforms, among which was a new statutory statement on directors' general duties, which came into force on 1st October 2007. One of the duties was the 'Enlightened Shareholder Value'. This broadly replaced the old duty to act in the company's best interest and requires directors to have regard to the longer term and to various 'corporate social responsibility' factors including the interests of employees, suppliers, consumers and the environment.

Although the ultimate course of action is a commercial matter for the client, the role of the lawyer is to seek to interpret the legal issues facing the client in the light of the changing societal circumstances and help the company adopt a principle of 'do no harm'.

2.5 CSR Obligations and Day to Day Business

Accounting for environmental performance in a transparent manner is core to CSR. However, some industries, such as the energy and extraction sectors, have a greater environmental impact and have historically a longer tradition of calibrating environmental performance. Further, some of the principles are somewhat inchoate and are still in the process of development with unintended consequences resulting from unexpected interaction with other legal instruments.

Nevertheless, a number of environmental concerns should be subject to consideration under any CSR policy. These include sustainable development, which enjoys a different interpretation in different jurisdictions, but the adoption of a CSR policy is seen as a positive contribution to achieving sustainable development.

The polluter pays principle is a long established principle of environmental liability that the polluter should make reparation for any harm, or detriment to the environment caused. An increasing number of developed states have established statutory liability for those who cause, when causing requires involvement in an active operation or chain of operations that results in the presence, or continued presence, of the contamination and can be either an act of commission or one of omission, or knowingly permit when knowingly permitting requires both knowledge of the presence of contamination and the power to prevent it being there. The definition is so wide that it can include not only the polluter but also future owners and occupiers once they become aware of the presence of the contamination.

The absence of any similar legislation in the jurisdictions in which the company operates will require consideration as to the potential for such issues to exist, the company obligations to report, and how the company intends to manage the issues arising.

2.5.1 Climate Change Issues

All parties to the UN Framework Convention on Climate Change (UNFCCC) are subject to the general commitments to respond to climate change. The 1997 Kyoto Protocol resulted in the industrial nations committing themselves to legally binding targets and timetables for the reduction of greenhouse gas (GHG) emissions with the use of flexible mechanisms to achieve these reductions. These flexible mechanisms include emissions trading, which involves the allocation of allowances to participants to emit GHG. Those participants are then permitted to trade those allowances between themselves, so that if they emit more than their allowances, they can purchase allowances from other participants in the market. In this way, reductions are achieved in the most cost effective way. A further mechanism is joint implementation which permits the industrialised nations to implement projects that reduce emissions in other industrialised nations. The investing party may then use the reductions effected to help meet its target and a corresponding subtraction is made from the host's emissions target, and clean development mechanisms. This mechanism allows the industrialised nations to implement projects that reduce emissions in less industrialised nations. The resulting emission reduction may then count toward the target of the investing nation. The host nation achieves sustainable development by the Annex I parties to meet their emissions targets.

These international developments are also driving national and supra-national initiatives that impact upon companies. The European Union adopted a Directive in July 2003, which established a mandatory emissions trading scheme (EU ETS). On a national level, the Climate Change Levy has been introduced as a major factor in the UK Government's initiative to reduce greenhouse gases emissions. This tax on businesses' use of energy generated from non-renewable sources is designed to encourage more efficient use of energy. In addition to the legislation outlined companies will also be affected by related policy and legislative developments in product liability and energy areas and the results of calls by stakeholders to improve social and environmental performance.

2.6 Compliance with Environmental Laws

Compliance is one of the fundamental objectives of CSR reporting as if a company does not comply with the legislation, they not only leave themselves open to prosecution by the regulators, but non-compliance is contrary to good governance. Compliance involves the identification and management of risks. Environmental laws encompass a wide range of issues including the condition of water, air and land in addition to the conservation of flora and fauna and the protection of human health. By identifying the relevant environmental laws that apply to a company's activities, the company can then claim due diligence and so avoid committing environmental offences and any corresponding harm to the company's reputation.

A recent line of case law involving foreign claimants seeking to argue that UK based parent companies should be liable for losses and damages suffered by them as a result of the acts and defaults of their foreign subsidiary companies also serves to illustrate that companies need to be equally alive to what is happening overseas in their name.

2.7 International Law of Human Rights

CSR obligations in the international treaties on human rights are often expressed in terms of broad principles. However, they are capable of very precise application and companies can easily be criticised for failing to comply with the expectations that the treaties raise. To choose a selective number of rights will demonstrate some of the issues that may face a modern international company.

2.7.1 The Right to Freedom from Discrimination

The obligation to avoid discrimination includes the prohibition of discrimination on the grounds of *inter alia* race, ethnic origin, nationality, religion, gender, political opinion, and physical disability. Many companies will have policies which address some of these sectors, but it is important that these policies are carried into effect. Especially where the company has subsidiaries and business partners in countries where local laws permits or entrenches discrimination on a gender, ethnic or other basis. Should the corporate social policy merely aim to comply with local law, this will not protect the company from criticism from international groups. In addition, particular problems may arise if the workforce includes indigenous peoples, who are entitled to recognition of their special rights and cultural identity. An ILO convention contains specific rules to be observed in relation to such groups.

2.7.2 The Prohibition of Slavery and Forced Child Labour

Sadly slavery within the meaning of the UN convention does still exist in several parts of the world and companies operating in those regions must have procedures in place to alert them to any indications that their local subsidiaries and their suppliers may be profiting from slave labour. This includes the practice of debt bondage which is not uncommon in some regions and industrial sectors. Debt bondage is a practice whereby the debtor agrees to work off a loan from his/her employer at ruinous rates of interest. Some countries use forced labour in public infrastructure projects or benefit from the labour of prisoners working in inhumane conditions. Migrant workers may be exploited in the labour market of the countries in which they work. Some agricultural societies still operate on a feudal basis. Employing a twelve year-old child in 'light work' may meet local laws, but is unlikely to be considered ethical elsewhere.

The International Labour Organisation (ILO) conventions also discourage the use of corporal punishment on workers. This practice is still used in some parts of the world by employers. Companies need to have procedures in place to detect such practices in their local subsidiaries or business partners.

2.7.3 The Right to Work

A further ILO convention requires the company to guarantee equal pay for equal work. Further the company needs a policy to provide protection against arbitrary or unjust dismissal in addition to one with regard to the even-handed hiring between different groups or communities.

2.7.4 Peaceful Assembly and Participation in Political Life

Although widely recognised in developed countries, trade unions and labour associations are treated much less sympathetically in some other regions. However, the ILO conventions impose strict requirements in this context. In some countries, failure to announce these rights in local languages may also result in a failure to eliminate discrimination. If union activities are unlawful or frowned upon in the country concerned then the major company may need to develop alternative mechanisms for meeting worker concerns.

In December 2003, the Business Leaders Initiative on Human Rights (BLIHR) was established by a leading group of international businesses that seeks to explore ways in which businesses can implement the principles of the Universal Declaration of Human Rights and the United Nations code of practice on business and human rights. BLIHR is a programme to help lead and develop the corporate response to human rights. It is a business led programme with 12 corporate members. The group is chaired by Mary Robinson, President of Realizing Rights: the Ethical Globalisation Initiative, former President of Ireland and former UN Commissioner for Human Rights. The programme will end in 2009.

2.8 Lawyers and CSR

The officially recognised organisation to represent the legal profession in Europe is the Council of the Bars and Law Societies of Europe (CCBE) which was founded in 1960. When the CCBE called for delegates to discuss guidelines for major international law firms and CSR, they were surprised to find that the lawyers were more interested in talking about how lawyers could advise the board-rooms of companies about their CSR responsibilities (Goldsmith, 2005). The delegates wanted the CCBE to help them to open up this developing area of work to lawyers. The general consensus was that this area of legal advice was dominated by non-lawyers. As a result the CCBE drew up 'A Guide for European Lawyers Advising on Corporate Social Responsibility Issues' in 2003. The aim of these guidelines was to explain the two main issues of why companies should be interested in CSR and why lawyers should advise on CSR. The Guidelines illustrate both of these aims by referring to the *Kasky v Nike* case in which Nike was sued under Californian State Law for false advertising.

Kasky claimed that information on Nike's social performance was false and did not reflect the poor working conditions in its foreign factories. Nike defended the claim by addressing the First amendment of the US Constitution on freedom of speech. However, the court of first instance ruled that the company's statements should be classified as 'commercial speech' and thus were subject to the stricter standard of truth required by advertising law. Although the US Supreme Court agreed to hear the case, they refused to decide it on procedural grounds. However, the case itself illustrates that companies' statements can be challenged for misrepresentation, and so the need for a corporate lawyer to be involved in CSR.

The CBBE Guidelines discuss in detail the need for each firm to draw up a code of practice which describes how sustainable development for the company is put into operation by the use of the triple bottom line, which is popularly described by the three Ps; 'People, Planet, Profit.' In other words, how the company will identify sustainable solutions for their relationship with human beings, which is in relationship with employees, suppliers, customers, local communities and other stakeholders; with the external environment, including bio-diversity and animal welfare; and with the economy, including the economy of the community. The Guidelines identify how the company code should be applied at every level of the organisation, be based on the UN Norms, be included in training for local management, workers and communities on implementation, have emphasis on gradual improvements to standards, and to the code itself. It should also include ongoing verification and enable benchmarking. As the code of conduct can take the form of a manual governing the day to day business of the company, it is the natural role of the lawyer to be involved in the drafting of such documents.

2.8.1 In-House Lawyers

Following the *Nike* case, in legal terms then, voluntary reporting on CSR issues entails both benefits and risks. As such reporting is relatively new, and mainly restricted to major international companies, the data is not sufficient to suggest that CSR reporting may increase the risk of litigation against a company, but what the *Nike* case suggests is that it may attract the attention of certain campaigning groups who will be keen to highlight any inaccuracies (Zerk, 2004). When Zerk reviewed a number of CSR reports it becomes apparent that a high proportion of them are more concerned with corporate image than giving actual information. Having identified that, some do report upon how the parent company involves itself in managing the social and environmental performance of its subsidiaries and also its supply chain.

This in itself could lead to legal liability without the careful intervention of the in-house lawyer. The courts, however, will give greater significance to the internal 'code of practice' when considering issues of due diligence and liability.

2.8.2 A Wider Role for In-House Lawyers

In a survey conducted by the UK law firm of CMS Cameron McKenna (Financial Times, 2005) one third of senior executives considered that although the chief executive has overall responsibility for CSR, it is the in-house lawyer who comes second, with over half of the respondents saying that it was the in house-lawyer who should in fact take the lead. However, the report also identified that in some corporations the legal departments can be very risk-averse and appear to restrict the company's efforts to address the social and environmental impacts of their activities (Murray, 2005). This is based on the perception that CSR aspirational principles may create binding legal obligations. This narrow interpretation is disappointing and does not take into account the broader risks of scrutiny of the company's activities by legislators and local communities including any pressure groups, who already use the existing legislation to bring legal actions. This risk averse approach can result in companies failing to identify problems that are beyond the immediate remit of legal compliance. The changing values of society lead to increasing demands for new regulations with regard to accountability for corporate actions, and the line between pure law and societal expectations are becoming a 'grey area', which the courts are left to interpret.

However, in the Cameron McKenna report other in-house lawyers claim that they are already helping companies take a broader approach to managing social and environmental risks by using their legal training and professional ethical code when they are operating as part of the management team. They claim that it is at board level that the in-house lawyer can make the greatest contribution as they have access to senior executives within a confidential environment. This also creates a responsibility to bring to the attention of the board and senior management all the situations that may create a risk, consider what might happen, and decide on how to deal with it before it happens.

2.8.3 Independent Law Firms

Independent law firms have historically taken on work on a *pro bono* basis. However, law firms are becoming more deeply involved in the communities in which they operate, with staff volunteering their time in areas beyond the purely legal Murray (2007). Accordingly, some legal firms have created dedicated teams and departments and mainstreamed such initiatives into the management of the firm. Many law firms consider that their offering of legal services *pro bono* to individuals, non-profit and charities, lies at the heart of their CSR strategies. Unsurprisingly, a key point for the legal profession is whether or not these *pro bono* hours can be included in individual lawyer's billable hours, and in one major international law firm they allow fee-earning lawyers to count 25 hours of *pro bono* work as part of their chargeable hours. Another major international law firm, Clifford Chance, is also working with one of its major clients via their *pro bono* work to develop an easy-to-use multi-jurisdictional legal template which will ultimately assist institutions world-wide to gain access to large-scale commercial funding. This approach goes far beyond the traditional *pro bono* work and demonstrates how major law firms are developing the concept of CSR as far as their own firms are concerned. According to Murray (2007) some law firms are also looking within their own organisations to consider the sustainability of their operations by diversifying their workforce, which is an area where law firms have been notoriously tardy.

2.8.4 Rankings of Major Law Firms and CSR

In July 2007 the Financial Times newspaper published a table of the rankings of major law firms with regard to their CSR. Four of the well-know firms stood out for their innovative approach to CSR. The project to develop a new legal product, in conjunction with Citigroup, which standardised legal documentation for accessing large-scale commercial funding put Clifford Chance at the top of the list with the model agreement having been translated into French, Spanish and Russian and will enable many transactions to happen without legal input. It is also estimated that the model agreement will be used as a vehicle for loans of more than $200 m in 30 countries. Second in the rankings came DLA Piper for their synchronised launch in a number of countries of an integrated international CSR strategy. This was one of the first firms to pioneer a major global CSR campaign at one time and involved the French Red Cross and Danish refugee efforts in Georgia. DLA Piper claims that the effect of the campaign has been to change the mind-set of their lawyers. The third law firm to stand-out was Linklaters who spearheaded the Shoreditch Project. This was collaboration between Linklaters, Deutsche Bank and UBS to regenerate local projects in conjunction with East London Business Alliance. This partnership stood out for using the different resources of the three large commercial firms, lawyers and bankers, combined with an NGO to focus on the local area. It was a grass-roots campaign that ensured sustainability. It has involved over 2,000 employees and Linklaters is the first law firm to collaborate in this way. The fourth law firm which stood-out was Weil Gotshal & Manges who introduced a goal in 2006 that every lawyer should perform 50 *pro bono* hours a year. Every new lawyer is encouraged to take on a *pro bono* project in their first 2 years and the total *pro bono* hours annually equals the total billing hours of a mid-sized law firm.

A further three law firms in the survey were Highly Commended. These included DLA Piper again who received an accolade for two of its projects which covered a partnership with the Prince's Trust to provide six-week apprenticeships to introduce young people to the construction industry through the many construction industry clients of the firm. The second project involved a strategy to reduce the firm's environmental impact worldwide. This was a comprehensive programme to make all of

its 62 worldwide offices compliant with ISO 14001. The other two law firms who
were Highly Commended were Lovells and Simmons & Simmons. The Lovells
project was an integrated CSR approach which involved a strong commitment to
CSR that offered a suite of activities. It was innovative in its work with young
Muslims and its global integrated *pro bono* programme. Simmons & Simmons provides free assistance to children in detention in Pakistan, who are held in appalling
conditions. They represent at least 92% of children in Lahore's juvenile detention
facility. The firm supported the initiative of a single lawyer and has made a real
impact in Pakistan's legal approach to the detention of children by also training
local lawyers.

The third category in the rankings was that of Commended and included a further
six top international law firms. These included Freshfields Bruckhause Deringer,
Allen & Overy, Uria Menéndez, Addleshaw Goddard, Authur Cox and Slaughter
and May. These projects have ranged from programmes to give homeless people
work experience to teaching copyright law to film students and employment law to
prisoners. They also include the more traditional *pro bono* work and formulating
CSR policies for more general use.

2.8.5 Regional Survey

To complement the international survey published by Financial Times.com, a survey
of the perceptions of local regional law firms was carried out by the author. This was
a qualitative survey of a selection of Partners who specialised in advising corporate
clients, and the results were markedly different from those found in the Financial
Times survey. The results reflected more those opinions of the European lawyers
when they were contacted by the Council of the Bars and Law Societies of the
European Union (CCBE). Their interest was less concerning the way the law firm
itself was involved with CSR, but more to do with the advice given by the lawyers
to their corporate clients on CSR. Indeed not all of the regional firms identified that
they had a CSR policy for their own firm, but all of the corporate lawyers gave
advice on CSR to their clients to a greater or lesser degree. The lawyers did not
always identify their advice specifically as CSR but more along the lines that it was
'the right thing to do' (Corporate Partner in Southampton Law firm. 2008).

A number of the regional law firms had a specific CSR policy for the firm even
though it was sometimes couched in employment and environmental terms. In fact
some were very specific as to their employment credentials with respect to diver-
sification and flexi-time. Others concentrated more on their environmental issues
particularly concerning recycling and energy efficiency. Few mentioned *pro bono*
work, but a number of the regional law firms do support activities in the local
community by giving time and some financial support to charities and non-profit
organisations. The Law Society of England and Wales seems somewhat ambiguous in its views on CSR and believes that lawyers are sufficiently bound by already
existing codes of practice.

When asked about advising corporate clients on their CSR the regional lawyers felt very much more on home ground. Most considered that they would bring up issues of CSR in the context of Board decisions and particularly when discussing the directors duties and their impact on the client company. However, some felt that not all corporate clients would welcome such an intervention and would not take any notice unless told specifically that any activity was unlawful. 'It is a delicate line which cannot be crossed over. If the client thinks it is my personal view and they are not there yet, then the financial issues will prevail.' However, most of those interviewed believed that their clients would take advice on specific issues which involved CSR if the lawyer approached the issues in the right way. When asked their opinions on the 2003 CCBE Guidelines, some, but not all, were aware of them and preferred to refer to the Law Society for England and Wales. All, however, considered that CSR was a growing area of advice that corporate lawyers are aware of. When asked if CSR extended the liability of corporations some had not considered the issue while others thought that it would only have an effect in extreme cases. However, all said that they would follow the case law from the English courts with interest and respond accordingly.

2.9 Voluntary or Compulsory?

There is currently much discussion on whether CSR should remain a voluntary principle or should aspects of CSR be legislated for on a mandatory basis? The view of the author is that much of the accepted CSR agenda is already a requirement under both international (as referred to above) and some national legislation. While the European Union believes in a voluntary approach to CSR, France has enacted legislation requiring all large companies to produce social reports on an annual basis. New legislation in both the USA (Sarbanes Oxley Act) and in the UK (Companies Act, 2006) imposes new duties upon Directors to ensure that elements of the CSR agenda are complied with.

So what are the benefits of a mandatory system? Firstly it would help to avoid excesses of the exploitation of labour, bribery, and corruption; companies would know what is expected of them and would produce a level playing field. Many aspects of CSR behaviour are in fact good for business inasmuch as it enhances reputation and may make it easier to locate in new communities. Non-compliant companies would be penalised for their lower standards and the wider community would benefit as companies reach out to address some of the key issues in underdeveloped countries.

The other side of the argument put forward by the International Chamber of Commerce on a number of occasions is that the additional bureaucracy and therefore costs of compliance would rise above those required for continued profitability and sustainability of the company.

From a personal point of view, clearly, one is not arguing for a 'no legislation stance'; because much legislation already exists, in particular concerning corporate governance. If there was legislation covering the full extent of CSR business could grind to a halt simply by attempting to be in compliance with legislation on every statute book. The most appropriate position would be sufficient legislation to create a level playing field which must apply to all corporations wherever they may be located. The major challenge here would be how to enforce such international legislation.

2.10 Conclusions

The understanding of the social, ethical and environmental impact of the activities of a business is becoming an increasingly important preoccupation of business managers. However, many of the most significant obligations are imposed on business as a direct result of the application of environmental and public international law principles. In fact CSR is part of an international drive towards transparency and accountability of business activities and a way of monitoring how businesses perform against environmental, ethical and social indices. Not only international law and principles but more specifically national legislation identifies the fact that the narrow path of delivering short term shareholder value has proved to be a short sighted policy. The new UK Companies Act 2006 which came into force in 2008 codifies the duties of the company director and obliges him/her to 'take account in good faith of all the material factors that it is practicable in the circumstances to identify'. Directors will need to consider both long term as well as the short term consequences of their actions in addition to foster the business relationships with its employees, suppliers and customers and have regard to the impact of the company's activities on both communities and the environment. However, this area of legal advice is dominated by non-lawyers. As CSR is developed within a legal framework and no other professional, than the in-house lawyer, has such ready access to Boardrooms and also enjoys legal privilege, who better to advice directors and senior management on these issues than lawyers along with other members of the managerial team.

The CCBE have recognised that CSR should be part of the lawyers' everyday activities and have issued guidelines for European lawyers in which they refer to the *Nike* case. The case identifies that CSR Reports can carry legal risks as well as benefits. The immediate risks can be dealt with through careful management of the information gathering and reporting process but the challenge will be to draft an understandable report without resorting to 'legal jargon' Zerk (2004). In the longer term CSR Reports help to build a new set of values and entrench the idea that parent companies have responsibility for the impacts of their subsidiaries, suppliers and contractors.

Independent law firms are beginning to embrace CSR both within their own firms and as a duty to advise their corporate clients. This is more obvious in the major international law firms but the local regional law firms will not be far behind, in particular if the English courts interpret the new Companies Act broadly.

References

Books

Goldsmith. (2005), Lawyers responsibility for advising on corporate social responsibility. In Mullerat, R. (Ed.), *Corporate Social Responsibility: The Corporate Governance of the 21st Century*, International Bar Association.
Odeleye, I. (2005), Corporate social responsibility and the in-house counsel. In Mullerat, R. (Ed.), *Corporate Social Responsibility: The Corporate Governance of the 21st Century*, International Bar Association.

Articles

Murray, S. (2005), A wider role for in-house lawyers. Financial Times, July 13th & 14th 2005.
Murray, S. (2007), Private practice: corporate social responsibility. Financial Times, July 6th 2007.
Ruckin, C. (2008), CSR winning more lawyer converts. *Legal Week*, Vol. 10, No. 4, 7.
Zerk, J. (Autumn 2004), Legal aspects of CSR Reporting: Panacea, Polyfilla or Pandora's Box? *New Academy Review,* Vol. 3, No. 3, pp 17–33.

Electronic Sources

CCBE, Corporate Social Responsibility and the Role of the Legal Profession. September 2003. www.ccbe.org
Freshfields Bruckhaus Deringer, Community and pro bono legal advice. www.freshfields.com/csr/community
International Unit. Corporate Social Responsibility A view from the Law Society, September 2002. www.lawsociety.org.uk/
Financial Times FT.com, July 13th 2005 www.ft.com/coms/s/4a7c84cc-0b4c-11dd-8ccf-0000779fd2ac.dwp_uuid=ebe33f
Modernising Company Law – draft clauses, vol II- Schedule II, 2 (b), (p 112). www.icaew.com/index.cfm/route/145195/icaew_ga/en/Technical_amp_Busines
Ruckin, C. CSR Winning More Lawyer Converts. www.legalweek.com/Navigation/24/Articles/1090741/Online+CSR+wi
Ruggie, J. Business and Human Rights: Mapping International Standards of Responsibility and Accountability for Corporate Acts. Report A/HRC/4/035. www.business-humanrights.org/Documents/RuggieHRC2007
The History of Corporate Social Responsibility and Sustainability, www.brass.cardiff.ac.uk

Legislation

Companies Act 2006 section 172.
UN Doc. E/CN. 4/Sub.2/2002/XX/Add.1 2002.
Modernising Company Law – draft clauses, vol II- Schedule II, 2 (b), (p 112).

Chapter 3
Corporate Social Responsibility from the Perspective of Corporate Secretaries

Samuel O. Idowu

> *Success is a ladder that cannot be climbed with your hands in your pockets*
> American proverb
>
> *Those that climb the tree deserve to pick the fruit*
> Aristotle

Abstract Corporate secretaries make a considerable contribution to corporate social responsibility (CSR) processes by the nature of the positions and responsibilities they hold in organisations. They act as a servant or full member of the board of directors, the body that formulates corporate strategies; which are subsequently executed by executive directors. When corporate secretaries become full members of the board, they pass on their duties as the secretary to someone else and take on the role of governance in directorship capacity.

The field of CSR has impacted on all professions that aspire to make a positive contribution to societies. For this reason, members of the chartered secretaries' professional body and those other chartered bodies in the UK who statutorily can become corporate secretaries have had to absorb all the challenges and opportunities that the field of CSR has thrown at them, albeit in collaboration with their other senior executive colleagues in organisations. This chapter seeks to analyse how corporate secretaries have contributed and continue to contribute to recent developments in the field of CSR. The chapter argues that modern stakeholders look on corporate entities to meet all their economic, social, ethical, legal and philanthropic responsibilities whilst remaining virtuous, Friedman (1962, 1970), Elkington (1997) and Carroll and Buchholtz (2003) even though meeting these responsibilities may at first sight appear contradictory and impossible, de Wit and Meyer (2004). Wood (1991) argues that business and society are interwoven rather than distinct entities. If this is so, then it is relevant to ask how today's professionals including corporate secretaries are coping with the task of meeting their CSR requirements to society.

S.O. Idowu (✉)
London Metropolitan University Business School, London, UK

S.O. Idowu, W.L. Filho (eds.), *Professionals' Perspectives of Corporate Social Responsibility*, DOI 10.1007/978-3-642-02630-0_4,
© Springer-Verlag Berlin Heidelberg 2009

There are numerous benefits that can emanate from following a good corporate citizenship strategy or being involved in several *pro bono publico* activities by an entity according to Jones et al. (2006), as this action is one of the variables that determine whether an entity survives and prospers or declines and fails in modern markets.

3.1 Introduction

During the last few decades an extensive coverage of issues relating to the field of corporate social responsibility (CSR), Sustainability (S), Sustainable Development (SD) and Corporate Governance (CG) has emerged in several countries around the globe both in literature and the media. There is similarly a significant increase in the number of advocates and supporters of the field of CSR, which has understandably led to a corresponding increase in corporate activities in the field. There is evidence to support these claims; scholars and practitioners in the field are suggesting that all this is happening. Vogel (2005) found 30,000 sites for CSR on Google, more than 15 million pages on the World Wide Web; addressing different dimensions of CSR including more than 100,000 corporate websites. Broomhill (2007) discovers 12,500 citations of CSR on Google Scholar, 12,900,000 phrases on CSR on internet Google and 97,800 of the same on Australian websites. Kotler and Lee (2005) from a survey of the Global Fortune Top 250 companies note a continued increase in the number of American companies reporting on corporate responsibility. The United Nations has organised several Climate Change Conferences – Rio (1992), Kyoto (1997), Johannesburg (2002), Bali (2007), Copenhagen (2009). Governments around the world are encouraging corporate entities operating within their jurisdictions to behave responsibly in ameliorating the adverse impacts of their operations on society, for example, to set CO_2 emissions reduction targets and meet them. Idowu (2008b) notes that 81% of FTSE100 companies are now actively reporting on their CSR activities either on their corporate websites and/or using paper copy of standalone annual CSR reports and 5% of these companies have their CSR activities reported on by related organisations. Grant Thornton (2007) in their annual corporate governance review argues that 94% of FTSE 350 firms included a reference to CSR in their annual reports; 84% of these firms claim to have a dedicated process in place for monitoring CSR activity, 40% of FTSE 100 now issue stand alone CSR reports and some of these companies are seeking to authenticate the validity of the information provided in their CSR reports by reference to some form of external verification of these reports by specialists in the field. All indications are suggesting that the growth in socially responsible activities will not abate but will continue to expand as the effects of the past corporate actions of years back unfold. These effects include global warming and climate change, the scarcity in some of man's natural resources including for example the world's petroleum reserves which we are constantly being reminded has between 40 and50 years from depletion Deming (2003), Schoen (2004) and the urge to find solutions to some of the social and environmental problems becomes more exigent in both the industrialised and emerging economies of the world.

Like all other professionals that work in corporate organizations, corporate secretaries are affected by all the happenings in the field of CSR. They have not been left unaffected by those issues relating to CSR which have been identified above. Whilst this chapter intends to focus its attention on corporate secretaries' contributions to the field of CSR, corporate social responsibility will be at its centre.

This chapter is structured as follows. It reviews the literature briefly on modern CSR, discusses the statutory duties of corporate secretary in the UK as specified in the Companies Act 2006 and a brief mention of the Corporations Act 2001; Australia, explores the role of *corporate governance* in the quest by corporate entities to be perceived as being socially responsible, takes a practical look at the involvements of corporate secretaries in the process of inculcating CSR in to corporate strategies as demonstrated in the findings of a UK study on the extent to which corporate secretaries are involved in the attempt to absorb CSR into their professional activities and provides a concluding remark to the chapter.

3.2 Literature Review

Since Bowen (1953) posited that business owes a responsibility to society and should pursue strategies which are desirable in meeting societal objectives and values and the ensuing disagreements over this issue between those scholars who are sympathetic to Bowen's idea – those who could be described as members *Bowen's camp* and the *other camp* notably Levitt (1958) and Friedman (1962), which dragged on until the 1980s and Wallich and McGowan's (1970) reconciliatory article. It is now no longer a question of whether CSR is a desirable activity or not – scholars such as Sethi (1975), Carroll (1979), Freeman (1984), governments' activities, e.g. the Commission of the European Communities (2002), international organisations, and the increased corporate activities in CSR since the 1990s have pragmatically answered the question. It must be noted however that there is still a very small minority of scholars who remain unconvinced about the need for CSR even though Jones et al. (2006) suggest that society stands to derive at least thirteen potential benefits from the actions of each socially responsible corporate entity. Lippeke (1996) for example argues that, like citizens; corporations pay their fair share of taxes to cover the cost of using these social resources and as such they should not be burdened with additional social responsibilities over and above those of other taxpayers. Similarly, Henderson (2001a) derides CSR as nothing more than 'global Salvationism' that will do nothing but lead to undesirable regulation of business, raising costs and diminishing both economic freedom and profits. Henderson (2001b) also argues that the apparent increase in commitments to CSR is deeply flawed since this action will result in a reduction in welfare and market economy being undermined. There are also others such as Lantos (2001) who still concur with Friedman (1962, 1970), even as recently as 2001 that philanthropic CSR is not a legitimate role of business but at the same time argue that strategic CSR is good for business and society. Despite these contradictory arguments, scholars have made some remarkable progress with regard to whether or not CSR is a legitimate role of business, see for example; Laine (2005), Idowu and Papasolomou (2007), Redmond et al. (2008). Supporters of CSR are in fact suggesting that corporations must demonstrate exceptionally high standards of responsibility in all their dealings with their stakeholders; and anything short of this will be unacceptable, Miller and Ahrens (1993).

McManus (2003) recites in the Social Market Foundation report – *Race to the top* the three broad types of relationship with CSR. The first type; the report refers to as *CSR Sceptics* – those who suggest that CSR is simply about complying with the law and making appropriate donations, the second; the report calls *CSR Utopians* – these hold the view that companies have an a priori duty to stakeholders rather than their shareholders and this moral duty ranks in priority to the one they owe their shareholders and the third type; which the report refers to as *CSR Realists* – these hold the view that what a company does in the course of its normal business should have a positive or at least neutral impact on the people and places it affects. It would appear from the advancements that CSR has made over the last twenty or so years that; the majority belongs to the third category – the *Realists* those who believe that corporate entities should ensure that the impact of their activities should affect all their stakeholders and the environment positively regardless of whether these stakeholders are near or in some remote part of the globe. The notion that corporate entities should affect all their stakeholders positively has been noted in studies McWilliams and Siegel (2001) and Idowu (2008a).

There are several watchdog organisations often referred to as non-governmental organisations (NGOs), which have diverse interests to protect, for example Green Peace, Friends of the Earth, the World Wildlife Fund, Amnesty International and others. These NGOs have been established in order to influence corporate entities to behave responsibly. Modern corporate entities are now aware that there are two classes of stakeholders they must recognise when formulating their corporate strategies, primary and secondary stakeholders, Clarkson (1995), Metcalfe (1998) and both classes are affected either directly or indirectly by the actions of corporate entities. Governments, Stock Exchanges, Standards Setters and Professional bodies around the world are also encouraging good governance either directly or indirectly to prevent corporate fraud and scandals and to ensure that companies engage in ethically acceptable behaviours, for example by investing only in environmentally friendly plant and machinery Idowu and Papasolomou (2007). Stakeholders can also be classified into Internal and External stakeholders.

Following some high profile corporate scandals and perhaps failures caused by the irresponsible actions of corporate senior managers, for example the Mirror Group (1991) and, the Bank of Credit and Commerce International (1991) some preventive actions have been put in place in the UK. The Cadbury Committee's – The Code of Best Practice (the Code), December 1991 was an attempt to establish good governance by UK listed companies. The Code recommends that the boards of all UK corporations whose shares are publicly traded should include at least three Non Executive Directors (NEDs) and the positions of the Chairman of the board and Chief Executive Officer (CEO) should not be held by a single individual. Following the publication of the Code, Dahya et al. (2002) note that the CEO turnover increased, the relationship between turnover and performance was strengthened and there was an increase in the sensitivity of turnover to performance amongst firms that adopted the Code.

Similarly, in the United States of America following a number of high profile corporate accounting scandals for example Enron (2001), Tyco (2002) and WorldCom (2002) the Sarbanes-Oxley Act 2002 (the Act) or the Public Accounting Reform and Investor Protection Act; popularly known as the SOX law was passed. The Act was enacted in order to protect shareholders and the general public from fraudulent accounting errors and practices in publicly owned companies. The Act established a Public Company Accounting Oversight Board (PCAOB) with which all public companies must now be registered. Despite some misgivings about the thoroughness of the Act, Perino (2002) argues that the increase in resources and enforcement authority accorded the Securities and Exchange Commission (SEC) would significantly increase the detection of securities fraud, in other words, the chances that corporate executives and others who would otherwise set out to engage in fraudulent acts would be discouraged from committing securities and other frauds against investors are high. Ribstern (2002) also argues that the US Congress has enacted the Act with the main objective of restoring confidence in the securities markets and improving the accuracy and reliability of accounting information reported to investors. All these are certainly socially responsible intentions which can only benefit society.

3.3 Companies Act and the Secretary

That a public limited company (Plc) should employ a secretary is a statutory requirement in the United Kingdom and its associated countries. In this section, we will briefly look at the relevant sections in the latest UK's Companies Act (CA) 2006 that deal with the position of secretary. The new Act received Royal Assent in November 2006 and its provisions must be implemented by October 2009. The Corporation Act 2001 in Australia will also be looked at briefly in order to see the similarities between the statutory requirement for quoted companies to have in post this corporate officer.

The requirement as to whether or not a company needs to employ a secretary is contained in Part 12 CA 2006 Sections 270–280. The Act describes a secretary as 'an officer of the company; at the centre of its decision making process, who shares legal responsibilities of running its day to day activities with the directors for certain specified tasks as contained in the CA 2006'.

The Act specifically states that a private limited company is not required to have a secretary in post; as such any communication that is required to be served on or given or sent to the secretary, may be served on, given or sent to the company itself. That communication will be deemed to have been properly served. Similarly, any act which the law requires or authorizes a secretary to perform may be performed by a director or anyone authorized generally or specifically by the director.

Section 271 states clearly that a Plc must have a secretary in post. Section 273 states that the secretary must have the required knowledge and experience to discharge the functions of a secretary and must be a member of one or more listed professional bodies specified in Section 273 sub-sections 3a–3 g as listed below:

(a) The Institute of Chartered Accountants in England & Wales
(b) The Institute of Chartered Accountants of Scotland
(c) The Association of Chartered Certified Accountants
(d) The Institute of Chartered Accountants in Ireland
(e) The Institute of Chartered Secretaries and Administrators
(f) The Chartered Institute of Management Accountants
(g) The Chartered Institute of Public Finance and Accountancy

3.3.1 Some Standard Duties of a Corporate Secretary Required by the CA 2006

The following are a few of the statutory duties of a corporate secretary, failure to meet these duties as and when specified by the Act could result in serious consequences. The secretary:

- Files Annual Returns to Companies House
- Establishes and maintains the Registered Office
- Maintains the Company's Statutory Books and Records
- Secures the Legal Documents of the company
- Informs the Registrar of Companies using the appropriate forms; any significant changes in the company's structures or management
- Arranges a board meeting if any director asks for one
- Arranges the Annual General Meeting (AGM) if the company is a publicly listed one (Plc)
- Has in addition to the above some administrative duties which are not necessarily statutory but important for the company to run smoothly and effectively

3.3.2 Corporate Secretary and Corporations Act (2001) in Australia

In Australia, understandably the requirement for a company to have a secretary in post is similar to that of the UK and it is also a statutory requirement in that country. Part 2D.4 of the Corporations Act 2001, Section 204A subsection 1 states clearly that 'a proprietary company is not required to have a secretary' but subsection 2 says that a public company must have at least 1 secretary; at least 1 of them must ordinarily reside in Australia.

Other issues relating to the office of the secretary are made explicit in sections 204C–204G.

Part 2D.5 of the Act deals with – Public information about directors and secretaries. Issues relating to this aspect are enumerated in detail in Sections 205A–205G.

3.4 CSR and Corporate Governance (CG)

3.4.1 Professional Institutions

In the UK, the Institute of Chartered Secretaries & Administrators (ICSA) is the professional body which assesses and certifies the competences of prospective chartered secretaries with a series of examinations and post qualification (CPD) programmes. The ICSA is the only body amongst the seven chartered bodies specified Section 273 subsection 3a–3 g CA 2006 which trains its members solely to become corporate secretaries, having said this; it must be noted that qualified members of the ICSA do end up in other senior executive positions in organizations which are not necessarily in company secretariat. There are two grades of membership of the Institute – Associate membership [a member becomes an Associate (having completed the Institute's examinations) after serving a period of time in their chosen industry] and Fellow membership (an Associate becomes a Fellow after a period of time in a senior management position in their chosen industry). The Institute represents the profession with all external bodies including governments and international organisations. Its American equivalent is the Society of Corporate Secretaries and Governance Professionals (SCSGP). There are also similar bodies in some other countries of the world for example the Chartered Secretaries, Australia, Canada, Hong Kong, India, Malaysia, New Zealand, Nigeria, Singapore, South Africa and Zimbabwe. These bodies are all affiliates of the ICSA, UK or had been related to it at some point in the past.

The ICSA in the UK, states that 'it promotes best practice in corporate governance, liaising with governments and regulatory bodies worldwide'. The SCSGP states that it recognises that 'the corporate secretary is a senior corporate officer who is expected to hold wide ranging responsibilities and is often the confidant and counsellor to the Chief Executive Officer and other members of senior management, especially on corporate governance affairs'. The Institute of Chartered Secretaries & Administrators in both the UK and in some of its other former colonies noted earlier for instance Australia, Canada, New Zealand and others consider that governance is one of the main duties of corporate secretaries. In fact, the Chartered Secretary Australia (CSA) describes its members as *Governance Professionals*. The CSA on their website describes itself as:

> The peak professional body committed to the promotion and advancement of effective governance and administration of organizations in the private and public sectors, CSA has developed its structure and reporting mechanisms to promote these ideals and principles.

Corporate governance therefore ranks highly in the roles corporate secretaries perform in organisations. Corporate social responsibility is part of governance, since the decision to embark on socially responsible actions whether this relates to strategic, altruistic, ethical and philanthropic Lantos (2001) or some other forms of CSR will start at the board level and works its way down the corporate ladder.

Because issues relating to CSR now rank highly on corporate agendas in the UK, several large UK companies now have a member of the Board in charge of CSR; in other words there are now CSR Directors. The UK Labour governments since March 2000 have had in post several Members of Parliament at different times that have held the position of CSR Ministers Idowu (2008b). It must be noted that a UK CSR minister does not spend 100% of their time on CSR duties; CSR issues are only part of what the minister does. For example, the current CSR Minister, Honourable Ian Pearson, MP who is a Junior Minister in the Department of Business, Enterprise and Regulatory Reform (BERR) (responsible to the Secretary of State for Business, Enterprise and Regulatory Reform, Lord Mandelson – current post holder) is responsible for seven ministerial activities including CSR and Sustainable Development.

As a result of the importance attached to the field of governance by professional bodies representing chartered secretaries around the world, corporate governance will be looked at in general terms in order to understand how the concept and the field of CSR are linked.

3.4.2 The Theory of Corporate Governance

This section begins with the theory of corporate governance (CG). A secretary is an executive officer of a corporate entity but act as a 'servant' of those involved in governance and he/she is therefore expected to be *governance professional*. A chapter on the secretary's contributions to CSR therefore requires an in-depth understanding of governance.

A search of the literature has revealed that because of the large number of areas covered by CG, it has been variously defined by scholars, committees and some international organisations that either work in the area or are affected by what it entails, perhaps to reflect their diverse interests in the field. A few of these definitions which we believe are relevant to the field of CSR are described in Table 3.1 below with their sources. This should enable readers to decipher how CG has been variously defined and perhaps make a better understanding it.

The above definitions demonstrate clearly that there is still no standard definition of CG albeit these definitions suggest that the field seeks to ensure that corporate entities are properly directed and controlled by those at the helm of their activities for the benefits of their stakeholders. Corporate scandals in several advanced nations around the world (for instance in the UK and USA noted above) which have resulted in financial and other losses by some sectors of stakeholder groups; notably investors, employees, suppliers, lenders and customers appear to have catalysed the need for governments', financial institutions' and professional bodies' actions in the field.

Table 3.1 Definitions of corporate governance by scholars and organisations

Author	Definition
Cadbury Report (1992)	The system by which companies are directed and controlled for the benefits of shareholders.
Fligstein and Freeland (1995)	The social organisation of firms and their relation to their environments including their relations to states.
Monks and Minow (1995)	Corporate governance is the relationship among various participants (Chief Executive Officer, Management, Shareholders, Employees) in determining the direction and performance of corporations.
Shleifer and Vishny (1997)	Corporate governance deals with the ways in which suppliers of finance to corporations assure themselves of getting a return on their investment.
Organisation for Economic Cooperation and Development (OECD) 1999	Corporate governance is the system by which business corporations are directed and controlled. The corporate governance structure specifies the distribution of rights and responsibilities among different participants in the corporation, such as, the board, managers, shareholders and other stakeholders, and spells out the rules and procedures for making decisions on corporate affairs. By doing this, it also provides the structure through which the company objectives are set, and the means of attaining those objectives and monitoring performance (April 1999).
World Bank (2000)	Corporate governance is concerned with holding the balance between economic and social goals and between individual and communal goals. The corporate governance framework is there to encourage the efficient use of resources and equally to require accountability for the stewardship of those resources. The aim is to align as nearly as possible the interests of individuals, corporations and society.
International Federation of Accountants (IFAC) (2001)	Corporate governance is the processes by which organisations are directed, controlled, and held to account. It is concerned with structures and processes for decision making, accountability, control and behaviour at the top of organizations.
Chartered Secretaries, Australia (CSA)	Governance encompasses the system by which an organization is controlled and operates, and the mechanisms by which it, and its people, are held to account. Ethics, risk management, compliance and administration are all elements of governance.

According to Katsoulakos and Katsoulacos (2007), 'corporate governance reflects the way companies address legal responsibilities and therefore provides the foundations upon which CSR and corporate sustainability practices can be built in order to enhance responsible business operations'. For any entity to be sustainable, it is now very important that its systems of government and control must be such that encourage transparency, reduce the adverse impact of its operations on both its stakeholders and the environment and be accountable to them and in addition; avoid strategies which may result in ethical compromises. A good number of the companies which were involved in some high profile corporate scandals noted earlier which led to preventive actions such as the Cadbury Committee 1992 and the Code of Best Practice (and others for example; the Greenbury Report 1995, the Hampel

Report 1998, the Turnbull Report 1999 and the Hicks Report 2001 that followed it) in the UK and the SOX law in the US failed to inculcate these principles in to their systems of governance. The governments of both countries were attempting to criminalize irresponsible behaviours on the part of executives who run the affairs of corporate entities.

Halal (2000) in the – *Evolution of corporate governance* posits that three models of corporate governance have evolved between 1900 and present date. Halal (2000) argues that CG originally evolved from the traditional 'profit-centred model (PCM)' during a period which he called the 'industrial age – 1900–1950', it metamorphosed into another model he called the 'social responsibility model (SRM)' during the 'Neo-industrial age – 1950–1980' and now the model is moving towards what Halal (2000) refers to as collaborative working relations phase – the 'corporate community model (CCM)' – the information age – 1980–date.

Let us now look at each of the three models as hypothesised by Halal (2000) with their accompanying diagrams in order to fully understand the relationship between corporate governance and society as seen by Halal (2000).

3.4.2.1 The Profit Centred Model (PCM)

Halal (2000), argues that the profit centred model (PCM) was prevalent over a fifty year period – 1900–1950 when those at the helm of the governance of corporate entities – that is; managers were expected only to focus on maximising the returns due to the providers of capital – shareholders with little or no regard for the adverse impact of the entities' actions on other stakeholders, ironically whilst working in collaboration with some of these stakeholders as depicted in Fig. 3.1 in order to achieve this single objective of profit maximisation. The interests of these other stakeholders were subordinated to that of the shareholders; in fact the law in some parts of the world assisted this to happen. Lee (2008) recounts how Henry Ford in 1917, stood in a Michigan courtroom (having been sued by the Dodge brothers who were shareholders in Ford Motor Company) defending his decision to reinvest Ford Motor company's accumulated profits on plant expansion whilst slashing the price of Model T vehicles in an attempt to demonstrate that corporations should encourage

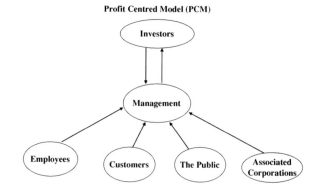

Fig. 3.1 Halal (2000) – Profit centred model – industrial age (1900–1950) Source: Halal, W. E. (2000, p. 11)

and build in their systems of governance some responsibility towards their other stakeholders. Lee (2008) argues that Ford's idea of business as a service to society was not only derided by the company's shareholders, but the court also granted the Dodge brothers' request for maximum dividends with no regard to the strategy the company was intending to embark on for the benefits of the company's other stakeholders. The court's decision in this case supports Halal (2000) conclusion of the profit-centred model which suggests that other stakeholders may probably benefit from the approach encouraged by the model but their interests are considered as 'means to the end of profitability rather than goals in their own right'. It is also interesting to note that the PCM appears to be in agreement with Friedman's (1962, 1970) argument that 'business managers are only employed by shareholders to pursue only those strategies which maximise owners' profits anything other than that is pure socialism after all businesses are not established for eleemosynary purposes'.

3.4.2.2 The Social Responsibility Model (SRM)

The SRM period falls within Bowen's (1953) *Social Responsibilities of the Businessman* book. It was during the time that Bowen (1953) attempted to theorise the relationship between business and society. Halal (2000), suggests that the SRM was introduced in an attempt to correct some of the anomalies of the profit centred model (PCM). Following Bowen's book, several corporations had opted to follow a different route from the PCM's period; they had identified the support and popularity the SRM was generating amongst some of the primary stakeholders notably their customers and employees. The SRM according to Halal (2000) was basically about 'doing good' if the entity aspires to do well. Even though the SRM was an improvement on the ethos and doctrines of the PCM, Halal (2000) argues that the two were mutually exclusive as depicted in Fig. 3.2 below, despite the interrelationship which

Social Responsibility Model (SRM)

Fig. 3.2 Halal (2000) –
Social responsibility model
Neo-industrial age
(1950–1980).
Source: Halal, W. E. (2000,
p. 11)

should coexist between them in order to bring about good governance, each was focusing in opposite direction of the spectrum; thus preventing the enormous benefits which could ensue if they were linked in some way. This made their goals to conflict and being at odds with each other. Profit was important for the corporation to survive but doing good would inevitably reduce profit, as such the desire to want to pursue and see the model through was lacking. The model failed to pass the test of time. It was therefore inevitable that a replacement to the model was sooner or later going to be necessary.

3.4.2.3 The Corporate Community Model (CCM)

By1980, the missing link between corporation and society had become apparent. The role corporate governance was expected to play in linking corporations and society together had also become obvious. Halal (2000) calls the period beginning in 1980 – the 'Information Age', Halal (2000), and describes the period as one which heralds a shift in focus from 'capital' to 'knowledge', since capital refers to tangible fixed assets which somehow wear out whether they are used or unused; knowledge on the other hand, refers to intangible fixed asset which does not depreciate in value but appreciates in value when shared with others. It is this quality of 'knowledge' that propels corporate managers to seek the sharing of information with their stakeholders since this course of action would contribute positively in meeting corporate strategies. Figure 3.3 below, depicts the flow of information between management and their various stakeholders. Managers provide information to these stakeholders and in return receive information from them. The result of which could only bring about a better understanding, a decrease in the level of mistrust of management's actions by these stakeholders and a better opportunity to jointly collaborate in order to solve both economic and societal problems. The CCM has continued to thrive since 1980 up until the present moment and there appears to be an unwritten memorandum of understanding between the two – community and corporations. The

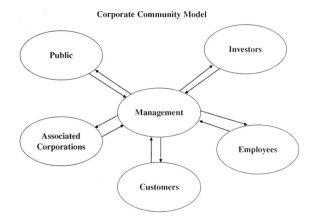

Fig. 3.3 Halal (2000) – Corporate community model Neo-industrial age (1980–date)

level of understanding has increased and a noticeable reduction in conflicts and frictions between the two sides now prevails. This perhaps explains why corporations are voluntarily following different strategies which are designed to the environment and activate sustainable development actions. Taking similar actions to these some thirty or forty years ago would have been perceived as creating unnecessary increase in costs thus reducing profits.

3.4.3 Stock Exchanges and Other Institutions Requiring CSR Reporting

Following the UK government's advice to the FTSE250 companies in 2001 to report on their environmental performance, socially responsible corporate entities have now adopted the policy of also reporting on the non-financial aspects of their operations on an annual basis. Thus; they provide information to their stakeholders on their achievements and those challenges they still need to work on in CSR by issuing annual CSR reports either on a stand-alone basis or by embedding it in their traditional annual reports Idowu and Towler (2004). Others are providing five development plans on CSR; see for example Marks & Spencer's Five Year 100 Plan 'A' Commitments, January 2007. Interestingly, CSR has now found itself included as part of those items that are required to be disclosed by companies for the purposes of risk and reputation management.

Stock Exchanges and other financial institutions around the world are also compelling listed companies to disclose information on their CSR activities, for instance in France, companies listed on the Paris Stock Exchange are required to provide information on their social and environmental performance, The Johannesburg Stock Exchange in South Africa requires listed companies to comply with a CSR based code of conduct, in the UK, several financial institutions are requesting listed companies to provide similar information; the London Stock Exchange, the Association of British Insurers (ABI), Pensions Fund Managers, FTSE4Good Index, the London Stock Exchange's Corporate Responsibility Exchange (CRE), in the United States of America; the Dow Jones Sustainability Index is a worldwide highly respected and used index which listed companies on the New York Stock Exchange must ensure that they comply with. It is now important for corporate managers to consider how CSR can support their corporate strategy. Corporate secretaries are actively involved in all the above noted governance matters. As far back 2002, the European Commission argues that the issue of CSR has gained prominence amongst corporate entities in recent times simply because these entities have realised that it is an important element of governance; it possesses the ingredients which enhance their ability to respond to fundamental changes in their business environments. Increased accountability is also a general expectation from corporate entities around the globe. It is therefore important that those at the helm of governance install appropriate mechanisms that will ensure that this happens in order to promote continued confidence in corporations and their activities by their stakeholders.

3.4.4 Combined CODES and the 8th Company Law Directive on Disclosure and Transparency

A chapter which talks about some aspects of Corporate Governance in the UK will certainly be incomplete without some reference to the Combined Code on Corporate Governance; an important document in corporate reporting in the UK. According to the Financial Reporting Council (the UK's independent regulator responsible for promoting confidence in corporate reporting and governance) 'the Combined Code on Corporate Governance sets out standards of good practice in relation to issues such as board composition and development, remuneration, accountability and audit and relations with shareholders'. The Combined Code was first issued in 1998 with some regular updating at intervals since that time. There are two versions of the code presently in operation: the Combined Code, June 2006 and Combined Code June 2008. All companies registered in the UK and listed on the main London Stock Exchange (LSE) Market are required to report on how they have applied the Combined Code in their annual report and accounts. Non-UK registered companies which are listed on the main market of the London Stock Exchange must disclose the significant ways in which their corporate governance practices differ from those set out in the Code.

In addition to the Combined Code on Corporate Governance which companies listed on the main market of the LSE must take cognisance of, there is also the Financial Services Authority (FSA) Corporate Governance Rules which UK companies listed on the main market of the LSE must also adhere to. The FSA rules implement the European Union Directive – the 8th Company Law Directive on Disclosure and Transparency. Basically, the FSA rules cover audit committees and governance statements and the rules are effective for accounting periods beginning on or after 29 June 2008 which coincidentally is the effective date of Combined Code 2008.

3.4.5 The Practice of Governance by its Professionals

The Chartered Secretaries Australia (CSA) on their website states that their members who are governance professionals have a variety of job titles apart from that of corporate secretaries. They might be given any of the following job titles depending on the circumstances of the entity which employ them: Chief Financial Officer, Chief Governance Officer or General Counsel.

They are called upon by their organizations to carry of the following functions:

- Drive and advice on best practice in governance.
- Champion the compliance framework to safeguard the integrity of the organization.
- Promote and sound the board on, high standards of corporate behaviour.
- Bridge interest of the board or governing body, management and stakeholders.

The CSA also argues that anyone who is referred to by his/her organization as 'governance professional' has a significant impact on the level and quality of the organisation's corporate governance and governance culture and often has a pivotal role in assisting the board to achieve the entity's vision and strategy. It concludes that the activities of the governance professional encompass legal and regulatory duties and obligations and additional responsibilities assigned by the employer.

3.5 A Study on Corporate Secretaries' Involvements in CSR in the UK

In an attempt to understand how UK corporate secretaries have absorbed the field of CSR in addition to their statutory duties for their various organisations and what parts they have played in their organisations' quest to join the 'CSR bandwagon' the author carried out a study in order to obtain information from UK companies' company secretaries using two methods – direct and indirect methods.

3.5.1 Direct Method

The author sent letters directly to thirty company secretaries of large listed UK companies asking them to 'explain in as much detail as possible their experiences of how their companies have absorbed the field of CSR into their professional activities giving both the pitfalls and benefits that have accrued from inculcating CSR into what they do'.

The direct method generated ten responses out of which only three provided the required information; the other seven stated that they were unwilling to participate in the study for different reasons; for example some companies stated that the time to provide the required information was not available to them.

3.5.2 Indirect Method

The author with the assistance of a practicing company secretary enlisted the assistance of a company which specialises in the recruitment of company secretaries for FTSE100, FTSE250 and other quoted companies in the UK. The company emailed 40 letters to these companies asking them to do exactly the same thing as contained in the letter sent out by the direct method.

The indirect method on the other hand generated eight responses with four of these companies providing the required information, the remainder stated that they did not have the time to participate in the study and wanted to wish the study every success. Table 3.2 below gives information about companies which provided information for the study.

The information provided by these seven companies from the two different methods was in different forms. Some companies provided detailed written explanations

Table 3.2 Companies
participating in the study

1.	Balfour Beatty Plc
2.	Bellway Plc
3.	Bovis Homes Plc
4.	Centrica Plc
5.	ITV Plc
6.	Lloyds TSB Plc
7.	Tesco Plc

as required by our letter; some sent their most recent CSR reports with some explanations, some sent an electronic version of their most recent CSR reports and one of these companies provided a link to their web address; where information about their most recent CSR report could be obtained.

3.6 Findings

The study reveals clearly that corporate secretaries in the UK and perhaps elsewhere working in collaboration with their other senior executive colleagues within their various organisations are actively involved in decisions about corporate involvements in corporate social responsibility activities. We were able to decipher from this study that several large UK companies now have Corporate Responsibility Committees which are chaired by one of their Executive Directors usually having the title of CSR Director or some similar titles. The Group Company Secretary of one of our seven participating companies stated that they had chaired this committee between 2003 and 2006. The Group Company Secretary of another of our companies currently chairs this committee. These Committees have an explicit remit to carry out several CSR activities within the particular company. It was also revealed that these companies' corporate secretaries are members of these Corporate Responsibility Committees.

The following is a summary of some of the CSR issues included in the explicit remit for which the committees in each of our participating companies are responsible:

- Assess and manage risk
- Develop corporate responsibility strategy
- Review social, ethical and environmental (SEE) policies and practices
- Encourage best practice throughout the business
- Identify opportunities to improve the effectiveness and sustainability of the business using community and environmental initiatives
- Review, agree, monitor and report on corporate responsibility Key Performance Indicators (KPIs)
- Increase internal awareness of corporate responsibility
- Improve stakeholder communication and engagement

- Ensure that the company's KPIs are meeting the needs of their stakeholders and the company continues to be good neighbours in the communities they serve
- Ensure that their KPIs are robust enough to reduce drastically their areas of adverse impact for example climate change, health and safety, local impact, employees
- Governance arrangements
- Reporting and disclosure of their non financial performance
- Stakeholder Engagement
- Increase employee engagement and customer satisfaction
- Conduct and Behaviours
- Better Corporate Responsibility Management

Apart from the above issues, the Group Company Secretary of a particular company which calls it own committee the Sustainability Working Group explains clearly that apart from being a member of the Sustainability Group, they are by virtue of their position in the Group personally responsible for the following activities:

- Coordinating the production of the CSR report
- Ensuring that its coverage accurately reflects the company's activities and provides a balanced view
- Provides information to various rating agencies and organisations
- The CSR report being a reputational tool is also used internally by the Company Secretarial Department to educate the business on the extent of initiatives
- Coordinating the quarterly meeting of the Sustainability Working Group.

3.7 Discussion

From the information which the study has elicited, it appears that corporate secretaries in their various organisations are not working in isolation in their quest to absorb the field of CSR into what they do whilst representing their profession in organisations. The field touches all professions that are required by corporate entities in order to ensure that they successfully achieve their missions, objectives and at the same time demonstrate to the world at large that they are socially responsible. The roles each of these senior managers (who are perhaps members of other professions and bring the knowledge and experiences of these profession(s) to the Board of corporate entities) play in order to ensure that the field of CSR is built into the corporate strategy are not explicit to non-insiders. There could be several reasons for this:

- There are still many things that are unclear about CSR. Lantos (2001) suggests that CSR has unclear boundaries; Idowu (2008b) argues that what falls under the umbrella of CSR in one political setting may probably be of little or no significance in another political setting.

- This field of CSR is not an exact art or science, corporations are only practicing it the way they believe it affects their core business or the way they understand it.
- Corporate entities that have chosen to adopt the requirements of the field are only doing so voluntarily, it must be noted that even though CSR is still voluntary; there are currently not many corporate entities which are not embedding the ethos of CSR into what they do. In most countries around the world, there appears to be no legal compulsion on the part of corporate entities to mandatorily practice CSR but some governments and international organisations are encouraging corporate entities to behave responsibly. In addition to this some NGOs and stakeholders are putting pressure on corporations to behave responsibly. Some companies are probably trying to stay out of trouble by adopting CSR ethos into their strategy.
- The field is still evolving, it is hoped that within the next ten to twenty years its situation would become clearer, the way to address some of the difficulties scholars and practitioners have identified up to now would also become clearer. It is also hoped that when the ISO26000 comes out in 2010 some of the obvious difficulties about the field would become easier to address.

It was also apparent to us that the roles executives play in an attempt by corporate entities to inculcate the field of CSR into their activities are unclear. These executives appear to innovate as they go along. Adopting a strategy of innovation is perhaps the best action they could take under the circumstances, since the field is neither an exact art nor science.

3.8 Conclusion

The objective of this chapter was to provide a framework that facilitates some understanding of the contributions corporate secretaries have made and continue to make in the development of the field of CSR using the United Kingdom as our main focus and case example. The issue of CSR, sustainability, sustainable development and corporate governance is one that corporate secretaries as 'the servant' of the Board of Directors cannot take lightly. This is so because most of the duties performed by corporate secretaries are statutory in nature. For our planet to stand the test of time; actions must start at the Board level. The secretary has a unique role here. S/he would need to direct members of the board's attention to aspects they need to deliberate on at board meetings.

Failure to take this issue on board at the Board level has serious implications and consequences not just for this generation but more importantly for future generations. Those at the Board level are aware that stakeholders; in particular Institutional Investors, Customers, NGOs etc are requesting that corporations take effective actions about those issues relating to CSR, apart from that, members of the board are aware that any corporation that takes the issue lightly will lose the trust, loyalty and advocacy of its stakeholders. These are important *sine qua non* which any corporation that aspires to prosper in modern markets cannot do without.

It is the responsibility of the corporate secretary to steer the Board to the path of formulating an effective CSR strategy on issues relating to CSR, and to similarly steer executive directors' attention to an effective path of executing the strategy. Formulating the strategy on paper or the corporate website for people to see will not suffice. Actions must be taken to ensure that their Key Performance Indicators on CSR are met in terms of measurable CSR initiatives across the business operations. One of the companies studied in the project for this chapter uses an Annual Business Plan based on Steering Wheel drivers made up of *Community, Customer, People, Operations and Finance*. At the beginning of the company's year, it sets out specific projects which they hope to deliver over the following twelve months in terms of the five wheel drivers in all its operations around the world. During the twelve months, it directs resources, energy, focus and vigour to delivering their expectations in these areas. At the end of the twelve months it measures its performance in the areas and asks a third party to take an independent examination of its performance in each of the five wheel drivers and reports on the strengths and weaknesses in terms of their actions during the operating period.

CSR is a field that will remain with us for the foreseeable future as long as business and society continue to co-exist and it will continue to cut across different organisational functions including that of the corporate secretary. Over time, it is hoped that all professions will become more equipped and effective to dealing with its requirements in order to make our world a better place to live in by this generation and future generations.

References

Bowen, H. R. (1953), Social Responsibilities of the Businessman, Harper Row, New York.

Broomhill, R. (2007), Corporate social responsibility: Key issues and Debates. In Orchard, L. and Matiasz, S. (Eds.), Dunstan Papers Series, Don Dustan Foundation, Adelaide.

Cadbury Report (1992), The Financial Aspects of Corporate Governance, Gee, London.

Carroll, A. B. (1979), A three-dimensional conceptual model of corporate social performance. Academy of Management Review, Vol. 4, No. 4, pp. 497–505.

Carroll, A. B. and Buchholtz, A. K. (2003), Business: Ethics and Stakeholder Management, 7th edition, South Western Pub, Cincinnati.

Clarkson, M. B. E. (1995), A stakeholder framework for analysing and evaluating corporate social performance. Academy of Management Review, Vol. 20, No. 1, pp. 92–117.

Dahya, J., McConnell, J., and Travlos, N. G. (2002), The Cadbury committee, corporate performance and top management turnover. The Journal of Finance, Vol. 57, No. 1, pp. 461–483.

Deming, D. (2003), Are We Running Out of Oil? Policy Backgrounder No. 159, of the National Centre for Policy Analysis, January 2003, Washington, DC.

Department of Business, Enterprise and Regulatory Reform (2006), Companies Act 2006, HM Stationery Office, London.

De Wit, B. and Meyer, R. (2004), Strategy: Process, Content, Context, 3rd edition, Thompson, London.

Elkington, J. (1997), Cannibals with Forks: The Triple Bottom Line of 21st Century Business, Capstone, Oxford.

Fligstein, N. and Freeland, R. (1995), Theoretical and comparative perspectives on corporate organization. Annual Review of Sociology, Vol. 21, pp. 21–43.

Freeman, R. E. (1984), Strategic Management: A Stakeholder Approach, Pitman, Boston, MA.

Friedman, M. (1962), Capitalism and Freedom, University of Chicago, Chicago, IL

Friedman, M. (1970), The Social Responsibility of Business is to Increase its Profits, The New York Times Magazine, September 13.

Grant, T. (2007) Grant Thornton's 6th FTSE 350 Corporate Governance Review December, http://ecomm.grant-thornton.co.uk/ve/zzj0097L929290B66Xe66 [Accessed 12 April 2008].

Halal, W. E. (2000), Corporate community: a theory of the firm uniting profitability and responsibility. Strategy & Leadership, Vol. 28, No. 2, pp. 10–16.

Henderson, D. (2001a), Misguided Virtue – False Notions of Corporate Social Responsibility, Institute of Economic Affairs, London.

Henderson, D. (2001b), The case against corporate social responsibility. Policy, Vol. 17, No. 2, pp. 28–32.

Idowu, S. O. and Towler, B. A. (2004), A comparative study of the contents of corporate social responsibility reports of UK companies. Management of Environmental Quality Journal, Vol. 15, No. 4, pp. 420–437.

Idowu, S. O. and Papasolomou, I. (2007), Are the corporate social responsibility matters based on good intentions or false pretences? An empirical study of the motivations behind the issue of CSR reports by UK companies. Corporate Governance, Vol. 7, No. 2, pp. 136–147.

Idowu, S. O. (2008a), An empirical study of what institutions of higher education in the UK consider to be their corporate social responsibility. In Aravosis, K., Brebbia, C. A., and Gomez, N. (Eds.), Environmental Economics and Investment Assessment II, WIT Press, Southampton.

Idowu, S. O. (2008b), Practicing corporate social responsibility in the United Kingdom. In Idowu, S. O. and Filho W. L. (Eds.), Global Practices of Corporate Social Responsibility, Springer Verlag, Berlin.

International Federation of Accountants (2001), Governance in the Public Sector: A Governing Body Perspective, Study 13, International Federation of Accountants (IFAC), August 2001, New York.

Jones, P., Comfort, D., and Hillier, D. (2006), Corporate social responsibility and the UK construction industry. Journal of Corporate Real Estate, Vol. 8, No. 3, pp. 134–150.

Katsoulakos, T. and Katsoulacos, Y. (2007), Strategic management, corporate responsibility and stakeholder management integrating corporate responsibility principles and stakeholder approaches into mainstream strategy: a stakeholder-oriented and integrative strategic framework. Corporate Governance, Vol. 7, No. 4, pp. 355–369.

Kotler, P. and Lee, N. (2005), Corporate Social Responsibility: Doing the Most Good for Your Company and Your Cause, John Wiley & Son Inc., Hoboken.

Laine, M. (2005), Meanings of the term 'sustainable development' in Finnish corporate disclosures. Accounting Forum, Vol. 29, No. 4, pp. 395–413.

Lantos, G. P. (2001), The boundaries of strategic corporate social responsibility. Journal of Consumer Marketing, Vol. 18, No. 7, pp. 595–632.

Lee, M-D. P. (2008), A review of the theories of corporate social responsibility: its evolutionary path and the road ahead. International Journal of Management Reviews, Vol. 10, No. 1, pp. 53–73.

Lippke, R. L. (1996), Setting the terms of the business responsibility debate in Ethics in the workplace, Selected Readings in Business Ethics, Larmer, R. A. (Ed.) West Publishing Co. St. Pauls, MN.

Levitt, T. (1958), The dangers of social responsibility, Harvard Business Review, Vol. 36, pp. 41–50.

McManus, J. (2003), Corporate Social Responsibility: Great Real, Chartered Secretary, October, pp. 12–15.

McWilliams, A. and Siegel, D. (2001), CSR: A theory of the firm perspective, Academy of Management Review, Vol. 26, No. 1, pp. 117–127.

Metcalfe, C. (1998), The stakeholder corporation. Business Ethics: A European Review, Vol. 7, No. 1, pp. 30–36.

Miller, F. D. and Ahrens, J. (1993), The social responsibility of corporations. In White, T. I. (Ed.), Business Ethics: A Philosophical Reader, Prentice Hall, Upper Saddle River, New Jersey.

Monks, R. A. G. and Minow, N. (1995), Corporate Governance, Blackwell, Oxford.

Organisation for Economic Cooperation and Development (1999), OECD Principles of Corporate Governance, OECD Publications, Paris.

Redmond, J., Walker, E., and Wang, C.(2008) Issues for small businesses with waste management. Journal of Environmental Management, Vol. 88, pp. 275–285.

Ribstern, L. E. (2002), Market versus Regulatory responses to corporate fraud: a critique of the SOX Act of 2002. Journal of Corporation Law, Vol. 28, No. 1, pp. 1–67.

Perino, M. A. (2002), Enron's Legislative Aftermath: Some Reflections on the Deterrence Aspects of the Sarbanes-Oxley Act of 2002, Columbia Law and Economics Working Paper Number 212, St John's Legal Studies Research Paper.

Sethi, S. P. (1975), Dimensions of corporate social performance: an analytical framework. California Management Review, Vol. 17, No. 3, pp. 5–9.

Shleifer, A. and Vishny, R. W. (1997), A survey of corporate governance. The Journal of Finance, Vol. 52, No. 2, pp. 737–783.

Smith, A. (1776), The Wealth of Nations, Book 1 Chapter II, Methuen & Co, London.

Vogel, D. (2005),The Market for Virtue: The Potential and Limits of Corporate Responsibility, Brooking Institution Press, Washington, DC.

Wallich, H. C. and McGowan, J. J. (1970), Stockholder and the corporations' role in social policy. In Baumol, W. J. (Ed.), A New Rationale for Corporate Social Policy, Committee of Economic Development, New York.

Wood, D. J. (1991), Corporate social performance revisited. Academy of Management Review, Vol. 16, No. 4, pp. 691–718.

Electronic Sources

Combined Code Financial Reporting Council, http://www.frc.org.uk/corporate/combinedcode.cfm site accessed 29 November 2008.

Schoen, J. W. (2004), How Long will the World's Oil Last? Energy Bulletin, http://www.energybulletin.net/2007.html site accessed 16 July 2008

World Bank (2000), Corporate Governance, Corporate Governance Defined http://www.corpgov.net/library/definitions.html site accessed 2 December 2008.

http://www.csaust.com/AM/Template.cfm?Section=CSA_governance&Template=/CM/HTMLDisplay.cfm&ContentID=12136 site accessed on the 6 April 2009.

Chapter 4
Mainsteaming Corporate Social Responsibility: A Triadic Challenge from a General Management Perspective

François Maon, Valérie Swaen, and Adam Lindgreen

Interplay and interaction are the integral parts of
music—they're as important as the notes

John McLaughlin

Abstract Based upon an examination of CSR initiatives of approximately 75 companies, this study examines how programs of corporate social responsibility (CSR) are designed, implemented, and monitored. Specifically, three key and interconnected challenges, which should be considered when companies embed CSR in their organizational processes, are identified: an action challenge, an activation challenge, and an aspiration challenge (referred to as the '3A framework for mainstreaming CSR in a company'). The objectives for mainstreaming CSR can be reached through the combination and interplay between the development of societal understanding and ongoing dialogue and engagement between the company and its stakeholders; the presence and maintenance of relevant skills and competencies at the various levels of the company; and CSR-related capacities linked to the existence of actual CSR leadership within the company.

4.1 Introduction

More than 50 years ago, Bowen (1953) argued that businesses have the duty 'to pursue those policies, to make those decisions, or to follow those lines of action which are desirable in terms of the objectives and values of our society' (op. cit., p. 6). Since then, CSR has come to constitute an important factor not only in the business world but also elsewhere, such as in economics, law, and politics (McKie, 1974). More recently, interest in CSR increased (Hopkins, 2006) turning it into a global trend that incorporates businesses, governments, non-governmental organizations, and civil society organizations (Matten and Moon, 2004; Sahlin-Andersson, 2006).

F. Maon (✉)
Université Catholique de Louvain, Louvain-la-Neuve, Belgium

S.O. Idowu, W.L. Filho (eds.), *Professionals' Perspectives of Corporate Social Responsibility*, DOI 10.1007/978-3-642-02630-0_5,
© Springer-Verlag Berlin Heidelberg 2009

Various factors are driving this interest in CSR, including the rising influence of pressure groups and activists (Amaeshi et al., 2008; de Bakker and den Hond, 2008), the media coverage of business responsibilities (Hogan, 2007; Tench et al., 2007), and the sympathy for ethical and ecological consumerism (Harrison et al., 2006). The mushrooming of agencies that report on CSR activities (Schäfer et al., 2006), the setting-up of initiatives in changing global business into a more sustainable system (e.g., the United Nations' Global Compact, the Organization for Economic Co-operation and Development's guidelines for multinational companies, and the Global Sullivan Principles), and the adherence to international standards testify to CSR's success. Many companies, not surprisingly, claim to adopt CSR management practices (Wilson and Bonfiglioli, 2002).

Although the literature is rich on insightful contributions regarding the design, implementation, and monitoring of CSR (cf. Lindgreen et al., 2009), at times the plethora of multifaceted CSR conceptualizations causes considerable disagreement among researchers (Frankental, 2001; Garriga and Melé, 2004). Common to the various conceptualizations, however, is the idea that companies should be not only concerned about making a profit but also engaged in 'actions that appear to further some social good, beyond the interests of the firm and that which is required by law' (McWilliams and Siegel, 2001, p. 117). Companies, it is said, need define their roles in society and apply social, ethical, legal, and responsible standards to their businesses (Lichtenstein et al., 2004; Lindgreen and Swaen, 2005). For the purposes of this chapter we concur with the European Commission (2001) that has defined CSR as a 'concept whereby companies integrate social and environmental concerns in the business operations and in their interactions with their stakeholders on a voluntary basis' (op. cit., p. 8).

Despite the spectacular growth of CSR – as reflected in managerial interest and investment in CSR activities – many companies still struggle with designing, implementing, and monitoring CSR. We contribute to literature by examining this issue; the development of the theoretical framework in this chapter is based upon the qualitative examination of a collection of more than 300 CSR initiatives and policies designed and implemented by approximately 75 companies, most of them being multinational.[1] Examined CSR practices were thematically coded according to a pre-established scheme in order to highlight key aspects and dimensions of CSR implementation processes. In the light of the existing literature on CSR implementation, the analysis leads to the identification of key challenges faced by companies in the CSR mainstreaming process. (To keep within the page limitations we deliberately decide not to provide details of the individual companies and their CSR activities; our discussion is based upon an aggregate analysis of these companies.) The remainder of this article is structured as follows: First, we provide a literature review, which we use to develop a theoretical framework. Second, we identify our

---

[1] Note: We have not ourselves investigated all of these companies and their programs. Instead we rely on CSR Europe that has organized the collection of the companies and their CSR initiatives before allowing them to be published on CSR Europe's Website.

study's contributions and managerial implications, and suggest avenues for further research.

4.2 Literature Review: Integration of Corporate Social Responsibility

Increasingly, companies seek to address CSR issues through systematic and organized processes: they revise policies and development programs, set up steering committees, evaluate particular programs' environmental and social performance outcomes, and publish annual sustainable development reports. In 2008, some 3,000 companies are expected to publish a report that will document the companies' CSR policy and performance outcomes (Corporate Register, 2008). The majority of these reports, however, will not be certified by a third party. Whether a company has engaged in factual CSR activities or not, therefore, becomes a real question (Laufer, 2003).

Companies demonstrate different levels of understanding of, commitment to, and integration of CSR. Various models of CSR development underline the strategic, organizational, and managerial capabilities required by companies in order to deal with environmental and social challenges and to implement a company-wide CSR orientation (Davis and Blomstrom, 1975; Mirvis and Googins, 2006; Van Marrewijk and Werre, 2003; Zadek, 2004). The level of CSR-related capacity and understanding determines the extent to which CSR principles have been embedded within a company's overall strategy and day-to-day practices. Table 4.1 summarizes the path that companies typically follow toward implementing a CSR orientation (Mirvis and Googins, 2006; Zadek, 2004).

To be successful, CSR needs to move from being a peripheral add-on to becoming an integrated core business function (Dickson, 2004; Pedersen and Neergaard, 2008); the way a company understands its business and the way it makes its decisions are made is essential (Lyon, 2004; Maon et al., 2008a; Zadek, 2004). The embedding of CSR in a company's strategy and operations in such a way that they support the company's core business is far from being an easy task. CSR embraces such dispersed concerns as sweatshops, workers' rights, supply chain partners, poverty alleviation, genetically modified food products, and climate change. These concerns are oftentimes unpredictable and also shift over time and place (Morsing and Schultz, 2006).

To ensure long-term environmental and social responsibility a company often will have to identify which issues are relevant to put in place appropriate procedures and technologies, to develop specific competencies, and to undertake arduous investment. As well, to anchor a company firmly around CSR steps must be taken, first, to internalize a CSR orientation in the company's various functional departments (Cramer et al., 2006; Nijhof and Jeurissen, 2006) and, second, to facilitate a dialogue between the company and its key stakeholders (i.e., groups or individuals that can affect or are affected by the achievement of a company's purpose;

Table 4.1 Stages of CSR embedment

Embedment stage	Corporate attitude toward CSR issues	Strategic rationale behind this attitude toward CSR issues	CSR performance objectives	CSR integration in organizational structure
Defensive	*Self-protective*: Denying practices, outcomes, or responsibilities	Limitation of potentially uncontrolled criticisms and attacks that in the short term could affect sales, recruitment, productivity and the brand	Resolution of problems as they occur	*Marginal*: Staff driven
Compliant	*Reactive*: Adopting a policy-based compliance approach as a cost of doing business	Mitigation of the erosion of economic value in the medium term because of ongoing reputation and litigation risks	Minimization of harmful externalities/respect of evolving norms and regulatory requirements	*Functional*: Ownership
Managerial	*Responsive*: Progressively embedding societal issue in core management processes	Mitigation of the erosion of economic value in the medium term and to achieve longer-term gains by integrating responsible business practices into their daily operations	Active management of CSR-related issues/definition of business-wide opportunities	*Cross-functional*: Coordination
Strategic/integrated	*Pro-active*: Integrating societal issues into core business strategies	Enhancement of economic value in the long term and to gain first-mover advantage by aligning strategy and process innovations with the societal issue	Leading of the pack/development of sustainable business leverages through CSR initiatives	*Organizational*: Alignment
Civil/transforming	*Defining*: Promoting broad industry participation in corporate social responsibility	Enhancement of long-term economic value by overcoming any first-mover disadvantages and to realize gains through collective action	Diffusion of expertise/maximization of positive externalities	*Institutional*: Business driven

Adapted from Mirvis and Googins (2006) and Zadek (2004).

Freeman, 1984) and the world at large (Basu and Palazzo, 2008). Only then can CSR values become deeply integrated in a company's management philosophy and culture and be the source of innovativeness and creativeness required for developing a sustainable business.

4.3 A Framework for Mainstreaming Corporate Social Responsibility

Existing management literature the qualitative analysis of CSR initiatives of more than 75 companies lead to consider that three key and interconnected challenges must be considered when companies are seeking to embed CSR in their organizational processes: an action challenge, an activation challenge, and an aspiration challenge. We refer to this idea (illustrated in Fig. 4.1) as the '3A framework for mainstreaming CSR in a company'; each of the three challenges is discussed next.

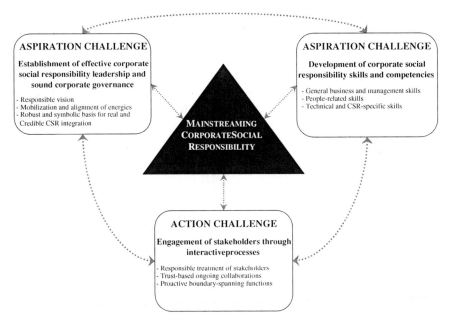

Fig. 4.1 3A Framework for mainstreaming corporate social responsibility in a company

4.4 The Action Challenge: Engagement of Stakeholders Through Interactive Processes

The action challenge is about developing specific competencies at the organizational level that allow the company to practically engage with its key stakeholders through dynamic collaborative processes. In line with Andriof and Waddock's (2002)

stakeholder engagement process, management needs first to identify which are relevant stakeholders and what are their claims before next assessing how to respond through dialogue and trust-based collaborative processes (in short referred to as interactive processes).

4.4.1 Stakeholder Identification and Stakeholder Claims

A company's stakeholders have previously been identified following Freeman's (1984) definition; stakeholders are further characterized as 'individuals and constituencies that contribute, either voluntarily or involuntarily, to its wealth-creating capacity and activities, and who are therefore its potential beneficiaries and/or risk bearers' (Post et al., 2002, p. 8). Stakeholders have some form of capital, either human or financial, that depends on the company's behavior (Clarkson, 1995), which implies a two-way highly dependent relationship between companies and their stakeholders (Gao and Zhang, 2006).

Companies will have to address the expectations of at least some of their stakeholders (Andriof and Waddock, 2002). Shareholders constitute a key category of stakeholders but 'are from being the only group who expect to benefit from and influence business activity and, accordingly, are just one of those groups that have a legitimate right to influence a company's strategic objectives' (Campbell et al., 2002, p. 26). From a normative perspective, companies have a moral obligation to consider more than just the interests of shareholders since stakeholders cannot be treated merely as a means to corporate ends, but are valuable in their own right, as ends in themselves (Evan and Freeman, 1988). As well, from an instrumental point of view, stakeholder management is crucial if a strategy is be effective and sustainable (Post et al., 2002) because 'stakeholders contribute to the organization's resource base, shape the structure of the industry in which the firm operates, and create the social/political arena in which the organization exists' (Miles et al., 2006, p. 199). The identification of relevant stakeholders is therefore crucial in order to consider and address the competing claims that companies face and to design appropriate CSR policies and programs.

Past research proposes various ways for classifying stakeholders. Such classifications include primary or secondary stakeholders; owners and non-owners of the company; owners of capital and owners of less tangible assets; actors and those acted upon; stakeholders engaged in voluntary relationships with the company and those that are not voluntarily engaged with the company; right holders, contractors, and moral claimants; resource providers to the company and dependents of the company; risk-takers and influencers; and, finally, legal principles to whom agent-managers bear a fiduciary duty (Greenwood, 2007). Among the most referred to is the stakeholder classification scheme that identifies which stakeholders requires most attention at particular points in time (Mitchell et al., 1997; this scheme is empirically tested in Agle et al. [1999]). Table 4.2 captures the classification scheme.

Table 4.2 Determination of stakeholder salience and type and emphasis on legitimate claims

Stakeholder category	Salience classes	Possessed or attributed attributes	Stakeholder type	Implications for Management
Latent *Possession or attributed possession of only one of the attributes*	Not highly salient stakeholders	**Legitimacy of the claim**	**Discretionary** stakeholders *Most likely to be recipients of corporate philanthropy*	No pressure on management to engage in an active relationship. However, managers could choose to do so in a CSR perspective (discretionary practices).
		Power to influence	**Dormant** stakeholders *Little or no interaction with the company*	Remaining cognizant of such stakeholders Dormant stakeholders can become more salient if they acquire either urgency or legitimacy
		Urgency of the claim	**Demanding** stakeholders *Bothersome but not critical*	Not warranting more than passing management attention
Expectant *Possession or attributed possession of two of the attributes*	Moderately salient stakeholders	**Legitimacy of the claim** Power to influence	**Dominant** stakeholders *Intrinsically influent*	Dominant stakeholders expect and must receive management attention and consideration
		Legitimacy of the claim Urgency of the claim	**Dependent** stakeholders *Need guidance of internal management values*	In a CSR perspective, management should definitely grant them attention and consideration since they depend upon others (such as managers) to carry out their legitimate will

Table 4.2 (continued)

Stakeholder category	Salience classes	Possessed or attributed attributes	Stakeholder type	Implications for Management
		Power to influence Urgency of the claim	**Dangerous** stakeholders *Possibly coercive and violent*	Failure to identify them can result in missed opportunities for mitigating dangers and in lower levels of preparedness, where no accommodation is possible
Definitive *Possession or attributed possession of all three attributes*	Highly salient stakeholders	**Legitimacy of the claim,** Power to influence Urgency of the claim	**Definitive** stakeholders *Member of a company's dominant coalition*	Management has a clear and immediate mandate to attend to and give priority to these stakeholders' claims

Adapted from Mitchell et al. (1997).

The degree to which managers give priority to competing stakeholder claims 'will be positively related to the cumulative number of stakeholder attributes–power, legitimacy, and urgency – perceived by managers to be present' (Mitchell et al., 1997, p. 873). These three stakeholder attributes can be summarized as follows (Preble, 2005). Legitimacy regards 'a claim on a firm, based upon a contractual or legal obligation, a moral right, an at-risk status, or a stakeholder having a moral interest in the harms and benefits generated by a company's actions' (op. cit., p. 411). Power concerns 'the ability to influence a firm's behavior, whether or not the stakeholder has a legitimate claim' (op. cit., p. 411). Finally, urgency relates to 'degree to which a stakeholder's claim calls for immediate attention, adding a dynamic component for a stakeholder to attain salience in the minds of managers' (op. cit., p. 411).

The Mitchell et al. (1997) classification scheme provides a strong basis for a dynamic typology of stakeholders and for a thorough analysis of their potential influence on the company achieving its stated objectives. Specific responses subsequently are developed by managers according to who the stakeholder is (i.e., which stakeholder type) and the nature of claims; in particular, stakeholders with legitimate claims must be granted special attention and consideration.

Identifying relevant stakeholders and claims requires skills and good judgment; this process can be further complicated when a company faces different stakeholders that aggregate into unique patterns of influence (Andriof and Waddock, 2002). That is, the company not only faces individual stakeholders but also the various constellations that come about through the way that the stakeholders relate to each other (Crane and Livesey, 2003). Such complicated stakeholder relationships, therefore, must all be understood before a company can make sound decisions regarding stakeholder claims.

4.4.2 Stakeholder Engagement Through Dialogue and Trust-Based Collaborative Processes

Stakeholder engagement is a process of consultation, communication, dialogue, and exchange that is inherently interactive and based on mutual interdependence and understanding between the actors (Preston and Post, 1975). The process aims at 'seeking stakeholder views on their relationships with the organization in a way that may realistically be expected to elicit them' (Institute of Social and Ethical Accountability, 1999, p. 91). Four different levels of stakeholder engagement are identified in the literature (Gao and Zhang, 2001):

1. A 'passive' level: information about the company's CSR activities are published in reports and various types of media outlets; both types are intended for mass stakeholders and the wider society.
2. A 'listening' level: selected stakeholders are consulted with through interviews and formal meetings; information is also obtained through suggestion boxes and questionnaires.

3. A 'two-way' process level: a limited number of key stakeholders engage in dialogue with the company through group discussions and feedback sharing, and stakeholder-driven performance measures are designed.
4. A 'proactive' level: a stakeholder council is typically created; this council is characterized by the integration of stakeholder representatives in decision-making processes and management.

The above continuum is characterized by an increasing corporate openness and a deepening of relationships with selected stakeholders (in terms of key areas of concern). The type of stakeholders and the reason for engaging with stakeholders could therefore influence the style of engagement along the continuum, as well as the nature of the stakeholders' expectations; both could change over time.

Stakeholder engagement does not automatically guarantee a responsible treatment of stakeholders and does not ensure that the company acts in the interests of legitimate stakeholders, 'Many of the stakeholder engagement practices that pass under the label of corporate social responsibility are in fact forms of strategic management where the company acts in its own interest and where the stakeholders are merely a vehicle for doing so' (Greenwood, 2007, p. 324). In theory, the strategic management of stakeholders ensures a better understanding of what the company's impact is; also, such a process helps the company to manage its social risk, avert and solve crises, get access to critical information, and facilitate regulatory approvals. Some companies, however, have been known to manipulate and deceive when managing their stakeholders strategically (Greenwood, 2007). In order for a company to develop stakeholder engagement practices that truly drive CSR development within the company through an involvement of stakeholders in decision-making processes and activities, the company will have to rely on genuine commitment, high integrity, and moral leadership – and be held accountable.[2] For stakeholder engagement practices to be constructive, companies must build up relevant skills and competencies with respect to the dialogue processes; develop boundary-spanning functions; and design and maintain collaborative strategies that ensure enduring stakeholder networks. The following box exemplifies how Vodafone, by developing specific managerial tool kits, has sought to identify, engage, and manage with their stakeholders.

---

[2]It should be noted that it is possible to act in the interests of stakeholders without actually engaging with them. Many contemporary companies carry out philanthropic activities and similar discretionary practices, such as employee volunteerism and donations to the local community. Whilst these initiatives certainly contribute, at least to some extent, to the improvement of societal well-being, they often do not entail stakeholder consultation.

Stakeholder Engagement Strategies at Vodafone[3]

We need to engage globally and locally, on single issues and more broadly, with single and multiple stakeholder groups, in structured and unstructured ways
                                                                                    (Vodafone, 2005)

At Vodafone, engagement with stakeholders is seen as an essential element of a responsible business. It is acknowledged that engagement helps to learn from stakeholders, to identify and manage risks, to build trust and strong relationships, and to identify ways to improve corporate performance. In this perspective, the company considers that stakeholder engagement needs to be tailored to the needs of specific circumstances, issues, and places and cannot therefore be described as a single process. At Vodafone, stakeholder engagement thus takes many forms, and it is believed "it will only be effective in helping companies to know, understand, and respond to stakeholder concerns if it takes place at the right level, in the right geography, and on the right subjects". Accordingly, Vodafone's engagement has been divided in five types: (1) broad local engagement across all CSR-related issues; (2) single issue local engagement; (3) single issue global engagement (e.g., digital divide and supply chain challenges); (4) engagement with specific stakeholder groups at global level (e.g., employee welfare); and (5) business and Industry-wide engagement (e.g., impact of mobile telephony on health). While the depth and breadth of engagement with the various stakeholder groups at the different levels may vary, focus on dialogue is key and the company's engagement focuses on interactivity in order to exchange views and build consensus on CSR issues. To ensure constructive dialogue processes with relevant stakeholders at all levels of engagement, Vodafone has developed a stakeholder engagement toolkit that helps operating companies understand the business benefits of engagement and that provides guidance on the mapping of stakeholder groups, the identification of stakeholder issues, the different suggested forms of dialogue, and the tracking of the engagement activity. Stakeholder feedback and learning is shared across the Group through twice-yearly global CSR workshops and a monthly teleconference for CSR managers around the world.

---

[3]This short abstract of Vodafone and its activities has been more or less taken as it appeared originally in Vodafone (2005).

4.5 The Activation Challenge: Development of Corporate Social Responsibility Skills and Competencies

The dynamic nature of CSR, and the complexity of the challenges, call for commitment, and planning, as well as particular skills and competencies (Maignan et al., 2006). It has been suggested that 'where they have to integrate it in their day-to-day management involving their whole supply chains, companies' employees and managers need training and retraining in order to acquire the necessary skills and competence' (Wilson and Bonfiglioli, 2002, p. 1). The literature, however, does not provide a significant body of work that comprehensively identifies the skills and competencies that are required in this process.

We suggest seven sets of organizational skills and competencies; our suggestions are based upon the literature (DTI, 2003; Dunphy et al., 2003; Maignan et al., 2006; Maon et al., 2009). These sets of skills and competencies are grouped into three broad categories: general business and management skills, people-related skills, and technical and CSR-specific skills; the three categories are strongly interrelated and complement each other (Table 4.3).

4.5.1 General Business and Management Skills

Any CSR activity must relate to the company's values, strategy, structure, and culture (Lyon, 2004; Mirvis and Googins, 2006). As a consequence, the development of CSR development is intrinsically linked to general business and management skills (DTI, 2003); these skills concern diagnosis, project management, and communication.

Diagnosis: To be socially and environmentally responsible a company must be aware of its internal and external environment through rigorous, pertinent, and regular environmental scanning and analysis (Jamali, 2008). The company needs to demonstrate a sound comprehension of the broader context of its activities and processes and also needs to acknowledge its social and environmental impact on the environment (CSR Academy, 2004). In this regard, and to reach sound and balanced judgments, the company must demonstrate an aptitude for questioning and listening to others for factual, value-based, and even emotional information, as well as an ability to using various information sources and analysis methods analysis (Dunphy et al., 2003). Knowledge about the company's environment constitutes the groundwork for developing strategies that allow the company adapting to environmental expectations or, alternatively, changing these expectations.

Project management: To seize new opportunities and pull off organizational changes in a focused, structured, and efficient manner the company must apply project management (Kezsbom and Edward, 2001); this has been defined as 'the application of knowledge, skills, tools and techniques to project activities in order to meet stakeholder's needs and expectations from a project' (Burke, 1999, p. 3). Ongoing technological change combined with ever-increasing market pressure have resulted in project management becoming critical in a company's bag of general

Table 4.3 Highlighting key corporate social responsibility skills and competencies

Skills areas	Key required competencies	Key features
General business and management skills	*Environment understanding and diagnosis establishment*	Ability to acknowledge the broader context of business activities and processes
		Ability to question and listen to others, to apply critical insights and to make balanced judgments
		Ability to use varied sources and method of analysis
	Project management	Ability to seize new opportunities
		Ability to flexibly mobilize resources
		Ability to pull of organizational changes in a focused and structured way
	Effective communication	Ability to adopt multiple viewpoints
		Ability to clearly convey ideas and information
		Ability to identify and adapt to distinct target audiences
People-related skills	*Employee and managers training and recruitment*	Ability to generate organization-wide knowledge and awareness
		Ability to educate specific groups of employees and managers to specialized issues
		Abilities to design effective hiring processes
	Capacity to leverage out-of-the box thinking	Ability to internally question business as usual
		Ability to generate open-minded organizational climate
		Ability to design institutionalized processes to foster creativity and innovative thinking
Technical and CSR-specific skills	*Stakeholder networks management*	Ability to build collaborative partnerships
		Ability to negotiate, influence without power and internally mobilize political savvy
		Ability to mentor and coach others
	Extra-financial reporting and performance evaluation	Ability to produce accurate, meaningful, and consistent data at all organizational levels
		Ability to conceptualize business activities and interactions into relevant indicators
		Ability to maintain measurement continuity and rigor in a changing business environment

business and management skills (Kerzner, 2003). As such, project management skills are essential for mainstreaming CSR within the company because this will often require new ways for organizing and working (Dawson, 2003). Companies have to design adequate strategies to mobilize resources flexibly in order to achieve the required changes efficiently (Cleland, 1990). Project management furthermore helps companies update their technical and organizational knowledge and allows them to develop problem-solving and resourcing abilities (Dunphy et al., 2003).

Communication: Skills under this banner relate to conveying ideas and information in a clear and appropriate manner to the intended audience – in writing, presentation, and public speaking (DTI, 2003). Effective communication skills may allow reconciling stakeholder conflicts early in the design and implementation processes, which means that the risk of CSR failure is minimized. To ensure a positive communicational effect on both internal and external stakeholders, the company and its management team should keep stakeholders informed and up to date; they should also demonstrate willingness to listen and ask skilful questions, as well as the abilities to adopt multiple viewpoints (Dunphy et al., 2003). This is especially true in the case of the company's employees and managers, who can be ambassadors for the company, advocate the company, and source information for the company; in contrast, if these stakeholders are not properly engaged it can be a problem for the company (Kolk and Pinkse, 2006). As well, companies increasingly use CSR activities to position their corporate brand in the minds of consumers and other stakeholders (Maignan and Ferrell, 2004; Maignan and Ralston, 2002). However, communicating about CSR is a delicate issue because stakeholders are often reluctant about receiving too much information about companies' CSR engagements (Morsing, 2003). One explanation for this is that many companies employ CSR to create a good corporate citizen image, sell a product or a policy, or try to rehabilitate their standing with the public and decision makers.

4.5.2 People-Related Skills

The development of CSR within a company is dependent upon people (Hemingway and Maclagan, 2004; Maon et al., 2008b); we include skills concerning recruitment and training and capacity to think 'out of the box.'

Recruitment and training: Companies need to ensure the presence of particular CSR-related knowledge and capacities within the organization. Therefore they need to demonstrate their ability to recruit and train employees and managers who are directly involved in CSR activities. It is essential to recruit the right people with the right skills and to provide them with subsequent tailored training (Gonzales et al., 1999). Personal characteristics identified as important for individuals involved in CSR management include adaptability, integrity, empathy, open-mindedness, problem-solving orientation, and strategic awareness (DTI, 2003). Guaranteeing organization-wide CSR training also helps creating employee awareness and understanding of how CSR issues affect them and their immediate environment (Maon et al., 2008b).

Capacity to think 'out of the box': A complex, yet crucial set of skills to be acquired in order to develop innovative and sustainable CSR initiatives that are deeply grounded in the company's strategic orientation are the skills to think 'out of the box', 'The transition to enduring advantage through CSR requires the dismissal of traditional operational goals and the development of innovative strategy' (Smith, 2007, p. 190). In order to internally generate new ways of thinking it is essential to critically reflect upon past company practices and their impact in relation to CSR principles (CSR Academy, 2004). The risk of staying the same or being ignorant of CSR in an evolving business environment is increasingly considered as damaging to the company (Cumming et al., 2005).

4.5.3 Technical and Corporate Social Responsibility-Specific Skills

Technical and corporate social responsibility-specific skills relate to, first, stakeholder network management and, second, extra-financial reporting and performance evaluation.

Stakeholder Network Management

Stakeholder network management implies companies building relations with their internal and external stakeholders, thereby engaging in consultation and balancing demands. Managers put themselves in their stakeholders' position and are thus able to acknowledge and take into account the stakeholders' interests when designing strategic CSR policies (Freeman, 1984). The objective is for the company to understand their stakeholders' agendas and perspectives and to recognize and weigh up expectations that it faces (DTI, 2003; Dunphy et al., 2003; Roloff, 2008). There is no standard approach to managing a stakeholder network (Burchell and Cook, 2006), but adapting behavior and communication to accommodate particular stakeholders and gaining stakeholders' agreement and ensuring their commitment constitute important prerequisites to successful network management. For example, managers should be able to negotiate 'softly,' network, team work, mentor, and coach; also, they should be humble and trustworthy, and they should have political savvy (DTI, 2003).

Extra-Financial Reporting and Performance Evaluation

A commitment to CSR requires a company's management team to address, for example, a 'triple bottom line' of economic, social, and environmental performance evaluation (Savitz and Weber, 2006). In this regard, a company designs methods, indicators, and reporting systems that allow for the evaluation of the company's CSR performance (O'Connor and Spangenberg, 2008). Extra-financial performance evaluation and reporting are, nonetheless, difficult, as they take place at different levels within the company; they must relate to the company's industry-specific context; and the company's CSR policy and activities are revised regularly. The company needs to demonstrate a clear commitment to transparency and accountability, together with a capacity to collaboratively identify relevant key performance indicators through a dialogue process with its external stakeholders. Adequate resources (human and financial), therefore, need to be allocated to the evaluation process.

Thus, the company should evidence rigor in order to be able to produce accurate, clear, meaningful, and consistent data at all relevant levels of the company and to summarize them into constructive statements.

Building CSR Capacity at STMicroelectronics[4]

Strategies lead nowhere without the men and women who will deploy and champion them.

Beyond the development of CSR-related knowledge and skills at the executive level, STMicroelectronics (2008) demonstrates a dedicated commitment to ensure that local and regional sites are adequately prepared to roll out CSR programs that potentially raises critical and delicate issues for discussion with stakeholders and that often requires a review of existing management systems and daily practices. In this sense, STMicroelectronics has developed and goes through an entire cycle of designing and deploying a cultural and competence framework to guide employee actions and behavior. More specifically, the company has taken a systematic approach to deploying CSR expertise and excellence within the company through a four-step process. It has started with (1) raising awareness among all employees about CSR through an e-learning course that prepared employees for CSR challenges faced by the company; 50,000 employees have been trained between 2006 and 2007. (2) STMicroelectronics' CSR principles were then launched and communicated to all employees through a variety of different communication channels and methods. (3) An assessment phase took a risk-and-opportunities management approach to compliance with the CSR principles, involving benchmarking and gap analysis workshops for local top management in all manufacturing sites and many medium and smaller sites across the world. (4) A new e-learning course has been developed and launched for around 10,000 managers and employees in critical functions with respect to CSR. This course takes a deeper look at the CSR principles of the company and how to ensure compliance through decision-making and actions in daily business life. The development of CSR competencies and skills at STMicroelectronics is decisively supported by the STM University that fosters the development of management and employees with existing learning solutions, but also new ones to respond to very specific strategic needs.

---

[4]This short abstract of STMicroelectronics and its activities has been more or less taken as it appeared originally in STMicroelectronics (2008).

4.6 The Aspiration Challenge: Establishment of Effective Corporate Social Responsibility Leadership and Sound Corporate Governance

To fully ensure that CSR is mainstreamed within a company the company must face the aspiration challenge, which concerns building strong organizational determination to achieve in CSR and to developing skills and competencies. The establishment of sound corporate governance and effective CSR leadership is identified as being essential in this regard.

4.6.1 Corporate Governance as a Critical Factor for Corporate Social Responsibility Mainstreaming

Increasingly, literature debates the need for CSR policies and activities to be based on sound corporate governance, even standards (Welford, 2007). To efficiently mainstream CSR within a company, CSR must be integrated into the company's management structures and processes 'so that as far as possible, all social responsibility issues are foreseen, covered by corporate policies, and dealt with in a way that shows an understanding of the issues involved and a willingness to help solve societal problems' (Shahin and Zairi, 2007, p. 766).

The development of more formal governance structures, such as CSR board committees, social, environmental, and economic risk registers, and CSR reports, evidence that companies are looking past short-term financial performance in order to take the company's long-term sustainability into consideration (Money and Schepers, 2007). By adhering to sound corporate governance that allows directors to play a constructive role in achieving CSR objectives and obtaining stakeholders' trust, companies demonstrate a real commitment to CSR. Corporate governance can provide a constructive, reinforcing, and emblematic basis for implementing relevant, efficient, and credible CSR policies through the creation of value-based stakeholder relationships (Beltratti, 2005; Welford, 2007). When corporate governance systems are efficient they can prevent illegal actions against stakeholders, whilst effective and socially endorsed CSR corporate codes can prevent actions that are legal but not appropriate (Beltratti, 2005).

On a practical level, board committee activity might helpfully address misaligned performance management systems and market failure that often stand in the way of achieving in CSR, '[...] boards should constructively address market failure by establishing board policies supporting government action on relevant issues; they should oversee implementation of these policies by the company's lobbying and government relations departments; and perhaps also keep a check on the lobbying activities of any relevant trade associations in which the company participates. They should also address PMS [performance management systems] incentives problems' (Mackenzie, 2007, p. 942). Problems of performance management systems incentives can be addressed by, first, examining the risks that are a result of these systems (and when market failure is a problem) and, second, modifying existing objectives and performance targets so that the risks are reduced or overcome (op. cit.).

It should be noted that organizational commitment – through the design of adapted corporate governance and organizational structures – cannot be achieved without the demonstration of a real willingness to embed CSR thoroughly within the company; this willingness should be tribute to a strong CSR leadership at the managerial level to ensure that CSR is embraced by the company's stakeholders (Maak, 2007).

4.6.2 The Need for Responsible Managerial Leadership

The management team is responsible for overseeing and guiding the company to succeeding with its long-term strategic decisions. The team plays a decisive role in articulating the strategic posture of the company (Thomas and Simerly, 1994) and, in this way, exerts a central influence on the development and implementation of a CSR orientation within the company (Banerjee, 2001; Maxwell et al., 1997; Waddock, 2002; Waldman et al., 2006). In the same vein, according to a McKinsey (2006) survey of global business executives, 74% of the 4,238 managers surveyed, believed that the CEO or the board chair should take the lead in the management of socio-political issues and social responsibility. The emergence of a strong leadership, therefore, appears as a key factor in fostering corporate ethics (Ciulla, 1999; Weaver et al., 1999) and improving the company's commitment to CSR.

Managers have a responsibility to 'mobilize and align the energy of different people for achieving common objectives and support the realization of a common and good vision' (Maak and Pless, 2006, p. 104). The ability to develop and maintain constructive and enduring relationships with relevant stakeholders then becomes a critical characteristic of responsible managers (George, 2003). As well, managers will have to work for integrating people from different cultures and backgrounds so that these work effectively together; for taking care of the well-being of the local communities in which the company is rooted; for understanding needs and values of different stakeholders; and for making dialogue possible between the stakeholders (Maak and Pless, 2006). A first set of skills for a responsible manager thus includes communicating with others, adopting a long-term perspective, and being open-minded. A second set of skills concerns acting with integrity and genuinely caring for people (Wilson et al., 2006).

Responsible managers must demonstrate both emotional intelligence and ethical intelligence (Maak and Pless, 2006). While the first allows the fostering of moral awareness and reflection and also serves as a source of imaginative and responsible CSR orientation, the latter is assumed to drive emotional awareness, reflection, and emotional regulation. The combination of said two qualities help leaders in efficiently influencing the orientation of their company through the sound understanding of trends in the business environment and the construction of positive interactions with the company's stakeholders.[5]

Inspirational Leadership at Interface[6]

I want to pioneer the company of the next industrial revolution.

In the mid-1990s, when founder and chairman of the world's largest commercial carpet manufacturer Interface, Ray Anderson, provided his global team with a mission – to develop an action plan to abolish any negative impact of Interface's activities on the environment by 2020 – everyone around him considered he was foolish (Anderson, 1999; Gifford, 2001). Since Anderson's sudden environmental epiphany, Interface is nearly 50% toward the vision of its 'Mission Zero.' The company has reduced costs, improved its products, developed a proactive approach to participation in external organizations and efforts focused on sustainability issues, empowered its people, and gained the goodwill of the marketplace. Anderson galvanized his people around a higher purpose: making CSR and growth becoming the same thing. Under Anderson's leadership, trying to make CSR a critical consideration in every business decision from the factory floor to the research and development laboratory has been the demonstrated a priority. Anderson evidenced dedication and zeal to the CSR embedment process. He and other company leaders redesigned the way business was viewed and conducted. 'They developed a vision and involved employees, encouraged their participation, and promoted new thinking. They communicated back and forth with employees and spoke of the big picture and each person's role within it. These leaders set up an environment that was conducive to change. They empowered teams and encouraged innovation. They also convened experts, both inside and outside the company, to assist in this great metamorphosis' (Gifford, 2001). At Interface, the considerable work of initiating sustainable practices throughout the whole company was thus made a practical reality first and foremost because of three key factors: (1) the definition of an inspiring common vision, (2) serious commitment and passion from company leaders, and (3) the empowerment and commitment of employees.

---

[5] Here we do not consider how power might intersect with these capacities, but instead refer to our subsequent discussion of the study's limitations.

[6] This short abstract of Interface and its activities has been more or less taken as it appeared originally in Anderson (1999) and Gifford (2001).

4.7 Synergies Between the Three Challenges

The three challenges of action, activation, and aspiration are mutually dependent; the way that a company tackles one challenge will bear on how it will need to tackle the other two challenges. First, the action challenge concerns stakeholder engagement through interactive processes, directly influences the development and diffusion of skills and competencies within the company. On the one hand, engagement activities generate knowledge exchange and organizational learning derived from the stakeholders' expertise, while an ongoing dialogue with stakeholders helps the company to build better relationships. Stakeholder engagement processes also affect CSR managerial leadership and commitment within the company, as interactions with stakeholders 'ask managers to articulate the shared sense of the value they create [. . .] It also pushes managers to be clear about how they want to do business, specifically what kinds of relationships they want and need to create with their stakeholders to deliver on their purpose' (Freeman, 1984, p. 364).

Second, CSR-related skills and competencies dramatically impacts a company's ability to develop constructive CSR actions and stakeholder engagement strategies. As companies deal with a growing range of complex factors relating to the economic, environmental, and social consequences of its business operations, successful implementation of CSR policies increasingly demands strong management and CSR-related skills, as well as an organization-wide awareness of CSR issues and their implications. Also, the existing level of CSR-related skills and competencies within the whole company will significantly moderate the timing and intensity of the influence of leadership on the organizational acknowledgment and enthusiasm with respect to CSR. To cultivate relevant CSR behaviors within the company, CSR leaders need valuable information sources with respect to the environment, worthy managerial support and expertise, and a knowledgeable internal audience to dialogue with.

Third, and finally, the establishment of a sound corporate governance structure and an effective CSR leadership deeply influences organizational CSR capabilities. Dedicated CSR leadership influences stakeholder engagement practices by shaping critical strategic decisions and actively developing and supporting the CSR vision of the company, as well as manifestly communicating and symbolizing the CSR commitments. Moreover, CSR leaders and sound corporate governance can significantly contribute to developing CSR-related skills and competencies within the organization through the development of dedicated CSR structures and functions, as well as by demonstrating the willingness to provide incentives and resources for organization-wide CSR sensitizing and training initiatives.

4.8 Closing Remarks

In the twenty first century, CSR is fast becoming the ticket for doing business (Altman, 1998) thus suggesting the requirement for a responsible management team. However, mainstreaming CSR within the company often remains an unclear and perplexing issue. This chapter offers some suggestions for dealing success-fully with this issue; the suggestions concern the challenges that companies face in having the idea of CSR embraced. More specifically, the challenges of action, activation, and aspiration are discussed in relation to the implementation of CSR within a company. The objectives for mainstreaming CSR can be reached through the combination and interplay between the development of societal understanding and ongoing dialogue and engagement between the company and its stakehold-ers; the presence and maintenance of relevant skills and competencies at the various levels of the company; and CSR-related capacities linked to the exis-tence of actual CSR leadership within the company. Finally, dealing with the three in a capable manner helps to ensure stimulating, learning, and implement-ing capabilities that all play a significant role in mainstreaming CSR within the company.

Despite these contributions, our study also contains several limitations that suggest some new research avenues. First, we have approached our examination from a top down and top out to the community approach. Positive leadership by senior management is critical to CSR implementation (Lyon, 2004; Werre, 2003): through change agents such as the executive board and line managers, CSR prin-ciples can be cascaded throughout the organization (Cramer et al., 2004). Our approach allowed us to focus on top management professionals' perspectives of CSR. However, we acknowledge that our approach is a simplistic view of how CSR is being mainstreamed within companies. For example, research has identi-fied the importance of employees (other than top managers) in the implementation of CSR (e.g., Lindgreen et al., 2008); also external stakeholders are central to the success of any CSR activities (Dunphy et al., 2003). Therefore, further research should examine how our suggested theoretical framework needs to be revised in order to accommodate for the inclusion of stakeholders other than top management. Also, we have relied upon secondary company sources; it is suggested that further research carries out primary research and involves the examination of companies' programs (including not successful ones). Finally, further research should include the opinions of stakeholders about these programs and relationships established with companies.

Second, with the inclusion of additional stakeholders further research needs to consider issues such as power differences between the company and, for exam-ple, community-based interest groups, as perhaps the company's CSR activities are not necessarily welcomed by such groups. Thus, learning about stakeholder expectations and the specifics of the context help ensure that changing to CSR is beneficial and supported by appropriate mechanisms (Burnes, 2004). Therefore, managers must understand and remain actively aware of both the context and expectations, as well as recognize that any changes they implement will shape the environment in turn (Mitleton-Kelly, 2003). The development of CSR activi-ties therefore can entail activity that acts on and reacts to and with the business environment.

Acknowledgments We wish to thank the editors and the reviewers for their helpful suggestions as to how to improve our chapter.

References

Agle B.R., Mitchell, R.K., and Sonnenfeld, J. 1999, 'Who Matters to CEOs? An Investigation of Stakeholder Attributes and Salience, Corporate Performance and CEO Values', *Academy of Management Journal*, Vol. 42, No. 5, pp. 507–525.

Altman, B. 1998, 'Transformed Corporate Community Relations: A Management Tool for Achieving Corporate Citizenship', *Business and Society Review*, Vol. 102–103, pp. 43–51.

Amaeshi, K.M., Onyeka, K.O., and Nnodim, P. 2008, 'Corporate Social Responsibility in Supply Chains of Global Brands: A Boundaryless Responsibility? Clarifications, Exceptions and Implications', *Journal of Business Ethics*, Vol. 81, No. 1, pp. 223–234.

Anderson, R. 1999, *Mid-Course Correction: Toward a Sustainable Enterprise. The Interface Model*, Peregrinzilla Press, Atlanta, GA.

Andriof, J. and Waddock, S. 2002, 'Unfolding Stakeholder Engagement', In Andriof, J., Waddock, S., Husted, B., and Rahman, S. (Eds.), *Unfolding Stakeholder Thinking: Theory, Responsibility and Engagement*, pp. 19–42, Greenleaf, Sheffield, UK.

Banerjee, S.B. 2001, 'Managerial Perceptions of Corporate Environmentalism: Interpretations from Industry and Strategic Implications for Organizations', *Journal of Management Studies*, Vol. 38, No. 4, pp. 489–513.

Basu, K. and Palazzo, G. 2008, 'Corporate Social Responsibility. A Process Model of Sensemaking', *Academy of Management Review*, Vol. 33, No. 1, pp. 122–136.

Beltratti, A. 2005, 'The Complementarity between Corporate Governance and Corporate Social Responsibility', *Geneva Papers on Risk and Insurance*, Vol. 30, No. 3, pp. 373–386.

Bowen, H.R. 1953, *Social Responsibilities of the Businessman*, Harper & Brothers, New York.

Burchell, J. and Cook, J. 2006, 'It's Good to Talk? Examining Attitudes Towards Corporate Social Responsibility Dialogue and Engagement Processes', *Business Ethics: A European Review*, Vol. 15, No. 2, pp. 154–170.

Burke, R. 1999, *Project Management: Planning and Control Techniques*, John Wiley, Chichester, UK.

Burnes, B. 2004, *Managing Change: A Strategic Approach to Organisational Dynamics*, 4th ed, Prentice Hall, Harlow.

Campbell, D., Stonehouse, G., and Houston, B. 2002, *Business Strategy: An Introduction*, Butterworth-Heinemann, Oxford, UK.

Ciulla, J.B. 1999, 'The Importance of Leadership in Shaping Business Values', *Long Range Planning*, Vol. 32, No. 2, pp. 166–172.

Clarkson, M.B. 1995, 'A Stakeholder Framework for Analyzing and Evaluating Corporate Social Performance', *Academy of Management Review*, Vol. 20, No. 1, pp. 92–117.

Cleland, D. 1990, *Project Management, Strategic Design and Implementation*, TAB Books, Blue Ridge Summit, PA.

Corporate Register. 2008, *Assure View: The CSR Assurance Statement Report*, http://www.corporateregister.com, last accessed August 2008.

Cramer, J., Jonker, J., and van der Heijden, A. 2004, 'Making Sense of Corporate Social Responsibility', *Journal of Business Ethics*, Vol. 55, No. 2, pp. 215–222.

Cramer, J.M., Van der Heijden, A.J.W., and Jonker, J. 2006, 'Corporate Social Responsibility: Making Sense through Thinking and Acting', *Business Ethics: A European Review*, Vol. 15, No. 4, pp. 380–389.

Crane, A. and Livesey, S. 2003, 'Are You Talking to Me? Stakeholder Communication and the Risks and Rewards of Dialogue', In Andriof, J., Waddock, S., Rahman S., and Husted, B. (Eds.), *Unfolding Stakeholder Thinking II: Relationships, communication, reporting and performance*, pp. 39–52, Greenleaf, Sheffield, UK.

CSR Academy. 2004, *The CSR Competency Framework*, Department of Trade and Industry, London, UK.

Cumming, J.F., Bettidge, N., and Toyne, P. 2005, 'Responding to Global Business Critical Issues: A Source of Innovation and Transformation for FTSE 350 Companies?' *Corporate Governance*, Vol. 5, No. 3, pp. 42–52.

Davis, K. and Blomstrom, R.L. 1975, *Business and Society: Environment and Responsibility*, McGraw-Hill, New York.

Dawson, P. 2003, *Understanding Organisational Change: Contemporary Experience of People at Work*, Sage, London, UK.

de Bakker, F.G.A. and den Hond, F. 2008, 'Activists' Influence Tactics and Corporate Policies', *Business Communication Quarterly*, Vol. 71, No. 1, pp. 107–111.

Dickson, T. 2004, 'CSR: Moving on to the Front Foot', *European Business Forum*, Summer, p. 2.

DTI. 2003, *Changing Manager Mindsets – DTI/CRG Report*, Department of Trade and Industry, London.

Dunphy, D., Griffiths, A., and Benn, S. 2003, *Organizational Change for Corporate Sustainability*, Routledge, London, UK.

European Commission. 2001, Green Paper *Promoting a European Framework for Corporate Social Responsibility*, Brussels, COM (2001) 416 final.

Evan, W.M. and Freeman, R.E. 1988, 'A Stakeholder Theory of the Modern Corporation: Kantian Capitalism', In Beauchamp, T.L. and Bowie, N.E. (Eds.), *Ethical Theory and Business*, pp. 97–106, Prentice Hall, Englewood Cliffs, NJ.

Frankental, P. 2001, 'Corporate Social Responsibility – A PR Invention?' *Corporate Communication: An International Journal*, Vol. 6, No. 1, pp. 18–23.

Freeman, R.E. 1984, *Strategic management: A Stakeholder Approach*, Pitman, Boston, MA.

Gao, S.S. and Zhang, J.J. 2001, 'A Comparative Study of Stakeholder Engagement Approaches in Social Accounting', In Andriof, J. and McIntosh, M. (Eds.), *Perspectives on Corporate Citizenship*, pp. 239–255, Greenleaf, Sheffield, UK.

Gao, S.S. and Zhang, J.J. 2006, 'Stakeholder Engagement, Social Auditing and Corporate Sustainability', *Business Process Management Journal*, Vol. 12, No. 6, pp. 722–740.

Garriga, E. and Melé, D. 2004, 'Corporate Social Responsibility Theories: Mapping the Territory', *Journal of Business Ethics*, Vol. 53, No. 1–2, pp. 51–71.

George, B. 2003, *Authentic Leadership: Rediscovering the Secrets to Creating Lasting Value*, Jossey-Bass, San Francisco, CA.

Gifford, M.A. 2001, *Operating a Sustainable Business – Where do We Start?* http://ese.colorado.edu/sustainable_development.htm, last accessed 15 August 2008.

Gonzales, B., Ellis, Y.M., Riffel, P.J., and Yager, D. 1999, 'Training at IBM's Human Resource Service Center: Linking People, Technology, and HR Processes', *Human Resource Management*, Vol. 38, No. 2, pp. 135–142.

Greenwood, M. 2007, 'Stakeholder Engagement: Beyond the Myth of Corporate Responsibility', *Journal of Business Ethics*, Vol. 74, No. 4, pp. 315–327.

Harrison, R., Newholm, T., and Shaw, D. 2006, *The Ethical Consumer*, Sage, London, UK.

Hemingway, C.A. and Maclagan, P.W. 2004, 'Managers' Personal Values as Drivers of Corporate Social Responsibility', *Journal of Business Ethics*, Vol. 50, No. 1, pp. 33–44.

Hogan, S.P. 2007, 'Toy Stories, Horror Stories and Fairy Tales: The Role of the Media in Highlighting Issues of Corporate Responsibility', *Young Consumers*, Vol. 8, No. 2, pp. 94–100.

Hopkins, M. 2006, 'What is Corporate Social Responsibility All About?', *Journal of Public Affairs*, Vol. 6, No. 3–4, pp. 298–316.

Institute of Social and Ethical Accountability. 1999, *Accountability 1000 (AA1000) Framework. Standard, Guidelines and Professional Qualification*, ISEA, London, UK.

Jamali, D. 2008, 'A Stakeholder Approach to Corporate Social Responsibility: A Fresh Perspective into Theory and Practice', *Journal of Business Ethics*, Vol. 82, No. 1, pp. 213–231.

Kerzner, H. 2003, *Project Management: A Systems Approach to Planning, Scheduling and Controlling*, John Wiley, New York, NY.

Kezsbom, D.S. and Edward, K.A. 2001, *The New Dynamic Project Management: Winning Through the Competitive Advantage*, John Wiley, New York.

Kolk, A. and Pinkse, J. 2006, 'Stakeholder Mismanagement and Corporate Social Responsibility Crises', *European Management Journal*, Vol. 24, No. 1, pp. 59–72.

Laufer, W.S. 2003, 'Social Accountability and Corporate Greenwashing', *Journal of Business Ethics*, Vol. 43, No. 3, pp. 253–261.

Lichtenstein, D.R., Drumwright, M.E., and Braig, B.M. 2004, 'The Effect of Corporate Social Responsibility on Customer Donations to Corporate-Supported Nonprofits', *Journal of Marketing*, Vol. 68, No. 4, pp. 16–32.

Lindgreen A. and Swaen, V. 2005, 'Corporate Citizenship: Let Not Relationship Marketing Escape the Management Toolbox', *Corporate Reputation Review*, Vol. 7, No. 4, pp. 346–363.

Lindgreen, A., Swaen, V., and Harness, D. 2008, 'The Role of 'High Potentials' in Implementing Corporate Social Responsibility', In Fleckenstein, M., Primeaux, P., Werhane, P., and Flanagan, P. (Eds.), *Proceedings of the 15th Annual International Conference Promoting Business Ethics: Business Ethics: Back to Basics*, October 22–24, the Vincentian Universities in the United States, New York.

Lindgreen, A., Swaen, V., and Johnston, W. 2009, 'Corporate Social Responsibility: An Empirical Investigation of U.S. Organizations', *Journal of Business Ethics* (forthcoming).

Lyon, D. 2004, 'How Can You Help Organizations Change to Meet the Corporate Responsibility Agenda?' *Corporate Social Responsibility and Environmental Management*, Vol. 11, No. 3, pp. 133–139.

Maak, T. 2007, 'Responsible Leadership, Stakeholder Engagement and the Emergence of Social Capital', *Journal of Business Ethics*, Vol. 74, No. 4, pp. 329–343.

Maak, T. and Pless, N.M. 2006, 'Responsible Leadership in a Stakeholder Society: A Relational Perspective', *Journal of Business Ethics*, Vol. 66, pp. 99–115.

Mackenzie, C. 2007, 'Boards, Incentives and Corporate Social Responsibility: The Case for a Change of Emphasis', *Corporate Governance: An International Review*, Vol. 15, No. 5, pp. 935–943.

Maignan, I. and Ralston, D.A. 2002, 'Corporate Social Responsibility in Europe and the U.S.: Insights from Businesses' Self-Presentations', *Journal of International Business Studies*, Vol. 33, No. 3, pp. 497–514.

Maignan, I. and Ferrell, O.C. 2004, 'Corporate Social Responsibility and Marketing: An Integrative Framework', *The Journal of the Academy of Marketing Science*, Vol. 32, No. 1, pp. 3–19.

Maignan, I., Ferrell, O.C., and Ferrell, L. 2006, 'A Stakeholder Model for Implementing Social Responsibility in Marketing', *European Journal of Marketing*, Vol. 39, No. 9–10, pp. 956–976.

Maon, F., Lindgreen, A., and Swaen, V. 2009, 'Designing and Implementing Corporate Social Responsibility: An Integrative Framework Grounded in Theory and Practice', *Journal of Business Ethics* (forthcoming).

Maon, F., Swaen, V., and Lindgreen, A. 2008a, 'Highlighting Change Motors at Play in Organizational Progress Towards Corporate Social Responsibility', *Academy of Management Meeting: Best Paper Proceedings*, Academy of Management, Anaheim, CA.

Maon, F., Lindgreen, A., and Swaen, V. 2008b, 'Thinking of the Organization as a System: The Role of Managerial Perceptions in Developing a Corporate Social Responsibility Strategic Agenda', *Systems Research and Behavioural Science*, Vol. 25, No. 3, pp. 413–426.

Matten, D. and Moon, J. 2004, 'Implicit and Explicit CSR: A Conceptual Framework for Understanding CSR in Europe', *ICCSR Research Paper Series*, Nottingham University, Nottingham, UK.

Maxwell, J., Rothenberg, S., Briscoe, F., and Marcus, A. 1997, 'Green schemes: Corporate Environmental Strategies and their Implementation', *California Management Review*, Vol. 39, No. 3, pp. 118–134.

McKie, J.W. (Ed.) 1974, *Social Responsibility and the Business Predicament*, Brookings Institution, Washington DC.

McKinsey and Company. 2006, 'Global Survey of Business Executives', *The McKinsey Quarterly*, January, pp. 1–10.

McWilliams, A. and Siegel, D. 2001, 'Corporate Social Responsibility: A Theory of the Firm Perspective', *Academy of Management Review*, Vol. 26, No. 1, pp. 117–127.

Miles, M., Munilla, L., and Darroch, J. 2006, 'The Role of Strategic Conversations with Stakeholders in the Formation of Corporate Social Responsibility Strategy', *Journal of Business Ethics*, Vol. 69, No. 2, pp. 195–205.

Mirvis, P. and Googins, B. 2006, 'Stages of Corporate Citizenship', *California Management Review*, Vol. 48, No. 2, pp. 104–126.

Mitchell, R.K., Agle, B.R., and Wood, D.J. 1997, 'Towards a Theory of Stakeholder Identification and Salience: Defining Who and What Really Counts', *Academy of Management Review*, Vol. 22, No. 4, pp. 853–886.

Mitleton-Kelly, E. 2003, *Complex Systems and Evolutionary Perspectives on Organizations: The Application of Complexity Theory to Organizations*, Elsevier, London.

Money, K. and Schepers, H. 2007, 'Are CSR and Corporate Governance Converging?', *Journal of General Management*, Vol. 33, No. 2, pp. 1–11.

Morsing, M. 2003, *Conspicuous Responsibility: Communicating Responsibility – to Whom?* http://www.kommunikationsforum.dk/Log/morsing.pdf, last accessed April 2007.

Morsing, M. and Schultz, M. 2006, 'Corporate Social Responsibility Communication: Stakeholder Information, Response and Involvement Strategies', *Business Ethics: A European Review*, Vol. 15, No. 4, pp. 323–338.

Nijhof, A. and Jeurissen, R. 2006, 'A Sensemaking Perspective on Corporate Social Responsibility: Introduction to the Special Issue', *Business Ethics: A European Review*, Vol. 15, No. 4, pp. 316–322.

O'Connor, M. and Spangenberg, J.H. 2008, 'A Methodology for CSR Reporting: Assuring a Representative Diversity of Indicators across Stakeholders, Scales, Sites and Performance Issues', *Journal of Cleaner Production*, Vol. 16, No. 13, pp. 1399–1415.

Pedersen, E.R. and Neergaard, P. 2008, 'From Periphery to Center – How CSR Is Integrated in Mainstream Performance Management Frameworks', *Measuring Business Excellence*, Vol. 12, No. 1, pp. 4–12.

Post, J.E., Preston, L.E., and Sachs, S. 2002, 'Managing the Extended Enterprise: The New Stakeholder View', *California Management Review*, Vol. 45, No. 1, pp. 6–28.

Preble, J.F. 2005, 'Toward a Comprehensive Model of Stakeholder Management', *Business and Society Review*, Vol. 110, No. 4, pp. 407–431.

Preston, L. and Post, J. 1975, *Private Management and Public Policy: The Principle of Public Responsibility*, Prentice Hall, Englewood Cliffs, NJ.

Roloff, J. 2008, 'Learning from Multi-Stakeholder Networks: Issue-Focused Stakeholder Management', *Journal of Business Ethics*, Vol. 82, No. 1, pp. 233–254.

Sahlin-Andersson, K. 2006, 'Corporate Social Responsibility: A Trend and a Movement, but of What and for What?' *Corporate Governance*, Vol. 6, No. 5, pp. 595–608.

Savitz, A.W. and Weber, K. 2006, *The Triple Bottom Line: How Today's Best-Run Companies Are Achieving Economic, Social, and Environmental Success and how You Can Too*, Jossey-Bass, San Francisco, CA.

Schäfer, H., Zenker, J., Beer, J., and Fernandes, P. 2006, *Who is Who in Corporate Social Responsibility Rating. A Survey of Internationally Established Rating Systems that Measure Corporate Social Responsibility*, Bertelsmann-Stiftung, Gütersloh, Germany.

Shahin A. and Zairi, M. 2007, 'Corporate Governance as a Critical Element for Driving Excellence in Corporate Social Responsibility', *International Journal of Quality and Reliability Management*, Vol. 24, No. 7, pp. 753–770.

Smith, A.D. 2007, 'Making the Case for the Competitive Advantage of Corporate Social Responsibility', *Business Strategy Series*, Vol. 8, No. 3, pp. 186–195.

STMicroelectronics. 2008, *Corporate Responsibility Report: A Culture of Sustainable Excellence*, STMicroelectronics, Geneva, CH.

Tench, R., Jones, B., and Bowd, R. 2007, 'Perceptions and Perspectives: Corporate Social Responsibility and the Media', *Journal of Communication Management*, Vol. 11, No. 4, pp. 348–370.

Thomas, A. and Simerly, R. 1994, 'The Chief Executive Officer and Corporate Social Performance: An Interdisciplinary Examination', *Journal of Business Ethics*, Vol. 13, No. 12, pp. 959–968.

van Marrewijk, M. and Werre, M. 2003, 'Multiple Levels of Corporate Sustainability', *Journal of Business Ethics*, Vol. 44, No. 2, pp. 107–119.

Vodafone. 2005, *Stakeholder Engagement in Practice at Vodafone*, Vodafone Group Plc, Newbury, UK.

Waddock, S. 2002, *Leading Corporate Citizens: Visions, Values, Value Added*, McGraw-Hill Irwin, New York.

Waldman, D.A., Siegel, D.S., and Javidan, M. 2006, 'Components of. Transformational Leadership and Corporate Social Responsibility', *Journal of Management Studies*, Vol. 43, No. 8, pp. 1703–1725.

Weaver, G.R., Trevino, L.K., and Cochran, P.L. 1999, 'Integrated and Decoupled Corporate Social Performance: Management Commitments, External Pressure, and Corporate Ethics Practices', *Academy of Management Journal*, Vol. 42, No. 5, pp. 539–552.

Welford, R. 2007, 'Corporate Governance and Corporate Social Responsibility: Issues for Asia', *Corporate Social Responsibility and Environmental Management*, Vol. 14, No. 1, pp. 42–51.

Werre, M. 2003, 'Implementing Corporate Social Responsibility: The Chiquita Case', *Journal of Business Ethics*, Vol. 44, No. 2/3, pp. 247–260.

Wilson, A. and Bonfiglioli, E. 2002, *Integrating CSR into Corporate Strategy, Management and Systems*, Proceedings of the Second International Global Compact Learning Forum Meeting, 11–12 December, Berlin, Germany.

Wilson, A., Lenssen, G., and Hind, P. 2006, *Leadership Qualities and Management Competencies for Corporate Responsibility*, Ashridge Business School and EABIS, Ashridge, UK.

Zadek, S. 2004, 'The Path to Corporate Social Responsibility', *Harvard Business Review*, Vol. 82, No. 12, pp. 125–132.

Chapter 5
The Company Directors' Perspective of Corporate Social Responsibility

Royston Gustavson

To every action there is an equal and opposite reaction.
Sir Isaac Newton

Abstract The role of a company director is, as a member of the Board of Directors, to create value for an organisation through both performance (direction) and conformance (control). Performance relates to setting the mission, values, and strategic direction of the organisation; a socially responsible director considers the impact of these on both stakeholders and the natural environment. Conformance relates firstly to accountability through setting internal policy and procedures, and adherence to both internal and external (such as laws) rules and procedures, and secondly to transparency through reporting to stakeholders; a socially responsible director supports high levels of each. Company directors realise their role through decision-making, and so it is essential to examine the impact of their experience, demographic characteristics, and personal values on their decision-making processes. Directors have access to a wide range of information and resources on CSR and its relationship to corporate governance, including legislation and case law, guidelines, reports, professional associations, corporate constitutions and codes of conduct, and professional and academic literature. An overview of the place of CSR in company directors' decision making is given through reference to empirical research.

5.1 Introduction

There is no universal definition of corporate social responsibility (CSR). Indeed, Idowu and Filho have stated that 'What falls under the umbrella of CSR in one country may perhaps be of little or no significance in another' (2009, p. 1). Company directorship as a profession is created by legislation, which is typically enacted at

R. Gustavson (✉)
The Australian National University, Canberra, Australia

S.O. Idowu, W.L. Filho (eds.), *Professionals' Perspectives of Corporate Social Responsibility*, DOI 10.1007/978-3-642-02630-0_6,

national level, and so it may be expected that a director will have her or his perspective significantly moulded by the legislative framework or frameworks within which he or she has practiced. This will interact with each individual director's corporate experiences and personal values. As such, the company directors' perspective of CSR will be a varied one.

It must be emphasised that this chapter examines company directorship as a profession, and how the individual members of that profession perceive and contribute towards CSR: that is, how a company director thinks about CSR and what a company director does about CSR. It is not about corporate governance and CSR, and so does not focus on the impact of an organisation's governance mechanisms on CSR, nor is it about corporations and CSR, and so does not discuss specific examples of CSR, as the practical implementation of CSR is a management role, not a governance role.

As corporate governance is the job of a company director, it is necessary to begin by defining this job. The reference point taken in this chapter is the predominant model of corporate governance, the Anglo-American model. Although there are important variants, especially those found in Germany and Japan, a discussion of them is beyond the scope of this chapter.

5.2 Company Directorship

5.2.1 Corporate Governance

Shleifer and Vishny, in a review of the corporate governance literature, state that 'Corporate governance deals with the ways in which suppliers of finance to corporations assure themselves of getting a return on their investment' (1997, p. 737). There is a very different definition – one that has CSR as a central focus – in a draft document issued by the New Partnership for Africa's Development: 'Corporate Governance is concerned with the ethical principles, values and practices that facilitate holding the balance between economic and social goals and between individual and communal goals. The aim is to align as nearly as possible the interests of individuals, corporations and society within a framework of sound governance and common good' (NEPAD, 2003, p. 20); the definition was changed significantly in the final document. Between these two definitions is the description of corporate governance in the *OECD Principles of Corporate Governance*: 'Corporate governance involves a set of relationships between a company's management, its board, its shareholders and other stakeholders. Corporate governance also provides the structure through which the objectives of the company are set, and the means of attaining those objectives and monitoring performance are determined' (OECD, 2004, p. 11). Unfortunately, legislation, corporate scandals and collapse, and litigation have led to the problem expressed in the opening statement of the *Hempel Report*, that 'The importance of corporate governance lies in its contribution both to business prosperity and to accountability. ... Public companies are now among the most accountable organisations in society. . ... But the emphasis on accountability has tended to obscure a board's first responsibility – to enhance the prosperity of the business over time' (Hempel, 1998, Sect. 1.1).

Alford, Gustavson, and Williams, in *Governing Australia's Courts*, focused on governance as '*categories of decisions* and who has power to make them. . .decisions affect performance and are in turn the mechanisms by which institutional power and authority are manifested in practice' (2004, p. 2). Shailer defined governance in essentially the same way: 'governance is decision-making in the exercise of author-ity for direction and control' (2004, p. 11). It is through the board's decision-making authority and resultant decision-making processes that the individual company director realises his or her perception of CSR; the director must not be involved in the implementation of CSR or the choice of specific CSR projects, both of which are management rather than governance tasks.

5.2.2 The Role of a Company Director

The role of director may be divided into two main categories: performance, which relates to setting the mission, values, and strategic direction of the organisation; and conformance, which relates to accountability through setting internal pol-icy and procedures, and adherence to both internal and external (such as laws and regulations) rules and procedures, and to transparency through reporting to stakeholders.

The *King II Report* (King, 2002, pp. 46–47) recommends ten roles for a director:

1. determine the company's purpose and values;
2. determine the strategy to achieve its purpose (that is, its strategic intent and objectives as a business enterprise) and to implement its values (that is, its organisational behaviour and norms to achieve its purpose) on order to ensure that it survives and thrives;
3. exercise leadership, enterprise, integrity and judgment in directing the company so as to achieve continuing prosperity for the company;
4. ensure that procedures and practices are in place that protect the company's assets and reputation;
5. monitor and evaluate the implementation of strategies, policies, management perfor-mance criteria and business plans;
6. ensure that the company complies with all relevant laws, regulations and codes of best business practice;
7. ensure that technology and systems used in the company are adequate to run the business properly and for it to compete through the efficient use of its assets, processes and human resources;
8. identify key risk areas and key performance indicators of the business enterprise in order for the company to generate economic profit, so as to enhance shareowner value in the long term (the wider interests of society should at the same time be recognized);
9. regularly assess its performance and effectiveness as a whole, and that of individual directors, including the chief executive officer; and
10. ensure that the company has developed a succession plan for its executive directors and senior management.

A company director can play an active role in ensuring that their organisation's purpose and values are consistent with, or promote, CSR, and can ensure that the strategy and, through setting policies and procedures, the implementation of that strategy are done in a socially responsible way. An ongoing convergence between CSR and corporate governance (Horrigan, 2007; Gill, 2008) is likely to see an increasing focus by directors on CSR.

5.2.3 Is CSR Permissible as a Value-Creating Activity?

Company directors are legally required to act in the best interests of, or promote the success of, the corporation, which is generally interpreted as a requirement to create value for the corporation. As such, directors may only act in a socially responsible way if they perceive it to be value-creating. From a review of the literature, Salzmann, Ionescu-Somers, and Steger didn't find a clear case for a relationship between CSR and financial performance, noting that the many instrumental studies suggest that the relationship 'is complex and contingent on situational, company- and plant-specific factors that are difficult to detect through most analytical approaches. Furthermore, the issue of the causal sequence...remains unresolved' (Salzmann et al., 2005, p. 30). Margolis and Walsh concluded that 'The clear signal that emerges from 30 years of academic research – indicating that a positive relationship exists between social performance and financial performance – must be treated with caution' as a result of methodological concerns (2001, p. 13). The only relationship that Dulewicz and Herbert found between board practice relating to responsibility to stakeholders and company performance was the effectiveness of communications (2004, p. 273). Steger, however, asks whether 'the laggards are more likely to be punished than the pioneers are to be rewarded' (2006a, p. 442), and Husted (2005), using real options theory, makes powerful arguments for the use of CSR as a risk management tool. The Australian Securities Exchange's *Corporate Governance Principles and Recommendations* (ASX, 2007) views stakeholder management as risk management. As such, individual directors do not need to agonise over whether or not CSR is in the best interests of the firm: its use as a risk management tool clearly justifies it. Indeed, it may be argued that, just as it is negligent not to manage some risks through insurance, it is negligent not to manage other risks through engaging in CSR.

5.2.4 How Should a Director Think About Stakeholders?

There is consensus that company directors should take stakeholders into consideration when making decisions. For example, the International Corporate Governance Network has stated that it 'concurs in the view that active cooperation between corporations and stakeholders is essential in creating wealth, employment and financially sound enterprises over time' (ICGN, 2005, Sect. 7.1). The New Zealand Securities Commission has stated that 'advancing the interests of other stakeholders, such as employees and customers, will often further the interests of an entity and its shareholders. . . .. Managing stakeholder interests should be viewed as simply good business' (NZSC, 2004, p. 25). This normative approach has empirical support from Wang and Dewhirst, who found that 'directors attach generally high importance to responding to stakeholder expectations' (1992, p. 120). Many examples of good stakeholder management are given in the two volumes edited by Andriof et al. (2002–2003). An excessive focus on stakeholders, however, is not good business. Directors may take comfort from the findings of Steger, that 'We cannot detect any massive discontent with corporate social and environmental performance; there is no evident opposition to the current basic (financially driven) business model. Those who are asking for more. . .are also those who are least important to companies, and companies have learned to manage them' (2006b, p. 120). Nevertheless, it has been found that one type of stakeholder does have a very significant impact: institutional investors (Aguilera et al., 2006).

5.2.5 Executive, Non-executive, and Independent Directors

A director is usually categorised as either an executive (or inside) director, that is, a director who is also an employee of the corporation (such as the Chief Executive Officer), or a non-executive (or outside) director, that is, a director who is not an employee of the corporation. The purpose of a non-executive director is to 'bring an external judgment on issues of strategy, performance, resources and standards of conduct and evaluation of performance to the board. Courage, wisdom and independence should be the hallmark of any non-executive director acting in the best interests of the company' (King, 2002, p. 56). The category of non-executive director is subdivided into independent directors and non-independent directors. The ASX *Guidelines* (ASX, 2007, p. 17) states that:

When determining the independent status of a director the board should consider whether the director:

1. is a substantial shareholder of the company or an officer of, or otherwise associated directly with, a substantial shareholder of the company;
2. is employed, or has previously been employed in an executive capacity by the company or another group member, and there has not been a period of at least 3 years between ceasing such employment and serving on the board;
3. has within the last 3 years been a principal of a material professional adviser or a material consultant to the company or another group member, or an employee materially associated with the service provided;
4. is a material supplier or customer of the company or other group member, or an officer of or otherwise associated directly or indirectly with a material supplier or customer;
5. has a material contractual relationship with the company or another group member other than as a director.

The ASX recommends a majority of independent directors (ASX, 2007, p. 16), and the *King II Report* recommends 'a majority of non-executive directors of whom sufficient should be independent of management for minority interests to be protected' (King, 2002, p. 47).

Different categories of directors have different perceptions of CSR. Wang and Coffee found that 'From the perspective of corporate social performance, free-spending insiders accomplish favourable results by contributing to the improvement of society's infrastructure and the long-term relationship between firms and communities. ... From the perspective of agency theory, however, if one is worried about unnecessary expense and waste, free-spending insiders should be monitored by independent outsiders' (1992, p. 776). In a later study, they concluded that 'increasing the number of outsiders on the board may actually have little effect on philanthropic behaviour' (Coffey and Wang, 1998, p. 1601). However, Ibrahim et al. found the opposite, that 'overall, outsiders are less economically driven and more philanthropically oriented than insiders' (2003, p. 398), concluding that 'by having outsiders on the board of directors, a firm in the service industry is more likely to engage in socially responsible activities' (2003, p. 399); Judge also found outsider representation to be 'positively related to social performance' (1994, p. 7). What is constant is that executive and non-executive directors perceive CSR differently.

5.3 Decision Making as a Company Director

The board is an ongoing body that makes a series of decisions. The directors' perceptions of the success or otherwise of a decision will feed back into the decision-making process, and as such will form part of the information or experience that is used in making later decisions. Board decision making has two particular characteristics. Firstly, the decision-makers are acting as agents: they are not making a personal decision, but are making a decision on behalf of the principals, that is, the owners of the corporation. Secondly, the decision is reached by a two-stage process: individuals, at least in theory, read the board papers before meetings and reach an initial position, and then the board uses group decision-making processes to reach a final decision which may be consensus or may be a majority vote. As such, both individual and group decision-making theories are relevant to the directors' perspective of CSR.

5.3.1 Individual Decision Making

How will an individual director take CSR into consideration when making a decision? Traditionally, decision making has been seen as a rational process, which Janis and Mann described as a 5-stage sequential process: (i) appraising the challenge, (ii) surveying alternatives, (iii) weighing alternatives, (iv) deliberating about commitment, and (v) adhering despite negative feedback (1977, p. 172). The chosen course of action is that which is expected to maximise utility, which in this case may be taken to be maximising the value of the corporation.

More recently, a number of theories have been developed that are categorised as naturalistic decision-making models. These take into consideration that decisions are 'frequently made under time pressure...in dynamic, uncertain, or ambiguous environments, making the notion of an 'expectation' problematic. Goals and

preferences may be unclear, with notions of stable, known utilities hard to apply'
(Connolly and Koput, 1997, p. 285) – typical characteristics of high-level corporate decision making. Two such theories are those of Klein and of Beach. Klein's
Recognition-Primed Decision Model states that experienced decision makers use
their experience as the basis for their decision making: 'the focus is on the way
they assess the situation and judge it familiar, not on comparing options' (1998,
p. 30). This implies that a director's past experience of CSR will have a significant impact on the role of CSR in her or his future decision making. Beach's Image
Theory contains an important insight: 'most decisions are made in an attempt to do
what is "right", rather than in an attempt to maximize – where "right" is defined in
terms of the decision maker's values, ethics, beliefs, and morals, not all of which
are necessarily admirable' (1990, p. xiii); he goes on to state that 'Whatever one's
principles may be, they are the foundation of one's decisions: potential goals and
actions must not contradict them or those goals and actions will be deemed unacceptable' (1998, p. 9). This implies that directors' personal principles will play a
key role in their decision making, including on CSR-related issues. Although not
studying company directors, Campbell found that, with regard to corporate giving,
'when the decision maker's personal sense of social consciousness was relatively
high, the firm was more likely to contribute' (1999, p. 382). The key role of personal values in business is made clear in the conference proceedings *Shareholder
Value and the Common Good* (Lutz and Mimbi, 2004), and pervades the writings of
Elegido (1996, 2003). The problems that may arise when a director's cultural values
are misaligned with the corporate governance framework is discussed in Gustavson
et al. (2009).

Another important factor in decision making is the director's perception of risk:
lay people and experts perceive risks differently (Slovic, 1987). This suggests that
different directors will perceive risks differently depending on their level of expertise in the area. Risk assessment is particularly important for environmental issues,
where decision makers may be required to make use of the precautionary principle
(see Peterson, 2006).

5.3.2 Board Diversity and Group Decision Making

Company directors do not make their final decisions in isolation: unlike most decision makers, they invariably make a joint decision with other company directors at
board meetings. As with any group decision-making process, it is important that
pathologies do not affect the process; a well known example is 'group think' (Janis
and Mann, 1977, pp. 129–133). Given the role of experience, values, and risk perception on the making of CSR-related decisions, it is important that a board has a
diverse group of people to maximise the range of experience, values, and risk perception that will be brought to the meeting and inform the discussion. Much research
has been done on board demographics and CSR. For example, female board members are more likely than male board members to support philanthropic community
service and cultural activities (Williams, 2003).

5.4 Guidance for the Company Director

The roles and responsibilities of a company director are highly codified and extensively researched, and so directors may develop their perspective of the place of CSR within their professional duties from a number of sources, including legislation and case law; international, regional, and national guidelines; reports on CSR and corporate governance; professional associations (Institutes of Directors); the constitutions and codes of conduct of individual organisations; and the professional and academic literature.

5.4.1 Legislation and Case Law

The profession of company director exists solely in the context of a corporation, and corporations are created by legislation, usually a Companies Act or Corporations Act. The role of the individual director is further defined by a wide range of other Acts and regulations dealing with, amongst other things, occupational health and safety, environmental protection, and discrimination. This legislation also imposes penalties – which may include imprisonment – on individual directors for breaches of their duties, which results in legislation being the single most influential source of guidance for company directors. The interpretation of legislation is found in case law, which gives directors insights into how the legislation should affect their perceptions and actions. As legislation will differ from country to country, and in some countries from state to state, a director sitting on multiple boards will have to comply with one set of laws when sitting on a board in one jurisdiction, and another set of laws when sitting on another board in another jurisdiction.

5.4.1.1 United Kingdom

In 1883, Lord Justice Bowen famously wrote in a judgment that 'The law does not say that there are to be no cakes and ale, but there are to be no cakes and ale except such as are required for the benefit of the company.... it seems to me charity has no business to sit at boards of directors *quâ* charity' (Bowen, 1883, p. 673). This view dominated directors' thinking about CSR throughout the Commonwealth until recently, and today is still the legislative position in many countries. One of the key events in the history of the development of the company directors' perspective of CSR was surely the introduction of the UK *Companies Act 2006*. Section 172, which relates to individual directors, not to corporations, is headed 'Duty to promote the success of the company' and states that:

> (1) A director of a company must act in the way he considers, in good faith, would be most likely to promote the success of the company for the benefit of its members as a whole, and in doing so have regard (amongst other matters) to –
>   (a) the likely consequences of any decision in the long term,
>   (b) the interests of the company's employees,
>   (c) the need to foster the company's business relationships with suppliers, customers and others,

(d) the impact of the company's operations on the community and the environment,
(e) the desirability of the company maintaining a reputation for high standards of business conduct, and
(f) the need to act fairly as between members of the company.
(2) Where or to the extent that the purposes of the company consist of or include purposes other than the benefit of its members, subsection (1) has effect as if the reference to promoting the success of the company for the benefit of its members were to achieving those purposes.
(3) The duty imposed by this section has effect subject to any enactment or rule of law requiring directors, in certain circumstances, to consider or act in the interests of creditors of the company (UK, 2006, p. 79).

This duty, especially the requirement to have regard to the impact on the community and the environment, will fundamentally alter British directors' perspectives of CSR, as it legitimises CSR in the corporate world in a way that no amount of theorising or stakeholder pressure could. Not everyone sees this as positive. A prominent Australian bank director has stated that 'Let me make a bold and serious prediction: if this British folly unfolds, as I think it will, the returns of UK companies will fall and their cost of capital will rise. Investors will see UK firms as a riskier repository for their mobile capital, and if it is more costly for most companies to raise capital but relatively cheaper for Australian firms unburdened by CSR, eventually Australians will be able to buy British companies cheaper – except we will not want to' (Green, 2007, p. 50).

5.4.1.2 Australia

Unlike UK legislation, Australian legislation does not require CSR. The *Corporations Act 2001* s.181(1) states that 'A director or other officer of a corporation must exercise their powers and discharge their duties: (a) in good faith in the best interests of the corporation; and (b) for a proper purpose' (COA, 2009, vol. 1, p. 219); it should be noted that, as in the UK, this applies to the individual director, not to the corporation. Austin, a Justice of the Supreme Court of New South Wales, has written that: 'If the directors apply the company's property in a manner that no reasonable person would regard as being for the benefit of the company, even though they might subjectively believe that it is, they are in breach of their duty of good faith. But considerable latitude is given to them because only the most extreme conduct will be found to fall outside the objective boundary to what is otherwise a subjective test' (2007, p. 8). Henley (2005, p. 155) and Wilson (2005, p. 279) have both argued that 'sincere' acts of CSR, defined by Parkinson as 'voluntarily sacrificing profits...[or] incurring additional costs ... in the belief that such behaviour will have consequences superior to those flowing from a policy of pure profit maximisation' (1993, p. 261), are technically illegal under current Australian law. However, the Australian Parliamentary Secretary to the Treasurer has stated that 'company directors need to take into account the interests of stakeholders when making decisions in the interests of companies. I think our current regulatory framework supports this goal well' (Pearce, 2007, p. 33). In practice, the difficulty in proving that a director did not expect a decision to be of benefit to the company – any decision will benefit at least one of the company's stakeholder groups – means that directors have, in practice, a lot of scope for exercising CSR.

To avoid this uncertainty, some have argued that Australian legislation should explicitly permit, or even require, CSR. For example, McConvill and Joy have recommended that a duty for environmentally sustainable behaviour 'be imposed on directors, rather than the company, to send a clear message to directors that they are responsible for ensuring that the culture within Australia's companies develops towards setting in practice systems and policies that are sustainable and respect Australia's natural resources' (2003, p. 130).

5.4.2 Guidelines

Directors have access to a wide range of guidelines relevant to both corporate governance and CSR that are international, regional, or country-specific. A number of those for Europe are listed in an appendix in Wieland (2005), for Latin America are listed in Table 2 of Bedicks and arruda (2005), and for Africa are given in the references to Rossouw (2005). Unlike legislation, guidelines are optional (some may be mandated by law in particular countries, in which case they are considered under legal requirements). They aim to improve corporate performance.

5.4.2.1 International Guidelines

International guidelines, by their very nature, need to be broad enough that they can be applied across a wide range of countries, legal frameworks, and cultures.

Arguably the best-known of the international corporate governance guidelines is the *OECD Principles of Corporate Governance*, which lists a number of responsibilities of the board (2004, pp. 24–25), but these focus very much, and possibly excessively, on accountability, and appear to place little importance on CSR. Environmental issues are limited to disclosure of 'risks related to environmental liabilities' (OECD, 2004, p. 53), and social issues are limited to disclosure of 'information on key issues relevant to employees and other stakeholders that may materially affect the performance of the company. Disclosure may include . . . relations with other stakeholders such as creditors, suppliers, and local communities' (OECD, 2004, p. 53). The International Corporate Governance Network's *Statement on Global Corporate Governance Principles* states that 'Corporations should adopt and effectively implement a code of ethics and should conduct their activities in an economically, socially and environmentally responsible manner' (ICGN, 2005, Sect. 7.5).

Many important international CSR guidelines have been collected and published by Leipziger (2003), who precedes each of the 27 selected full-text documents with an introduction and analysis, and by Tully (2005), although some of the 116 full-text documents are national guidelines. The best known international CSR-related guidelines have been prepared by or for the United Nations, including the *Global Compact* (Fussler et al., 2004; Tully, 2005, pp. 3–4); *Agenda 21*, subtitled

'A blueprint for action for global sustainable development into the 21st century' (UN, 1993, p. 13), which includes the justification, objectives, activities, and means of implementation for each programme area; and the various publications of the United Nations Environment Program (www.unep.org).

There is a number of organisations that produce standards; a standard may be defined as a 'Document, established by consensus and approved by a recognized body, that provides, for common and repeated use, rules guidelines or characteristics for activities or their results, aimed at the achievement of the optimum degree of order in a given context' (ISO, n.d.). The International Organization for Standardization, which consists of 157 national standards bodies, has, as at 31 December 2008, produced 17,765 standards (ISO, 2009). For the purposes of CSR, its key standards are those of the ISO14000 series, which relate to environmental management, including life cycle assessment; and ISO26000 *Social Responsibility*, a draft of which was released in December 2008, which aims 'to integrate socially responsible behaviour into existing organizational strategies, systems, practices and processes. . ... [It] emphasizes the importance of results and improvements in performance' (ISO, 2008, p. v). There is much published on the ISO14000 series that will help directors to decide whether or not to adopt the guidelines (for example, Prakash and Potoski, 2006), or that will give directors an overview of best practice to help them to assess their own organisation's policies and their implementation. Social Accountability International has released *Social Accountability 8000* which aims to 'protect and empower all personnel within a company's scope of control and influence, who produce products or provide services for that company' (SAI, 2008, p. 4).

5.4.2.2 Regional Guidelines: The African Peer Review Mechanism

An important and interesting document of relevance to directors in Africa, from which directors worldwide can learn much, is the *African Peer Review Mechanism* (APRM) created by the New Partnership for Africa's Development (NEPAD). Each country that is a member of NEPAD is to undertake a voluntary self assessment in four areas, one of which is corporate governance. The five objectives for corporate governance (NEPAD, 2004, pp. 59–75), and the indicators that are most relevant to CSR, are:

- Objective 1: Promote an enabling environment and effective regulatory framework for economic activities.
- Objective 2: Ensure that corporations act as good corporate citizens with regards to human rights, social responsibility and environmental sustainability.
    - o Are there measures in place to ensure that corporations recognise and observe human and labour laws?
    - o To what extent are corporations responsive to the concerns of the communities in which they operate?
    - o What measures have been put in place to ensure sustainable environmental management on the part of corporations?
- Objective 3: Promote adoption of codes of good business ethics in achieving the objectives of the corporation.
- Objective 4: Ensure that corporations treat all their stakeholders (shareholders, employees, communities, suppliers and customers) in a fair and just manner.

    o To what extent does the corporate governance framework protect shareholder's rights?
    o Does the corporate governance framework recognise the rights of stakeholders (other than shareholders)?
- Objective 5: Provide for accountability of corporations, directors and officers.

By September 2008, reports had been published for Ghana (2005), Rwanda (2006), Kenya (2006), South Africa (2007, www.aprm.org.za), Algeria (2007), Benin (2008), and Uganda (2008, www.nepaduganda.or.ug). The APRM is important in ensuring that company directors in Africa give CSR a high priority in their decision making, and in helping to legitimise acts of CSR in the minds of stakeholders including shareholders and directors themselves.

5.4.2.3 National Guidelines: Australia

Australian directors may turn to a number of guidelines; those issued by the Australian Securities Exchange are discussed by Gustavson (2009, pp. 471–472). The Australian Institute of Company Directors has issued *A Guide to Sustainability in your Company* as part of its Directors' Checklist Series. The *Guide* is based around a four-part sustainability framework: Define what it means for your company, Commitment, Make it happen, and Report, review and perfect (AICD, 2003, p. 8). The *Guide* provides practical advice to directors; for example, to 'Make it happen', directors should: 'Make sustainability a fixed board agenda item; Recognise what you do already; Establish systems for measurement, and review and quantify the actual benefits of such systems; Establish criteria by which your company will measure its performance; [and] Revise incentive and reward systems to include sustainability performance criteria' (AICD, 2003, p. 15). Under each of these headings is a set of dot points that give further guidance on implementation.

An internationally groundbreaking series of Standards on Corporate Governance was issued in Australia beginning in 2003. *Organizational Codes of Conduct* (Standards Australia, 2003a) focuses primarily on the control of fraud and corruption, which may encourage directors to perceive a code of conduct as being only incidentally related to CSR, but the standard does recommend that each code should include a section dealing with stakeholders and a section dealing with the environment. That there is a separate standard entitled *Corporate Social Responsibility* (Standards Australia, 2003b) signals the importance of CSR in corporate governance. As it relates to governance, it gives no guidance on how to be socially responsible, which is a management task: it explains the structure for setting up a system to implement and document CSR.

5.4.3 Reports

There are many reports on corporate governance and corporate social responsibility, often commissioned by governments, that may either inform or represent the views of company directors. Internationally, the most famous and influential report to clearly place corporate social responsibility as an integral function of corporate governance is arguably the *King Report on Corporate Governance for South*

Africa – 2002 (King, 2002). It sets the scene by opening with Sir Adrian Cadbury's definition: 'Corporate governance is concerned with holding the balance between economic and social goals and between individual and communal goals...the aim is to align as nearly as possible the interests of individuals, corporations, and society' (King, 2002, p. 5), with the final paragraph of the introduction stating that 'The company must be open to institutional activism and there must be greater emphasis on the sustainable or non-financial aspects of its performance' (King, 2002, p. 19). To this end, the longest and most detailed of the report's six sections, Sect. 4, is devoted to 'Integrated Sustainability Reporting', and the report's appendices include the full texts of the *United Nations Global Compact*, the *Global Sullivan Principles of CSR*, and the *Recommendations of the Global Reporting Initiative – Draft 2002*, and the executive summary of the *AA1000 Standard*; together these account for more than a third of the length of the report, clearly indicating the importance of CSR within it.

Australia has produced a number of important reports on CSR (Gustavson, 2009, pp. 468–470). Of these, *Corporate Responsibility: Managing Risk and Creating Value* (Chapman Report, 2006) gives a director perhaps the clearest overview of current experiences of CSR in Australia: not only from the report itself, but also from some 800 pages of official Committee Hansard and 146 substantial public submissions, including from company directors, in addition to the many form letters (Chapman Report Documentation, 2006).

5.4.4 Institutes of Directors

Many company directors are members of a relevant professional association. Like most professional associations, directors' associations play an important role in forming the perspectives of their members through, for example, publications, training, and advice. The oldest and largest of these is the Institute of Directors (www.iod.co.uk), established in the UK in 1903. Since then, directors' associations have been founded in many countries. Globalisation has seen the rise of international associations, two of which were founded in 2004. The Global Director Development Circle (www.globaldirectors.org) has, as its founding members, the Institute of Directors (UK), the Australian Institute of Company Directors, the Institute of Corporate Directors (Canada), the Institute of Directors in New Zealand, the Institute of Directors in Southern Africa, and the National Association of Corporate Directors (USA). The European Confederation of Directors' Associations (www.ecoda.org) consists of ten nationally-based directors' institutes from throughout Europe.

Institutes may have specific policies relating to CSR. The Australian Institute of Company Directors' policy on sustainability (AICD, 2002) states that:

> Australian Institute of Company Directors supports the generally accepted definition of sustainable development – meeting the needs of the present generation without compromising the ability of future generations to meet their own needs.... It is Australian Institute of Company Directors policy to inform its members of the benefits of treating sustainability as a priority business objective. We will do this through the provision of information and resources and the facilitation of appropriate and practical programs and responses.

This policy is promoted, for example, by its publications: the cover story of the AICD's magazine, *Company Director*, for March 2006 was 'The Good Corporate Citizen: Negotiating the legal and ethical tensions of corporate social responsibility', and for November 2008 was 'The new green guard: Investors square in on climate change'. The Institute of Directors – Kenya has as the second of its corporate values: 'Leadership that upholds courage, transparency, accountability, fairness and zero tolerance to corruption, while taking responsibility through the adoption of social responsibility and environmentally sustainable practices' (IOD-K, 2008).

Other types of organisations may fill the role generally taken by Institutes of Directors, or may support the role of Institutes of Directors. For example, the Nairobi-based Centre for Corporate Governance has a mission 'To develop and promote the adoption of sustainable best practices in corporate governance through training, education, research, advocacy, monitoring and evaluation' (CCG, 2008); before the founding of the IOD-K it filled the role, and since the founding of the IOD-K it has supported the role.

5.4.5 Corporate Constitutions/Codes of Conduct

Company directors will be strongly influenced by documents prepared by their own organisation, or to a lesser extent other organisations, that deal with CSR. Such documents may include value or mission statements, the terms of reference of board CSR committees (examples are given in Mackenzie, 2007, pp. 939–940), or codes of conduct (examples are given in Bondy et al., 2008, pp. 306–311). There is also a growing move towards sustainability reporting, an influential framework for which is the Global Reporting Initiative (www.globalreporting.org).

An example is the multinational company BHP Billiton. One of its board committees is a 'Sustainability Committee' which, according to its terms of reference, examines health, safety, environment and community matters (BHP Billiton, 2007), which immediately signals to board members the importance to the corporation of these issues. It also publishes an annual sustainability report detailing the company's commitment to CSR, the 2008 report running to 190 pages (BHP Billiton, 2008): again, this document will inform directors' perceptions of the organisation's approach to CSR. The power of path dependency means that the history of an organisation's engagement with CSR will send a powerful signal to its directors.

5.4.6 The Literature

Company directors may turn to the professional literature to inform and shape their perception of CSR. There is a plethora of books on company directorship, but most have little, if anything, explicit to say about CSR. There are some notable exceptions. Mervyn King's *The Corporate Citizen: Governance for All Entities* (King, 2006) is infused with a sense of the social responsibility of a corporation and the key importance of a corporation's relationship with its stakeholders. King's reputation as Chairman of the King Committee on Corporate Governance, President of the Commonwealth Association of Corporate Governance, and a Governor of the International Corporate Governance Network, surely gives this book an unusually high standing with practitioners. Another notable book is Willard's *The Next Sustainability Wave: Building Boardroom Buy-in* (Willard, 2005). Additionally, Institutes of Directors publish professional magazines or newsletters which they distribute to their members.

Directors may read the academic literature for guidance and models, such as the 'Sustainable Corporate Governance Model' developed by Ricart et al. (2005). Anecdotal evidence, however, suggests that company directors generally do not read academic literature.

5.5 How Important is CSR to Practicing Directors?

The question discussed earlier, whether or not CSR creates value, is a crucial one when considering the incentives or disincentives for a director to take a proactive role in CSR. Yermak found 'statistically significant evidence that outside directors receive positive performance incentives from compensation, turnover, and opportunities to obtain new board seats' based on the company's financial performance (2004, p. 2282). As such, a director's stance on CSR may have personal financial consequences: if it raises organisational value, it may raise a director's personal wealth; if it decreases organisational value, it may decrease a director's personal wealth. A director therefore has a *personal* interest in urging socially responsible policies that increase the value of a firm; the stance of a director on policies that are of neutral value will therefore presumably depend on the director's personal values. If an organisation's CSR is perceived by the market as decreasing value and so decreasing the share price, with the cessation of CSR therefore increasing value and so increasing the share price (although Mackey et al., 2007 demonstrates that the market for socially responsible investment may mean that maximising value is not the same as maximising the present value of future cash flows), then the market for corporate control may be activated and the new owners may remove the incumbent board. In such a case, directors' pursuit of CSR may cost them their jobs (see Gustavson, 2008). This is a disincentive for undertaking CSR unless it creates value.

Surprisingly, a survey by CPA Australia found that directors had a less positive attitude to CSR than shareholders; the percentage of company directors who agreed with each statement is given, followed by the percentage of shareholders who agreed (CPA Australia, 2005, pp. 6, 23):

- A company exists only to build shareholder value (58, 43%);
- Australian company directors adequately balance the financial performance of the company with its social and environmental concerns (58, 46%);
- Financial performance is more important than social and environmental concerns (53, 34%);

- The interests of the shareholders and other stakeholders should be of equal importance to the company (66, 87%);
- Australian company directors have adequate regard to the interests of all stakeholders (54, 31%); and
- Companies social and environmental reporting is just a public relations exercise (51, 60%).

As shareholders also receive a gain or suffer a loss of value from CSR, then either financial reward is more important to directors than to shareholders, or there must be some other explanation.

An Australian Government survey (AGT, 2008) found that a majority of directors felt a high risk 'for being found personally liable (under any law) for decisions you or your board(s) of directors have made in good faith'. The legal requirement for directors to act solely in the best interests of the corporation may be assumed to focus them on profit maximisation. The greatest concern expressed by directors was with derivative liability laws, which include CSR issues such as the environment and occupational health and safety (AGT, 2008). As such, when issues such as environmental impact are under consideration, the primary focus may too easily become one of acting in the way that minimises the possibility of legal liability, rather than acting in the way that minimises environmental damage.

In New Zealand, a study found that only 12.3% of directors considered it very important to review social responsibilities (Ingley, 2008, p. 26), the author concluding that 'With regard to CSR in the New Zealand context it would seem that the concept has yet to move from the margins to the mainstream in corporate thinking and be taken seriously as a strategic issue' (Ingley, 2008, p. 33). In a Canadian survey asking for 'the three major issues facing boards and directors today as they attempt to constructively engage with their managements in setting the strategic direction of their organisations', CSR was not among the 13 identified broad categories of issues (Bart, 2007), suggesting that CSR may not currently be regarded in Canada as a primary strategic issue.

5.6 Conclusion

The company directors' perspective of CSR is a broad one; the perspective of an individual director could fall anywhere within the entire gamut of possibilities from considering CSR irrelevant through to a passionate commitment to society and the environment. The key influences on how those perceptions are realised in boardroom decision-making processes are the legislative frameworks within which the organisation operates, which will differ from country to country (and in some countries from state to state); the boardroom demographics and culture; the organisation's history of CSR; and the individual's personal values and experiences. The nature of the first three of these means; that a director who holds multiple board positions may have a slightly different perception of CSR when acting in each of those positions. There is a wide range of guidance available to directors to assist them in forming, reinforcing, or changing their perception of CSR, ranging from legislation and guidelines to professional education and professional literature, all of which change over time. As at 2009, many directors, at least in some countries, still have more of a shareholder focus than a stakeholder focus, presumably as a result of their interpretation of their fiduciary obligation to act in the best interests of the corporation; indeed, an Australian survey (CPA Australia, 2005) found directors to be more profit focused than the shareholders themselves. If the recent and continuing convergence of CSR and corporate governance results in CSR being a precondition of value maximisation, it will result in a fundamental shift in the typical company director's perception of corporate social responsibility.

References

Aguilera, Ruth V., Cynthia A. Williams, John M. Conley, and Deborah E. Rupp. (2006). "Corporate governance and social responsibility: A comparative analysis of the UK and US." *Corporate Governance* 14(3): 147–158.

AGT. (2008). Australian Government Treasury. *Survey of Company Directors*. Online at: www.treasury.gov.au/content/Company_Directors_Survey/SurveySummary.html. Accessed 23 December 2008.

AICD. (2002). Australian Institute of Company Directors. *Sustainability*. Policy Document. Online at: www.companydirectors.com.au/Policy/Policies+And+Papers/2002/Sustainability. htm. Accessed 15 October 2007.

AICD. (2003). *A Guide to Sustainability in your Company*. Directors' Checklist Series. Sydney: AICD. Also available for purchase as an E-Book at www.companydirectors.com.au

Alford, John, Royston Gustavson, and Philip Williams. (2004). *The Governance of Australia's Courts: A Managerial Perspective*. Melbourne: Australian Institute of Judicial Administration.

Andriof, Jörg, Sandra Waddock, Bryan Husted, and Sandra Sutherland Rahman (Eds.). (2002–2003). *Unfolding Stakeholder Thinking*, 2 Vols. Sheffield: Greenleaf.

ASX. (2007). Australian Securities Exchange. *Corporate Governance Principles and Recommendations*, 2nd edition. Sydney: ASX Corporate Governance Council. Online at: asx.ice4.interactiveinvestor.com.au/ASX0701/Corporate%20Governance%20Principles/EN/ body.aspx?z=1&p=-1&v=1&uid=. Accessed 4 September 2007.

Austin, Robert P. (2007). "Commentary: Australian company law reform and the UK Companies Bill." In: *Company Directors and Corporate Social Responsibility: UK and Australian Perspectives*, Robert P. Austin (Ed.). Sydney: Ross Parsons Centre for Commercial, Corporate and Taxation Law, pp. 3–18.

Bart, Chris. (2007). "Improving the board's involvement in corporate strategy: Directors speak out." *International Journal of Business Governance and Ethics* 4(3): 382–393.

Beach, Lee Roy. (1990). *Image Theory: Decision Making in Personal and Organizational Contexts* (Wiley Series in Industrial and Organizational Psychology). Chichester: Wiley.

Beach, Lee Roy (Ed.). (1998). *Image Theory: Theoretical and Empirical Foundations*. London: Lawrence Erlbaum Associates.

Bedicks, Heloisa B. and M. Cecilia Arruda. (2005). "Business ethics and corporate governance in Latin America." *Business & Society* 44(2): 218–228.

BHP Billiton. (2007). *Terms of Reference: Sustainability Committee*. http://www.bhpbilliton.com/ bbContentRepository/sustcommitteetor.pdf. Accessed 23 December 2008.

BHP Billiton. (2008). *Resourcing the Future: Sustainability Report 2008*. Online at: www.bhpbilliton.com/bbContentRepository/docs/fullSustainabilityReport2008.pdf. Accessed 23 December 2008.

Bondy, Krista, Dirk Matten, and Jeremy Moon. (2008). "Multinational corporation codes of conduct: Governance tools for corporate social responsibility?" *Corporate Governance* 16(4): 294–311.

Bowen, Lord Justice. (1883). "Judgment 3 (pp. 669–678) of 'Hutton *v.* West Cork Railway Company'." In: *The Law Reports. . .. Supreme Court of Judicature. Cases Determined in the Chancery Division and in Bankruptcy and Lunacy, and on Appeal Therefrom in the Court of Appeal,* George Wirgman Hemming (Ed.). London: William Clowes, Vol. 23, pp. 654–684.

Campbell, Leland, Charles S. Gulas, and Thomas S. Gruca. (1999). "Corporate giving behaviour and decision-maker social consciousness." *Journal of Business Ethics* 19: 375–383.

CCG. (2008). Centre for Corporate Governance. *Values, Vision and Mission of the Centre.* www.ccg.or.ke/index.php?option=com_content&task=view&id=3&Itemid=10. Accessed 2 December 2008.

Chapman Report. (2006). Parliamentary Joint Committee on Corporations and Financial Services. *Corporate Responsibility: Managing Risk and Creating Value.* Online at: www.aph.gov.au/Senate/committee/corporations_ctte/completed_inquiries/2004-07/corporate_responsibility/report/report.pdf. Accessed 14 June 2007.

Chapman Report Documentation. (2006). Online at: www.aph.gov.au/Senate/committee/corporations_ctte/completed_inquiries/2004-07/corporate_responsibility/index.htm. Accessed 14 June 2007.

COA. (2009). Commonwealth of Australia. *Corporations Act 2001.* Online at: http://www.comlaw.gov.au/comlaw/management.nsf/lookupindexpagesbyid/IP200401854?OpenDocument. Accessed 9 March 2009.

Coffee, Betty S. and Jia Wang. (1998). "Board diversity and managerial control as predictors of CSP." *Journal of Business Ethics* 17: 1595–1603.

Connolly, Terry and Ken Koput. (1997). "Naturalistic decision making and the new organizational context." In: *Organizational Decision Making,* Zur Shapira (Ed.), Cambridge Series on Judgment and Decision Making. Cambridge: Cambridge University Press, pp. 285–303.

CPA Australia. (2005). *Confidence in Corporate Reporting 2005: Detailed Findings.* Melbourne: CPA Australia. Online at: http://www.cpaaustralia.com.au/cps/rde/xbcr/SID-3F57FECA-36953E3F/cpa/CICR.pdf. Accessed 31 October 2007.

Dulewicz, Victor and Peter Herbert. (2004). "Does the composition and practice of Boards of Directors bear any relationship to the performance of their companies?" *Corporate Governance: An International Review* 12(3): 263–280.

Elegido, Juan Manuel (1996). *Fundamentals of Business Ethics: A Developing Country Perspective* (LBS Management Series). Ibadan, Nigeria: Spectrum.

Elegido, Juan Manuel (2003). *Business Ethics in the Christian Tradition* (LBS Management Series). Ibadan, Nigeria: Spectrum.

Fussler, Claude, Aron Cramer, and Sebastian van der Vegt (Eds.). (2004). *Raising the Bar: Creating Value with the United Nations Global Compact.* Sheffield: Greenleaf.

Green, John. (2007). "Should the Corporations Act require directors to consider non-shareholder 'stakeholders'?: Two perspectives." In: *Company Directors and Corporate Social Responsibility: UK and Australian Perspectives,* Robert P. Austin (Ed.). Sydney: Ross Parsons Centre for Commercial, Corporate and Taxation Law, pp. 44–50.

Gill, Amiram. (2008). "Corporate governance as social responsibility: A research agenda." *Berkeley Journal of International Law* 26(2): 452–478.

Gustavson, Royston. (2008). "Market for corporate control." In: *Encyclopedia of Business Ethics and Society,* Robert W. Kolb (Ed.). Thousand Oaks, CA: Sage, Vol. 3, pp. 1333–1335.

Gustavson, Royston. (2009). "Australia: Practices and experiences." In: *Global Practices of Corporate Social Responsibility,* Samuel Idowu and Walter Leal Filho (Eds.). Berlin: Springer, pp. 463–495.

Gustavson, Royston, Nicholas Ndegwa Kimani, and Donald Atieno Ouma. (2009). "The Anglo-American model of corporate governance in Sub-Saharan Africa: Exploratory and normative dimensions." In: *Corporate Governance and Development Reform, Financial Systems and Legal Frameworks,* Thankom Gopinath Arun and John Turner (Eds.), The CRC Series on competition, Regulation and Development, Cheltenham, UK: Edward Elgar, pp. 23–42.

Hempel, Ronnie. (1998). *Committee on Corporate Governance: Final Report.* London: Gee.

Henley, Peter. (2005). "Were corporate tsunami donations made legally?" *Alternative Law Journal* 30(4): 154–158.

Horrigan, Brian. (2007). "21st century corporate social responsibility trends – An emerging comparative body of law and regulation on corporate responsibility, governance, and sustainability." *Macquarie Journal of Business Law* 4: 85–122.

Husted, Bryan W. (2005). "Risk management, real options, and corporate social responsibility." *Journal of Business Ethics* 60: 175–183.

Ibrahim, Nabil A., Donald P. Howard, and John P. Angelidis. (2003). "Board members in the service industry: An empirical examination of the relationship between corporate social responsibility orientation and directorial type." *Journal of Business Ethics* 47: 393–401.

ICGN. (2005). International Corporate Governance Network. *ICGN Statement on Global Corporate Governance Principles Revised July 8, 2005 at the Annual Conference in London.* Online at: www.icgn.org/organisation/documents/cgp/revised_principles_jul2005.pdf. Accessed 17 August 2007.

Idowu, Samuel and Walter Leal Filho. (2009). "Global practices of CSR in context." In: *Global Practices of Corporate Social Responsibility*, Samuel Idowu and Walter Leal Filho (Eds.). Berlin: Springer Verlag, pp. 1–7.

Ingley, Coral B. (2008). "Company growth and Board attitudes to corporate social responsibility." *International Journal of Business Governance and Ethics* 4: 17–39.

IOD-K. (2008). The Institute of Directors – Kenya. *Guiding Principles.* www.iodkenya.co.ke/menu.php?abid=3. Accessed 2 December 2008.

ISO. (n.d.). International Organization for Standardization. *Glossary of Terms and Abbreviations used in ISO/TC Business Plans.* Online at http://isotc.iso.org/livelink/livelink/fetch/2000/2122/687806/Glossary.htm?nodeid=2778927&vernum=0. Accessed 15 March 2009.

ISO. (2008). *Committee Draft ISO/CD26000 Social Responsibility.* 15 December 2008. Online at: http://isotc.iso.org/livelink/livelink/fetch/2000/2122/830949/3934883/3935837/ISO_CD_26000__Guidance_on_Social_Responsibility.pdf?nodeid=7795973&vernum=0. Accessed 15 March 2009.

ISO. (2009). *ISO in Figures for the Year 2008.* Online at: http://www.iso.org/iso/about/iso_in_figures/iso_in_figures_1.htm. Accessed 15 March 2009.

Janis, Irving L. and Leon Mann. (1977). *Decision Making: A Psychological Analysis of Conflict, Choice, and Commitment.* New York: The Free Press.

Judge, William Q. (1994). "Correlates of organizational effectiveness: A multilevel analysis of multidimensional outcomes." *Journal of Business Ethics* 13: 1–10.

King, Mervyn. (2002). *King Report on Corporate Governance for South Africa – 2002.* Johannesburg: Institute of Directors in Southern Africa.

King, Mervyn. (2006). *The Corporate Citizen: Governance for all Entities.* Johannesburg: Penguin.

Klein, Gary. (1998). *Sources of Power: How People make Decisions.* Cambridge, Mass: MIT Press.

Leipziger, Deborah. (2003). *The Corporate Responsibility Code Book.* Sheffield: Greenleaf.

Lutz, David and Paul Mimbi (Eds.). (2004). *Shareholder Value and the Common Good: Essays on the Objectives and Purposes of Business Management.* Nairobi: Strathmore University Press and the Konrad Adenauer Foundation.

Mackenzie, Craig. (2007). "Boards, incentives, and corporate social responsibility: The case for a change of emphasis." *Corporate Governance* 15(5): 935–943.

Mackey, Alison, Tyson B. Mackey, and Jay B. Barney. (2007). "Corporate social responsibility and firm performance: Investor preferences and corporate strategies." *Academy of Management Review* 32: 817–835.

Margolis, Joshua Daniel and James Patrick Walsh. (2001). *People and Profits?: The Search for a Link Between a Company's Social and Financial Performance.* Mahwah, NJ: Laurence Erlbaum Associates.

McConvill, James and Martin Joy. (2003). "The interaction of directors' duties and sustainable development in Australia: Setting off on the uncharted road." *Melbourne University Law Review* 27(1): 116–138.

NEPAD. (2003). New Economic Partnership for Africa's Development. *Objectives, Standards, Criteria and Indicators for the African Peer Review Mechanism ("The ARPM")*, NEPAD document NEPAD/HSGIC-03-2003/APRM/Guideline/OSCI, 9 March 2003. Online at: www.nepad. org/2005/files/documents/110.pdf. Accessed 19 March 2007.

NEPAD. (2004). *Country Self-Assessment for the African Peer Review Mechanism*. Midrand, South Africa: NEPAD and the African Union. Online at: www.nepad.org/2005/files/documents/156. pdf. Accessed 19 March 2007.

NZSC. (2004). New Zealand Securities Commission. *Corporate Governance in New Zealand: Principles and Guidelines. A Handbook for Directors, Executives, and Advisers*. Online at: www.sec-com.govt.nz/publications/documents/governance-principles/ corporate-governance-handbook.pdf. Accessed 25 November 2005.

OECD. (2004). Organisation for Economic Co-operation and Development. *OECD Principles of Corporate Governance*. Paris: OECD.

Parkinson, John E. (1993). *Corporate Power and Responsibility: Issues in the Theory of Company Law*. Oxford: Clarendon.

Pearce, Chris. (2007). "Directors' duties in Australian law; the Government's response to the CSR debate." In: *Company Directors and Corporate Social Responsibility: UK and Australian Perspectives*, Robert P. Austin (Ed.). Sydney: Ross Parsons Centre for Commercial, Corporate and Taxation Law, pp. 29–33.

Peterson, Deborah C. (2006). "Precaution: principles and practice in Australian environmental and natural resource management." *The Australian Journal of Agricultural and Resource Economics* 50(4): 469–489.

Prakash, Aseem and Matthew Potoski. (2006). *The Voluntary Environmentalists: Green Clubs, ISO 14001, and Voluntary Environmental Regulations*. Cambridge: Cambridge University Press.

Ricart, Joan Enric, Miguel Ángel Rodríguez, andPablo Sánchez. (2005). "Sustainability in the boardroom: An empirical examination of Dow Jones sustainability world index leaders." *Corporate Governance* 5(3): 24–41.

Rossouw, Deon. (2005). "Business ethics and corporate governance in Africa." *Business & Society* 44(1): 94–106.

SAI. (2008). Social Accountability International. *Social Accountability 8000*. New York: SAI. Online at: http://www.sa-intl.org/_data/n_0001/resources/live/2008StdEnglishFinal.pdf. Accessed 15 March 2009.

Salzmann, Oliver, Aileen Ionescu-Somers, and Ulrich Steger. (2005). "The business case for corporate sustainability: Literature review and research options." *European Management Journal* 23(1): 27–36.

Shailer, Gregory E.P. (2004). *An Introduction to Corporate Governance in Australia*. Frenchs Forest, NSW: Pearson.

Shleifer, Andrei and Robert W. Vishny. (1997). "A survey of corporate governance." *Journal of Finance* 52: 737–783.

Slovic, Paul. (1987). "Perception of risk." *Science* 236(4799), 17 April: 280–285.

Standards Australia. (2003a). *Organizational Codes of Conduct*. Sydney: Standards Australia. AS 8002—2003.

Standards Australia. (2003b). *Corporate Social Responsibility*. Sydney: Standards Australia. AS 8003—2003.

Steger, Ulrich. (2006a). "Building a business case for corporate sustainability." In: *Managing the Business Case for Sustainability: The Integration of Social, Environmental and Economic Performance*, Stefan Schaltegger and Marcus Wagner (Eds.). Sheffield, UK: Greenleaf, pp. 412–443.

Steger, Ulrich. (2006b). "What is it with stakeholder pressure." In: *Inside the Mind of the Stakeholder: The Hype behind Stakeholder Pressure*, Ulrich Steger (Ed.). Houndmills: Palgrave Macmillan, pp. 120–127.

Tully, Stephen (Ed.). (2005). *International Documents on Corporate Responsibility*. Cheltenham, UK: Edward Elgar.

UK. (2006). United Kingdom. *Companies Act 2006*. London: The Stationery Office. Online at http://www.opsi.gov.uk/acts/acts2006/pdf/ukpga_20060046_en.pdf. Accessed 20 November 2008.

UN. (1993). United Nations. "Agenda 21: A blueprint for action for global sustainable development into the 21st century." In: *Agenda 21: Programme of Action for Sustainable Development. Rio Declaration on Environment and Development. Statement of Forest Principles. The Final Text of Agreements Negotiated by Governments at the United Nations Conference on Environment and Development (UNCED), 3–14 June 1992, Rio de Janeiro, Brazil*. New York: United Nations Department of Public Information, pp. 13–288. The text of Agenda 21 is also available online at: http://www.un.org/esa/sustdev/documents/agenda21/english/agenda21toc.htm. Accessed 15 March 2009.

Wang, Jia and Betty Coffey. (1992). "Board composition and corporate philanthropy." *Journal of Business Ethics* 11: 771–778.

Wang, Jia and H. Dudley Dewhirst. (1992). "Boards of directors and stakeholder orientation." *Journal of Business Ethics* 11: 115–123.

Wieland, Josef. (2005). "Corporate governance, values management, and standards: A European perspective." *Business & Society* 44(1): 74–93.

Willard, Bob. (2005). *The Next Sustainability Wave: Building Boardroom Buy-in*. Gabriola Island, Canada: New Society Publishers.

Williams, Robert J. (2003). "Women on boards and firm philanthropy." *Journal of Business Ethics* 42: 1–10.

Wilson, Therese. (2005). "The pursuit of profit at all costs: Corporate law as a barrier to corporate social responsibility." *Alternative Law Journal* 30(6): 278–282.

Yermack, David. (2004). "Remuneration, retention, and reputation incentives for outside directors." *Journal of Finance* 59: 2281–2308.

Chapter 6
The Need to Reconsider Societal Marketing

Timothy T. Campbell and José-Rodrigo Córdoba

> *Marketing's raison d'être is eminently noble; it alone has the*
> *power to align the interests of corporations and their customers*
> *directly (and, by extension, society as a whole)...Used wisely*
> *and with restraint, marketing can harness and channel the vast*
> *energies of the free market system for the good of consumers,*
> *corporations, and society as a whole. Used recklessly, it can*
> *cause significant harm to all those entities.*
>
> Sheth and Sisodia (2005, p. 160)

Abstract Marketers have every right to be proud of their field and the contribution they have made to raising standards of living around the world. Yet, despite encouraging the development of beneficial products and services globally, marketing has increasingly become the target of criticism, largely due to the assumptions of the marketing concept. This philosophy advocates satisfying customer needs for profit and has remained dominant for over half a century. Critics question whether this orientation, with a lack of consideration of marketing's social impacts, is in the best interests of consumers or society in the longer-term. This chapter begins by arguing that the business environment has fundamentally changed since the emergence of the marketing concept as the dominant marketing paradigm. There is a far greater awareness and sensitivity to social and environmental issues. The Societal Marketing Concept (SMC), despite being developed at least 40 years ago, is advocated as being more able to meet both business and social objectives for the long-term. The SMC extends marketing considerations beyond company profits and consumer wants, to include society's interests. An examination of the history of the SMC reveals that the concept has had little impact on marketing literature or practice because of criticisms that have also been apparent, but largely dealt with, in the corporate social responsibility (CSR) literature. The chapter concludes by examining the CSR journey to address the criticisms of the SMC and thereby provide direction on how the SMC can be advanced.

T.T. Campbell (✉)
Hull Business School, Hull, UK

S.O. Idowu, W.L. Filho (eds.), *Professionals' Perspectives of Corporate Social Responsibility*, DOI 10.1007/978-3-642-02630-0_7,
© Springer-Verlag Berlin Heidelberg 2009

6.1 Introduction

Marketing is the primary interface between the organisation and society, and as such, has an important role to play in Corporate Social Responsibility (CSR). The function has the ability to align the needs of society with the resources of the business for lasting social and economic benefits. Despite the capacity to aid social improvement, and examples of marketing excellence in this regard, critics argue that by and large practitioners appear to be either powerless or reluctant to consider the 'greater social good'. They point to the fact that marketing stands out amongst the functional areas of business as a target of criticism and source of controversy and over recent years this has only intensified (Smith et al., 2005). A range of disapproval has been advanced from deceptive practices and high-pressure selling to creating false wants and targeting the disadvantaged.

The public image and professional reputation of marketing has suffered, its antagonists claim, because of the marketing concept that focuses on satisfying often short-term consumer wants for profit with little or no regard to the social impacts. There is some evidence to support these assertions. A survey of 607 marketing executives revealed 'marketing basics' (customer satisfaction, customer retention, segmentation, brand loyalty and return on investment) was the concept of greatest interest to marketers in 2008. At the bottom of the list, apart from the miscellaneous 'other' category was social issues. The proposition being that social issues, of all the main concepts, are of least interest to marketers (Marketing Trends Survey, 2007).

Since the emergence of the marketing concept more than 50 years ago, society has become more aware and responsive to the social impacts of business. For example, the consequences of the business decisions of a few on society as a whole was particularly noticed during the global financial market crisis that began to be significantly felt in 2007. Reckless lending practices by some financial institutions to provide short-term customer satisfaction for profit directly resulted in, for instance, unemployment, falling house prices, and more expensive and difficult to access mortgages and credit. The marketing concept philosophy may be insufficient for the new environment in which organisations find themselves. Thomas (2000) agrees that the marketing profession must define itself in its 'social trustee' role, as opposed to mechanical, market driven professionalism, if it's going to survive (Murphy and Crowther, 2002). Marketers may have no choice. In response to the financial crisis, U.K. Prime Minister Gordon Brown called for an end to the 'age of irresponsibility' by tighter global financial regulation (Pickard, 2008). There has already been widespread governmental action on issues such as packaging, waste, safety standards, product warranties, credit practices and ongoing debates about regulating various promotional devices and marketing activities. These actions pose serious questions about marketing's social role. If marketers ignore the social implications of their activities, others will act, and probably in an unpleasant and unrealistic manner.

There is a need for marketing to build on its solid foundations and contributions. The next stage in the development of marketing is advocated as being one that takes into account not just customer satisfaction, but also long-run societal well-being to achieve both the company's goals and its responsibilities. The following section briefly traces the history and criticisms of the marketing concept before exploring the 'next' stage of marketing development, the Societal Marketing Concept (SMC). The second section draws on the CSR debate to help provide guidance on how the SMC can be advanced.

6.2 The History and Criticisms of the Marketing Concept

Modern conceptions of the marketing function are usually traced back to the beginning of the twentieth century. During this period, marketing has gone through a number of developmental stages. Originally marketing was concerned with improving production and distribution at a time when mass production technologies aimed to provide the wants of increasingly affluent consumers. This *production orientation* emphasised marketing as a technical process, dealing primarily with physical distribution and the economic and legal aspects of transaction. At around the time of the great depression when consumer spending and business investment declined, and saturation was reached in production, the *sales orientation* emphasised aggressive selling and distribution. In the 1950s as competitive pressures intensified, the *market orientation* refocused efforts outwards, towards the markets (Abratt and Sacks, 1988). The marketing concept philosophy 'holds that achieving organizational goals depends on determining the needs and wants of target markets and delivering the desired satisfactions more effectively and efficiently than competitors do' (Kotler et al., 2005, p. 16, Fig. 1). This notion remains the dominant model of marketing. The purpose of marketing remains largely technical, to translate demand in to production. The U.K. Chartered Institute of Marketing's (2008) official definition of marketing reflects this orientation: (Fig. 6.1)

> Marketing is the management process responsible for identifying, anticipating and satisfying customer requirements profitably

This dominant view of marketing with the focus on satisfying often short-term wants for profit has been questioned as not always being in the best interests of consumers or society in the longer term. For example, despite increasingly restrictive

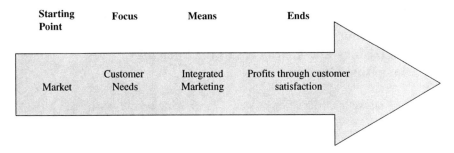

Fig. 6.1   The marketing concept (Kotler et al., 2005, p. 16)

legislation, the tobacco industry has been accused of playing a central role in the global spread of tobacco use and addiction due to sophisticated and manipulative marketing strategies (Anderson et al., 2002). Although the marketers are providing customer satisfaction at a profit, the longer-term consumer interest in terms of health problems and financial drain are not considered. Nor are the interests of society which is likely to be required to pay the costs of healthcare or that of the emotional distress of families of those suffering from tobacco related diseases. Similar claims have been advanced for the alcohol and fast food industries. Although these are obvious examples, there are many products and services that may not be in the consumer or society's long term interests such as automobiles (pollution), high sugar cereals, or potentially hazardous toys.

Although criticisms of marketing began as soon as the field emerged (Wilkie and Moore, 1999), these criticisms, controversies and problems have become more prominent. A study by Yankelovich in 2004 (Smith et al., 2005) found that more than 60% of respondents believe that marketing and advertising are 'out of control,' and 70% try to tune out as much marketing and advertising as possible. These negative attitudes are much stronger than those found by Bauer and Greyser (1968) in an early academic assessment of public attitudes toward advertising. These authors revealed that 15% of consumers were 'serious resisters' of advertising, whereas, Yankelovich's 2004 research finds that 60% of the population are serious resisters, and approximately 70% are interested in products that help them skip, block, or opt out of marketing and advertising (Sheth and Sisodia, 2005). The lack of concern for wider social issues has led to consequences for the public image and professional reputation of marketing. Paradoxically, what Wilkie and Moore (2003, p. 145) term era IV (1980-present) has 'brought the most significant decline in mainstream interest in this topic [marketing and society] during the entire history (nearly a century) of marketing thought'.

The contribution of marketing to economic growth, prosperity and consumers over the period of almost a century must be recognised. However, the current dominant marketing concept needs to be revised. Not because the basic aim of business has changed, but because the environment in which it is pursuing its aims has changed. The rationale for embracing the SMC is not only to safeguard marketing's future freedom of action, but to ensure the survival of business itself in an increasingly hostile social environment (Abratt and Sacks 1988, p. 504).

6.3 The History and Criticisms of the Societal Marketing Concept

The 'new' marketing orientation of *societal marketing* actually emerged nearly 40 years ago as a result of an increased awareness of CSR developing in the 60s and 70s. Writers like Dawson (1969), Feldman (1971) and Kotler and Levy (1969) criticised the emphasis on material consumption without consideration of societal benefit. Kotler (1972) articulated societal marketing as:

A *customer orientation* backed by *integrated marketing* aimed at generating *customer satisfaction* and *long-run consumer welfare* as the key to attaining long-run profitable volume (p. 54 Italics in original).

Kotler (1972) writes that the addition of long-run consumer welfare requires social and ecological considerations within an organisations product and market planning. Importantly, not only is this a requirement to meet social responsibilities, but Kotler (1972) also claims that failure to do this may hurt the long-run interests of the business. The reason being that a concern for consumer well-being can be turned into a profitable opportunity through the introduction of needed new products and through the adoption of a total concern-for-the-consumer attitude leading to trust and goodwill. Societal marketing is regarded as the next stage in the evolution of enlightened marketing. Just as the sales concept propounded sales as all-important, and the original marketing concept said that customer satisfaction was also important, the societal marketing concept has emerged to say that long-run consumer welfare is also important. Later, the concept moved beyond long-run consumer welfare to include society's well-being. The basic rationale for this extension was that the well-being of consumers could be achieved at the expense of other groups. For example, artificially low prices for desirable products (those which combine high immediate satisfaction and high long-run benefits) such as tasty, nutritious breakfast foods may be at the expense of suppliers and employees.

The SMC advocates that marketers balance three considerations in setting marketing policies: company profits, consumer wants and society's interests (Kotler et al., 2005). The concept has broadened the responsibility of marketing from a customer focus in the interests of profits to a responsibility to include wider social issues. In doing so, the emergence of societal marketing can be likened to the arguments being put forward by the 'modern' beginnings of CSR literature such as Bowen (1953) who advocated business as having social obligations beyond making profits. Despite some gains in popularity, there has been relatively little advancement in the discussion of societal marketing since the early 1970s. Crane and Desmond (2002, p. 551) recognised that the contribution of the SMC could be gained by its widening of attention away from the satisfaction of individual desires to longer term social and individual interests. They note that the continued preoccupation of marketing texts on customer satisfaction and profitability suggests that the SMC has yet to have anything more than, at best, a marginal impact on the traditional principles of marketing theory. Kang and James (2007) made a similar observation that modern business thinking and writings have mainly concentrated on managerial aspects that are important for producing a product to satisfy immediate customer desires in order to help organizations generate profits. The current understanding and practices of marketing remain narrowly focused on the individual consumer and the gratification of immediate wants, with little concern for long-run consumer interests and/or the interests of others in society. The practice of societal marketing remains heavily outweighed by the traditional marketing orientation of generating revenue by providing customer satisfaction.

6.3.1 Demarcating the Societal Marketing Concept

It is necessary to distinguish the SMC from social marketing and other related concepts and interpretations because there has been a lack of clarity or consistency in the use of the term. For instance, societal marketing has been used as an umbrella term to encompass various marketing types that *involve* social issues such as cause-related marketing, ethical marketing, or green marketing.

Social marketing refers to the use of commercial marketing concepts and tools to promote social ideas and causes. The motive is not profit, but rather social change. Social marketing programmes include, for example, safe driving, anti-smoking, prevention of crime, and prevention of skin cancer. *Cause-related marketing* joins business with non-profit organisations for mutual benefit. For example the U.K. supermarket chain Morrison's has joined with Asthma U.K. with a contribution being given to the charity when certain products are bought. *Green marketing* can be broadly defined as the marketing of products that are environmentally friendly such as energy efficient light bulbs. *Ethical marketing* refers to products that have considered issues such as working conditions or paying suppliers a living wage, for example, Bodyshop products.

With reference to the marketing concept, organizational goals are being met by determining the wants of the target markets and delivering the desired satisfactions profitably. These types of marketing cannot be considered to be anything beyond the marketing concept. This in no way is to denigrate the social good that the majority of these programmes undoubtedly achieve. The Anglo-American cause-related marketing (CRM) programme with Sightsavers, a charity that works to combat blindness in developing countries, has demonstrated undeniable benefits in providing eye care to the disadvantaged. However, CRM it is not a fundamental reconstruction of the moral base of marketing, neither has it refocused the goals of marketing away from primarily consumer satisfaction and organisational profits. CRM plays on the social conscience of the target market in return for increased sales and loyalty.

Kotler et al. (2005) refer to the SMC as a new philosophy, as such it requires a revision to a more explicit social orientation, rather than being a new marketing tactic. It can be argued that these tactics are transitory as social values are in a constant state of flux, vary globally, and are sensitive to the mass media. For example, not using genetically modified products has been a major issue in the U.K., but barely registered in the U.S. Furthermore, for how long will it continue to be a social issue in the U.K. before science proves the concept safe (or otherwise), or society simply moves on to other issues. Although the SMC may use techniques such as CRM or green marketing, SMC is a more holistic approach that is sensitive, responsive and focused on social issues. It emphasizes communication between the business and its environment in the form of feedback mechanisms, consultations and negotiations between a wider range of stakeholders such as competitors, consumers, and government agencies (Abratt and Sacks, 1988). As such, organizations that adopt the SMC are more likely to be profitable in the long term because they will be more responsive to new product and service opportunities and likely to gain

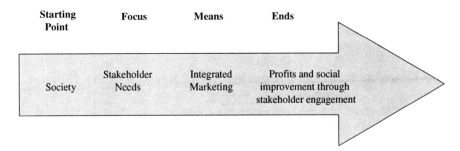

Fig. 6.2 The societal marketing concept

the loyalty and trust of stakeholder groups beyond the consumer. The societal orientation means they are also more likely to make a lasting beneficial contribution to society. Figure 6.2 presents the authors conceptualization of the SMC by utilizing the marketing concept framework.

As previously noted, these arguments have not been influential in marketing literature or practice. The SMC has little in terms of theoretical models, theory constructs, concepts, relationships or testable propositions. Nor has the notion of societal marketing found its way into common business language. Other marketing terms such as social marketing, green marketing, ethical marketing and cause related marketing, have received far greater attention than societal marketing (Crane and Desmond, 2002).

Why has societal marketing not been wholeheartedly embraced? Opponents of societal marketing claim that social objectives are the realm of public policy makers, the concept undermines the economic role of marketing, and marketers cannot be relied upon to decide societal 'good' and nor are they likely to have the abilities to do so. For example, Gaski (1985) asserts that for marketers to act in the public interest as societal marketing dictates, they first must decide what is in the public interest. In doing so, they are arbitrarily and unilaterally usurping a public policy making role that they never were elected or designated to perform. He claims, 'Although marketing managers are experts at satisfying their customers at a profit, they are not experts at defining and acting in the public interest' (p. 44). These criticisms are not unique to marketers but have been a basic premise of the 'against' CSR brigade. Friedman (1970), as well as other criticisms of CSR, claimed social causes are best served by the function of government. He also advised that corporate executives are not experts in solving social issues when he wrote in the New York Times, '. . .suppose he [corporate executive] could get away with spending the stockholders' or customers' or employees' money [on social causes]. How is he to know how to spend it?...'.

Here we find a disjunction between CSR and societal marketing. Despite the criticisms CSR 'has been transformed from an irrelevant and often-frowned upon idea to one of the most orthodox and widely accepted concepts in the business world during the last twenty years or so' (Lee, 2008, p. 53). Societal marketing has not demonstrated anywhere near the same degree of acceptance and remains on the periphery of marketing practice. For societal marketing to be advanced, it can learn from the history and lessons of the CSR literature.

6.4 Learning from the Corporate Social Responsibility Journey

Despite a 'modern' history dating back more than 50 years (Carroll, 1999), there is still much debate apparent in the CSR literature. Many conceptualizations of CSR exist, none of which are universally accepted (Garriga and Melé, 2004) and many of which are contested (Matten and Moon, 2008). It has been claimed that the complexities apparent in CSR theory and practice have led to a veritable CSR labyrinth (Cordoba and Campbell, 2008). However, these theoretical deliberations have not hindered the general acceptance and growth of CSR practice. As the arguments against societal marketing mirror those of the CSR critics, examining the key CSR debates and recognising how CSR has been actioned despite these contentions provides lessons on how the SMC can be progressed.

6.4.1 Criticism of the SMC #1: The SMC Threatens the Very Foundation of the Economic System

In response to the rising attention towards CSR in the 1950s and 1960s, the 'against' CSR proponents began to vocally advance their arguments, most notably by Milton Friedman (1962, 1970). A fundamental argument against CSR was that it was 'anti-business'. By doing business properly (i.e. ignoring social responsibilities) jobs are created, standards of living are increased, competitive pressure mean we get products and services that we want which are constantly being improved, and by being a profitable business unit taxes are paid to the Government which administers the money to the social causes that are most in need. The 'for' CSR proponents (e.g. Freeman, 1984; Mintzberg, 1983) countered that, as well as other arguments, corporations rely on a wide range of stakeholders for their existence and therefore must have some responsibility to them as well as shareholders. Further, the strategic decisions of large organisations inevitably involve social as well as economic consequences, inextricably intertwined. Business cannot operate outside of society. The argument for social responsibilities being the province of governments alone neglects that policy makers are often weak in regulating business due to the possibility of stifling economic activity. In addition, globally many nations do not have 'good' governance.

Despite the fact that these debates continues to rage, CSR is practiced by the vast majority of business organisations. One study concluded that 90% of large corporates have adopted socially responsible practices into their mainstream business strategies, with 71% investing heavily in CSR programmes (IVCA, 2004). In practice, it has been realised that business and social objectives need not be at odds. Mackay et al. (2007, p. 817) write, 'One way to resolve this conflict is to observe that at least some forms of socially responsible behavior may actually improve the present value of a firm's future cash flows. . .', thereby business and society can both benefit.

This debate has been mirrored in the marketing management literature since the early marketing and society writings. Lazer (1969, p. 56) wrote that the more traditional view has been that marketing management fulfills the greater part of its responsibility by providing products and services to satisfy consumer needs profitably and efficiently. Those adopting this view believe that, as a natural consequence of its efficiency, customers are satisfied, firms prosper, and the well-being of society follows automatically. They fear that the acceptance of any other responsibilities by marketing managers, particularly social responsibilities, tends to threaten the very foundation of the economic system. He then recognizes an emerging view as one that does not take issue with the ends of customer satisfaction, the profit focus, the market economy, and economic growth. Rather, its premise is that the tasks of marketing and its responsibilities are much wider than purely economic concerns. This view parallels the 'for' CSR arguments that business has wider responsibilities beyond profits. A perspective that Lazer (1969, p. 56) advocates; 'Because marketing is a social instrument through which a standard of living is transmitted to society, as a discipline it is a social one with commensurate social responsibilities that cannot merely be the exclusive concern of companies and consumers'.

Critics of the SMC (e.g. Gaski, 1985) present only two choices, either marketing managers alone decide what is in our interests, or they must not even consider such questions. However, as the previous discussions have revealed, a middle ground is possible where marketing managers can begin with the long-term interests of society (how they do this will be discussed later) and meet (or exceed) economic goals. For example, Cadbury's, a company with a long tradition of attention to employee and community welfare, provides schemes to aid the homeless back to work. The activity is part of numerous initiatives that have helped Cadbury's become one of the U.K.'s most attractive employers and has provided benefits for the community. This may be considered a societal marketing orientation because the starting point was the long-term needs of society (the issue was identified as being important by market research). The company then oriented its practice to fit societies need in a way that did not compromise the company's survival, but in fact, contributes to its success. This example can be juxtaposed with another initiative by the same company. In 2003 Cadbury's launched a 'Sports for Schools' promotion that attempted to emulate the highly successful 'Computers for Schools' promotion by the retail chain Tesco. The promotion offered to buy fitness equipment for schools in exchange for tokens from Cadbury's confectionery. After scathing criticism the promotion was withdrawn because it was seen to be a perverse incentive to eat more of a product associated with obesity, the condition the fitness equipment was intended to reduce. The promotion also drew unwelcome attention to the potential adverse health effects of eating confectionery (Smith, 2007). In this case, the company did begin with a pressing social issue, obesity, but failed to choose the marketing practices to fit with the business and social objectives.

The lesson for marketers is that carefully chosen practices can benefit the long-term interests of society and the business. This resolves the dilemma of whether the SMC threatens the very foundation of the economic system by advocating that economic imperatives are not neglected, but rather may be enhanced by carefully considered marketing practices that are also in society's long term interests. This lesson is further advanced in the strategic CSR literature. An influential article by Porter and Kramer (2006) stated that organizations should focus on a fewer number of carefully targeted CSR programs which are tightly linked to core business objectives. These authors reason that by linking the CSR approach with strategy these programs will provide a greater impact on both the organization and society. By implication, societal marketing practices need to align with core business objectives for the most benefit.

6.4.2 Criticism of the SMC #2: Meeting Social Obligations is Too Broad to be Actionable

The emergence of the stakeholder perspective of CSR recognised that meeting societal obligations may be too broad a challenge for practice. These proponents advocate responsibilities to stakeholders rather than society as a whole as these are the groups that affect, and are affected by, a firm's activities (e.g. Clarkson, 1995). Stakeholders include those that are absolutely necessary for a firms survival (e.g. employees, customers, investors, suppliers) and those that are not, but may still be particularly influential (e.g. media, trade associations, special interest groups). The implication for marketing is that actioning a societal orientation requires a focus not only on customers, but also on the important stakeholder groups that hold the firm accountable for its actions. This concept has demonstrated some acceptance by the marketing community. Maignan et al. (2005 p. 956) cite the 'new' definition of marketing developed by the American Marketing Association (2004) which states that:

> Marketing is an organizational function and a set of processes for creating, communicating, and delivering value to customers and for managing customer relationships in ways that benefit the organization and its stakeholders.

This definition emphasizes the importance of delivering value and the responsibility of marketers to be able to create relationships that provide benefits to all relevant stakeholders. Maignan et al. (2005) note that this 'new' definition of marketing was the first to include 'concern for stakeholders'.

Stakeholder issues often compete, for example, employees may want higher wages and customers lower product costs. Balancing and prioritising stakeholder issues is not a simple task, however, the CSR literature provides a framework. Mitchell et al. (1997, p. 854) propose that classes of stakeholders can be identified by their possession or attributed possession of one, two, or all three of the following attributes: (1) the stakeholder's *power* to influence the firm, (2) the *legitimacy* of the stakeholder's relationship with the firm, and (3) the *urgency* of the stakeholders claim on the firm. The occurrence and magnitude of these three elements increases organizational attractiveness to stakeholder concerns. Understanding and addressing stakeholder demands involves gathering data about the groups, distributing the information throughout the firm, and responding in appropriate ways (Thorne et al., 2008). The role of the marketer is at the forefront of these activities and necessarily elevates the role of the marketing function to being integral to organisational strategy.

6.4.3 Criticism of the SMC #3: Marketers do Not Have the Expertise to Address Social Problems

The adoption of a stakeholder orientation means that the business manager does not need to be skilled in social policy. They do, however, need to understand and respond appropriately to the issues identified by stakeholders. The same is true for marketers who need to be able to understand how to align their activities with the various stakeholder issues. There have been numerous examples of marketers not fully appreciating social issues. Coca-Cola's £7 million U.K. launch in 2004 of a new bottled water backfired because the company misunderstood public sentiment on bottled water, especially when it became known that the £1.90/litre bottled water was purified tap water. The often cited outcry over poor working conditions in Nike supplier factories was famously underestimated by the company. Smith (2007) writes that the cause of marketing failure in these examples is not primarily product quality or poor execution of a marketing promotion, but marketing mistakes that reflect a misalignment with societal expectations. He concludes that these marketing failures are set to multiply unless marketers become more attuned to societal issues.

For the marketer the lesson is to understand and be able to prioritise stakeholder issues which requires stakeholder engagement and often involves compromise and creativity to identify the most appropriate practices to provide the most benefit for business and society.

6.4.4 Criticism of the SMC #4: Marketers are Unable to Exercise Individual Moral Responsibility and Action

Marketers often work in large corporations (or they may be external to the organisation) where their decisions may be evaluated according to purely economic criteria rather than economic and social criteria. If this is the case, then how can marketers make socially responsible decisions unless they are for profit maximisation reasons alone? CSR literature again provides some direction. Embedding CSR requires that it emanates from the organisations values and norms. It is not the realm of a few individuals with a moral agenda, but a commitment from the organisation as a whole. For example, Herman Miller, a multi-national provider of office furniture and services crafted a statement that it calls the Things That Matter. The statement includes, along with performance, aspects such as 'a better world', 'inclusiveness', 'relationships', and 'engagement'. The statement declares Herman Miller's philosophy and the way it will fulfil its responsibilities to stakeholders. The statement provides guidance for the entire organisation (Thorne et al., 2008). The marketing function of Herman Miller has considerable licence to act in ways that meet both economic and social needs. Robin and Reidenbach (1987, p. 48) write that, 'When implemented and communicated to all involved parties, these values define the profile or "face" of the organization and become an integral part of the organizational mission. Because the mission or broadly defined objectives of an organization direct all marketing strategy, social responsibility and ethics can be successfully integrated if they become part of the marketing mission. The profile, relying heavily on these core values, should permeate the entire strategic planning process as well as the implementation of the final plan.'

Marketing values are constructed directly from corporate values and are internal guidelines for marketing practices. For example treat customers with respect, concern, and honesty and market products you would feel comfortable and safe using. These core values are more than a code of ethics, they have a controlling function in the design of marketing programs, specifically overseeing the development of the marketing mix. Robin and Reidenbach (1987, p. 55) cite two contrasting examples that demonstrate the importance of core values in marketing. The Ford Motor Company's Pinto was linked to more than 500 deaths and accidents resulting from collisions that ruptured the fuel system of the automobile and produced fires. Ford was aware of this problem even before the large number of accidents revealed it (Dowie 1977, pp. 26–55). Ford management conducted a cost/benefit analysis of the situation and decided it was more cost effective to deal with the accidents than to institute a recall and repair the problem. The company's reaction is a good example of marketing plans conceived in the absence of well-developed ethical core values. Johnson & Johnson demonstrates the type of response that would be expected of a company that has a well developed system of ethical core values. After the deaths of seven individuals who had consumed contaminated Tylenol capsules, Johnson & Johnson, within the week, had instituted a total product recall costing an estimated $50 million (Gardner, 1982, p. 71). This action was taken even though the deaths were not the fault of the company but were attributable to the actions of some unknown individual outside the company. The company also spearheaded an industry-wide move to develop tamper proof packaging.

Organizational commitment to social responsibility through core values is essential for marketers to be able to act in socially responsible ways themselves. The uptake of CSR by business demonstrates that most organizations already adhere to socially responsible values. If this is the case. then marketers need only to align marketing practices with the organization's values. However, Kotler (2004) provides recommendations for those marketers whose organizations are more dismissive regarding their social responsibilities. He writes that, 'Some of us, in fact, are independent enough to tell these clients that we will not work for them to find ways to sell more of what hurts people. We can tell them that we're willing to use our marketing toolkit to help them build new businesses around substitute products that are much healthier and safer. But, even if these companies moved toward these healthier and safer products, they'll probably continue to push their current "cash cows". At that point, marketers will have to decide whether to work for these companies, help them reshape their offerings, avoid these companies altogether, or even work to oppose these company offerings.' (p. 35).

6.5 Conclusion: The Need to Reconsider Societal Marketing

The lessons from the CSR literature are that the SMC need not compromise the foundations of the economic system, or indeed the economic foundations of individual organisations. Carefully considered marketing practices that focus on pressing social issues and then align with the organisations strategy, values and norms can bring about long-term business success and social improvement. Identifying and thoroughly engaging with stakeholders will identify social issues and the most salient of these can be determined according to the power, urgency, and legitimacy (or similar) framework. This process also means that the marketing manager need not be an expert in social policy, but remain a marketer who is able to understand social imperatives and recognise the most appropriate marketing tool to align social improvement with business objectives.

The business environment has fundamentally changed since the emergence of the marketing concept as the dominant marketing paradigm. There is a far greater awareness and sensitivity to social and environmental issues. It is advocated that the marketing concept, with the focus on satisfying consumers often short-term wants for profit, with no consideration of the social impacts, no longer fits with this new environment. The SMC broadens the focus to recognising wider social issues and acting in ways that improve society. In being understanding and responsive to these issues trust, loyalty, and innovation develop to serve the interests of the firm. By embracing the SMC, organizations can benefit both themselves and society, for the long-term.

References

Abratt, R. and Sacks, D. (1988) The Marketing Challenge: Towards Being Profitable and Socially Responsible. *Journal of Business Ethics*, 7(7), 497–507.

Anderson, S., Hastings, G., and Macfadyen, L. (2002) Strategic Marketing in the UK Tobacco Industry. *The Lancet Oncology*, 3(8), 481–486.

Bauer, R. and Greyser, S. (1968) *Advertising in America: The Consumer View*, Boston, Harvard University.

Bowen, H. (1953) *Social Responsibilities of the Businessman*, New York, Harper & Row.

Carroll, A. (1999) Corporate Social Responsibility: Evolution of a Definitional Construct. *Business and Society*, 38, 268–295.

Chartered Institute of Marketing U.K. (2008) Available at: http://www.cim.co.uk/KnowledgeHub/MarketingGlossary/GlossaryHome.aspx [accessed 20/09/2008].

Clarkson, M. (1995) A Stakeholder Framework for Analyzing and Evaluating Corporate Social Performance. *Academy of Management Review*, 20(1), 92–117.

Cordoba, J. and Campbell, T. (2008) Editorial: Special Issue Systems Thinking and Corporate Social Responsibility. *Systems Research and Behavioural Science*, 25(3), 359–360.

Crane, A. and Desmond, J. (2002) Societal Marketing and Morality. *European Journal of Marketing*, 36(5/6), 548–562.

Dawson, L. (1969) The Human Concept: New Philosophy for Business. *Business Horizons*, 12, 29–38.

Day, G. and Montgomery, D. (1999) Charting New Directions for Marketing. *Journal of Marketing*, 63, 3–13.

Dowie, M. (1977) How Ford Put Two Million Firetraps on Wheels. *Business and Society Review*, 23(3), 46–55.

Feldman, L. (1971) Societal Adaptation: A New Challenge for Marketing. *Journal of Marketing*, 37(3), 54–60.

Freeman, R. E. (1984) *Strategic Management: A stakeholder Approach*, Boston, Pitman.

Friedman, M. (1970) The Social Responsibility of Business is to Increase its Profits. *The New York Times Magazine*.

Friedman, M. and Friedman, R. (1962) *Capitalism and Freedom*, Chicago, University of Chicago Press.

Gardner, J. (1982) When a Brand Name Gets Hit by Bad News. *U.S. News & World Report* 71.

Garriga, E. and Melé, D. (2004) Corporate Social Responsibility Theories: Mapping the Territory. *Journal of Business Ethics*, 53(1/2), 51–71.

Gaski, J. (1985) Dangerous Territory: The Societal Marketing Concept Revisited. *Business Horizons*, 28, 42–47.

IVCA. (2004) The IVCA Launch Clarion Awards 2004 to Promote the Effective Communications of Corporate Social Responsibility. Available at: http://www.nomensa.com [accessed 13/09/2008].

Kang, G. and James, J. (2007) Revisiting the Concept of a Societal Orientation: Conceptualization and Delineation. *Journal of Business Ethics*, 73, 301–318.

Kirby, T. (2008) Over The Limit *The Guardian*, available at: http://www.guardian.co.uk/responsibledrinking/over.limit [accessed 20/09/2008].

Kotler, P. (1972) A generic Concept of Marketing. *Journal of Marketing*, 36(4), 46–54.

Kotler, P. (2004) Ten deadly Marketing Sins: Sign and Solutions, John Wiley & Sons, Hoboken, N.J.

Kotler, P. and Levy, S. (1969) Broadening the Concept of Marketing. *Journal of Marketing*, 33(1), 10–15.

Kotler, P., Wong, V., Saunders, J., and Armstrong, G. (2005) *Principles of Marketing*, Harlow, Pearson.

Lazer, W. (1969) Marketing's Changing Social Relationships. *Journal of Marketing*, 33, 3–9.

Lee, M. (2008) A Review of the Theories of Corporate Social Responsibility: Its Evolutionary Path and the Road Ahead. *International Journal of Management Reviews*, 10(1), 53–73.

Mackey, A., Mackey, T., and Barney, J. (2007). Corporate Social Responsibility and Firm Performance: Investor Preferences and Corporate Strategies. *Academy of Management Review*, 32(3), 817–835.

Maignan, I., Ferrell, O., and Ferrell, L. (2005) A Stakeholder Model for Implementing Social Responsibility in Marketing. *European Journal of Marketing*, 39(9/10), 956–977.

Marketing Trends Survey. (2007) Fielded by Anderson Analytics, available at: http://www.marketingcharts.com/interactive/marketing-executives-identify-top-marketing-trends-concepts-in-2008-2565/ [accessed 12/08/2008].

Matten, D. and Moon, J. (2008) "Implicit" And "Explicit" CSR: A Conceptual Framework for a Comparative Understanding of Corporate Social Responsibility. *Academy of Management Review*, 33(2), 404–424.

Mintzberg, H. (1983) The Case For Corporate Social Responsibility. *Journal of Business Strategy*, 4(2), 3–16.

Mitchell, R., Agle, B., and Wood, D. (1997) Toward a Theory of Stakeholder Identification and Salience: Defining the Principle of Who and What Really Counts. *Academy of Management Review*, 22(4), 853–887.

Murphy, R. and Crowther, D. (2002) Social Responsibility and Marketing: An Agenda for Research. *Management Decision*, 40(4), 302–309.

Pickard, J. (2008) Brown Blasts Age of Irresponsibility. *Financial Times*, available at: http://www.ft.com/cms/s/0/42cc6040-8bea-11dd-8a4c-0000779fd18c.html [accessed 14/08/2008].

Porter, M. and Kramer, M. (2006) Strategy & Society: The Link Between Competitive Advantage and Corporate Social Responsibility. *Harvard Business Review*, 84(12), 78–92.

Robin, D. and Reidenbach, R. (1987) Social Responsibility, Ethics, and Marketing Strategy: Closing the Gap Between Concept and Application. *Journal of Marketing*, 51, 44–58.

Sheth, J. and Sisodia, S. (2005) A Dangerous Divergence: Marketing and Society. *Journal of Public Policy and Marketing*, 24(1), 160–162.

Smith, J., Clurman, A., and Wood, C. (2005) *Coming to Concurrence*, Evanston, IL, Racom Communications.

Smith, N. (2007) Out of Left Field. *Business Strategy Review*, 18(2), 55–59.

Thomas, M. (2000) Marketing Paradise: Citizen Professionals on the Road to Paradise (via Damascus). *Marketing Intelligence and Planning*, 18(6/7), 321–327.

Thorne, D., Ferrell, O., and Ferrell, L. (2008) *Business and Society: A Strategic Approach to Social Responsibility*, Boston, Houghton Mifflin Company.

Transparency International: Corruption Perceptions Index. (2008) available at: http://www.transparency.org/policy_research/surveys_indices/cpi/2008 [accessed 12/09/2008].

Wilkie, W. and Moore, E. (1999) Marketing's Contributions to Society. *Journal of Marketing*, 63, 198–218.

Wilkie, W. and Moore, E. (2003) Scholarly Research in Marketing: Exploring the '4 Eras' of Thought Development. *Journal of Public Policy and Marketing*, 22(2), 116–146.

Chapter 7
An Analysis of Corporate Social Responsibility, Trust and Reputation in the Banking Profession

Sallyanne Decker and Christopher Sale

*Let us remember that if this financial crisis taught us anything,
it is that we cannot have a thriving Wall Street while Main Street
suffers.*

Barack Obama 4th November 2008

Abstract Bankers and other financial services professionals play a fundamental role in determining the economic fortunes, stability and sustainability of modern economies. Using Carroll's (1991) four part model of CSR and evidence from a small interview survey and desk study of documented interviews, CSR reports and other representations from bankers, the chapter explores bankers' understanding of and approach to CSR in a global environment and in a variety of contexts. Secondly, bankers' involvement in CSR is analysed from a variety of sociological perspectives. We suggest that trust, reputational and regulatory risks are of particular concerns in bankers' efforts to engage with CSR. While bankers may have made some advancement in embedding CSR through reporting initiatives and at a firm and strategic level, such an approach has shortcomings when the role and place of the banking profession is considered from a wider sociological perspective. For bankers to engage meaningfully with and embed CSR, they must look beyond their functional role in society.

7.1 Introduction

Bankers and other financial services professionals play a fundamental role in determining the economic fortunes, stability and sustainability of modern economies. The financial services sector is viewed as a central pillar of modern capitalist economies, performing core functions that facilitate economic activity (Merton, 1995; Levine, 1997; 2005). Bankers recognise the industry's significance in this

S. Decker (✉)
London Metropolitan University Business School, London, UK

S.O. Idowu, W.L. Filho (eds.), *Professionals' Perspectives of Corporate Social Responsibility*, DOI 10.1007/978-3-642-02630-0_8,
© Springer-Verlag Berlin Heidelberg 2009

way, acknowledging in CSR reports that their functions are necessary for sustainable economic growth and progression.

The 2008 financial crisis brought CSR in this industry dramatically into public consciousness and also highlights the importance of trust and reputation as part of the CSR agenda of bankers. Many countries have followed the UK government's move to introduce a package of restructuring, recapitalisation and support to tackle a wider lack of confidence in banking. In terms of social responsibility, the crisis also shows that no other profession has a comparable ability to privatise gains and socialise losses (Wolf, 2008).

The aims of this chapter are twofold. Firstly, given the unique features of the financial services sector, we explore bankers' perceptions of CSR and the nature of bankers' social responsibilities, considering the impact of these on their efforts to absorb CSR. Secondly, from a sociological perspective we provide a critical commentary on CSR within banking. In writing, we draw insights from documented and original interviews with bankers and banking experts, bankers' CSR initiatives and banks' CSR reports. As pointed out by Bennet and Durkin (2002) and Shreeve (2008), twenty first century bankers operate more and more within financial services and not just banking. Hence, valuable insights into the way in which financial services professionals in general can engage with CSR may be drawn from exploring CSR from a banking perspective.

The chapter is structured as follows: Section 7.2 outlines briefly the literature on CSR and reputation. Section 7.3 presents findings on bankers' perceptions of CSR and of the parallels between CSR and regulation. Using Carroll's 4 part model, Sect. 7.4 examines the various dimensions of bankers' social responsibilities and explores some of the steps that have been adopted to absorb CSR into banking. Given the central role of bankers and banking in modern societies, Sect. 7.5 provides a critique of CSR by reviewing the CSR agenda of bankers from a sociological perspective. Section 7.6 concludes.

7.2 CSR, Trust and Reputation

CSR is a widely contested concept (Crowther and Rayman-Bacchus, 2004; Broomhill, 2007). From an industry or professional perspective, CSR can be understood as a systemic expression of the context and drivers in which the businesses and the professionals involved in a sector operate (Commission of the European Communities, 2001; Nelson, 2004).

The financial contracts that bankers execute are characterised by information asymmetry and uncertainty which makes trust a necessary condition for doing business (Beck, 2006; Schanz, 2006). Although this trust is often taken for granted, it is a central strategic issue for financial services firms (Llewellyn, 2005; Olsen, 2008). A lack of trust in bankers and banking can have widespread damaging consequences for the industry and macro-economy. It is the understanding that trust is a functional prerequisite to the operations of bankers that provides a justification for the regulation of the industry on the grounds of market failures such as information asymmetry, the nature of financial contracts and externalities.

Ethically responsible conduct gives rise to trust and reputational outcomes that contribute positively to developing the effective informational frameworks which are part of the essential underpinnings of a sound financial system. Reputation represents trust capital that is acquired through addressing corporate performance, addressing society's concerns and meeting or exceeding stakeholders' expectations (Schanz, 2006). Since the players in the sector operate as a system, reputation is a shared asset Gaultier-Galliard and Louisot (2008). Similarly, like ethical responsibility in banking, reputation is both individual and collective and can give rise to positive as well as negative externalities (Bozovic, 2007).

Although evolutionary trends such as financial innovation, deregulation and the growth of universal banking have eroded the distinct identity of bankers and the definition of bankers through membership of a professional body, Bossone (2000) and Olson (2006) argue that trust and confidence in banking will continue to be important and vital to society's financial well being. Key CSR principles such as accountability and transparency are at the heart of regulatory efforts to ensure banks and bankers operate with trust. Since regulation creates mandatory legal responsibilities, some professionals and commentators have suggested that increased and committed engagement with CSR may make further regulation of CSR unnecessary and counterproductive (Australian Bankers Association, 2006; Broomhill, 2007).

Regulatory concerns aside, reputation is recognised as a key motivator for engagement with CSR by firms seeking to defend or maintain legitimacy. These same reputation concerns extend to professions. Rossier (2003) highlights a number of reasons why bankers, in particular, have to consider issues of reputation. Apart from the fact that bankers trade money which represents other people's security and well being, they are also involved in a profession that has been held in contempt, since medieval times because of usury, a practice which was prohibited at that time by Christianity. Rossier argues that bankers suffer from an image problem that has largely been ignored by the profession. Reputation is built on the trust that is established with all stakeholders and as an intangible asset it directly affects the value of financial services firms and is crucial to their sustainability and to the economic sustainability of society. As most of the value of financial firms is based on intangibles, a strong reputation is essential for the sustainability of the sector and the profession (Csiszar and Heidrich, 2006; Gaultier-Galliard and Louisot, 2008; The Banker, 2007).

Industry wide CSR initiatives that involve banking bodies and which seek to engage with CSR systematically within the financial services sector are fairly recent. In particular, Vigano and Nicolai (2006) found that European bankers have been slow in considering issues of sustainability. The UK's FORGE guidance (2002) on CSR was published to assist bankers and other financial services professionals in their efforts to engage with CSR and to develop CSR management and reporting frameworks that were appropriate for a range of financial businesses. This document acknowledged that in spite of the sector's efforts to manage components of

CSR, defining the concept and determining an appropriate and integrated response to CSR issues posed significant challenges. Furthermore, CSR issues in the marketplace were identified as particularly challenging because of demands for increased transparency, ethical practices and value for money in the sector. For retail bankers, Decker (2004) argues that these marketplace social responsibilities include trust, customer knowledge, prudent management of funds, proximity and accessibility. The work of the FORGE group is ongoing. In 2007, the consortium published a new set of guidelines on how the financial services sector can address climate change.

7.3 Bankers' Perceptions of CSR

Although, the industry specific nature of CSR is recognised in the literature, less attention is paid to the extent to which heterogeneity within industries can impact on CSR. A review of the corporate responsibility and sustainability reports of the UK's leading banks shows that UK bankers do not share a common baseline definition or understanding of CSR and that definitions of CSR vary across banks and over time. However, there are some areas of commonality. One observation is that banks see reputation as a source of competitive advantage. Even those banks that do not make explicit their definition of CSR state that their goal is to be a leader or leading brand in CSR. Where there is a high level of heterogeneity, organisational factors could have a strong influence on perceptions. Organisational commitments to ethics and CSR have been shown to affect professionals' perceptions (Vittel and Paolillo, 2004).

7.3.1 Results of Study of Bankers' Perceptions

Similar to Fenwick and Bierema's (2008) methodology in a study of human resource development professionals' engagement with CSR, we undertook an interpretive qualitative study to explore the views of bankers from different sectors of the banking industry. The study sought, from the experiences of bankers who have involvement with CSR, an understanding of how CSR is perceived and undertaken by bankers. This phenomenological approach is suitable to the exploratory nature of the study. The strategy of investigation was based on semi-structured interviews with banking personnel based in the UK at the time of the study. Non-probability purposive sampling was used in order to enable the researchers to approach respondents who have had or currently have involvement with CSR in their professional lives, as those experiences would permit an understanding of the phenomena under investigation and would therefore be valuable. Given the diverse nature of banking, the study was limited to the retail aspects of the banking sector.

Since the retail sector is itself heterogeneous, it was decided to widen the scope to include bankers with mutual, co-operative and Islamic backgrounds so as to gain insights of CSR from a variety of retail contexts. Leading retail financial institutions were identified from league tables obtained through internet search engines.

Suitable bankers who had been identified through phone calls to banks and recommendations, were approached initially by means of an email that outlined details of the study's goals and objectives. They were also provided an aide-memoir of the issues on which they were to be consulted later by means of face to face and telephone interviews.

As the study was undertaken in a period of extreme environmental turbulence, it was perhaps not surprising that the researchers experienced reluctance from many of those approached to participate in the study. We were referred to CSR reports and company websites for information from the majority of bankers approached who stated that everything on CSR was available from these sources. Although 9 bankers agreed to participate in the study initially, only 6 were eventually interviewed as 3 subsequently withdrew. All those consulted requested anonymity. Creswell (1998), Groenwald (2004) suggest researchers conduct interviews with between 2 and 10 subjects for studies of a phenomenological nature. The final sample consisted of 5 respondents from banks and 1 from a building society. Although, the small sample size is in keeping with exploratory qualitative studies of this nature which seek to surface deeper issues, the main limitation lies in the limited generalisability of the findings which may not be applicable to a wider population of banking professionals.

The study was originally set up to explore bankers understanding of CSR and views of efforts to embed CSR in their professional practice, given the regulated nature of the industry. A number of insights were gained from these consultations. In discussing these findings, we also draw from documented interviews with bankers on CSR.

The findings with regards to bankers' perceptions indicate that considerable variation exists as to their personal understanding of CSR and that these perceptions appear to have organisational cultural dimensions. This suggests a view of CSR as a means of institutional differentiation and promotion. Some respondents preferred to talk of sustainability because this was the term used by their organisation while others spoke of corporate responsibility or corporate social responsibility.

One respondent from a large high street bank interpreted sustainability as being *'about maintaining your reputation and improving it'*. This definition of sustainability focuses on the long term success of the bank's business and the role of reputation in achieving sustainability. Another respondent, a private banker, saw CSR as a vehicle for cohesion as it embodied the organisation's CSR values, provided employees with a vision of what the organisation represented and established the ethical boundaries and a common yardstick for the bank's employees in any geographic location. The respondent noted that *our culture matters, we deal with high net worth individual individuals so we do not have a corporate/corporate environment with an aggressive culture. We focus more on the client, on the individual and on giving a service.*

Similarly, respondents from a co-operative and mutual culture perceived CSR as a natural extension of their traditional values. A respondent from a building society felt that CSR was an extension of the building society's mutual status and that engagement with CSR was *natural* for his organisation especially in terms of community involvement: *CSR is about recognising that we need to put something back into the communities where we look to do business. We stick to what we know best and we have a what's in it for me mentality as well. Through mutuality we are spending our members' money. We are careful about sponsorship and focus on encouraging personal responsibility in finance. We are also not here to replace things that government should be supporting.* This view of CSR reveals how, in this instance, mutuality defines the boundaries within which bankers operate and how bankers are looking to create shared value through CSR, hence adopting a strategic approach to CSR as advocated by Lantos (2001), Porter and Kramer (2006) and Zappi (2007). Although, these views suggest an increasingly strategic approach to CSR, the Islamic banker highlighted that *in Islamic banking, community welfare is the essence of CSR, the bank is not seen as separate from society.* In this sense, there is no need to create shared value so as to secure a competitive advantage through CSR.

The respondents' largely strategic view of CSR echoes a similar trend evident in documented interviews. Perceptions of CSR as a source of competitive advantage are not uncommon amongst bankers. In a panel discussion on CSR, published in The Banker (2007), leading bankers and banking experts world-wide identified issues relating to reputation and a recognition of CSR as a source of value as primary motivators for bankers engagement with CSR. The discussants noted that CSR strengthens corporate reputation, helps to earn and keep the trust of stakeholders, and helps to meet customers' expectations of wanting a 'bank with a conscience'. Hence it appears there is a general consensus amongst bankers that CSR is strategically important because the competitive advantage of their business lies in integrity, transparency, good risk management and the motivation of customer facing employees.

To further explore bankers' perception of CSR, we asked them for their views on the relationship between CSR and regulation. Respondents from our interview survey agreed unanimously that CSR was different from regulation and expressed a desire for CSR to remain largely if not totally voluntary. One respondent noted that some aspects of CSR that relate to customers were already regulated such as equitable treatment of customers because the *[Financial Services Authority's] Treating Customers Fairly initiative comes close to what you see as CSR.*

The main difference that respondents highlighted between CSR and regulation was in terms of the voluntary nature of CSR and that CSR did not set 'standards' except those that were outlined in guidelines such as the Global Reporting Initiative (GRI). A number of reasons were given as to why the respondents objected to the legislation of CSR. These included the argument that if CSR is regulated, those regulatory requirements would now become targets which firms would have no incentive to exceed. *Once regulation is introduced, it will become the maximum.* Regulation would therefore limit CSR performance, as imposed standards become the ultimate targets and not the baseline.

Another concern was that engagement with CSR would become a mere tick box exercise that would be limited to the department given responsibility for CSR and would not be an undertaking in which the whole organisation would be engaged.

Responsibility will be taken away from the masses, making it difficult to embed CSR within the organisation. A third objection was that CSR could no longer be used as a source of differentiation as CSR practice would become the same across all businesses with no scope for *flair.* One respondent compared the impacts of legislating for CSR to the problems associated with the Basle 1 Accord on Capital Adequacy: *the problem with legislating for CSR lies with the issue of the typical scenario or the typical company. It would be just like what happened with the Basle Capital adequacy ratio. Every bank's business is so different.*

As many banks across the world have accepted government funds to recapitalise their balance sheets, these bailouts are most likely to have implications for cultural influences of CSR and for the for the balance between banks mandatory legal responsibilities and voluntary ethical responsibilities. Deal and Kennedy (1982) define culture as consisting of underlying core values shared by members of an organisation which gives rise to symbols, rituals and practices within the organisation and argue that it affects every aspect of an organisation's functions. CSR is a value driven concept and the practices adopted evolve from the definition and understanding of CSR and from the CSR values embraced by organisations (Grayson and Hodges, 2004; Carrasco, 2007). One factor that has been cited in analyses of the crisis is that retail bankers were increasingly adopting the bonus remuneration culture of investment banking. Unlike retail bankers, investment bankers have a mainly corporate client base and transactions orientation. Hence they may have different reputation concerns compared with retail banking which traditionally has a relationship orientation. To date, responsibility for ensuring integrity in the area of remuneration has been ethical and not legal.. The notion that culture affects bankers' understanding of CSR will have implications for embedding CSR in large financial conglomerates where professionals are engaged in retail and investment banking as well as insurance and other types of financial activity.

7.4 Banking and Bankers' Social Responsibilities

Carroll's (1991) CSR pyramid provides a useful framework for discussing the social responsibilities of banks and bankers and their efforts incorporate these into their business. Crane and Matten (2004) point out that the model is pragmatic since it structures social responsibilities into different dimensions and recognises the interrelationships between them. Within this four-part model, Carroll argues that while economic and legal responsibilities are required by society, ethical responsibility is only expected and philanthropy is desired by society.

7.4.1 Economic Responsibility

The fundamental layer of economic responsibility relates to why banks and bankers exist and provides the foundations for other levels of responsibility. In the narrowest sense this can be viewed as improving the wealth of the owners within the context of free market competition. The market imposes constraints on professionals within banks to deliver profitability and growth. One of the ways in which this responsibility is executed is through financial innovation. As the financial needs of individuals and firms change, bankers create new opportunities for risk management and the efficient transfer of funds. Financial innovation involves creating new products as well as redefining existing products and developing new delivery channels (Verweire and van der Berghe 2008). In addition, many banks have won CSR awards for innovations that include credit cards that incorporate and mainstream environmental concerns.

Yet, recent experience of subprime lending and the use of risk-transferring financial innovations such as asset backed securities and collateralised debt obligations, while profitable in the short term, widen the scope of stakeholders to which a banker is responsible. The global financial crisis raises questions about bankers' judgment and sense of economic responsibility, particularly in the light of their damaging effect on trust and reputation. There is considerable debate surrounding whether bankers' practices in these areas reflect shareholder, stakeholder or the personal motivations of bankers. Freeman (1984 cited in Walsh, 2005) argues that CSR strategy should be oriented around managing bilateral stakeholder relationships. These relationships, however, are more complex and organic in nature than simple bilateral relationships with immediate or primary stakeholders. While a stakeholder view may appear inconsistent with an instrumental orientation that puts long-term wealth production for the firm's owners as an economic imperative, it recognises the overt or tacit 'contractual relationships' that exist with other parties on whom the long-term strategic goals of the firm may depend. Managing these relationships is considered as *good management sense* and also secures trust and reputation.

Banks and bankers determine their corporate responsibility priorities and commitments through stakeholder engagement processes. However as banking becomes global, this process is becoming complex, increasingly requiring world-wide consultation in the case of large, global operators such as Hong Kong and Shangai Banking Corporation (HSBC). Table 7.1 shows the issues that HSBC's worldwide consultation identified as the most important to stakeholders. The ranking is based on consolidated scores from stakeholders in North America, Asia-Pacific, Europe and Latin America. The table shows sustainable lending and finance as stakeholders' primary concern. Strandberg (2005) defines sustainable finance as the provision of financial capital and risk management products and services in ways that promote or do not harm economic prosperity, ecological and community wellbeing. In project finance, bankers have responded to this concern by developing the Equator Principles, which provide a benchmark for managing social and environmental issues in project financing. Established in 2003 by 10 institutions, there are some 63 Equator Principles Financial Institutions as at November 2008.

Table 7.2 shows how through stakeholder engagement, HSBC and Royal Bank of Scotland (RBS) have been able to identify and prioritise CSR issues for engaging with CSR. The list of issues identified is representative of those with which all bankers are generally concerned. A breakdown of concerns by HSBC according to

Table 7.1 Outcomes of global stakeholder engagement

What are the most important issues that HSBC's sustainability reporting should address?

Rank	Issue
1	Sustainable finance/lending
2	Treatment of staff
3	Community impacts
3	Climate change
5	Sustainable profit growth
6	Implementation of sustainability strategy
6	Business ethics
8	Community investment in education
9	Financial Inclusion
9	Transparency
9	Governance and prioritisation issues
9	Treating customers fairly
9	Green products
14	Capturing revenues linked to sustainability
14	Sharing best practice community programmes

Source: HSBC Holdings plc Sustainability Report 2007

business area again highlights that depending on the type of banking activities in which a banker is involved, perceptions and the focus of CSR may differ.

In addressing these issues, bankers' strategies are not simply concerned with recognising and reacting to stakeholder influence; there is an ethical and moral obligation to stakeholders. One example of this is the agreement between the major UK

Table 7.2 CSR issues facing bankers

HSBC Key sustainability issues	RBS CSR priorities
Personal financial services	1. Financial crime
1. Financial inclusion and consumer debt	2. Customer service
2. Secure and convenient delivery channels	3. Selling and lending practices
3. Customer satisfaction	4. Employee practices
Commercial banking	5. Environmental impact
1. Environmental credit risk needs to be managed carefully to minimise ecological damage caused indirectly through financing	6. Community investment
	7. Global lending and project finance
2. Emerging markets pose certain regulatory and ethical risks	8. Financial education
	9. Financial inclusion
Private banking	10. Small business support
1. Money laundering and financial crime	
2. Determining the legitimacy of the source of an individual's wealth	

Sources: HSBC n.d.
Royal Bank of Scotland. n.d.

banks not to charge customers for use of their own or other banks' Automated Teller Machines (ATM's). Managing the relationship with the customer to use banking services has been adopted by a consortium of banks. Another example is the provision of basic bank accounts since 2003 by high street banks following criticisms of 'financial desertification and exclusion' attributed to bankers' purely economic decisions to close branches in certain areas (Thrift and Leyshon, 1997; Mayo, 1997). These basic accounts do not only provide access to banking services but have features that prevent these customers from overdrawing their accounts and facing bank charges that may exacerbate their financial vulnerability. Over time, customers become culturally acclimatised to the provision of such services. Social pressures to conform are so strong that exit costs in terms of lost reputation and revenue are likely to be high as a result of media and activist attention. Sustaining such services also sustains bankers' reputations and the reliability, visibility and integration of the banking system in society.

7.4.2 Legal Responsibility

For bankers, legal responsibility is determined largely by regulation. Maintaining confidence in the financial system is a public good and there is a long history of government intervention in the financial system to limit risk taking, arbitrate relationships between the financial sector and society, through prudential and conduct of business regulations, as well as provide safety net arrangements. The UK financial services sector is governed by the Financial Services Authority's risk based and principles based approach to regulation which aims at improving efficiency by allowing institutions the flexibility to decide how best to align their business objectives and processes with the outcomes specified by the regulator. The aim of this approach is to ensure that regulation becomes an integral, rather than a marginal, part of business decision making. The Australian Bankers Association, (2006) argues that bankers could adopt a compliance approach to CSR in which, although they may meet their legal obligations, such compliance does not foster ethical business practices or an ethical corporate culture and thereby fails to ensure sustainable performance. Although CSR is largely voluntary in the UK, the FORGE guidance noted areas of cross-matching with regulation such as complaints handling and money laundering which together with reputation underpin the business case for bankers' engagement with CSR.

It is possible to draw parallels between principles based regulation and CSR. For example, as part of its principles based approach to regulation, the FSA recently introduced the Treating Customers Fairly Initiative (TCF). The initiative does not define what constitutes treating customers fairly, but provides management of individual firms with the flexibility to determine what practices would achieve this outcome. Like banks' CSR agenda, the TCF initiative needs to be embedded into the culture of a firm at all levels, so that over time it becomes business as usual.

It has been suggested that the FSA's 'light touch' approach to regulation was too loose and that tighter regulation, including product regulation, might have prevented or reduced the impact of the financial crisis of 2007 and 2008. A familiar pattern in banking is for further and costly regulation to be introduced, following a financial crisis, to combat unethical practices and unethical aspects of innovations. Undoubtedly, given the impact of the crisis and subsequent bailouts efforts on society, the regulation of banks, particularly in terms of their global operations and connection with other sectors of the financial service industry will undergo significant reform so as to rebuild trust not only in the banking profession but in regulation itself as a pillar of responsibility.

7.4.3 Ethical Responsibility

Legal and ethical responsibilities are not necessarily mutually exclusive. Regulatory agencies operate within a framework of ethical drivers which determine the purpose and nature of regulation. Neo-liberal ideology in the west has been significantly influenced by the utilitarian ethic that an ethical decision should provide *the greatest happiness for the greatest number* (Bentham, 1789). As in the case of principles-based regulation, the basis for policy-making is therefore based entirely on the expected outcome (teleological ethics). Nevertheless, societies typically impose some constraints on the level of freedom awarded to individuals and corporations. These are moral absolutes (deontological ethics) that define right or wrong, independently of outcomes. Kant cited in (Paton, 1948) referred to this code of actions (or inactions) as social obligations or duties, as the *categorical imperative* and argued that such duties extended to truthfulness, theft, charity, laziness, cruelty to animals and even suicide. Regulation is one mechanism by which such ethical codes are imposed in banking.

Lantos (2001) has argued that of all the different conceptualisations of CSR it is the issue of ethical responsibility that is most relevant to the professional as an individual. He also highlights that the financial community has always embraced the view that businesses do have a social responsibility that goes beyond economic responsibility to include values such as honesty and good faith. The motto of the London Stock Exchange *My word is my bond* captures the ethical values of honesty and sincerity that are traditionally associated with financial services and form the foundations of trust which is of significant importance in the financial services sector. Within Carroll's framework, ethical responsibility derives from expectations. Confident expectations, usually about the intentions and behaviour of others form the basis of trust (Olsen, 2008).

The Worshipful Company of International Bankers, a representative body for professionals in the banking and financial services community, reiterates that expectations about bankers include honesty, professional integrity, transparency and accountability, a lack of which can impair the ability of financial services providers to fulfil their role (www.internationalbankers.co.uk). Consequently, financial service firms and their officers and employees have both a public good (collective) and an individual commercial interest in the maintenance of high standards of behaviour and of their professional reputation.

The main UK professional bodies, the Institute of Financial Services, formerly, the Chartered Institute of Bankers (CIB), Chartered Institute of Bankers in Scotland (CIOBS) and the Chartered Insurance Institute require members to pass a programme of professional educations, engage in continuing professional development and adhere to the institutes' code of ethics. CIOBS, which in 2008 introduced a Professionalism and Ethics module as part of its Chartered Banker qualification cites its vision and standards as follows:

> Our vision is for real professionalism in the financial services market. We want people with integrity, responsible to their customers, who know their jobs inside out and behave ethically. (www.ciobs.com)

Yet, professional bodies do not seem to be primary vehicles through which ethical responsibilities are absorbed into the banking profession. Furthermore, as noted by the Cooperative Bank in its 2007 Sustainability Report, unlike ecological sustainability, there is much less consensus in banking as to what constitutes the ethical elements of CSR. In this respect, the Co-operative Bank states it is guided by stakeholder dialogue and the established values of the co-operative movement.

Since the legal relationship between a lending banker and a customer is one of creditor and debtor, and is not fiduciary, trust falls under realms of voluntary responsibility. Instead, the relationships and accountability implied in trust between bankers and their customers and stakeholders are captured in banks' voluntary codes of conduct. In the UK, bankers subscribe to the Banking Code and Business Banking Codes which outline principles for doing business and generally cover areas that include the treatment of clients, customers and counterparties; execution of responsibilities; observation of laws, codes and standards and, market dealings and conflicts of interest. Their effectiveness can be marred by lack of stakeholder engagement in code development, lack of integrity in organisational practice and lack of stakeholder activism (Painter-Morland, 2006). In November 2008, the FSA published proposals to take over elements of the Banking Code regime from the Banking Code Standards Board (BCSB). These relate to the regulation of retail banking conduct of business. Reasons given for this decision include an acknowledgement that it was anomalous for the FSA to now have responsibility for regulating payments services but not core retail services, which may reduce the FSA's regulatory effectiveness. Furthermore, the FSA noted that should regulation of this business remain voluntary, there may be scope for consumer detriment since the regulator was not enforcing, in these core retail areas, one of its key principle No 6 that a firm must pay due regard to the interests of its customers (FSA, 2008).

7.4.4 Philanthropy

Corporate philanthropy is additional to the responsibilities that the corporation has to its owners and the minimal regulatory factors that constrain its activities imposed by law within the jurisdiction in which it operates. It implies that managerial behaviour may not be limited to the concepts implicit in the traditional liberal economic model of the firm to increase shareholder wealth. These altruistic acts are not required of the firm and can be seen as an ethical extension of the firm's social role. The social reputation of the industry is further enhanced by the social activities supported by the financial services industry. This can be interpreted as a *social* distribution of a proportion of profit. All large UK banks have CSR activities of this nature. The institutions in the UK banking industry engage in philanthropic activities such as funding charitable and community organisations.

Increasingly bank employees are taking part in corporate philanthropy through their employers' charitable donations' matching schemes and volunteering. For most bankers, this is how they have their most direct and only engagement with CSR. In this way, philanthropy has a bottom up element. Bankers', however, are not confined to philanthropic donations. They are becoming more strategic in their philanthropy, with a recognition that it is essential for bankers to distinguish between charity and community support. However the specific choices as to where contributions are made using a top down approach are not immediately apparent. From a strategic perspective, banks' foundations such as that of Halifax Bank of Scotland (HBOS) will consider grant applications related to *Money advice and financial literacy* and *Developing and improving local communities* from registered charities or not-for-profit local community groups. The foundation further states that:

> In order to make a real difference within the community the Foundation remit is tightly focused. Unfortunately, therefore, anything falling outside the Foundation's key themes is unlikely to be supported.

Such prescribed activities include: animal rights or welfare organisations; sponsorship of fundraising events for registered charities; medical research; political appeals or organisations; any group which discriminate on the basis of age, race, colour, religion, gender, disability or sexual orientation. Two issues worth considering are why some activities are seen as to be acceptable and also whether the choices of sponsorship reflect an allocation to where charitable need is most acute.

The discussion in this section has highlighted how bankers, through the various dimensions of social responsibility, seek to manage multiple stakeholders and engage with the concerns of those with whom they have relationships and regular interactions. In managing these relationships, bankers have to develop trust and a positive reputation to be able to address a complex range of CSR issues within appropriate regulatory, ethical and economic boundaries.

7.5 Sociological Perspectives on CSR Within the Financial Services Industry

Olsen (2008) describes trust as a sociological issue because it is a device to reduce the complexity in social relationships and the uncertainty of the natural world. In this section, we use alternative and contrasting sociological interpretations of professionalism theories to assess and comment on the developments in CSR within the banking industry. We argue that the commonly adopted focus on professionalism limits the understanding of the interactions between bankers, banking and society.

7.5.1 Functional Perspectives

The economic and social role of the banking industry is typically defined in terms of a functionalist sociological paradigm. This perspective creates an image of an industry which is integrated into capitalist society in terms of economic benefits, broader social benefits and as a figurehead of trust. Functionalist frameworks view institutions in society as operating in a systematic and harmonious way for the net benefit of its members. Dysfunctional institutions that fail to provide economic and social value will fail to adapt to a changing society and cease to exist. The popular economic roles of the banking system as described by Merton (1995) and Levine (1997, 2005) are functionalist models. The banks themselves diligently reiterate these functions in their literature. Lloyds TSB's mission statement emphasises its social role by stating:

> Our vision is to be the **best** financial services company, first in the UK, then in other markets. To be a **great** place to work, to be a **great** place for our customers to do business and to generate **great** returns for our shareholders. Emphasis added

Functionalist perspectives on the nature of professionals (Carr-Saunders, 1928; Goode, 1960; Perks, 1993) outline the characteristics of professional workers as typically having extensive business education (usually involving tests of professional competence), institutionalised training, membership of an exclusive self-regulating professional body with a (code of ethics and influence over remuneration). These attributes of professionalism are associated with high social status, respect and the notions of public service. They also provide professionals with other privileges such as relative autonomy over their own work, mobility of employment and above average levels of remuneration. This is apparent within the banking profession. The Courses Careers UK website (accessed March 2009) cited starting salaries for graduate management trainee programmes in banking ranging from around £19,000 to £25,000. After a year's experience, salaries could have risen to between £26,000 and £29,000. At more senior levels, salaries (including sales commission), were typically quoted at £40,000–£100,000. These initial salaries are relatively good in comparison with the national average wage at the time of £23,000. However, the total annual remuneration for Executive Directors of banks is significantly higher than this and typically of the order of £1,000,000–£3,000,000 (see Table 7.3).

Structural developments have led bankers to acknowledge that they now operate within the financial services industry which has implications for professional status and for relationships with stakeholders. Gavin Shreeve, Chief Executive of the UK's Institute of Financial Services (IFS), argues that membership of a professional body may be captured by the profession to the detriment of society as professions become elitist and protectionist gentlemen's clubs that are separate from as opposed to being

Table 7.3   Directors remuneration in Lloyds TSB

Executive directors	Salaries/ fees	Other benefits		Performance-related payments	2007 Total	2006
		Cash	Non cash			
	£000	£000	£000	£000	£000	£000
Group Chief Executive	960	105	8	1,811	2,884	2,444
Deputy Group Chief Executive	600	35	7	798	1,440	1,885
Group Executive Director, UK Retail Banking	625	285	4	1,081	1,995	1,719
Executive Director Insurance and Investments	550	20	20	787	1.377	1,252
Group Executive Director Wholesale and International Banking	600	21	27	738	1,386	1,303
Group Finance Director	575	83	19	909	1,586	1,310

Source: Extracted from Lloyds TSB annual report 2007

part of society. In such cases, the dominant ideologies are prestige and exclusivity and not social responsibility (Shreeve, 2008).

The CSR literature is also dominated by a functionalist orientation (Scherer and Palazzo, 2008). Carrol's four part model (1991), discussed earlier in this article is consistent with this way of thinking. The emphasis is on the *corporate role* in terms of the way business strategy, the management of stakeholder relationships and profit orientation which are consistent with CSR and the needs of society as a whole. The emphasis is on the relationship between business and society. However broader questions as to *what firms should be responsible for*? Or *to whom they should be responsible*? remain ambiguous when the focus of CSR research is on the corporation and not on society as a whole or on the globalised world of banking.

7.5.2 Alternative Perspectives

The weakness of the functionalist approach is that CSR is viewed primarily from the business perspective rather than the social. Alternative perspectives in social science are largely not explored within the literature. We argue that the predominant functionalist orientation in the CSR literature fails to consider Socio-Political,

Cultural and Socio-Cognitive perspectives and hence that the theory underlying CSR is incomplete. Indeed, interpretations of the 2008 crisis in the banking industry cannot be fully understood without an understanding of conflict, culture and symbolism.

We explore this by looking at two issues relating to CSR in the banking industry.

a. Power relationships between banking professionals.
b. Religious and cultural differences in the interpretation of CSR within banking

a. Power relationships between banking professionals. The functional perspective on professionalism fails to recognise the tensions and contradictions implicit in the role. The concept of *professional trust* in the financial services industry assists in managing the expectations of clients with respect to hidden information and hidden action. The size and global reach of the institutions also pose a challenge for embedding CSR. While it may be the responsibility of management to initiate a CSR agenda that is tailored to fit the size, geographical location and scope as well as cultural, political and economic context of the organisation, management cannot successfully embed a CSR agenda in an organisation without the appropriate structures and political support from professionals within the organisation.

The functionalist paradigm does not reveal the conflict and struggle in the competitive environment in which professionals operate on an intercompany and at the intracompany level. Pressures from the firm, the client and the individual's moral judgment affect the decision making process of a professional (Sweeney and Roberts, 1997). In the banking industry, the professional has greater power than the client through information asymmetry. The extent to which this power is exercised is influenced by the power of superiors in the corporate hierarchy and the profession to reinforce ethical values and control material benefits of financial incentives. Intercompany competition may lead to a stronger focus on incentive schemes with a consequential increase in risk exposure and weaker ethical orientation. In recent years, salaries for top executives have become inflated with bonuses and other performance related incentives (see Table 7.3). However, bonus structures may create perverse incentives, encouraging risk taking disguised as value creation since there is an asymmetry of risk to the professional as their risk exposure is largely oriented around the achievement of additional bonuses and not the loss of the basic salary. Hence media attention in the early twenty first century has focused significantly on the disparities between the apparent levels of performance and the level of remuneration.

At the professional/client interface there is a fundamental informational asymmetry. From the client perspective, the decisions to engage in a contract with the institution cannot be made with complete knowledge of the cost and risks involved. This decision is constrained by a bounded rationality (Simon, 1972; 1957). As Roberts and Dietrich (1999) points out, the quality of the decision is not simply the availability of information but also the ability of the user to make use of it. This may vary significantly from one individual to another since the concepts of monetary values; return and risk are complex and for many clients not understood or even misunderstood. Unlike the consumption of tangible products for which the client is likely to have more experience, the conceptualising of financial services and products is more abstract. The contractual agreement may also involve legal conditions that are under the direct control of the institution such as variable interest rates. Professionals in the financial services, as with many other professions, have a power advantage in managing the information asymmetry and sustaining the corporate reputation with clients. The professional/client interface can be successfully sustained if: (1) the professional provides appropriate reassuring guidance to the client to enable a decision to be made; (2) the corporate reputation is managed and communicated to the client; (3) there is public confidence in the integrity of the industry as a whole.

It is revealing that in our interviews with banking professionals, all respondents unanimously wished to remain anonymous and frequently referred us to publicly available statements on their company websites. We interpret this to mean that there are political or cultural constraints on the extent to which professionals believe that CSR policies can be openly debated. The *social* is not for open social discussion. The cultural aspect may relate to the traditional bureaucratic or process culture associated particularly with the banking industry (Deal and Kennedy, 1982). It could also reflect the close association of CSR with broader strategic issues and the management of reputation. We note the different interpretations of CSR amongst professionals of different banking organisations. Hence we suggest that the management of CSR is a political process which involves a complex set of dimensions related to competition, political power, inequality and remuneration.

   b. Religious and cultural differences in the interpretation of CSR within banking. The evolutionary trends that have taken place in the industry over the last three decades have implications for the way in which CSR has been conceptualised and adopted in the western banking industry. Traditionally, structural regulations served to impose clear lines of demarcation between the different sectors of the sector. Liberalisation of capital flows and deregulation of the banking system throughout the 1980s and 1990s created greater freedoms for financial institutions to exploit new opportunities but has also exposed the banking system to greater risks. This is manifested in a move away from the traditional prudent approaches of banking professionals to a more overt sales-oriented approach and business models that have not anticipated broader economic developments. At the same time, business ethics have become blurred. One of the reasons for this lies in the cultural differences that exist between different types of financial institutions. In particular, attention has been drawn to the traditional relationship orientation of commercial bankers and the transactions and deals focus of investment bankers. One factor that may be responsible for the confusion that currently exists in western banking is the *blurring* of distinctions between retail and investment banks which have different corporate cultures. The bonus culture is an inherent part of investment banking. One outcome of universal banking is that the nature of western banking itself has changed in recent years in terms of attitude to risk. With widespread adoption of the universal banking model, investment banks and capital markets are playing an increasing role in meeting the financing and risk management needs of the world. Furthermore, in a deregulated and global environment where the boundaries between institutions and nations have been eroded, financial innovations that are designed to diversify risk spread quickly across the globe.

In contrast to conventional western banking, Islamic banking operates within the framework of Sharia'a law. This imposes theocratic ethical constraints on banking strategy that require: prohibition of interest and speculation; sharing of profits and losses; asset-backing for all contracts, restriction on the financing of projects which conflict with the moral values of Islam and ensuring the sanctity of contracts (Kettell, 2008). Development of community oriented, ethical strategy is more overt in this context. Decision-making is ethically constrained by 'Kantian' *categorical imperatives* rather than the utilitarian ethical framework associated with western capitalism.

Therefore there is a significant divergence between conventional and Islamic banking systems regarding ethics, morality and the concept of fairness and justice. In Islamic banking, religion and the assumption of shared values allow for viewing society as an organic whole. In the West, the pursuit of wealth has become the social goal. In Islamic economics, based on advocacy of co-operation within a community with shared goals, social interest takes precedence over personal ones and stresses harmony and co-operation. At the heart of Islam is a promotion of co-operation between individuals who can be motivated to be generous. The main process of decision-making is *Shoora* or consultation which has parallels with stakeholder engagement view of CSR. Within conventional economics and banking, the strategic approach to CSR focuses on the concept that good ethics is good business. However, this is denounced in Islam where the value of an action is judged the intention and not the outcome (Zaman, 2008). Hence CSR activities undertaken for reputation benefit to favourably impact on the business bottom line this is condemned in Islam.

The Islamic banking system is afforded some protection from risk by its deontological ethics. It tends to have a greater dependence on retail deposits rather than money markets for funding. Islamic banks have tended to avoid complicated debt-backed securities whereas western institutions have been less conservative and are more exposed as a result of a teleological ethical orientation for which the outcome is only certain in its final occurrence.

However, as Wigglesworth (2008) observes the globalisation of the financial services industry and inter-bank mutual dependency for liquidity still exposes Islamic banks to contagion arising from falls in global liquidity. In addition, the propensity to adopt an asset-backed investment strategy exposes these institutions to risk in equity and real estate markets.

7.6 Conclusions

The dichotomy between private interest and public good that results from the capacity for bankers to privatise gain and socialise losses adds a unique dimension to CSR in the banking profession. It is clear that there are significant variations in the definitions of CSR adopted in their CSR reports as well as in terms of day to day working definitions. As employees within large organisations, bankers do not only draw from their own morals and ethics but also from regulatory principles and institutional policies and CSR agendas to formulate their understanding of CSR. Bankers face underlying tensions that exists between strategies of profit-orientation, social responsibility, regulation and reputation management. In the banking industry CSR activities are high profile and can be seen as a key aspect of 'trust' management. This strategy is integral to the nature of the client-professional relationship and organisational goals.

Yet of greater concern is the fact that in the current global financial crisis, bankers have failed to protect the interests of a significant proportion of their stakeholders. The magnitude of the financial crisis and its wider social implications place bankers under significant public scrutiny. Prior to these events public debate about the banking system was more muted. High remuneration packages were periodically debated in the media but trust in banking professionals was not under the same level of public scrutiny. Whilst all leading players try to address the key CSR issues of their industry, they are not of equal strategic importance and priority. For all banks however, trust and reputation are key issues. However, strategically the focus is on individual reputation to gain competitive advantages while the systemic and collective aspects of reputation seem to be ignored. Where ethical values are fundamental to the culture and regulation of parts of the industry, such as in Islamic banking, it is still not immune from the consequences of the economic contagion arising from their more risk-taking western counterparts. The banking system could sustain its social reputation on the basis of its responsible integration into the social framework. The perceived role of the banking system in the economic crisis will necessitate a significant re-evaluation of CSR goals and the role of banking in society.

Key aspects of trust and reputation are formed in crisis and change situations. In this respect, the global financial crisis of 2007 and 2008 presents a major challenge to bankers to rebuild reputations that have been damaged by a breakdown of trust and confidence in bankers' ability to execute their economic, legal, ethical and philanthropic responsibilities. In spite of the current wave of cost cutting in banking, it is unlikely that efforts to embed CSR into banking will be halted or significantly curtailed. However, those strategies that were meant to favour the 'corporate', by using CSR as a tool to promote the progressiveness of a bank will diminish and there will be a more careful assessment of economic responsibilities and a more committed acceptance of ethical responsibilities by bankers at a collective level. As the crisis marks another phase in the emergence of CSR, an introduction of more rigorous screening procedures and mechanisms into CSR efforts and genuine integration of CSR into risk management and decision-making processes can contribute towards a more effective deconstruction, filtering and consideration of economic, social and environmental risks. The emphasis will be on how CSR can play a role in re-establishing credibility and regaining legitimacy. We suggest that such credibility and legitimacy can only be achieved if the 'Social' in CSR is awarded high priority.

References

Australian Bankers Association (2006) *'CAMAC Discussion Paper, Corporate Social Responsibility'*, available at http://www.bankers.asn.au/ArticleDocuments/ABA-6867-v1C-CAMAC_Discussion_Paper-CSR.DOC.

Beck, T. (2006) *Creating an Efficient Financial System: Challenges in a Global Economy*, World Bank Policy Research paper WPS 3856.

Bennett, H., Durkin, M.G. (2002) *'Developing relationship-led cultures – a case study inretail banking'*, International Journal of Bank Marketing, 20(5) 200–211.

Bentham, J. (1789). *'An introduction to the principles of morals and legislation'*. in Ryan A. (ed.) (1987), *'Utilitarianism and other essays/J.S. Mill and Jeremy Bentham*; Penguin, London, 1987.

Bossone, B. (2000) *'What makes banks special? A study of banking, finance andeconomic development,'* World Bank Policy Research Paper 2408.

Bozovic, J. (2007) *'Business ethics in banking'*, Economics and Organisation, 4(2) 173–182.

Broomhill, R. (2007) *'Corporate Social Responsibility: Key issues and debates'* DunstanPaper Series No 1, available at www.dunstan.org.au.

Carrasco, I. (2007) *'Corporate social responsibility, values and cooperation'*, International Advances in Economic Research, 13(4) 454–460.

Carroll, A.B. (1991) *'The pyramid of corporate social responsibility: toward the moralmanagement of organisational stakeholders'*, Business Horizons, 39(4) 39–48, July–Aug.

Carr-Saunders, A.M. (1928). *'Professionalism in historical perspective'*, in Vollmer, H.M and Mills, D. (eds.), *Professionalization*. Prentice Hall, Englewood Cliffs, NJ.

Commission of the European Communities (2001) *'Promoting a European Framework for Corporate Social Responsibility'*, COM (2001) 300 Brussels.

Courses Careers UK, *'Careers Advice and Job Vacancies – Banking Executive.'* [online] n.d. Available at: http://www.ca.courses-careers.com/articles/banking.htm.Accessed 12 March 2009.

Crane, A., Matten, D. (2004) *'Business ethics; a European perspective,'* Oxford University press, Oxford.

Creswell, J.W. (1998) *'Qualitative inquiry and research design: Choosing among five traditions'* Sage, Thousand Oaks, CA.

Crowther, D., Rayman-Bacchus, L. (2004) *'Perspectives on CSR'*, Ashgate, London.

Csizar, E., Heidrich, G. (2006) *'The question of reputational risk: perspectives from an industry'*, Geneva Papers on Risk and Insurance, 31 382–394.

Deal, T., Kennedy, A. (1982) *'Corporate cultures'*, Addison Wesley, Reading, MA.

Decker, O.S. (2004) *'Corporate social responsibility and structural change in financial services'*, Managerial Finance 19(6) 712–728.

Fenwick, T., Bierama, L. (2008) *'Corporate social responsibility: issues for human resource development professionals'*, International Journal of Training and Development, 12(1) 24–35.

FORGE Group (2002), *'Guidance on corporate social responsibility management and reporting for the financial services sector'*, [online] available at: www.abi.org.uk/ForgeText, accessed 12 March 2009.

FORGE Group (2007) *'Managing climate change in financial services: a guidance framework'* available at http://www.bba.org.uk/content/1/c6/01/16/92/FORGE%20V%20Guidance%20Framework%20FINAL.pdf accessed 12 March 2009.

FSA (2008) *Regulating retail banking conduct of business*, Consultation Paper CP 08/19 available at http://www.fsa.gov.uk/pubs/cp/cp08_19.pdf.

Freeman, R.E. 1984. *'Strategic management: a stakeholder approach'*, Pitman/Ballinger, Boston, MA.

Gaultier-Galliard, S., Louisot, J. (2008) *'Risks to reputation: a global perspective'*, Journal of Financial Transformation, 22 171–185.

Goode, W.J. (1960) *'Encroachment, charlatanism and the emerging professions: psychology, medicine and sociology'*, American Sociological Review, 25 902–14.

Grayson, D., Hodges, A. (2004) '*Corporate social responsibility: 7 steps to make corporate social responsibility work for your business*', Greenleaf, London.

Groenewald, T. (2004). '*A phenomenological research design illustrated*', International Journal of Qualitative Methods, 3(1). Article 4. Available at http://www.ualberta.ca/~iiqm/backissues/3_1/pdf/groenewald.pdf.

HSBC '*Key Sustainability Issues*' [online] n.d. available at http://www.hsbc.com/1/2/sustainability/sustainability-at-hsbc/key-sustainability-issues.

HSBC Holdings plc., '*Sustainability Report 2007.*' [online], available at http://www.investis.com/reports/hsbc_sr_2007_en/pdf_cache/hsbc_sr_2007_en_extract_11-12.pdf

Kettell, B. (2008) '*Introduction to Islamic banking*', Harriman House, London.

Lantos, G. (2001) '*The boundaries of strategic corporate social responsibility*', Unpublished Paper, Stonehill College, North Easton MA.

Levine, R. (1997) '*Financial development and economic growth: views and agenda,*' Journal of Economic Literature, 35 688–726.

Levine, R. (2005) '*Finance and growth: theory and evidence*'. in Aghion, P and Durlauf, S. (eds.), *Handbook of economic growth*. Elsevier Science, The Netherlands.

Llewellyn, D. (2005) '*Trust and confidence in financial services: a strategic challenge*', Journal of Financial Regulation and Compliance, 13(4) 333–346.

Mayo, E. (1997) '*Policy responses to financial exclusion*', in Rossiter J. (Ed) *Financial exclusion: can mutuality fill the gap?* New Policy Institute, London.

Merton, R.C. (1995) '*A functional perspective of financial intermediation*', Financial Management, 24(2) 23–41.

Nelson, J. (2004) *Leadership, accountability and partnership: critical trends and issues in corporate social responsibility*, Report of the CSR Initiative Launch Event, CSR Report No 1. Cambridge, MA: John F Kennedy School of Government, Harvard University.

Olsen, R. (2008) '*Trust as risk and the foundation of investment value*', Journal of Socio Economics, 37(4) 2189–2200.

Olson, M. (2006) *Are banks still special*? Remarks at the Annual Washington Conference of the Institute of International Bankers, Washington DC, available at www.bis.org.

Painter–Morland, M. (2006) '*Triple bottom line reporting as social grammar: integrating corporate social responsibility and corporate codes of conduct*', Business Ethics: A European Review, 15(4) 352–364.

Paton, H.J. (1948) '*The moral law, or, Kant's groundwork of the metaphysic or morals*', Hutchinson's University Library, London.

Perks, R.W. (1993) '*Accounting and society*', Chapman and Hall, London.

Porter, M.E., Kramer, M.R. (2006) '*Strategy and society: the link between competitive advantage and corporate social responsibility*', Harvard Business Review, 1–14, December.

Roberts, J., Dietrich, M. (1999) '*Conceptualizing professionalism: why economics needs sociology*'. American Journal of Economics & Sociology, 58(4) 977–998, October.

Rossier, J. (2003) '*Ethics and money: what is required of the banking profession*', Geneva Private Bankers Association, La Lettre, No 23, pp 1–8.

Royal Bank of Scotland. '*What our stakeholders think.*' [Online] n.d. Available at http://www.rbs.com/corporate03.asp?id=CORPORATE_RESPONSIBILITY/WHAT_OUR_STAKEHOLDERS_THINK/ISSUE_DEFINITIONS. Accessed 12 March 2009.

Schanz, K. (2006) '*Reputation and reputational risk management*', The Geneva Papers on Risk and Insurance, 31 377–381.

Scherer, A.G., Palazzo, G. (2008) '*Globalisation and social responsibility*', in Crane A., McWilliams, A., Matten, D. , Moon, J. , Siegel, D., (eds.), '*The Oxford handbook of corporate social responsibility*', Oxford University Press, Oxford, pp. 413–431.

Shreeve, G. (2008) *Leader*, Financial World, June, Institute of Financial Services.

Simon, H.A. (1957) '*Models of man*' John Wiley & Sons Inc, London.

Simon, H.A. (1972) '*Theories of bounded rationality,*' in McGuire C. and Radner R. (eds.), *Decision and organization*. Amsterdam, North-Holland.

Strandberg, C. (2005) *Best practices in sustainable finance,* Standberg Consulting available at http://www.corostrandberg.com/pdfs/Sustainable%20Finance%20%20Best%20Practices.pdf.

Sweeney, J.T., Roberts, R.T. (1997) *'Cognitive moral development and auditor independence',* Accounting, Organizations and Society, 22(3/4) 337–352.

The Banker (2007) *'The right principles – what does a socially responsible company mean and how are successful banks integrating the principles of responsibility and accountability into their business models'?,* CSR Roundtable, February.

Thrift, H., Leyshon, A. (1997) *Financial desertification,* in Rossiiter J. (Ed) *Financial exclusion: can mutuality fill the gap?* New Policy Institute, London.

Verweire, K., Van den Berghe, L. (2008) *'Strategic innovation in the financial services industry – opportunity or threat?'* Journal of Financial Transformation, 23, 69–76 available at www.capco.com.

Vigano, F., Nicolai, D. (2006) *'CSR in the European Banking Sector: evidence form a sector survey',* A research project within 6th framework programme, available at http://www.rareeu.net/fileadmin/user_upload/internal/project_documents/Sector_Survey/RARE_CSR_Survey_Banking_Sector.pdf

Vitell, S., Paolillo, J. (2004) *'A cross-cultural study of the antecedents of the perceived role of ethics and social responsibility',* Business Ethics: A European Review, 13(2/3) 186–199.

Walsh, J.P. (2005) *Review book review essay: 'taking stock of stakeholder management'.* Academy of Management Review, 30(2) 426–437 April.

Wigglesworth, R. (*2008*), *'Islamic banks exposed to property risk',* Financial *Times* (London, England), October 27 p. 13.

Wolf, M. (2008) *Regulators should intervene in bankers pay'* Financial Times, January 15.

Zaman, A. (2008) *Islamic economics, a survey of the literature,* MRPA paper No 11024, available online http://mpra.ub.uni-muenchen.de/11024/.

Zappi, G. (2007) *'Corporate social responsibility in the Italian banking industry: creating value through listening to shareholders',* Corporate Governance, 7(4) 471–475.

Chapter 8
An Analysis of Corporate Social Responsibility (CSR) and Sustainability Reporting Assessment in the Greek Banking Sector

Konstantinos I. Evangelinos, Antonis Skouloudis, Ioannis E. Nikolaou, and Walter Leal Filho

> *Economic advance is not the same thing as human progress.*
> John Clapham, *A Concise Economic History of Britain* (1957)

Abstract This paper aims to examine implementation of CSR in the banking sector by means of an analysis of the incorporation of environmental and social concerns into financial institutions' decision-making, in order to evaluate the content of annual environmental (social or sustainability)[1] reports published by Greek banks. It also analyses the various reporting strategies Greek banks adopt, as well as the emerging trends they tend to follow. A sustainability report assessment was implemented according to scoring systems based on the Global Reporting Initiative guidelines and the Deloitte Touché Tohmatsu sustainability reporting scorecard. The study has identified the fact that Greek banks finished in exactly the same position in the overall ranking with both scoring systems. However, the GRI requirements are very demanding for Greek banks while they seem to cover a greater number of the Deloitte Touché Tohmatsu requirements. The paper concludes by reporting on future CSR trends of the Greek banking sector, especially in the field of environmental and social strategies, as well as outlines some steps banks need to take in order to promote sustainability and thereby fulfil their stakeholders' demands.

8.1 Introduction

Financial markets at present monitor several social and environmental issues associated with financial risks (Labatt et al., 2002) to the point that an environmental risk assessment of financial products is becoming common practice.

K.I. Evangelinos (✉)
Department of Environment, University of the Aegean, Mytilene, Greece

[1] For the purpose of this study, the terms environmental reports, social reports, sustainability reports and corporate social responsibility reports are considered simultaneous.

S.O. Idowu, W.L. Filho (eds.), *Professionals' Perspectives of Corporate Social Responsibility*, DOI 10.1007/978-3-642-02630-0_9,
© Springer-Verlag Berlin Heidelberg 2009

This state of affairs is partly due to the contemporary trend of globalization, which requires transparency and access to information that may directly or indirectly affect the robust operations of the financial system. Such vital information may be linked with organizations' environmental and social strategies. It is widely accepted that this information is linked with financial markets and the operations of those organizations working within it such as banks, insurance companies and the stock exchange. In this respect, Goldstein (2001) notes that the lack of relevant information causes two significant drawbacks:

i. the under-funding of economic activities and
ii. the increase of productive capabilities among organizations in the private sector as well as limiting the competitive advantage of environmentally and socially responsible organizations.

Based on the relevance of this theme, Richardson et al. (1999) developed a model for examining the effect of corporate social responsibility and relevant information on capital market operations and found that these strategies affect firms' cash flow and investors' discount rates. Moreover, numerous authors claim that social and environmental issues may offer opportunities to develop new financial products or to avoid hidden financial risks from related players. Furthermore, some authors such as Labatt et al. (2002), Lanoie et al. (1998) and Dasgupta et al. (2001) claim that financial markets could play a critical role in achieving the goals of sustainable development in both developed and developing countries.

In general terms, those organizations involved in the financial markets could indeed play an important role in sustainable development according to their strategic management. Specifically, the banking sector, an important player in the financial markets, has developed specific environmental strategies in order to confront contemporary challenges such environmental risks assessment and risk management strategies. The interface between banking, environmental strategies and sustainability is outlined in Fig. 8.1.

Most banks perceive environmental issues not only as threats, but also as an opportunity to gain financial benefits or to foresee potential future financial risks that should be avoided. Taking this into account, banks' environmental strategies could be classified in two general approaches: those aiming at developing new

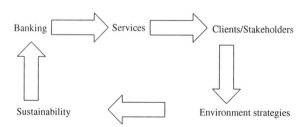

Fig. 8.1 Interface between banking, environmental strategies and sustainability

financial products, and those related to environmental management strategies for improving their environmental performance and reputation. According to the former approach, banks have designed new financial tools and loans to finance cleaner technology (Thompson, 1998). Such tools are often called 'green' lending, 'green' funds, 'green' bond and other 'green' financial products. The overall purpose of these strategies is that they support banks not only by gaining benefits or avoiding risks, but also by playing the role of motivator for firms and other organizations to implement environmental and corporate social strategies and to achieve the ultimate goal: sustainable development.

Additionally, banks have been implementing different environmental strategies such as energy efficiency and waste management programs and Environmental Management Systems (i.e. ISO 14001 and EMAS). These strategies assist banks in gaining financial benefits such as energy cost reduction, minimization of water and material use (McCammon, 1995).

It is widely known that banks' financing decisions affect and are affected by the level of environmental performance of the corporations they lend money or associated with. Thompson and Cowton (2004) for example, recognize the fact that banks should incorporate in their lending decisions specific environmental criteria mainly to ensure that borrowers repay loans and in order to improve their environmental status by contributing to environmental preservation. These strategies and their results are usually communicated by separate reports such as environmental reports or as part of formal annual reports (Ferreira, 2004; Branco and Rodrigues, 2006). These reports are very important for informing stakeholders about the environmental and social performance of the organizations. However, despite the body of information available today, there are few studies on banks' environmental and social reporting analyzing and assessing this information in different categories such as energy consumption, waste management, human resources issues and community issues (Tarna, 1999; Hamid, 2004). This paper will attempt to do by focusing on the Greek bank sector as a case study.

It should at this stage be stated that, at present, only a few Greek banks have adopted environmental and social strategies and attempt to communicate relevant information. Such information focuses mainly on environmental, social and cultural issues. However, hardly any attempts are made to analyze this information (Skouloudis et al., 2007a). Thus, this study aims to fill this gap by contributing to the current literature as follows: by analyzing the various categories of social and environmental information of Greek banks' environmental and social reports (also referred to as Corporate Social Responsibility reports or sustainability reports) based on the Global Reporting Initiative and the Deloitte Touché Tohmatsu guidelines and to depict the current trends in Greek banks' environmental and social strategies. Specifically, the aim is to highlight the environmental and social issues for which Greek banks implement corresponding strategies and to analyze the sector's trends concerning the environment.

This paper is organized as follows: Section 8.2 gives a short literature review about banks and the environment, the current scoring methods of reporting strategies and a content analysis for the banking sector. Section 8.3 discusses the status of Greek banks' environmental reports and analyzes the methodology for scoring these reports. Additionally, in this section the results of the study are also presented. Finally, Sect. 8.4 discusses the results and draws the relevant conclusions.

8.2 The Relationship of Banks with the Environment: A New Trend

Due to both peer pressure and the strong emphasis now given to environmental matters in banking, the efficient operation of the banking sector may be associated with the state of environment. This relationship is considered either as symbiotic or antagonistic. Banks may confront environmental issues as potential risks or as opportunities to develop new financial products. Environmental risks found for example in polluting firms (e.g. the chemical industry) might generate financial liabilities to banks, if they had lent money to those firms. These risks are classified into three types (Thompson, 1998):

a) direct risk (e.g. legal liability for cleaning up contamination transferred from the insolvent borrower),
b) indirect risk (e.g. the weakness of borrowers to repay their loan due to their financial responsibilities after environmental damage), and
c) reputation risks (e.g. negative public relations due to doing business with environmentally unfriendly firms).

Coulson and Monks (1999, p. 5) state that '*environmental management activities of companies also provide investment opportunities for banks*'. Indeed, banks face the challenge of making new funding products to finance companies' capital equipment for abatement pollution strategies with high returns and reduced financial risks.

Numerous banks are now implementing strategies in order to face these contemporary challenges. Generally, these strategies could be separated in the following categories:

a) bank lending environmental criteria,
b) environmental management strategies, and
c) 'environmental' financial products. The former category of strategies is based on the idea that the environment has significant impacts on financial institutions' operations (Thompson and Cowton, 2004).

Banks may certainly face financial liabilities from environmental damages caused by borrowers, whose extent depends on the severity of the damage and the prevailing environmental legislation ((Thompson, 1998). In such circumstances, several authors underline the necessity of the banking sector to introduce environmental concerns in their lending decisions (Sarokin and Schulkin, 1991; Smith, 1994; Coulson and Monks, 1999). The second category of strategies is based on the view that banks consume significant amounts of paper, energy, water, plastic and other resources. For this purpose, banks may implement environmental strategies for managing these resources from an economic and environmental point of view. According to Weiler et al. (1997), such environmental strategies may be the implementation of ISO 14001 and EMAS. Finally, the last category derives from the assumption that the physical environment has a symbiotic relationship with banks. For example, this view is adopted by some banks in connection with new financial products aiming to explore the tendency of firms to invest in new environmental management strategies including cleaner technology. Such products include loans for investments in new environmentally friendly technology and equipment, 'environmental' mutual funds, green charge cards, and specific bonds (Boyer and Laffont, 1997; Laundgren and Catasus, 2000; Schmitt and Spaeter, 2005).

These strategies are also driven by the new perception of policy makers and the management of financial markets of an emerging role that the financial institutions could play in the implementation of the general goals of sustainable development. As a result of this perception, several researchers have conducted relevant studies to analyze these prospects. For example, Mezher et al. (2002) attempted to develop an accurate picture of Lebanese financial institutions' strategies aimed at achieving the main goals of sustainable development. Similarly, Haque (2000) analyzed the potential new role that the financial institutions could play in Bangladesh in order to promote sustainable development. Although several authors support the idea that banks can incorporate environmental concerns into their decision making to gain benefits, other authors consider these strategies as a result of the growing demand of financial stakeholders to protect their investment.

8.3 Evaluating Methods of Environmental and Social Reports (ESR)

Today, numerous methods have been developed to evaluate the quality and quantity of environmental disclosures in either corporate annual reports or in separate environmental reports. Indeed, this kind of information is considered very important for informing stakeholders on social, environmental or corporate social responsibility (CSR) performance.

In this respect, Igalens and Gond (2005) analyzed current measuring methods across the five categories, namely: measurement methods based on environmental reporting content, indices, questionnaire surveys, corporate reputations indices, and data produced by external organizations (environmental auditing reports). These methods use environmental and social information for measuring CSR performance in a comparable and compatible manner over a number of years and across various industries. Nevertheless, several researchers utilize some of these methods for quantifying the types of information taken from environmental and social reports in order to compare the level of corporate practices among different countries and industries. Indeed, several studies analyzed the usefulness of this information. Gray et al. (1995) classified it in three categories such as decision usefulness studies, economic theory studies and social and political theory studies.

However, to evaluate the content of environmental and social reports, the current well-known methods could be classified in three general categories: content analysis methods, scoring methods and questionnaire surveys. The first category of methods attempts to analyze the different types of information disclosed in corporate annual reports and environmental reports (social, sustainability or corporate social responsibility) (Idowu and Towler, 2004). In particular, Abbott and Monsen (1979) considered that these methods give the analytical techniques for classifying environmental and social information into separate categories and, furthermore, to quantify these categories in comparable scales. In this context, several studies have been undertaken to assess the types of social and environmental disclosures (Table 8.1).

The majority of these studies use the following measuring methods in order to quantify social and environmental information in a consistent and comparable manner: number of documents (e.g. reports, advertising brochure), number of sentences per page, words per page and number of pages of annual reports associated with any type of environmental information (e.g. energy conservation, waste management, water treatment). Apart from the different measuring methods described above, these methods can be categorized by other characteristics such as the type of information they disclose (e.g. monetary and non monetary information) the frequency of the publication (e.g. annual or bi-annual reports) and the type of the report (environmental, social, CSR, sustainability). (Table 8.1).[2]

The second group of measuring methods contains the scoring methods which classify environmental and social information into different types and quantify this information by using scoring systems (e.g. on a scale of 0–4). Over the last decades, several scoring surveys have been conducted based on different guidelines and scoring criteria (Table 8.2). Some widely-accepted guidelines used to evaluate these reports, have been developed by international organizations such as the Global Reporting Initiative (GRI), the United Nations Environmental Program (UNEP), Sustainability, Deloitte Touché Tohmatsu, ISO (ISO 14031), Ernst & Ernst and KPMG.[3] These surveys differ on measuring methods, guidance or scoring criteria which they use and finally, by themes (Table 8.2).

Table 8.1 Environmental and social disclosures content analysis studies

Authors	Measuring methods	Themes
Roberts (1991)	No of documents	54 themes
Tsang (1998)	% sentences	5 categories
Tilt (2001)	% sentences	10 categories
Gao et al. (2005)	% words	6 categories – 30 themes
Raar (2007)	% sentences of A4 page	GRI themes

[2]For more detail about the conducted surveys of this category, see Unerman (2000).

[3]For more detail about the criteria of these guidelines see Morhardt et al. (2002).

Table 8.2 Environmental and social disclosures scoring studies

Authors	Scoring scale	– Guidance; – Criteria measurement	Themes
Wiseman (1982)	0–3	Synthesis of prior research	18 themes
Frekrat et al. (1996)	0–3	Synthesis of prior research	4 categories – 18 themes
Davis-Walling and Batterman (1997)	0–2	Synthesis of prior research	6 categories – 29 themes
Stanwick and Stanwick (1998)	Scoring system	Synthesis of prior research	5 themes
Morhardt et al. (2002)	0–3	GRI and ISO 14031	GRI: 8 categories – 129 themes, 3 categories – 197 themes
De Villers and Staden (2006)	0–3	Synthesis of prior research	18 themes
Van Staden and Hooks (2007)	0–5	Sustainability index and synthesis with prior researches	6 categories – 32 themes
Bolivar (2009)	0–1	Synthesis of prior research	3 categories
Daub (2007)	1–3	GRI guidance	21 themes

Scoring methodologies mostly rank environmental and social reports for comparability reasons. Moreover, such surveys use quantified information for measuring social and environmental performance[4] (Ilinish et al., 1998; Jung et al., 2001; Igalens and Gond, 2005), for comparing the quality and quantity of relevant information among firms of the same sector (Hammond and Miles, 2004; van Staden and Hooks, 2007), as well as among different sectors and different countries (Kolk, 1999; Adams and Kuasirikum, 2000), and to examine the compatibility of reports with the recommendations of international guidelines (Morhardt, 2001; Morhardt et al., 2002).

Finally, there are many questionnaire surveys to evaluate social and environmental information (Table 8.3).

Table 8.3 Environmental and social disclosures questionnaire surveys

Authors	Measuring methods
Deegan and Rankin (1997)	Questionnaire survey
Stray and Ballantine (2000)	Questionnaire survey
O' Donovan (2002)	Questionnaire survey

---

[4]However, it is very interesting to note that Wiseman (1982) and Morhardt (2001) have clearly stated that scoring methods are not connected with corporate environmental performance.

For example, Deegan and Rankin (1997) investigated the views of many different categories of stakeholders on the social and environmental information using questionnaires. Additionally, Stray and Ballantine (2000) attempted to elicit the preference of firms on environmental and social disclosures conducting a questionnaire survey among different industries (e.g. automobile, banking, electronics, energy, food and drink and water sectors in the UK). Finally, O' Donovan (2002) investigated the disclosure choices of firms on environmental and social information in their reports with questionnaires.

8.4 Evaluation Assessments for ESR in the Banking Sector

There is a limited number of studies for content analysis or the scoring of banks' environmental and social reports. These surveys can be classified in two general groups. Firstly, surveys which exclusively assess banks' reports (Weiler et al., 1997; Laundgren and Catasus, 2000; Billiot and Daughtrey, 2001; Douglas et al., 2004; Hamid, 2004; Coupland, 2006; Branco and Rodrigues, 2006) and secondly surveys examining banks' environmental disclosures as a part of surveys with a wider scope (e.g., as one industry among other industries – Zeghal and Ahmed, 1990; Tsang, 1998; Tarna, 1999; Cerin, 2002; Idowu and Towler, 2004).

These surveys mainly analyze the banks' disclosure patterns on social and environmental issues and examine the content of banks' environmental and social reports. In this respect, Branco and Rodrigues (2006) compared the content of the environmental and social disclosure among the web sites and annual reports of Portuguese banks. They used a content analysis method and found that banks focused on the following themes: environmental management, human resources, product development, consumers and community involvement. Similarly, Douglas et al. (2004) focused on financial institutions' environmental and social reports during a 3 year period (from 1998 to 2001). Their sample consisted of ten Irish banks and four international financial institutions. Their findings showed that these institutions disclosed information in relation to corporate governance, human resources and community involvement; they also found that Irish banks did not disclose any environmental policy information.

Similarly, Hamid (2004) examined social and environmental disclosures of the banks and financial firms of Malaysia. It was shown that these institutions have frequently revealed information related to the environment, human resources and community issues. Additionally, they examined determinants which either positively or negatively affect the level of their disclosures such as size, listing status and age of business.

Other studies assess the content of these firms and compare the results with firms of different sectors. For example, Tsang (1998) analysed social and environmental disclosures among three sectors: (banking, food and beverages and tourist industries) in Singapore from 1986 to 1995. He stressed that these industries focused mainly on two general categories; human resources and community involvement. Similarly, Idowu et al. (2004) analyzed CSR reports published by companies of nine different sectors including banks. They underlined that the commonly disclosed issues among all sectors were environmental issues, community, marketplace and workplace. In their survey, Zeghal and Ahmed (1990) used Ernst and Ernst's data classification scheme to assess monetary, quantitative and qualitative environmental and social information and revealed that banks tended to present mostly information in relation to human resources, products, and community involvement.

8.5 Research Development

8.5.1 Greek Bank System Structure – SER Statues – Sample Selection

Until the mid-1980s, the Greek banking system operated under a strong regulatory regime. There was a complex system of credit rules within a context of administrative fixed interest rates (Hondroyannis et al., 1999). Later, several European directives and international developments motivated the Greek banking system to operate in a new financial environment and to take into consideration some new parameters within its strategies to face the newly deregulated environment. Specifically, the important directives on the Greek banking system is the law 1266/1982 which enhanced the role of the Central Bank of Greece in conducting monetary policy and the Second European Banking Directive (1992) which commits credit institutions to make specific provisions.

The main changes in the banking system after 1992 included the liberalization of the interest rate determination, the abolition of cautious credit rules, the free flow of capital and increased competition from banks of the European Union (Halkos and Slamouris, 2004; Athanasoglou et al., 2008). In this new environment, the Greek government eliminated its interventions and control role in the national banking system. Thereby, some state banks were privatized (e.g. Attica, Cretabank, Macedonia-Trace, Central Greece, Ionian), while several others were merged (for more details see Christopoulos et al., 2002).

These structural changes shaped new conditions in the banking system and several changes in the structure of the Greek banking system. Indeed, by 1995 fifty two credit institutions were established, of which twenty were commercial banks, twenty branches of foreign banks, two investment banks, three housing banks, one saving bank, one specific purpose bank and five co-operatives (Hondroyannis et al., 1999). In 1998, the credit institutions numbered three fewer than in 1995 (Christopoulos et al., 2002) while today; there are sixty-three in total (Association of Greek Banks, 2006).

Among the sixty-three Greek credit institutions, only six disclosed information associated with environmental and social issues, two have developed 'green' products and one branch of a foreign bank published a sustainability report of its activities in all countries-activity together. Only 5% of banks, which disclosed information, publish separate environmental reports, while 33% disclose relevant information via the internet and 16% as a part of annual reports. It is important to point out that the disclosures on websites and in annual reports extend to no more than one page.

For the requirements of this study, we used all the reports of the Greek banks published in 2005: Eurobank, Piraeus Bank and the Commercial (Emporiki) Bank.

8.6 Methodology Used

The evaluation of banks' sustainability reports were based on two scoring systems: the Deloitte Touché Tohmatsu (DTT) system and a scoring system developed by the Centre for Environmental Policy and Strategic Environmental Management of the University of the Aegean based on the Global Reporting Initiative (GRI) guidelines and requirements. The proposed scoring system follows the 142 indicators of the GRI which are separate measurable parameters. Each indicator could be evaluated as follows: 0 when no information connected to environmental matters appears in the report; 1 when a general mention is made concerning the environment; 2 when the organization discloses incomplete information about environmental and social parameters; 3 when the recording and disclosing of information is done with clarity, and 4 when relevant information is recorded and disclosed in a consistent, transparent and methodical manner. Additionally, it is assumed that each measurement parameter of GRI has the same weight in the measuring of the final degree.

Analytically, topics and possible points of each parameter are: vision and strategy of firms (2 topics – 8 possible points), profile (22 topics – 88 possible points), governance (20 topics – 80 possible points), economic indicators (13 points – 52 possible points), environmental indicators (35 topics – 140 possible points), social indicators (49 points – 196 possible points), labour practices (17 topics – 68 possible points), human rights (14 points – 56 possible points), society (7 topics – 28 possible points), product and services (11 points – 44 possible points) (Appendix 1).

The other scoring system of DTT used contains the following general categories of measuring thematic areas: corporate profile, report design, environmental impact, environmental management, finance/eco-efficiency, stakeholder relations, communications and third party statement In particular, these categories are analyzed in 30 additional parameters and evaluated by a system of measures from 0 to 4 as previously outlined. Consequently, each parameter could take a total of four possible points and the total degree would be equal to 120 (Appendix 2).

8.7 Results

The overall results of these methodologies are presented in Table 8.4. This table shows the banks examined (column 1), the type of report that they publish (column 2), the year when these reports were published (column 3), the scoring

Table 8.4 Greek banking sector environmental and social performance scoring

Bank name	Kind of reports	Year	GRI scoring method	Percentages	Deloitte Touché Tohmatsu	Percentages
Piraeus	Corporate Social Responsibility	2005	114	20	54	45
Eurobank	Corporate Social Responsibility – Sustainability	2005	109	19	43	36
Commercial/ Emporiki	Corporate Social Responsibility	2005	96	17	28	23

methods used (columns 4 and 6) as well as the percentage covering of disclosed information with the two different scoring systems (column 5 and 7). It is noteworthy that these banks finished in exactly the same position in the whole ranking with both scoring systems. Indeed, the ranking with the two scoring systems is as follows: first, Piraeus Bank (114 points), second, Eurobank (109 points) and third, the Commercial/Emporiki Bank (96 points).

The other important result is that these banks show different percentage covering with the requirements of the GRI and DTT guidelines. Pireous Bank covers 20% of GRI requirements, while it covers 45% of DTT. Similarly, Eurobank covers 19% of GRI requirements and 36% of DTT requirements. Finally, the Commercial/Emporiki Bank covers correspondingly 17 and 23% of each guide's requirements.

The GRI requirements are very demanding for Greek banks. Indeed, Greek banks cover a small percentage of the GRI requirements, while they cover a greater number of DTT requirements. This may be attributed to the fact that the DTT requirements are more general while the GRI indices are much more specific. However, no banks exceed 50% of the requirements of either of these guides, a fact that may indicates both lack of sustainability strategies as well as ineffective communication initiatives.

8.8 Discussion and Conclusions

The evidences obtained from this study are related to trends from Greece, but its basic principles apply to other countries and contexts. Indeed, as stated earlier on this paper, it is commonly accepted nowadays that banks should incorporate environmental and social issues into their decision-making in an effort to minimize their impact on both the environment and the society.

In this respect, few banks in Greece – and in other countries to this matter – implement such strategies in order to promote sustainability and thereby fulfil their stakeholders' demands. However, the communication of information related to these strategies in a credible, transparent, consistent and standardized manner through environmental and social reports is important in order to gain the confidence of clients and business-partners alike and to engage stakeholders in the decision-making process.

Indeed, such reports can provide important information and form the basis for a sound comparison of environmental, social and economic performance of banks within a country as well as across different countries. However, there is no one standardized commonly accepted reporting framework. Rather, several scoring systems are used. This paper has discussed the GRI and DTT reporting systems and their implementation in all Greek banks with social and environmental reports. Furthermore, through this discussion, it has examined the current trend of the Greek banking sector in the areas of environmental and social strategies.

The results gathered from this study indicate that information disclosed by Greek banks in relation to these issues has been fragmentary in nature. Additionally, it shows that Greek banks do not cover these issues widely while they have low compliance level with the GRI and the DTT, with the Greek banks scoring less than 50% by each scoring systems.

It is necessary however, to point out the limitations of this research effort. Firstly, the methodologies here employed only examine the completeness and clarity of these reports, not the linkage between social and environmental information with banks' environmental performance. Secondly, a significant issue is that these banks have not adopted GRI or used DTT guidelines. In fact, these banks implement environmental strategies according to their necessities and on a voluntary basis. Thirdly, the current study is based on the analysis of 1 year reports (2005).

Nevertheless, an increase in the publication of non-financial reports by Greek banks within the next few years can be expected, as they feel the pressure from their foreign competitors that already produce such reports. In this context, Greek financial institutions which already have experience in sustainability, social and environmental reporting have a competitive advantage at a national level, and can potentially urge their peers to follow their example. Without doubt, the firms sampled are pioneers in Greece, being the first to promote sustainability reporting in the Greek banking sector. But while the first step has been made, it is crucial to further endorse corporate transparency by producing balanced and effective reports following globally accepted standards and guidelines.

Appendix 1: GRI Scoring System

Criteria of GRI	Possible measures	Pieraous bank	Eurobank	Commercial/Emporiki bank
Vision and strategy	8	2	1	1
Profile	88	28	29	24
Corporate governance	80	24	15	23
Economic indicators	52	4	17	7
Environmental indicators	140	13	12	15
Labour practices	68	23	25	16
Human rights	55	5	1	0
Society	28	7	4	7
Product and services	44	8	5	3
Overall score	564	114	109	96
Percentage covering (%)	100	20	19	17

Appendix 2: DTT Scoring System

Criteria of DTT	Possible measures	Pieraous bank	Eurobank	Commercial/Emporiki bank
Corporate context	4	2	1	1
Basic principles of reporting	4	1	1	1
Qualitative reporting characteristics	4	3	3	2
Report structure	4	2	2	2
Readability	4	3	2	1
Quick reading options	4	2	2	1
Key stakeholders and their concerns and challenges	4	3	3	1
Relevant issues	4	2	2	1
Sustainable development vision and strategy	4	0	1	0
Top management commitment	4	2	0	1
Responsibilities and organizational structure	4	4	0	1
Improvement action	4	2	1	1
Management system and integration into business process	4	2	2	1
Managing risk and opportunity	4	1	0	1

Criteria of DTT	Possible measures	Pieraous bank	Eurobank	Commercial/Emporiki bank
Innovation for more sustainability	4	2	3	1
Sustainable value/supply chain	4	1	1	1
Financial implication and wider economic impacts	4	1	2	1
Employee involve-ment/relationship	4	1	3	1
Interaction with civil society	4	1	2	1
Framework conditions and public policies	4	1	1	1
Use of metrics/indicators	4	2	1	1
Data quality and accuracy	4	0	0	0
Trends over time	4	3	3	0
Targets	4	4	1	0
Interpretation and benchmarks	4	2	1	1
Engagement with stakeholders	4	1	2	1
Balance of issues and suitability	4	3	2	2
Connection to readily	4	2	0	1
Accessibility and interactivity	4	1	1	1
Assurance and services	4	0	0	0
Overall score	120	54	43	28
Percentage covering (%)	100	45	36	23

References

Abbott, W.F. and Monsen, R.J. (1979), "On the measurement of corporate social responsibility: self reported disclosures as a method of measuring corporate social involvement", *Academy of Management Journal*, Vol. 22, No. 3, pp. 501–515.

Adams, C. and Kuasirikum, N. (2000), "A comparative analysis of corporate reporting on ethical issues by UK and German chemical and pharmaceutical companies", *European Accounting Review*, Vol. 1, pp. 53–79.

Association of Greek Banks (2006), "Catalogue of Greek Credit Institutions", available at http://62.1.43.74/Hebic/UplPDFs/banks_2007-1/Kodikos_All%2006.pdf [accessed 15 May 2007].

Athanasoglou, P.P., Brissimis, N.S. and Delis, D.M. (2008), "Bank-specific, industry-specific and macroeconomic determinants of bank profitability", *Journal of International Financial Markets, Institutions & Money*, Vol. 18, No. 2, pp. 121–136.

Billiot, J.M. and Daughtrey, W.Z. (2001), "Evaluating environmental liability through risk premiums charged on loans agribusiness borrowers", *Agribusiness*, Vol. 17, No. 2, pp. 273–297.

Bolivar, M.P.R. (2009), "Evaluating corporate environmental reporting on the internet: the utility and resource industries in Spain", *Business and Society*, Vol. 48, No. 2, pp. 179–205.

Boyer, M. and Laffont, J.J. (1997), "Environmental risk and bank liability", *European Economic Review*, Vol. 41, No. 1, pp. 427–459.

Branco, C.M. and Rodrigues, L.L. (2006), "Communication of corporate social responsibility by Portuguese banks: a legitimacy theory perspective", *Corporate Communications: An International Journal*, Vol. 11, No. 3, pp. 232–248.

Cerin, P. (2002), "Characteristics of environmental reports of the OM Stockholm exchange", *Business Strategy and the Environmental*, Vol. 11, pp. 298–311.

Christopoulos, K.D., Lolos, E.G.S. and Tsionas, G.E. (2002), "Efficiency of the Greek banking system in view of the EMU: a heteroscedastic stochastic frontier approach", *Journal of Policy Modelling*, Vol. 24, pp. 813–829.

Coulson, B.A. and Monks, V.C. (1999), "Corporate environmental performance considerations within bank lending decisions", *Eco-management and Auditing*, Vol. 6, pp. 1–10.

Coupland, C. (2006), "Corporate social and environmental responsibility in web-based reports: currency in the banking sector?" *Critical Perspectives on Accounting*, Vol. 17, pp. 865–881.

Dasgupta, S., Laplante, B. and Mamingi, N. (2001), "Pollution and capital markets in developing countries", *Journal of Environmental Economics and Management*, Vol. 42, pp. 310–335.

Daub, C.H. (2007), "Assessing the quality of sustainability reporting: an alternative methodological approach", *Journal of Cleaner Production*, Vol. 15, pp. 75–85.

Davis-Walling, P. and Batterman, S.A. (2007), "Environmental reporting by the fortune 50 firms", *Environmental Management*, Vol. 21, No. 6, pp. 865–875.

De Villers, C. and Staden, J.C. (2006), "Can less environmental disclosures have a legitimising effect? Evidence from Africa", *Accounting, Organizations and Society*, Vol. 31, pp. 763–781.

Deegan, C. and Rankin, M. (1997), "The materiality of environmental information to users of annual reports", *Accounting, Auditing and Accountability Journal*, Vol. 10, No. 4, pp. 562–583.

Deloitte Touché Tohmatsu (2006), "Deloitte Sustainability Reporting Scorecard", Deloitte Touché Tohmatsou Global Sustainability Group, available at http://www.deloitte.com/sustainability [accessed 12 June 2007].

Douglas, A., Doris, J. and Johnson, B. (2004), "Corporate social reporting in Irish financial institutions", *The TQM Magazine*, Vol. 16, No. 6, pp. 387–395.

Ferreira, C. (2004), "Environmental accounting: the Portuguese case", *Management of Environmental Quality: The International Journal*, Vol. 15, No. 6, 561–573.

Frekrat, A.M., Inclan, C. and Petroni, D. (1996), "Corporate environmental disclosures: competitive disclosures hypothesis using 1991 annual report data", *The International Journal of Accounting*, Vol. 31, No. 2, pp. 175–195.

Gao, S.S., Haravi, S. and Xiao, J.Z. (2005), "Determinants of corporate social and environmental reporting in Hong Kong: a research note", *Accounting Forum*, Vol. 29, pp. 233–242.

Goldstein, D. (2001), "Financial sector reform and sustainable development: the case of Costa Rica", *Ecological Economics*, Vol. 37, pp. 199–215.

Gray, R., Kouhy, R. and Lavers, S. (1995), "Corporate environmental reporting: a review of the literature and a longitudinal study of UK disclosure", *Accounting, Auditing & Accountability Journal*, Vol. 8, No. 2, pp. 47–77.

Global Reporting Initiative (2002), "Sustainability Reporting Guidelines", Global Reporting Initiative, Boston, available at http://www.globalreporting.org [accessed 9 September 2006].

Halkos, E.G. and Salamouris, S.D. (2004), "Efficiency measurement of the Greek commercial banks with the use of financial rations: a data envelopment analysis approach", *Management Accounting Research*, Vol. 15, pp. 201–224.

Hammond, K. and Miles, S. (2004), "Assessing quality assessment of corporate social reporting: UK perspectives", *Accounting Forum*, Vol. 28, pp. 61–79.

Hamid, F.Z.A. (2004), "Corporate social disclosure by banks and finance companies: Malaysian evidence", *Corporate Ownership and Control*, Vol. 1, No. 4, pp. 118–130.

Haque, T. (2000), "New roles for finance in the race to sustainability: the experience of Grameen Bank, Bangladesh", *Corporate Environmental Strategy*, Vol. 7, No. 2, pp. 228–234.

Hondroyannis, G., Lolos, S. and Papapetrou, E. (1999), "Assessing competitive conditions in the Greek banking system", *Journal of International Financial Markets, Institutions &Money*, Vol. 9, pp. 377–391.

Idowu, S.O. and Towler, B.A. (2004), "A comparative study of the contents of corporate social responsibility reports of UK companies", *Management of Environmental Quality: An International Journal*, Vol. 15, No. 4, pp. 420–437.

Igalens, J. and Gond, J.P. (2005), "Measuring corporate social performance in France: a critical and empirical analysis of ARESE data", *Journal of Business Ethics*, Vol. 56, pp. 131–148.

Ilinish, Y.A., Soderstrom, S.N. and Thomas, E.T. (1998), "Measuring corporate environmental performance", *Journal of Accounting and Public Police*, Vol. 17, pp. 383–407.

Jung, E.J., Kim, J.S. and Phee, S.K. (2001), "The measurement of corporate environmental performance and its application to the analysis of efficiency in the oil industry", *Journal of Cleaner Production*, Vol. 9, pp. 551–563.

Kolk, A. (1999), "Evaluating corporate environmental reporting", *Business Strategy and the Environment*, Vol. 8, No. 4, pp. 225–237.

Labatt, S., White, R.R. and Cooper, G. (2002), Environmental Finance: A Guide to Environmental Risk Assessment and Financial Products, Wiley & Sons, London.

Landgren, M. and Catasus, B. (2000), "The banks' impacts on the natural environment- on the space between 'what is' and 'what if'", *Business Strategy and the Environment*, Vol. 9, pp. 186–195.

Lanoie, P., Lamplante, B. and Roy, M. (1998), "Can capital markets create incentives for pollution control?", *Ecological Economics*, Vol. 26, pp. 31–41.

McCammon, A.L.T. (1995), "Banking responsibility and liability for the environment: what are banks doing?", *Environmental Conservation*, Vol. 22, No. 4, pp. 297–305.

Mezher, T., Jamali, D. and Zreik, C. (2002), "The role of financial institutions in the sustainable development of Lebanon", *Sustainable Development*, Vol. 10, pp. 69–78.

Morhardt, J.E., Baird, S. and Freeman, K. (2002), "Scoring corporate environmental and sustainability reports using GRI 2000, ISO 14031 and other criteria", *Corporate Social Responsibility and Environmental Management*, Vol. 9, pp. 215–233.

Morhardt, J.E. (2001), "Scoring corporate environmental reports for comprehensiveness: a comparison of three systems", *Environmental Management*, Vol. 27, No. 6, pp. 881–892.

O'Donovan, G. (2002), "Environmental disclosures in the annual report extending the applicability and predictive power of legitimacy theory", *Accounting, Auditing and Accountability Journal*, Vol. 15, No. 3, pp. 344–371.

Raar, J. (2007), "Reported social and environmental taxonomies: a longer-term glimpse", *Managerial Auditing Journal*, Vol. 22, No. 8, pp. 840–864.

Richardson, J.A., Welker, M. and Hutchinson, R.I. (1999), "Managing capital market reactions to corporate social responsibility", *International Journal of Management Review*, Vol. 1, No. 1, pp. 17–43.

Roberts, B.C. (1991), "Environmental disclosures: a note on reporting practices in Mainland Europe", *Accounting, Auditing and Accountability Journal*, Vol. 4, No. 3, pp. 62–71.

Sarokin, D. and Schulkin, J. (1991), "Environmental concerns and business, banking", *Journal of Commercial Bank Lending*, Vol. 74, No. 5, pp. 6–19.

Schmitt, A. and Spaeter, S. (2005), "Improving the prevention of environmental risks with convertible bonds", *Journal of Environmental Economics and Management*, Vol. 50, pp. 637–657.

Skouloudis, A., Evangelinos, K. and Kourmousis, F. (2007), "Benchmarking Greek sustainability reports according to the GRI reporting guidelines", First Conference on Environmental Management, Engineering, Planning and Economics, June 24–28, Skiathos Island, Greece.

Skouloudis, A., Kourmousis, F. and Evangelinos, K. (2007), "Development of an evaluation Methodology for sustainability reports Using International Standards on Reporting", 10th International Conference on Environmental Science and Technology, September 5–7, Kos Island, Greece.

Smith, D.R. (1994), "Environmental risk: credit approaches and opportunities, an interim report", United Nations Environment Programme, McGraw Hill, Geneva.

Stanwick, D.S. and Stanwick, A.P. (1998), "A descriptive analysis of environmental disclosures: a study of the US chemical industry", *Eco-Management and Auditing*, Vol. 5, pp 22–37.

Stray, S. and Ballantine, J. (2000), "A sectoral comparison of corporate environmental reporting and disclosure", *Eco-Management and Auditing*, Vol. 7, pp. 165–177.

Tarna, K. (1999), "Reporting on the environment: current practices in the financial services sector", *Greener Management International*, Vol. 26, pp. 49–64.

Thompson, P. and Cowton, J.C. (2004), "Bringing the environment into bank lending: implications for environmental reporting", *The British Accounting Review*, Vol. 36, pp. 197–218.

Thompson, P. (1998), "Bank lending and the environment: policies and opportunities", *International Journal of Bank Marketing*, Vol. 16, No. 6, pp. 243–252.

Tilt, A.C. (2001), "The content and disclosure of Australian corporate environmental policies", *Accounting, Auditing and Accountability Journal*, Vol. 14, No. 2, pp. 190–212.

Tsang, K.W.E. (1998), "A longitudinal study of corporate social reporting in Singapore: the case of the banking, food and beverage, and hotel industries", *Accounting, Auditing and Accountability Journal*, Vol. 11, No. 5, pp. 624–635.

Unerman, J. (2000), "Methodological issues: reflections on quantification in corporate social reporting content analysis", *Accounting, Auditing and Accountability Journal*, Vol. 13, No. 5, pp. 667–680.

Van Staden, J.C. and Hook, J. (2007), "A comprehensive comparison of corporate environmental reporting and responsiveness", *The British Accounting Review*, Vol. 39, pp. 197–210.

Weiler, E., Murray, C.B., Kelly, J.S. and Ganzi, T.J. (1997), "Review of environmental risk management at banking institutions and potential relevance of ISO 14000", Research Triangle Institute, Working Paper, RTI Project Number 5774-4.

Wiseman, J. (1982), "An evaluation of environmental disclosures made in corporate annual reports", *Accounting, Organizations and Society*, Vol. 7, No. 1, pp. 53–63.

Zeghal, D. and Ajmed, A.S. (1990), "Comparison of social responsibility information disclosure media used by Canadian firms", *Accounting, Auditing and Accountability Journal*, Vol. 3, No. 1, pp. 38–53.

Part II
Engineering

Chapter 9
Industrial Engineering's Perspective of CSR

Velázquez Luis, Munguía Nora, Zavala Andrea, Esquer Javier,
and Marin Amina

*One of the most highly developed skills in contemporary
Western civilization is dissection: the split-up of problems into
their smallest possible components. We are good at it. So good,
we often forget to put the pieces back together again.*
Alvin Toffler, foreword to Order out of Chaos

Abstract Industrial engineering is one of the five main fields of engineering that
endeavour to improve the quality of life in society; ironically, actual production
and services patterns have created unintended side effects such as environmental
pollution and human health problems.

This chapter seeks to provide an introduction to the early developments in the field
of industrial engineering, and explore what the industrial engineer is capable of
doing in order to promote the field of Corporate Social Responsibility (CSR) or, in
other words, to explore how he attempts to secure a long-term productivity growth
while improving the quality of life for the stakeholders and environment.

Industrial engineers face very complex problems daily because the issues they
deal with involve human beings who are generally unpredictable. It is therefore
important to emphasize the need for a new industrial engineer's profile with an
interdisciplinary and trans-disciplinarity knowledge that is not usually present in
the traditional engineer's profile.

The purpose of this chapter is to provide some directions as to what an industrial
engineer is capable of doing in order to secure a long-term productivity growth
while improving the quality of life for workers and communities by adopting the
principles and ethos of CSR.

Initially, readers are provided with a brief overview of some early engineering
developments with some explanations of the main branches of engineering science.

One of the major challenges for future engineers is fulfilled with the principles
embedded in sustainable development which go together with those entrenched in

---

V. Luis (✉)
Industrial Engineering Department, University of Sonora, Sonora, Mexico

S.O. Idowu, W.L. Filho (eds.), *Professionals' Perspectives of Corporate Social
Responsibility*, DOI 10.1007/978-3-642-02630-0_10,
© Springer-Verlag Berlin Heidelberg 2009

CSR. For this reason, it is necessary to absorb a systems thinking that encourages industrial engineers to function under the ethos of sustainability and CSR that provide them with a vision to operate well beyond the traditional focus on production, services and consumption.

9.1 Introduction

It is generally believed that the ultimate goal of engineers is to improve the quality of life in society Cross (1950); however, the role of the industrial engineer in implementing CSR initiatives has been blurred by his desire for a higher productivity and quality at any cost. It should be noted that CSR is a concept that is not easily found in industrial engineering literature, since this profession has traditionally focused on technical and managerial decisions to increase efficiency and effectiveness in technical operations.

The lack of CSR experiences in industrial engineering scenarios has led to a discussion on how engineers are taught in higher education institutions. Based on the engineering curriculum content from two top ranked American universities, it is suggested that industrial engineers are formed by mastering a reductionist thinking which leads to something that scholars have termed 'engineering myopia'. As consequence of this myopia, engineers are even still largely unaware that society is being affected by the by-products resulting from industrial processes; sometimes adversely. Some authors have argued that CSR can be seen as an opportunity for improving and strengthening the field; nevertheless, there is a need for a change in the old paradigms in industrial engineering that results in a new profile of engineer who can deal with problems that are not just technical but also those that are social and ethical in nature. This new engineer will have the capacity to improve operations that result not only in increasing productivity and quality but also environmentally friendlier.

The chapter ends by presenting several sustainability tools which are used to conclude that Sustainable Development can be the lever for introducing CSR in industrial engineering applications because the two pursue similar the same goal, of effecting a better quality of life for people.

9.2 Understanding Engineering

There are five main branches of engineering: Civil, Mechanical, Electrical, Chemical and Industrial Engineering. All early engineering developments were associated with military activities; for obvious reasons, the urge to want to involve ordinary citizens in such matters was lacking. From about 1750, some of the principles and tools designed to be used in the army were borrowed from the military engineering and used by civilians; it was then that civil engineering flourished. This could be described as 'the mother of current civilian engineering professions', the engineering field that deals with aspects such as construction, water and wastewater, geotechnical, hydraulics, mechanics of materials, and transportation issues amongst others (Chen and Richard, 2002).

The emergence of steam engines and other mechanical devices that could perform mechanical work were the predecessor mechanical engineering. This branch of engineering involves the study of statics and strength of materials, dynamics, and heat transfer and fluid mechanics (Bird and Ross, 2002).

The knowledge derived from the field of magnetism and electricity fostered the discovery of electrical engineering. This engineering field is considered to deal mainly with the problems associated with circuit theory, electromagnetism, digital systems, and control and systems (Chen, 2005).

Advances in physics, mathematics and chemistry helped to understand the nature of matter. Chemical engineering was created for using these sciences into the process of converting raw materials or chemicals into more useful or valuable forms. Chemical engineering comprises of topics such as mass transfer, energy balances, thermodynamics, and reactions among others (Ogawa, 2007).

Finally, the industrial engineering field appeared with the rapid growth in technology in the developed nations during the transition from agricultural to industrialized economies. This profession determines the most effective methods of using resources in a production or service system. Industrial engineering often deals with problems related to productivity, quality, ergonomics, facilities planning, manufacturing technologies, Statistics, operations research, optimization, and engineering economics (Zanding, 2001).

While industrial engineering was originally linked to manufacturing, now, this profession has grown to encompass services and other organizations as well (Institute of Industrial Engineers, 2008).

9.3 Understanding Industrial Engineering

Industrial engineering emerged in the context of the industrial revolution when there was a need for engineers who had the competence for increasing productivity to use their knowledge. According to Sumanth (1994, p. 3), productivity was initially mentioned in the literature in 1776, mathematically, productivity is the ratio of outputs to inputs. Of course, the methods for ensuring higher productivity have changed a lot over time; from its crude and less efficient administration to its modern strategic administration. Several great men have been credited for this industrial engineering development. One of the most brilliant minds of all the times was Frederick Winslow Taylor – (described as the father of modern scientific management) who applied the scientific method to management in order to increase productivity and conserve resources. He succeeded in increasing worker productivity by analyzing work content and designing the job. He is considered as the father of scientific management because prior to him, production was carried out by poorly trained workers with crude methods.

Many other industrial engineering advocators also made significant contributions to this profession; it is impossible to mention all, but some of them were Adam Smith, Henry Gantt, H. Ford, Frank and Lillian Moller Gilbreth (mother of modern management).

Quality is a key concept within industrial engineering that is related to productivity; while quality is a term applied to products and services, productivity is a term applied to organizations. There is a cause-effect relationship between both. To understand quality, it is necessary to examine Juran and Deming's influential legacy. Juran defines quality as those features of products which meet customers' needs and thereby provide customer satisfaction. He also defines quality as freedom from deficiencies. Perhaps, one of the most important contributions he made was the addition of the human dimension to quality management (Juran, 2000). Edwards Deming is recognized by his work in Japan where he improved the Japanese economy by using statistical methods applied to the management of quality. His philosophy is summarized in his famous 14 points (Deming, 1988).

9.3.1 Industrial Engineering Courses

At this stage, it is worthy to know how industrial engineers are actually educated to respond to the demands of societies. It would be impossible to provide an exhaustive list of industrial engineering curricula to analyze their content; nevertheless, it is useful to review the contents of the best undergraduate and graduate industrial engineering programs in the United States. Since these are perceived as the leader in industrial engineering programs; there is little reason to believe that curricula would be significantly different in other zones of the United States or even around the globe.

Students who enroll on the bachelor's industrial engineering program in the best undergraduate engineering programs in the United States (US News and World Report, 2008) could choose to focus on human factors and ergonomics, operations research, simulation, quality engineering, facilities planning and design, and sustainability. Students who enroll on the bachelor's manufacturing engineering program could choose to focus on electronics manufacturing, manufacturing process design, automation, manufacturing systems, and sustainability. Their major courses are: introduction to industrial and manufacturing engineering, manufacturing processes: net shape, introduction design and manufacturing, basic electronics manufacturing, work design and measurement, industrial costs and control, operations research I, II and III, engineering economics, human factors engineering, computer aided manufacturing I, manufacturing automation, engineering test and analysis, inventory control systems, simulation, manufacturing organization, ergonomics lab, quality engineering, among others. They also have to choose some support and general education courses; support courses such as electric circuits' theory, calculus, mechanics of materials, linear analysis physics, among other and general education courses such as English, literature, philosophy, political economy among others (Cal Poly Website, 2008).

At the graduate level, the best ranked graduate program in the United States (US News and World Report, 2008) offers eight degree options: industrial engineering, operations research, statistics, quantitative and computational finance, health systems, international logistics, computational science and engineering, and human-integrated systems. The core courses required for a master of science in industrial engineering degree are: manufacturing systems, warehousing systems, transportation and supply chain systems. Students need to pick three courses for the following pool: deterministic optimization, probabilistic models and their applications, simulation, statistical modeling and regression analysis, engineering economy or financial engineering. Two electives – technical and free courses are also required to complete the grade. There are five PhD programs: industrial engineering, operation research, algorithms, combinatorics, and optimization, computational science and engineering, bioinformatics.

As it is possible to observe, engineering curricula are concerned with the application of knowledge to the solution of particular problems with emphasis on mathematics, physics and sciences. Most engineers are taught to solve problems by breaking them down into smaller pieces and then quantitatively analyzing each of the pieces. This is known as reductionist thinking or analytical thinking. Reductionist thinking works especially well for technical problems; however, this fails with complex problems that include social concerns. As engineers carry out their tasks, there will be times when their activities will ultimately lead to a product that is unsafe or less than useful (Martin and Schinzinger, 1996).

As mentioned before, industrial engineers are involved with improved quality and productivity. It is not unusual for the obsession of industrial engineers to increasing quality and productivity at any cost to create unintended occupational and environmental risks. For instance, in 1920, engineers and scientists put lead, tetraethyl lead (TEL), in gasoline in order to increase the octane rating of gasoline and consequently to make car engine work more efficiently. However, 50 years after, TEL was phased out because of its extreme toxicity that caused air pollution, serious health problems, and failures in catalytic converters.

Some decades ago, engineers used chlorofluorocarbons (CFC) mainly as refrigerants, aerosol propellants and industrial cleaners, but in 1995, it was discovered that CFCs were destroying the protective ozone layer. This led to the banning of CFC-based products.

In 2004, it was discovered that industrial processes generated, as by-products, resulted in 5% of total U.S greenhouse gas emissions. See Fig. 9.1.

The above examples illustrate the consequences of making decisions just for the sake of efficacy and efficiency. They also show the need to educate engineers with a holistic approach. This does not mean that the analytical thinking should be rejected, but highlights that the whole is greater than the sum of the parts.

Industrial and systems engineering is a specialty field study derived from industrial engineering, but that integrates knowledge from the other four engineering sciences. Industrial and systems engineering also uses knowledge from Social Sciences. Although social courses are necessary to provide engineering students

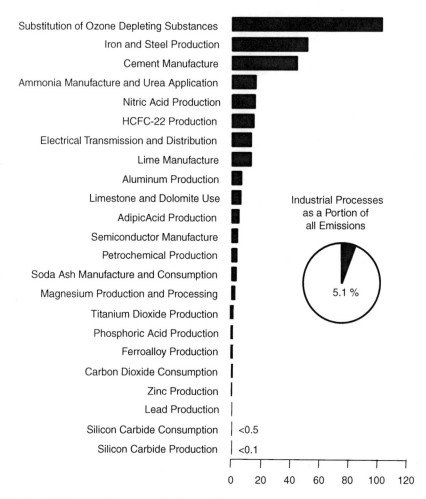

Fig. 9.1 2004 Industrial processes chapter greenhouse gas sources
Source: US Environmental Protection Agency, 2008

with some background of the importance of social values, albeit they often hesitate to take social science courses.

In a simple way, it is possible to say precisely that what industrial and system engineers do is to design and improve systems; usually, complex systems. Complexity lies in the involvement of human beings who are not predictable such as physical systems.

Industrial and systems engineers use numerous strategies for attaining quality and productivity through techniques such as benchmarking, continuous improvement, training in managing for quality, partnering, employee empowerment, motivation, total quality management, etc.

At the beginning, the systems were manufacturing organizations; nowadays, industrial and systems engineers perform not only within factories but also within any organizations such as, hospitals, hotels, governmental agencies, banks, insurance and other service providing organisations.

9.4 Industrial and Systems Engineering and CSR

In order to understand the role of an industrial and systems engineer in promoting CSR initiatives, it is necessary to review the concept of CSR.

Although there are several definitions of CSR United Nation (2000), World Business Council on Sustainable Development (2000), CEPAL (2004), Idowu (2008); most of them agree that the field encompasses common topics, such as: ethics, environment, sustainability, and human rights among others.

The European Commission considers CSR from two dimensions: internal and external (European Commission, 2001). From the internal dimension, the Commission mentions those practices that take into consideration employees' welfare; issues such as health and safety, training, education, etc. It is also considers environmentally responsible practices from the stand point of the use and management of natural resources. The external dimension involves partnership with local or regional stakeholders in communities to enhance well-beings of these stakeholders.

Traditionally, the performance of industrial engineers falls within the internal dimension of CSR but their responsibilities have now extended to include external dimension. They do not have any problem in their quest to improve operations that result in safer ways for workers; however, fostering initiatives within the external dimension of CSR require breaking old paradigms and barriers of industrial engineering or perhaps returning to basics: 'improving society's welfare'.

Performing within the external dimension of CSR demands a new industrial engineer profile with an interdisciplinary and trans-disciplinarity knowledge that is not usually present within a traditional industrial engineer's profile. See Fig. 9.2.

The main characteristic that distinguishes industrial and systems engineers from other professionals is their systems thinking. Students who enroll in industrial and systems engineering programs are familiarized with the General Systems Theory. This theory outlines the essential elements for understanding factors in the context of a dynamic system Bertalanffy (1968). The General Systems Theory is very useful

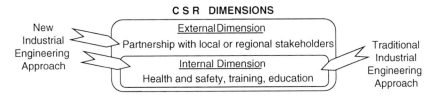

Fig. 9.2 Industrial engineers' approaches within CSR dimensions

in understanding the context of a system with its levels of complexity through the study and conceptualization of each essential element or subsystem as well as their interrelations and interactions with the others subsystems within the whole system Van Gigch (1972).

Industrial and systems engineers are expected to solve problems considering everything by studying extensively beyond a traditional field. For achieving that, it is necessary to visualize the whole of the life-cycle of a product, because raw materials may generate environmental and occupational risks during different stages of their cycle.

9.5 Sustainability and Corporate Social Responsibility

In 1987, the World Commission on Environment introduced in the very well known Brundtland Report (1987) the phrase 'sustainable development' defining it as 'development that meets the needs of the present without compromising the ability of future generation to meet their own needs' (WCED).

Sustainable Development and Corporate Social Responsibility are similar in that they both seek a better quality of life for people (see Fig. 9.3). Reaching sustainability requires a systems perspective focused on the relationships among key stakeholders Edwards (2005) so does CSR; yet, sustainability is more complex. In fact, CSR can be considered as a way of reaching the goals of Sustainable Development.

CSR is related with what the World Business Council for Sustainable Developments (WBCSD, 2000) describes in its definition of the field as 'the continuing commitment by business to contribute to economic development while improving the quality of life of the workforce and their families as well as of the community and society at large.'

Engineers have been unjustly criticized of being pragmatic doers that focus on fast and short-range solutions to problems causing unintended by-products just because they are not aware of the risks along the life cycle of raw material they use. This behavior can be called 'engineering myopia'. This term is used to describe

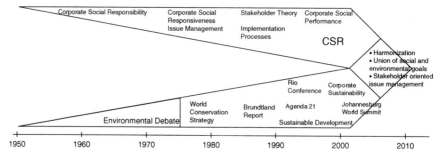

Fig. 9.3 Historical development of the CSR and sustainability debate
Source: Loew et al., 2004

the failure to foresee environmental, social or even economic negative impact of their decisions along the life cycle of their products or services.

Life cycle thinking (LCT) can be considered as a treatment for engineering myopia. This is a sustainability concept, very close to systems thinking that helps conceptualize environmental – and occupational-problems as a system-level issue Mont and Bleischwitz (2007). UNEP recognizes LCT as an appropriate tool for CSR (2007). Life cycle thinking implies that everyone in the whole chain of a product's life cycle, from cradle to grave, has a responsibility and a role to play, taking into account all the relevant external effects (UNEP, 2004). See Fig. 9.4.

An industrial engineer that develops and practices LCT will be in a better position to going beyond the traditional focus on production/services site in order to take account of the triple bottom line. It implies that industry has to expand the traditional economic focus to include environmental and social dimensions, in order to create a more sustainable business (Elkington, 1998).

Industrial Ecology, Cleaner Production and Pollution Prevention are used in industry to foster the triple bottom line. The literature refers to these concepts in several ways such as philosophies, methods, strategies, or simple tools. Especially, Industrial Ecology is described as a field of knowledge very close to systems thinking (Allenby, 1999).

The two concepts; industrial metabolism (Ayres, 1989) and industrial ecosystems (Frosch and Gallopoulos, 1989) were the foundation for Industrial Ecology which is defined as 'the multidisciplinary study of industrial systems and economic activities, and their links to fundamental natural system' (IEEE, 1994). The idea

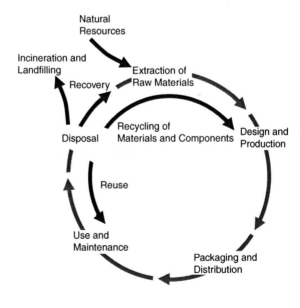

Fig. 9.4 LCT conceptual framework
Source: United Nation Environment Programme, 2004

is to make industrial systems perform analogously to natural ecosystems (Erkman, 1997). Industrial ecology emphasizes the interconnectivity of industrial activity as a system and promotes action at the regional or industrial level (Oldenbung and Geiser, 1997).

Currently, the terms Cleaner Production and Pollution Prevention are used indistinctively; they can be described as: the continuous application of an integrated, preventive environmental strategy to both processes and products to reduce risks to human and environment (Baas, 2005). For both, source reduction is a priority in the hierarchy of options for reducing risks to environment and human health (Quinn and Kriebel, 1998).

Cleaner production and pollution prevention is the antithesis of the end-of-pipe approach (Keoleian, 1995). End-of-pipe practices have been the traditional approach used by engineers for environmental management. This is a reductionist approach that attempts to control pollution by isolating contaminants from the environment or workers and by using end of the pipe technology, usually filters (Hirschhorn et al., 1993).

Dematerialization and detoxification (Geiser, 2001) are pathways of clean production to promote a sustainable material system. The first seeks the reduction of the material flow through those processes, cycles and activities without loss of efficiency. And the second is the reduction and the substitution of toxic materials by several techniques such as: chemical substitution or product redesign, reforming production processes to use less hazardous substance, or recycling of toxic substances.

There are a number of benefits to industry by implementing Cleaner Production and Pollution Prevention initiatives including: improving the firm's bottom-line, make compliance with legislation, improving image (Freeman, 1995). There are also benefits for society since pollution will be totally eliminated and the environment will be cleaner for citizens.

9.6 Conclusions

The ultimate goal of industrial engineering is to improve the quality of life in society; for that reason, industrial engineers must foster and embrace CSR initiatives. Traditionally, industrial engineers perform their roles within the internal dimension of CSR which are easily achievable and which do not require a lot of extra effort, at least when comparing these requirements with those that fall within the external dimension. Initiatives within the external dimension are often not performed by engineers perhaps because their educational background is deficient in this regard which causes engineering myopia.

Industrial engineers are trained to apply knowledge to the solution of particular problems by using analytical thinking which constitutes an essential feature of industrial engineering education. Consequently, their curriculum is overloaded with mathematics and physics knowledge rather than with applications of scientific knowledge. It is not being implied that something is seriously wrong with the engineering education. Rather, it implies that a holistic approach needs to be taken cognizance, which entails incorporating social concerns to the engineering curricula. This should hopefully prepare them to function more effectively in the modern business environment.

For the sake of productivity and quality, industrial engineers have made remarkable achievements; unfortunately, history has recorded unintended side effects such as environmental pollution and human health problems, which have to some extent clouded these achievements. To avoid unintended byproducts, hard-science knowledge in engineering should be applied in a broader sense rather than a narrower sense. Productivity should not be the only goal itself; it should the route to reaching the ultimate goal of engineering.

It is worthy to mention that the nature of the problems faced by engineers is not just technical but also social, economic and ethical. Engineering education needs a change its paradigm in line with these extended responsibilities. New breed of engineers; different from those from traditional breed engineers who were less equipped to cope with society's social concerns is what the modern business environment needs.

Systems thinking can really encourage industrial engineers to perform in a sustainable and CSR aware way by thinking beyond the traditional focus on production, services, and consumption. This will require a reorientation in terms of the whole of the life cycle of products and services to reduce and/or eliminate the adverse environmental and occupational impacts without creating negative side effects to society.

References

Allenby, BR 1999, *Industrial ecology: policy framework and implementation*, Prentice-Hall, Inc., Upper Saddle River, NJ.

Ayres, R 1989, 'Industrial metabolism'. *Technology and environment*, National Academy Press, Washington, pp. 23–49.

Baas, L 2005, *Cleaner production and industrial ecology*, Eburon Academic Publishers, The Netherlands.

Bertalanffy, LV 1968, *General system theory: foundations and development applications*, George Braziller, Inc., New York.

Bird, JO, Ross, CT 2002, *Mechanical engineering principles*, Butterworth-Heinemann, Woburn, MA.

Cal Poly Website 2008, *Industrial and Manufacturing Department*. [Internet] viewed 11 October 2008 available from: http://ime.calpoly.edu/about/

Chen, WF, Richard, JY (eds) 2002, *The civil engineering handbook*, 2nd edn. CRC press, Boca Raton, FL.

Chen, WK 2005, *The electrical engineering handbook*, Elsevier, Boston, MA.

Comisión Económica para América Latina y el Caribe (CEPAL) 2004, *Responsabilidad social corporativa en América Latina: una visión empresarial*. Serie: Medio ambiente y desarrollo No. 85 [Internet] viewed 13 August 2007 available from: http://www.cepal.org/cgi-bin/getProd.asp?xml=/publicaciones/xml/4/14904/P14904.xml&xsl=/dmaah/tpl/p9f.xsl&base=/tpl/top-bottom.xslt

Cross, H 1950, *Engineers and ivory towers*, Mc Graw-Hill Book Company, New York.

Deming, WE 1988, *Out of crisis: quality, productivity and competitive position*, MIT Press, Cambridge, MA.

Edwards, AR 2005, *The sustainability revolution: a portrait of a paradigm shift*, New Society Publishers, Canada.

Elkington, J 1998, *Cannibals with forks: the triple bottom line of 21st century business*, New Society Publishers, Gabriola Island, BC.

Environmental Protection Agency 2008, Inventory of US Greenhouse Gas Emissions and Sinks: 1990–2006, [Internet] viewed 19 August 2008 available from: http://www.epa.gov/climatechange/emissions/downloads/08_CR.pdf

Erkman, S 1997, 'Industrial ecology: an historical view'. *Journal of Cleaner Production*, Vol. 5, No. 1–2, pp. 1–10.

European Commission 2001, Promoting a European framework for corporate social responsibility Green Paper [Internet] viewed 13 August 2007 available from: http://www.jussemper.org/Resources/Corporate%20Activity/Resources/greenpaper_en.pdf

Freeman, H 1995, *Industrial pollution prevention handbook*, McGraw-Hill, Inc., New York.

Frosch, RA, Gallopoulos, NE 1989, 'Strategies for manufacturing'. *Scientific American*, Special Issue, Vol. 261, pp. 144–152.

Geiser, K 2001, *Materials matter: toward a sustainable materials policy*, MIT Press, Cambridge, MA.

Hirschhorn, T, Jackson, T, Baas, L 1993, 'Towards prevention: the emerging environmental management paradigm'. In Jackson, T (ed), *Clean production strategies*, Lewis Publishers, Boca Raton, FL.

Idowu, SO 2008, 'Practicing CSR in the United Kingdom and Northern Ireland'. In Idowu, SO and Leal Filho, W (eds), *Global practices of CSR*, Springer Verlag, Berlin.

Institute of Electrical and Electronics Engineers, Inc 1994, *Sustainable development and industrial ecology*, IEEE Inc., Washington, DC.

Institute of Industrial Engineers 2008, What does an industrial engineer really do? [Internet] viewed 11 September 2008 available from: http://www.iienet2.org/Details.aspx?id=716

Juran, JM (ed) 2000, *Juran's quality handbook*, 5th edn. Mc Graw-Hill, New York.

Keoleian, G 1995, Pollution prevention through life-cycle design'. In *Industrial pollution prevention handbook*, Freeman, H (ed), McGraw-Hill, Inc., New York.

Loew, T, Ankele, K, Braun, S, Clausen, J 2004, *Significance of the CSR debate for sustainability and the requirements for companies: summary*, Future e.V. and Institute for Ecological Economy Research GmbH (IÖW), Berlin.

Martin, MW, Schinzinger, R 1996, *Ethics in engineering*, 3rd edn. The McGraw-Hill Companies Inc., New York.

Mont, O, Bleischwitz, R 2007, Sustainable consumption and resource management in the light of life cycle thinking'. *European Environment*, Vol. 17, pp. 59–76.

Ogawa, K 2007, *Chemical engineering: a new perspective*. Elsevier, Amsterdam.

Oldenbung, K and Geiser, K 1997, Pollution prevention and or industrial ecology'. *Journal of Cleaner Production*, Vol. 5, No. 1–2, pp. 103–108.

Quinn, MM, Kriebel, D, et al. 1998, Sustainable production: a proposed strategy for the work environment'. *American Journal of Industrial Medicine*, Vol. 4, No. 34, pp. 297–304.

Sumanth, DJ 1994, *Productivity engineering and management*, 3rd edn. McGraw-Hill, New York.

The World Commission on Environment and Development 1987, *Our common future*. Oxford University Press, Oxford, NY.

US News and World Report, American's Best College 2009. [Internet] viewed 11 October 2008 available from: http://colleges.usnews.rankingsandreviews.com/college/spec-industrial

United Nation 2000, Global compact [Internet] viewed 13 August 2007 available from: http://www.unglobalcompact.org/AboutTheGC/index.html

United Nation Environment Programme 2004, Why take a life cycle approach. [Internet] viewed 13 September 2008 available from: http://www.unep.fr/shared/publications/pdf/DTIx0585xPA-WhyLifeCycleEN.pdf

United Nation Environment Programme 2007, Life cycle management: a business guide to sustainability. [Internet] viewed 13 September 2008 available from: http://www.unep.fr/shared/docs/publications/LCM_guide.pdf?site=lcinit&page_id=F14E0563-6C63-4372-B82F-6F6B5786CCE3

Van Gigch, JP 1972, *Applied general systems theory*, Harper & Row Publishers, New York.

World Business Council on Sustainable Development (WBCSD) 2000, Corporate social responsibility, [Internet] viewed 13 August 2007 available from: http://www.wbcsd.org/DocRoot/hbdf19Txhmk3kDxBQDWW/CSRmeeting.pdf

Zanding, KB (ed) 2001, *Maynard's industrial engineering handbook*, 5th edn. McGraw-Hill, New York.

Chapter 10
An Exploratory Study of the Corporate Social Responsibility Practices in the Greek Manufacturing Sector

Nikolaos A. Panayiotou, Konstantinos G. Aravosis, and Konstantinos Saridakis

> *Dare to be naive.*
> —Buckminster Fuller

Abstract This paper sets out to describe the level of corporate social responsibility of the Greek manufacturing sector. While the level of corporate socially responsible behaviour has been widely explored in the context of Northern European industry, analysis concerning the level of CSR practices of the Greek manufacturing industry is underdeveloped. An empirical study is performed based on the identification of CSR practices of the most active companies in the industrial sector in Greece. Their CSR orientation is recognized by their published annual CSR reports and the performance indicators they use in order to demonstrate their corporate responsibility. The analysis of their CSR behavior is based on an eight-category framework, which is a decomposition of the three typical CSR views recognized in the literature, these being economy, environment and society. The results are critically commented and conclusions are made for the CSR future of the manufacturing companies operating in Greece.

10.1 Introduction

Over the last decade, there has been an apparent shift from adopting more responsible business practices as a result of regulatory citations, consumer complaints, and special interest group pressures, to proactive research exploring corporate solutions to social problems and incorporating new business practices that will support these issues (Business for Social Responsibility Education Fund, 2000). In fact, it is only in recent years that the number of organisations engaging in social behaviours

N.A. Panayiotou (✉)
Section of Industrial Management and Operational Research, Faculty of Mechanical Engineering, National Technical University of Athens, Zografos, Athens, Greece

S.O. Idowu, W.L. Filho (eds.), *Professionals' Perspectives of Corporate Social Responsibility*, DOI 10.1007/978-3-642-02630-0_11,
© Springer-Verlag Berlin Heidelberg 2009

and activities has increased markedly (McWilliams et al., 2006; Stainer and Stainer, 2003; McIntosh et al., 2003). According to Pryce (2002), the current focus, is driven by five forces: customer pressure, changes in business procurement, government legislation and pressure, the rise of socially responsible investment, and the changing expectations of employees.

However, despite the interest that CSR has generated, a number of issues have not yet been satisfactorily addressed. Whilst the rhetoric encourages organisations to aspire to be more socially responsible, there is not a sufficiently explicit or detailed description of what it is they should be aiming for, nor is there a well developed or convincing body of literature that can clearly articulate the value to organisations of engaging in such behaviours (Van Marrewiijk, 2003). Indeed, much of the current interest in CSR Centres on the need to engage in such behaviours as a matter of course but there is none, or very little, consideration of the incidence and types of initiatives that are seen in practice, or of why CSR initiatives are undertaken in some organisations and not in others. As a result, the meaning of CSR and the issues surrounding it remain clouded for many organisations (Webley, 2001; McWilliams et al., 2006).

With a lack of a commonly agreed definition of CSR (something being reported by many articles, such as these of Carroll (1999), Jones (1995, 1999), McWilliams and Siegel (2001), and Idowu and Papasolomou (2007)) the formation of a performance measurement framework for its evaluation and the communication of the results to the stakeholders of the organisation become very difficult. Whilst organisations have generally recognised a responsibility to society (Boatright, 2003), the implementation of this at a strategic level is much more problematic (Idowu, 2008). To many, CSR remains "a vague and intangible term", with "unclear boundaries" (Frankental, 2001; Lantos, 2001). Therefore, although the debate about CSR has continued to grow, we remain far from consensus on what it means and its value. Some companies see it as a source of business opportunity and improved competitiveness, while others view it as simply good business practice.

Trying to demonstrate their CSR orientation, some companies have started to publish annual CSR reports. These reports do not follow a clear standard. The Global Reporting Initiative (GRI, 2006), is a framework offering companies guidance on the categories that should be explained in their reports (Global Reporting Initiative). This group of companies, accounting experts, investors, unions, NGOs and other stakeholder groups has set itself the objective of formulating globally applicable guidelines for sustainability reporting that are relevant for all sectors (Hennigfeld et al., 2006). However, he GRI permits a high degree of flexibility in how efforts in these categories should be measured, so the variations in CSR report details reflect this flexibility. Similarly, the United Nations Global Compact and the Global Sullivan Principles of Social Responsibility are occasionally referenced standards for what categories constitute responsibility, but they are not as well used or as useful as the GRI (United Nations Global Compact; Global Sullivan Principles). In 2003, UK-based non-profit business institute Account-Ability launched its AA1000AS international standard for sustainability assurance in an effort to improve the quality of assurance statements by independent auditors.

The AA1000AS recommends that assurors assess reports against the principles of materiality, completeness and responsiveness. Social Accountability International (www.sa-intl.org), a human rights organization, created SA800, which is based on international workplace norms in the ILO conventions and the UN's Universal Declaration of Human Rights and the Convention on Rights of the Child. Issues measured and reported according to SA800 include child labour, forced labour, health and safety, freedom of association and right to collective bargaining, discrimination, discipline, working hours, compensation and management systems. Other internationally recognised standards include environmental standard ISO 14001, which is popular with the manufacturing sector, the GHG Protocol, and the Global Compact. Organisations, such as Business in the Community, have also developed their own reporting guidelines in addition to CR benchmarking indices (Fahy et al., 2004).

Although GRI seems to be the most influencing CSR framework world-wide (Vogel, 2005), it most often only serves as a reference point to which corporations map their report details, not as a framework for the report itself. CSR initiatives are still largely seen as competitive differentiators, and with no agreed-upon standard, companies choose to primarily highlight their strengths and explain their stance on issues relevant to their business. For example, a consumer product retailer's version of "responsibility" is likely to include product safety, while for a manufacturing company; environmental protection will be a larger focus. As it is understood by the above, the sector in which companies operate is a prominent factor (but still not the only one) responsible for the differentiation of CSR issues considered as of great importance that are reported to the public.

10.2 The Manufacturing Sector in Greece

Increasingly, society expects businesses to have an obligation to the environment and the community in which they operate, to the people they employ and their customers, beyond their old-fashioned narrow shareholder concerns. While such expectations concern all aspects of all kind of businesses, many advocates of CSR argue that, the greenhouse effect and other similar irreversible environmental impacts resulting from the avaricious growth of the manufacturing sector, are the primary forces that have boosted SCR to one of the most important management notions of the twenty first century. As an example, Maltby (2004) argues that CSR reporting has been practiced proactively by several UK manufacturing companies since the earlier part of the 1900s.

The concept of "sustainable development", that embodies mainly the environmental perspective of CSR, has lead manufacturing corporations to be among the first businesses to addresses CSR issues and adopt CSR practices, in an attempt to confront the first massive waves of public pressure and discomfort, and to comply with the emergence of the first environmental regulations. As a result, nowadays the manufacturing sector is considered to be among the leading areas regarding the development and adoption of good CSR methods and practices. Hence, this paper will focus on the CSR reports published by the companies of the manufacturing sector in Greece.

Manufacturing in Greece is one of the economic sectors faced with challenges connected with the globalized business reality. The emergence of Asian states, most notably China, along with ever-increasing domestic production costs, have cost Greek industrial manufacturers dearly, and translated into numerous job losses.

On the other hand, a few enterprises have found themselves more able to withstand the competition, and have actually gained international access- as well as larger profit margins. These select companies are to be found in all areas of Greek industrial production and some have aspirations to become key players in niche markets worldwide. Most successful of these Greek firms have shown they have the abilities and the potential to play an important international role.

According to the Economist Intelligence Unit (The Economist Intelligence Unit, 2007), the Greek manufacturing sector is small by European standards, accounting for an estimated 9.7% of GDP in 2005, including mining. In 2004 the sector employed 570,000 people, 13.2% of employment.

The majority of manufacturing firms are small family businesses. Data for 2004, aggregated by a business information company, ICAP, and covering 4,684 companies publishing balance sheets (for example, limited companies or corporations), show 78% of firms employing fewer than 50 people; 18.2% employing between 50 and 249 people; and 3.9% employing more than 250. The firms with fewer than 50 staff employed 63,459 (25%), while the others employed 186,386 (75%), but the larger firms generated nearly 89% of the total profits, and their earnings per employee were 2.7 times higher than those of their smaller counterparts, at €11,512 per head, compared with €4,315 per head.

The largest and generally most profitable sectors produce either consumer goods or intermediates based on local raw materials. As an example, the top 20 companies in 2004 included firms in the cement and aluminum, olive oil, brewing and tobacco, oil refining and telecommunications sectors. The clothing and footwear industries, which used to be important, have gone into decline in recent years because of competition from low-wage countries in Asia and Eastern Europe, although a few large firms have shifted their focus towards providing higher-value-added garments in order to restore profitability. Many Greek firms in the clothing sector now subcontract their labour-intensive processes to Balkan countries.

The manufacturing sector is the largest sector in Greece concerning employment. This fact is responsible for the close connection of the sector with the local community, as the companies operating in it offer employment opportunities. Moreover, its relationship with environmental issues is particularly strong because of the nature of its operations (use of raw materials, energy consumption and use of heavy pieces of equipment). As a result, the sector is usually found in the center of criticism concerning issues related to Corporate Social Responsibility.

Manufacturing companies in Greece have been the first to take CSR seriously, following CSR practices in areas such as the internal environment (employee issues), as well as the external environment (customers, local community, nature).

The above is supported by the fact that the majority of the establishing members of the Greek Network for Corporate Social Responsibility belong to the manufacturing sector. However, the number of the active companies in CSR is still very small and is restricted to large corporations with global presence.

Highlighted CSR areas in the Greek manufacturing sector are hygiene and safety in the working environment, environmental protection, consumer protection, employees' competences' continuous improvement through continuous learning schemes and suppliers and sub-contractors sensitivity in CSR matters. Previous research in Greece, concerning CSR (such as this by Panayiotou et al., 2008) shows that CSR is in its infancy stage in Greece, however, some remarkable examples of good CSR practices can be found in the manufacturing sector. In some cases these practices are followed by companies having the role of supplier or sub-contractor of large Greek or international corporations. Although these companies are not as much sensitive in CSR issues as their customers, they are aware of many aspects of it and they have succeeded in adopting some practices by themselves, in order to guarantee their flawless and continuous cooperation with them. This somehow "coercive" behavior has provided them with a competitive advantage in the market they operate.

The synthesis of the Greek manufacturing sector by small and medium enterprises (SMEs) is an inhibitory factor for the adoption of CSR mentality.

This paper tries to identify the adoption of CSR by the Greek manufacturing companies through an empirical analysis. The small number of active companies in Greece does not permit a meaningful statistical analysis, so emphasis is put on the qualitative analysis of the issues that are perceived of importance by the existing companies. Possible differences compared to CSR practices of other sectors are investigated and conclusions are made for the role of CSR in the strategies of the Greek manufacturing companies.

10.3 Methodological Framework for the Analysis of CSR Practices in the Greek Manufacturing Sector

According to the World Business Council for Sustainable Development, CSR reports are public reports released by organizations to provide internal and external stakeholders with a picture of corporate position and activities on economic, environmental and social dimensions. In short, such reports attempt to describe the companies' contribution towards sustainable development. Most reporting frameworks are based on three distinctive views (Vogel, 2005), as these are depicted in Table 10.1.

In order to analyse the CSR practices of manufacturing companies in Greece, the companies publishing a CSR report were identified, making the assumption that companies that do not report on CSR issues do not have a substantial CSR orientation. As a result, the CSR reports of the Greek companies were collected and examined in order to identify the CSR performance measures each company uses.

Table 10.1 CSR reporting commonly used views

View	Issues
Economic	Profitability, wages and benefits, resource usage, job offerings, outsourcing
Environmental	Processes, products and services related to the environment
Social	Health and safety issues, employee relations, ethics human rights, working conditions

The lack of standards and the fact that the report has no defined audience but is aimed at the world at large has led to a wide variation in what is reported. In order to overcome this problem, an attempt was made to categorize the corporate social responsible behaviour of the companies in Greece according to which categories were more common among the CSR reports published by the companies. Care was taken in order to define categories compatible with the three views identified in the literature.

The analysis of the results revealed eight distinctive categories of CSR performance measures mostly used (in a non-formal way) by companies operating in Greece. These categories are as follows:

- Economy.
- Internal business processes.
- Learning and growth.
- Environmental impact.
- Human resources.
- Society.
- Marketplace.
- Health and safety.

The correlation of the identified categories with the three main CSR views recognized in the literature is depicted in Fig. 10.1.

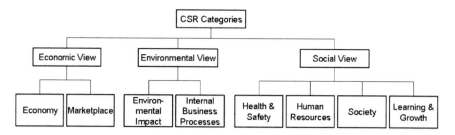

Fig. 10.1 CSR views and categories

The analysis of the CSR reports generated by the Greek companies operating in the manufacturing sector was based on the above framework.

Furthermore, in order to quantify findings and allow a company's CSR performance subjective evaluation as well as the ability for any comparisons and conclusions to be made, a CSR performance scale from 1 to 5 was introduced to be used as a point of reference. The scale seeks to provide a correlation between what is generally perceived as good CSR practices in literature and by widely accepted reporting standards, and the degree of disclosures on CSR performance and goals on each of the aforementioned CSR views and categories, as identified in the CSR reports of the examined companies. The CSR performance scale used in the analysis of the reports is presented in Fig. 10.2.

Finally, in an attempt to complement the Methodological Framework for the Analysis of CSR Practices in the Greek Manufacturing Sector, CSR reports were further examined in order to identify any qualitative correlation between CSR performance and a company's approach to CSR from a managerial and organizational point of view. The latter was accomplished by examining the following perspectives:

- **CSR and Communications**: seeks to provide insight on the degree of a company's will for CSR accountability and transparency, as far as the general public is concerned. In this perspective the following aspects of the reports were inquired:

  - Stand alone CSR report
  - Statement from the CEO
  - Online CSR report
  - Interim CSR report
  - Number of previous reports

˙Disclosures on Performance and Goals	
●	Advanced disclosures balanced across all organizational divisions, regions and business units, in accordance to International best practices and widely accepted reporting standards.
◕	Advanced disclosures that cover major organizational divisions, regions and business units and meet most reporting requirements of International best practices and widely accepted reporting standards.
◑	Concise disclosures on a sufficient number of widely accepted performance indicators compared to predetermined targets and previous performance.
◔	Unstructured disclosures on random performance indicators.
○	No disclosures.

Fig. 10.2 CSR performance correlation with CSR reports' disclosures on performance and goals

- **CSR and Management**: seeks to provide insight on the degree at which CSR is embedded in the organization's day-to-day decision-making process. In this perspective the following aspects of the reports were inquired:

  - CSR mentioned in corporate vision/mission
  - CSR appointed director/department
  - CSR strategy and objectives explicitly defined
  - CSR practices in the Supply Chain
  - CSR risks and opportunities identified

- **CSR and Governance**: seeks to provide insight on the degree of engagement of shareholders and other stakeholders in the process to design and implement a company's CSR practices. In this perspective the following aspects of the reports were inquired:

  - SCR committee in the BoD
  - Degree of establishing Stakeholder engagement policies
  - External assurance

10.4 Identification and Description of CSR Issues

In order to identify the companies that are active in CSR issues in Greece, we found the listed companies in the Athens Stock Exchange or in a Stock exchange outside Greece, operating in the greater area of manufacturing that generate an annual CSR report, making the hypothesis that it would be very unlikely for a company to prepare a CSR report if it is not public. Moreover, manufacturing companies that are active in CSR without publishing an annual report were identified through the directories of the following Greek organizations:

- Hellenic Network for Corporate Social Responsibility (CSR Hellas): CSR-Hellas is a business-driven non-profit organisation with the mission of promoting the meaning of CSR to both the business community and the social environment. CSR-Hellas includes ninety-six members. It is one of the most active organisations promoting CSR in Greece.
- Centre for Sustainability and Excellence (CSE): The CSE is an advising and leading organisation and a Think Tank with offices in Athens, Brussels and Dubai, specialized in CSR and Sustainable Development.
- Eurocharity: Eurocharity is a non-profit company that donates 25% of its annual revenues to charity. It operates a comprehensive CSR directory in Greece.

Although the number of companies participating in a Greek CSR network has been substantially increased in the last two years, the available information included in their sites relating to CSR is still not worth analyzing. As a result, the remaining part of this chapter will focus on the CSR reports of the companies identified based on the aforementioned criteria. In this section we have answered the question – what do the reports reveal about CSR policies and practices adopted by companies operating in the Greek manufacturing sector? The order below is of no significance but primarily a matter of convenience.

10.4.1 Titan S.A.

Company Profile: Founded in Greece in 1902 and listed in the Athens Stock Exchange since 1912, TITAN is a vertically integrated group of wholly-owned affiliated companies and joint ventures that operates in 12 countries. Its activities cover the production of cement, concrete, aggregates, mortars and other building materials, transportation and distribution of products, as well as processing and industrial utilization of fly ash.

Analysis Results: The CSR report clearly shows the Executive's high level of commitment to embed CSR practices within the organization and in accordance to international guidelines such as the GRI, the UN Global Compact, the Cement Sustainable Initiative of the World Business Council for Sustainable Development (WBCSD/CSI) and the AA1000 Accounting Standards. Moreover, the report has been externally assured by an independent organization which confirms that the GRI "A+ application level" has been met, while another external firm undertook to provide assurance on the company's carbon dioxide emission data and safety data performance. In line with the previous, disclosures underscore that while performance in all CSR categories is thoroughly unfolded, environmental and social aspects appear to receive more gravity. Additional disclosures on past performance provide the ability to assess progress accomplished whereas negative performance is noted and discussed rather than overshadowed. In conclusion, while levels of awareness, capability and implementation may vary across Divisions, Regions and Business Units, the company has sought to identify and adopt good CSR practices and policies in line with the overall corporate strategy.

10.4.2 Hellenic Petroleum S.A. (ELPE)

Company Profile: Founded in 1975 by the Greek Government, the company was listed in the Athens and London stock exchanges in 1998, following its privatization. Today, Hellenic Petroleum (ELPE) has presence in 11 countries and aims to transform into a major regional, internationally competitive energy Group. The Group's principal activities are refining of crude oil and marketing of refined petroleum products, while there is also involvement in the production and marketing of petrochemicals, exploration development and production of hydrocarbons and other related activities.

Analysis Results: The CSR report reveals that Hellenic Petroleum has a high level of awareness with regard to the concepts of CSR and sustainable development. While the report is not assured by an independent party, it has been structured taking into consideration best practice standards such as the principles of the UN Global Compact and the indicators of the GRI. Although programs, policies and activities cover adequately all relevant categories, the levels of disclosure vary significantly across CSR views. Extensive reporting focus has been given on local communities and employee safety, highlighting in this way the company's CSR orientation. As ELPE is subject to occasional internal and external audits imposed by strict safety and environmental regulations, it appears to have embedded sophisticated performance management systems yet relevant disclosures are limited within the report. Overall, the company's active support to CSR practices is evident nevertheless additional effort is required in order to accomplish a full integration of CSR as a management framework for improving economic, social and environmental performance.

10.4.3 S&B Industrial Minerals S.A.

Company Profile: The company started its operations in Greece in 1934 and is listed in the Athens Stock Exchange since 1994. Today, S&B has become a multinational group of more than 40 companies, with extensive operations in 23 countries in 5 continents. The Group's principal activities are the extraction and wholesale of precious metals and minerals while secondary activities include import of motorbikes, spare parts for motorbikes, accessories and lubricants, earth moving equipment, forklifts, warehouse machinery, diesel motors and generators.

Analysis Results: S&B Group has been publishing social reports for the past six years which indicates that its commitment to business development and growth is coupled with the practice of sustainable development. The report has been compiled according to the GRI guidelines and has been self-declared as "B" in the relevant scale of application levels. CSR practices and policies are apparent in all categories yet their systematic and comprehensive undertaking concern primarily areas directly related with employee health and safety and the negative impact on the environment. Reporting in these areas is sufficiently accompanied with targets and previous performance while the company has made additional efforts to further evaluate material issues and challenges for sustainable development at both Group and local level. Among other practices, risk assessments by external firms and the implementation of two-way communication schemes between stakeholders and management reveal the company's commitment to improve performance in all areas of social responsibility and sustainability.

10.4.4 Vivartia S.A.

Company Profile: Vivartia was formed in 2006 through a series of acquisitions and is now the largest food manufacturing group of companies in Greece and one of the largest in Europe, as its recognized brands are reaching consumers in 30 countries. Through its subsidiaries the Group is actively involved in the dairy business, ice-cream market, fresh juices market, frozen food market and processing of ready-made meals and milk.

Analysis Results: While Vivartia is conducting a broad program of initiatives and activities compatible with typical CSR practices followed by international companies publishing CSR reports, it seems that it lacks the appropriate monitoring and reporting mechanisms that would allow better CSR performance management as well as better tracking and communication of results. As the company operates in a "greener" and "safer" industry in comparison to the cement or the petroleum refinery industries, reporting focus on environmental and health and safety aspects has not been as thorough as encouraged by the GRI and other international reporting standards. Focus is given mainly on product safety as well as on contributions to the society and the employees through the provision of financial assistance, additional benefits and the launching of training, educational and cultural initiatives.

10.4.5 The Coca-Cola Hellenic Bottling Company S.A.

Company Profile: Coca-Cola Hellenic was formed in 2000 through the merger of Hellenic Bottling Company S.A. and Coca-Cola Beverages plc and is the second largest bottler of products of the Coca-Cola Company by revenue. Coca-Cola Hellenic serves 550 million people across 28 countries by manufacturing and distributing soft drinks, juices, waters, teas and functional beverages. The company is primarily listed in the Athens stock exchange and also in the London, the New-York and the Australian stock exchanges.

Analysis Results: With its fifth consecutive report, Coca-Cola Hellenic shows that it continues to strengthen its approach to sustainability, by embedding sustainability considerations into business processes and by deepening its engagement with stakeholders. The report follows most international best practice guidelines and has been externally assessed as GRI application level "B" by the GRI organization itself. As a Food and Beverages company, reporting weight has been given to the key social and environmental issues associated with its business and thus, adopted CSR practices derived from the company's priorities that represent the greatest risks and opportunities for the business and the most significant stakeholder concerns such as employee safety, product health and quality and environmental impact. With regard to the latter, a considerable part of the report concerns the adoption of CSR policies in the supply chain as Coca-Cola Hellenic's supply chain accounts for more than double the environmental impact of the Company's own operations. However, the use of metric data and indicators illustrate sufficiently the results achieved in the aforementioned areas and provide clear conclusions on progress achieved.

10.4.6 Italsementi S.p.A.

Company Profile: With an annual production capacity of approximately 70 million tons of cement, Italcementi Group is the world's fifth largest cement producer. With activities in 22 countries, the company operates in Greece through its international subsidiary Xalyps Building Materials S.A., a Greek company with over 70 years of experience in production of cement that was acquired by the Group in 1992.

Analysis Results: The report provides valuable insight into the company's thinking and performance on sustainability issues. It has been documented in accordance to the GRI guidelines as well as with those defined by the Cement Sustainability Initiative (WBCSD/CSI); however it has not yet undergone an overall independent assurance process. An engagement with an external auditor to provide verification on key environmental and safety performance indicators, for the second consecutive year, highlights the Group's increasing awareness for adopting best practices and achieving greater transparency and accountability of results. Sustainability challenges and the Group's strategies and activities with targets achieved and areas where further improvements are possible are well addressed, yet environmental and safety issues outshine other views where reporting focus and scope appear to be bounded.

10.4.7 Siemens S.A.

Company Profile: With more than 100 years of active presence in Greece, Siemens Hellas is an international subsidiary of the German giant that has evolved to a large group of electronics and industrial engineering companies involved in the areas of manufacturing and distribution of electrical and electronic equipment, telecommunications, information technology and system implementation, technical support, consulting and medical diagnostic solutions.

Analysis Results: The report revealed very interesting findings with regard to CSR practices not only due to the parent company's enormous size that embodies over 600 companies in nearly 190 countries but also due to the corruption and bribery cases at Siemens that dominated the public's awareness during the fiscal year 2007. In contrast to other manufacturing companies, the company has published a report that is not based on the GRI guidelines but has its own unique structure and aims to regain and strengthen the trust and acceptance of customers, society and the financial markets. While the environmental portfolio is externally assured and social aspects are sufficiently covered with disclosures on targets and performance, extensive reporting gravity is given to the principles of the UN Global Contact and the company's adopted policies and procedures to uncover misconduct and to heighten all employees' responsiveness for lawful, ethically irreproachable behavior. Siemens has set the goal to become the industry benchmark for transparency and as stated by its higher governance body, CSR reporting should make an important contribution toward this goal.

10.4.8 BP Hellas S.A.

Company Profile: BP Hellas, a wholly owned subsidiary of the British conglomerate BP plc. is one of the largest distributors of petroleum and oil products in Greece with 1,500 service stations selling BP and Castrol branded products. The company also provides aviation fuels and lubricants to 22 airports, while each year supplies around 380,000 tonnes of products to the shipping industry.

Analysis Results: BP's report shows that the Group is very conscious of the need to manage its business in a way that contributes to long-term sustainability and promotes responsibility for society and the environment. The report has been externally assured by two independent organizations, including the GRI which ascertains that requirements of the "A+" application level have been met. Furthermore, the AA1000 Accounting Standards have been followed as well as the International Petroleum Industry Environmental Conservation Association Oil and Gas Industry guidelines (IPIECA/API) and the UN Global Contact principles. Disclosures cover sufficiently all CSR views with extensive coverage on those that concern people's safety and the climate change; however they also reveal BP's greater interest in developing and implementing appropriate management systems and in achieving greater transparency and accountability of results. The latter appears to be a consequence of the severe 2005 Texas City refinery accident that triggered a number of governmental investigations in BP's facilities and raised significant concerns on process safety risks and regulation compliance issues.

10.4.9 Shell Hellas S.A.

Company Profile: Shell Hellas was established in 1926 and comprises a part of the Royal Dutch Shell Plc, the second largest oil company in the world. The company's main activities include the import, distribution and marketing of a wide range of oil and chemical products, including fuel oil, petrol, diesel, lubricants and LPG, through a network of over 1,000 service stations across the country.

Analysis Results: The company's 2007 report utilizes innovative communication methods in explaining Shell's view of a sustainable energy future and its role in achieving it. The description of two strategic energy scenarios and their use to frame the dialogue on future energy needs and climate change reflects the most important sustainability issues facing the company. While with this approach significant insight is provided with regard to the company's strategy to offset the greenhouse effect and to meet the energy challenge, other topics such as local environmental impacts and social performance receive less attention. However, Shell asserts that its CSR report meets the "A+" application requirements of the GRI and has followed other international reporting standards such as the UN Global Contact, the AA1000AS and the International Petroleum Industry Environmental Conservation Association Oil and Gas Industry guidelines (IPIECA/API).

Based on the analysis of the reports, the following paragraphs seek to describe the key findings with regard to the CSR methods and practices adopted by the examined companies of the Greek Manufacturing Sector.

As presented in Fig. 10.1, the methodological framework for the analysis incorporates three CSR views and eight distinctive categories of CSR performance, according to which the evaluation of each company is based on. In each of these distinctive categories, a company's CSR performance is assessed by applying the CSR performance scale presented in Fig. 10.2, which relates a company's CRS performance, as demonstrated in their reports, with what is generally perceived as good CSR practices in literature. The analytical results for each company are presented in the following Fig. 10.3:

	Economic View		Environmental View		Social View			
Company	Economy	Market place	Environ-mental Impact	Internal Business Processes	Health & Safety	Human Res. (HR)	Society	Learning & Growth
Titan	◕	◔	●	◔	●	◕	◔	◔
Hellenic Petroleum	◕	◔	◐	◔	◕	◔	◔	◔
BP	●	◕	●	●	●	◕	◕	◔
Shell	●	◕	●	●	◕	◔	◕	◔
S&B	◕	◔	◔	◔	◕	◕	◔	◔
Vivartia	◕	○	◔	◔	○	◔	◔	◔
Siemens	●	◔	◐	◕	◔	◕	◕	◔
Coca-Cola HBC	◕	◔	◕	◔	◔	◔	◕	◔
Italcementy	●	◕	◕	◔	◔	◔	◔	◔

CSR Categories

Fig. 10.3 Results of CSR views and categories analysis

Based on the previous analysis, the following summary results can derive regarding the CSR performance demonstrated by all companies in the economic, environmental and social views:

- Economic performance was partially described mainly through the presentation of key financial indicators and the breakdown of revenues according to the relevant groups of stakeholders. The latter is due to the fact that companies perceive CSR reports as complementary to their annual reports and thus urge readers to review both reports in case a holistic view about economic performance is required. Furthermore, as companies are familiar with economic performance reporting, most CSR relevant reporting criteria, as defined by best practice standards, were already satisfied by their annual bulletins. Consequently, economic reporting among the examined companies showed a high degree of similarity.
- Environmental indicators identified in the examined reports fall into two different categories. The first contains established measures that were present in all reports and expresses the global concerns to offset climate change and control the use of natural resources such as carbon dioxide and other greenhouse gases' emissions, energy and water consumption and efficiency, waste management and recycling and the use of alternative materials. The second includes metrics tailored to the industry's specific attributes that track environmental performance in operations

with disparate results and thus do not allow comparability as they are usually guided by different international standards such as the Cement Sustainable Initiative (WBCSD/CSI) for the cement industry and the International Petroleum Industry Environmental Conservation Association (IPIECA/API) for the oil and gas industry.

- While economic and environmental indicators seek to measure more or less the same aspects (in the environmental category of performance measures, mostly due to the fact that legal requirements are common in nature for all companies), performance tracked by social indicators among the examined companies showed significant similarities but also great variation. Similarities concerned employ health and safety (an area where a national legal framework exists), decent labor, training and financial assistance though donations, charities and sponsorships. On the other hand, variations were apparent according to the type of industry. The cement and mining companies appeared to focus more on employee health and safety and quarry rehabilitation. The three petroleum and oil companies were giving more gravity on local communities' safety, the beverage companies on product development and customer health while Siemens utilized extensive metrics on work ethics.

Following the analysis of the CSR performance on each of the CRS views and categories, the study is completed by presenting additional findings on the approach demonstrated by the examined companies regarding the issues of CSR communications, management and governance in Fig. 10.4.

		Titan	Hellenic Petrol-eum	BP Hellas	Shell Hellas	S&B	Viva-rtia	Siemens Hellas	Coca-Cola Hellenic	Italce-menty
CSR & Communications	Stand-alone CSR report	✓	✓	✓	✓	✓	✗	✓	✓	✓
	Statement from the CEO	✓	✗	✓	✓	✓	✗	✓	✓	✓
	Online CSR report	✓	✓	✓	✓	✓	✗	✓	✓	✓
	Interim CSR report	✗	✗	✗	✗	✗	✗	✗	✗	✗
	# of pervious reports	4	2	9	10	6	n/a	n/a	4	3
CSR & Management	CSR mentioned in corporate Vision/Mission	✓	✗	✓	✓	✗	✓	✓	✓	✓
	CSR Director / Department	✓	✓	✓	✓	✓	✗	✗	✗	✓
	CSR strategy and objectives explicitly defined	✓	✗	✓	✓	✓	✗	✓	✓	✓
	CSR practices in the Supply Chain	✓	✗	✓	✓	✓	✗	✓	✓	✓
	SCR risks and opportunities identified	✓	✓	✓	✓	✓	✗	✓	✓	✓
CSR & Governance	SCR committee in the Bod	✓	✗	✓	✓	✗	✗	✗	✓	✓
	Degree of establishing Stakeholder engagement policies	High	Low	High	High	High	Mod/te	High	High	Mod/te
	External assurance	✓	✗	✓	✗	✗	✗	Partial	✓	Partial

Fig. 10.4   CSR in relation to communications, management and governance

Based on the findings, it appears that:

- All companies apart from Vivartia provide extensive focus on communicating their CSR performance.
- At management level, most companies demonstrate adequate efforts to embed CSR in the day-to-day decision making.
- At governance level, all companies seem to encourage stakeholder engagement however about half of them only have appointed CSR roles in the BoD or have requested external assurance so as to ensure that what is being said is being done.
- Companies with operations affecting more the environment such as the petroleum and cement ones appear to utilize more sophisticated CSR practices.
- Companies that are a part of a giant foreign group appear to be more CSR oriented in comparison to the ones initially established in Greece.

10.5 Conclusions

The very small number of manufacturing companies officially reporting CSR issues on an annual basis proves that CSR-orientation is found in an infant stage in Greece. This small number implies that CSR practice is still regarded as an optional and costly additional task affecting core business activity. The analysis of the companies in Greece, that are active in CSR shows that the existence of business performance criteria has been the reason for such a behavior. As a result, companies operating in an international environment, where social responsibility is translated in business efficiency and customer satisfaction, were the first to adopt a CSR-oriented approach, gaining a competitive advantage.

Materiality of CSR reports, meaning issues which have a non-financial risk at an operational level, is still without a sound definition, making it difficult for organisations to decide on what constitutes as an actual or potential corporate responsibility "risk" in the Greek marketplace. Furthermore, the global growth of corporate responsibility has led to an explosion of ethical league tables and benchmarks, all offering a different perspective of the discipline, causing confusion to the companies operating in the Greek market. This confusion was obvious in the CSR reports of the companies operating in the manufacturing sector in Greece. The identification of rather few common environmental and social indicators among the companies supports the above conclusion. However, it has to be stated, that to a certain degree, the sector a company operates determines the nature of the CSR indicators used.

The study of the performance measures used by the Greek manufacturing companies in their CSR reports and their comparison with their everyday business practices shows that was is being reported is actually being performed (although this assumption is mostly based on the results of external assurance which exists only in half of the cases). However, the question which still remains is whether enough is being reported. Although the quality and comprehensiveness of Greek CSR reports has improved in the last three years, it remains uneven. As a result, some include quantitative measures of nonfinancial performance, such as changes in carbon dioxide emissions. But not surprisingly, since the firms themselves choose what to report, they can tout their strengths and ignore their potential weaknesses.

The confusion surrounding CSR reporting may be affected by the lack of a single standardised reporting framework, which has led to the creation of numerous initiatives, codes, and guidelines. Although GRI seems to be the dominative framework in CSR issues of companies operating in Greece, the lack of a unified and well-defined approach by all companies raises concerns over future consistent clarity.

The European Union is also encouraging companies within its member states to adopt corporate responsibility policies, however there is still a vague suggestion of making it a mandatory reporting requirement. A first good step would be the legal obligation, at least of listed companies, to report on influential performance factors including employees, customers, supplies, and impact on the environment and the wider community will have to be detailed and explained. The development of new regulatory structures, providing minimum standards for activities covered by CSR, remains an effective means through which the behaviour of manufacturing SMEs will be changed in the short to medium-term, following the example of most successful and international companies presented in this paper. All of the above, together with the increased Greek societal demand for corporate social responsibility initiatives will help in the substantial professionalization of CSR work in Greek companies. CSR reporting is a means towards this professionalization by providing a more structured and spherical use of CSR principles. However, the small number of companies that are active in CSR issues in Greece proves there is still a long way to go.

References

Boatright, J.R., 2003. *Ethics and the Conduct of Business*, 4th edn. Hemel Hempstead: Prentice Hall.

Business for Social Responsibility Education Fund, 2000. *Corporate Social Responsibility: A Guide to Better Business Practices*. San Francisco: Business for Socially Responsible Education Fund, p. 179.

Carroll, A.B., 1999. Corporate social responsibility: evolution of a definitional construct. *Business and Society*, 38 (3), 268–295.

Fahy, M., Roche, J., Weiner, A., 2004. *Beyond Governance: Creating Corporate Value Through Performance and Responsibility*, New York: John Wiley & Sons, Ltd.

Frankental, P.G., 2001. Corporate social responsibility. *Corporate Communications*, 6 (1), 18–24.

Global Reporting Initiative, http://www.globalreporting.org.

Global Sullivan Principles, http://www.thesullivanfoundation.org/gsp/default.asp.

GRI, 2006. *Sustainability Reporting Guidelines*. Amsterdam: Global Reporting Initiative (GRI).

Hennigfeld, J., Pohl, M., Tolhurst, N., 2006. *The ICCA Handbook on Corporate Social Responsibility*, New York: John Wiley & Sons, Ltd.

Idowu, S.O., 2008. An empirical study of what institutions of higher education in the UK consider to be their corporate social responsibility. In: K. Aravossis, C.A. Brebbia, N. Gomez (Eds.), *WIT Transactions on Ecology and the Environment*, vol. 108, Southampton: WIT Press.

Idowu, S.O., Papasolomou, I., 2007. Are the corporate social responsibility matters based on good intentions or false pretences? An empirical study of the motivations behind the issuing of

CSR reports by UK companies. *Corporate Governance: International Journal of Business in Society*, 7 (2), 136–147.

Jones, T.M., 1995. Instrumental stakeholder theory: A synthesis of ethics and economics. *The Academy of Management Review*, 20, 404–437.

Jones, T.M., 1999. The institutional determinants of social responsibility. *Journal of Business Ethics*, 20 (2), 163–179.

Lantos, G.P.G., 2001. The boundaries of strategic corporate social responsibility. *Journal of Consumer Marketing*, 18 (7), 595–630.

Maltby, J., 2004. Hardfields Ltd: its annual general meetings 1903–1939 and their relevance for contemporary corporate social reporting. *The British Accounting Review*, 36 (4), 415–439.

McIntosh, M., Leipziger, D., Thomas, R., and Coleman, G., 2003. *Living Corporate Citizenship: Strategic Routes to Socially Responsible Business*, Prentice Hall, London.

McWilliams, A., Siegel, D., 2001. Corporate responsibility: a theory of the firm perspective. *The Academy of Management Review*, 26 (1), 117–127.

McWilliams, A., Siegel, D.S. and Wright, P.M., 2006. Introduction – corporate social responsibility: strategic implications. *Journal of Management Studies*, 26 (1), 1–18.

Panayiotou, N., Aravossis, K., Moschou, P., 2008. Contents of corporate social responsibility reports of companies in Greece. In: S.O. Idowu, W.L. Filho (Eds.), *Global Practices of Corporate Social Responsibility*. Berlin: Springer Verlag.

Pryce, V., 2002. CSR – should it be the preserve of the usual suspects? *Business Ethics: A European Review*, 11 (2), 140–142.

Social Accountability International, www.sa-intl.org.

Stainer, A. and Stainer, L., 2003. Editorial: business performance and corporate social responsibility. *International Journal of Business Performance Management*, 5 (2/3), 107–108.

The Economist Intelligence Unit, Greece, 2007. Country Profile, November 8.

United Nations Global Compact, http://www.unglobalcompact.org.

Van Marrewiijk, M., 2003. Concepts and definitions of CSR and corporate sustainability: between agency and communion. *Journal of Business Ethics*, 44 (2/3), 95–105.

Vogel, D., 2005. *The Market for Virtue: The Potential and Limits of Corporate Social Responsibility*, Washington, DC: Brooking Institution Press.

Webley, S., 2001. *Business Ethics: A European Review*, London: Blackwell Publishers Ltd.

Part III
Environment, Estate Management and Valuation and the Built Environment

Chapter 11
Corporate Social Responsibility: The Investor's Perspective

Céline Louche

The cynic knows the price of everything and the value of nothing.

Oscar Wilde

Abstract Investors are increasingly realising that a proactive approach to the management of a firm's social and environmental risks can result in considerable opportunities in both financial and sustainable value creation. This trend is being reflected in a significant increase in the number of corporations that are involved in what is called 'Responsible Investment' (RI) – that is approaches which integrate environmental, social, governance and ethical factors into investment processes.

This chapter explores the investor's perspective of the field of corporate social responsibility and more specifically on the practice of Responsible Investment (RI). The aim is threefold: firstly to provide a general background on Responsible Investment – definition, history, actors and trends, secondly, to give an overview of the existing practices of responsible investment and its key characteristics and finally to discuss some critical issues that may shape the future of RI.

RI is still a developing and changing activity which is expected to keep growing in the future. But responsible investors can play a major role in transforming the concept of investing by integrating social and environmental dimensions whilst simultaneously pushing up the issue in a company's CSR agenda.

11.1 Introduction

Investors like any other members of society have not remained indifferent to the concept of Corporate Social Responsibility (CSR). According to the Economist Intelligence Unit 2005 survey 85% of the investors consider CSR as a 'central' or 'important' consideration in investment decision (Economist Intelligence Unit,

C. Louche (✉)
Vlerick Leuven Gent Management School, Gent, Belgium

S.O. Idowu, W.L. Filho (eds.), *Professionals' Perspectives of Corporate Social Responsibility*, DOI 10.1007/978-3-642-02630-0_12,
© Springer-Verlag Berlin Heidelberg 2009

2005); a number which has almost doubled in five year (44% in 2000). This trend has been confirmed by other surveys that show that fund managers and financial analysts do not only believe in the relevance of CSR to assess companies' potential viability but also effectively use CSR related information in valuing firms (Taylor Nelson Sofres, 2003; Ambachtsheer, 2005; Guyatt, 2005; PLEON, 2005; Jaworski, 2007). Indeed CSR related information is believed to help to better manage investment risks and bolster long-term shareholder value as well as investment returns (CSR Europe, Deloitte et al., 2003; Jaworski, 2007).

As a result investment vehicles with specific CSR objectives have emerged. One of such prominent vehicles is Responsible Investment (RI). Responsible investment combines investment strategies to bring together the three dimensions of CSR, namely social, environmental and economic responsibilities. RI does not only seek to maximize financial returns but also to contribute to social betterment.

This paper provides insights into investors' perspective on and practices of corporate social responsibility and more importantly, it y focuses on the activity of Responsible Investment.

The paper is structured as follows. The first part provides background information on the history and development of the responsible investment it also gives an overview of the current trends and the actors involved in the field of RI. The second part focuses on the implementation of responsible investment. It introduces the three dimensions of RI, namely materiality focus, long term orientation and stakeholder perspective and then moves on to the consider different strategies and tools used in the RI industry. And finally, the last two parts present some discussion points and conclusions.

11.2 Introducing Responsible Investment

11.2.1 Investors and CSR

Investors constitute one of the core stakeholder groups that can affect companies' (Donaldson and Preston, 1995; Freeman, 1984; Freeman et al., 2007; Mitchell et al., 1997). As such they can play a major role in encouraging companies to engage in CSR. Nonetheless CSR concerns and adoption have been a neglected area of inquiry within the investment community. But changes have been taking place over last decade and a number of signs suggest a growing interest and implementation of CSR among members of the investment industry:

- Some investment management firms are presenting the CSR argument as a tool of competitive advantage. For example Generation IM believes that sustainability research integrated into a rigorous traditional investment process can strengthen fundamental investment analysis and deliver superior long term results (Generation IM, 2009).

- Studies are suggesting that worldwide, money managers are convinced that the adoption of RI practices and strategies will become a commonplace (Taylor Nelson Sofres, 2003; Ambachtsheer, 2005; Jaworski, 2007).
- Launch of several initiatives promoting responsible investment within the investment community. One of the most prominent initiatives is the Principles for Responsible Investment (PRI) launched in 2006, the PRI is a coalition of more than 400 institutional investors and asset managers with some $15 trillion dollars under management (Hobbs, 2008).
- An increasing number of studies on the link between corporate social performance (CSP) – and – corporate financial performance (CFP) have emerged (see for example (Pava and Krausz, 1996; Preston and O'Bannon, 1997; McWilliams and Siegel, 2000; Orlitzky et al., 2003). Margolis and Walsh (2003) counted 127 studies devoted to exploring the relationship between CSP-CFP in the period 1972–2002 (Margolis and Walsh, 2003).
- A large number of academic research has looked at the impacts of social and environmental aspects on stock valuation (see for example (Klassen and McLaughlin, 1996; Jones and Murrel, 2001; Bauer et al., 2002, 2007)

In December 2008, Günter Verheugen, Vice President of the European Commission, emphasised the importance of investors in boosting CSR during his speech at the CSR Alliance event. He also stated that 'there is indeed no other powerful incentive to consider the strategic role of corporate responsibility than an investor being able to value the role that it plays for the future prosperity and sustainability of a business' (Verheugen, 2008).

11.3 Defining Responsible Investment

Responsible Investment (RI) can be described as an investment strategy which seeks to generate both financial and sustainable value. It consists of a set of investment approaches that integrate environmental, social and governance (ESG) and ethical issues into financial analysis and decision-making (Hutton et al., 1998; Cowton, 1999; Eurosif, 2003; 2006; Mercer and UNEP Financial Initiative, 2007). The 2005 World Economic Forum's report specifies that it takes 'into account the impact of investments on wider society and the natural environment, both today and in the future' (World Economic Forum, 2005).

Over the past four decades, Responsible Investment has mainly focused on the equities market, where it has been variously described. Names such as ethical investing, socially responsible investing, sustainability investing, triple-bottom-line investing and best-of-class investing have been used. However, as we will discuss in the last part, RI can be implemented in different investment asset classes.

RI is a product and a practice. It is a product in the sense that investors acquire, hold or dispose of company's shares that are estimated to be sustainable. It is a practice in the sense that RI is a way to identify the best performing, sustainable and responsible companies (Boxenbaum and Gond, 2005). Based on ESG and financial criteria fund managers evaluate and judge the corporate sustainability performance of firms.

11.4 History

The definition and practices of RI have evolved and changed over time. Three main periods can be identified, each of them showing an increasing complexity in the methods used to practice RI, and a change in terms of actors involved.

The first period, relatively long period and deeply anchored in the United States, dates back to the eighteenth Century (Domini, 2001). The first embryonic forms of RI were dominated by the use of negative exclusion criteria. For hundreds of years, many religious investors whose traditions embrace peace and non-violence have actively avoided investing in certain kinds of enterprises, the so-called 'sin' stocks – alcohol, tobacco, weapons and gambling. Church groups like the Methodists and Society of Friends (Quakers) have long imposed certain social screening of their investment activity. However this form of RI attracted limited attention.

The *second period* can be traced back to the 1970s. It marks the beginnings of contemporary RI with new issues and new actors driving the movement but also the start of RI in Europe. It grew in large part from political roots and the major protest movements. The Vietnam War and apartheid in South Africa are examples of such issues fuelled by the RI community especially in the US. A number of investors refused to support the war and such a regime. Other citizen movements such as the civil rights movement, women's right and environmental protestors joined RI to lobby against industrial activities seen as non ethical (Louche and Lydenberg, 2006). RI reached a major milestone in 1970 when the US consumer advocate and environmentalist; Ralph Nader succeeded in getting two socially-based resolutions on the General Motors annual meeting proxy ballot. The first so-called RI fund was launched in 1971 in the US, the Pax World Fund.

In the 1980s, RI started to develop also in Europe. The first UK RI fund was launched in 1984 by Friends Provident Stewardship Unit Trust. It began to develop more broadly in Europe towards the end of the 1980s and early 1990s with a clear emphasise on environmental issues. Many RI funds were based on a positive and restrictive approach which encourage investing only in very specific sectors usually linked to the environment; such as renewable energy. It is also called the 'green funds'.

During the second period, RI spread in an impassioned political climate and was transformed from a clerical activity (attempts to use ethical principles in the construction of investment portfolios) into a public awareness of 'ethical' investment (the self-conscious phenomena of RI) (Sparkes, 2001). RI was used as a vehicle to coerce corporations to change their strategy towards responsible and ethical practices.

The beginning of the twenty first century heralded a turning point for RI both in terms of approach and growth. The *third period* has been characterised by the main-streaming of the activity on RI. As a result of its embracement by major financial institutions, RI has shifted its image away from activism to becoming a commer-cial project (Déjean et al., 2004; Louche, 2004). As a consequence, not only did the name used for this activity change but there was also a resurgent of a new approach to RI. 'Responsible Investment', as used in this chapter, is a recent phenomenon. During the previous periods, the activity was referred as 'ethical', 'mission based' or 'socially responsible' investment. The new RI approach is based on a more diver-sified, positive and quantified approach. One of the key developments in terms of methodology is the best in class approach. It consists of benchmarking companies in terms of their corporate sustainability performance. Companies are not excluded or included on the basis of pure involvement in certain activities or sectors (the neg-ative and positive approach) but on the basis of their performance. Companies from the same sector are compared and only the best performing ones are selected for the investment universe. The objective of RI products is not only to promote cer-tain principles and values but also to create value. Although the exclusion approach is still in use today, often in combination with the best in class, the tendency is to reduce or even eliminate negative screens.

11.5 Trends

RI has grown dramatically especially since the 2000s. A number of factors can be used to explain this dramatic growth from both the supply and demand side of the financial markets – e.g. legislative imperatives and requirements of funds, mar-ket opportunities, personal preferences and believes of investors (Cullis and Lewis, 1992; Michelson et al., 2004).

Although RI has diffused and spread worldwide (see Fig. 11.1), its growth is best illustrated in the US and European contexts. In the U.S., the first RI fund was launched in 1971 by 2007; it had expanded to the extent of reaching a target of more than 260 RI funds. In 2007, RI assets under management were of $2.71 trillion, representing an increase of 324% since 1995. It means that one out of every nine dollars under professional management is using a RI Strategy, – 11% of the $25.1 trillion in total assets under management (US SIF, 2008). According to the US SIF, RI is growing at a much faster pace than the broader universe of all investment assets under professional management: an increase of 18% against 3% between 2005 and 2007.

In Europe, the first RI fund was created in 1984 in the UK. At the end of 2007, there were 447 RI funds available (Lipper FERI, 2008). Between 2002 and 2007, the number of RI funds has increased by 150%. Eurosif has valued the RI market[1] at €2.665 trillion as at December 31, 2007, an increase by 102% between 2005 and

---

[1] This estimation include the broad and core RI as defined by Eurosif (2008).

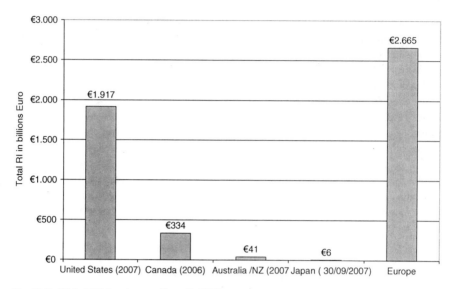

Fig. 11.1 Global RI data (source Eurosif, 2008)

2007 (Eurosif, 2008). Institutional investors represent a very significant part of the RI market as they hold 94% of RI assets under management. The Core RI represents a total of €511.7 billion and €2.154 trillion for Broad RI.[2] RI accounts for 17.6% of total European funds under management (Eurosif, 2008). Although there is a general growing trend towards RI in Europe, the leading countries are by far UK and the Netherlands (Eurosif, 2008). But the most proactive countries for new RI funds launched in 2007 were Belgium, France and the UK (Lipper FERI, 2008). It is also interesting to note that in Norway, the UK and Netherlands, the State Pension Funds are clearly taking the lead in RI.

The recent trend in the RI market is the development of the thematic funds. Thematic funds focus either on sectors or issues such as energy efficiency, climate change, renewable energy, water or health and nutrition. Thematic funds have multiplied over the last couple of years. According to Lipper FERI, 13 out of 20 top RI funds in Europe by estimated net sales were thematic funds. The top 10 thematic funds represented a total of €22 billion in March 2008.

---

[2]Eurosif defines Core RI as all funds that include either ethical exclusions (more than two negative criteria applied), positive screening, including Best-in-Class and RI, Theme Funds, or a combination of ethical exclusion and positive screening. Broad RI consists of all funds including simple screening, including norms-based screening (up to two negative criteria), engagement, or integration.

11.6 Actors Involved in RI

Actors involved in the Responsible Investment field can be classified into three categories:

- Investors: this group refers to the different types of investors investing in responsible investment funds.
- Rators: this group refers to rating organisations and Responsible Investment indices.
- Connectors: it refers to initiatives and platforms related to responsible investment that bring together actors of the field (all or some of them) in new combinations and venues.

11.6.1 Investors' Type

There are two main groups of investors: retail and institutional investors. Retail investors are individuals who purchase small amounts of equities for him/herself, as opposed to institutional investors who are corporate entities that invest large amounts, such as investment companies, mutual funds, brokerages, insurance companies, pension funds, investment banks and endowment funds.

The US and Japan RI markets are dominated by retail investors while the dominant type of investors in Europe are institutional (Louche and Lydenberg, 2006; Sakuma and Louche, 2008). Historically, isolated individuals within the world of finance and small institutions have been the most involved in the RI field. Institutional investors represent 11% of the total assets in all RI funds in 2007 (US SIF, 2008). Compared to Europe, the government has not played an active role in promoting RI. In several European countries, law and regulations have been enacted requiring especially pension funds to publicly state the degree to which they take into consideration social and environmental aspects in their investment decisions. The precursor legislation was the U.K. Pension Act issued in 1999 and implemented in 2000. Since then regulations have flourished in a number of other European countries: Sweden (2001), Germany (2001), Belgium (2004), Italy (2004), Austria (2002), Netherlands (2001), France (2001), and Spain (2003). Those legislations have been significant drivers in the growth of RI in Europe (Solomon et al., 2002) and explain the importance of institutional investors in the European RI landscape (for more detailed information see Eurosif (2003)).

11.6.2 Rators

Reliable information on social, environmental and governance performance is an important prerequisite for investment decisions in line with RI principles. That explains why raters are such important actors in the RI field. Two main groups can be distinguished among the raters: the rating organisations and the Responsible Investment indices.

Rating organisations play a very central role in the RI field. They are rating agencies that screen companies using social, environmental, corporate governance and ethical criteria. They act as providers of information services (e.g. company profiles, ranking, sector analysis, etc). Information is used mainly for investment decisions or shareholder engagement activities. While there are commonly applied standards for financial reporting, non financial information like ESG information is rather inconsistent among companies making the evaluation of the CSR performance of companies a difficult task and requiring some expertise. In 2003, ORSE counted 33 rating organisations (ORSE, 2003).

Responsible Investment indices are stock market indices to measure and benchmark companies' performance on ESG indicators. Many of the major stock markets have established RI indices. There are more than 30 RI indices around the world but the most popular are the Domini Social 400 (US) created in 1990, the Jones Sustainability Index (DJSI) launched in 1999 and the FTSE4Good Index (UK) launched in 2001.

11.6.3 Connectors

Connectors are all type of venues facilitating networking, meeting, and exchange. They are very important as they enable actors to connect, share and develop knowledge, and build an identity. The platforms and initiatives bring together professionals, academics or a mix of the two. Two of the earliest actors in this group are the US based organisation the Council on Economic Priorities (CEP) and Interface Centre in Corporate Responsibility (ICCR) both created in the early 1970s. In 1991 the first Social Investment Forum was set up in the US. As at December 2007, twelve SIFs were in existence throughout the world including one European SIF, the Eurosif. Those membership associations are dedicated to advancing the concept, practice, and growth of responsible investing. SIF's membership includes more than 500 social investment practitioners and institutions, including financial professionals, analysts, portfolio managers, banks, mutual funds, researchers, foundations, community development organizations, and public educators. Those initiatives are both national and international. The most prominent and influential initiative that has been set in 2006 is the Principle for Responsible Investment (Section 11.2 above). In relation to RI, there are also, a range of new organisations that have emerged which have been described as part of an emerging 'Civil Economy'. Those organisations seek to influence investors and the ultimate owners of the funds to factor in the externalities of business and seek the integration of ESG factors. These include organisation like Enhanced Analytics Initiatives and others like Carbon Disclosure Project, and Fair pensions.

Next to the more professional platforms, are a number of academic RI initiatives that have been created. Just to mention a few: the Moskowitz award, an initiative created in the United States in 1996, the Sustainable Investment Research Platform, initiated in 2006 in Sweden, and the European Center for Corporate Engagement (ECCE) based in the Netherlands and was officially launched in 2007 (Table 11.1).

Table 11.1 Classification of the actors involved in responsible investment

Actors' category	Description	Examples
Investors	• Retail investors • Institutional investors	*Pension Funds with RI strategies*: ABP (NL), AP2 (SE), ARIA (AU), Caisse de dépôt et placement du Québec (CA), CalPERS (US), CIA (CH), The Environment Agency Pension Fund (UK), ERAFP (FR), Fonds de Réserve pour les Retraites (FR), Government Pension Fund (TH), Metallrente (DE), Norges Bank (for Government Pension Fund) (NO), PGGM (NL), PREVI (BR), TIAA-CREF (US) (*Source: Insight Investment*)
Raters	• Social rating agencies • Responsible Investment indices	• *Rating agencies*: Vigeo (FR); KLD (US); EIRIS (UK); Innovest (US); Good Bankers (JP); Jantzi Research (CA), Centre Info (CH), DSR (NL), SAM (CH), Trucost (UK), Scoris (DE), SIRIS (AU) • *Indices*: FTS4Good, Domini 400 Social Index, Dow Jones Sustainability Index Family, MS-SRI, ASPI, DAXglobal Sarasin Sustainability, Ethibel Sustainability Index, ECPI Index Family, HSBC Global Climate Change Benchmark Index
Connectors	• Responsible Investment initiatives & Platforms	• *Practitioner platforms & initiatives*: Social Investment Forum (SIF), Principles for Responsible Investment (PRI), Enhanced Analytics Initiative (EAI), Carbon Disclosure Project (CDP), Fair Pensions, Pharma Futures • *Research platforms*: European Centre for Corporate Engagement (ECCE), Moskowitz award, Sustainable Investment Research Platform

11.7 Implementing Responsible Investment

11.7.1 Key Dimensions

There are three main aspects which characterise RI, namely the focus on materiality, the long term orientation and the stakeholder perspective. They are all three participants playing an important role in shaping the implementation of RI. Although there is a variation in the understanding and translation of these three aspects, they are definitively at the core of RI.

11.7.2 Materiality Focus

Investors have a very specific approach to CSR in the sense that they focus on factors that generate value. There is an increasing believe among investors that responsible corporate behaviour can have a positive influence on the financial performance of companies – particularly over the long term (McKinsey, 2009). ESG information helps investors to be better placed to manage risk and make better informed investment decisions (Lydenberg, 2007). But the challenge for investors is to identify the relevant information and understand which forms the myriad of issues that companies are confronted with might significantly affect companies.

As pointed out by the SustainAbility report in 2002, companies communicate increasingly ESG information but they sometimes over-communicate information on ESG, which makes it difficult for investors to decipher what they are looking for (SustAinability, 2002). Indeed what investors are looking for are issues that are of material nature.

The concept of materiality comes from the field of financial auditing, and relates to the 'impacts that would cause an informed person to reach a different conclusion to make a different decision about representations shown in financial statements' (in Beloe et al., 2004). The focus is on identifying information that might be useful to decision making. In the context of CSR, the scope of materiality needs to be widened and its definition revisited to bridge the gap between the narrow focus of financial materiality and the wide lens of stakeholder perspective (Forstater et al., 2006).

Materiality requires identifying issues that (1) matter and are significant for the company and (2) are of importance to stakeholders. According to AccountAbility, 'an issue or concern becomes material if it can influence the decisions, actions and behaviour of stakeholders or the organization' (Forstater et al., 2006). Judgements are based on relevance (what matters) and significance (how much it matters), meaning that some relevant issues may not be material because they are not sufficiently significant. 'Issues that are material to key stakeholder groups can very quickly become financially material to a company' (Beloe et al., 2004)

However, it is important to differentiate between financially and non-financially material ESG factors (Lydenberg, 2007). Some ESG factors can be directly related to the individual price of stocks or the market valuation of whole industries. This is due to the fact that environmental, social and governance factors inherently require a long term perspective. Risks and reward which are related to CSR issues are best measured in years or even decades, not months or quarters. Environmental issues like climate change, resource depletion, but also environmental legislation or implementation an environmental management systems need to be looked at over several years. Social issues similarly require assessment in the long term such as adequacy of working conditions within the supply chain or implementation of a diversity policy. Those long term issues are not captured by the short term price speculation of the stock market but they do inform on the future value of the company in the long term. Therefore non financial material issues do add value to the investments with a long term appreciation.

11.7.3 Long Term Perspective

Excessive focus on quarterly earnings and incentives structures encourage corporations and investors to pursue short-term gain with inadequate regard to long term effects (Aspen Institute, 2008), which ultimately has various detrimental effects. It causes misallocation of assets; introduce dangerous volatility into financial markets; generate social and environmental damages (Tonello, 2006; Lydenberg, 2007).

RI provides an alternative to the excessive short-termism. They are long term in their perspective.

> Long term investors speculate on the value of corporations to society and the environment, while simultaneously seeking to enhance that value at the company, industry and society level (Lydenberg, 2007)

Long term investing has been encouraged by a number of organisations like CFA Institute, the Conference Board, the United Nations, the World Economic Forum and the Aspen Institute. In 2007, the Aspen Institute with an influential group of CEOs, business organisations, institutional investors, labour unions, corporate lawyers, accountants and consultants has produced guiding principles for corporations and investors, the 'Guidelines for Long Term Value Creation' (Aspen Institute, 2008). These principles seek to introduce long term bias in corporate and investment decision-making.

As mentioned earlier in this paper, many ESG issues require a long term perspective as it is looking at the long term societal and environmental impact of businesses. There are two additional arguments. RI is not meant to condemn business but rather to engage in a process of dialogue with businesses to help and encourage them to improve their CSR performance. For this purpose it is important to establish a trust relationship between investors (or shareholders) and companies and to give companies the opportunity to change. The other argument is more pragmatic as it has to do with financial performance. RI is based on the assumption that the financial performance gains from improved CSR performance accrue in the long term. Although there is not a general consensus on this, but research suggests that the relationship between CSR and financial performance is more likely to be positively correlated in the long term because of the potential favourable impact of CSR issues upon long run risk and return (Graves and Waddock, 2000; Cox et al., 2004) Cox et al., Hillman and Keim (2001) argue that good CSR activities can contribute positively to 'long term value creation'. A number of studies have argued that corporate social performance (CFP) and corporate financial performance (CFP) might be positively related in the long run (Moskowitz, 1972; Cochran and Wood, 1984; Hart, 1995; Waddock and Grave, 1997; Ruf et al., 2001). Others have shown that a low CSR performance may increase financial risks (Alexander and Buchholz, 1978; Ullman, 1985; McGuire et al., 1988).

11.7.4 Stakeholder Approach

At the core of RI is the stakeholder approach. RI evaluates firms in terms of the company's response to multiple stakeholders. Indeed as Clarkson (1995) argues, that the business world can be considered as responsible towards society as a whole, however corporations can only be held responsible towards their stakeholders (Clarkson, 1995).

Stakeholders have been broadly defined in the literature as different groups that could be affected and/or could affect the deployment of its operations (Freeman, 1984). They are characterized by a set of three key attributes: power, legitimacy and urgency (Mitchell et al., 1997).

As suggested by the stakeholder theory, RI is based on a presentation of corporations centred on management and captured by the various relationships between managers and stakeholder groups, including typically: employees, customers, suppliers, shareholders, the ecological environment and the local community. CSR requires companies to consider and balance the social and environmental interests of its stakeholders. Therefore RI has a direct interest in the specific nature of the firm's interactions with society and with its multiple stakeholders.

As a consequence and to ensure a multi-stakeholder evaluation, RI analysts base their evaluation on multiple sources including the firm itself but also a wide range of stakeholders and the media.

11.8 RI Approaches

Responsible investors are not a homogenous group. They have different expectations, interests and motivations to implement RI. As a result RI is being implemented through a variety of approaches which are not necessarily exclusive but could be combined. Table 11.2 provides an overview of the different strategies and tools used for the different strategies.

Table 11.2 RI strategies

Strategies		Tools
Avoidance	Avoid investing in companies engaged in certain business areas or practices	Negative screening e.g. tobacco, alcohol, gambling
Support	Support certain sectors or exceptional practices	Positive or thematic screening e.g. environmental technologies, bicycles, but also water, energy
Comparative	Benchmark companies' performance and take the leading ones.	Best-in-class Includes a broad range of ESG criteria (see Table 11.3)
Engagement	Engage with companies on ESG issues	Shareholder activism, dialogue e.g. shareholder resolutions, proxy voting, or closed door dialogue

11.8.1 Avoidance

This approach aims to avoid investing in companies that are engaged in business areas or practices which are morally unacceptable, or problematic. It is based on the exclusion of certain sectors or activities.

Avoidance uses negative screening. It includes in a number of screens that serve to exclude companies or sectors from the investment universe based on criteria relating to their products, services, policies, or actions; e.g. tobacco, alcohol, gambling, human rights violation and child labour. In general, the types of exclusions applied are tailored to the value sets of individual and institutional investors targeted by the fund manager. These may vary considerably from one fund to the next.

According to some recent reports, as much as 70% of the American and European RI industries may employ some kind of avoidance strategy, which makes it the dominant strategy in RI (Eurosif, 2008; US SIF, 2008).

11.8.2 Support

This approach aims to seek out and invest in companies engaged in business areas or practices which in some way benefit society.

Support is based on positive or thematic screening. Those screens seek out investments in companies engaged in activities with positive social or environmental benefits. It includes companies that demonstrate a significant involvement in business activities that are seen to be inherently beneficial to society. Positive screens can differ a lot among funds. For example Triodos Meerwaardefondsen, a Dutch RI fund, has defined a number of 'sustainable' activities which are regarded as positive screen such as environmental technology and bicycles.

This strategy is less employed than the avoidance strategy– according to Eurosif < 10% of the European RI industry employs it (Eurosif, 2008).

11.8.3 Comparative

This approach aims at selecting sector leaders on Environmental, Social and Governance criteria. Table 11.3 provides examples of ESG criteria used by the RI industry.

Table 11.3 Examples of environmental, social and governance (ESG) issues

Environmental (E)	Social (S)	Governance (G)
• Emissions	• Stakeholder relations	• Board structure
• Environmental policies	• Working conditions	• Independent directors
• Environmental management system	• Respect of human rights	• Independent leadership
• Toxic chemicals	• Diversity	• Separation of Chairman and CEO
• Genetic engineering	• Health and safety	• Remuneration
• Pollution	• HIV/AIDS	• Shareholder rights
• Water	• Product safety	• Accounting quality
• Use of resources	• Treatment of customers	• Audit quality
• Waste	• Labour relations	• Board skills

Comparative approach uses the best in class method. Companies are compared to their sector or industry group peers. It aims to invest across all industry sectors, but to select the best performing companies in each sector.

11.8.4 Engagement

This approach aims at entering into a dialogue with companies. This can be done by investing in companies which are engaged in business areas or practices which are regarded as morally unacceptable and use shareholder influence to make them change. The engagement approach can be done via confrontative or soft actions.

Confrontative actions are also called shareholder activism. It refers to shareholders' actions to exercise their rights to raise issues with management by introducing and voting on resolutions at companies' annual general meetings.

> They [the shareholders] loudly demand more environmental protection, more social justice, and the maintenance of human rights in the annual general meetings of shareholders (Critical Shareholders, 2002).

Owning stocks in a publicly traded corporation brings with it the responsibilities of ownership, as well as the opportunity to influence corporate behaviour. Over the last 30 years, shareholder activism has emerged as a popular strategy for those seeking to influence corporate behaviour on a broad range of issues. Shareholders actively invest and use their positions to affect corporate behaviour. Shareholders have the right to align directors' interests with those of shareholders and hold them to account for the management and performance of the company (Forum for the Future, 2002). Shareholders can act independently but often they charge an organisation to represent them as a group. By gathering their voices they have more impact. In the Netherlands, VBDO engages with companies in order to direct corporate polices and behaviour towards the goal of sustainable performance. In the US, Interfaith Centre on Corporate Responsibility, an international coalition of 300 institutional investors mainly religious investors with combined portfolios worth an estimated $45 billion, have been primary proponents of shareholder resolutions on social issues in recent years. Although few proposals on social issues earn a majority of votes, shareholders' engagement is an important tool in reaching management and initiating dialogue (Forum for the Future, 2002).

A softer approach is to start a dialogue with corporate managers (direct engagement conducted privately), writing letters to companies (cf. Carbon Disclosure Project) or to institutional investors and sending out press releases.

Between 30 and 40% of the US and European RI industry is engaged in some kind of shareholder activism (Eurosif, 2008; US SIF, 2008) but activities under the dialogue strategy differ a lot in the US and Europe. While the US RI industry is very active in shareholder resolution and public engagement, Europe is more active in direct private engagement (Louche and Lydenberg, 2006).

Although the avoidance strategy is still one of the dominant approaches in the RI industry, it is increasingly criticised for being too limited in its impact and scope and also for conveying the wrong message (too negative rather than stimulating companies to improve their CSR commitments) (Cowton, 1999). During these last few years, RI strategies have shifted from a negative to a more positive approach based not solely on avoidance. The trend is to develop a combined strategy based on a combination of tools–positive screening, negative screening as well engagement– to achieve a variety of objectives.

11.9 Discussion

RI has not only grown over time but it has also gained recognition among the financial as well as the boarder business community. But RI is not yet a mature field. The practice and definition of RI are still a work in progress to some extent. Changes and development are expected in the future and numerous questions still need to be debated and answered. In this section three issues are addressed: the first relates to the mainstreaming of RI, the second to fiduciary duties and the third to RI across all asset classes.

11.9.1 RI: A Niche or Mainstream?

The globalisation and intensification of the RI industry has led to the conclusion that RI is becoming mainstream (Friedman and Miles, 2001; Sparkes and Cowton, 2004; World Economic Forum, 2005; Zadek et al., 2005). A study led by Mercer Investment Consulting shows that 84% of European investment managers surveyed expect the integration of ESG factors to become mainstream within 6–10 years (Ambachtsheer, 2005). As already claimed in this chapter, RI has become a source of competitive advantage and differentiation for many financial institutions. But also the new regulatory pressures, the emerging collaborative initiatives such as the PRI or the Enhanced Analytics Initiatives (EAI), the growing shareholder activism and engagement, and the increase transparency of companies making evaluation possible are stimuli to mainstream RI.

There are clear progress being made towards mainstreaming, however the RI industry remains a relatively small activity within the financial sector and still seems to struggle to get fully accepted by the financial mainstream community. If RI is to become mainstreamed it still has to overcome a number of barriers such as:

- The lack of tools and models allowing the quantification of ESG data into stock valuation practices. The 2005s WBCSD YMT and the UNEP FI survey showed that young financial analysts felt unequipped to incorporate ESG issues into mainstream company analysis (WBCSD and UNEP Finance Initiative, 2005; Jaworski, 2007).
- The need for a cross-fertilisation between mainstream RI and ESG specialists in order to create new knowledge and new understandings is very paramount. A cross fertilisation would also help to facilitate a more holistic picture of the firm

rather than dividing on one side social and environmental issues and on the other financial factors.

- The communication gap between companies and investors. Although companies may be very active with regard to CSR, it seems that there is a communication problem between companies and investors: companies do not always communicate the information to investors in a way that would enable these investors to use the information in to evaluate the firm's performance and also firms do not communicate clearly the information investors expect from companies in terms of their CSR activities. A joint project has been established between the European Academy of Business in Society (EABIS) and the European Alliance for CSR with the backing from the European Commission[3] to develop a European framework for improved company and investor dialogue on ESG issues.
- The need to change the conventions of the investment community (Guyatt, 2005). A number of investment practices are 'conventional' meaning that they are recognised and accepted by all. For example, practices such as stock valuation models used by financial analysts are generally accepted and implemented by investment agents. In this context the diffusion of new practices such as RI is very difficult.
- The behavioural impediments. One of the dominant impediments is the short-termism of the financial market (Guyatt, 2006; Juravle and Lewis, 2008) which is going against the long term orientation of RI.

11.9.2 RI: Contradictory to Fiducially Duties?

Financial institutions are influenced by some long-established legal principles on how to manage the capital of their investors. Professional managers of investment funds such as pension funds, pension plan, or all others entrusted with management of other people's investments are legally bound to meet their fiduciary duties. They are obliged by these duties to invest carefully in the best interests of their beneficiaries (not to cause harm to the best interests of their beneficiaries or clients) and in accordance with the purposes of the particular fund. Interests usually are usually assessed using financial measures.

One may wonder whether or not fiduciary duties hinder the practice of RI. This argument has been used to restrict the use of social and environmental issues in investment decisions. A study on capital markets undertaken in Canada for the National Round Table on the Environment and the Economy concluded that 'current interpretations of the fiduciary duties of pension fund managers may unnecessarily constrain their ability to address the full range of relevant corporate responsibility considerations related to prospective investments'.[4]

---

[3] The EU laboratory is led by Lloyds TSB and Telecom Italia with participation from the business network CSR Europe. The research is being coordinated by Cranfield School of Management together with Vlerick Leuven Gent Management School and Bocconi School of Management. For more information www.investorvalue.org.

[4] Stratos Inc. (2004).

Indeed as an investment intermediary does not have the mandate to invest their clients' money according to a CSR perspective, the assumption there is that they must choose investments that maximize financial returns for their beneficiaries. A breach of the fiduciary duties is liable calls for the intermediary to compensate beneficiaries for losses attributable to this breach of duty (Richardson, 2007).

However, recently the debate has been re-opened on the definition of the scope of these duties and whether or not ESG issues should drive the consideration of large institutional investors (Lydenberg and Sinclair, 2009). In 2005, Freshfields Bruckhous Deringer, a law firm, concluded that investment managers' fiduciary duties should not necessarily preclude or overly hamper RI (Freshfields Bruckhaus Deringer, 2005). According to this report ESG information should be taken into account whenever it is relevant to the investment strategy. As the link between ESG factors and financial performance is increasingly being recognised, the integration of ESG is not only permissible but even advisable. Therefore fulfilling fiduciary obligations can actually require careful attention to corporate social and environmental performance. But the fundamental question about understanding the 'best interest' of the beneficiaries still remains to be debated. Is the best interest simply based on the price performance or does it also involve the broader societal implications which indirectly or directly may affect their non financial interests? (Lydenberg and Sinclair, 2009).

11.9.3 RI: A Practice for all Asset Classes?

The main focus of RI has been on equities –stock of quoted companies. But the concept of responsible investment can be applied equally across all asset classes (Lydenberg, 2008; UK SIF, 2008; Lydenberg and Sinclair, 2009). In 2007, the Institute for Responsible Investment published a Handbook on Responsible Investment across Asset Classes (Wood and Hoff, 2007). The handbook provides an overview for investors on how they can implement responsible investment in practices, across a wide range of asset classes and investment opportunities.

A number of new approaches and products in other asset classes have been developed embedding the RI concept such as microfinance that use cash to empower the poorest, venture capital to support alternative business models or real estate that emphasise on green building and sustainable communities. These initiatives show that there is a huge potential to widen the scope of responsible investment and thereby increase the RI market.

11.10 Conclusion

This paper has provided some insight into the investor's perspective on CSR. Investors, as a key stakeholder group, can be important catalysts for change towards sustainability. Interest of investors in CSR is reflected in the significant increase in the number of Responsible Investment practices. The expectation is that RI will keep growing and evolving in the near future. Although the focus has been essentially on equities, RI is starting to infiltrate a broader range of assets classes. The practices of RI are not homogenous. Indeed RI can be based on different strategies which can be combined in a variety of ways. In this chapter we have identified four types of strategies; namely avoidance, support, comparative and engagement. RI is still in a work in progress stage; it is still evolving. There are a number of issues and questions which still remain unanswered leaving the door wide open for creativity and innovation as well as to social, environmental and economic opportunities to take place over the next few years or even decades in this field.

References

Alexander, G. J. and T. A. Buchholz (1978). "Corporate social responsibility and stock market performance." *Academy of Management Journal* **21**(3): 479–486.

Ambachtsheer, J. (2005). *SRI: what do investment managers think?* Toronto, ON: Mercer Investment Consulting.

Aspen Institute (2008). Long-Term Value Creation: Guiding Principles for Corporations and Investors. http://www.aspeninstitute.org/atf/cf/{DEB6F227-659B-4EC8-8F84-8DF23 CA704F5}/FinalPrinciples.pdf.

Bauer, R., J. Derwall, et al. (2007). "The ethical mutual fund performance debate: new evidence from Canada." *Journal of Business Ethics* **70**(2): 111–124.

Bauer, R., K. Koedijk, et al. (2002). "International evidence on ethical mutual fund performance and investment style."

Beloe, S., J. Scherer, et al. (2004). *Values for money: reviewing the quality of SRI research.* London: SustainAbility and Mistra.

Boxenbaum, E. and J. -P. Gond (2005). "Importing 'socially responsible investment' in France and Quebec: work of contextualisation across varieties of capitalism."

Clarkson, M. B. E. (1995). "A stakeholder framework for analyzing and evaluating corporate social performance." *Academy of Management Review* **20**(1): 92–117.

Cochran, P. L. and R. A. Wood (1984). "Corporate social responsibility and financial performance." *Academy of Management Journal* **27**(1): 42–56.

Cowton, C. J. (1999). "Playing by the rules: ethical criteria at an ethical investment fund." *Business Ethics: A European Review* **8**(1): 60–69.

Cox, P. B., S. Brammer, and A. Millington (2004). "An empirical examination of institutional investor preferences for corporate social performance." *Journal of Business Ethics* **52**(1): 27–43.

Critical Shareholders (2002). "Association of critical shareholders in Germany." Retrieved 16 April 2002.

CSR Europe, Deloitte, et al. (2003). *Investing in responsible business.* Brussels: Corporate Social Responsibility Europe.

Cullis, J. G. and A. Lewis (1992). "Paying to be good? U.K. ethical investments." *Kyklos* **45**(1): 3–23.

Déjean, F., J.-P. Gond, et al. (2004). "Measuring the unmeasured: an institutional entrepreneur's strategy in an emerging industry." *Human Relations* **57**(6): 741–764.

Domini, A. L. (2001). *Socially responsible investing: making a difference in making money.* Chicago, IL: Dearborn Trade.

Donaldson, T., and Preston, L. (1995). The stakeholder theory of the corporation: Concepts, evidence, and implications. *Academy of Management Review*, 20(1): 65–91.

Economist Intelligence Unit (2005). *The importance of corporate responsibility.* London: Economist Intelligence Unit.

Eurosif (2003). Socially Responsible Investment among European Institutional Investors: 2003 Report. Paris.

Eurosif (2006). European SRI Study.

Eurosif (2008). European SRI Study.

Forstater, M., S. Zadek, et al. (2006). *The materiality report – Aligning strategy, performance and reporting*. London, UK: AccountAbility.

Forum for the Future (2002). "Sustainability pays." http://www.cis.co.uk/socacc2002/pdf/SusPays.pdf.

Freeman, R. (1984). *Strategic management: a stakeholder perspective*. Englewood Cliffs, NJ: Prentice-Hall.

Freeman, R. E., Harrison, J. S., and Wicks, A. C. (2007). *Managing for Stakeholders: Survival, Reputation, and Success*: Yale University Press.

Freshfields Bruckhaus Deringer (2005). A legal framework for the integration of environmental, social and governance issues into institutional investment, UNEP FI.

Friedman, A. L. and S. Miles (2001). "Socially responsible investment and corporate social and environmental reporting in the UK: an explorative study." *Brithish Accounting Review* **33**: 523–548.

Generation IM (2009). Generation Investment Management LLP. www.generationim.com.

Graves, S. B. and S. A. Waddock (2000). "Built to last and then some. An evaluation of stakeholder relations in 'built-to-last' companies." *Business and Society Review* **105**(4): 393–418.

Guyatt, D. J. (2005). "Finance and accounting: meeting objectives and resisting conventions. A focus on institutional investors and long-term responsible investing." *Journal of Corporate Governance* **5**(3): 139–150.

Guyatt, D. J. (2006). Identifying and Overcoming Behavioural Impediments to Long Term Responsible Investments – a Focus on UK Institutional Investors. Department of Psychology, University of Bath.

Hart, S. L. (1995). "A natural resource-based view of the firm." *Academy of Management Review* **20**(4): 986–1014.

Hillman, A. J. and G. D. Keim (2001). "Shareholder value, stakeholder management and social issues: what's in the bottom line?" *Strategic Management Journal* **22**(2): 125–139.

Hobbs, M. (2008). UN PRI enlists 400 firms. *Financial Standard*. http://www.financialstandard.com.au/news/view/23618/. 28 July 2008.

Hutton, R. B., L. D'Antonio, et al. (1998). "Socially responsible investing." *Business and Society* **37**(3): 281–306.

Jaworski, W. (2007). Use of extra-financial information by research analysts and investment managers, European Center for Corporate Engagement (ECCE).

Jones, R. and A. Murrel (2001). "Signaling positive corporate social performance. An event study of family-friendly firms." *Business & Society* **40**(1): 59–78.

Juravle, C. and A. Lewis (2008). "Identifying impediments to SRI in Europe: a review of the practitioner and academic literature." *Business Ethics: A European Review* **17**(3): 285–310.

Klassen, R. D. and C. P. McLaughlin (1996). "The impact of environmental management on firm performance." *Management Science* **42**(8): 119–124.

Lipper FERI (2008) From niche to mainstream. *Hot Topics* Volume, DOI: http://www.feri-fmi.com/FERIFMI/Information/Files/Hot%20Topics%20SRI%200807.pdf.

Louche, C. (2004). Ethical investment: processes and mechanisms of institutionalisation in the Netherlands, 1990–2002. *PhD dissertation, Erasmus University Rotterdam*. Rotterdam, Optima Grafische Communicatie: Available at: https://ep.eur.nl/retrieve/3259/ESM-dissertation-003.pdf.

Louche, C. and S. Lydenberg (2006). "Socially responsible investment: difference between Europe and United States." *Vlerick Leuven Gent Management School Working Papers*.

Lydenberg, S. (2007). *Long term investing*. 2007 summit on the future of the corporation, Paper No.5.

Lydenberg, S. (2008). Form and Function: Research on Responsible Investment across Asset Classes.

Lydenberg, S. and G. Sinclair (2009). "Mainstream or daydream?" *Journal of Corporate Citizenship* June.

Margolis, J. D. and J. P. Walsh (2003). "Misery loves companies: rethinking social initiatives by business." *Administrative Science Quarterly* **48**(2): 268–305.

McGuire, J. B., A. Sundgren, et al. (1988). "Corproate social responsibility and firm financial performance." *Academy of Management Journal* **31**(4): 854–872.

McKinsey (2009). Valuing corporate social responsibility. McKinsey Global Survey Results.

McWilliams, A. and D. Siegel (2000). "Corporate social responsibility and financial performance: correlation or misspecification?" *Strategic Management Journal* **21**: 603–609.

Mercer and UNEP Financial Initiative (2007). Demystifying Responsible Investment Performance: A review of key academic and broker research on ESG factors.

Michelson, G., N. Wailes, et al. (2004). "Ethical investment processes and outcomes." *Journal of Business Ethics* **52**(1): 1–10.

Mitchell, R. K., B. R. Agle, et al. (1997). "Toward a theory of stakeholder identification and salience: defining the principle of who and what really counts." *Academy of Management Review* **22**: 853–886.

Moskowitz, M. R. (1972). "Choosing socially responsible stocks." *Business and Society Review* **1**: 71–75.

Orlitzky, M., F. L. Schmidt, et al. (2003). "Corporate social and financial performance: a meta-analysis." *Organization Studies* **24**(3): 403–441.

ORSE (2003). *Guide to sustainability analysis organisations*. Paris: EDEME, EPE, ORSE.

Pava, M. L. and J. Krausz (1996). "The association between corporate social-responsibility and financial performance: the paradox of social cost." *Journal of Business Ethics* **15**: 321–357.

PLEON (2005). Accounting for Good: the Global Stakeholder Report 2005, Pleon Kohtes Klewes GmbH/Pleon b.v.

Preston, L. E. and D. P. O'Bannon (1997). "The corporate social-financial performance relationship." *Business & Society* **36**(4): 419–429.

Richardson, B. J. (2007). "Do the fiduciary duties of pension funds hinder socially responsible investment?" *Banking and Finance Law Review*, **22**(2): 145–201.

Ruf, B. M., K. Muralidhar, et al. (2001). "An empirical investigation of the relationship between change in corporate social performance and financial performance: a stakeholder theory perspective." *Journal of Business Ethics* **32**(2): 143–156.

Sakuma, K. and C. Louche (2008). "Socially responsible investment in Japan: its mechanism and drivers." *Journal of Business Ethics* **82**(2): 425–448.

Solomon, J., A. Solomon, et al. (2002). "Socially responsible investment in the UK: drivers and current issues." *Journal of General Management* **27**(3): 1–13.

Sparkes, R. (2001). "Ethical investment: whose ethics, which investment?" *Business Ethics: A European Review* **10**(3): 194–205.

Sparkes, R. and C. J. Cowton (2004). "The maturing of socially responsible investment: a review of the developing link with corporate social responsibility." *Journal of Business Ethics* **52**(1): 45–57.

Stratos Inc. (2004). *Corporate disclosure and capital markets*. Ottawa: National Round Table on the Environment and the Economy.

SustAinability (2002). *Trust us: the global reporters 2002 survey of corporate sustainability reporting*. London: SustaAinability.

Taylor Nelson Sofres (2003). Investing in responsible business – The 2003 Survey of European fund managers, financial analysts and investor relations officers, CSR Europe, Deloitte, Euronext.

Tonello, M. (2006). Revisiting Stock Market Short-Termism. Available at SSRN: http://ssrn.com/abstract=938466. The Conference Board Research Report: No. R-1386-06-RR.

Ullman, A. A. (1985). "Data in search of a theory: critical examination of the relationships among social performance, social disclosure and economic performance of U.S. firms." *Academy of management* **10**(3): 540–557.

UK SIF (2008). *Sustainable alternatives*. London: UKSIF Sustainable Pensions Project.

US SIF (2008). *2007 Report on socially responsible investing trends in US – executive summary.* Washington, DC: US Social Investment Forum.

Verheugen, G. (2008). Speech at CSR Alliance event. 4 December 2008., http://www.csreurope.org/data/files/press/20081204_verheugen_equippedforcsr.pdf.

Waddock, S. A. and S. B. Grave (1997). "The corporate social performance-financial performance link." *Strategic Management Journal* **18**(4): 303–319.

WBCSD and UNEP Finance Initiative (2005). Generation lost: young financial analysts and environmental, social and governance issues. Perspectives.

Wood, D. and B. Hoff (2007). *Handbook on responsible investment across asset classes,* Institute for Responsible Investment.

World Economic Forum (2005). *Mainstreaming responsible investment.* Cologny/Geneva, Switzerland: World Economic Forum.

Zadek, S., M. Merme, et al. (2005). *Mainstreaming responsible investment.* Geneva: Accountability & World Economic Forum.

Chapter 12
Corporate Social Responsibility: The Estate Surveyors and Valuers' Perspective

Olatoye Ojo

Not life, but good life, is to be chiefly valued.
– Socrates

Abstract As society's expectations for business continue to rise, the societal role and perception of professionals in their respective fields need to be investigated. This paper undertook a discussion of corporate social responsibility (CSR) of business institutions from the perspective of a specific professional – the Estate Surveyors and Valuers (ESVs).

Pursuant to the above and in order to establish a link between CSR and the Estate Surveying and Valuation profession, the paper undertook a review of relevant literature on the concerns of CSR that have one bearing or the other either directly or indirectly on the conduct or behaviour of Estate Surveyors and Valuers and in the discharge of their specific professional duties. The paper also undertook a review of relevant literature on real estate education, the mission statements, code of ethics and conduct, objectives and activities of several Estate Surveying and Valuation professional bodies across the globe with a view to bringing out issues of concern to CSR. The identified issues of common concern include – ethics, the environment, sustainable development, infrastructure, capacity building and manpower development, and good governance.

The paper showed that with respect to their professional conduct and behaviour, Estate Surveyors and Valuers operate in the domain of ethical CSR while in the discharge of their specific professional duties, it is the strategic and altruistic CSR that hold sway. It concluded that in the efficient and effective discharge of their professional duties, ESVs need to be committed to the ideals of CSR in its entirety. The paper suggested that the curriculum of real estate education should be reviewed to accommodate CSR as a relevant topic. Finally, the paper made a case for further research and empirical studies on CSR from the perspective of the ESVs across the globe with a view to shedding more light on this emerging subject area.

O. Ojo (✉)
Obafemi Awolowo University, Ile Ife, Nigeria

S.O. Idowu, W.L. Filho (eds.), *Professionals' Perspectives of Corporate Social Responsibility*, DOI 10.1007/978-3-642-02630-0_13,
© Springer-Verlag Berlin Heidelberg 2009

12.1 Introduction

It is a firmly entrenched notion that business owes the society some duties or responsibilities. These have been documented in literature to cover-economic, legal, ethical and altruistic responsibilities (Carroll, 1979, 2000). Carroll and other scholars (Waddock and Smith, 2000; Lantos, 2001) believe that corporations should not only be judged on their economic success but also on non-economic criteria. Economic responsibility seeks to be profitable for stockholders by delivering a good quality product at fair price to consumers. Legal responsibilities entail complying with the law and playing the rules of the game although the limitations lie in not being able to cover every possible contingencies. Ethical responsibilities overcome the limitations of legal duties as the focus is on being moral, doing what is right, just, and fair, respecting peoples' moral rights and avoiding harm or social injury as well as preventing harm caused by others (Smith and Quelch, 1993). Ethical responsibilities derive their root of authority from religious convictions, moral traditions, humane principles and human rights commitments (Novak, 1996). Altruistic or philanthropic responsibilities involve 'giving back' time and money in the forms of voluntary service, voluntary association and voluntary giving. Over the past half century, business increasingly has been judged not only by its economic and moral performance but also by its social contributions. All these perceived expectations of society from business institutions today underlie the concept of corporate social responsibility.

Several definitions of CSR now abound in literature which tend to reflect the background of the respective scholars or authors (Bloom and Gundlach, 2001; European Union, 2001; The World Bank, 2006). For example, according to Nottingham University Business School, International Centre for Corporate Social Responsibility (2006), CSR refers to the social, environmental and ethical responsibility and accountability of companies for their impacts – including impacts on the communities where they operate. For our purpose here, three types of CSR will be discussed – ethical, altruistic and strategic. Ethical CSR is based on the socially aware view and stakeholder model of CSR that business should be sensitive to potential harms of its actions on various stakeholder groups (Freeman, 2001). Altruistic CSR is based on the community service view or corporate social performance perspective that business must use its vast resources for social good (Carroll, 2001). Strategic CSR or 'strategic philanthropy' (Carroll, 2001, p. 200) is done to accomplish strategic business goals – good deeds are believed to be good for business as well as for society. From the definitions given and foci of the various types of CSR identified, the concerns of CSR can be broadly classified as touching on the following – environment, sustainable development, ethics, infrastructure, good governance and capacity building among others.

While the society's expectations for business continue to rise as enumerated above, the societal role of professionals and the way corporate social responsibility is perceived in their respective fields need to be investigated. This is due to the fact that professionals occupy a pride of place in the operations of business institutions (that are supposed to be socially responsible) and have privileged position within the society. The privileges accruing to professionals in the business world and within the society in turn carry with them various special duties or social responsibilities. Society expects professionals to conduct themselves in a way that will yield some benefits to society beyond economic and legal duties, to moral and quality-of-life obligations (Lantos, 2001, p. 20). This implies that professionalism carries with it an extra burden of accountability – the social responsibility of 'professional reciprocity', i.e. the social obligation to act in ways that benefit society. Thus, it can be reasonably argued that the corporate social contract theory of business which holds that business and society are equal partners, each enjoying a set of rights and having reciprocal responsibilities (Bowie, 1983; Davis, 1983; Lippke, 1996) can also be used to justify the expected social duties of professionals as individuals within those business institutions.

A critical review of codes of conduct in the various professions will confirm the significant role attached to the concept of social service in professional life. Each code enumerates the social aspects of professional assignments, suggesting that rendering service to society should be a high priority in the professions. In the context of the foregoing exposition therefore, an understanding of and insight into the concept of corporate social responsibility in the professions will appear imperative and inevitable. Herein lies the justification for this work. It is against the foregoing background that this paper undertook a discussion of corporate social responsibility from the perspective of a specific professional – the Estate Surveyors and Valuers. The focus is on the concerns of CSR that are perceived to have direct or indirect bearing on the conduct or behaviour of ESVs and in the discharge of their specific professional duties.

Real estate is the physical land and appurtenances affixed to the land (such as – buildings, site improvements, utilities and infrastructure, trees and minerals) while real property on the other hand includes all interests, benefits, and rights inherent in the ownership of physical real estate (Reinold, 2003). According to Reinold, real estate is immobile and tangible, hence the use of the term 'real' and that a right or interest in real estate is also referred to as an estate, while the subject of investigation, analysis and reporting by appraisers is real property. The total range of all ownership interests in real estate is called the bundle of rights which contains the right to – occupy, use, lease, mortgage or assign. Much of the private, corporate and public wealth of the world consists of real estate and the magnitude of this fundamental resource creates a need for informed appraisals to support decisions pertaining to the use and disposition of real estate and the rights inherent in ownership (The Appraisal Institute, 2007).

Estate Surveyors and Valuers, also known by different names in other countries of the world: e.g. Chartered Surveyors (UK), Appraisers (US and Canada) and Valuers (Australia and New Zealand) belong to a profession which is also equally known by several names across the globe e.g. Surveying, Appraisal, Valuation, Real Estate Valuation and Real Estate Appraisal. In Nigeria, they are called Estate Surveyors and Valuers while the profession is known as Estate Surveying and Valuation. By definition, an appraisal is 'the act or process of developing an opinion of value' while value is 'the monetary relationship between properties and those who buy, sell or use those properties' (The Appraisal Foundation, 2003). Estate Surveyors and Valuers (or Real Estate Appraisers) perform useful functions in society and offer a variety of services to their clients in the following regards: transfer of ownership (estimating a property's value when buying or selling real estate), financing and credit (determining the value of property for mortgage loan and insurance purposes), litigation (assessing the value of property for compensation, arbitration and environmental disputes) and tax matters (rating and probate) (The Appraisal Institute, 2001). Their services are also required in investment counselling, decision making and accounting such as: setting of rent schedules and lease provisions, feasibility studies of new projects or renovation schemes, assisting in property purchase, facilitating corporate mergers or revision of book value and assisting in preparation of financial reports and accounts.

In many countries, valuation is a distinct profession while in others it forms part of a package of services offered to clients by multidisciplinary practices which include other wider property services like agency, management and investment (Gilbertson and Preston, 2005). Under the first model (which is typical of US), valuers work as sole practitioners, in government departments, firms of valuers or other valuation related employments and the market is unwilling to accept, the provision by valuers of wider property services like agency and investment. Indeed, separate licences are required for brokerage services in the US while the licensing of appraisers is controlled on a state by state basis and the recognition of licences between states is very limited. Under the second model (which is typical of UK and many Commonwealth countries), training to become a valuer is much more rigorous requiring a broader university education in property, period of supervised experience, further examinations and peer assessment and valuation as a discipline tends to be more highly regarded by clients and institutions (Wyatt, 2001). In the UK, a regulatory framework is set by the leading professional body, the RICS. The situation of valuation profession in Nigeria falls under the second model discussed above.

Around the world, there are differences in valuation practice, fundamental valuation concepts, terminology and methodology (Milgrim, 2001). The development of international valuation standards is however a major step in avoiding conflicts, promoting harmony and facilitating global valuation practice (Ndungu et al., 2002). The principal objectives of international valuation standards are:

- To facilitate cross-border transactions and contribute to the viability of international property markets by promoting transparency in financial reporting as well as the reliability of valuations performed to secure loans and mortgages, for transactions involving transfers of ownership, and for settlements in litigation or tax matters;
- To serve as a professional benchmark, or beacon, for Valuers around the world, thereby enabling them to respond to the demands of international property markets for reliable valuations and to meet the financial reporting requirements of the global business community; and

- To provide Standards of valuation and financial reporting that meet the needs of emerging and newly industrialized countries.[1]

This work which is principally based on review of relevant academic and professional literature and data obtained from websites of several national, regional and global real estate professional bodies is divided into four broad sections. After the introduction, it gives a broad overview of the Estate Surveying and Valuation profession. This is followed by a treatment of issues perceived to be of common concern to CSR and the Estate Surveying and Valuation profession. The last section contained the concluding remarks and suggestions for further research.

12.2 The Estate Surveying and Valuation Profession

The focus of this section will be on a discussion of the Estate Surveying and Valuation profession. Unlike many professions such as: medicine, nursing, law, engineering and accountancy, the estate surveying and valuation profession is bedeviled by lack of a universally accepted nomenclature. This in the opinion of this author is due to the fact that real estate education evolved along geographic regional lines (UK, USA etc) and at different periods. For example, three diverse approaches to real estate education around the world can be identified namely – 'interdisciplinary approach' (which is practiced e.g. in Continental Europe), 'surveying approach' (typically found in the UK and other Commonwealth countries like Nigeria) and the 'investment and finance approach' (dominant in the USA) (Schulte, et al., 2005). This has led to differences in – valuation practice, fundamental valuation concepts, terminology and methodology around the world (Milgrim, 2001). For example, in the UK, Australia and New Zealand, appraisers work closely with accountants on financial reports, whereas in North America, financial reporting is left to the domain of accountants. Also, in some countries, 'market value under existing use' is an established concept whereas in others, practitioners recognize only 'market value under highest and best use' (Ibid). These are part of the main challenges that served as impetus for the development of international valuation standards referred to earlier under introduction.

Real estate as an academic discipline has an identity problem. This is because efforts to delimit and define the territory of real estate are confronted by a confusing thicket of diverse activities – lending, investing, governing, developing, consuming, marketing, appraising, and more (Diaz, 1993). Perhaps nothing accounts so much for the lack of consensus among real estate academics as does this challenging richness. In view of the above, the establishment of a common body of knowledge in the field of real estate will need to be very broad and all encompassing (Rabianski and Black, 1999). The regional nature of its evolution has also led to different countries emphasizing different fields of real estate education (Schulte, et al., 2005).

---

[1] IVS (2000), Objectives and Scope, p. 15.

The course of study in real estate education in tertiary institutions across the globe carries different nomenclatures depending on the country and institution. Institutions in the UK and many Commonwealth countries use such titles as: Land Economy, Land Management, Estate Management, Estate Surveying and Real Estate Management. In Nigeria (a British Commonwealth country), the Universities and Polytechnics use the title – Estate Management. In the USA, titles used include – Land Economics and Real Estate, Urban Land Economics, Real Estate, and Real Estate and Finance. In Continental Europe, the titles Real Estate and Real Estate Management are commonly used. The titles estate and real estate are used interchangeably in real estate education and the profession without prejudice to their legal connotations. In spite of the differences in titles, there is a growing global concern that there should be consensus of opinion on what should constitute real estate body of knowledge both on a national and international level (Epley, 1996). The various countries have in place, professional and government regulatory bodies that oversee real estate education and practice in their respective domains.

There are national, regional and international bodies and associations that regulate and control real estate education, research and practice (including all transactions in landed property) in the different countries and regions of the world. The International Real Estate Society (IRES) was formed in 1992 as an international umbrella organization to provide a global forum for the exchange of real estate research ideas, education, students, and faculty (Worzala, 1996). In order to pursue the same goal at regional levels, the following bodies were also constituted as part of IRES Network – American Real Estate Society – ARES, European Real Estate Society – ERES, African Real Estate Society – AfRES, Pacific Rim Real Estate Society – PRRES and Asian Real Estate Society – AsRES. Other regional real estate professional bodies that can be identified include – The Royal Institution of Chartered Surveyors (RICS) and The Commonwealth Association of Surveying and Land Economy (CASLE). At the national levels, several associations across the globe can be identified. Some of these include – Appraisal Institute (USA), The Appraisal Institute of Canada, The Singapore Institute of Surveyors and Valuers, The Australian Property Institute, The New Zealand Institute of Valuers and The Nigerian Institution of Estate Surveyors and Valuers.

The various national, regional and international real estate associations and bodies have their respective mission statements, objectives, codes of conduct, scope of professional activities as well as clearly defined policies on membership and discipline. A brief discussion of some of these associations in the above contexts will now be undertaken here:

(i) The International Real Estate Society (IRES) was established in 1992 as an international umbrella organization to provide a global forum for the exchange of real estate research ideas, education, students, and faculty (Worzala, 1996; Schulte, et al., 2005).

(ii) The American Real Estate Society (ARES) was founded in 1985 as an association of real estate thought leaders drawn from academia and the profession at large, both in the United States and internationally. The objectives of the

Society are 'to: encourage research and promote education in real estate, improve communication and exchange of information in real estate and allied matters among college/university faculty and practicing professionals, and facilitate the association of academic, practicing professional, and research persons in the area of real estate.'[2] The society publishes five journals which provide relevant and timely research of interest to real state academics and practitioners worldwide.[3]

(iii) The European Real Estate Society (ERES) was 'established in 1994 to create a structured and permanent network between real estate academics and professionals across Europe.'[4] Affiliated with the International Real Estate Society, ERES is dedicated to promoting and advancing the field of real estate research throughout Europe. The specific objectives of ERES are 'to:

- encourage research and promote education in real estate and closely allied areas, especially in European Countries,
- improve communication and exchange information in real estate and allied matters among college/university faculty members and practitioners, who are teaching or engaging in property, real estate and land use,
- facilitate the association of academic, practicing professional, and research persons in the area of real estate and closely allied areas,
- encourage professionalism in practices related to real estate and closely allied areas as well as other activities promoting the purposes of the foundation,
- organize events where researchers and educators in the broad area of real estate can interact,
- organize events where researchers and decision-makers from both academia and practice can exchange their views with respect to the research needs in the field of real estate, but also discuss the best ways of using research results to enhance decision-making in the field to promote in any other feasible way, the development of real estate research and education in Europe.'[5]

(iv) The Asian Real Estate Society (AsRES) was established in 1996 with 60 founding members with the aim of producing and disseminating real estate related knowledge with particular emphasis on Asia. AsRES offers 'a great opportunity for anyone who wants to learn more about Asian real estate markets and interact with real estate educators and professionals in Asia.'[6]

(v) The Royal Institution of Chartered Surveyors (RICS) – 'is the pre-eminent organization of its kind in the world and as such, it represents everything that

---

[2] ARES: http://www.aresnet.org/

[3] Ibid

[4] ERES: http://eres.ua.es/privat/estatico.php?c=1

[5] Ibid

[6] AsRES: http://www.asres.org/about_1.htm

is good in the property profession. RICS has 140,000 members who operate out of 146 countries around the world.'[7] Its members offer advice on diverse range of land, property, construction and related environmental issues. As part of its role, RICS helps to set, maintain and regulate standards as well as provide impartial advice to governments and policy makers. The RICS represents a strong self-regulating body for the property profession in the UK. Given the fact that the RICS has continued to expand its activities around the globe, the organization seems well positioned to play an important role in the promotion of international real estate education (Schulte et al., 2005). Parsa (1999) had earlier noted that the RICS has a fundamental role to play in ensuring that appropriate standards in course design and content are developed in relation to international real estate.

(vi) The Commonwealth Association of Surveying and Land Economy (CASLE) was formed in 1969 as a federation of independent professional societies representing surveying and land economy in Commonwealth countries. CASLE's Mission Statement is as follows: 'We are committed to the advancement of the profession of Surveying in the Commonwealth, and to the enhancement of the skills of Surveyors in the management of the natural and built environments for the common good.'[8] It currently comprises over 40 societies in 32 countries and it has approved Associate Members and correspondents, some of whom are in 19 other countries. The objectives of CASLE have 'been defined as:

- fostering the development of the profession in all Commonwealth countries.
- fostering appropriate standards of education for surveying and land economy and the establishment of appropriate facilities for education and training.
- helping to develop professional techniques and practices attuned to national needs.
- facilitating the transfer of technology within the Commonwealth and assisting national programmes of continuing professional development designed to keep surveyors up-to-date.
- encouraging dialogue between its member societies and national governments on all matters of national policy on which the profession is competent to offer informed opinions and advice'.[9]

The profession of surveying and land economy as envisaged by CASLE includes the three but kindred disciplines of land surveying, land economy and quantity surveying. The land economy component which is the focus of this work is concerned with the management and development of land and property, in an economical and sustainable manner, and involves a range of disciplines which form the basis of a number of professional specialisms. It 'covers:

---

[7]RICS: http://www.rics.org/Aboutus/spotlight.htm

[8]CASLE: http://www.awestcott.freeserve.co.uk/casle/about.htm

[9]Ibid

– advice on policies relating to land ownership, land use, land reform and related aspects of national development programmes.
– land use planning, land transactions, and project implementation, including advice on the sourcing of development finance.
– the development and management of rural and agricultural land, the development of mineral resources and advice on terms of occupation or disposal of land.
– the development of urban land, the provision and updating of buildings for residential, industrial or commercial purposes; and the management of land and buildings, including handling property transactions, valuation of property, auctioneering, building surveying, building maintenance and facilities management'.[10]

CASLE is committed to the ideals and principles of sustainability because it believes that many of the problems facing the world in respect of the use of scarce resources may be mitigated by careful planning. It believes that the modification of the environment to serve human needs can and must be more sensitively managed. CASLE has collaborated with other stakeholders in addressing issues relating to sustainability as part of its initiative to encourage the development of constructive attitudes towards sustainability, at all levels in public and private sector clients and their professional advisers, throughout the Commonwealth.

(vii) Appraisal Institute (USA) was organized in 1932 and is now a global membership association of professional real estate appraisers, with nearly 23,000 members and 92 chapters throughout the world. Its mission is 'to support and advance its members as the choice for real estate solutions and uphold professional credentials, standards of professional practice and ethics consistent with the public good'.[11] All Appraisal Institute members adhere to a strictly enforced Code of Professional Ethics and Standards of Professional Appraisal Practice. Majority of Appraisal Institute members are practicing real estate appraisers and property analysts who provide valuation-related services to such clients as mortgage lenders, financial institutions, government agencies, attorneys and financial planners as well as home owners and other individual consumers.[12]

(viii) The Appraisal Institute of Canada is the country's 'professional organization that designates, and represents professional real estate appraisers, and valuation consultants nationwide'[13] The Institute certifies and registers members who meet its quality standards of professional practice, adhere to the Code of Professional Ethics, and submit to a peer-driven discipline and enforcement process. It is also responsible for developing and maintaining the Canadian

---

[10] Ibid

[11] Appraisal Institute: http://www.appraisalinstitute.org/about/

[12] Ibid

[13] AIC:http://www.aicanada.ca/e/aboutaic_areas.cfm?print22=1&

Uniform Standards of Professional Appraisal Practice to ensure the public is protected and that the Institute members are well served.[14]

(ix) The Australian Property Institute (API) which was originally formed in 1926 as the Commonwealth Institute of Valuers has undergone several name changes over the last century as the array of services offered by its members expanded. With present membership strength of over 7,500 property, professionals throughout Australia, the Institute's primary role is 'to set and maintain the highest standards of professional practice, education, ethics and professional conduct for its members and the broader property profession'.[15] Members of the Institute subscribe to and are bound by – a Code of Ethics, Rules of Conduct and Professional Practice Standards.[16]

(x) The New Zealand Institute of Valuers (NZIV) which was established by the country's Valuers Act, 1948 has merged its operations with the Property Institute of New Zealand (PINZ) but it still represents Valuer members as an occupational community within PINZ. The general functions of NZIV are 'to:

- promote and encourage ethical conduct among valuers and other members of the Institute
- preserve and maintain the integrity and status of valuers and other members of the Institute generally
- provide opportunities for the acquisition and communication of knowledge in relation to the valuing of land and related subjects
- consider and suggest amendments to the law relating to the valuing of land and related subjects
- provide means for the amicable settlement of professional differences
- protect and promote the interests of the public in relation to valuations of land and related subjects'.[17]

(xi) The Nigerian Institution of Estate Surveyors and Valuers (NIESV) was established in 1969 as a non-profit voluntary professional organization to cater for the interests of landed profession in Nigeria. Six years after its establishment, the Institution was accorded official recognition with the promulgation of The Estate Surveyors and Valuers Registration Board Decree No. 24 of 1975. The profession of Estate Surveying and Valuation is defined as 'those engaged in the arts, science and practice:

a. determining the value of all description of the property and of the various interests therein,

---

[14] Ibid

[15] API: http://www.propertyinstitute.com.au/printfriendly.aspx?MenuID=1&SubMenuID=1
[16] Ibid

[17] NZIV: http://www.property.org.nz/AM/Template.cfm?Section=About_NZIV&Template=/CM/H...

   b. managing and developing estates and other business concerned with the management of landed property,

   c. securing the optimal use of land and its associated resources to meet social and economical needs,

   d. determining the structure and condition of buildings and their services and advising on their maintenance, alteration and improvement,

   e. determining the economic use of the resources by means of financial appraisal for the building industry,

   f. selling (whether by auction or otherwise), buying or letting as an agent, real or personal property or any interest therein'.[18]

The objects of The Nigerian Institution of Estate surveyors and Valuers as contained in Chapter One of its constitution (NIESV, 2005) are to:

a. establish high and reputable standards of professional conduct and practice in the landed profession throughout the Federal Republic of Nigeria

b. secure and improve the technical knowledge that constitutes Land Economy, Real Estate and Allied Matters, Valuation and Appraisal of Plant, Machinery and Bussiness Assets, Land and Facilities Management, Building Maintenance, Property Development and Investment and Town and Country Planning, as well as Land administration Systems.

c. facilitate the acquisition and dissemination of such knowledge by establishing Training Institutions and working in close collaboration with universities, other institutions of higher learning and other professional bodies

d. promote the general interests of the profession and to maintain and extend its usefulness for the public good by advising, educating and informing members of the public, government departments, statutory bodies, local governments, associations, institutions and such like bodies on all matters coming within the scope of the profession

e. initiate and consider any legislation relevant to the objects of the Institution.

f. endeavour to acquaint the public with the role of the Estate Surveyor and Valuer in the economic development of the country

g. engage in any other lawful activity (ies) which may be conducive to the promotion of any or all the objects of the Institution mentioned above for profit or nonprofit purposes.

Chapter 15 of the Institution's constitution on discipline contains adequate provisions on – Rules of Conduct (Section 67), Disciplinary Offences (Section 68), Disciplinary Powers of The Council (Section69) and Disciplinary Procedure (Section 70).

---

[18] NIESV: http://www.niesv.org/pages.php?page_id=2&site_id=2

A number of inferences could be drawn from our discussion of the estate surveying and valuation profession under introduction and in this section. First, the real estate profession could be perceived as a very important public interest profession in view of the significance of real estate and the array of services rendered by appraisers/valuers to businesses, the society, governments and individuals in the various countries of the world. This perception puts the profession and its members in a position of obligation to their clients (i.e. stakeholders) in the performance of their professional duties. This is because the clients are affected by corporate policies and practices of these appraisers/valuers as envisioned by their respective professional bodies. Second, the various professional bodies at various levels are committed to the ideals of capacity building for their members as well as good governance. For example, CASLE's mission statement and objectives evidently show the body's commitment to the ideals of capacity building.

Third, the concern of the estate surveying and valuation profession for the environment, sustainable development and infrastructure is very clear and understandable. From the definition of real estate, all development on land (buildings, site improvements, utilities and infrastructure) take place within the setting of the environment in accordance with relevant statutory regulations. As will be shown later, the environment, sustainable development and infrastructure have direct impact on property and property values in respect of which appraisers are often called upon to express professional opinion. According to Boyd (2002), environmental issues have a direct impact on property and property value. RICS and CASLE are committed to the ideals and principles of sustainability. Fourth, the issue of ethics occupies a pride of place among all the real estate professional bodies discussed. The bodies expect their individual members to adhere to a strictly enforced Code of Professional Ethics and Standards of Professional Appraisal Practice in the discharge of their professional assignments. The code is also intended to inform the general public, the business community and government agencies of the ethical standards of the various associations. From the foregoing, real estate profession could be perceived as a public interest profession with great concern for – ethics, the environment, sustainable development, infrastructure, capacity building and manpower development, and good governance.

12.3 CSR and the Estate Surveying and Valuation Profession

We have undertaken a discussion of the estate surveying and valuation profession from several dimensions in the preceding section. We shall focus our attention in this section on a discussion of CSR and the estate surveying and valuation profession with a view to identifying areas of common grounds between the two. A distillation of our discussion in the two preceding sections will reveal the following areas of common grounds or concerns between CSR and the estate surveying and valuation profession namely – ethics, the environment, sustainable development, infrastructure, capacity building and manpower development, and good governance. These issues will now be discussed hereunder.

12.3.1 Ethics

Our discussion of the activities of the various real estate professional associations across the globe in the preceding section revealed that all these bodies place a very high premium on the conduct and behavior of their respective members by expecting them to be committed at all times to the ideals of highest standards of professional practice and ethics that are consistent with the public good. Members of these professional bodies are expected to adhere strictly to and be bound by- Code of professional ethics, Rules of conduct and standards of professional practice applicable in their respective countries. These bodies are also committed to ensuring that the interests of the patronizing public are well protected. Appropriate sanctions abound for any erring member(s) by the professional associations.

Taking this into the realm of CSR will show that Estate Surveyors and Valuers (Chartered Surveyors, Appraisers or Valuers as they might be called in their country of operation) are presumed to owe their clients and the public at large ethical duties or responsibilities. The Code of ethics, rules of conduct and professional practice standards give a summary of what the practitioners should do, what they should not do and how they should relate to their clients and the public at large. In the light of all these, they must always be seen to do that which is right, just and fair without causing harm or injury to their clients or others. Their professional conduct and behavior must be seen to be above board. Adherence to the ideals of good moral conduct and ethical behavior as expected by their professional associations shows that Estate Surveyors and Valuers are embracing or practicing CSR either knowingly or unknowingly. It can therefore be said that with respect to their professional conduct and behavior, Estate Surveyors and Valuers operate in the domain of Ethical CSR.

12.3.2 The Environment and Sustainable Development

Several professional activities of Estate Surveyors and Valuers (such as the development and management of rural and urban land for various purposes – residential, commercial, industrial, agricultural, recreational and mineral resources etc) take place within the natural and built environment. These activities call for adequate programmes and policies on – land use and land use planning, zoning, development control, land ownership and land reform among others. This is why the profession of land economy (estate management, estate surveying and valuation or real estate) is concerned with the management and development of land and property, in an economical and sustainable manner. For example, one of the professional bodies – CASLE is expressly committed to the ideals and principles of sustainability as a result of its belief that many of the problems facing the world in respect of the use of scarce resources may be mitigated by careful planning. Its belief that the modification of the environment to serve human needs can and must be more sensitively managed led to its pursuing and collaborating with other stakeholders in embarking on and embracing several initiatives on sustainability of the environment.

There is increasing evidence of the environmental damage affecting real estate appraisals and a number of challenges facing the Chartered Surveyor (Wilbourn, 2008). First, there is the challenge of how to integrate other professionalisms into core business activities. Second, there is the challenge of embracing the practical implications of sustainability by the wide variety of disciplines that make up the surveying profession. Third, clients of the surveying fraternity expect that the profession will provide them with relevant and most current advice on all aspects of sustainable developments. In response to these issues and challenges in the UK, the RICS has tried to integrate a number of initiatives into core work of Chartered Surveyors through the Specialist in Land Condition and Society for the Environment projects (Ibid). The issues for the property professional are that sustainability must be considered throughout the property life cycle because the process of sustainable built asset management is continuous throughout the life cycle of the property. In the context of property and construction, it is a time horizon which commences with land acquisition, includes the design and construction of buildings, and continues with the ongoing operation of the property and ceases with the ultimate demolition or deconstruction and recycling of the property (Robinson, 2005). Successful sustainable development considers the 'triple bottom line' of environmental, economic and social issues (Wilbourn, 2008).

The Bathurst Declaration (UN-FIG, 1999) established a powerful link between appropriate land administration and sustainable development. FIG is the International Federation of Surveyors and the Bathurst Declaration is an outcome of the workshop organized in 1999 by FIG in conjunction with the United Nations. Land administration comprises an extensive range of systems and processes to administer (namely – land tenure, land value and land use) while the combination of an efficient land market and an effective land-use administration should form the basis for a sustainable approach to economic, social and environmental development (Enemark, 2003). Land administration systems, and particularly their core cadastral components, are an important infrastructure which facilitates the implementation of land policies in both developed and developing countries (UN-FIG, 1999). These systems are concerned with the administration of land as a natural resource to ensure its sustainable development (Enemark, 2003). It is reasonable therefore to infer from the above that sustainable development is not attainable without sound land administration.

The emerging global concept of green building is another area that is bringing sustainability into prominence in the real estate profession. A green building may be defined as a building which is designed, constructed and managed in a way that significantly reduces or eliminates its negative impact on the environment and its occupants (Yuan, 2008). The goal of green building is to minimize the impacts of buildings on the environment and create healthier spaces in which to live and work while the terms 'green' and 'sustainable' are often used interchangeably (Pitts and Jackson, 2008). Among the real estate practitioners, concerns are expressed how sustainability and the green movement may impact on real estate developments and values (Yuan, 2008). This is why real estate professional bodies in the UK, US, Canada and Australia have introduced a sustainability policy to emphasis the importance of the concept. Green buildings are changing the landscape of commercial and residential construction around the world with 'green' becoming very visible in construction markets in every global region (Shalley, 2008).

In March 2007, valuation professionals and others from international organizations concerned with green building and sustainability met in Vancouver, British Columbia, to create the Vancouver Accord (Pitts and Jackson, 2008). This document is a commitment from signatories to the Accord to facilitate sustainability and valuation through education, standards creation and practices. By 2010, participants in the Vancouver Accord intend to collaborate on agreed valuation practices and standards, participate in a consensus to create consistent approaches to valuation and sustainability, and create education tools and resources to improve knowledge and skills in this area (Bergsman, 2007). The US Green Building Council has developed a certification programme- Leadership in Energy and Environmental Design, to promote sustainable development based on six criteria – sustainable site, water efficiency, energy efficiency, use and reuse of materials and resources, indoor environmental quality, and innovation and design (Pitts and Jackson, 2008). Australia and Singapore have similar programmes which are however called by different names (Yuan, 2008). While empirical work on the whole concept is very limited, some of the existing published works revealed that the impact was greater in improving the image and well-being of occupants rather than impact on values while for now, the income approach will be one to rely heavily on by valuation experts (Shalley, 2008; Yuan, 2008).

In the realm of CSR, the concern for the environment and sustainable development has always occupied a very central stage. This is evidently clear from the various definitions of CSR given earlier where the need to integrate social and environmental concerns in the business operations of corporations and contribute to sustainable economic development of the local communities where they operate and the society at large featured very prominently. In this context, it is reasoned that a firm's social welfare responsibilities create a win-win situation in which both the corporation and one or more stakeholder groups benefit. This is strategic CSR or strategic philanthropy which is done to accomplish strategic businessman goals on the premise that good deeds are good for business as well. Some of the strategic CSR initiatives pursued by corporations that border on the environment and sustainable development which have been identified earlier include – water conservation, environmental protection, greening the environment; transforming, managing wastes and garbage handling among others. By paying due attention to various environmental concerns in the discharge of their professional duties as enumerated earlier, Estate Surveyors and Valuers could rightly be perceived as operating as individuals or on behalf of the corporation in the domain of strategic CSR.

12.3.3 Infrastructure

The concept of infrastructure in this context relates to provision of – roads, electricity, portable water, health and educational facilities among others. The comfort of using and enjoying various types of real estate (residential, commercial, industrial etc) is greatly influenced by the availability of the aforementioned types of infrastructural facilities. In the discharge of their professional duties – property valuation, giving advice on leasing and purchase decisions, property and facilities management, Estate Surveyors and Valuers are concerned about the degree and quality of infrastructure in the neighbourhood where the property is located. This is because the factor of infrastructure affects property value and can also affect leasing and purchase decisions as well among others.

Besides their concern for existing infrastructure, Estate Surveyors and Valuers also have a major role to play in the provision of new infrastructure. Specifically, they can through feasibility appraisal advise on economic desirability of providing any type of infrastructure. Furthermore, they could also by virtue of their training act as project managers in the construction of these facilities. Infrastructure is therefore an issue of concern to Estate Surveyors and Valuers in the discharge of their professional duties.

The community service view of CSR expects companies to use their vast resources for social good and specifically help in alleviating identified 'public welfare deficiencies', though not caused or created by them. This is the domain of altruistic CSR where companies are expected to embrace and subscribe to the ideals of philanthropic responsibilities which involve 'giving back' time and money thereby making the world a better place through solving of social problems. Lack of infrastructure constitutes a notable public welfare deficiency in many rural and urban centres especially in the developing countries. This is why it offers a good attraction for altruistic CSR initiatives by many corporations. While infrastructure is an issue of concern to Estate Surveyors and Valuers in the discharge of their professional duties as enumerated earlier, it is also an issue of concern to corporations in the area of altruistic CSR. Where the services of Estate Surveyors and valuers are required either as individuals or as agents of corporations in the provision of infrastructure, they could be perceived as operating in the domain of altruistic CSR.

12.3.4 Capacity Building, Manpower Development, and Good Governance

The various real estate professional bodies across the globe have as part of their mission statements, aims or objectives, the achievement of capacity building and manpower development while they are also committed to the ideals and principles of good governance. These they intend to pursue by encouraging research and promoting education in real estate and closely allied areas both in their respective countries/continents and internationally. For example, CASLE is committed to transfer of technology and fostering the development of the profession throughout the Commonwealth. These bodies are also poised to making contributions to policies bordering on economic development of their respective countries.

In addition, this concept has great relevance in land administration systems which are concerned with the social, legal, economic and technical framework within which land managers and administrators must operate (UN-ECE, 1996). The three levels of capacity building (the system, the entity and the individual level) can be considered in the context of land administration systems (Enemark, 2003). At the broader system/societal level, the purpose is to build, identify and ensure land rights, to build efficient land markets, and to ensure effective and sustainable management of the use of land. The organizational level (the entity) is about building infrastructure that will pave way for administrative policies, good governance and capable government that will be able to perform key functions effectively. At the individual level of capacity building, land administration is about people – from politicians, senior and middle level personnel, to lower cadre – whether in public or private sector. At the senior level, a broad vision and understanding is required while at the more practical level, the players in the system need to have some understanding of the overall system but will have much more detailed and specific skills that need to be developed. For example, the Land Administration Programme in Ghana was intended to build capacity for Ghana Survey Department (GSD) (Dotse, 2006). The programme which is of long-term nature being undertaken by six land sector agencies including GSD was aimed at enhancing economic and social growth by improving the security of tenure and simplifying prudent land management by establishing an efficient system of land administration in Ghana.

According to Magel and Franke (2007), good governance is a central issue, considered and implemented by nearly all professionals, particularly those in surveying and that sustainable development is not attainable without sound land administration and good governance. According to them, all surveyors' work should follow the five principles of good governance namely – legitimacy and voice, direction, performance, accountability and fairness. The concept of good governance as it affects surveyor's profession had earlier been alluded to by Septh (1997) when he emphasized that there is no real sustainable human development without strong, effective and participatory government. Participatory government, or in other words governance, is the key for the future – it is related to civil society, youth, human rights, capacity building and role of the State, including decentralization and social cohesion. Implementing good governance principles in the daily work of surveyors guarantees or at least tries to guarantee that political, economic, ecological and social priorities and decisions are based on a broad and balanced consensus that targets a more just, equitable and peaceful world. That is the ethical basis of FIG, 'the mother of all surveying and surveyors', and of many of its member associations (Ibid).

Capacity building and manpower development, and good governance constitute another noticeable area of 'public welfare deficiencies' especially in the developing countries. Interestingly this has been identified earlier as a notable area of attraction for altruistic CSR. Many corporations have engaged in several altruistic CSR initiatives that are aimed at achieving capacity building and manpower development, and good governance. It is therefore highly commendable that the real estate professional bodies also have these initiatives as part of their mission statements, aims and objectives, and are committed to these ideals and principles. Embracing the concept of capacity building in land administration amounts to strategic CSR in the opinion of this author while good governance is altruistic CSR.

12.4 Concluding Remarks and Suggestions for further Research

This work examined the place of CSR in the context of the professional conduct of Estate Surveyors and Valuers as well as in the discharge of their professional duties. Starting with a discussion of society's expectations from businesses and the professions, it presented a brief introduction of the Estate Surveying and Valuation profession and CSR under introductory section. This was followed by a discussion of the estate surveying and valuation profession covering aspects such as – real estate education, national, regional and international real estate professional bodies and their respective mission statements, code of conduct and objectives. The section that followed identified areas of common concern between CSR and the estate surveying and valuation profession. The identified areas of common concern include – ethics, the environment, sustainable development, infrastructure, capacity building and manpower development and good governance.

It was shown that with respect to their professional conduct and behavior, Estate Surveyors and Valuers operate in the domain of ethical CSR while in the discharge of their specific professional duties, it is the strategic and altruistic CSR that hold sway. In the efficient and effective discharge of their professional duties, Estate Surveyors and Valuers need to be committed to the ideals of CSR in its entirety because of the society's rising expectations not only from the corporations but also from the professionals.

In view of the several identified areas of common concern between CSR and the real estate profession and the growing global concern for CSR, it is hereby strongly advocated that the curriculum of real estate education worldwide should be reviewed to accommodate CSR as a very relevant topic. Also, further research and empirical studies would have to be undertaken on several aspects of CSR from the perspective of Estate Surveyors and Valuers across the globe in order to shed more light on this emerging subject area which is fastly gaining global attention.

References

Bergsman, S. (2007), "Sustainable by all accords". Valuation, (Second Quarter 2007): 25–27.

Boyd, T. (2002), "Thirty years later – is there a 'new school' of appraisal thought". Paper delivered at the PRRES Annual Conference, January, 2001, Christchurch, New Zealand.

Bloom, P.N. and Gundlach, G.T. (2001), "Handbook of Marketing and Society", Sage Publications, Inc., Thousand Oaks, CA.

Bowie, N.E. (1983), "Changing the rules", in Beachamp, T.I. and Bowie, N.E. (Eds), Ethical Theory and Business, Second Edition, Prentice-Hall, Inc., Englewood Cliffs, NJ.

Carroll, A.B. (1979), "A three dimensional model of corporate performance". Academy of Management Review, 4, 497–505.

Carroll, A.B. (2000), "The four faces of corporate citizenship", in Richardson, J.E. (Ed), Business Ethics 00/01, Dushkin/McGraw-Hill, Guilford, CT, pp. 187–191.

Carroll, A.B. (2001), "Ethical challenges for business in the new millennium: corporate social responsibility and models of management morality", in Richardson, J.E. (Ed), Business Ethics 01/02, Dushkin/McGraw-Hill, Guilford, CT, pp. 187–191.

Davis, K. (1983), "An expanded view of the social responsibility of business", in Beachamp, T.L. and Bowie, N.E. (Eds), Ethical Theory and Business, Second Edition, Prentice-Hall, Inc., Englewood Cliffs, NJ.

Diaz, J. (1993), "Science, engineering and the discipline of real estate". Journal of Real Estate Literature, 1(2), 183–195.

Dotse, J. (2006), "GSDI capacity building requirements of national mapping agencies in developing countries", Electronic copy available at http://creativecommons.org/licenses/by/3.0/us/

Enemark, S. (2003), "Understanding the concept of capacity building and the nature of administration systems", FIG Working Week April 13–17, 2003, Paris, France.

Epley, D.R. (1996), "The current body of knowledge paradigms used in real estate education and issues in need of further research". Journal of Real Estate Research, 12(2), 229–236.

European Union (EU) (2001), Green Paper on promoting a European Framework for Corporate Social Responsibility.

Freeman, R.E. (2001), "Stakeholder theory of the modern corporation", in Hoffman, W.M., Frederick, R.E., and Schwartz, M.S. (Eds), Business Ethics: Readings and Cases in Corporate Morality, Fourth Edition, McGraw Hill, Boston, MA.

Gilbertson, B. and Preston, D. (2005), "A vision for valuation". RICS Leading Edge Series: London.

International Centre for Social Corporate Responsibility, Nottingham University Business School (2006), An Evaluation of Corporate Community Investment in the UK.

International Valuation Standards (IVS) (2000), Electronic copy available on the IVS Committee web site (www.ivsc.org).

Lantos, G.P. (2001), "The boundaries of strategic corporate social responsibility". Journal of Consumer Marketing, 18(7), 595–630.

Lippke, R.L. (1996), "Setting the terms of the business responsibility debate", in Larmer, R.A. (Ed), Ethics in the Workplace: Selected Readings in Business Ethics, West Publishing Company, St. Paul, MN.

Magel, H. and Franke, S. (2007), "Good governance, - what does it mean for surveyor's profession and contributions?" Technische Universitaet Muenchen, Institute of Geodesy, GIS and Land Management, Muenchen, Germany.

Milgrim, M.R. (2001), "International valuation standards for global property markets". Paper delivered at the Japan Real Estate Institute, Tokyo, 31 January, 2001.

Ndungu, K., Makathimo, M., and Kaaria, M. (2002), "The challenges in globalisation of valuation profession – lessons from Nairobi, Kenya". FIG XXII International Congress, Washington DC, USA, April 19–26.

NIESV (2005), The Constitution of The Nigerian Institution of Estate Surveyors and Valuers, Lagos.

Novak, M. (1996), Business as a Calling: Work and the Examined Life, The Free Press, New York

Parsa, A. (1999), Globalisation and real estate education. RICS Research Paper Series: London.

Pitts, J. and Jackson, T.O. (2008), "Green buildings: valuation issues and perspectives". The Appraisal Journal, Spring 2008, 115–118.

Rabianski, J.S. and Black, R.T. (1999), "An international perspective on the importance of real estate concepts and topics". Journal of Real Estate Practice and Education, 2(1), 13–32.

Reinold, D.P. (2003), "Real estate appraisals". Electronic copy available at: www.arkansastimber.info.

Robinson, J. (2005), "Property valuation and analysis applied to environmentally sustainable development". Pacific Rim Real Estate Society (PRRES) Conference, 2005.

Septh, J.G. (1997), "Challenges for sustainable human development: governance and democratization". Speech at the Bruno Kreisky Forum on International Dialogue, Austria, April 15, 1997 (as quoted in Angola NHDR, 1998, UNDP).

Schulte, K., Schulte-Daxbok, G., Holzmann, C., and Wiffler, M. (2005), Internationalisation of Real Estate Education. FIG Working Week 2005 and GSDI-8 Cairo, Egypt. April 16–21.

Shalley, M.J., Jr. (2008), "Green buildings: a new paradigm in real estate". IPT Property Tax Symposium, November 2–5, 2008.

Smith, N.C. and Quelch, J.A. (1993), Ethics in Marketing, Irwin, Homewood, IL.

The Appraisal Foundation (2003), "Uniform standards of professional appraisal practice (USPAP)". Electronic copy available at: www.appraisalfoundation.org

The Appraisal Institute (2001), "The appraisal of real estate". Twelfth Edition, Chicago.

The Appraisal Institute (2007), "Understanding the appraisal". Electronic copy available at: www.appraisalinstitute.org

The World Bank (2006), World Development Report.

UN-ECE (1996), Land Administration Guidelines, UNECE, Geneva.

UN-FIG (1999), The Bathurst Declaration on Land Administration for Sustainable Development. FIG Office, Copenhagen, Denmark.

Waddock, S. and Smith, N. (2000) "Relationships: the real challenge of corporate global citizenship". Business and Society Review, 105(1), 44–62.

Wilbourn, P. (2008), "Building the environmental capacity of the surveyor". FIG Working Week, 14–19 June, 2008, Stockholm, Sweden.

Worzala, E. (1996), "ARES and the formation of the international real estate society". The Journal of Real Estate Research, 12(2), 167–181.

Wyatt, P. (2001), "An investigation of the nature of the valuation service offered to business occupiers". Journal of Property Investment and Finance, 19(2), 100–126.

Yuan, L.L. (2008), "Perceptions of sustainable developments on real estate values". Paper presented at The 24th Pan Pacific Congress of Real Estate Appraisers, Valuers and Counselors, 22–25 September, 2008, Seoul, Korea.

Electronic Sources

AIC: About AIC: Areas of Responsibility within Canada http://www.aicanada.ca/e/aboutaic_areas.cfm?print22=1& ; site accessed 5/20/2008

API: Australian Property Institute Overview http://www.propertyinstitute.com.au/printfriendly.aspx?MenuID=1&Su menuID=1 site accessed 5/20/2008

APPRAISAL INSTITUTE: About Us http://www.appraisalinstitute.org/about/ site accessed 5/20/2008

ARES: About Us http://www.aresnet.org/AboutUs.htm site accessed 5/20/2008

AsRES: About Us http://www.asres.org/about_1.htm site accessed 5/20/2008

CASLE: About CASLE http://www.awestcott.freeserve.co.uk/casle/about.htm site accessed 5/20/2008

ERES: About ERES http://eres.ua.es/privat/estatico.php?c=1 site accessed 5/20/2008

NZIV: About New Zealand Institute of Valuers http://www.property.org.nz/AM/Template.cfm?Section=About_NZIV&Template=/CM/H site accessed 5/20/2008

NIESV: http://niesv.org/pages.php?page_id=2&site_id=2 site accessed 5/20/2008

RICS: Who we are http://www.rics.org/Aboutus/spotlight.htm site accessed 5/20/2008

Chapter 13
Corporate Social Responsibility and Ethics in Real Estate: Evidence from Turkey

Berna Kirkulak

Water, everywhere over the earth, flows to join together. A single natural law controls it. Each human is a member of a community and should work within it

Tao I Ching

Abstract Many countries have experienced real estate bubbles due to unethical appraisal practices and a limited base of real estate industry skills. Since the real estate industry is subject to a series of uncertainties and therefore speculation, a responsible method of real estate appraisal reduces the risk involved in property transactions. In the absence of a credible real estate appraisal method, investors are prone to experience swings in property values and suffer as a result.

Financial crises tend to have an adverse impact on the real estate industry. This is more so when a country's financial system relies too heavily on its banking sector, the chances of systemic vulnerabilities increase. Social change can be achieved through the quality of the service provided by the financial markets. Banks which are aware of the importance of CSR in their lending decisions are more likely to operate in a more socially responsible manner. Turkey, as a bank oriented country, suffered from the last banking crisis of 2001. The economy started to recover in 2003 and since then the rate of inflation has increased and interest rates have declined. This provided a basis for a mortgage lending market and consequently the need for improving the standards of real estate appraisal emerged. This can be accomplished by establishing professional standards of appraisal, education requirements, and ethics in developing real estate markets.

This paper attempts to evaluate the current state of real estate appraisal process in Turkey from an ethical view point. It provides a case study of real estate appraisal in Turkey. It points out the consequences of fraudulent practices that could have a devastating impact on the economics of real estate investment. It seeks to draw attention to the role of real estate agents and real estate appraisers who could contribute

B. Kirkulak (✉)
Dokuz Eylul University, Izmir, Turkey

S.O. Idowu, W.L. Filho (eds.), *Professionals' Perspectives of Corporate Social Responsibility*, DOI 10.1007/978-3-642-02630-0_14,
© Springer-Verlag Berlin Heidelberg 2009

to society in a responsible manner. It is hoped that this paper provides some insights into CSR practices and ethics for real estate investment in emerging markets, namely Turkey.

13.1 Introduction

Real estate is a broad term and it covers not only commercial real estate but also residential real estate. Although real estate is often considered to be a profitable investment tool, it provides people's basic housing needs and hence, has substantial implications for society. Ethical values and practices in real estate business are important for the stakeholders such as investors, real estate agents, real estate appraisers, financial institutions, and government bodies who are involved in real estate transactions. In order to build a respectful environment, market players of real estate business should embed the principles of corporate social responsibility (CSR) into their operations.

There is a growing awareness of the principles of CSR in the financial markets around the globe; in particular in the real estate market due to occasional financial crises. A better understanding of the ethos of CSR can contribute to the prevention and resolution of conflicts in financial transactions such as mortgages. In particular, the lending process has had a great impact on real estate. Examples include the Asian financial crisis and the recent credit crunch which emanated from the US. All these show that irresponsible lending in the industry the real estate booms often ended in bank failures. Almost a decade ago, most of the Asian countries including Japan, Thailand, Korea, Indonesia, and Malaysia faced a financial collapse due to the imbalances in real estate which resulted in banking busts. Recently, the US experienced a severe financial crisis in similar circumstances which stemmed from the real estate boom, triggered by the failure of banks. Both experiences underline the importance of a strong bank regulatory system and CSR. Poorly supervised financial markets and legal loopholes may induce fraudulent practices that lead to misallocation of high-risk credits. In order to prevent this, a strong ground for regulations, supervisory standards and comprehensive education should be established.

CSR deals with issues which should facilitate mutual understanding between the company and its stakeholders with the aim of building trust. The current crisis emerged due to the collapse in trust; perhaps between the two sides. The recent event in the global money markets and real estate industry heightens the need for qualified real estate appraisers to operate in the industry. This is because the absence of qualified and trustworthy appraisers could make it difficult if not totally impossible to promote market transparency. Lack of credible appraisal speeds up the speculation process and this is reflected in real estate prices. It is believed that a market with more responsive regulatory environment tend to experience less volatility as well as less appraisal and mortgage frauds characterized by speculation. Malpezzi and Wachter (2005) argue that the effects of speculation depend on supply conditions including the regulatory framework for real estate. Lending processes form bubbles through speculative pricing. Hence, it is important to minimize the risks associated with housing loans faced by the banks. Pomerleano (2005) notes that countries with qualified professionals in real estate business respond more quickly to asset bubbles in comparison with the countries which have no solid foundation. The differences may stem from the nature of the legal traditions. In his paper, it is argued that common law reacts quickly to new circumstances; however, civil law does not react in the same manner in adapting to the changing needs of the economy. While common law practices rely on independent jury and judges, civil law practices rely on legal codes. In terms of real estate appraisal, civil law practices may require additional regulations such as insurance policies.

The size of the company is another important issue for CSR practices. Without having institutional settings, it is a hard task to fulfill the required CSR responsibilities to all stakeholders. In general, large companies undertake initiatives to foster CSR through donations, sponsorship, training programmes, and implementing new standards etc. Lepoutre and Heene (2006) argue that due to financial constrains, small and medium sized enterprises (SMEs) have difficulties becoming involved in CSR practices. In particular, CEO duality (owner-manager) in small businesses becomes an important issue resulting in a degree of conflict between self interest and social priority. From the view point of CSR, real estate agencies need careful attention. In Turkey, most of the real estate agents are relatively small business and they are self-employed. Heavy competition in the market and lack of customers' expectations make real estate agents unconcerned about taking issues relating to CSR seriously. It is important that real estate agencies take an active role in improving the neighborhoods and commit themselves to sustainable development. Turkey provides a unique ground to examine the ethical sense of real estate agents when it comes to fulfilling CSR criteria.

In Turkey, the stable economic and political environment created a stimulus for real estate and financial instruments such as housing loans over the last couple of years. Housing loans have increased considerably following the recovery of the economy from the 2001 financial crisis. However, developments in real estate do not facilitate good reputation for the real estate business and its market players. The *Ethical Values Foundation of Turkey* (TEDMER) conducted a survey about ethics indicators in 2007. The survey was pooled among 84 CEOs and high level managers in leading Turkish firms. According to survey results, the construction industry is ranked as the 5th industry that needs to make significant progress in terms of ethical issues (TEDMER, 2007). Another survey, the Real Estate Transparency Index, conducted by Jones Lang LaSalle (2008) reveals that Turkey is part of the low-transparency group. Among the 81 countries which participated in the study, Turkey is ranked 67th, reflecting the fact that the real estate industry is opaque. It is stated that the uncertainty associated with Turkey's EU application membership has resulted in a low transparency market. Furthermore, the survey documents that transparency is high in Europe but it is low in MENA (Middle East and North African) countries. However, the MENA region has been receiving increased attention from international investors.

To the author's best knowledge, there is presently no study about real estate investment from an ethical and CSR perspectives. This paper therefore attempts to correct this imperfection and examines the real estate appraisal process in Turkey. The paper seeks to attract attention to the need for training and legal regulations in order to promote CSR activities in the real estate industry in emerging markets such as Turkey. In order to achieve this objective, the current study focuses on the market players such as real estate agents and appraisers. The paper discusses the intermediary function of real estate agents and it presents a case study regarding real estate appraisal practices in Turkey.

The remainder of this paper is structured as follows; Section 13.2 describes the real estate market including real estate agents, real estate appraisers and mortgage systems in the country. Section 13.3 discusses the mortgage and appraisal fraud Section 13.4 concludes the paper.

13.2 Real Estate Market in Turkey

Real estate is the preferred investment method for many Turkish people. This can be explained with the economic circumstances. In their paper, Gur et al. (2002) argue that the inadequacy of the Turkish social security system and the country's unstable economic conditions have brought about people's involvements in real estate transactions.

Turkey has experienced hyper inflation over the last two decades and its citizens have attempted to prevent their savings from being eroded by this unacceptable economic problem. Hence, many people have tended to invest in real estate. Inflation and political uncertainty have made the country's financial market vulnerable due to the high cost of borrowing. Table 13.1 shows the annual inflation rate from 1998 through to 2001. Although the inflation rate started to decrease steadily over the years, it remained high compared with most other countries. In 2003, there was a sharp decline in the inflation rate showing a recovery in the economy and success of the disinflation programme. As of 2007, the inflation rate reduced to one figure number. Table 13.1 further presents the devaluation of the Turkish Lira (TL) against the US dollar. In particular, there was a sharp depreciation of the TL during the 2001 financial crisis.

There is a close relationship between the value of the domestic currency and the interest of foreigners in real estate. When a country's domestic currency depreciates in value, it becomes more attractive and cheaper for foreigners to purchase goods and services including real estate in that country. Balkir and Kirkulak (2009) studied the economic and social impacts of the retired migrants in Turkey namely in Antalya. They noted that most Mediterranean countries such as Spain, Italy, Malta etc. are losing their attractiveness for foreign retirees due to the overvaluation of properties. Recently, Turkey emerged as a new retirement destination and this new trend has resulted in an increasing number of foreign retirees immigrating to Turkey. In particular, Balkir and Kirkulak (2009) note a close relationship

Table 13.1 Major economic indicators from 1998 through 2007

Year	Inflation rate %	USD $/TL (YTL)
1998	84.6	314,230
1999	64.9	542,703
2000	54.9	675,004
2001	54.4	1,446,510
2002	45.0	1,642,384
2003	25.3	1,402,567
2004	10.6	1,348,600
2005	10.14	1.34950
2006	10.51	1.41990
2007	8.76	1.17030

Source: Turkish Statistical Institute (TUIK) (2008) Inflation and Price, Available at http://www.tuik.gov.tr As of January 2005, six zeros were omitted from the Turkish Lira. The new currency is called the New Turkish Lira (YTL). Hence, the values are in TL from 1998 to 2004 and in YTL from 2005 to 2007.

between the time of purchasing property and the financial crisis. They argue that during the 2001 financial crisis when the Turkish local currency depreciated, there was a sharp increase in property purchases by foreigners. However, the intensive interest of foreigners in the real estate market created unethical profits. In their paper, they discussed that the increasing number of property purchases by foreigners was accompanied by an increase in the property prices. This resulted in a situation where the country's local people could no longer afford buying houses.

The Turkish real estate market was affected by several factors over the years. In 1999, there was a severe earthquake and it was the turning point for the real estate industry. The human loss and the economic damages of the earthquake were enormous. This led to a need for good quality and sustainable housing. This necessitated for the country's policy makers to implement measures desired to reduce the risks inherent in any future earthquake risk. These measures understandably increased the construction costs. Following the earthquake, the Turkish economy was badly shaken by a severe financial crisis. The 2001 financial crisis adversely impacted on the construction industry. While some people suffered in bother financial and other terms by the crisis, it created several opportunities for others. The financial crisis provided some benefits to those who had enough liquidity and could afford to purchase real estate at discounted prices. The prolonged recession continued until the economy recovered in 2003. Accordingly, the construction and real estate industries were positively affected from the optimisms created by the recovery. The real estate industry peaked in 2005.

There were numerous reasons for the peak in the industry in 2005, three major events occurred. First, the real estate acquisition law for foreigners was liberalized. Real estate acquisition by foreigners is regulated in article 35 of the Land Registry Law No. 2644. According to this law, foreigners were not allowed to own property.

In 2003, this law was modified and the restrictions were removed (Article 19 of Law No. 4916), allowing foreigners to buy real estate if there would be a reciprocal agreement. This modification accelerated property purchases by foreigners. However, in 2005, the Constitutional Court abolished this article suspending all purchases by foreigners. In 2008, foreigners were again allowed to purchase property imposing some restrictions for foreign firms. Second, the real estate boom gained momentum following Turkey's accession talks with the EU in 2004. This increased foreigners' appetites to want to own real estate with comparatively lower prices to their home countries. They hope to earn substantial returns on their investments when Turkey eventually becomes a full member state of the EU. Investing in real estate became a rising investment dynamic driven by optimism about Turkey's full EU membership. Third, the Turkish economy recovered from the financial crisis and started to take off in 2003. This resulted in an increasing trend in real estate. The economic and political instability, low interest rates, high economic growth rate, and the positive atmosphere created in the economy provided unique grounds to extend credit maturities. The availability of long-term credits significantly changed the consumption patterns of the investors, such as buying a house through mortgages. Furthermore, a new Mortgage Law was introduced in 2007. This law aims to improve real estate finance and to promote a primary mortgage market. It is expected that the new mortgage law will help boost the property market and also bring new standards for the construction industry, in such a way that only qualified houses would be eligible for mortgage financing.

The report prepared by the Banking Regulation and Supervision Agency (BRSA) (2007) shows a development in housing loans between 2002 through to 2007. The restoration of economic and political stability after the 2001 financial crisis had a positive effect on the real estate industry. Table 13.2 indicates that there is clear evidence that the housing loans increased significantly during the period. In particular, the increase in the amount of housing loans reached its peak of up to 371.5% in 2005. This has led to some commentators questioning whether or not a real estate bubble actually took place. In their study, Binay and Salman (2008) examined the real estate prices in Ankara between 2002 through to 2005 and argued that there was probably a real estate price bubble. They came to the conclusion that real estate prices have recently picked up to the pre-2001 crisis levels. Therefore, they argue that it is too early to say that the Turkish economy experienced a real estate price bubble during 2005. Table 13.2 further shows that although the amount of mortgage loans increased over the period, there was a decline in the percentage increase of the housing loans since 2006. This could be attributed to the recession in the global economy. In 2006, increasing interest rates slowed down the housing loans and curbed customers' willingness to buy properties. The increase in housing loans declined from over 371.5 to 88.4%.

Turkey lacked the mortgage market and financial infrastructure for a long time due to hyper inflation. The absence of a proper mortgage market reduced the importance of real estate financing and its education. Onder (2002), who studied real estate education in Turkey, argued that there was no adequate interest in real estate education by the country's universities. Most of the courses were offered at undergraduate

Table 13.2 The development of mortgage loans in Turkey

Year	Housing loans (million YTL)	Percentage (%) increase	Percentage (%) in total loans	Non-accruing housing loans (million YTL)
2002	460	–	0.9	11
2003	786	70.9	1.2	10
2004	2,631	234.8	2.7	14
2005	12,407	371.5	8.4	16
2006	23,377	88.4	10.7	56
2007	32,448	38.8	11.4	218

Source: Banking Regulation and Supervision Agency (2007) Financial Markets Report, No. 8, Available at http://www.bddk.org.tr/turkce/Raporlar/ Finansal_Piyasalar_Raporlari/4816FPR-Aralik2007.pdf

level and they mainly focus on city and regional planning, and urban economics. However, some universities have started offering real estate financing courses as electives in recent years. This could be attributed to the increasing popularity of real estate in the country. The availability of the mortgage system has not only increased the number of property acquired but displayed a need for real estate education in terms of financing and appraisal.

13.2.1 Real Estate Agents

In Turkey, there is no specific legislation which regulates the activities those who operate as real estate agents. The real estate agencies can be in the form of either merchant real estate agencies or tradesmen real estate agencies, with each type being subject to different regulations. Most of those who operate as real estate agents are relatively small and self-employed. A family member can keep the office open during the absence of the person who runs the firm. Children follow in their fathers' footsteps and therefore the agency can be passed on from father to son. There is no regulation preventing this process from taking place. In particular, during the 1980s and 1990s, the social security system encouraged people to retire in their late 30s and early 40s. Retirement disbursements, particularly for government officers, are usually not enough to survive on with a high quality of life. Retirement is perceived in Turkey as a chance to have a second job such as being a real estate agent. Therefore, it is a common case that many retired high school teachers or retired army officers become real estate agents. This kind of situation accompanied with the lack of knowledge and experience in the industry often result in adverse impacts on the reputation of those who practice the real estate profession. For this reason, it is important that people, who are in the business of real estate agents, should commit themselves to the profession as a lifetime profession instead of treating it as a fall-back secondary profession after retirement from their primary professions.

In recent years, there have been a few attempts by foreign owned real estate agents to enter into the real estate market in the country by providing consulting services, feasibility and investment analysis, and property valuation.[1] These firms have franchised agreements with domestic real estate agents. Under the franchise agreement, domestic agents pay a fee for the privilege of using the well established franchised label. Brand reputation plays a crucial role in the franchised agreements and CSR consequently is a driver for brand reputation. It therefore makes perfect sense for franchised real estate firms to maintain their brand images. Nourick (2001) argues that the presence of a franchised agreement contributes to social responsibility. The agreement, with an institutional setting, provides a variety of training brings more high quality standards to bear on the profession and franchisors being generally from Western countries are more likely to integrate CSR ethos into their business strategy. However, it is important to bear in mind that being attached to a well established foreign real estate firm is not the equivalent of being an accredited real estate agent. The franchisee real estate agents bear the full responsibility for the failure or fraudulent actions of their firms.

An important issue regarding real estate agents is commission. Real estate agents play an active role at each stage of the real estate transaction and they are paid commission fees when the deal is finally brought to a successful close. The commissions are typically a percentage of the sales price of the property. In Turkey, the 'Compulsory Standard Communiqué for Real Estate Agencies' was issued by the Ministry of Industry and Trade in 2003, and it came into force in 2004. According to the communiqué, real estate commissions are specified by the relevant professional body. The commissions on real estate transactions are not negotiable, and as such the real estate agents charge a fixed fee, which is determined by the Real Estate Professional Chamber. It is unethical to charge a *commission* according to the value of the property. Real estate agents charge a commission of 3% of the total value of the property which both seller and buyer pay.

The absence of regulations and control mechanisms in the industry in Turkey has encouraged unfair competitive practices. In some cases, real estate agents often offer buyers and sellers services at a price lower than the prevailing commission fees. This suggests that albeit; professionals in the industry make people believe that their commissions are not negotiable but this is certainly not the case. An OECD report of 2007, in fact mentioned that in Turkey, being a merchant or a tradesman in the real estate business means that different pricing practices are in operation in terms of the tariffs and commissions charged. There is no regulation to discourage the activities of low-cost agents. The real estate transactions need to be mortified and unfair competition restrictions should be effected in order to avoid unfair business practices.

---

[1] The most well-known franchise brands among real estate agents are twenty first Century, Remax, TURYAP, and EskiDJ. The first two firms are foreign owned real estate franchise labels and the other two firms are domestic franchise labels.

13.2.2 Real Estate Appraisers

Turkey, as an emerging market, still lacks qualified and trained appraisers to apply the generally accepted standards in the industry. In general, real estate appraisal practices depend heavily on past experiences. The real estate market is not transparent, and there is no property value index. There are three methods widely used for real estate appraisal: sales comparison, income approach, and cost approach methods. The income approach method is applied to commercial properties such as offices, houses for rent, agricultural lands, etc., which provide incomes. In the absence of proper data, the values these properties are estimated by the cost approach. There is a great need for independent real estate appraisers who are eligible and qualified to assess the real value of properties.

The real estate market is being regulated by several laws such as city planning, tax, expropriation, and capital market laws. The legal framework for real estate appraisal has been recently formed. The government appointed the Capital Markets Board of Turkey (CMBT) to regulate the real estate market. The CMBT is the regulatory and supervisory authority which certifies appraisers. The real estate appraisal firms operate in accordance with the 'Communiqué on Principles Regarding Pertaining to Companies Offering Valuation Services according to Capital Markets Legislation and the listing Rules of these Companies to be used by the Board', Serial No. VIII, No. 35. The regulation took effect in 2001. The communiqué also regulates the duration of the services obtained. According to the regulation, firms can obtain services from the same real estate appraisal firm for up to 5 consecutive years. After 5 years, the firms should wait at least 2 years in order to get appraisal services from the same appraisal firm (Communiqué Serial: VI, No: 20). The logic behind this regulation can be attributed to ethical concerns. Long ongoing business relations between companies and the appraisal firms may lead to conflicts of interest and this may distort the real estate transactions in the long-run.

The Mortgage Law was enacted to improve the standards in real estate industry. The Mortgage Law was prepared by the CMBT and it was passed by the Parliament in 2007. The new regulations made significant amendments and strengthened the legal grounds for real estate appraisal. According to the Mortgage Law, appraisal services are defined as a profession and the appraisal process should be done by certified real estate appraisers. The law also states that secured loans by mortgages cannot exceed 75% of the total value of a property and the loan cannot exceed 50% of the total value of the property in question. A mortgage fraud occurs when the appraiser's report inflates the value in order to help their customer to obtain a loan which is over and above what the lender would normally wish to lend the borrower in order to cover all expenses with the excess loan. As a result, the customer may not even pay the compulsory 25% of the total value of a house due to the property's inflated value. This gives rise to a bubble in the real estate industry in Turkey. Therefore, it is important to have independent, accredited professional real estate appraisers to carry out the appraisal process. Being aware of the fragility of the market and this unethical practice, some banks have recently attempted to protect their lending transactions by obtaining professional services from real estate appraisers.

There is also evidence that some banks have already established their own appraisal firms.

In Turkey, the Real Estate Appraisal Association was established in 2001. It is a member of The European Group of Valuers of Fixed Assets (TEGOVOFA) and International Valuation Standards Committee (IVSC). The association plays a leading role in coordinating the activities of real estate appraisers. In pursuant to the Mortgage law, the appraisers are required to register with the association within three months after they obtain their licences. It is important to note that the association is not in charge of the certification of appraisers. Appraisal experts are licensed and regulated by the CMBT. The requirements for real estate appraisers are listed below:

- to have graduated from a 4-year university
- to have professional experience of at least three years in the relevant fields such as law, construction, banking and finance etc.
- to pass the written examinations in five subjects including the Professional Legislation and Ethics Code

13.3 Mortgage and Appraisal Fraud

In general, the most common fraudulent practices in real estate are often related to mortgages and appraisals. The success of the appraisal firms heavily depends upon the accuracy and the competence of the reports they provide. Bad practices of appraisers may damage the financial markets and result in huge losses. Therefore, the appraisal process and the duties performed by appraisers need great attention.

The real estate industry is subject to speculative practices. Risk is associated with mispricing, insufficient investigations, and compromises in the independence of the appraisers. Agency problem is a key issue in real estate appraisal and mortgage lending. There is a conflicting interest between the principal and agent. While vendors, buyers, and lenders can be considered principals in the appraisal process, appraisers act as agents. The structure of the relationships between the principals and the appraiser can affect the outcome of the appraisal process. There is a large body of literature examining the mortgage and appraisal fraud in real estate. Among them, Smolen and Hambleton (1997) carried out a survey in the US and reported that almost 80% of appraisers had been pressured by lenders to modify their appraisal reports. Lentz and Wang (1998) note that appraisers are constantly under pressure to estimate the value of the property at the agreed price between the vendor and buyer. Worzala et al. (1998) found a similar conclusion reflecting the fact that most of the appraisers experience pressure to overestimate real estate value. There are also supporting evidence of appraisal fraud from emerging markets. The recent study of Chen and Yu (2009) shows that there is significant pressure on valuation practices in both Taiwan and Singapore. They attribute this outcome to the lack of transparent market information. In their paper, Amidu and Aluko (2007) examine the client influence on valuation in Nigeria and they note that individual borrowers are the primary source of pressure on appraisers.

One of the shortcomings of the appraisal process in Turkey is its ineffective monitoring. When competition warms up in the market, there is the tendency for real estate appraisal firms to get involved in providing insufficient appraisal investigations and careless practices. Roberts et al. (2007) note that unreported real estate appraisal fraud is a very common practice in the real estate market. They analyzed real estate fraud from a broad perspective and argue that most of the real estate professionals encounter fraudulent deals at one time or the other during their professional lives. Since some appraisers often refuse to be a part of such deals, they are generally unwilling to report such cases. This argument partly explains the causes of the real estate bubble and burst that triggered the recent financial crisis which drew attention to the subprime mortgage defaults. It seems that in light of this turmoil, real estate appraisal fraud investigations would gain more prominence in the market around the world.

The case study given below provides evidence about the incident of an incompetent appraisal report. It is the first reported real estate appraisal fraud in Turkey and it highlights some of the shortcomings of real estate appraisal process in that part of the world.

13.3.1 Case Study

In 2006, the CMBT delisted one of the real estate appraisal firms named Turyap Appraisal Corporation (TAC) and cancelled the licenses of 7 practitioners working in the industry in Turkey. Among these experts whose licenses were revoked, 4 of them worked for TAC and the rest worked for other firms. The firm was accused of violating some professional ethics and was delisted due to its provision to clients inadequate investigation services and incorrect appraisal reports. This resulted in loss of reputation and confidence in the real estate market. The reason was that TAC was known as one of the leading firms involved in appraising not only real estate but also a wide range of tangible fixed assets including machines and vehicles.

Indeed, TAC was an affiliate of Turyap, its holding firm whose history goes back to 1980s. Turyap was established as a real estate agent in 1986 and expanded its franchise business over a number of years. The growth potential of the market and the expansion in the requirement for valuation encouraged Turyap to expand its scope and establish TAC in 1992. The firm gained reputation over the years having been successful in appraising a large number of real estate in both the domestic and international markets.

In Turkey, the CMBT is authorized to delist and revoke the appraisal licence of any real estate appraisal firm found to have contravened the rules and regulations prescribed in the Mortgage Law Act 2007. Listing, delisting and relisting conditions for real estate appraisal firms are clearly described by legislations (Communiqué Serial No. VIII No. 35, Article 4 and 9). Delisted real estate appraisal firms can apply to the CMBT for being relisted. However, they have to wait for at least 5 months which is a relatively short period of time before being eligible to do so. At the end of 5 months, a real estate appraisal firm should ensure that the condition(s) or violation(s) which led to its delisting have been eliminated. The CMBT takes the reapplication into account and gives the decision for relisting according to the evidence provided which indicates that those conditions or circumstances which led to the decision to delist have changed. The delisting conditions in Article 9 provide the following criteria:

(a) Failure to fulfill the requirements of Article 4 (g) or (h) and a continued existence of this situation for at least 6 months.
Article 4 (g) – states that at least 51% of the paid up capital of the real estate appraisal firm should belong to 2 responsible real estate appraisal experts.
Article 4 (h) – states that in order to establish a real estate appraisal firm, there must be at least 2 full-time employees responsible to real estate appraisal experts and 5 real estate appraisal experts must be employed by the firm.
(b) Appraisal reports have been signed by unqualified and uncertified people.
(c) Inadequate investigations during the appraisal process.
(d) Failure to comply with the expected appraisal standards and appraisal professional ethics described in the capital market legislation framework.
(e) Inadequate level of information given in the reports to conclude the appraisal exercise.
(f) Provision of incorrect, incomplete, misleading and fake appraisal reports or information.
(g) Failure or delay to submit the information to CMBT when required or to report to CMBT.
(h) Notification of the firm's violation of the independency principle.
(i) Failure to comply with stipulated regulations for real estate appraisal firms as provided in the capital market legislation.

TAC's delisting was as a result of a complaint made by Halkbank which received an appraisal service from TAC for a building used as collateral for a loan advanced by it. When the loan became delinquent, Halkbank attempted to convert the collateral into cash. The bank was not able to sell the building at the price appraisal valued noted by TAC. The appraisal value was not similar to the general prices in the locality of the property (Karamuk, 2006). This was the genesis of the problem. The bone of contention was basically on the two reports prepared by TAC for Emlak Real Estate Investment Trust (EREIT). Emlak REIT asked 3 real estate appraisal firms including TAC to prepare real estate appraisal reports for two lands located in Ataşehir in Istanbul. Emlak REIT used the appraisal reports prepared by TAC which valued the land at a relatively lower price level. Emlak REIT presented these reports in a tender; unfortunately the reports failed to comply with the expected requirements (Guven, 2006). After having investigated the case, the CMBT declared that TAC did not comply with the standards required of a professional real estate appraisal practice as stated in the rules in Article 9 (c), (d) and (e). Furthermore, the

CMBT considered TAC as acting contrary to the provisions of Article 10 and Article 14 which describes the responsibilities and code of professional ethics, respectively. This was the first case of an appraisal licence revocation in Turkey and TAC was delisted from the CMBT's real estate appraisal firms' register. Thus, the number of real estate appraisal firms reduced to twelve in 2006.

After being delisted, TAC stated that the company was delisted due to improper appraisal report format. TAC further argued that Emlak REIT did not inform them that the requested appraisal reports were for tender. The officials of TAC critical of the CMBT's way handled the situation. TAC was also critical of CMBT's failure to provide adequate notice prior to the public declaration of its delisting (Guven, 2006). Indeed, it is the responsibility of a real estate appraisal firm to prepare its reports in accordance with the required standards. It is a general understanding that all appraisal companies should comply the standards specified by the CMBT guidance notes for each single report they provide to their clients even when the report is to be used for private purposes.

This evidence clearly indicates that in Turkey, the concept of real estate appraisal is in its initial stages. There is a need to link the appraisal exercise with the field of social responsibility as many of the 'ingredients' for the interrelationship between business and society are present. Appraisal firms and appraisers should identify risks inherent in their activities and they should ensure that they integrate CSR principles into their strategies. This should hopefully demonstrate that they are socially responsible and consequently protect their corporate reputation. The authorities should also tighten the licensing procedure; impose operational curbs to discourage malpractices, as well as stipulate criminal penalties to dissuade potential criminal actions being taken by practitioners in the sector. There are still gaps in the sector waiting to be fulfilled. For example: in the case of fraud, the CMBT may censure a certified real estate appraiser or impose an administrative fine which is a common practice in the USA. Upon conviction of a subsequent violation, the appraisal firm or appraisers may be punished in different ways such as revoking their licence. It is also important that the board should notify the licensee of the punishment decision prior to its public announcement.

A key issue that often arises in the sector and needs to be addressed is how to compensate vendors when the suffer losses following the failure of a real estate appraisal firm. Professional liability insurance system can be a partial solution to this problem. In developed countries, the insurance for real estate appraisals provides secure and efficient protection against consequential losses which could arise as a result of an unforeseen mishap. As a matter of fact, this experience allowed TAC to initiate the professional liability insurance for errors and omissions which emanated from its failure for the first time in the real estate industry in Turkey. However, a mandatory professional liability insurance coverage should be designated as one of the preconditions for licensing of all appraisal firms.

The remaining question relates to how individual landlords and investors' confidence as to the accuracy of the valuation services that they receive can be restored. This is even more so as it has been suggested that even some reputable firms in the sector are not totally exonerated from real estate appraisal fraud. In response to growing concern over the problem of appraisal frauds, governmental bodies should increase the number of their inspection watchdogs and mandate professional liability insurance coverage for both errors and omissions on the part of appraisal experts. Having said this, it is important to note that regulations and threats of criminal proceedings can only be successful to dissuade fraudulent practices up to a given limit. Individual consciousness and public attention will certainly be required to ensure compliance.

13.4 Conclusion

Issues relating to CSR have been of increasing concern not just in Turkey but globally, see for example Idowu and Filho (2009). The concern has heightened following the recent financial crises in real estate investments around the globe triggered by both irresponsible lending and over-valuation of real estate properties in some parts of the world. This chapter has examined the issue of ethics in real estate investment and discusses the roles of real estate agents and appraisers in their attempt to make some positive contributions to what goes on in society focusing principally on Turkey.

After the recovery from the financial crisis in 2001, the Turkish economy has started to strengthen. The passing of regulations relating to the financial market has led to a more stable economy. In particular, Turkey has managed to keep inflation under control and this has resulted in low borrowing costs and a considerable increase in the amount of housing loans advanced by financial institutions. Furthermore, Turkey's accession talks on its proposal to join the EU and the legislation enabling foreigners to purchase real estate properties in the country has increased the interest and confidence of global investors. In terms of the price bubble, it is too early to state that Turkey has experienced real estate price bubble. However, it is a striking fact that the Turkish real estate market has developed as a result of its stable economic and political environment of the past few years. Its consecutive regulations in different areas have also encouraged good quality standards to real estate appraisal sector since 2001. Furthermore, the Mortgage Law was a turning point the regulation of the lending process in real estate sector. Accordingly, banks in Turkey like their counterpart elsewhere are under pressure to take issues relating to social responsibility seriously. However, it should be said that it is not enough only to seek solutions all problems through regulations and legislations. An ongoing education for personal and professional skills and encouraging individuals to understand their responsibilities to themselves and society and to equally behave virtuously are crucial ingredients when implementing CSR related strategies. Therefore, the real estate professionals at each level in the process; including financial institutions, real estate agents and real appraisers should voluntarily put in maximum efforts to bring about the best CSR practices to their professions and society.

This paper is a good starting point to attract attention to the importance of CSR in the real estate industry in an emerging market, such as that of Turkey. The paper mentions not only common deficiencies in the real estate industry but it also emphasizes that regulations and as well as supervision in the financial market are necessary in order to avoid ills such as speculations, fraudulent practices, and which could result in enormous economic losses. Furthermore, it is important that the real estate agents as well as appraisers are committed to high ethical standards not just for their own reputation but for society as a whole. This can be achieved through regulation, education, and training in the field of CSR. Considering the population growth and urbanization in Turkey, the real estate industry needs some structural reforms now and in the future. A growing economy will give some impetus to commercial real estate management which requires professional multidisciplinary actions. There are still some shortcomings and gaps to be filled, for example the insurance system against inaccurate evaluation methods needs to be revamped. It is hoped that this paper has been successful to draw the attention of readers to this piece about an in-depth understanding of ethics and CSR in the real estate industry in Turkey.

References

Amidu, A. and Aluko, B. 2007, 'Client Influence on Valuation: Perceptual Analysis of the Driving Factors', *International Journal of Strategic Property Management* Vol. 11, 77–89.

Balkir, C. and Kirkulak, B. 2009, 'Turkey, the New Destination for International Retirement Migration' in *Migration in Europe – Threat or Chance?*, eds. H. Fassmann, M. Haller, D. Lane, Edward Elgar, Cheltenham, UK (forthcoming).

Binay, S. and Salman, F. 2008, 'A Critique on Turkish Real Estate Market', *Turkish Economic Association*, Discussion Paper, Ankara.

BRSA 2007, Financial Markets Report, No: 8, Available at http://www.bddk.org.tr/turkce/Raporlar/Finansal_Piyasalar_Raporlari/4816FPR-Aralik2007.pdf.

Chen, F.Y. and Yu, S.M. 2009, 'Client on Valuation: Does Language Matter? A Comparative Analysis between Taiwan and Singapore', *Journal of Property Investment and Finance*, Vol. 27, 25–42.

Gur, M., Cagdas, V., and Demir, H. 2002, 'A General Overview of Real Estate Applications in Turkey', *FIG XXII International Congress*, Washington, DC, USA, April 19–26.

Guven, A.A. 2006, 'SPK Formata Takıldı Sektörde TURYAP'a Güven Sarsıldı', *Hürriyet Gazetesi*, Kasım 15.

Jones Lang Lasalle 2008, 'From Opacity to Transparency', *Global Real Estate Transparency Index*, Jones Lang Lasalle Publication, London.

Idowu, S.O. and Filho, W.L. (eds.) (2009), *Global Practices of Corporate Social Responsibility*, Springer Verlag, Berlin.

Karamuk, O. 2006, '50 Bin Gayrimenkul Bir Anda Değersiz Kaldı', *Vatan Gazetesi*, Ekim 11.

Lentz, G.H. and Wang, K. 1998, 'Residential Appraisal and the Lending Process: A Survey of Issues', *Journal of Real Estate Research*, Vol. 1/2, No. 15, 11–39.

Lepoutre, J. and Heene, A. 2006, 'Investigating the Impact of Firm Size on Small Business Social Responsibility: a Critical Review', *Journal of Business Ethics*, Vol. 67, No. 3, 257–273.

Malpezzi, S. and Wachter, M. 2005, 'The Role of Speculation in Real Estate Cycles', *Journal of Real Estate Literature*, Vol. 13, No. 2, 141–164.

Nourick, S. 2001, *Corporate Social Responsibility: Partners for Progress*, Organisation for Economic Co-operation and Development (OECD) Publishing, Paris.

OECD 2007, 'Improving Competition in Real Estate Transactions', Working Paper, (OECD) Publishing, Paris.

Onder, Z. 2002, 'Real Estate Research and Education in Turkey', in *Real Estate Education Throughout the World: Past, Present and Future*, ed. K.W. Schulte, Kluwer Academic Publishers, Norwell, MA.

Pomerleano, M. 2005, 'The Morning After: Restructuring Aftermath of an Asset Bubble', in *Asset Price Bubbles: The Implications for Monetary, Regulatory, and International Policies*, eds. W.C. Hunter, G.G. Kaufman, and M. Pomerleano, MIT Press, Cambridge.

Roberts, R.R., Dollar, R., and Kraynak, J. 2007, *Protect Yourself from Real Estate and Mortgage Fraud: Preserving the American Dream of Homeownership*, Kaplan Publishing, New York.

Smolen, G.E. and Hambleton, D.C. 1997, 'Is the Real Estate Appraiser's Role too Much to Expect?', *The Appraisal Journal*, Vol. 65, No. 1, 9–17.

TEDMER 2007, 'The Ethic Barometer in 2007', Ethical Values Foundation of Turkey, Working Paper, Istanbul.

TUIK 2008, Inflation and price statistics, Available at http://www.tuik.gov.tr .

Worzala, E.M., Lenk, M.M., and Kinnard, W.N. 1998, 'How Client Pressure Affects the Appraisal of Residential Property', *The Appraisal Journal*, Vol. 66, 416–427.

Part IV
Not-for Profit Organisations and Leisure

Chapter 14
Does 'Corporate' Responsibility Apply to Not-for-Profit Organizations?

Elizabeth Hogan

> *NGOs are diverse in terms of their missions, strategies,*
> *methods, and organizational forms, and the NGO world as a*
> *whole is anarchic. Quite appropriately, there are a number of*
> *distinguishable views and approaches within the NGO world.*
> ~ Morton Winston (2002)

Abstract This chapter begins by exploring the different approaches to Corporate Social Responsibility (CSR) between the standard practitioners, i.e. large multinational corporations (MNCs), and the not-for-profit sector, focusing on large-scale international NGOs. While it is assumed that not-for-profit organizations, given the very nature of their existence, are likely to meet the same social standards as the corporate sector, very little research has been done as to whether such organizations are practicing what they preach. Despite the fact that most of the well-known international NGOs have the organizational layout, funding, branding, and public relations of a large MNC, the expectations of these entities are less clearly defined. Are their resources better spent on the mission of their organization, or are they to be held to the highest standards of social conduct given their position as role models? Or is the most beneficial role of the NGO that of consultant to the corporate sector, regardless of whether they conduct such practices themselves? If not, how can CSR be incorporated into the business plan of a not-for-profit organization? The attempt to initiate these relatively new expectations of socially conscious behavior into the standard daily operations of a not-for-profit organization is viewed in the context of the similarity of NGOs to the MNCs which they position themselves to lead in the dawn of the CSR revolution.

Looking specifically at the World Resources Institute, the International Labor Rights Forum, and the International Fund for Animal Welfare, the study then goes on to examine the incentives behind CSR, and whether those goals are best met by current practices. Ultimately, the study revealed that the integration of

E. Hogan (✉)
David Gardiner & Associates, LLC, Washington, DC, USA

S.O. Idowu, W.L. Filho (eds.), *Professionals' Perspectives of Corporate Social Responsibility*, DOI 10.1007/978-3-642-02630-0_15,
© Springer-Verlag Berlin Heidelberg 2009

socially responsible business practices into everyday operations is best met when the endeavor is in line with the central goal of the organization, and socially conscious practices which fall outside of this scope are of a lesser concern.

14.1 Introduction

The phrase 'Corporate Social Responsibility' has in recent years become one of the most popular corporate catchphrases used throughout the global marketplace to distinguish the virtues of one company from another. The popularity of the practice has grown in sync with public awareness of and standards for corporate operational conduct and practices. Greater media exposure of large business practices, particularly those of multinational corporations (MNCs), has led to rising expectations of these wealthy and resourceful entities. It is becoming common practice now for large companies to initiate their new 'socially responsible' operating plans by turning directly to non-governmental organizations (NGOs) for guidance and expertise, as well as joining forces with these former opponents to lobby for stricter legal standards in order to level the commercial playing field. Many of the more well-known non-profits such as Environmental Defense and Conservation International have entire programs within their organization devoted solely to working with multinational corporations on implementing more socially palatable operating standards.

The idea that a company or organization is in fact a member of the surrounding community whose obligations extend beyond their own four walls is not new in itself, but the rising expectations of the public and the media in recent years have created new impetus among the business community to raise their standards of citizenship. While the expectations of governments do not appear to have risen in tandem with other stakeholders in the form of legislative obligation, a 'soft' network of standards and accountability is beginning to take shape in the form of corporate and industry codes, stakeholder initiatives, and private standard-setting bodies.

What then of the operational practices of the non-profit organizations themselves? The concept of a non-profit organization committing to socially responsible behavior may seem a foregone conclusion. However, a large-scale NGO has many of the same concerns and objectives as a for-profit corporation, and to that end frequently operates in a surprisingly similar manner. Those that are international in scope have far-reaching impacts – as intended given the nature of the work that they perform. That being the case, how does their approach toward responsible operations contrast – if at all – with the approach taken by for-profit corporations? What are their own standards of conduct for themselves and their peers in the non-profit sector, and how do those differ (if at all) from public perception?

CSR presents a unique lens through which to view the differences between the actual business practices of – and consumer standards for – non-profit organizations and for-profit business. The overall purpose of this chapter is to examine the impact of rising CSR expectations on the large-scale non-profit; to discern patterns in the ways that NGOs approach corporate social responsibility and to look at the similarities and differences between multinational NGOs and companies through the lens of CSR. Are NGOs then any more or less susceptible to those incentives than corporations? Do NGOs receive a 'free pass' for non-socially responsible business operations, based merely on the fact that their entity is not-for-profit? Or are expectations and standards exponentially higher for these organizations given the altruistic nature of their business?

The relative novelty of CSR as a practice leaves open many possible paths for growth. In which directions will the practice evolve? In order to address these questions, it is also necessary to examine the driving forces behind CSR: what incentives exist to change the status quo?

14.2 Methodology

The methodology utilized for this chapter is comprised of three separate components, divided into a study of NGO behavior contrasted with that of corporations, a series of interviews focused on international NGO operational practices, and a literature review of the subject for contextual purposes. Initially, I utilized firsthand case studies and interviews in order to draw a comparison amongst members of the NGO sector. The objective was to observe individually held approaches, methodologies, and standards within this sector by investigating the already established corporate social responsibility programs of three large-scale global NGOs, each covering different areas of the non-profit world. In addition to a three-month case study conducted with the Green Team at the International Fund for Animal Welfare, interviews were procured with Cindy Milburn, head of the CSR initiative for IFAW, Samantha Putt del Pino and Nancy Kiefer of the World Resources Institute, and Timothy Newman of the International Labor Rights Forum.

In order to provide contrast with the CSR initiatives of the for-profit sector, interviews were conducted with David Stangis, former Global Director of Corporate Responsibility of Intel, Patricia Leiva, Director of Public Relations of Microsoft Costa Rica, and Richard D'Amato, former Executive Director of Corporate Philanthropy at America Online. The ability to compare their responses to those of the NGO community was particularly useful in evaluating the approaches of three multinational corporations within the same sector to those of three multinational non-profits. Similar answers to identical questions provided visible patterns within the relationship between social responsibility and the overall benefit to the entity itself; the end result of this interconnectivity being the incentive to operate in a socially sustainable manner.

Another essential component to the research was an examination of the similarities between MNCs and NGOs. In the interest of accurate comparison, companies and non-profits that are compared are of similar size, structure, name recognition, and international scope. Strategies employed by MNCs were examined as well as NGOs, in order to discern any patterns or differences.

A literature review was also conducted, inclusive of several academic journal articles and books from both for-profit and non-profit perspectives. This review focused on standards held throughout the non-profit sector, both self-imposed and maintained via an internal checks-and-balances system existing within various fields, according to demands of the clientele and operational necessities of their specific marketplace. The theories put forth in this collection of literature were evaluated in the context of current events in the field of CSR as reported by mainstream media.

To balance the literature review, documented case studies were also utilized. These case studies examined new business practices adopted by different companies in order to compare current efforts to address this relatively new component of business strategy. As will be demonstrated, the cases focused on context-appropriate measures for the companies in question and primarily attempted to distinguish between legitimate efforts at improving citizenship, as opposed to minimal efforts for the sake of marketing or public relations purposes.

14.3 NGOs vs. MNCs

Given the similarity of objectives, it seems only natural that the evolution of Corporate Social Responsibility should emulate certain elements of non-profit organization practices. The issues taken up under the guise of CSR are typically the domain of the non-governmental/non-profit organization realm. Such organizations are typically built around a single cause: human rights, wildlife conservation, social justice, global poverty, etc. Within these areas of expertise, most NGOs operate in a project cycle format, developing individual ventures that cater specifically to the unique needs and circumstances of each individual location where they operate. These organizations can grow to the same size – and in some cases, degree of brand name recognition and public influence – as a multinational corporation, as in the cases of Amnesty International or the World Wildlife Fund. That being the case, their capacity for raising funds can parallel the profit margins of a multinational corporation. Goodwill Industries earned revenue in the amount of $2.21 billion in 2003; this profit margin ranked among the top fifteen discount retailers in the United States in that year (Austin et al., 2007). How then is Goodwill different from Wal-Mart?

NGOs and MNCs operate in very similar fashions. Both have financial responsibilities to meet, employees to take care of, a client base to respond to, and both rely on customer satisfaction expressed in the form of financial contributions, called either donations or investments. Branding and rivalry are as much of a factor amongst the NGOs which compete for donors and media recognition within their sector in the same way that their MNC counterparts compete for clientele and advertising. In their article 'Capitalizing on Convergence', authors James E. Austin, Roberto Gutierrez, Enrique Ogliastri, and Ezequiel Reficco have even determined that 'business and nonprofit sectors have so much in common that it is difficult to tell them apart' (Austin et al., 2007). That being the case, what then can NGOs gain from the MNC model of social responsibility, and how can it be appropriately applied in a non-profit context?

14.3.1 Lessons to Be Learned from the NGO Model

An MNC has a primary function – to earn revenue by means of providing a good or a service at a profitable rate. CSR represents the most holistic means of performing that primary function. Large scale non-profit organizations can easily be looked upon as MNCs whose product is some form of social responsibility. That being the case, could not the private sector stand to improve their contributions to social welfare by emulating the methodologies of these organizations? One of the fundamental principles of the non-profit world is specialization; to assess local needs and contexts within the realm of their area of expertise and dedicate their outward CSR efforts – those that are intended to primarily impact the surrounding community rather than the business itself – toward those needs.

14.3.2 Contrasting Approaches

Three seemingly different approaches to CSR are those of three global conglomerates: GE, Intel and Microsoft. Microsoft chose to focus on community development via their global program called Unlimited Potential, functional in all countries where they operate. This program creates community centers where children can have free access to computers and training classes after school. While this may appear to be straightforward philanthropy rather than CSR, the program is actually equal parts community outreach and future market growth. By providing a local good which benefits the local community, Microsoft is simultaneously introducing their product to potential future users. In a different example, Intel has been able to promote social responsibility within host countries where they operate by raising the local labor safety standards. When opening a new subsidiary, or having maintenance work performed on an existing one, Intel utilizes local contracting firms and employs their own labor safety regulations and equipment, which are among the most stringent in the industry and typically exceed those mandated by the local government. Given the time required to obtain permits for various components of their operations, Intel has discovered that money invested in worker safety routinely provides a competitive advantage in their time-to-market turnaround; by having high safety standards and using the safest equipment available, they receive work permits faster and get their product out more quickly than their competitors. Additionally, such precautions have lowered their insurance premiums and reduced their compensation outlay to the lowest in the industry (Stangis, 2006).

GE, on the other hand, has elected to incorporate CSR directly into their product line. The 400+ appliances that GE now introduces to the marketplace have all been adapted to incorporate energy-saving and (when relevant) water-saving technologies. In addition to altering the mechanics of their products, GE has also developed a wastewater management and filtration system, which they now market to public utilities. Rather than merely adding recycling or rideshare programs to their core business in an effort to showcase their environmental responsibility, GE adapted their product line to alleviate the carbon footprint of their customers, and simultaneously gained a market share advantage in efficient appliances.

While each of these three companies selected different areas of CSR to focus on (community relations, labor, and the environment), they each incorporated the initiative directly into the mainstream of their core business. The most vulnerable CSR programs are typically those that are isolated from the primary function of the company. According to a recent World Bank report on Corporate Social Responsibility, 'Traditional top-down strategies do not achieve sustainable CSR. By adopting a more holistic approach to CSR, one can observe that capacity-building ... can lead to sustainable improvements'. In other words, successful CSR methodologies incorporate the mission of a corporation.

According to Richard D'Amato, former Executive Director of Corporate Philanthropy at America Online, the first step for a MNC to take when beginning to address CSR practices for the first time is to look to their own local employees – determine what issues impact them where they live, and what areas of concern exist in that community. The second step is to establish best practices to address those concerns (D'Amato, 2007). Stakeholder identification and impact, as well as best practice establishment and refinement, are literally the business of the NGO. And as the very subjects of CSR are their areas of expertise, not only do MNCs stand to learn a great deal from them, but can literally use such organizations as partners in their endeavors (Pedersen, 2005). Given their 'goal congruence', as the overlap in CSR objectives between MNCs and NGOs is described by Esben Pedersen in 'Guiding the Invisible Hand', such a partnership has the potential to be fruitful for all three parties – company, non-profit, and stakeholders – given the combination of resources, expertise, and dedication (Pedersen, 2005).

14.3.3 MNCs and NGOs – Similar Ends Call for Similar Means

Businesses succeed by filling a consumer need in the marketplace. Where there is competition to fill that need, companies are compelled to produce their product at a higher quality and more efficiently than the alternatives. As MNCs are presumably efficiency-seeking in all other components of their business operations, why should their efforts at CSR be conducted any differently? By emulating the best practices established by successful NGOs, companies that would like to contribute to social welfare may do so in a manner which has been demonstrated to function effectively for both the implementing agency and the stakeholders. The same is often true in the non-profit world. Organizations with similar causes often compete with one another for donors, members, and recognition. In order to maintain their very existence, they must be able to demonstrate that they are able to meet the objectives of their cause. Hence they have developed both expertise and efficiency in achieving the objectives of CSR. Given the multiple similarities between NGOs and MNCs in other areas, the ability of a NGO to design socially-minded solutions which meet business needs clearly demonstrates that such an endeavor can succeed in the non-profit community as well.

As a proponent of this methodology of CSR, Pedersen even describes corporate citizenship as 'development done by the private sector', or PSD (Pedersen,

2005). In many cases, such corporate programs consist of partnerships with development agencies. While such community interaction goes beyond the scope of merely employing sustainable business practices, it addresses obligation to stakeholders by the most efficient means available: the utilization of available expertise. However, PSD can also serve as a two-way street; by participating outright in development work, companies stand to lower a portion of their investment risk in that certain of their costs are likely to be covered, such as field visits or market research (Pedersen, 2005). Partnership with a local NGO can also include access to free consulting and legal advice as well as both financial and bureaucratic assistance in obtaining the necessary licenses and approvals, all of which reduces time-to-market costs. Such partnerships serve to alter the manner in which the company does business as the NGO and MNC increase both their utilization of and reliance upon each other.

This is not to suggest that NGOs and MNCs are becoming indistinguishable, or that CSR will eventually make NGOs redundant. Ultimately, there is a role for both of these entities. As Austin et al. (2007), pointed out: 'Nonprofits should continue to serve as watchdogs, making sure that businesses and governments do as little harm as possible. And businesses should continue to perform their core economic functions efficiently, because they are the engines of a healthy economy' (Austin et al., 2007). The ability and willingness of both organizations to learn from each other and work together is paramount to the progress of global social welfare.

14.4 Incentive for CSR Among NGOs

One of the reasons for the interest in the non-profit sector is that based almost solely on the very nature of their existence, higher ethical standards are impugned. According to Margaret Gibelman and Sheldon Gelman in their article 'NGOs are defined as 'self-governing and non-profit distributing, have some degree of voluntarism, and are expected to produce a public benefit' (Gibelman and Gelman, 2001).

For a NGO, reputation is currency. The overwhelming majority of non-profits are largely, if not exclusively, funded by private donations. The slightest hint of impropriety on the part of a non-profit will bear a direct negative impact on their income and therefore their ability to carry out their mission. As succinctly phrased in Walsh and Lanihan (2006), 'Accountability and Effectiveness of NGOs', 'donors want to see value for money and positive outcomes'. Therefore a reputation for social responsibility carries significantly more weight for a NGO than it does for a corporate entity. For example, Nike received a great deal of negative publicity and media attention after reports of child labor and sweatshop conditions were broadly publicized in 2004. Yet that negative publicity had almost no effect on Nike sales or their stock share price. The company reported that they were most impacted in their diminished ability to recruit top talent and retain valuable employees; however, their financial impact was negligible (Vogel, 2005). Likewise, interviews conducted with leading CSR officers for Microsoft, Intel, and America OnLine revealed a similar lack of correlation between social reputation and profit margin. When asked to describe the impact of a (hypothetical) negative news story revealing non-socially conscious behavior, each corporate representative reported that it would not affect company sales or stock price, regardless of the prominence of such a story (Leiva, 2006; Stangis, 2006; D'Amato, 2007).

However, consumer expectations for NGOs are higher because the standards affiliated with the non-profit sector are higher. The public expects that a for-profit entity will always act in their own best interests, whereas NGOs are purported to have a high ethical standard. But the similarities between NGOs and MNCs extend beyond the daily costs and demands of operating. As much as MNCs are capable of achieving altruistic goals, NGOs are also capable of falling to corruption. While there has been a great deal of attention of late focused on the many corporate scandals that have had dramatic impacts on Wall Street and the retirement funds of their employees, the non-profit sector, despite their magnanimous aura, is equally prone to corruption. In a snapshot as narrow as a three-year window, multiple prominent NGOs have had to exercise damage control on their own less-than altruistic scandals, highlighted in Table 14.1 (Gibelman and Gelman, 2001):

As noted by Gibelman and Gelman, 'The excesses and misdeeds associated with private enterprise and even government have long been fertile territory for the press. But in the [NGO] sector, public trust is a key component. When this public trust is compromised, the costs to status, reputation, and funding can be significant'. (Gibelman and Gelman, 2001) Likewise, the consequences of impropriety for a NGO are astronomical.

The need to avoid the appearance of any impropriety has led the NGO sector to begin their own quest for CSR at the same starting point as many a MNC: transparency of information. One crucial element of CSR is the amount and transparency of the data which is reported (Stangis, 2006). Over the course of the last ten years, pressure has risen across industry sectors to meet a growing standard of disclosure, leading to an increase in corporate citizenship publications. When one company within any given industry reports data on their social impact, other companies within that sector are compelled to offer their shareholders the same figures. Thus the available information on CSR gradually increases. This trend is gradually taking hold in the non-profit sector as well.

An interview with David Stangis, Global Director of Corporate Responsibility with Intel Corporation, revealed that transparency is the primary step for any business or organization to take in an attempt to establish social responsibility in that it dictates all other action (Stangis, 2006). It also serves as a self-perpetuating standard; the more data and information that the public has access to, the more they will continue to demand. Only when data is readily available can benchmarks for all components of social responsibility be established and then assessed by analysts and utilized by investors. This standard has taken root for the NGO sector as well. Public attention given to scandals within the NGO sector as well as some criticism of NGOs for the recent trend of partnering with for-profit companies on certain endeavors –

Table 14.1 Documented corruption in the NGO sector

Year	Country	Organization	Allegation	Wrongdoer
2000	Australia	Wesley Mission	False Billing	Board of Directors
2000	Australia	Youth Motor Sport Foundation	Fraud	Board Members
1998	Ecuador	Fundacion Perez Pallares	Fraudulent Investments	Financial Advisors
1999	England	L'Chaim Society	Misuse of Funds	Director
2000	England	Women's Royal Voluntary Service	Embezzlement, Fraud	Controller
1999	France	Association for Cancer Research	Embezzlement, Fraud, Forgery	Founder, Director
2000	Germany	Bavarian Red Cross	Bribe acceptance, Fraud, Tax Evasion	Director, Manager
1999	Ireland	Irish Society for the Prevention of Cruelty to Children	Embezzlement	Chief Executive Officer
2000	Israel	Kupat Holim Health Fund	Harassment/ Exploitation	Director
2000	Scotland	Order of the Eastern Star	Embezzlement	Secretary, Acting Treasurer
1998	South Africa	Foundation for Peace and Justice	Embezzlement	Director, Bookkeeper
2000	United States	American Cancer Society (OH)	Theft	Chief Financial Officer
1999	United States	Baptist Foundation of Arizona	Fraudulent investments	Officers
1998	United States	Goodwill Industries (CA)	Embezzlement	Director and Six Confederates
1999	United States	Head Start (NY)	Embezzlement	Director
2000	United States	Operation Smile	Misappropriation of Funds	Founder, Chairman
2000	United States	Toys for Tots	Theft	Founder, CEO

charitable or profitable – has driven an increased demand for transparency among donors and members (Townsend and Townsend, 2004).

14.5 The Evolving Relationship of NGOs to CSR

As previously discussed, the emergence of CSR over the course of the past few years as both a prominent media topic and a matter of consumer and investor expectations has pushed corporations from philanthropic gestures toward the incorporation of responsible practices into the substance of their business. As a result, the role of the NGO within the space of CSR has shifted from that of critic, to guide or consultant, and now to that of partner and colleague.

Historically, NGOs have played the role of watchdog to MNCs; monitoring behavior and using the publicity they command by virtue of their reputations and expertise to shame companies into adopting more responsible practices. This methodology routinely took place across multiple sectors of the non-profit industry including components of CSR such as labor rights, animal welfare, the environment, local community welfare, and even democracy, as demonstrated in the case of the Southern Christian Leadership Conference orchestrating boycotts against Coca-Cola for operating in South Africa during the reign of apartheid (Pendergast, 2000).

Such a watchdog role catapulted the NGO into a status not far from that of Caesar's wife – in order to be able to critique for-profit organizations in their approach to social responsibility, the NGO must themselves be beyond reproach. Given the competition among the international NGO sector, there is as much to lose for an NGO not deemed to be living up to their responsibility as that of a MNC, if not more. To a non-socially-conscious consumer, the value of a product is unchanged regardless of whether the company producing it invokes socially responsible operations. However, a donor is not likely to continue devoting money to a NGO to produce altruism if they no longer feel confident in the social performance of the recipient. Hence the rise of transparency and increased reporting among NGOs preceded other forms of CSR. And as with the private sector, the increase in available data has prompted a rise in other tenets of CSR, many of which have focused on environmental efforts such as energy efficient office space. Such efforts grew in tandem with an evolving role in the private sector.

With the growth of CSR and rising expectations of consumers, corporations switched from a defensive stance to offensive, enlisting the help of the very entities that had previously monitored and evaluated their impact on society. While companies initially took the step of hiring consultants with NGO backgrounds to guide them in their efforts toward a more responsible business operation – and reputation – they eventually moved in the direction of joining forces. Rather than react to public criticism from the NGO community, or pre-empt negative publicity by instituting the simplest policy changes in order to appease the 'name and shame' advocates, companies are now adopting more progressive strategies. In recent years large-scale multinational corporations have begun to form partnerships within the non-profit sector, harnessing the expertise of the large-scale, multinational NGO such as Environmental Defense to lead their CSR (and PR) efforts. Coca-Cola, for example, was previously criticized by numerous NGOs for social indiscretions ranging from supporting apartheid in South Africa, to human rights abuses in Columbia, to unsustainable water procurement in India (Center for Media and Democracy, 2007). However, Coca-Cola is now a corporate partner of both the World Wildlife Fund and Conservation International.

But should the position of the NGO be that of consultant to the corporate sector, without conducting such practices themselves? Many have turned from critic, to consultant, and emerged as partner, offering guidance and expertise, as well as joining forces with their former opponents to push for mutually beneficial legal standards; raising a given social standard such as minimum wage, animal treatment or emissions regulations in order to level the commercial playing field. Such alliances can be seen in the creation of groups such as the United States Climate Action Partnership, a joint collaboration of prominent environmental NGOs and top-tier companies focused on lobbying the United States legislature to enact stricter emissions standards. According to John Garrison in his article 'From Confrontation to Collaboration' on the changing relationship between these two entities: '[NGOs] are key opinion makers in society and can help mobilize community interest around the project and disseminate useful information about the projects to the beneficiary population.' (Garrison, 2000)

There is a correlation in the size and overall wealth of the organization with its ability and willingness to participate in socially responsible behavior typically – just as in the case of a for-profit business. The visibility of a large company or organization makes it more susceptible to public pressure, and larger profits make expenditure on initial cost outlay for social measures possible. Throughout the course of the interview process, the single greatest point of contention was the question of whether socially responsible practices were a greater obligation for the NGO or for the for-profit entity. Opinions of CSR on the part of the non-profit ranged from an obligation to a luxury. In the case of the International Labor Rights Forum, Newman stated that CSR was a luxury; an initiative to be attempted only after the initial costs and primary objectives of the organization had been met. In that case, CSR is viewed as an obligation according to the income level of the entity in question, rather than their profit-earning status.

In contrast, Cindy Milburn of the International Fund for Animal Welfare stated that there is an additional obligation for a non-profit entity to operate in a responsible manner given the public expectation for an NGO to live up to their altruistic missions. From this perspective, profit status determined obligation more than size, scope, or revenue. Still others feel that it is incumbent upon businesses to contribute more than non-profits because they have the means to do so, whereas all earned income at a non-profit organization is already being dedicated to a specific social cause.

14.6 Case Studies

Given the wide variety of large-scale NGOs operating throughout the globe, I chose to examine three different non-profit fields, all relevant to the concept of CSR. For animal welfare, I interviewed Cindy Milburn of the International Fund for Animal Welfare, and also joined IFAW's organization-wide 'Green Team', to observe their progress over a four month timespan. In the labor rights field, I interviewed Timothy Newman, a campaign officer at the International Labor Rights Forum. Lastly, representing environmental responsibility, I was able to interview Nancy Kiefer and Samantha Putt del Pino at the World Resources Institute.

14.6.1 World Resources Institute

The amount of large-scale MNCs seeking to enhance their brand name and corporate image by improving their environmental track record, both in terms of daily operations, supply chain management, and creation of more environmentally-sound products, is literally too large to name, and the majority of this self-improvement was initiated within the last five years. The World Resources Institute (WRI) is a think tank whose stated goal is to 'to move human society to live in ways that protect Earth's environment'. (WRI, 2007) WRI, along with the World Wildlife Fund, the Natural Resources Defense Council, Conservation International, and several other environmental NGOs all boast large lists of corporate 'clients' which have turned to them in their capacity as experts to assist them in the pursuit of environmentally sustainable business operations. Each of these organizations (as well as others like them) has an established department dedicated solely to the reform of the corporate sector. However, the decision to focus on their own carbon footprint and other environmental side effects of operating a multinational organization often evolved after the role of the NGO morphed from critic, to consultant, to partner with members of the private sector.

For WRI, this transition took place sooner than for most of their peers. WRI is one of the leading global organizations operating today in the field of environmentally sustainable business practices, and their efforts at 'greening' their own operations precede even the establishment of LEED standards. Samantha Putt del Pino, Project Manager within the Climate and Energy Program at WRI, described the efforts at WRI to reduce their own emissions as a 'walking the talk' initiative: 'It's about implementing our own values. If we are going to work to reduce "corporate" climate change, we have to lead by example and make the effort ourselves.' (Putt del Pino, 2008) Hence the efforts to reduce their own carbon footprint grew directly out of WRI's mission to reduce the carbon footprint of the corporate world; one of the very foundations of the organization.

Nancy Kiefer, Director of Facilities and Office Services for the entire organization, notes the positive element of the competitive atmosphere among NGOs with similar missions. Like the private sector, competition within the same space forces all contenders to improve their performance. By driving each other with constantly climbing standards, better practices will continue to evolve.

While Kiefer acknowledged the role of CSR in positioning the organization against other NGOs within the environmental non-profit market, she did stipulate that it was not a blatant PR measure as much as a result of having 'like-minded staff'. Given the propensity of their employees to espouse responsible business standards, NGOs have the dual advantages of research professionals and in-house expertise, in addition to a staff devoted to such principles. It is much easier for an organization to adopt environmentally friendly business policies when their staff is comprised of experts within that very field.

However, while any expenditure on the elements of CSR that pertain directly to the mission of the WRI, i.e. environmental and natural resource protection are not just accepted but *expected* by members, other elements of CSR, such as labor rights, are not as readily addressed. Areas of CSR that directly pertain to the organization's mission are readily supported, but other areas of CSR do not always receive the same attention. When asked if labor practices were factors in procurement and supply chain considerations, Kiefer's response was no.

14.6.2 International Labor Rights Forum

The stated mission of the International Rights Labor Forum (ILRF) is to achieve just and humane working conditions for all workers throughout the globe. For corporations, proactively responsible labor practices typically involves independent monitoring of labor conditions and union safety by independent third-party contractors or certification from internationally recognized human rights organizations (Gereffi et al., 2001). ILRF does routinely partner with companies, tending to focus on large-scale, multinational businesses, given the 'trickle-down' ability of larger companies to pressure their suppliers to change their ways. According to Tim Newman, a Campaign Associate at ILRF, the ability to shape corporate policies and practices is the ideal role for ILRF acting in a CSR capacity within the private sector.

According to Newman, the ILRF has a high level of accountability for reporting purposes. Monthly and annual reports as well as annual campaign summaries, all with extremely detailed data on procurement practices, are regularly distributed to members, supporters, an advisory council, and a board of directors. The desire to meet donor expectations and to embody the very mission of their organization were driving factors behind establishing any CSR policy, and the need for transparency played a significant role in the decision to adopt CSR reporting measures. The little funding that was available to devote to the initiative was dedicated to the creation of a donor coordinator position, charged with assessing the variety of data that donors and supports are beginning to expect.

When asked if environmental, community, democratic, or animal welfare concerns were a factor in the decisions made regarding any of the suppliers that the organization utilized, the response from Newman was no. However, when that same question was proposed concerning labor standards, the response was a vehement yes. All supplies utilized by the organization are carefully procured from union-represented companies with strong track records of fair trade and fair labor practices. When asked what represented the essential components of 'legitimate' labor practices, Newman promptly answered with 'healthcare and the right to organize'. In particular, adherence to the Employee Free Choice Act was an essential qualification for any supplier within the United States.

Newman sited lack of sufficient funds as the major reason, stating that their supporters would prefer to see funding go directly to the mission of the organization rather than any non-related efforts. However, he stated that ILRF saw the need for NGO participation, and that it was only due to a lack of resources that they 'could not do as much as they would like' (Newman, 2008). Given their restrained resources, CSR was a luxury, rather than an obligation, for a NGO. Therefore, according to Newman, companies, as profit-generating entities, have a greater responsibility to engage in CSR due to their financial capacity to address the issues. He further stated that because it is typically companies that produce the items causing environmental side-effects, abusing animals, or creating unfair labor environments, that there is a greater responsibility incumbent upon the corporate sector to resolve them, and the role of the NGO is to guide them in that capacity.

14.6.3 International Fund for Animal Welfare

Animal welfare is not as publicized in the media as a component of CSR as labor rights or environmental conservation, but has recently begun to grow in prominence. Factory farming practices in particular have received the greatest amount of media attention of late within this sector. Some of the most globally successful and well-known MNCs are in the food and beverage industry, and well-known restaurant chains including Burger King and McDonalds have been adopting animal-friendlier policies. Last year, Burger King announced that they would begin buying eggs and pork from suppliers that did not confine their animals in cages and crates, and used only humane methods of slaughter. While the plan is to start applying this standard slowly to only a low percentage of suppliers, the plan is to gradually increase the percentages until any supplier wishing to work with Burger King must meet these standards of animal treatment (Martin, 2007). Thus the company is able to disseminate their social standards not only throughout their company, but throughout their supply chain and their consumer base as well, reaching well beyond their own operations.

This component of CSR is the realm of The International Fund for Animal Welfare (IFAW). IFAW has the capacity for worldwide impact, with offices established in seventeen countries throughout the world and operations that are global in scope. While the focus of the organization is on wildlife protection, they also provide relief to livestock and companion animals, particularly in disaster situations. Almost since inception, there has been an organization-wide policy that food at any IFAW-sponsored event or meeting be vegetarian, in keeping with the mission of the organization to promote the wellbeing of animals. However, in the past year IFAW has decided to take their animal protection initiative further into the basic functionality of daily operations, and is aiming to protect not only the animals themselves but also their habitats. While habitat protection has been a goal of the organization for years, the incorporation of habitat protection into daily operating procedure by means of carbon emissions reduction has only recently been initiated. The organization has set in motion a plan to become carbon neutral, donating carbon offsets to a reforestation project in India, in order to recreate lost habitat in an area with several species in decline due to habitat loss. According to Cindy Milburn, lead advisor on the CSR initiative at IFAW, 'Animal welfare is our ultimate goal; this primary objective pulls together all other factors of CSR.'

As often the case with for-profit companies, the initiative grew out of efforts toward transparency and full disclosure. Ethical gift policies, an ethical investment policy, and transparent reporting initiatives all preceded the CSR program, but are now all conjoined under a CSR umbrella policy. Like the ILRF, the importance of transparency as a tenet of CSR has emerged and shaped significant operating procedures, particularly budgets. IFAW has recently extended this concept even to their employees' means of transportation to commute to the office. However, supply chain management is not yet a factor here, as the majority of supplies used by the organization pertain to localized disasters such as severe weather or oil spills, which necessitate immediacy over procurement standards.

Like WRI and ILRF, Milburn also cited member/donor expectations as a secondary incentive for the adoption of CSR policies relevant to animal welfare. Credibility with those who make the organization possible is a clear motivation to promote socially responsible policies, including means such as the large press event held at the opening of the new energy-efficient headquarters building. Another similarity to the other two organizations is the exclusive focus on the elements of CSR which pertain to their field. Rather than adopting a holistic approach to all elements of socially responsible operating practices, IFAW has chosen to focus their efforts on a component of CSR which will speak to the legitimacy of the organization.

14.7 Lessons Learned – How NGOs Can Benefit from the MNC Example

What the large-scale NGOs appear to have learned in recent years regarding the public and media-driven demands for social responsibility is that the easiest route to follow is that which is most closely aligned with their end product or service. In the case of the non-profit sector, the end product is an ideal, be it human rights, labor standards, animal welfare, environmental stewardship, democracy, or myriad other goals. While the evolving NGO model may not be as all-encompassing as one might expect from an altruistic organization, the ability to incorporate ethical operations with the actual product is the most efficient way to carry out their mission and to meet the constantly increasing expectations of an informed audience and a scandal-driven media.

For example, according to the World Resources Institute, more than 50% of the World Bank's $1.8 billion energy-sector portfolio did not include any climate change considerations as recently as 2007 (WRI, 2008). Operationally, opportunities to mitigate emissions and reduce climate risk are still not systematically incorporated into development strategies throughout the globe. Given the wide scope of projects undertaken by NGOs around the world, the incorporation of the basic principles of CSR, such as carbon emissions reduction, has the potential to prevent multiple harmful practices that will then have to be remedied at a later date. The stakeholders that are the designated beneficiaries of the World Bank project portfolio are likewise negatively affected by greenhouse gas emissions. Would the project not accomplish more if it were held to the same high social standards as the entity conducting it? (Fig. 14.1).

Hence the next logical step for the NGO to take on the CSR spectrum is to incorporate responsible practices not only in their day-to-day operations, but in their global project work as well. In this respect, it will likely be the MNC providing the functioning model for the NGO to emulate, rather than the other way around.

Evolving past the role of providing assistance to the for-profit sector in achieving socially responsible operations, the NGO is coming full circle and may soon be seeking guidance on how to incorporate other facets of CSR into their operations. Hence the position of the non-profit entity moves beyond that of critic, to consultant, to partner.

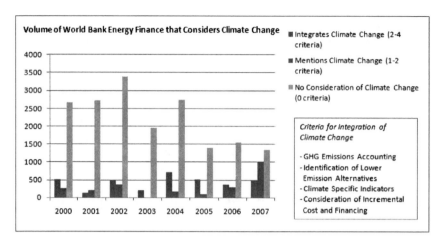

Fig. 14.1 Climate and energy correlation in world bank projects
Source: *World Resources Institute*

14.8 Conclusion

Is the obligation to operate in a socially responsible manner more incumbent upon the profitable, or the altruistic of purpose? Interviews across both sectors revealed that ultimately, each are obligated because they both have their own means to do so. The difference lies within those means: the NGO has the will and the knowledge at their disposal, and the for-profit entity has the capital to buy it.

The case studies utilized in this research revealed a clear tendency among NGOs to incorporate CSR as a component of the overall mission of their organization, whereas the corporate approach tends to focus more on industry-specific efficiency, cost savings, and time-to-market advantages. As the interviews and case studies revealed, NGOs displayed the greatest interest in areas of CSR corresponding to their sector. This tendency belies both a commitment to their cause as well as a primary interest in their perceived legitimacy and reputation amongst competitors within the same sector. Where there is no financial profit, other forms of currency fill the void in the forms of clout, money, donors, press, and influence – all currency in the non-profit world. Competition for prestige and media coverage are of significant value within this sector, because they lead directly to the ability to raise funds and for the organization to carry on their work – of legitimate importance – and grow as an organization.

However, the purpose of these organizations is after all to focus on their stated mission. They are naturally concerned with doing their part to contribute to the cause which defines their existence. To what extent are they obligated to branch into other elements of CSR? Is a holistic approach the exclusive domain of the private sector, or will the practice of CSR evolve to a point where an animal welfare organization can do their part to further labor rights, or an environmental organization can focus on community development?

CSR could also be viewed as an obligation according to not the profit status of the entity in question, but rather their income level. NGOs such as Goodwill and the World Wildlife Fund have vastly more capital than most businesses. Does a struggling midsize business have the same social obligations as a global-scale organization earning millions per year, merely because they are a for-profit entity? Or do these variations in income, status, and mission all speak to a shared obligation, varying only in tactical approach?

Partnerships between non-profit organizations and corporations, such as the United States Climate Action Partnership, embody this new regime. The very existence of such joint ventures shifts the strategy of corporate responsibility from defensive to offensive in nature by raising the profile of efforts made by companies and organizations alike with active CSR agendas. It further serves to shift the role of the NGO from critic, to guide, to colleague. While NGOs will continue to lead by example in many fields of social responsibility, they have demonstrated that they capable of learning within this field as well.

References

Austin, JE, Gutierrez, R, Ogliastri, E, and Reficco, E (2007), "Capitalizing on Convergence", *Stanford Social Innovation Review*, 24–31. Stanford University, Palo Alto, CA

Center for Media and Democracy (2007), *WWF Greenwashes Coca-Cola*, Environment News Service, Beijing, China

Garrison, J (2000), *From Confrontation to Collaboration*, The World Bank, Washington, DC

Gereffi, G, Garcia-Johnson, R, and Sasser, E (2001), "The NGO Industrial Complex", *Foreign Policy*, 125, 56–65

Gibelman, M, and Gelman, SR (2001), "Very Public Scandals: Nongovernmental Organizations in Trouble", *Voluntas: International Journal of Voluntary and Nonprofit Organizations*, 12(1), 49–66

Martin, A (2007), "Burger King Shifts Policy on Animals", *The New York Times*, New York

Pedersen, ER, (2005), "Guiding the Invisible Hand", *The Journal of Corporate Citizenship*, 20, 77–91. Copenhagen Business School, Denmark

Prendergast, M (2000), *For God, Country, and Coca-Cola: The Unauthorized History of the Great American Soft Drink and the Company that Makes It*, Basic Books, New York

Townsend JG and Townsend, AR (2004), "Accountability, Motivation, and Practice: NGOs North and South", *Social and Cultural Geography*, 5(2), 271–284

Vogel, D (2005), *The Market for Virtue*, Brookings Institution Press: Washington, DC

Walsh, E and Lanihan, H (2006), "Accountability and Effectiveness of NGOs", *Development in Practice*, 16(5), 412–424

Winston, M (2002), "NGO Strategies for Promoting Corporate Social Responsibility", *Ethics & International Affairs*, 16(1), 71–87

Interviews

D'Amato, Richard; former Director of Corporate Philanthropy, America Online, Inc; Interview conducted on June 8, 2007

Kiefer, Nancy; Director, Facilities & Office Services, World Resources Institute; Interview conducted on April 30, 2008

Leiva, Patricia; Director of Public Relations, Microsoft Costa Rica; Interview conducted on August 14, 2006

Milburn, Cindy; Senior Advisor and Green Team Lead, International Fund for Animal Welfare; Interview conducted on April 04, 2008

Newman, Timothy; Campaign Associate, International Labor Rights Forum; Interview conducted on April 29, 2008

Putt del Pino, Samantha; Project Manager, Climate and Energy Program, World Resources Institute; Interview conducted on May 22, 2008

Stangis, David; Global Director of Corporate Social Responsibility; Intel Corporation; Interview conducted on August 21, 2006

Websites

Conservation International (*as of August 31, 2009*):
http://www.conservation.org/discover/centers_programs/business/Pages/overview.aspx
http://www.conservation.org/discover/partnership/corporate/pages/default.aspx

International Fund for Animal Welfare (*as of August 31, 2009*):
http://www.ifaw.org

International Labor Rights Forum (*as of August 31, 2009*):
http://www.laborrights.org/

Natural Resources Defense Council (*as of August 31, 2009*):
http://www.nrdc.org/greenbusiness/

World Wildlife Fund (*as of August 31, 2009*):
http://www.panda.org/about_wwf/how_we_work/businesses/index.cfm

United States Climate Action Partnership (*as of August 31, 2009*):
http://www.us-cap.org/

World Resources Institute (*as of August 31, 2009*):
http://www.wri.org/about
http://www.wri.org/project/capital-markets
http://www.wri.org/chart/volume-world-bank-energy-finance-considers-climate-change

Chapter 15
A Hotelier's Perspective of CSR

Diana Luck and Jean Bowcott

*"The great thing in this world is not so much where we are, but
in what direction we are moving"*
Oliver Wendell Holmes (1809–1894)

Abstract Over the years different activities have been associated with the topic
of Corporate Social Responsibility. In line with much of the business environment,
the hotel industry also embraced the concept. Although, discussions and activities in
general have tended to revolve primordially around the environment and the community, there has been a disparity in the extent to which the concept has been embraced
within companies. The level at which hotel chains have engaged in CSR has also
understandably been varied.

Rather than offer a synoptic overview of how the hotel industry has engaged in
CSR over the past decade, this chapter instead attempts to offer an insight from
within the industry. Accordingly, it discusses the perspective of a key internal
employee about how a specific company, namely Accor, has been engaging in CSR
within the UK and internationally. Consequently, although issues discussed in the
chapter occasionally refers to key debates, the chapter is based on a case study and
hence is arguably subjective. Indeed, this chapter is merely intended to provide a
hotelier's perspective about CSR rather than presume to be an objective overview of
the changing dimensions of engagement of hotel companies with the concept.

15.1 Introduction

Scholars including Carroll (1999) and Broomhill (2007) have argued that CSR has
been formally and academically written about since the 1950s. All too often the
work of Bowen (1953) is quoted. However, the term CSR as a much more global

D. Luck (✉)
London Metropolitan University, London, UK

S.O. Idowu, W.L. Filho (eds.), *Professionals' Perspectives of Corporate Social
Responsibility*, DOI 10.1007/978-3-642-02630-0_16,
© Springer-Verlag Berlin Heidelberg 2009

theme has only come to prominence in recent years. Accordingly, long practiced activities such as recycling and looking after the environment for instance are now considered under the banner of CSR.

Various academics including Adams et al. (1998) and Idowu and Towler (2004) have explored how companies should meet their social responsibilities to the surrounding society or community and do the right things at all times. Although the latter contention in particular could debatably be considered to be merely part of business ethics (Carroll and Buchholtz, 2000), much attention has increasingly been given to these aspects of business conduct; both internally and externally. Accordingly, over the years, a variety of activities and concerns have been developed. Due to their plausible connection with the theme of Corporate Social Responsibility, social responsibilities to the surrounding society or community and doing the right things are now often been discussed in terms of the latter. This arguable shift in discussion and terminology has not evaded the hotel industry.

As is clearly demonstrated by most hotel chains' marketing communications, websites and press releases, the hotel industry has in general for many years engaged in altruistic or environmentally friendly practices. When the objective was to help the world, the focus was laid on the environment or recycling. When the target was the community, schools and colleges were discussed, built and supported. Although in the past these activities were not defined as CSR, such practices or activities would nowadays undoubtedly be considered to be linked to Corporate Social Responsibility.

However, as is emphasised in such trade magazines as The Caterer and Hotelkeeper and organisations such as Green Hotelier (www.greenhotelier.org), ten years ago very few hoteliers talked about Corporate Social Responsibility. Instead, people talked about the community and the environment. As a matter of fact, the term Corporate Social Responsibility arguably did not even exist in the hotel industry then. Notwithstanding, based on contemporary definitions of corporate social responsibility (Carroll, 1991, 1999; Goyder, 2003), CSR had indeed, albeit perhaps not in such specific terms, been practiced within the hotel industry for decades.

15.2 The Changing Dimensions of Engagement

In general, the consensus is that hotel industry has somehow moved on from its early engagement with CSR (www.greenhotelier.org). This of course varies from company to company. Although NGOs and organisations such as Tourism Concern (www. tourismconcern.org.uk) would highlight that there is room for much improvement within the hotel industry at both the internal and external level, such companies as the multinational chain Accor have been increasingly engaging in CSR. Accordingly, the company is presently involved with a wide range of projects ranging from working with children in communities where their hotels are based, to attempting to tackle environmental concerns at construction level. Indeed, arguably as means to be effective in real terms or plausibly in an attempt to differentiate itself from its competitors (Lantos, 2001a; Luck, 2006), Accor has in evidence been trying to engage in CSR somehow differently.

In contemporary terms, most hotels probably display something in their bathrooms about re-using towels. Invariably the explanation given or implied to guests is that such an action will help that hotel company save water and energy, and consequently therefore help the environment. Cynical guests could possibly think that hoteliers are simply trying to save on the cost of laundering towels. However, although it cannot be denied that if guests re-use their towels, laundering costs are indeed reduced, it is argued that most hotel companies do not ask guests to re-use their towels just because of their intention to reduce operating costs.

For instance, in an attempt to help their guests fully understand how the re-using of towels would ultimately have an effect on the environment, Accor has an initiative in the UK whereby in addition to putting cards about re-using towels in the bathrooms, the company also displays on the back of these cards everything else that it is doing with regards to its CSR initiatives. As the card stands in front of the bathroom mirror, the back is reflected in the mirror and hence attracts the guest's attention. The rationale is that guests are usually drawn to pick the card up and read what is on the back.

Although such a practice could highlight how Accor is attempting to demonstrate to guests the implications of re-using towels, it could arguably also be seen as a subtle ploy of marketing communications and public relations. Indeed, in addition to showing how re-using towels can help reduce the taxation of hotel guests' consumption on the environment, this card is also unquestionably used to showcase some of the company's CSR activities. By means of this card, Accor can emphasise to its guests that asking them to re-use their towels is just one of several CSR practices that the company is currently engaged in. It could be argued that Accor is not only attempting to inform its guests about its CSR activities but that it is using this simple means of communication from the company to the guests to actively support the brand's image in terms of CSR credibility (Aaker, 2002). As a matter of fact, in this case this basic means of marketing communications is serving as a platform to inform as well as to create interest (De Pelsmacker et al., 2007).

The succinct choice of practices is arguably also demonstrative of how Accor is attempting to differentiate itself in terms of CSR. For instance, there is currently an international initiative that the company is testing in a couple of hotels in UK whereby it is making a commitment to plant trees and help the environment with the money that it is saving from guests re-using their towels. Such an initiative could be indicative of two distinct changes. Firstly, it is revealing how significant it is increasingly becoming for companies to engage in *real* campaigns, to which guests can additionally relate to. Secondly, and perhaps even more importantly for its competitive edge, despite the fact that as a company Accor have been engaging in environmentally-friendly and even CSR practices for a long time, it is nonetheless now trying to find innovative yet measurable ways in which to engage in CSR. Such practices will undoubtedly strengthen the brand positioning of the company in terms of its engagement in CSR (Keller, 2003; Olins, 1994).

15.3 CSR in Contemporary Terms

Companies currently operate in a business environment that is not only global and complex, but that additionally is more demanding than ever before. Indeed, companies appear to no longer only be judged on their profitability, but also on their behaviour within the societies within which they operate. As such they face an array of economic, social and environmental pressures.

Arguably indicative of the increasing significance that CSR is representing within the business environment, in their latest annual corporate governance review published in December 2007, the UK based chartered accountants firm Grant Thornton revealed that 94% of FTSE 350 companies refer to CSR in their annual reports (http://ecomm.grant-thornton.co.uk/ve/zzj0097L929290B66Xe66). Interestingly, 88% of these 350 companies emphasized that they have a special process within their organisation to monitor their engagement in CSR. 40% of the FTSE 100 companies even compiled specific CSR reports. Such findings are arguably indicative of a shift in consciousness as well as in practices. Indeed, it appears that CSR is no longer considered to be something that companies engage in as a peripheral activity. Instead, CSR appears to be increasingly regarded as part of a company's primary activities. Such a shift could have emerged from attempts within the companies to have more monitoring processes. However, just as plausibly, it could have been engendered by the shift in consciousness of consumers, who are not only becoming savvier about CSR practices, but also becoming more demanding in terms of companies engagement in CSR (www.greenhotelier.org).

Based on the growing engagement in CSR, it could be concluded that the latter is becoming increasingly important to hotel organisations. However it appears that hotel clients are also aligning themselves to this growth of interest. As revealed by Accor, CSR is currently demanded by some of corporate clients. When companies contract hotels for their employees or partners to use during their travels, they used to always enquire about health and safety procedures such as fire procedures for instance. However, now prior to approving any business to business contractual agreement, many large companies, such as IBM for example, are additionally asking what the hotel company is currently doing for the environment and for the community.

Within Accor, similar monitoring and reporting processes have been embraced. For instance, the company has had an environment charter for years and every year there is an audit to ensure that hotels are conforming to the charter. There is a minimum set of criteria, which each hotel must comply with. The monitoring is done within the company and there is a self-audit for the hotel. The fact that the general manager controls the Accor internal self-audit and inputs the results into a central database on the intranet once a year could be considered to be problematic. However the company strives to keep this database transparent. Thus, if anyone wants to come and check the inputs, they can.

In addition to having to abide by the environment charter, general managers within the Accor group of hotels have to do a report every month where they have to discuss their unit's performance. In addition to sections on occupancy levels and

Human Resources Management, this three-page long report also contains a section on CSR. Accordingly, yearly targets are set and monitored. In fact, the general managers have a target as to how many days a year they must make a commitment to doing something related to CSR. Additionally, not only do they have to update this report every month, they also have to indicate their actual achievement compared to their target and explain any disparity. Such complex yet concrete processes are arguably indicative of the significance that CSR currently represent within Accor.

Although the Grant Thornton review's findings are in line with the increasing significance of corporate governance within the business environment, what is considered arguably most interesting in Grant Thornton's latest annual corporate governance review is the shift towards independent audit (please see the link in the bibliography). Indeed, the report highlighted that some of the FTSE 100 companies are now also seeking to authenticate the validity of their engagement in CSR by form of external verification of their reports and practices.

The additional practice to obtain external verification of reports and practices could arguably be considered to be aligned with a search for transparency and external objective validation. Indeed, external validation not only enables concrete associations to be reaped (De Pelsmacker et al., 2007) but just as importantly, it enables the strengthening of a pre-intended image (Aaker, 2002). Such a conjecture can arguably be made about Accor's current initiative to obtain the Green Globe accreditation for its Novotel hotels globally (http://www.ec3global.com/).

The Green Globe Company Standard is designed for organisations within the travel and tourism industry and sets out the criteria to attain certification. It provides an environmental management framework for organisations to achieve sustainability. In an attempt to align itself with a globally accredited environmental management framework as well as arguably be associated with highly respected international organisation, all Novotel hotels within the Accor portfolio are intended to be connected with the Green Globe accreditation. Novotel London Tower Bridge was the 1st hotel to be accredited with Green Globe Accreditation. However to date, three hotels in the UK received the accreditation.

Even though individual hotels initially conducts a self-audit and sends it off to Green Globe, auditors from the latter organisation then come to inspect each hotel unit. As such, the accreditation is done independently. If there are gaps, then the individual hotel has to follow up on these and address them before further inspection. Only then, can accreditation be granted. The complete process is multi-levelled and includes such dimensions as policy, benchmarking, compliance, approach, performance and communication (http://www.ec3global.com). Ultimately, not only will the hotels be accredited with a global and significant accreditation, but just as importantly, they would have overtly been objectively and independently assessed; thereby consolidating the dimension of transparency and validation sought.

Idowu (2008) reported that 81% of the FTSE 100 companies currently report on their CSR activities. This is done either on the company's websites or within standalone CSR reports. Furthermore it was reported that 5% of the FTSE 100 companies have enlisted related organisations to report on their CSR activities. The increasingly structured approach to corporate governance may arguably be considered to be reflective of a shift which the business environment in general has been favouring more and more. Additionally, it could be indicative of the significance that stakeholders are increasingly attributing to CSR.

15.4 An Insight into Accor's Multi-Levelled Engagement in CSR

Arguably in response to the combined shift in demand, significance and indeed even consciousness, Accor appears to have adopted a multi-levelled yet structured and formalised approach to CSR. Although it is difficult to determine whether the company is engaging in conviction CSR (Goyder, 2003) or merely in convenience CSR (Mintzberg, 1983; Moore, 2003) or indeed in its own strategic CSR hybrid, it is nonetheless evident that varied external as well as internal engagement has been embraced.

As discussed by Kitchin (2002), CSR is sometimes equivalent to charitable donations. In line with the current trend to select a nominated charity, Accor is associated with the charity Plan. Plan is an international development agency, which works with children and for children. Accor hotels carry out a range of projects to support Plan throughout the year. At times, fundraising events are conducted. At other times, specific projects or children are sponsored. While some projects have been sponsored by the company, Accor, others have been sponsored by a group of hotels such as Novotel or London West hotels. For example, London West hotels have for a long time been engaged in the scheme whereby part of the savings incurred from guests re-using their towels is donated to Plan.

Supporting the earlier contention that there has been an increasing consciousness about CSR, the staff at Accor has wholeheartedly participated in the various projects to raise money for Plan. Events have included football tournaments and CSR awareness days. According to internal employees, the fact that they are kept informed and updated with photographs and regular communications briefs undoubtedly helps maintain the connection among the company, the employees and the stakeholders of Plan. Furthermore, the fact that employees see for themselves how their contribution is just not going into a big pot somewhere but towards something specific, may indeed help maintain their bond with the charity. Indeed, they see the schools that they have helped build.

Accor hotels and guests have over many years helped raise money for Plan. However as a company, Accor did give money to any specific project for Plan. In fact, Accor Head Office did not allocate any budget to their nominated charity. In an attempt to also engage financially in CSR at a company level (Carroll, 1991); the company has recently launched a trust, Foundation. Although Accor is allocating a fixed initial budget, which is not a percentage of its yearly profits, for a period of 5 years, the trust is detached from the company. Foundation will be managed by a board of trustees and any organisation may put in a bid to the trust. Indeed in line with Mintzberg's (1983) philosophical stance about CSR, the company expects nothing for its efforts. Instead, its activities will benefit society and the world.

Accor's engagement in CSR has not been limited to the financial level, there have been several projects with regards to energy saving whether water, electricity or gas. Cost effective and energy efficient light bulbs are now widely used throughout the company. That is however an evolving process. Meanwhile, the company has arguably been proactive and over the years improved such things as shower flow and toilet flushes in attempts to be more environmentally friendly. In future, in particular in its newly built hotels, the company hopes to include the use of solar panels and of using rainwater to flush toilets among its CSR environmental initiatives. As a matter of fact, Accor intends to increase its focus on its newly built hotels as although improvements on existing hotels can be made, much more significant changes can be embraced in new buildings.

Consequently, from the onset, new hotels are being built to be energy and environmentally efficient.

In line with its aim to be more environmentally friendly, Accor has specific recycling processes within its offices. In order to incorporate its CSR practices holistically throughout the company, Accor has additionally been trying to also engage the guests to recycle in their bedrooms. The initial scheme of putting recycling canvas bags in the bedrooms for guests to put their recyclable paper in backfired as rather than filling these with recyclable paper, guests instead walked off with the bags. Notwithstanding this initial unpredictable outcome, the company is currently seeking new means to encourage guests to recycle in their bedrooms.

CSR has been referred to as just the right way for companies to behave (Novak, 1996; Trevino and Nelson, 1999). Although the adequate treatment of employees is traditionally associated with human resources management and indeed with the fact that it is something that should be done as part of business, academics such as Kitchin (2002) have nonetheless referred to CSR as being akin to the treatment of employees.

The training of employees has traditionally been considered fundamental to welfare within the hotel industry. In line with the contentions of such academics as Rogers et al. (1994) and Reichheld et al. (2000), this is expected to not only be beneficial for the employees themselves but also for the organisation in the long-term. However in addition to providing ample training opportunities for its internal employees, in line with Brotherton's (2004) discussion about the significance of identifying critical factors, Accor has been attempting to offer further benefits to support its employees.

In contrast to some hotel companies such as Thistle Hotels, which only offer pension schemes to their heads of department or higher ranked employees, Accor's pension scheme is available to all staff members at any levels. However due to the relatively low interest of its transient and young workforce in the scheme, at present the company is reviewing how to encourage engagement from the younger staff members. In an attempt to enhance staff welfare, employees have free access to a helpline through another company, to which Accor pays a yearly subscription. Employees can thus call, anonymously if they wish, to get advice on any concern. This may range from problems with finances, to being new to a country, to seeking help with finding childcare, to seeking help to deal with domestic violence or even grief. Counselling can be done on the phone. Alternatively, face-to-face counselling can be arranged. Furthermore, an employee can ask to speak to someone in their own language. Additionally, the helpline can be used free by any friend or relative of that member of staff.

As these practices may indeed be categorised as "the treatment of employees", they thus fall within the remit of CSR as defined by Kitchin (2002). However Accor does not consider the treatment of its employees to be part of CSR but rather part of its business duties and responsibilities. Indeed, for the company the treatment of its employees is a human resources management function. Accordingly, general managers should be responsible to take care of their staff when there is no human resource manager employed within a hotel unit to do so. Such a viewpoint strengthens the relevance of the Virtuous Circle (Reichheld et al., 2000) to Accor's success. Indeed, by focusing on internal service quality by via the nurturing of its employees, the level of external service quality is enhanced. As a result, the performance of the company is bound to be positively affected.

Furthermore, if it wants to retain its employees, then the company unquestionably needs to find ways of making them happy in their work environment. If financial incentives cannot be given (Rogers et al., 1994) then other creative means to maintain a positive and nurturing relationship with staff need to be sought so that the latter will remain loyal. Thus, even though as part of the hotel industry, Accor too is not renowned for being the greatest payers, it has striven to provide employees with pertinent benefits such as meals, uniforms and the cleaning of uniforms; all which would be rather costly for the staff to pay for.

15.5 CSR Within Accor: Much More than a PR Conundrum But Still a Business Strategy

Such academics as De Pelsmacker et al. (2007) have argued how public relations can be used to enhance the image of brands as well as to strengthen marketing and positioning objectives. More succinctly, Lewis (2003) has contended that CSR should be used to enhance the image of brands. As such, many CSR initiatives have attracted criticisms about being mere disguised PR ploys. Yet, Lantos (2001b) and Luck (2006) have argued that if used properly, in addition to being an effective PR element, CSR can indeed be an important tool for companies.

Some CSR initiatives can obviously get a company PR coverage. It would be futile to pretend otherwise. In view of the competitive marketing environment within which most hotels operate, getting positive publicity is unquestionably something which hotel companies want. However in general hotel companies such as Accor maintain that they do not engage in CSR just for publicity. Notwithstanding, the company is also acutely aware that it is also operating in a very competitive marketing environment. As such no positive opportunity for publicity can be ignored. Accordingly, when Novotel London Tower Bridge was the first hotel in the UK to be accredited with the Green Globe, the PR company that represents the company was asked to see if any publicity could be gained around this event. When the Green Globe Project is rolled out across the Novotel hotels, Accor will undeniably conduct a PR campaign to support this association. This is not only a normal marketing communications practice, but it may even be considered foolish to miss out on this commendable opportunity. Nonetheless, the company is adamant that regardless of its public relations campaigns and events, publicity or mere public relations was and is still not the first reason for its engagement in the Green Globe accreditation.

Simply put, the Green Globe Novotel project is not deemed to be a PR stunt. Nonetheless, as Accor is a business operating in a very competitive environment, if it can get publicity about this initiative, then it should by all means take advantage of any opportunity to do so. Still, it depends on how the publicity and PR is managed. In order not to seem to be indulging in compliance CSR (Mintzberg, 1983; Moore, 2003) but to assert its engagement in conviction CSR (Goyder, 2003), the company endeavours to behave ethically and consciously in terms of its publicity and PR coverage too. In line with its ethical stance about publicity and PR, even though the company will by all means seek publicity with regards to the newly launched Foundation discussed earlier, the company is adamant that PR is unquestionably not the reason why the company created the trust. Accordingly an integrated marketing communications campaign, which is aligned to its CSR objectives and strategies, is intended to be maintained.

Academics including Jones (2003), Mintzberg (1983) and Moore (2003) have compared CSR to a business strategy to boost a company's self-interest. It cannot be denied that the engagement in CSR can directly influence marketing and indeed branding strategies. However, it is argued that rather than be merely a business strategy for self-interest, a CSR business strategy is unquestionably needed by any company, which intends to engage in effective and sustainable CSR (Luck, 2006).

Hotel companies have a sales strategy, a cost strategy, an HR strategy to help them achieve their specific objectives. Accordingly, a CSR strategy is not only needed but highly recommendable. As a company, Accor now also have a specific CSR strategy alongside its various other strategies. Indeed, if a hotel company wishes to engage in CSR properly, and not just as a philosophy (Carroll, 1991, 1999), how then can its initiatives be productively and effectively conducted without any strategy?

15.6 Conclusions and the Way Forward

Ten years ago, hoteliers were not well versed in CSR. Indeed, the term or concept was arguably not even heard of. In its early stages within the hotel industry, CSR revolved around the environment and the community. However, although in contemporary terms, engagement in CSR is much more structured and formalised, the focus still appears to remain on the focal areas of previous years: environment and community. For instance, Accor's nominated charity Plan is still very much about the community while the company's commitment to planting trees and building energy efficient new hotel units is indeed very much still about the environment.

The hotel industry is renowned for not being the most progressive industry. Notwithstanding, as is demonstrated by the overview of the engagement of Accor in CSR depicted in this chapter, an improvement in the embracing of the concept is evident.

Furthermore, according to the academic definitions of the concept, whether the company labelled it so or not, Accor appears to have been engaging in external as well as internal CSR activities.

On the external level, there have been increasingly more focused and successful projects with regards to energy saving whether water, electricity or gas. New buildings have been and are being planned and constructed to be more energy efficient and environmentally friendly from the onset. Altruistic activities have included financial support to the charity, Plan. The newly launched Foundation fund is undoubtedly going to considerably strengthen the company's engagement in financially helping others.

Meanwhile CSR has also been evident on the internal level. Although the company does not forthrightly consider the support of its employees to be part of its CSR engagement but rather of its HR function, several of its schemes such the pension scheme, the staff helpline, the provision of meals and the cleaning of uniforms have in fact contributed to the positive treatment of its employees. Indeed, these schemes have been refined to actively support staff welfare. Consequently, if the definitions of internal CSR were to be acknowledged, then it would be undeniable that Accor has in fact been engaging in CSR internally too.

CSR can sometimes be considered to be little more than a philosophical stance. However as a hotel company, Accor is clearly demonstrating how far from being a mere philosophy, not only can hotel companies engage in CSR initiatives but perhaps just as importantly, CSR can also be integrated in hotel operations. Indeed, in view of the company's initiative to not only continue to recycle in its offices but also to engage their guests to do so in their bedrooms, it is clear that the company is slowly but surely seeking new avenues to incorporate its CSR practices holistically throughout the company. Moreover, not only is the engagement of the company at the corporate level evident, but just as commendably, operational staff who may not be earning very high salaries seem to be as enthusiastic and engaged in the CSR initiatives of the company.

In brief, even though Accor hotels represent a busy work environment, which is all too often short-staffed, CSR appears to be increasingly embraced holistically. However, the engagement of the company in CSR is an evolving process. Indeed, although this chapter provides a hotelier's perspective about CSR rather than presume to be an objective overview of the changing dimensions of engagement of hotel companies with the concept, it nonetheless clearly illustrates how like its current ongoing search to engage its guests to partake in recycling in their bedrooms, Accor appears to be striving to refine its CSR activities in line with the changing dimensions of engagement.

References

Aaker D.A. (2002), *Building strong brands*, Free, New York; London

Adams C.A., Hill W.Y., and Roberts C.B. (1998), "Corporate social reporting practices in Western Europe: legitimating corporate behaviour", *British Accounting Review*, Vol. 30, No. 1, pp. 1–21

Bowen H.R. (1953), *Social responsibilities of the businessman*, Harpen & Row, New York

Broomhill R. (2007), "Corporate social responsibility: key issues and debates", in Orchard L. and Mathiasz S. (Eds.), *Dunstan paper series*, Don Dunstan Foundation, Adelaide

Brotherton B. (2004), "Critical success factors in UK budget hotel operations", *International Journal of Operations and Production Management*, Vol. 24, No. 3, pp. 944–969

Carroll A.B. (1991), "The pyramid of corporate social responsibility: towards the moral management of organisational stakeholders", *Business Horizons*, Vol. 34, No. 4, pp. 39–48

Carroll A.B. (1999), "Corporate social responsibility: evolution of definitional construct", *Business and Society*, Vol. 38, No. 3, pp. 268–295

Carroll A.B. and Buchholtz A.K. (2000), *Business and society: ethics and stakeholder management*, 4th Ed., South-Western College Publishing, Cincinnati, OH

De Pelsmacker P., Geuens M., and Van den Bergh J. (2007), *Marketing communications: a European perspective*, 3rd Ed., FT Prentice Hall, Harlow

Goyder M. (2003), *Redefining CSR: from the rhetoric of accountability to the reality of earning trust*, Tomorrow's Company, London

Idowu S.O. and Towler B.A. (2004), "A comparative study of the contents of corporate social responsibility reports of UK companies", *Management of Environmental Quality*, Vol. 15, No. 4, pp. 420–437

Idowu S.O. (2008), "Practicing corporate social responsibility in the United Kingdom", in Idowu S.O. and Filho W.L. (Eds.), *Global practices of corporate social responsibility*, Springer Verlag, Berlin

Jones C. (2003), "As if business ethics were possible within such limits", *Organization*, Vol. 10, No. 2, pp. 223–248

Keller K., (2003), *Strategic brand management*, Pearson, London

Kitchin T. (2002), "Corporate social responsibility: a brand explanation", *Brand Management*, Vol. 10, No. 3, pp. 312–326

Lantos G.P. (2001a), The boundaries of strategic corporate social responsibility", *Journal of Consumer Marketing*, Vol. 18, No. 2, pp. 595–630

Lantos G.P. (2001b), "Corporate socialism masquerades as CSR: the difference between being ethical, altruistic and strategic in business", *Strategic Direction*, Vol. 19, No. 6, pp. 31–35

Lewis S. (2003), "Reputation and corporate social responsibility", *Journal of Communication Management*, Vol. 7, No. 4, pp. 356–394

Luck D. (2006), "Customer relationship marketing and corporate social responsibility: not just ethical standpoints or business strategies", *Social Responsibility Journal*, Vol. 2, No. 1, pp. 83–87

Mintzberg H. (1983), "The case for corporate social responsibility", *The Journal of Business Strategy*, Vol. 4, No. 2, pp. 3–15

Moore G. (2003), "Hives and horseshoes, Mintzberg and McIntyre: what future for corporate social responsibility?" *Business Ethics: A European Review*, Vol. 12, No. 1, pp. 41–53

Novak M. (1996), *Business as a calling: work and examined life*, The Free Press, New York

Olins W., (1994), *Corporate identity*, Thames and Hudson, London

Reichheld F., Mirkey R. Jr., and Hopton C. (2000) "The loyalty effect – the relationship between loyalty and profits" *European Business Journal*, Vol. 12, No. 3, p. 134, Autumn

Rogers J.D., Clow K.E., and Kash T.J. (1994), "Increasing job satisfaction of service personnel", *Journal of Service Marketing*, Vol. 8, No. 1, pp. 14–26

Trevino L.K. and Nelson K.A. (1999), *Managing business ethics: straight talk about how to do it right*, 2nd Ed., John Wiley and Sons, New York

Websites

http://www.accor.com
http://www.ec3global.com
http://www.ecomm.grant-thornton.co.uk/ve/zzj0097L929290B66Xe66accessed
http://www.grant-thornton.co.uk/pdf/CGR-2007.pdf
http://www.greenhotelier.org
http://www.tourismconcern.org.uk

Chapter 16
Emphasizing the 'Social' in Corporate Social Responsibility: A Social Work Perspective

Dyann Ross

It was a spring without voices
Carson (1962)

United we stand, divided we fall
Lyric to popular song

Abstract Social work is a profession that stands for social justice and protection of human rights for individuals, communities and societies. As such it has an invaluable knowledge and skills set that can inform debates and practice in the area of CSR. The paper will draw indirectly on lessons derived from research, funded by a multi-national mining company in regional Western Australia, to address conflict between the company and an impacted neighbouring community. Social work knowledge directed the research towards enabling dialogue and mutual respect, with due attention to power issues and the need for social justice for people and sustainability for the local environment. Profit unhinged from these parallel considerations of people and place threatens sustainability as well as social justice.

A key insight is the creative potential of stakeholder relationships in collaboratively dialoguing about the conflict to find common ground and ways forward. Legalistic strategies, media coverage and government policies and inquiries were inadequate to address the conflict. Local supported dialogues with company managers and impacted people can make a difference for the better. This difference for the better has important implications for CSR being a public responsibility, not solely owned and driven by corporations or government. Additionally, the social dimension of sustainability concerns contains the creative potential when competing agendas, conflict and power issues are embraced.

D. Ross (✉)
Edith Cowan University, Perth, Australia

S.O. Idowu, W.L. Filho (eds.), *Professionals' Perspectives of Corporate Social Responsibility*, DOI 10.1007/978-3-642-02630-0_17,
© Springer-Verlag Berlin Heidelberg 2009

16.1 Introduction

Social work is a profession that stands for social justice and protection of human rights for individuals, communities and societies (AASW, 2002; Solas, 2008). As such it has an invaluable knowledge and skills set that can inform debates and practice in the area of corporate social responsibility (CSR). The paper draws on lessons from research, funded by a multi-national mining company in regional Western Australia, to address conflict between the company and an impacted neighbouring community. Social work knowledge directed the research towards enabling dialogue and mutual respect, with due attention to power issues and the need for social justice for people and sustainability for the local environment. Profit unhinged from these parallel considerations of people and place threatens sustainability as well as social justice.

There is a life and death struggle occurring between vested interest groups who appear to stand on opposite sides of the sustainability challenge (Dunphy and Griffith, 1998). The sustainability challenge simultaneously and differently confronts ecosystems, communities, civil governance, and industry profitability. This struggle is most evident in the business practices of mining industries (MMSD, 2002a) as these variously impact on neighbouring communities and environments (Holliday et al., 2002). There is also a largely silent struggle occurring regarding who is seen to be a stakeholder (Cooper, 2004), how they are valued and who therefore has a legitimate right to have a say and influence the agendas of governments and extractive industry.

To explore the potential of social work in these internationally significant issues, a link is made between social work's mission of enabling social justice for disadvantaged groups and the idea of an ethic of love (hooks, 1994; Ross, 2002). In this case the disadvantaged groups are residents in impacted communities adjacent to the Alcoa World Alumina bauxite mine site & alumina refinery at Wagerup in the south west of Western Australia.

> *Alcoa is a large multi-national mining company whose operations at Wagerup have been in the headlines of local and national newspapers since early 2002. At this time many frustrated and aggrieved local residents spoke out publicly about their experiences of being negatively impacted by air borne pollution from the refinery which was for some less than 2 kilometres from their homes. There were claims of serious health impacts and that attempts to talk about their concerns with Alcoa were unsuccessful. Alcoa had also recently begun to buy up properties in the immediate area to gain more control over their operations (Alcoa, 2002). This had the unintended serious consequence of de-stabilising the local towns, causing extreme social impacts which are now subject to a class legal action, and led to perceptions that Alcoa was deliberately trying to buy off troublemakers (Hahn, 2002). Many of the details of resident's claims and Alcoa's position are on the public record as a result of a Parliamentary Inquiry (Sharp, 2004) that was initiated at around the same time I was contracted by Alcoa.*

After outlining the value in linking CSR and an ethic of love, this paper proceeds to describe the elements needed for industry/community partnerships which are sustainability focussed, civilly engaged and socially just. To this end I explore the key social work ideas and practices of:

1. The need for a critical analysis to unpack the power issues & unequal relationships – that is, who are the winners and losers?
2. The importance of enabling equalising strategies in partnerships
3. The value of listening to the powerless and engaging the powerful stakeholders
4. The idea of dialogue as meetings between stakeholders to achieve socially just outcomes which are free from exploitation and control
5. The need for the more powerful partners to act ethically and be accountable to the less powerful
6. The value of measuring the success of the partnership in terms of maintaining warrants or agreements of engagement.

These elements are integral to a social work approach to addressing the failure of corporate social responsibility. I show how a social emphasis must inevitably embrace power imbalances and struggles if it is to address matters of harm, loss and injustice. Further, there appears to be a yawning gap between the theory and the practice of managing outrage and responding to viability threats at the intersections of individual, community and corporate interests. I found that the theorising needed expanding to better explain the deep emotionality and complex lived experiences that the stakeholders grapple to understand. The classic text by Carson (1962), Silent Spring, is a relevant backdrop to this case study & I suggest that not only are her warnings of environmental catastrophe not yet being heard at Wagerup but also the social catastrophe will perhaps not be recognised at all, if the impacted residents give up or go away. I add my voice here to show some aspects of a way forward which didn't persist when we tried it in 2002 but could still work if given a fair chance.

16.2 A Case Study

Sustainability is the new buzz word in the business literature but risks being a hollow promise if, for example, the Western Australian Government's vision, as enshrined in their Sustainability Report (Newman and Rowe, 2003), is not backed by licensing regulations that hold the mining industry accountable. Also, universities, industry think tanks and research centres have a crucial role to play in providing the stakeholders with relevant knowledge to inform their attempts at sustainability. Through my involvement as a university researcher, I found the premises of sustainability thinking needed to be strengthened with a social justice and human rights emphasis. The paper shows how such an emphasis puts power differences and un-reconcilable vested interests at the centre of partnership strategies to seek fairer outcomes as far as possible within the constraints of the situation.

Alcoa approached Edith Cowan University for help in resolving the controversy after a local resident explained how they were not seeing the sociological aspects and needed to listen to the people. From the outset being an outsider coming to do research which was paid for by Alcoa was a challenge on many fronts. But I firmly believed social work had something to offer and proceeded by being open and accountable, especially to the more vulnerable stakeholders. Alcoa gave a commitment that all papers created by the research could be provided to the community as well as part of this openness. Additionally, the research brief was re-designed from one of gathering data about the community to an action research approach to engage stakeholders & enable dialogue about the issues. At this time neither side in the conflict nor the state & local governments were very keen to talk to other parties, but all parties separately were keen to tell their story to me. So this is where I started.

I soon became aware that something more is asked of multi-national companies than meeting often inadequate government regulations for operating within production levels and licensing requirements (Sharp, 2004). At a local level, I was hoping to contribute towards enabling a more civil corporation where:

> Corporate citizenship can become a significant route for overcoming global poverty, inequality and environmental insecurity. This requires that it evolves to a point where business becomes active in promoting and institutionalising new governance frameworks that effectively secure civil market behaviour, globally ... to address, effectively and without contradiction, the aspirations underpinning sustainable development (Zadek, 2001, p. 13).

I also discovered that something more is also to be asked of civil society as it interfaces with government and industry interests where these interests seem to adversely affect viability of towns, the sustainability of ecosystems and the social justice of locally impacted people. In Western Australia, lay people were already raising concerns in various forums across a range of industry issues – for example: The Brookdale contamination issue, the Alcoa Wagerup pollution claims & Iluka's mining of Ludlow tuart forest (The West Australian 2003/2004). But little change was evident as a result of activists groups' efforts. Linking social justice with sustainability seemed to be necessary & was a way I could draw on my social work background. As I will show this linkage commits all parties to a civil regard for each other, a mutual willingness to seek fairer outcomes, to focus on relevant matters and to give a substantive contribution to the work of the partnerships this requires (Fox and Miller, 1995).

> *As I interviewed and met with people in the company & community it became clear that there were intensely contested views of the issues and who was at fault and what should be done. Some areas were "no go" for me as a social researcher (for example: the Alcoa worker compensation claims for health injuries due to pollution claims and the legal case being developed by some residents). One area where there was enough scope to engage all the stakeholders was the controversial impact the Alcoa's land management policy was having on the adjacent towns. This policy outlined the rules for Alcoa buying private properties around the refinery for their business purposes. The purchases treated parts of the town of Yarloop differently and was contested from the outset as damaging to the town as many people sold to Alcoa and moved away. This was all happening at the same time people were trying to be heard about their health concerns. Alcoa publicly stated the land purchases were not related to health concern claims & that it did not want people to leave but people kept selling & leaving deepening the crisis.*

An excerpt from a resident's story (name changed) as told to the Parliamentary Inquiry into the Wagerup issue is presented here to convey some of dimensions of the case study:

Submission Against Alcoa, Wagerup's Expansion

The Browns

23/7/05

We wish to let our views and concerns be known about Alcoa's efforts to get an expansion at its Wagerup refinery. This is totally unacceptable to us and threatens our sense of safety and well-being after what has already been years of adverse social and health impacts from the refinery.

We lived in the northern fringe of Yarloop happily for many years until Alcoa installed the liquor burner in 1996. Since that time Kay has suffered quite debilitating health effects from direct exposure to air borne pollution from the refinery. Alcoa staff have even witnessed her vomiting and her distress when responding to our complaints. We have kept a detailed log book of all the times we have lodged a complaint with Alcoa each time corresponding with personal suffering on my part in witnessing my wife's failing health. There was a period when I was really concerned I was going to lose Kay due to the deterioration in her health. She became trapped in the house which is no way to live.

Neither of us wanted to move from our home and close contact with long term friends in Yarloop. But as Kay was so unable to lead a normal life we had no choice to eventually take up Alcoa's offer to sell to them. We bitterly resent having had to do this and haven't yet recovered from the loss of our home in Yarloop. We are now living in Cockernup and with all this talk of an expansion at Wagerup are experiencing a heightened fear that we will now be impacted here as well.

In the last month I have had several nose bleeds which is very alarming as I haven't had any since leaving Yarloop. One of the nose bleeds occurred when I was visiting a friend in Yarloop. We are worried that it will continue and get worse for us and it doesn't make sense that Alcoa says the expansion will not result in an increase in noise, air pollution and the like. As it currently is, it's a problem so we can't in good conscience believe them that it won't be in the future.

Not only have we lost many of our friends who felt they had to leave for their own safety and to protect their financial interests but we still find many of our conversations in the community dominated by talk of Alcoa. This industry is much too impacting on our everyday lives and much too determined to have its own way at our expense. There is already plenty of evidence that Alcoa and the Government are aware of the social impacts of the refinery operations on these communities. What seems to be happening is a quick patch up by throwing some money to some community groups and thinking this fixes everything. It is much too soon to be expecting those of us who have been so seriously threatened by Alcoa to be presuming an expansion is acceptable. People and communities need to feel safe and able to survive with the current levels of production before an expansion is even considered. That there is an increase in their production already happening at the moment of large proportions leaves us disturbed. How is this happening even before the current application is heard?

We are also alarmed at the West's (newspaper) report of a spill at Wagerup this week. This is no surprise to us and we suspect the delay in them reporting and their claim that it wasn't according to their judgment a risk is political as the last thing they want at the moment is such adverse public attention.

We are concerned that the little people who are most impacted and least able to run weekly advertising programs about our experiences (compared with Alcoa in recent months, promoting their credentials and how good the expansion will be for us all) will not be heard. Alongside this we have no confidence that Alcoa knows how to be good neighbours to those of us who are badly impacted.

It can't be left to them to say what we need and what the social initiatives they can provide are. They have yet to fix the problem and yet are pushing for an expansion for purely economic reasons. This feels to us like a blatant disregard for recent history and the continuing controversy about the social impact in this area. We are just one example of how the situation is still affecting local folks

Yours sincerely
Greg Brown (Cockernup resident)

16.3 CSR as Practised from an Ethic of Love

Hooks explains why an ethic of love is relevant for concerned citizens struggling to gain social justice and also for good corporate business practices in these situations:

> Domination cannot exist in any social situation where a love ethic prevails. It is impor-tant to remember Jung's insight that if the will to power is paramount love will be lacking. When love is present the desire to dominate and exercise power cannot rule the day. All the great social movements of freedom and justice in our society have promoted the love ethic. Concern for the collective good of our nation, city, or neighbourhood rooted in the values of love makes us all seek to nurture and protect that good. If the public policy was created in the spirit of love, then we would not have to worry about unemployment, home-lessness, schools failing to teach children or addiction (and severe company/community conflict because these things would cease to exist) (2000a, p. 98).

> *At a critical point in the research when my legitimacy was being questioned by Alcoa, I attempted to convey to them the main ideas that were influencing my actions to make them aware of residents' perceptions of Alcoa's misuse of power and the need to embrace a caring regard in their business activities as it intersected with the local communities. This was a radical approach but derives from a strong tradition in social work of standing up for the downtrodden and disadvantaged. Here though I was seriously trying to maintain the dialogue that had begun around the land management meetings with the community over the preceding 12 months. The clash of world views and agendas between stakeholders was most evident when I tried to use language that accents the social aspect of issues, especially when I argued for the need for care, compassion, shared wisdom and respect to guide company decisions. Up to this time there was a guarded appreciation that much was being lost due Alcoa's deteriorating community relations but a more active embrace of ethics to do with loving your neighbours was hard for them to hear.*

It had become clear that an 'us versus them', tit for tat dynamic (Axelrod, 1997) was more prevalent as a business ethic and there remained a desire for Alcoa as the dominant party in the contestation to resume control for deciding the rules & terms for settling the dispute. The research and previous history between the government, community and company were showing though that Alcoa's approach was a recipe for domination not partnership. Solutions gained through domination are not sustainable or just and in fact will not be solutions, as disaffected groups will continue to resist what they perceive as unfair treatment (Sandman, 2002a). A research insight was that industry stakeholders involved in conflict with local communities could gain by shifting to a more rigorous ethical capacity to ensure their own agendas are not pursued at the expense of local communities, or at the expense of some less desirable (to the company) elements within the community.

This is where the dialogue that was attempted as part of my research between the communities, Alcoa and at times the state government became tested and eventually broke down. The practice of love as I understand it is inextricably linked with working towards social justice and challenges us as individuals, collectivities & companies to integrate our values, thinking and actions:

> Embracing a love ethic, means that we utilize all the dimensions of love which are shown in society in different forms for example – care, commitment, trust, responsibility, respect, and knowledge – in our everyday lives (hooks, 2000a, p. 94).

These are all capacities that traditional social work values and seeks to enable in their clients but what was confronting in the research were the attempts to get government officials, politicians and company managers to embrace the challenges of the love ethic. For me this is at the heart of emphasizing the social in CSR that was not written about in the literature that I went to for help. As the research proceeded I became more convinced that problem-solving in relationship and partnerships with those who feel impacted upon, aware of the abuses of power that cause disadvantage and loss, is a key aspect of an ethic of love:

> Until we are all able to accept the interlocking, interdependent nature of systems of domination and recognize specific ways each system is maintained, we will continue to act in ways that undermine our individual quest for freedom and collective liberation struggle. The ability to acknowledge blind spots can emerge only as we expand our concern about politics of domination and our capacity to care about the oppression and exploitation of others. A love ethic makes this expansion possible (hooks, 1994, p. 244).

16.3.1 Social Work Skill No. 1: Critical Analysis

The skill of critical analysis involves questioning and appreciating the patterns of power and control that are occurring in a situation (Fook, 2000). Thus, a critical analysis of the case study excerpt would not naively assume the residents are imagining the health issues or just stirring up trouble for Alcoa. Residents are less able to influence Alcoa's operations and even with the authority of a Parliamentary Inquiry their ability to be heard and influence decisions remained minimal. This type of dynamic points to power differences which are clear to many residents that Alcoa had enormous ability to influence the government to maintain its operations and in fact increase production during this troubled time.

A critical analysis of the issues also required an active seeking and protecting of the interests and human rights between the parties regarding each others' experiences and understandings. It should be noted though that companies do not have human rights, yet this is being claimed in some cases with profound implications for impacted communities (Achbar, 2003). In this case study the community and company interests were irreconcilable as Alcoa's operations were perceived to be threatening the very survival of neighbouring towns. So there were many losses as people begun to sell and leave the area which had a compounding effect on the sustainability of the towns. The adoption of a critical analysis in the research takes the literature on corporate social responsibility one step further by refusing to allow the debates, strategies and definitions of what counts as problematic remain in the hands of the company managers, government bureaucrats, and even university academics. Impacted residents had non-dominant, often unwelcome, perspectives on the issues and were affected by the impact of Alcoa's actions and yet were not being treated as legitimate stakeholders. From the outset this was a warning sign of unequal power relationships that were serving to keep things under cover and unanalysed. The research unsettled these relations of domination and control and recognised that:

> Debates over sustainable development require equal and adequate representation of communities affected by mining . . . one of the key challenges facing [the mining industry] today is putting in place mechanisms to ensure that communities can effectively engage in decision-making on issues that affect them. There is a great need to strengthen community-based organisations and their ability to represent their views effectively at all levels.

> Key issues being addressed [in international forums] include: codes of conduct for the mining industry, appropriate modes of dialogue between mining companies and communities, the role of central and local government, relationship between mine workers and communities and the impacts of mining [especially] on women and youth (Mining, Minerals and Sustainable Development (MMSD), 2002a, p. 70).

16.3.2 Social Work Skill No. 2: Equalising Strategies in Partnerships

By emphasing the social dimensions and the impacts of failures in CSR in this manner, it opens up relationship based ways of responding to injustice and harm. It puts the focus on the importance of minority stakeholder engagement which goes beyond representation & consultation to what some author's have called 'co-creative stakeholder engagement' (Svendsen, 2008). These social emphases to CSR allow us to accent the central importance of 'human sustainability' interlinked with ecological sustainability (Dunphy and Benveniste, 2000, p. 6).

> *The research attempted to establish a space where stakeholders could meet as equals to discuss their shared concerns but for this to work, Alcoa had to let go of their control over key decisions that affected local people. The weekly meetings I facilitated, relating to the land management issues, thus, worked to develop some agreements about changes to Alcoa's land management policy which would make it fairer for local people and give them a say in what was happening in their towns. A key goal for many locals was to gain a guarantee*

from Alcoa of protection against loss of property values for the life of the refinery. This was eventually achieved, not by the space created by the research, but by government intervention. However the groundwork laid by the research showed how supported discussions with Alcoa could establish the shared concerns and what each party was willing to do about it. These supported discussions ensured people were treated respectfully and that really sensitive matters were talked about in a safe environment. For it to work though key decisions made by Alcoa needed to also occur in line with agreements made at these meetings.

I found much of the literature on CSR of limited value in guiding the research as it tends to be 'top down' theorising with a bias toward convincing big business that it is in their interests to be socially responsible (for example, Grayson and Hodges, 2004). Much of the impetus and scope to define what will count as their appropriate exercise of social responsibility is also at the instigation of the dominant stakeholder, namely industry. Many people spoke of Alcoa's exercise of social responsibility as a form of selective philanthropy, sometimes referred to as corporate philanthropy (Porter and Kramer, 2002). They believed that philanthropy on Alcoa's terms served only Alcoa and from a social work perspective it seemed to reinforce relations of domination and subservience.

Industry stakeholders are increasingly keen to secure support from local communities, so that they might claim a 'community licence to operate'. See for example, the effort of Alcoa in regional newspapers to promote their good neighbour image as part of their agenda for expanding their refinery at Wagerup (Bunbury, 14th April 2005). This community licence to operate needs to be about more than giving of charity in the form of sponsorships to community services & groups, although it can include this type of 'gifting' (Titmus, 1970). Promises of job creation when plans for an expansion of operations was announced, can be enticing but also may hide bigger issues of increased environmental degradation and/or increased pollution and impacts on nearby communities. A social justice and sustainability emphasis puts the onus on negotiated gifting, negotiated areas of mutual interest and negotiated preferred outcomes. Significantly, this negotiating in turn needs to be informed by sustainability principles, natural justice in how all stakeholders are listened to and treated and social justice in the equality and relevance of the outcomes.

16.3.3 Social Work Skill No. 3: Listening to the Powerless and Engaging the Powerful

Actually engaging with local towns as equals was a research goal that remained elusive in its substantive outcomes. The stories told by many people in neighbouring communities showed that it is dangerous to accept Alcoa as the arbiter of all matters to do with CSR as the best possible starting point for enabling sustainability. This is because industry stakeholders have disproportionate power and are also arguably the greatest beneficiaries of the status quo (Brueckner and Ross, 2010). Thus, they are unlikely to want change that might threaten their monopoly over: resources; definitional control over what constitutes good business practice, and what is perceived as the proper role of outraged communities in the affairs of their business. Despite a serious attempt at dialogue, the research found this control by the company in question to ultimately be non-negotiable. Texts which offer some valuable ideas for engaging stakeholders in corporate social performance matters (Cooper, 2004) tend to downplay the complexity of power issues I observed which were facing the non-dominant or minority stakeholders, in this instance, members of the small communities adjacent to Alcoa's Wagerup refinery.

A finding of the research was that a without engaging the senior members of Alcoa management though it was not going to be possible to progress a power sharing model of company/community relations. Social work skills alone were not enough to move the stakeholder relationships onto a more equitable footing. State government legislative authority was also found to not make a difference in the conflict. It was also very difficult to have frank discussions about power imbalances in a climate of calls for compensation and legal cases by some aggrieved members of the adjacent towns.

My idealism as a social worker was sorely tested over the months of seeking to engage company personnel, community members and government officials. I had believed there was a contribution social work ideas could make, for example as hooks writes:

> A genuine feminist politics always brings us from bondage to freedom, from lovelessness to loving. Mutual partnership is the foundation to love [and the opposite to domination]. And feminist practice is the only movement for social justice in our society which creates conditions where mutuality can be nurtured (2000b, p. 104).

Strength of the research orientation was that it was people (relational) and power sensitive as well as very responsive to the shifts and pulls of the socio-political context in which the stakeholders are situated. It also involved a valuing of local, embodied, emotional and subjective knowledge as well as technical, (seemingly) objective and 'imported' knowledge. Yet these very elements were also the battle grounds – people were pitted against profits; new ideas against traditional business management practices and blame was prevalent instead of taking responsibility.

For example, it was a challenge to convey the idea that a social justice lens is not about being 'pro' the community at any cost to the company or vice versa. There were differences, nevertheless, in power to influence 'the other' when the industry stakeholder is part of a multi-national company, and as such has the advantage of enormous resources to draw upon to serve, and if necessary, defend its business interests. A feminist lens alongside social work skills of engaging stakeholders and facilitating dialogue and problem-solving also alerted me to the need to work respectfully and inclusively with differences of relevance to the conflict. Thus, holding on to the idea of 'together-in-difference' (Young, 1995) ensured all voices, perspectives and solutions were genuinely engaged and placed on the table for consideration. The community members stepped up to the table and took many risks and many local Alcoa managers also stepped forward to try to sort out the issues. But the most senior members of Alcoa's management did not come to the dialogue table and if they came they did not stay. Engaging the powerful remains a challenge for advancing lasting changes that benefit the local people while maintaining a profitable company.

Nevertheless the partnership approach (Tennyson, 2003; Tennyson and Wilde, 2000) allowed many of the ideas which underpin my approach to social work to be drawn productively together to achieve some agreements between Alcoa and the local residents.

> *A range of meetings were conducted in the town of Yarloop during 2002 and 2003 and allowed many residents to have their say in a public forum for the first time. Further, the strongly facilitated meetings required of all participants that they observe basic rules of respectful interaction so that people could talk openly without being attacked or disparaged. Issues and agreements were carefully documented and notes from the meetings were made widely available. This openness and inclusion of all interested parties was a radical change from the secrecy and separate meetings behind closed doors that had been happening. The researcher role became one of a third party broker (Tennyson and Wilde, 2000) and as such much of the possibility for dialogue and valued outcomes to these meetings rested on maintaining credibility with both the community and Alcoa. This was perhaps always going to be a fraught and short term strategy because of the powerful vested interests within sectors of the community but more so within the government and Alcoa which variously sought to maintain the status quo and not concede too much to the impacted locals.*

The research approach arose from a notion of social justice as being about how decisions are made, how people are treated, who speaks and for whom and what the institutional structures are that influence how people act (Young, 1990). This idea of social justice is more sophisticated than the usual notion of re-distribution of resources (Rawls, 1973) yet should, nevertheless, show outcomes that move towards a fairer treatment of people and a more sustainable use of disputed resources. The added benefit of the more elaborate notion of social justice is that it is more likely to spur stakeholders on to find less damaging processes to settle disputes so that human rights, especially of the most vulnerable, can be re-instated or upheld.

16.3.4 Social Work Skill No. 4: Building Dialogue Without Exploitation

The literature is weak on how to build true dialogue across differences of power, interests and values, although there are many case studies of efforts globally that have elements of interest for this paper (see Holliday et al., 2002). The theory and these practice examples, though, have not adequately spoken to the complexity where an escalation of conflict and public counter/attacks are being played out in an uneven power struggle between stakeholders. Sustainability and capacity building literature and outrage/risk management manuals suggest a range of strategies and models for responding to less overt conflict and struggles on the one hand and more extreme conflict involving violence on the other (MMSD, 2002a, b; Sonn et al., 2002; Hermanti, 2002; Sandman, 2002a). The literature tends to assume it is the community stakeholder who needs capacity building to be self sufficient and the industry stakeholder who needs to provide leadership toward more socially responsible behaviour (up to a point that tends to stop short of ensuring social justice is attained for the most aggrieved parties).

The hope of the research was that if the meetings between the community and the company could model how issues could be raised and resolved together that confidence would be built to keep using less confrontational, exclusionary and win/loose strategies that had prevailed to this time. Alongside the weekly open meetings, there were various other conversations some of which were part of the research. For example, regular debriefs were conducted with the Alcoa managers to enable them to avoid reactive, short sighted behaviour as a result of what they heard or felt arising from the meetings. It became clear that the company needed to learn new ways of engaging their neighbours and this was not going to be easy when they felt so threatened by much of what was being raised in the meetings. One Alcoa representative said that Alcoa was just beginning to grasp that they needed to embrace the social aspects of their CSR much as they came to realise with the inter-related environmental aspects 20 years earlier.

Another manager from Alcoa stated:

The impacts of this project are being dealt with and felt at all levels of the organisation. [It] would be good if the human side to Alcoa could come across [in your paper]. My personal view is that as an individual working on this project I am very much affected by everything that is done, said, felt, etc. by Alcoa as well as the community and media. So too are the people from head office who have never even visited Wagerup. All the people from Alcoa dealing with this issue are human and all feel very much for the people of Yarloop and the impacts on them. . . . [We are] humans with feelings working on behalf of Alcoa rather than as a giant corporation that has no feelings.

The research attempted to enable behaviours that were not about seeking the upper hand in the key decisions that arose from long and often painful conversations in the community based meetings. The risk remained high that those with power in other spaces – for example, company boardrooms or government ministerial inquiries – would undermine the small local experiment in dialogue. The main challenge remained one of ensuring the impacted residents were part of conversations and decisions that affected them. The power imbalance shifted to a more equal footing every time the less powerful stakeholders were involved and listened to and their ideas taken seriously as part of the solution. A finding of the research though, was that it was the powerful stakeholders who needed the most assistance in building their capacity to engage in dialogue not the community members.

16.3.5 Social Work Skill No. 5: Enabling Ethical Actions by the Powerful

Is it an ethical company? What does an ethical company look like? Who is doing the looking, with what vested interests and agendas? At times to ask the first question of people in the impacted town where I did some research on these issues, the resounding answer was – NO! One person said at the time, 'Are they stupid, or what?' This was said in the context of the person not being able to understand why Alcoa had acted as it had, if it has been sincerely wanting what was best for their town.

At its most fundamental, examples like this point to a questioning of the ethical behaviour of the industry stakeholder. What Lagan (2000) says is that, among other things, an ethical company works hard to be a neighbour of choice. However, more typical are adversarial situations where much of a company's energy is dedicated to talking about the town in question, without the town's people present. When individuals step toward the company with a complaint or to raise an issue, they can quickly become scapegoats and not taken seriously. This dynamic is what Pettman (1992) calls 'invisible absence or pathological presence'. When the besieged company has contact with the outraged community in some form, the community are constructed as problematic. On the other hand, when the company considers its business concerns the community are neither present nor visible. The reverse may also be true although there is less organised power available for the community to utilise & a lesser level of responsibility for creating the problem (for example in the case of industrial pollution impacting nearby resident's health).

Additionally, it is likely there will be resistance by industry stakeholders to relinquishing control over what the interaction looks like when attempts at dialogue happen (Freire, 1970). Control over the terms of engagement and key decisions which affect an impacted town are at base ethical challenges for the industry stakeholder. Clearly these challenges are also deeply steeped in power issues. The dialogic partnership proposed here has much to offer any serious attempt to shift the ethical underpinnings & power dynamics of industry stakeholders' relationships with their nearest neighbours. As Lagan notes:

> An ethical company is not afraid to discuss the undiscussable, promotes a culture of openness, trust, dialogue & disclosure. . . . It recognises that fundamental human values of social & environmental responsibility, community commitment & dignity can sit alongside profit maximization – (& enable it) (2000, p. 195).

Hass, the CEO for Levi Strauss & Co., suggests:

> Ethics is about character and courage. How we meet the challenge when doing the right thing will cost more than we want to pay (quoted in Lagan, 2000, p. 149).

Hass was not talking only about individual character and courage or purely financial costs. Lagan (2000) goes on to say that the focus should not only be on the specifics of a company's decision-making but also the values which inform it. Many industry stakeholders proudly profess to being values based, global companies where the values of integrity, people and accountability (among others) are highly cherished. See for example: Rio Tinto's (2006) WA Future Fund which they describe as 'our partnerships working together for a sustainable future'; Alcoa's (2006) stronger communities projects & values statement, and; Shell's (2006) claim 'everyone's a winner' in their perfect partners magazine segment.

The ongoing challenge involves aligning professed values with day to day actions, especially in contexts of threat to the company. This is very hard to do if you are an individual in a complex multinational company but it is also very hard in a different way for an individual in the complex, voluntary and informal relationships of a community. Thus, for the company or the community to move to an agreed collectivist position for its constituency requires highly sophisticated engagement & governance processes. When such sophisticated collectivising is required is probably when stakeholders feel least inclined to participate.

I became convinced during the research that the best company in the world will be the one which practices all aspects of its business from an ethic of love. It seemed to be in everyone's interest to encourage an expansion of valuing of what constitutes good business practices beyond narrow rationalistic, technical and profit driven considerations. This is being recognised by some leaders in the extractive industry (Holliday et al., 2002) but there is a high risk that their grand statements will get stuck in rhetoric in the absence of a willingness to warrant respectful engagement and dialogue with stakeholders. This willingness to engage becomes more crucial and less likely when conflict is threatening or occurring. This is because a defensive or aggressive action by the conflicted parties is a more likely response (Chetkow-Yanoov, 1997; Sandman, 2002b). A leap of faith and some amount of goodwill is required to engage in dialogue between the conflicted parties, and the longer and more entrenched the conflict, the harder it is to change the dynamics, voluntarily and non-violently.

16.3.6 Social Work Skill No. 6: Working to Maintain the Partnership Warrants

Underpinning the commitment to business in partnership with other stakeholders from within a love ethic is a need to pursue a cultural shift in industry practices. The cultural shift needs to involve a valuing of non-scientific knowledge (head); knowledge gained through relationships (heart) and lived experience (hand) (Kelly and Sewell, 1988). The social work and community development literature is replete with the value of these capacities for communities and vulnerable groups (Ife and Tesoriero, 2006; Kenny, 2006; Muirhead, 2002) yet the same principles and practices can serve in the cultural change needed in the management of big business.

Social work practice often occurs in highly contested and conflictual settings, although not usually in company boardrooms and as submissions to ministerial inquiries. The significance of focussing on industry/community conflict in exploring social work's contribution in this case study is that the dynamics of conflict 'write large' dominant power plays that exist in the situation. Similar dynamics also occur in a range of other relationships, both in nation states, organizations and families (Goldie et al., 2005). Also the stakes are very high in terms of the sustainability of the planet's ecosystems and industries and in terms of the sovereignty of elected governments to act in the public interest. Much can be learned about the health of our system of governance from how the government positions itself in conflicts between community rights and industry claims on resources (Brueckner, 2007).

Additionally, it is possibly also the case that conflicts of this type highlight the lack of sustainability and social justice in the situation (and other similar situations). Careful consideration of these types of conflicts may show the limited mechanisms for those most adversely impacted to protect their interests and influence the dominant stakeholders to be accountable and socially responsible. This has to become a bigger issue in public debates if we wish for our democratic system of government to have any credence (Achbar, 2003).

These points notwithstanding, when the stakes in industry/community conflict are so high and converge into the specific demands of the stakeholders, it can bring a moral and political pressure to bear to 'sort it' that might not otherwise be possible. There are examples internationally where conflict has resulted in a negative spiral of tit for tat with serious abuses of human rights and damage to local environments (Rees and Wright, 2000). There are few examples of conflict that have been peacefully, justly and sustainably negotiated.

The challenge for the stakeholders is very complicated and interconnected, with the risk and losses likely to be borne unequally and to a greater extent by the least powerful members in the partnership. The most crucial finding of the research was that a particular rigour is needed to guard against further exacerbating existing inequities and harm. Adapting Fox and Miller's (1995) ideas, it is possible to suggest that ethical, sustainable partnerships require the securing of specific warrants or agreements around key aspects of the conflict resolution process.

This involves four capacities by both parties to the partnership, namely:

1. To be sincere in building relationships
2. To stay focussed on relevant shared issues
3. To do so with willing attention, especially to the effects of power, and
4. To ensure substantive contributions are made by both parties (Fox and Miller, 1995).

These qualities are necessary for obtaining a *warrant* or legitimacy to claim one's own position/interests – because it is done with a refined regard for others' interests and a willingness to pursue equitable, sustainable and relevant solutions. The downward spiral of tit for tat can be turned *at any time* into a virtuous upward spiral by warranting those responsible to address the issue to act in partnership with those affected by it.

In deciding to orient the research as outlined it was apparent very early on that Alcoa would have to change its thinking and practices and as a result the research work would sooner or later become threatening to their usual way of doing business. In such circumstances spending more time earlier on in establishing the terms of engagement, what Fox and Miller (1995) called "warrants" with senior, non-involved company executives may have flagged the limits regarding what changes they might be willing to undertake. As it became apparent that each of the warrants were not being upheld by Alcoa, I decided to stop all the meetings as it was asking too much of the most powerless to try to keep the dialogue going. While this closed the space for shared decisions it was already evident that there were not going to be shared decisions on the details of the land management issues that mattered most to the residents.

Other mechanisms undertaken by local residents such as formal submissions to the Ombudsman about Alcoa's operations and recently the results of independently analysed air samples from sites around the impacted towns have had more success (see the Community Alliance for Positive Solutions (CAPS, 2008) website). The Western Australian Attorney General is now on the public record as saying there is evidence of pollution from Alcoa's refinery. The story is not finished and the research and community activism of locals continue to provide important lessons about CSR for the company if it were to listen.

16.4 Loving Your Neighbour

Multi-national mining companies desire to be 'good neighbours' to surrounding towns and businesses. This desire needs to be based on more than their perceptions of having gained a licence to operate from neighbouring communities. Licences to operate are often purchased through the exercise of selective corporate philanthropy. Being a good neighbour needs to embrace practices of social justice where:

> Justice (is) primarily the virtue of citizenship wherein persons collectively deliberate problems and issues facing them within their institutions and actions, under conditions free from oppression and domination, with reciprocity and mutual tolerance of differences (Young, 1990, quoted in Mullaly, 1997, p. 142).

Partnerships without genuine dialogue and substantial contributions to matters of social justice and sustainability are not in reality partnerships. A business case for an ethic of love challenges industry stakeholders to lead with their hearts as well as an eye for profits when trying to understand and negotiate mutually beneficial outcomes with impacted neighbouring communities. Conflict, depletion of the environment, including the human environment, over-focus on profit at the expense of people are very costly for big business and little towns.

The alternative is to practice the politics of loving y/our neighbours. Social work ideas and skills have much to offer stakeholders in this regard. The first step in building trusting partnerships is listening:

> The transition to a listening mode, which is shorthand for a lot of underlying activities – (was) the way we broke the (traditional) corporate mould . . .. I am very proud of that. We demonstrated that transparency works, as does sharing dilemmas and difficult and sensitive issues where we were not certain how to proceed. Sharing this with the outside world was not a sign of weakness but a sign of strength. (Shell's Vice President for sustainable development, quoted in Holliday et al., 2002).

Social work in western countries such as Australia has been slow as a profession to recognise the importance of love (Ross, 2002) as an integral dynamic of social justice, but making this link has much to contribute to CSR related concerns.

> *It has been difficult to describe the research because much of how it was constructed and enacted was not ultimately, from my perspective, what Alcoa thought it was going to get. In turn, it has been more a professional responsibility, after the ceasing of the research contract, to distil the insights and to try to understand how it might have worked better. The specific case study details of: the claims of negative social and other impacts by residents; Alcoa's claims that there was no evidence of pollution or harm to people, and; the government's subsequent actions to manage a larger buy up of properties by Alcoa of people who felt impacted by Alcoa's operations, are all matters that need more dialogue even now several years later.*
>
> *More as a bystander now, the continuing conflict has made me realise how important it is to also focus on the rules of engagement when attempts are made to intervene, especially where there are such unequal power dynamics. I would go so far as to suggest there needs to be a clear legislative basis to the warrants being followed to avoid further injustices to the powerless stakeholders in conflicts of this nature. Even with a legal basis to the rules of negotiations it will not be a certainty that the least powerful will be treated fairly and included in matters which affect them. Such is the way of unchecked corporate power.*

References

AASW, 2002. *Code of ethics*. Barton: Australian Association of Social Workers.

Achbar, M., 2003. *The corporation*. England: Metrodome Distributions.

Alcoa World Alumina Australia, 2002. *Visions and values: Principles*. [Online]. Available at: http://www.alcoa.com.au/governance/values.shtml. [accessed 11th September 2002].

Alcoa World Alumina Australia, 2006. *Partnering stronger communities*. [Online]. Available at: http://www.alcoa.com/australia/en/info_page/partnering_stronger_communities.asp. [accessed 29th August 2008].

Axelrod, R., 1997. *The complexity of co-operation*. Princeton: Princeton University Press.

Brueckner, M., 2007. The western Australian regional forest agreement: economic rationalism and the normalisation of political closure. *Australian Journal of Public Administration*, 66(2), 148–158.

Brueckner, M. and Ross, D., 2010. *Under corporatised skies: A struggle between people, place and profit*. Perth: Fremantle Arts Press.

Bunbury H., 2005. *Helping build a sustainable future*. Mining and Minerals Supplement. Bunbury: South Western Times Newspapers, p. 136.

Carson, R., 1962. *Silent spring*. Boston: Hougthon Mifflin.

CAPS, 2008. http://www.caps6218.org.au/index.php

Chetkow-Yanoov, B., 1997. *Social work approaches to conflict resolution*. New York: Hawthorn Press.

Cooper, S., 2004. *Corporate social performance: A stakeholder approach*. Burlington: Ashgate.

Dunphy, D. and Benveniste, J., 2000. An introduction to the sustainable corporation. In D. Dunphy, J. Benveniste, A. Griffiths, and P. Sutton (Eds.), *Sustainability: The corporate challenge of the 21st century*. St. Leonards: Allen & Unwin.

Dunphy, D. and Griffiths, A., 1998. *The sustainable corporation: Organizational renewal in Australia*. St. Leonards: Allen & Unwin.

Fook, J., 2000. *Social work in changing times: new ways for new challenges*. Paper presented at the Australian Association of Social Workers, State Branch Conference, Bunbury: AASW.

Fox, C. and Miller, H., 1995. *Postmodern public administration: Toward discourse*. Thousand Oaks: Sage Publications.

Freire, P., 1970. *Pedagogy of the oppressed*. New York: Herder and Herder.

Goldie, J., Douglas, B., and Furnass, B. (Eds.), 2005. *In search of sustainability*. Collingwood: CSIRO Publishing.

Grayson, D. and Hodges, A., 2004. *Corporate social opportunity: 7 steps to make corporate social responsibility work for your business*. Sheffield: Greenleaf Publishing.

Hahn, T. 2002. *In the loop*. A video. Bunbury: Edith Cowan University.

Hemmati, M., 2002. *Multi-stakeholders processes for governance and sustainability – Beyond deadlock and conflict*. London: Earthscan.

Holliday, C., Schidheiny, S. and Watts, P., 2002. *Walking the talk: The business case for sustainable development*. San Francisco: Greenleaf Publishing.

hooks, b., 1994. *Outlaw culture: Resisting representations*. New York: Routledge.

hooks, b., 2000a. *All about love*. London: New Visions.

hooks, b., 2000b. *Feminism is for everybody: Passionate politics*. Cambridge: South End Press.

Ife, J. and Tesoriero, F., 2006. *Community development: Community based alternatives in an age of globalism*, 3rd edition. French's Forest: Pearson Education Australia.

Kelly, A. and Sewell, S., 1988. *With head, heart and hand: Dimensions of community building*, 2nd edition. Bowen Hills, Qld: Boolarong.

Kenny, S., 2006. *Developing communities for the future*, 3rd edition. South Melbourne: Nelson Thompson Learning.

Lagan, A., 2000. *Why ethics matter: Business ethics for business people*. Melbourne: Information Australia.

Mining, Minerals and Sustainable Development (MMSD), 2002a. *Breaking new ground*. London: Earthscan.

Mining, Minerals and Sustainable Development (MMSD), 2002b. *Seven questions to sustainability: How to assess the contribution of mining and minerals activities*. Winnipeg: IISD.

Muirhead, T., 2002. *Weaving tapestries: A handbook for building communities*. Mt. Hawthorn: Local Government Community Services Association.

Mullaly, B., 1997. *Structural social work: Ideology, theory and practice*. Toronto: Oxford University Press.

Newman, P. and Rowe, M., 2003. *Hope for the future: The Western Australian state sustainability strategy*. Perth: State Government of W.A.

Pettman, J., 1992. *Living in the margins: Racism, sexism and feminism in Australia*. North Sydney: Allen & Unwin.

Porter, M. and Kramer, M., 2002. The competitive advantage of corporate philanthropy. [Online]. Available at: *Harvard Business Review On Point*, December. [accessed 29th August, 2008].

Rawls, J., 1973. *A theory of justice*. London: Oxford University Press.

Rees, S. and Wright, S. (Eds.), 2000. *Human rights, corporate responsibility: A dialogue*. Sydney: Pluto Press.

Rio T., 2006. [Online]. Riotinto.com.partnerships. asp. Available at: http://www.wafuture fund. [accessed 29th August, 2008).

Ross, D., 2002. Enacting my theory and politics of an ethic of love in social work education. Unpublished doctoral dissertation. Bunbury: Edith Cowan University.

Sandman, P., 2002a. Laundry list of 50 outrage reducers. [Online]. Available at: http://www. psandman.com/col/laundry.htm. [accessed 7th November, 2003].

Sandman, P., 2002b. Accountability. [Online]. Available at: http://www.psandman.com/col/ account.htm. [accessed 7th December, 2004].

Sharp, C., 2004. *Report for the standing committee on environment & public affairs in relation to the Alcoa refinery at Wagerup Inquiry*. Perth: Government of Western Australia.

Shell, 2006. Everyone's a winner. Impact. Issue 2; p. 18. [Online]. Available at: http://www.shell.com/globalsolutions. [accessed 7th December, 2004].

Solas, J., 2008. Social work & social justice: What are we fighting for? *Australian Social Work*, 61(2), pp. 124–136.

Sonn, C., Drew, N., and Kasat, P., 2002. *Conceptualising community cultural development: The role of cultural planning in community change*. Cloister's Square: Community Arts Network.

Svendsen, A., 2008. *Co-creative stakeholder engagement*. Melbourne: Australian Centre for CSR, 1st & 2nd May.

Titmus, R., 1970. *The gift relationship: From human blood to social policy*. London: Allen & Unwin.

Tennyson, R., 2003. The partnering toolbook. [Online]. Available at: http://www.google.com. au/search?sourceid=navclient&aq=t&ie=UTF-8&rlz=1T4ADBF_enAU233AU233&q=The +partnering+toolbook. [accessed 29th august, 2008].

Tennyson, R. and Wilde, L., 2000. *The guiding hand: Brokering partnerships for sustainable development*. Geneva: United Nations Office of Public Information.

Young, I.M., 1990. *Justice and the politics of difference*. Princeton: Princeton University Press.

Young, I.M., 1995. Communication and the other. In Wilson, M. and Yeatman, A. (Eds.), *Beyond deliberative justice and identity: Antipodean democracy practices*. Wellington: Bridget Williams Books.

Zadek, S., 2001. *The civil corporation: The new economy of corporate citizenship*. London & Stirling: Earthscan Publications.

Chapter 17
Democratic Gains in Public Administration at Local Level in Terms of CSR: Theory and Practice-Based Approaches at Izmir Metropolitan City, Turkey

Zerrin Toprak Karaman

In the middle of difficulty lies opportunity
Albert Einstein

Abstract Cooperation is of great importance in ensuring social responsibility. Thus, the democratic indicators, which are important in the realization of governance, were given precedence in this study. How much attention do 'central and local governments' pay to issues relating to the presence of democracy? And how much does society claim ownership of these issues at any given level? In relation to this, how many of the democratic indicators have been expressed numerically? All these questions are closely related to issues concerned with the sustainability of any society and constitute the dynamics of urban life. Furthermore, the fact that citizens and other foreign settlers in a city play a role in the development of that city is closely related to ensuring solidarity from them. In a sound urban structuring, the existence of different cultural groups is considered to be crucial in ensuring the existence of social peace. However, these issues are not observed on the agenda at local level. This is indicated by their absence in the strategic planning of municipalities in the context of Turkey.

This chapter seeks to provide answers to a series of questions which relate to CSR, for example it provides answers to questions such as: What is the role of individuals and the community in the development of a city? How much do individuals as 'women and men' share in the feeling of solidarity brought about by democracy?

To develop and sustain the ability of any society to make decisions and collectively implement strategies with the help of ongoing learning tools in order to develop democratic gains; are important ingredients which could lead to an ideal social form. How ready are the legal decision makers in Turkey to accept new ideas affecting the

Z.T. Karaman (✉)
University of Dokuz Eylül, Izmir, Turkey

S.O. Idowu, W.L. Filho (eds.), *Professionals' Perspectives of Corporate Social Responsibility*, DOI 10.1007/978-3-642-02630-0_18,
© Springer-Verlag Berlin Heidelberg 2009

government structure? The degree of success in social responsibility can be more or less monitored by the democratic indicators developed concretely to this end.

17.1 Introduction

The approaches in new government strategies, interpreted under the headings of good government or governance based on participation in the decision making process and execution mechanisms at both central and local levels in state admin-istration, direct us to the concept of 'social capital'. In addition, issues relating to social responsibility have to be evaluated holistically along with negotiation democ-racy. Briefly, successful sustainability of the CSR activities in society is closely related to the development of the components of social capital and negotiation democracy. This subject is examined further below.

17.1.1 Social Capital

Social capital is interpreted as the ability of human beings to work together (Sargut, 2006, pp. 1–13) as individuals or in groups or organizations for their common purposes. Social capital is regarded as a value that puts all elements of business life, economy, organizational behavior, political science and sociology at its centre. Having reached the present state of affairs by the process of transformation which is also stated as 'the whole of material and moral values', the phenomenon of 'human and social capital' in a sense defines the general framework of public administration. Social Capital in fact is not a new concept in social sciences; however, in the mod-ern sense, the word 'social capital' was defined by the political researcher Robert D. Putnam (1970) (Putnam, 1995, p. 67) and sociologist James Coleman (1988) (Karagül and Dündar, 2006, pp. 61–78) in their studies.

Bourdieu (1985) associated 'social capital' with social duties and this in a sense is the direct association of economic capital and the pride of belonging to a society with new government strategies (Bourdieu, 1985, pp. 241–258). Fukuyama (2005) attached importance to the phenomenon of enabling (Fukuyama, 2005, p. 26) human beings to do business through groups and organizations acting for a common pur-pose. In summary, the interrogators of social capital have drawn attention to social organization as it connects to the network of relationships where norms, social con-fidence, coordination and cooperation are widely ensured. In order to make use of social capital efficiently, firstly, human capital is required. The social values mentioned enable the effective operation of democracy. These opinions, where the authors stress the importance of socialization by using the means of participatory democracy, suggest the connection between 'social capital and participatory democ-racy'. The approach by the interest groups in society to 'cooperation' is an essential step for social cooperation. The development of the capacities for ensuring social consensus is of importance for the sustainability of the cooperation concerned. The importance of negotiation democracy is mentioned below.

17.1.2 Negotiation Democracy

The belief that democratic institutional regulations, which are based solely on a voting system and dependent on the methods of calculating individual interests and preferences, are unable to create political consequences for the whole society has continued to be widely accepted in society.

The democratic institutions, which intermediate the distribution of goods and services, have not resulted in satisfaction. The idea that it is required to look for a better solution in operating a more effective negotiation system and ensuring stronger social consensus than is present in a democracy, where votes are collected, is becoming increasingly evident. The address for this preference is the existence of a negotiation medium that will enable individuals and institutions to reach consensus automatically and without pressure.

The amendments intended for the development of dialogues between different parties only in the assemblies are not considered satisfactory by many political thinkers. In support of this, a model is needed where citizens share relevant information, talk about social affairs, form opinions about society and participate in political processes. As a system 'based on social consultation' that will support the participatory mechanisms of democracy, the practices of 'negotiation democracy' (Sitembölükbaşı, 2005, pp. 139–162) are gradually becoming popular.

Negotiation democracy claims that the information obtained on politics and political speeches improves the capacity of individuals. In connection to this, it is considered that their social contributions will enhance the quality of negotiations. The opinions, developing within the structuring of an information society and formed by consensus, will naturally affect the quality of decision mechanisms as well.

Being effective in ensuring corporate cooperation and being the instruments of democracy, participation and good government, along with governance practices require a multidimensional analysis. The common features of these terms are the internalization of democracy and maturation of political culture. In literature, the evaluations according to each country practices and depending on the development of the understanding of participatory democracy, cause concepts to intertwine. With a view to clarifying the concepts, it is of importance to put forth the philosophical grounds of the bases for their connections to each other.

There are organizations at national and local levels for the fulfillment of rules and duties specified in state administration. In modern public administration, 'effectiveness in services' and 'democratic participation' are basic references of the activities of these organizations which provide services at local and central levels. In order to develop the operation of these two basic elements for the benefit of the society and to make them functional, studies are continuously made on the mechanisms which enable participation.

17.2 What is the Place of Turkey in Negotiation Democracy? – Democratic Indicators

The important factors of negotiation democracy, participation indicators and governance indicators have only recently begun to be included in the area of public interest administration in Turkey. The Participation Indicators can be summarized as follows:

1. Adoption of new techniques and making use of services and facilities;
2. Use of local resources and foreign aids in order to solve community problems;
3. Development of local entrepreneurship and leadership;
4. Participation of the local community in elections and their voluntary attendance in working groups.

Furthermore, monitoring all interest groups in society and their preference for participating in decision mechanisms demonstrate various dimensions of governance. These dimensions of governance can be stated as follows:

- An effective, independent and transparent 'administrative governance' capable of being monitored.
- 'Social governance' preserved and shaped by the political and socio-economic interest of citizens and surrounded by the cultural and moral values for environmental health, freedom, security and a better social life.

The administrative procedures, developed to enable interest groups to gather and increase their effectiveness and performance in public services, are included among governance indicators. The broad extension of social cooperation indicators can be listed as follows:

- Informing the public and exchanges of opinion;
- 'Performance Monitoring and Evaluation Committees' institutionalized by Functioning Local Development Council and members of technical non-governmental organizations;
- Programmes and activities made up by the participation of the private sector, NGOs and citizens; and programmes and processes (Brillantes et al., 2007, p. 13) in which beneficiaries can always participate.

Governance indicators and participation indicators are listed together in the study by the Ministry of Public Works and Settlement (Bayındırlık and Bakanlığı, 2008, p. 109). As interconnected, the six dimensions (http://info.worldbank.org/governance/wgi/index.asp, accessed on: 17.02.2009) of governance during 1996–2007 period were listed as accountability, control of corruption, political stability and absence of violence in the country, government effectiveness, regulatory quality and rule of law in 212 countries and regions in the Worldwide Governance Indicators (WGI) project for the formation of the sustainable democratic state.

The issues mentioned are directly connected with the necessity for structuring in the institutional supervision of the sustainable democratic state government. The elimination of irregularities resulting from poor government makes the ombudsman institution outstanding (Abdioğlu, 2007, pp. 79–85). 'The Ombudsman Institution Law' No. 5548 dated October 13, 2006 came into force; however, the execution of the Interim Article 1, the basic article of the Law, was terminated (Constitutional Court P. No: 2006/140 and D. No: 2006/33 dated 27.10.2006) and finally, the Constitutional Court unanimously cancelled the Law (December 2008) and 'an uphill struggle' was lost.

Urban sustainability is closely related to human capital. 'Human capital variables' constitute a basic group among the indicators used in measuring the level of competitiveness on country scale. The International Institute of Management Development (IMD) recommends a number of variables likely to be used within the framework of the methodical approaches it has developed through analysis http://www.imd.ch/research/centers/wcc/research_methodology.cfm, accessed on: 23.02.2009). 'Social Framework' has been put forth as a sub-indicator within the Efficiency of State. In addition, the indicators of a Social Framework have been demonstrated as the provision of justice in the country, the protection of personal security and private property, of age distribution in society, political instability, social cohesion, income distribution, granting of equal opportunities by legislation, the right of women to take part in local council and decision making mechanisms and income rates adjusted according to gender.

In Turkey, the State Planning Organization (SPO) prepares the socio-economic development ranking for provinces by taking into consideration other welfare indicators such as Population, Gross Domestic Product (GDP), Numbers of Schools, Students and Teachers, Health Indicators and Number of Vehicles (http://ekutup.dpt. gov.tr/bolgesel/gosterge/1999/, accessed on: 23.02.2009). The issues pointed out by these indicators do not provide basic information on social capital. In general, they are indicators of economic and employment progress.

Considering the data 'that can be published regularly' at provincial level; in a study published by the International Competitiveness Research Institute (URAK), four main variables have been identified in order to provide a measure of inter-provincial competitiveness index in Turkey. These variables are Human Capital and Life Quality, Innovation, Branding and Commercial Skills and Accessibility.

Variables on Human Capital and Life Quality are measured in terms of increasing: 'the number of people with higher education qualifications, the number of students receiving technical education, the rate of success in gaining university places (with Student Selection and Placement Examination for University), the number of hospital beds per capita, the number of automobiles per capita, deposits per capita, crimes committed in provinces per capita, urbanization rate, the presence/absence of super league and upgrading league teams and 5-star hotels in the province' (Aklin et al., 2007, p. 226). The development level of provinces (Uluslararası Rekabet

Araştırmaları Kurumu 'URAK', 2008, pp. 14, 64) was determined on the grounds of the current numerical values on the above-mentioned subject areas.

As can be seen, both participation and governance indicators are explained in various evaluations in the institutional briefings in Turkey. The numerical values of these indicators show the success or failure of public administration. However, the pertinent question is: how many of these indicators capable of being measured continuously and expressed in figures? Turkey is just in the process of evaluating indicators which are related to the quality of life. There have been numerous determinants of factors on quality of life, and the indicators used to represent these factors are: material wellbeing, purchasing power, economic climate, health, political participation, urban security, political stability, social activities, gender equality, cemeteries and etc. The model of quality of life examines not only personal and socio-cultural and economic-political aspects but also the natural environment. Indeed, indicators of quality of life (the model of quality of life: http://www. utoronto.ca/qol/concepts.htm, accessed on: 06.03.2009) are open-ended and can be developed. Due to the use of a limited number of easily-accessible indicators, the quality of life in cities and in total in Turkey is believed to be lower than it really is.

17.3 The Practice of Negotiation Society and Turkey

The Department of Public administration provides services to citizens in accordance with the stages of planning, organizing, directing, staffing, coordinating, supervising, reporting and budgeting which has been abbreviated using the mnemonic 'PODSCoRB' with, Gulick and Urwick (1973) who are leading scholars in the theory of this aspect. Making various consensus mechanisms outstanding at local and national levels together with negotiation and representation constitutes the basis for structuring studies in public administration.

17.3.1 International Interaction Networks

International agreements are an ethical guideline in the development of national democracy. Accordingly, participation in these common studies (whether a member or not) more or less demonstrates the democratic-political atmosphere of the country concerned.

Although voting and participation in elections are important elements in any society, participation in democratic life is worth considerably more. Participation in decisions on city policies and activities aimed at supporting the establishment of a better society require the ownership, human rights, political instruments, freedom of movement and opportunities in that society.

Indicators of quality of life underlie international agreements as essential factors affecting development of settlements are multi-dimensionally. In international approaches focusing on urban development, 'social development' is stated to be an important factor in dealing with almost every subject such as the conservation of historical works and cultural heritage and spatial planning (strategic approach to planning). A series of rules become outstanding for urban development. These rules seem to depend on:

- creating economic values and taking decisions collectively in administration;
- providing and being able to sustain sectoral cooperation for resource efficiency;
- determining the threats and opportunities created by multiculturalism and being able to turn threats into gains using opportunities provided by cooperative projects;
- strengthening the constitution of an information society and evaluating information and endeavors from various groups of the informed society such as the youth, the elderly, women and men;
- being able to meet and use past and present information and experiences in attaining objectives;
- being able to carry the responsibility of success and failure in programmes, where results are obtained, and realizing the conditions for using the programmes many times (compare with Landry, 2006, p. 244).

In the basic approach of international agreements, the connection of the feasibility of these rules with sectoral and interest groups are put forward on the network of global relations. The gains for social development by the implementation of integrated action plans targeted by international agreements or targeted outputs are as follows:

- Creating political determination and administrative facilitation of central and local governments;
- Forming innovative and creative strategies envisaging effective participation to ensure monitorability;
- Forming and sustaining social and economic development as well as integrating government and action plans which also include other sectors;
- Enhancing social sensitivity by creating awareness;
- Sharing information for developing inter-institutional and inter-organizational cooperation, making citizens conscious and informed and involving them in dialogues;
- Strengthening local administrative units and local service units by participatory mechanisms and local, regional and cross-border cooperation;
- Strengthening public, civil-academic-private sector relationship networks and ensuring that they trust each other;
- Looking at the Concepts of Youth, Children, the Handicapped and Senior citizens (the elderly) and introducing the expectations of these groups to society;
- Attaching importance to individualism with all its social and cultural aspects for the sound sustainability of society; preparing the public for a productive and peaceful life and establishing social partnerships for good government;
- Developing the social dynamics of participation in government at local level.

The relationship between the sustainability of urban life and democratic sustainability leads to the willingness to create common action plans for the development of common strategies by countries and for their applicability. Citizens' satisfaction is associated with the integration of democratic participation and the provision of service effectiveness. For creating sustainable and sound cities, access to city-dweller rights and the ownership of rights and obligations are being made widespread to the settled foreigners just as they are available to citizens.

Making social cooperation widespread, joining uninformed and disconnected practices, preventing the waste of labour, time and money and attaining peace underlie all these objectives outstandingly. International agreements bring 'local participation' and 'national and international cooperation' to a partnership, the ownership of which is required to be acknowledged at state/national and local levels. In local governments, the philosophical approach of 'subsidiarity' is undoubtedly structured depending on the pre-acceptance of state and government powers. This makes it important to train legal decision makers for the development of governance practices.

It is not statistically easy to examine the development of the operation of legally-secured participatory mechanisms in Turkey since, as is also mentioned above, the statistics of this operation of participatory mechanisms in the whole country has not been thoroughly carried out. Furthermore, the recent harmonization of the legislation on the activities of Turkish associations and foundations within the legislation of the European Union has also accelerated the process of change and development of nongovernmental organizations. These developments are more acceptable for the participation of civil society. It is considered that both international factors and the economic and social crises experienced have created the medium in Turkey required for discussing the practices of CSR (UN Coordinator of Turkey and United Nations Development Program, 2008, p. 7).

In line with this, 80 programs have been conducted in Turkey by the United Nations Development Program (UNDP) since 1986. Three basic spheres, namely, (i) the capacity for development of democratic government, (ii) the reduction of poverty and (iii) the environment and the provision of sustainable development, corporate social project practices and policy recommendations were determined in the 2006–2010 strategic plan of the UNDP (UN Coordinator of Turkey and United Nations Development Program, 2008, pp. 8, 9). International support transforms the development of social capital in a positive way.

17.3.2 Local Politics and Democratic Practices

The participation of people in services directly affecting urban space is ensured by means of local governments in Turkey. The 1982 Constitution of the Republic of Turkey has shaped Local Governments in three ways, namely, Special Provincial Administrations, Municipalities and Villages. The question of governance in Special Provincial Administration and Village administration is not included in the subject of this paper. It is indeed so comprehensive that it contains a separate subject for examination. The instruments necessary for democratic Municipalities to be able to implement 'governance practices' are worth examining first in terms of the Municipality Law No. 5393 dated 2005 as well as the Metropolitan Municipality Law No. 5216 dated 2004.

The performance of city councils formed by voluntary participation other than elections, in comparison to municipality councils which are formed through election in provincial and municipal administration, is undoubtedly important in the evaluation of cooperation in social responsibility. Nevertheless, it has not been examined administratively in the whole country nor has it been used as a subject for performance indicators.

The examination of variables such as the right to elect and to be elected (voting right), participants' satisfaction, participation intensity and representation, and public confidence are the first elements that come to mind in participatory democracy (Lijphart, 2002, pp. 107, 108). It is the phenomenon of protectionism or favoritism developed over time within the practices of politics that drags down representative and pluralist democracy in Turkey. Those people, wanting to control power within parties, distribute opportunities to party members and supporters 'in return for political loyalty' when they obtain power. Accordingly, the parties, which behave in this way, are no longer an organization, in which the staff are shaped by political success, but turn into organizations shaped by intra-party loyalties (http://www.stksempozyumu.org/15sempozyum/ilhantekelikonusma.htm, accessed on: 08.02.2009). Therefore, it can be readily stated that democracy has not reached a mature level and that, in their current state, political parties do not undertake any 'supportive' functions in the creation of social cooperation networks. Under these conditions, the party organization in Turkey remains insufficient for social negotiation studies and corporate social responsibility (CSR). Another important indicator in the democratization is that women are almost nonexistent in decision mechanisms of public life and they have an insignificant participation in politics.

In Turkey, the participation of women in determining political power is extremely weak both in the parliament and in local government. In the history of the Republic, we have had only one female governor (province of Muğla) (1991–1995) and one female prime minister (1993). In the general elections of 2007, there were 48 female deputies out of 550 deputies. In the last local elections in 2004, the number of female mayors was only 18 out of 3,225 mayors, only 0.56% of the total. Representation therefore was at the rate of 2.42% with 834 female members out of a total of 34,477 members in municipality councils and a percentage rate of only 1.81% with 58 female members out of 3,208 members in the Provincial General Council (http://www.undp.org.tr/Gozlem3.aspx?WebSayfaNo=1577, accessed on: 07.02.2009, http://min.avrupa.info.tr/QA/forum/viewthread.php?lang=0&forum_id=63&thread_id=3135, accessed on: 07.02.2009).

In terms of women, the situation appearing in preparations for the local elections held in March 2009 is not brilliant either. Fatma Şahin, the head of the women's branch and Gaziantep Deputy of Justice and Development Party (AKP), the ruling party, during the meeting of provincial presidents presided by the Prime Minister Tayyip Erdoğan, stated, 'you praise women when they are successful; however, you do not nominate women seats, but you should'. These words of Şahin were applauded, mostly by men, leading, the female deputy to react by saying that: 'The actions do not go beyond applause' (Hurriyet Newspaper, February 08, 2009, p. 17).

Considering 2009 Local Elections, there were only 5 female members out of 547 (72) Metropolitan Municipality members in Izmir Metropolitan Municipality Council. In the 2009 local elections, all the mayors elected from 21 district municipalities within Izmir metropolitan area are men. Out of a total of 547 municipality members of these municipalities, there are 72 female municipality members. There are only 5 female members out of (128) people in the metropolitan municipality council, which is made up representatives from the councils of municipalities. The overall picture in Turkey shows that, there are 2,947 municipalities as of 2009. In 81 provinces, only 2 female mayors have been elected from the provincial central municipalities while only 15 female mayors have been elected from other municipalities. The proportions of male and female voters in the election are uncertain. This prevents making accurate analyses in connection with the female members' participation in political parties.

The most important problem in individual participation is that women are unable to use their rights to elect or vote independently. Surveys demonstrate that women (50%) vote under the influence of men. Furthermore, the rate of participation of women in the workforce is very low in Turkey and the rate of participation of women in employment in 2008 was 26.1% whereas the rate of participation of men in employment was 73.5%. (http://www.tuik.gov.tr/PreTablo.do?tb_id=25&ust_id=8, accessed on: 10.03.2009).

In addition, among the indicators that determine whether participation is democratic, the following participatory mechanisms are examined: how the council (*whether democratic processes are used or not in electing members to local councils*) and mayor are elected (*whether the mayor is chosen by being directly elected among the public or among the council members elected by the public or directly by being appointed*), voting percentages of men and women in the last elections, the function of participatory mechanisms such as city councils and urban consultation councils as well as the determination of indicators of associations per 10,000 people.

Information on the general elections held on July 22, 2007 ranging from the number of registered voters (42,376,953) to the ratio of voters to population (79.10%), the total number of ballot boxes (172,143) and photographs of the ballot boxes can be accessed via internet and published documents. The point, to which readers' attention should be drawn, is that the percentage of women and men among voters is conspicuously absent in the statistical information regarding the elections. It is understood that there are no accessible records regarding this lack of information and there is no awareness to this end in the country. When democratic indicators are listed one under the other, it is possible to comprehend the reason why Turkey occupies the lowest position in world ranking.

Furthermore, the rate of voting in Turkey was approximately 85% in the general elections of 2007. It may be supported that this percentage does not represent voluntary participation but is due to the legal pressure of 'compulsory voting'.

Nevertheless, it is also stated by the authorities that, despite a fine-based legal regulation, fines have never been imposed in practice and, therefore, participation is not actually compulsory. There are no field studies verifying this claim in literature.

The rules of 'competitive democracy' are more valid in a political medium where presidents of political parties patronize. Negotiation democracy is generally not used in determining political power. In local governments, municipal organization and election models depend upon a 'powerful presidency'. Accordingly, as Lijphart discusses (Lijphart, 2002, pp. 107–108, 112),[1] democracy in Turkey is not fully susceptible to a type of democracy (consociational democracy), where socialization is encouraged, in terms of the type of assembly, the network of relationships between executive and legislative bodies, party structuring and election systems. Undoubtedly, this structure is also effective in the government process following elections despite the legal regulations putting participatory mechanisms in force in preferring urban services. In other words, the habit created in the society after election by competitive democracy negatively affects 'democracy of ideas' that will determine the actions which may in turn have a multidimensional effect on participation.

However, democracy should be evaluated within the whole area of interrelated activities. In a democracy encouraging socialization, the corporate cooperation between political parties and groups is considered as an integrative security system in 'loose' social structures (Armingeon, 2002, pp. 81–105). The party members in Turkey do not create any social projects that involve people other than their own party members. In other words, attracting voters to the party indirectly while meeting individuals in a social project is not included in the agenda of inclined Parties yet. Indeed, they are not inclined to cooperation, either. Nevertheless, although local governments in Turkey are political bodies, they have corporate functions that will enable meetings and solidarity among different cultural groups in society and that are independent of politics since they have integrated responsibilities pertaining to the city, and they can operate them with reasonable success.

Innovative and creative ideas have a specific shelf life. Innovations are initiated, their ownership is claimed, they become a useful part of life; however, in time they may become obsolete. Even though this phenomenon does not need any constant change, it reminds us of the fact that 'evaluation requires continuity'. Maybe some things will remain the same and the difference will be the revision of 'what has remained the same' (Landry, 2006, pp. 204–205). The revisions mentioned also provide the continuation of social 'negotiation'. On the network of developing global relations, social cooperation studies cannot be solely limited to the citizen. However, to what extent can the conditions for forming partnerships based on cooperation in social responsibilities among citizen groups be provided? This issue is examined

---

[1] Lijphart states that he does not consider the phenomenon of 'consensus democracy' to be different from 'the negotiation democracy' of Armingeon, but expresses it with a different terminology. Negotiation democracy has three types. Armingeon describes these types as 'consociational democracy', 'corporatism' and 'regimes with strong veto players'.

briefly below in terms of 'confidence' and 'neighborhood', the important elements in the provision of social integration.

Both domestic and foreign cooperation, partnership studies are closely related to 'the feeling of confidence'. However, in domestic and cross-border (Toprak Karaman, 2005, pp. 70–73) studies, it has been found that the citizens in our society have a low level of confidence regarding each other and also their cross-border neighbours. In Turkey, there is bi-directionality, where people do not trust each other and confidence only depends on proof, in individual relationships as much as in public affairs. A similar approach took place in a research by Bjørnskov (2006, pp. 26, 27) where the level of confidence in Turkey was determined as 15.72%.

In the operation of democracies, 'social capital' and even 'foreign social capital' entering a foreign country from cross-border areas (Toprak, 2008a, pp. 98, 102) are evaluated as primary socio-cultural gains (Toprak Karaman, 2008, pp. 16–18). Individualities and 'confidence', components identified by Esmer, are indispensible elements in providing sustainability (Esmer, 1999, pp. 22–25, 66, 85) of different cultures and affected societies (http://www.hurriyet.com.tr/english/domestic/10381452.asp accessed on: 06.03.2009).

In terms of the Council of Europe, considerable importance is attached to the fact that different cultural and ethnic groups are able to live peacefully and to participate in public life. Local integration is evaluated on the basis of 'education of good quality, organization in social sphere and mutual cultural expansions of institutions' and together with a series of policies establishing 'participation' and a medium for connecting on a network of mutual interaction (Council of Europe, 2004, p. 26). The provision of cultural integrations is of importance in the international political arena particularly where the conditions for foreign settlers to participate in administration and to use political mechanisms together with the local people are developed. In summary, the importance of coming together as projects to be developed particularly in public-private-civil partnerships at local level is becoming more and more outstanding in the development of confidence at local level and in international relations.

17.3.3 Weak Social Dialogue Networks: Associations of Kinsmen and Foreigners

The most important factor that affects urban integration is the overall movement of population. It is suggested that migration is not limited only to domestic migration from rural areas to urban areas and vice versa. Migrations in Turkey which occur for different reasons and present different profiles such as the cognate migrations from abroad (foreigners with Turkish Cognation) and migrations of foreigners with European origin also create various socio-cultural problems and economic effects among the newly-arrived settlers. New arrivals bear features that may create opportunities and/or threats to Turkish cities.

The most important effect of this is that new foreign immigrants form gated communities separate from the rest of society. These communities are criticized since they lead to segregation and thus prevent social integration and cooperation. There are many examples particularly in coastal settlements such as Antalya and Izmir that make this criticism valid.

Kinsmen associations were previously established in order to create opportunities for newcomers to get used to the city. Today the basic purpose of associations is generally shown as a 'gathering of citizens', 'gathering them under the roof of the association', 'preserving local values', 'preserving the cultural values of the place from which they came', 'supporting the people with financial difficulties and granting scholarships to the children of poor families' and 'forming a medium where they can express themselves easily'. Kinsmen associations are mainly groups of people other than the people of that particular area and are distinguishable from the local people in terms of profile and other features.

Are citizen-oriented integrations an acceptable change with a positive effect on social solidarity in the name of sustainable cities? It is necessary to look for the answer to this question in kinsmen's associations, which search for corporate success in 'maintaining their differences' and in their willingness to sustain this. Studies have noted that the identity citizens is becoming vital in expressing ideological and political opinions for example (Aktaş et al., 2006, pp. 9–13). In addition, this phenomenon is also an important indicator that citizens; kinship has become a means of opportunity in the city. The changes mentioned, in a sense, also suggest the reason why common decision making mechanisms (governance) in public administration or at least good government mechanisms do not operate optimally.

According to the information by the Department of Associations in the Ministry of Interior, it was found out that 12% (8,595,176) of the Turkish population (71,517,100) were members of the NGOs (association) as of 2008. Only 16% (1,363,303) of the members of NGOs were females. Depending on data, it was observed that there is one NGO for every 106 people in Turkey. The low level of membership to associations weakens social dialogues and cooperation. While complaining about the low level of membership to associations, it is necessary to consider 'kinsmen associations' as a separate group.

In 2006, the number of kinsmen associations in Turkey was observed to be 8,135. Nearly 5% of the total number of NGOs was the kinsmen associations (Department of Associations of Ministry of Interior, 2006). In time, the number of NGOs increased. As at February 2009, a total of 204,186 associations have been registered, out of which only 80,642 of them continue to be active. 123,544 NGOs were annulled. Moreover, 8,360 associations, classified in the category of 'kinsmen associations', carry on their activities in Turkey. (http://www.dernekler.gov.tr/_Dernekler/Web/Gozlem2.aspx?sayfaNo=74, accessed on: 04.02.2009). In March 2009, a total of 4,359 NGOs were registered in İzmir and the number of kinsmen associations was announced to be 507 (Department of Associations of Ministry of Interior, 2009).

To sum up, kinsmen associations have been organized in metropolitan cities such as Istanbul, Izmir and Ankara and they are influential in local politics. Because of this, they are perhaps not a part of social cooperation projects. Against the hypothesis that associations of citizens will automatically disappear within the urban process, it is observed that these associations in time have turned into organizations that could tie their interest relations to the network of protective political relations. Thus, it seems very unlikely that associations of citizens will be closed automatically. In other words, in terms of their above-mentioned features, 'associations of citizens' are 'the weak links' in the process of cooperation to provide social responsibility.

When the results of 2009 local elections in Izmir were examined, it was noted that the heads of migrant associations such as the Secretary General of Izmir Balkan Federation (Buca), Head of Buca Salonikan Association (Buca), Western Thracian migrant (Buca), Head of Association of Migrants from Macedonia (Karşıyaka) and Head of Bornova Branch of Association of Migrants from Macedonia (Bornova) have become members of the local council in the districts concerned. Under the conditions in which the mayor and municipality councils are appointed, the decision of the heads of parties in Turkey, is vital in making a choice about who is eligible to become a council member, this decision is even more important when it involves 'the citizens who are the heads of associations of migrants'. This phenomenon clearly indicates that corporate responsibility for the integration of migrant citizens with the city is not developed within public bureaucracy. In other words, for the settlement of the problems of migrants, the personal success of the heads of associations is transformed into votes and this, in a sense, politicizes these associations.

What strategies would one consider as being ideal in order to direct the associations of citizens, in terms of social responsibility, to encourage them to cooperate with local people? In the event that citizen organizations undertake active roles in operating the mechanisms formed at the local level such as city councils and specialization commissions directed at shaping local politics, it is possible to state that their existence may turn into an opportunity and they may be influential in developing dialogues among social groups.

In Turkey, there are 139 associations with members who are foreign nationals, with the three highest ranking cities being Ankara with (32), Istanbul (18) and Izmir (29) (the Department of Associations in the Ministry of Interior, 21 March 2007). As at February 2009, there were 53 associations of foreigners established with various statuses except for foundations (6) and, out of this figure, 23 are nonprofit making foreign institutions open to representations, 9 are foreign associations open to representations and 12 are foreign associations with open branches. These associations and nonprofit institutions are not allowed to register members. However, 'branches and federations' are permitted to register members (Department of Associations in the Ministry of Interior, 20 February 2009). Associations of foreigners also bear features based on similar 'weak' relationships 'with citizen associations' in terms of social relationships. However, their existence is not supported strongly by society.

According to the data of the Ministry of Interior, the number of foreigners in Turkey with residential permits, stood at 163,018 as at the middle of 2005. This has increased to 202,085 as at March 1, 2007. In the present and near future scenarios in terms of social development indicators, the exploitability of foreigners can be developed on local and national levels as 'foreign social capital' (Toprak, 2008b, pp. 99, 103, 116). It is of importance to run the following process in order to ensure

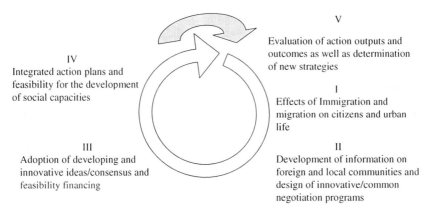

IV
Integrated action plans and
feasibility for the development
of social capacities

V
Evaluation of action outputs and
outcomes as well as determination
of new strategies

I
Effects of Immigration and
migration on citizens and urban
life

III
Adoption of developing and
innovative ideas/consensus and
feasibility financing

II
Development of information on
foreign and local communities and
design of innovative/common
negotiation programs

Fig. 17.1   Cycle of effective elements in ensuring social cooperation and dialogue

social dialogue which includes the contribution of social capital and also of foreign social capital (Fig. 17.1).[2]

The evaluation of ideas from local and foreign communities also serves towards the development of social capacities by creating synergy. Unofficial meetings are targeted so as to stimulate creative potentials without getting bogged down by 'corporate bigotry'. These studies can be organized in cities under various names. The development of media in order for people in cities to acquire new information from each other and for them to catch opportunities for co-learning constitutes the modern approaches dwelt upon by public administration.

The meeting media among various groups namely: public, private and civil partners (organizations of Local Agenda 21, city councils, development agencies and etc.), placed normatively inside institutional practices for providing the continuation of information of the organizational structures of local governments, have existed widely in Turkey since 2004. The practices supported by participant experiences are transferred into the information pool of the society through the participatory mechanisms nourished by these voluntary contributions.

17.4 Negotiation Media: Activities of Local Agenda 21

As international participatory programmes, the activities of Local Agenda 21 are important instruments in ensuring CSR at national level. Being the target output of the 1992 United Nations Rio Conference, Agenda 21 is qualified as an action

---

[2]The author defines 'foreign social capital' as the reflection of the intellectual accumulations (human capital) by foreigners on the society they are present in and as the socio-cultural externalities leading to positive effects. The economic power connoted by the word 'capital' does not have any primary positions; however, its effect is taken into consideration.

plan for the materialization of the concept of 'sustainable development' that aims at establishing balance between development and the environment. It has been internationally accepted that it is a successful programme based on participation at local level (Emrealp, 2007, pp. 75, 79).

Within the framework of 'global partnership', the ground for Local Agenda 21, the common approach to projects is based on the understanding of 'governance' based on participation and partnership. In accordance with this, it is aimed to take permanent steps for the development and settlement of a democratic and participatory government (governance) understanding that is supported by the 'facilitative' and 'feasible' role of local administration, that is based on the power of town people and that encourages cooperation and 'equal partnerships' with local interest groups. Its slogan is A New Awareness: 'claiming the ownership of one's city'; A New Understanding: 'partnership in solution'; A New Behavior: 'active participation'.

Activities of Local Agenda 21 constitute an important action plan that serves for the development of social dialogues 'within the framework of global partnership'. Turkey is also affected positively by the activities of Local Agenda 21 (http://www.tepav.org.tr/sempozyum/bildiriler/4_3_Toprak.pdf accessed on: 06 March 2009). While sample practices were initiated in 23 cities in 1999, it was observed that the number of partners of the Program reached 52 cities as of November 2005 and 70 cities as of 2008. This numerical development shows willingness towards participation.

The adoption of the United Nations Millennium Goals (MDG) by the decision taking bodies of a minimum of 200 local governments by the end of 2008 and the establishment of participatory mechanisms by municipalities in 150 new cities of various sizes, features, and geographical structures, were among the objectives envisaged (Development Report on the Project of Localization of UN Millennium Development Goals via the Governance Network of Local Agenda 21 in Turkey, 2007, p. 14).

Meetings with wide sectoral participation and which are open to interest groups enable the negotiation of a variety of social issues and the feasibility of social activities by ensuring social consensus. Nevertheless, how ready is the whole public for the integrated operation of these structures that will constitute 'the learning city'? In particular, the activities of Local Agenda 21 are criticized by a small number of opposing academics, who have never taken part in any voluntary activities aimed at this purpose and by some civil organizations. The 'rejection side' concerned are generally known to be against the studies of structuring in public administration. The national studies (United Cities and Local Governments, Middle East and West Asia Organization Millennium Development Goals Report, 2009) and the studies developed by a Local Agenda in Izmir under cooperation in social responsibility are doubtlessly one ring of the efforts for developing social capital through democratic practices (http://www.izmir-yerelgundem21.org.tr/strateji.htm, accessed on: 27 February.2009).

The positive effect of studies on social cooperation on legal regulations for the country as a whole is shown below.

17.4.1 The Experience Gained in Terms of Local Democratic Organization Between 1996 and 2009

The following phenomena developed in connection with each other can be regarded as gains:

- There has been an increase in the 'confidence threshold', one of the main components of political participation among public, private and civil partners both with each other and mutually;
- The call for meetings as required by the activities of Local Agenda 21 (LA21), made by the Mayor, who is the chairman of the LA21 project, and the authorized bodies of LA21 in his name has not been regarded as a subject for 'local political opposition'. Participation was attained exclusive of the subject to which nongovernmental organizations, public and private sectors are related and also in subjects with general content.
- The establishment o 'City Councils' in order to provide information for the activities of the council, which have the status of being the decision taking body of municipalities (Law No. 5393, dated 2005, art. 76). With the above mentioned structuring, a subsidiary body was established that was not formed by election and was fundamentally based on institutional representation. This subsidiary body was empowered at the same time to propose agendas to the Municipality Council composed by Election.
- The regulation of 'Voluntary Participation in Municipal Services' of the Municipality Law (No. 5393, dated 2005, art. 77) also provided intellectual and action participation in decisions about the city. With this development, the regulations concerning rights and obligations (1580, art. 13) on 'the citizenship law', which was not implemented although mentioned in the Municipality Law, which is no more in effect, No. 1580 dated 1930, became more perceivable and applicable.
- The re-regulation of participation and submission of opinions within the 'specialization commissions' on the scale of the Municipality (5393, art. 24), the Metropolitan Municipality (5216, art. 15) and the Special Provincial Administrations (5302, art. 16/4) to include all interest groups was also put in place.
- The determination of the working principles of the Regulation of City Council (the unelected participants and other actors) (Regulation of City Council, 2009).

The integrated development of social practices on the basis of the power of local people that will answer the expectations and outputs of interest groups in this 'equal partnership' (United Cities and Local Governments, Middle East and West Asia Organization, 2009) is becoming more and more important. In social partnership, 'national and international civil-social solidarity' (Toprak, Palabıyık, 2000, pp. 101–106) is of importance. Depending on the success by the activities of Local Agenda 21 particularly in provincial central municipalities which exceeded 70 in number as of the end of 2008, the organizational models of participation have been brought to national scale institutionally. As of 2009, only 52 out of 2,947 municipalities have had a 'youth council' established due to local agenda 21 program. Other components making participation difficult can be summarized as the weakness of participants in affecting decisions, time insufficiency and intolerance of different opinions.

In conclusion, as stated before the 2000s, revelation of the ability of people to compose local agenda by participatory programmes partially made 'the fear of inability to affect government' anymore a 'strong' factor. However, even if 'opinions formed by social negotiation' in councils composed of unelected people are included in the agenda of municipality councils, it is probable that a decision of 'not to decide' is taken in the council composed of the elected in line with expectations. Undoubtedly, it should be possible to research whether this result is objective.

How certain are the elected members in the local council about their new roles and responsibilities? One is still unsure as to whether the Ministry of Interior is aware of its role in the implementation of routine training programs to council members and mayors in order to implement the norms stated in the legal regulation. In this way, governance will be able to rid itself of being a paradigm and a concrete governance (meta-governance) model can be realized.

17.5 The Effect of Local Agenda 21 on Democratic Life in Izmir

Izmir is a settlement established on the western coast of Turkey. Recorded as having a population 3,370,866 according to the results of 2000 General Census, the population of Izmir reached 3,795,978 in 2008 according to the latest data from the Turkish Statistical Institute. The total population of Turkey is 71,517,100, with 5.3% living in Izmir. The annual rate of population increase is 1.50%. According to official records, it is understood that the total number of foreign settlers in Izmir has exceeded 6,000 mark as of October 2007.

According to the 'Research on Socio-Economic Development Ranking by Province', conducted by the SPO in 2003, Izmir ranks in 3rd position among 81 provinces. According to the development indicators of provinces formed by the URAK, the Index Value of Izmir regarding Human Capital and Life Quality amounts to 44.34 and it ranks in the 4th position in Turkey. Table 17.1 shows Izmir in terms those other provinces in the 1st–3rd positions.

Table 17.1 Human capital and life quality index

Province	Index value
Ankara	67.05
Istanbul	60.01
Eskişehir	52.13
Izmir	44.34

Source: Interprovincial Competitiveness Index (2007–2008), URAK, p. 14.

Unclear participatory indicators and a low rate of membership to civil organizations are important factors which indicate that social capital is weak in Izmir. 'The phenomenon of governance' becomes significant in Izmir in terms of developing ideas in the activities of Local Agenda 21. It is understood that Turkish city councils are more notable in the urban strategic plans in cities such as Adana and Antalya (Interviews, 2009). There is no doubt that the support from mayors is influential in this phenomenon.

Positive effects to be brought about by negotiation democracy are not present in the participatory mechanisms, where unelected people take part within the organization of Municipality and Special Provincial Administration in Izmir. The 'general and open invitation' made in the respective laws with respect to participation of both municipality and special provincial administration in 'specialization commissions' is not implemented. It is monitored that neither local governments nor the interest groups required to contribute at local level are ready to run the participation mechanisms stated in the legislation.

CSR studies were carried out with 3 Metropolitan mayors during the preparations for the 1996 Istanbul Habitat Summit and a similar study is currently in process in the Metropolitan Municipality of Izmir. In an attempt to implement in the City Councils related activities to Local Agenda 21, development has so far been sustained 'in terms of producing ideas, providing awareness and participation'. However, despite this 13-year experience in participation in social activities, social participation and functionality, in the organization of Municipality and Special Provincial Administration in general term, it was not possible to effect the provision in Izmir by the start of 2009. Also published in a book as the outputs of city councils of Local Agenda 21, the action plans had a limited effect on the strategic plans of the metropolitan municipality.

The main problem in the targeted services to be developed in an integrated way in corporate-social activities is the lack of cooperation in the supply of information among all components prior to the final user. Therefore, it is necessary to attach importance to cooperation that will provide integration. In order for the governance programs to provide social cooperation appropriate for their purpose, informing citizens by means of written and visual media, receiving their support and enabling them to claim ownership through their participation and contributions are among urgently required actions. It is projected that these activities will be facilitated by the technological developments in communication opportunities.

It was also assumed that the Development Agency, established in Izmir on the '31st May 2006', would play an important role in the process of integrating the development of social studies. The fundamental purposes of Development Agencies are to develop cooperation among the public sector, private sector and non-governmental organizations, to accelerate regional development in harmony with the principles and policies envisaged in the national development plan and programs, to ensure its sustainability and to reduce interregional and intraregional development differences. Development Agencies are composed of representatives sent by public institutions and organizations as well as private sector and nongovernmental organizations. The development council is composed of a maximum of a hundred members in a structure aimed at providing a balanced representation of the province/provinces.

The activities of the Izmir Development Agency were discontinued in March 2007 by a claim that they were acting against the Constitution but they were reinitiated in April 2008. Concentrating on social projects, the Agency put out a request for planned projects. Within the framework of the *Social Development Financial Support Program*, financial support is granted for projects from public institutions and organizations, local governments, nongovernmental organizations, universities, trade unions, vocational chambers, vocational schools and social centers within the borders of Izmir which are concerned with the development of human resources and social capital and the improvement of the quality of life (http://izka.org.tr/index.php?option=com_content&task=view&id=94&Itemid=37 accessed on: 07.03.2009). Recent studies on economic activities have been carried out but their effects are still unclear.

The other CSR programme on the study of 'healthy cities' which includes 'Izmir' can be shown as a programme for developing social dialogues. Izmir Metropolitan Municipality became a member of the Healthy Cities Association in September 2006. Studies for Healthy Cities are strategies for enhancing the physical, mental, social and environmental capacities of people who live and work in cities (www.sagliklikentlerbirligi.org.tr / accessed on: 17.10.2007).

The objectives for the working plan are as follows:

- to form a supportive social environment;
- to enable the proper use of resources;
- to increase and develop the participation of society;
- to develop and encourage individual capacities;
- to make the elements of redefining health services outstanding;
- to prepare integrated urban health programmes and plans;
- to form national and international project partnerships.

While the activities of the working groups of Local Agenda 21, Healthy City and Development Agency continue in the Izmir metropolitan area, it is clear that it is important to ensure the integration of all these activities. The kind of an Integrated City Administration model required for Izmir was discussed in 2007 with the support of the Izmir Governorship and within the framework of the studies of the City Council of Izmir Local Agenda 21. In fact, all public institutions and organizations have to make their strategic action plans by 2010. For this general objective, Izmir has to support its activities for Integrated Strategic Governance by corporate and social dialogues.

The Integrated Strategic City administration model for Izmir is seen below. It is based on an enlargement of the working philosophy of Local Agenda 21 by considering it together with the Development Agency. In this model,[3] the participators

---

[3] 'Integrated City Governance Model of Izmir' was developed by Zerrin Toprak, Gökhan Tenikler and Yunus Emre Özer to consider the activities of Local Agenda 21.

from the councils which include elected bodies and from the hierarchical structure of public administration bring together the various mechanisms including public, private and civil partners that are formed in order to create integrated social dialogues such as the City Council and the Development Agency. Thus, a medium is created where issues relating to the city (integrated coastal zone management, integrated solid waste management and etc.) are discussed. These activities are 'governance practices'.

Izmir Local Agenda 21 has held '10 city council meetings' on average annually since 1996 (April, 2009). In addition, on the basis of these activities, working groups on 'city', 'environment' and 'migration' have come together. The experience of urban negotiation, conducted during the City Council meetings, has been shaped as follows. At 15.00 p.m. on the third Wednesday of every month, the public, private and civil participants in the city meet at the Metropolitan Council Hall in order to discuss the issues specified a year earlier. The City Council can also meet when an extraordinary agenda is presented. Initially, awareness is raised among the Council participants by offering opinions from universities and specialists. Then information regarding the issues, which have been submitted to the court, but not negotiated, is shared; and a peaceful medium is created where local people/interest groups participate in discussions.

The primary objective of every participant from public, private and civil actors is to refrain from endangering the sustainability of these negotiation media that have already been accepted socially and gained trust in the city. It is of importance to repeat the briefing on the working method as the opening speech for participants during each City Council meeting and the preparatory meetings for the meeting. The meetings of the City Council of Local Agenda 21 are held in order to provide the continuation of interest in issues such as 'domestic migration, handicapped people, street children and environmental problems' and sometimes simply for attracting attention to a new phenomenon. The best examples to this end are 'the foreign settlers who were not born in Turkey' and sometimes an impending social problem, such as 'water crisis'. The rate of participation in the meeting may vary depending on the issue. In general, a minimum of 60 and a maximum of 150 or more people attend the meetings.

As can be seen from Fig. 17.2 above, apart from the people and institutions, who attend every meeting but who are not directly a part of the issue, specialists and directly-related institutions also attend depending on local agenda issues. These issues may relate to areas such as the conservation of the environment, problems specific to women, and building. Participation in solving common problems of the city (such as earthquake, water scarcity and climatic change) which are of interest to the crisis management team and which are considered to be more intensive. The 'briefings for public opinion' apart from the participants in meetings, cooperation with a large mass is provided through technological networks.

This suggested model is based on gathering the participatory mechanisms individually taking part in the laws of local governments on a provincial scale. 'Good governance', the application of the issues evaluated within governance practice developed with urban stakeholders by being transformed into decision by the

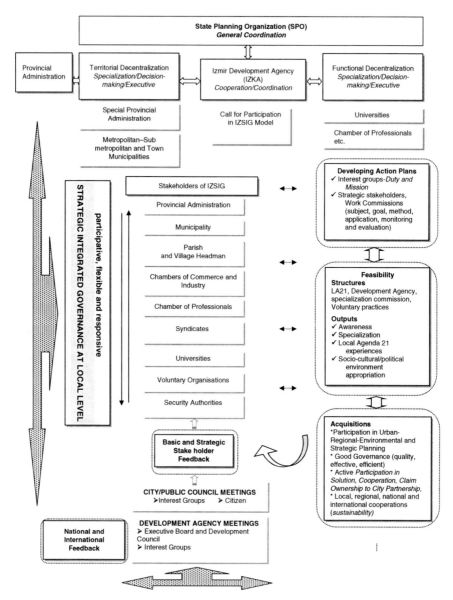

Fig. 17.2 Izmir strategic integrated governance (IZSIG) model (planning, implementation, monitoring, evaluation and reporting)

Administration (provincial and municipal administrations), is envisaged in the Model. In summary, the model alone does not fully change the traditional decision making process of public administration. Nevertheless, it stands for the internalization of the opinions adopted by public, private and civil partners within 'governance' mechanisms and for the improvement of its acceptability by the administration.

The model is planned to democratize the operation of the traditional mechanisms, which are decided at the central level in the organization of public administration in Turkey, and to create positive social effects.

17.6 Conclusion

For social cooperation, overcoming the bureaucratic social structuring in Turkey is an urgent problem which requires an urgent solution. To eliminate this problem, legislators and public administrators in their decision making process should take into consideration public opinions based on deliberative democracy. In support of this, the roles and responsibilities of citizens/interest groups/sectors in enhancing both democratic participation and the efficiency of urban services should be 'diagnosed'. The confidence of the members of society should hopefully be enhanced. For this change, the social cooperation activities including negotiation models bear a feature that will play an important role in the related issues.

The concern as to whether the meetings participated in by the public will be developed in a consensus medium based on knowledge as can be expected from the logic of negotiation democracy is one of the most important evaluations. Will prejudices and corporate bigotries lose their dominance in these media? These issues have become topical in Turkey.

The provision of sustainability of such structuring transferred in a normative sphere at the central level is undoubtedly largely dependent on the consideration of social activities. Attention should be paid to the participation of young people in these activities.

Motivation of integrated action (coordination and provision of consensus in objectives) with the support of legislation is also important. For the applicability of legislative regulations, it should be planned to revise the job definitions of administrators, directing their dialogues with local citizens, in accordance with daily conditions and needs. Since participation also means rapid access to information and the control of decisions and activities of the administration, it is probable that administrators may behave hesitantly towards participators. However, provided that the benefits of working together are perceived properly, this can result in a positive outcome claiming ownership of administration by the public.

The training programs for the internalization of roles required by the philosophy of governance in legal decision makers are expected to contribute positively. Developing and sustaining society's ability to decide and work together by means of ongoing learning tools and developing social capacities and the democratic gains are regarded as good strategies for an ideal society. For the political and administrative authorities running decision mechanisms, an administrative approach, which continuously controls and monitors social benefit, which always takes measures in sustaining social security without being oppressive, seems ideal.

Solidarity brought about by democracy bears a strong emotional profile. The role played by citizens in the development of cities is of importance in providing integration brought about by solidarity. We can state that the process of encouraging administrative structuring towards participation will strengthen democracy by creating an alleviating effect on psychological tensions and stresses in society. To sum up, the presence of negotiation democracy in a society demonstrates a characteristic of a 'political atmosphere' that anesthetize 'interest and fear' indicated by the Machiavelli's approach.

References

Abdioğlu, Hasan, "Yönetişim İlkelerinin Uygulanmasında Kamu Denetçiliği (Ombudsmanlık) Kurumu ve Avrupa Birliği Sürecinde Türkiye Açısından Önemi", İstanbul Ticaret Üniversitesi Sosyal Bilimler Dergisi, Year: 6, Issue: 11, 2007.

Aklin, Kerem, Melih Bulu ve Hüseyin Kaya, "İllerarası Rekabet Endeksi: Türkiye'deki İllerin Rekabetçilik Seviyelerinin Göreceli Olarak Ölçülebilmesi İçin Bir Yaklaşım", İstanbul Ticaret Üniversitesi Sosyal Bilimler Dergisi, Year: 6, Issue: 11, 2007.

Aktaş, Erkan, Asiye Aka ve Murat Cem Demir, "Kinship(Hemşehri) Association and Rural Transformation in Turkey", http://mpra.ub.uni-muenchen.de/8646/accessed on: 05.02.2009, 2006

Armingeon, Klaus, "The Effects of Negotiation Democracy: A Comparative Analysis", European Journal of Political Research, Vol. 41, No. 1, pp. 81–105, 2002.

Bayındırlık ve İskân Bakanlığı, Kentsel Göstergeler Kılavuzu, Bayındırlık ve İskân Bakanlığı Yayını, Ankara, 2008.

Bjørnskov, Christian, "The Multiple Facets of Social Capital", European Journal of Political Economy, Vol. 22, No. 1, pp. 22–40, 2006.

Bourdieu, Pierre, "The Forms of Capital", In J. Richardson (Ed.), Handbook of Theory and Research for The Sociology of Education. New York: Greenwood Press, 1985.

Brillantes Jr, Alex B., Mila A. Reforma ve Danilo R. Reyes, "Philippine Governance Indicators Survey Tools", 10th National Convention on Statistics (NCS)EDSA, Shangrila Hotel October 1–2, 2007.

Council of Europe Publishing, Foreigners' Integration and Participation in European Cities, 15–16 September 2003, Studies and texts no: 90, Strasbourg, 2004.

Decision by the Constitutional Court, P. No.: 2006/140 and D: 2006/33 dated 27.10.2006 (O.G. No. 26.333 dated November 1), 2006.

Department of Associations in the Ministry of Interior, 2006.

Department of Associations in the Ministry of Interior, 21.03.2007.

Department of Associations in the Ministry of Interior, 20.02.2009.

Emrealp, Sadun, Yerel Yöneticinin 1 Nisan Rehberi, UCLG-MEWA Yayınları, İstanbul, 2007.

Esmer, Yılmaz, Devrim, Evrim, Statüko, Türkiye'de Sosyal, Siyasal, Ekonomik Değerler, TESEV Yayını, İstanbul, 1999.

Fukuyama, Francis, (2005) Güven Sosyal Erdemler ve Refahın Yaratılması, A. Buğdaycı (Translator), 3.Baskı İstanbul: Türkiye İş Bankası Kültür Yayınları.

Hürriyet Gazetesi, "Kadın Aday Az Sitemi" February 8, 2009.

Karagül, Mehmet, Süleyman Dündar, "Sosyal Sermaye ve Belirleyicileri Üzerine Ampirik Bir Çalışma", Akdeniz İİBF Dergisi, Vol. 12, pp. 61–78, 2006.

Landry, Charles, The Creative City. London: Earthscan, 2006.

Lijphart, Arend, "Negotiation Democracy Versus Consensus Democracy: Parallel Conclusions and Recommendations", European Journal of Political Research, Vol. 41, pp. 107–113, 2002.

Putnam, Robert, "Bowling Alone", Journal of Democracy, Vol. 6, No. 1, pp. 65–78, 1995.

Sargut, A. Selami, "Sosyal Sermaye: Yapının Sunduğu bir Olanak mı, Yoksa Bireyin Amaçlı Bir Eylemi mi?", Akdeniz İİBF Dergisi, Vol. 12, pp. 1–13, 2006.

Sitembölükbaşi, Şaban, "Liberal Demokrasinin Çıkmazlarına Çözüm Olarak Müzakereci Demokrasi", Akdeniz İ.İ.B.F. Dergisi, Vol. 10, pp. 139–162, 2005.

The Quality of Life Model, http://www.utoronto.ca/qol/concepts.htm, accessed on: 06.03.2009.

Toprak Karaman, Zerrin, "Willingness of Foreign Retired Residents to Participate in Local Public Life and Strategic Approaches to Relationship Networks Within the Local Community; Example of Antalya, Turkey", European Journal of Economic and Political Studies (EJEPS), Vol. 1, No. 2, 2008.

Toprak Karaman, Zerrin, "Avrupa Konseyi'nde Sınırötesi İşbirliği Stratejileri Açılımında Sınır ve Sınırötesi Komşularımıza Bakış", Uluslararası Hukuk ve Politika, Uluslar arası Stratejik Araştırmalar Kurumu Yayını, Year: 1, Issue: 4, 2005.

Toprak, Zerrin, "Yerelde Yönetişim Olgusunda Demokratik Kazanımları Teorik Ve Pratik Temelli Yaklaşımlar- Türkiye ve İzmir", 2.Bölgesel Kalkınma ve Yönetişim Sempozyumu Bildiri Kitabı, Matsa, Ankara, Ekim, 2008-a.

Toprak, Zerrin, Hamit Palabıyık, "Participation and Civil Society: The Experiences of İzmir Local Agenda 21 (1995–2000)", Turkish Public Administration, Annual, Vol. 24–26, pp. 59–76, 2000.

Toprak, Zerrin, Kent Yönetimi ve Politikası, Birleşik Matbaacılık, İzmir, 2008-b.

Türkiye'de Yerel Gündem 21 Yönetişim Ağı Kanalıyla BM Bin Yıl Kalkınma Hedeflerinin Yerelleştirilmesi Projesi, Gelişme Raporu, No.4, 1 Temmuz 2007-30 Eylül, 2007. Development Report on the Project of Localization of UN Millennium Development Goals via the Governance Network of Local Agenda 21 in Turkey, No.4, July 1, 2007–September 30, 2007.

Uluslar arası Rekabet Araştırmaları Kurumu(URAK), İllerarası Rekabetçilik Endeksi (2007–2008), İstanbul, 2008.

United Cities and Local Governments, Middle East and West Asia Organization, "Localizing the UN Millennium Development Goals in Turkey through the Local Agenda 21 Governance Network; 1 October 2008 to 31 December 2008"(2009) Progress Report No.9 Project No.: 00053165, Istanbul, 2009.

UN Coordinator of Turkey and United Nations Development (UNDP), Türkiye'de Kurumsal Sosyal Sorumluluk Değerlendirme Raporu-CSR Rapor (Turkish), Ankara, 2008.

Interviews, Adana(Fevzi Acevit); Antalya(Sema Kurt) (Secretaries General of Local Agenda 21/Urban Council) 2009.

Electronic Sources

http://www.dernekler.gov.tr/_Dernekler/Web/Gozlem2.aspx?sayfaNo=74, accessed on 04.02.2009.

http://ekutup.dpt.gov.tr/bolgesel/gosterge/1999/, accessed on: 23.02.2009.

http://www.hurriyet.com.tr/english/domestic/10381452.asp, accessed on: 06.03.2009.

http://www.imd.ch/research/centers/wcc/research_methodology.cfm, accessed on: 23.02.2009.

http://info.worldbank.org/governance/wgi/index.asp , accessed on: 17.02.2009.

http://www.izmir-yerelgundem21.org.tr/strateji.htm, accessed on: 27.02.2009.

http://izka.org.tr/index.php?option=com_content&task=view&id=94&Itemid=37, accessed on: 07.03.2009.

http://min.avrupa.info.tr/QA/forum/viewthread.php?lang=0&forum_id=63&thread_id=3135, accessed on: 07.02.2009.

http://www.sagliklikentlerbirligi.org.tr, accessed on: 17.10.2007.

http://www.stksempozyumu.org/15sempozyum/ilhantekelikonusma.htm, accessed on: 08.02.2009.

http://www.tepav.org.tr/sempozyum/bildiriler/4_3_Toprak.pdf, accessed on: 06.03.2009.

http://www.tuik.gov.tr/PreTablo.do?tb_id=25&ust_id=8, accessed on: 10.03.2009.

http://www.undp.org.tr/Gozlem3.aspx?WebSayfaNo=1577, accessed on: 07.02.2009.

Legal Arrangements

5393, dated 2005; Municipality Law.
5216, dated 2004; Metropolitan Municipality Law.
Regulation of City Council 2009.

Part V
Education, Consultancy, Research and Human Resource Management

Chapter 18
An Academic's Perspective on the Role of Academics in Corporate Responsibility

Ralph Hamann

Be the change you want to see in this world.

Mahatma Gandhi

The trouble with the rat race is that even if you win, you are still a rat.

Lily Tomlin

Abstract This chapter begins by emphasising its personal nature. This is because my thoughts on this subject are necessarily based on personal experience, and because my work on corporate responsibility is premised on two disconcertingly questionable assumptions: first, that business can make a positive contribution to sustainable development, even in southern Africa (where I live and work), and second, that the academic practice of research and teaching assists to this end. This is in the context of opposing perspectives, also among academics, on whether business can, indeed, make a decisive difference. To some extent the tensions between these perspectives have led to important research and debates, but the chapter argues that there are significant constraints to the realisation of the academic ideal of open and informed debate. These constraints relate to the social and cultural context in which academics work and they pertain to the resource base of academic work, including access to finances and information, as well as the socialisation of researchers in peer groups and wider social networks. At the root of these challenges, are increasing cultural and economic pressures to perform according to particular standards, coupled to personal ambition driven by broader social trends. Hence, just as we academics are emphasising the development of business decision-makers as 'whole persons' – capable of transcending self-interest and instrumental rationality – it is questionable whether we are able to teach by example. The implication is that we, as academics, ought to revisit what whole personhood means and how we can foster it within ourselves, as we seek to foster it within the business community.

R. Hamann (✉)
University of Cape Town, Cape Town, South Africa

S.O. Idowu, W.L. Filho (eds.), *Professionals' Perspectives of Corporate Social Responsibility*, DOI 10.1007/978-3-642-02630-0_19,

18.1 Introduction

Writing this chapter is very personal. Hardly a day goes by in which I do not ask myself whether my work on corporate citizenship really does what it aspires to do – to contribute towards lasting improvements in poor people's lives on the basis of human rights and environmental stewardship. Nowhere is this overarching objective more pressing than in southern Africa, the only region in the world where the proportion of extremely poor people increased during the final decades of the previous century (though the proportion has been decreasing more recently) (see Sachs, 2005; United Nations, 2007).

My work on corporate responsibility has been based on the assumption that business can play an important role in poverty alleviation and sustainable development, also in southern Africa. Even though I have adopted a critical stance in some of my writing, highlighting possible underlying motives for big business to adopt the responsibility rhetoric and warning against undue expectations that corporations will make a decisive difference, a recurring theme has been that business can, in the right circumstances, be a partner to governments and civil society for the achievement of common objectives in the public interest. A second assumption, of course, is that my work as an academic can make a difference, based on contributions to be made by sound research – that is, the systematic collection, analysis and interpretation of information, including primary data and secondary sources – as well as effective teaching and policy advice.

Let us focus first on the assumption that business has a positive role to play in society. This view is in contrast to some of my colleagues, whose predominant approach to business, especially multinational corporations, is opposition and critique. A powerful illustration of this occurred recently at a sociology conference here in South Africa. At the end of a panel discussion on research priorities, one of my fellow panelists, a well-known South African sociologist, declared, 'Each of us has to make the fundamental choice: To be co-opted by the forces of capitalist exploitation or to join us in fighting for the rights of the poor and the environment!' Despite its resemblance to one of the infamous statements of George W. Bush ('You are either with us or against us!'), this argument's simplicity and clear delineation of good and evil was clearly compelling and attractive to many of the conference participants. As someone who ventured the opinion that business can in some instances play a constructive role I found myself branded an apologist for capitalism, even a traitor to the cause.

One of the ironies in this is that just 1 week earlier, at an international conference of business ethics and management scholars, I was the one who was criticising the role of business. In my view, many of the presenters at that conference paid too little attention to the power imbalance between large corporations and others and the potential for business decision-makers to abuse their power for their own advantage.

Is this just a case of being contrarian, of seeking to generate the academic's currency of disagreement and critique? Or, worse, is it akin to sitting on the fence, unable to give a decisive answer to one of the big questions of this time, whether the force of private enterprise can be harnessed for the collective good? I do not think that either concern is fundamentally valid. With regard to the former, it is true that critique is an underlying aspect of most scholarly work and that it is often over-zealous, but in general it takes place against the backdrop of an effort to develop a common understanding of what questions matter and how to go about answering them. Critique of the constructive kind is vital in challenging scholars to improve their argument and in bringing new information to the discussions.

On the second charge, my response would be that broad, challenging questions on the role of business in society are a good point of departure for classroom discussion, but researchers need to go further to investigate more nuanced questions. More fundamentally, we need to go beyond black-and-white caricatures of business decision-makers as either the bogeymen, driven by obsessive greed, or the saviours, based on the mythology of efficient markets and enlightened self-interest.

18.2 Creative Tensions

Of course, it is a vital feature of academia for there to be diverging perspectives and methodologies. Hence the contrasting views of the sociologists and the management scholars mentioned above ought to give rise not only to interesting debate but also more rigour in the compilation of evidence and the design of arguments. Furthermore, the differences between academics reflect and in some instances inform different social groups' perspectives and paradigms influencing policy makers around the world. This is particularly true with regard to issues related to corporate citizenship, given that the role of big business in sustainable development is highly controversial.

On the one hand, for instance, the United Nations (UN) Global Compact argues, 'Through responsible business practices, business is making a unique and significant contribution to implementing the Millennium Development Goals' (www.unglobalcompact.org, accessed 16 September 2005). Prominent business leaders are no less ambitious and optimistic in expecting decisive contributions from big business (see, for instance, World Business Council for Sustainable Development, 2005). On the other hand, critics see the corporate citizenship discourse as a measure by big business to emphasise voluntary approaches and to pre-empt stricter government regulation by diverting attention from the negative impacts business activities have on the poor and the environment (e.g., Christian Aid, 2004). The rhetoric of corporate citizenship, in this analysis, involves an opportunity cost, because corporate citizenship efforts by business and others, including government and multilateral organisations, may preclude other ways of addressing the negative consequences of economic activity.

Indeed, in the context of slow progress towards achieving the MDGs, particularly in sub-Saharan Africa, we have little evidence that corporate citizenship efforts are indeed fulfilling their promise. Current development trajectories are clearly unsustainable and a more committed transition is required, characterised by a co-evolutionary process involving many diverse role-players – with a special responsibility for governments – and demanding particular attention to innovation and fairness. 'Many companies seem more involved in this journey than many governments are' (Kemp et al., 2005: 23), and companies and the markets they operate in play a crucial role in innovation and the efficient allocation of resources.

Nevertheless big business, in particular, has been a key beneficiary and protagonist of globalisation, responding to critics by developing the concept and practice of corporate citizenship. Current uncertainties as to whether corporate citizenship efforts are making a difference in the sustainability transition thus strike at the heart of broader debates surrounding globalisation and our quest for a sustainable future. To 'make a difference', any effort and its impacts need to be commensurate to the scale of the challenge that is to be addressed. However, we have very little evidence to suggest that corporate citizenship efforts are, on the whole, making a significant, systematic impact on the challenges facing poor communities in southern Africa or elsewhere (Hamann, 2007).

In the absence of compelling evidence that either supports or contradicts the argument that business can proactively support sustainable development, there are – in simplistic terms and broadly speaking – three perspectives on the role of business. Depending on his or her personal trajectory, a young scholar is likely to be socialised into feeling more or less at home in any one of these 'conceptual camps' or paradigms, famously defined by Thomas Kuhn as 'universally recognized scientific achievements that for a time provide model problems and solutions to a community of practitioners' (Khun, 1970: viii). These perspectives are schematically illustrated in Fig. 18.1, using illustrative quotes for representation purposes.

Figure 18.1 suggests that advocates of corporate citizenship are flanked on both sides by critics, which, though they share some characteristics, come from contrasting vantage points with opposing assumptions and diverging interpretations of sustainable development. The first critique is that of the liberal economists, who are – superficially speaking – more likely to believe that a corporation operating within the law in a competitive market is inherently contributing to sustainable development because it is contributing to the most efficient and effective allocation of resources. The liberal economists' concern is that business decision-makers are not mandated or capacitated to devote attention and resources to anything other than the company's core purpose of making money. The most well-known statement to this effect was Nobel laureate Milton Friedman's argument in 1970 that 'the social responsibility of business is to increase its profits' (Friedman, 1970). More recent proponents of this view include David Henderson, former chief economist at the OECD, who argues: 'The case against CSR is... that it would make people in general poorer by weakening the performance of business enterprises in their primary role' (Henderson, 2005: 31).

Finding a decisive rebuttal to the liberal economists' perspective has provided a purpose for many scholars working on corporate responsibility. Especially in the North American management literature, these efforts have involved arguments about what is called the 'business case' for sustainable development or CSR – that is, that contributing to social objectives will also benefit a company's financial performance. Margolis and Walsh surveyed 127 studies on this topic published between 1972 and 2002. They write that 'a simple compilation of (these studies') findings

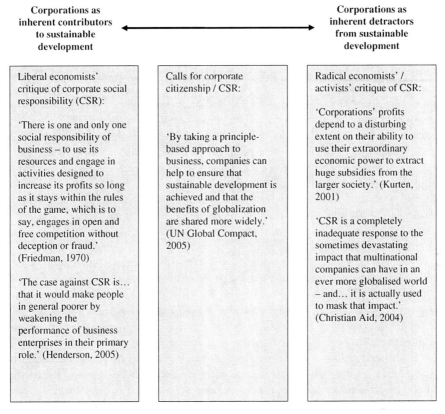

Fig. 18.1   Perspectives on the role of big business in sustainable development
Source: Author, using quotes from various sources (the figure is taken from Hamann, 2008: 19)

suggests that there is a positive association, and certainly very little evidence of a negative association, between a company's social performance and its financial performance' (Margolis and Walsh, 2003: 278). However, they also note that these various studies are plagued by diverse methodological shortcomings, so the debate over the business case arguably remains unresolved and thus may well provide ample opportunity for researchers in years to come. Furthermore, much work needs to be done to better understand the business case in developing economies' contexts (an attempt in this regard based on anecdotal evidence was made by International Finance Corporation et al., 2002).

An enduring concern, however, is that the business case alone is not a sufficient motivation for responsible business practices. Hence, Chris Avery, the coordinator of the Business and Human Rights Resource Centre, argues, 'While there is a strong "business case" for respecting human rights, companies are obliged to respect human rights at all times, not just when it suits them' (Avery, 2006: 4). In many instances, such arguments have been made on ethical grounds. Nobel laureate economist Amartya Sen has argued in this vein that the conventional view of economic self-interest as the primary or even the only motivation for business is out of place, noting that economic transactions themselves rely to a large extent on social norms and values (Sen, 1999).

A further response to the liberal economists' critique of CSR is to focus on the changing context in which companies find themselves. Friedman himself emphasised that the business manager's responsibility is generally 'to make as much money as possible *while conforming to the basic rules of the society, both those embodied in law and those embodied in ethical custom*' (Friedman, 1970, emphasis added). These rules of the society are bound to change, including legal requirements and ethical custom, and it may be argued that the current emphasis on CSR and business contributions to development and respect for human rights is part of a broader shift that has taken place since 1970. From a scholarly perspective, one of the most fruitful analytical frameworks for this has been institutional theory. For instance, Hoffman (1999) used an analysis of the changing institutional context of the US chemical industry to better understand the way companies in that industry adopted environmental policies and practices.

This brief overview of the tensions between liberal economists and scholars seeking to defend a cause for corporate responsibility illustrates how these tensions have given ample opportunity for scholars from different disciplines and perspectives to engage in these debates, and how they have contributed important arguments and a better understanding of the issues at stake (without, by the way, resolving the tensions).

The second critique of corporate responsibility is that of the radical economists or advocacy groups, who believe the ideal free market conditions assumed by the liberal economists are far from the current reality and that, generally speaking, corporations *detract* from sustainable development because in their quest for profits they seek to externalise the costs to society (for example by decreasing real wages) and the environment (for example by causing air and water pollution). These critics argue that business leaders' emphasis on voluntary corporate *responsibility* initiatives is a means to pre-empt or limit mandatory government regulations to ensure corporate *accountability* that would make corporations answerable for the negative consequences of their actions.

Activist NGOs are not the only ones to have raised such concerns. Analysts and academics of diverse persuasions have agreed that there is a danger of CSR becoming dominated by companies' public relations departments. Even prominent business management scholars, such as Porter and Kramer (2006), lament the precedence of image over substance in the approach of most companies to CSR.

It is apparent that the activist NGOs and radical critics have very different perspectives on the role of business than the business leaders and the management scholars who are espousing corporate citizenship principles and initiatives such as the UN Global Compact. Elsewhere, we have argued that the polarisation of the debate between CSR protagonists (in business and elsewhere) and anti-CSR activists may prevent the acknowledgement of strengths or weaknesses in the arguments in each of the respective camps (Hamann et al., 2003). Since then, there have been numerous initiatives and organisations established to create something approaching a middle way between these contrasting perspectives. This middle way consists of a more differentiated assessment of the current role of business in sustainable development, in that it is both a contributor to and a detractor from sustainable pathways, and much depends on the strategies adopted and decisions taken by business leaders and the broader institutional context in which business operates.

18.3 Challenges to the Academic Ideal

So it is apparent that to a large extent the critical voices on both sides of the corporate citizenship field provide important impetus for reflection and adaptation, both in scholarly research and teaching, and in policy debates. However, despite the lofty ideals of academia – the term *academy* is linked to Plato's school of philosophy, premised on the ideal of a free exchange of ideas – academics are not always very good at creating what the German sociologist Jurgen Habermas (1997: 105) called the 'public sphere', in which 'citizens . . . deal with matters of general interest without being subject to coercion.'

Hence over and above the epistemologists' realisation that science – social science in particular – is unlikely to arrive at objective truths, but at best imperfect approximations awaiting further refinement or even contradiction (see, for instance, Popper, 2002), sociologists of science have long pointed out that the practice of science occurs within and is circumscribed by a social and political context. Without necessarily agreeing with the claims of the more radical, so-called relativist or constructivist approaches to science (which see scientific arguments as having little inherent advantage over other perspectives), it is nevertheless important to acknowledge that science is undertaken by people who rely on finances, offices and computers, who conduct their research as part of teams and organisations, and who are part of social networks that link their peers and others.

At the most basic level, this context pertains to the resource base of academic work. The vital resources include finances to support academics' salaries, buildings and other overheads, as well as access to information. The academic ideal, again, is that research and teaching is supported by public funds and hence unencumbered by the need to raise money. However, even in those instances in which public funding organisations support universities and research institutes, research priorities are generally influenced by the resource providers. Furthermore, academic organisations around the world are adopting business oriented management models and rely increasingly on business sponsorship. This is particularly so in business schools, which often pride themselves in obtaining large grants or sponsorships from companies. It is also these business schools, especially in North America and Europe, but also in Africa, where much of the research and teaching on matters related to corporate responsibility takes place (Matten and Moon, 2004; Barkhuysen and Rossouw, 2000).

With regard to academic independence, this also becomes problematic as more and more researchers (like me, incidentally) rely on so-called 'soft money'. This means they need to raise money to cover some or all of their salary, plus overheads.

This obviously influences the kind of research that is done, because funding from the private or public sector is generally easier to obtain if it will help private or public organisations achieve their objectives, as opposed to critiques of the social or environmental damages inflicted by them.

As mentioned, access to funding is not the only form of resources required by scholars. They also need access to information. Especially for researchers in business schools, who often focus on the business organisation as their primary or even only object of analysis (a point of contention even among business scholars – see Ghoshal, 2005), this of course means that they rely on access to interviewees and documents within companies. Gaining access to senior business people, in fact, is one of the most significant challenges especially for young researchers in the corporate responsibility field. A key requirement is establishing suitable credentials and ensuring the interviewee that any information she or he is willing to share will be considered with due regard to its integrity. For instance, the interviewee must trust the researcher not to misquote or misrepresent her or him. In other words, due process, methodological rigour and intellectual honesty are vital for gaining access, rather than – as is sometimes assumed – a sycophantic attitude.

However, there is a risk especially for young researchers to become overly impressed by their interviewees in business, who are generally in positions of authority, well educated and situated in organisations and buildings designed to make an impression. These early encounters can give way to more frequent interactions in the course of ongoing research, at conferences and business school events. In other words, researchers with frequent interactions with business representatives are likely to become involved in personal networks characterised by business oriented discussions and perspectives. Such networks can provide important benefits in terms of access to information, but they will also influence the kinds of discussions and perspectives a researcher will be exposed to.

This social networking can thus socialise a researcher and influence her or his research in particular ways. A researcher interviewing or interacting predominantly with business representatives is likely to become accustomed to their way of seeing the world. She or he may disagree here or there, but a common framework of meaning will determine what kinds of questions and possible answers are feasible. On the other hand, the anthropologist studying communities impacted upon my mining through ethnographic research, living in their villages for weeks on end, will perceive the role of business very differently and she or he will ask different questions and propose different answers to the management scholar conducting interviews in the corporate head-office many miles away.

This social context of a researcher is not only relevant with regard to access to information and the thematic content of discussions. It also pertains to the researcher's desire for acknowledgement and recognition. As a researcher develops relationships with her or his contemporaries in business or elsewhere, she or he will be receiving – consciously or unconsciously – continuous feedback on whether the arguments emanating from the research are considered valid, intelligent or helpful. Most people desire some form of affirmation from others, so the social networks in which researchers find themselves will influence the way researchers develop and frame their arguments.

Of course, the most directly relevant group for researchers in terms of affirmation is their academic peer-group. The quality of academic work is judged and a researcher's career prospects are to some extent determined by their peers. This is most clearly manifest in the system of peer-review, in which accredited journals require that submitted manuscripts go through 'double blind peer review', that is, they are reviewed by two assessors and neither the author not the reviewers are aware of each others' identity. The key criteria guiding the reviewers are related to methodological rigour, which means that a paper should not be disqualified because of unexpected or counter-intuitive conclusions, as long as it relies on reliable information and sound argument. Contrary views ought to be fostered in order to stimulate and improve the quality of debate. However, though there are some very dynamic academic societies, the system of peer review runs the risk of reinforcing 'group think', as researchers learn to 'play by the rules' to get their manuscripts published in particular journals. This includes making reference to an established canon of material and reproducing a hierarchy of recognised authorities in particular fields. Using methodological or theoretical approaches from other disciplines or fields is risky because it may well challenge the reviewers' assumptions. Attempts at inter-disciplinary innovation are thus generally avoided.

Academics' research is also determined by the prevailing system of rewards. The imperative of 'publish or perish' is well known. Publishing in recognised journals is a key to career advancement. However, the thematic and methodological criteria applied by these journals are also framed by their socio-economic context. Most of the high ranking journals are North American and cater for North American academics that operate in a particular institutional context. These academics are generally tenured researchers situated in academic departments organised around subsidies, working schedules and discussion groups that make possible the kind of theoretically and methodologically focused research that is likely to be published. Researchers in other parts of the world, especially in developing countries, do not have this kind of organisational context and thus operate at a disadvantage in terms of their academic development and publishing success. Furthermore the division of labour between academic research and more practical work is not as clearly defined in most developing countries, because the prevalent skills gaps lead to expectations that academics also contribute to issues such as policy making or organisational development especially in the public sector or civil society. All this leads to the predominance of North American or European academics' perspectives taking centre stage in most established academic journals.

Not only does this prevailing international order in academia create an unfair distribution of opportunities and arguably a distorted representation of perspectives, but it also influences the kind of research that is considered legitimate and thus rewarded. High ranking journals generally emphasise 'objective' methodologies in which the researcher is meant to have as little influence on the object of study as possible. Furthermore, research based on survey data with large samples to ensure statistical rigour are generally preferred. In methodological terms, the predominant emphasis is on nomothetic research focused on identifying generalisable conclusions based on large samples, rather than understanding the role of context in influencing more particular manifestations of the phenomena under investigation.

However, even on a practical level, this methodological approach is less feasible in developing country contexts. For a start, large sample sizes are not always easy to come by and much greater effort is needed to obtain data for such large samples. Instead of readily available datasets on the Fortune Top 500 companies, for instance, it is difficult to obtain data on companies beyond the top 50 in South Africa, let alone other African countries. More fundamentally, many of the theoretical assumptions underlying a quantitative, nomothetic research approach are not appropriate especially in developing countries (bearing in mind that these assumptions have been thoroughly criticised in general, as well). This is especially pertinent in research on corporate responsibility, in which the role of historical, socio-economic, political and environmental context is vital to understanding the drivers, manifestations and impacts of corporate activity.

Finally, the quality criteria of the high ranking journals – and as a result the incentive schemes adopted by most universities – oppose the kind of research that seeks to develop innovative approaches to dealing with the complex problems faced by society. Action research, in this vein, is a methodological approach that suggests that researchers can become intricately involved in effecting change in the organisations or social systems under investigation. Such intervention can not only lead to positive social change, which is so pressing in developing countries in particular, but can – based on a rigorous and systematic approach – also lead to theoretically valid and innovative discoveries (see, for instance, Whyte, 1989). Arguably there is a particularly strong case for action research in corporate responsibility, as there are vital opportunities for researchers to understand the nuances of organisational change when they are involved in making these changes. Admittedly it is not always easy to interpret the data arising from this kind of research in a manner that avoids parochialism and is of broader theoretical relevance, but it is possible. However, academic institutions, spearheaded by the conventions of the ranked journals, are stacked against such innovations in method and research practice.

18.4 Beyond Narcissism to Whole Person Innovation

In the above, I have argued that the academic ideal of objectivity and reasoned debate is circumscribed by the socio-economic context in which research takes place, more so and often more subtly than is generally recognised and acknowledged. Of course this positioning in a broader social and cultural context is common to all professions and, indeed, all individuals. With particular reference to our socio-economic class position, the French sociologist Pierre Bourdieu referred to this as *habitus*, or the manner in which our inclinations and choices are shaped by our social context (see Bourdieu and Wacquant, 1992). In other words, our *position* shapes our *disposition*.

This link between economic interests, power, culture, and individuals' motivations was the mainstay of the Frankfurt School of sociologists, who created a potent link between social and economic analysis, on the one hand, and psychoanalysis, on the other. In 1972, Theodor Adorno and Max Horkheimer argued that culture – and by extension, much of academic research – had lost its potential for true expression and social emancipation and was primarily about the production and consumption of commodities, premised on economic calculations. By the same token, commodities are fetishised; they provide individuals with a semblance of sense and purpose in a life that is dominated by menial and monotonous work in the corporate economy. Aggressive advertising promotes and perpetuates this commodity fetishism, linked to sex and prestige. Adorno felt that economic processes and their implications for family life were negatively impacting the development of people's personality. Rather than provide a healthy and strong model for a child's ego-development, parents' subservience to the corporate economic system creates a vacuum. The result is the development of a personality that is obsessed with the self and especially the appearance of the self.

These ideas were developed most explicitly in a book by Christopher Lasch called *The Culture of Narcissism* in 1979. Narcissus is the Greek god who was so proud of his beauty that he ridiculed the advances of suitors. One day he saw his image reflected in a magically calm pool of water and instantly fell in love. He became so captivated by his own reflection that he eventually fell into the water and drowned.

> What makes modern culture narcissistic is its overwhelming emphasis on *appearances*. The appearance of things, of success, of sexiness, of celebrity, is what matters more than its substance (How, 2003: 97–98).

In addition to consumption, narcissistic culture is expressed in individuals' productive behaviours. The corporate economy forces us – those with jobs – into increasingly stressful and intensive work patterns. We do this not only because we need to earn more money for increased consumption. It is also the aspired image of high-performing, hard-working achiever, which is an intrinsic part of the narcissistic culture. The monk and writer Thomas Merton (1966: 73) put it potently: 'The rush and pressure of modern life are a form, perhaps the most common form, of its innate violence.'

Narcissistic culture serves dominant economic interests. To some extent, it is even consciously perpetuated by these interests. The increasingly aggressive use of advertising and its effects on our consciousness and identity is a case in point. It is also manifest in international politics. Lasch's book is subtitled 'American Life in an Age of Diminishing Expectations' and he is particularly scornful of what he identifies as rampant self-absorption, historical ignorance, and corporate domination in the United States. This coincides with lingering questions about the 'Americanisation' of global cultures. Indeed, the culture industry, which incorporates academia, is identified as a powerful tool to proactively expand the United States' global influence, as argued by David Rothkop (1997) in *Foreign Affairs*: 'The United States dominates [the] global traffic in information and ideas . . . Aspects of

American culture will play a critical role in helping to ensure the continuation of that leadership.'

The key point here is that narcissism is an important theme in the study of corporate responsibility. John Roberts (2003: 263) identifies the following forms of corporate conduct with reference to the role and motivations of individual decision-makers within these organisations:

> The first, negative, [manifestation of corporate conduct] suggests that ethical sensibility is routinely occluded in the way that exclusively financial interests, advertised and enforced by disciplinary processes both within and beyond the corporate hierarchy, have the effect of rendering us defensively or assertively preoccupied with the self. The second, more positive, form of corporate social responsibility I have termed the ethics of narcissus. Stimulated by new forms of negative external visibility, the corporate response has been to seek to manufacture the appearance of its own goodness through the production of corporate ethical codes and new forms of social and environmental reports. The third form of the attempt to manufacture corporate social responsibility seeks to give more than local reach to sincere moral sensibility within the corporation through the creation of new forms of internal social and environmental controls, with associated rewards and incentives, as a complement to existing management accounting. The final form suggests the necessity and potential of a dialogue across the corporate boundary with those most vulnerable to the effects of corporate conduct.

The culture of narcissus is prevalent in academia, as well. Though the benefits of career progress are perhaps not as clearly demarcated in job positions and material reward as in the business sector, ambition manifests itself in forceful ways in academia. The academic ideal is to contribute innovation and original knowledge, but an academic's standing is determined by her or his highly ranked publications and peer recognition. Not only does ambition hence countervail the kind of teamwork that is often the source of real innovation, but it can have even more pernicious effects, as argued in 1957 already by Robert Merton (1957: 659):

> The more thoroughly scientists ascribe an unlimited value to originality, the more they are in this sense dedicated to the advancement of knowledge, the greater is their involvement in the successful outcome of inquiry and their emotional vulnerability to failure. Against this cultural and social background, one can begin to glimpse the sources, other than idiosyncratic ones, of the misbehaviour of individual scientists. The culture of science is, in this measure, pathogenic. It can lead scientists to develop an extreme concern with recognition which is in turn the validation by peers of the worth of their work. Contentiousness, self-assertive claims, secretiveness lest one be forestalled, reporting only the data that support an hypothesis, false charges of plagiarism, even the occasional theft of ideas and in rare cases, the fabrication of data, - all these have appeared in the history of science and can be thought of as deviant behaviour in response to a discrepancy between the enormous emphasis in the culture of science upon original discovery and the actual difficulty many scientists experience in making an original discovery. In this situation of stress, all manner of adaptive behaviours are called into play, some of these being far beyond the mores of science.

The irony, hence, is that scholars of corporate responsibility and business ethics bemoan the greed and narcissism of decision-makers in business and highlight the social and environmental fallout, but at the same time such forces are at play among us, as academics, as well. The immediate outcomes of academic narcissism may not be as directly visible as in the business world, but they are also profound.

This irony becomes more pertinent and interesting as we see academics identifying a role for ourselves in not only focusing attention on the dangers of greed and social disregard among business decision-makers, but also in developing teaching programmes that are meant to foster 'whole person' learning among future business people. Such learning should, ostensibly, transform the narcissistic, conformist and competitive self bemoaned by Lasch and others into a more reflective, empathetic, collaborative and emotionally and socially conscious person (Rogers, 1983; for a discussion on whole person learning in the context of corporate responsibility, see Prinsloo et al., 2006). Such ideas have found their way from what were once considered radical pedagogues, including well known ones such as Paulo Freire (1976), to mainstream initiatives, such as the Globally Responsible Leadership Initiative, which argues in its manifesto:

> We need more responsible leadership to implement a more comprehensive model for sustainable development. This requires a profound change in individual mindsets and behaviours as well as overall corporate culture. What is necessary is that both individuals and corporations assume their responsibility towards the Common Good ... Importantly, it also implies a necessary re-thinking of the way business, political and social leaders are educated and trained. Concretely, [the Globally Responsible Leadership Initiative] believes that business schools should focus on educating the whole person as entrepreneurs, leaders, and corporate statesmen. Leadership is the art of motivating, communicating, empowering and convincing people to engage with a new vision of sustainable development and the necessary change that this implies. Leadership is based on moral authority (http://www.grli.org, accessed 9 December 2009; see also Swanson, 2004).

These are important developments, yet we may ask ourselves, as academics, whether we are in a good position to educate and train business leaders as 'whole persons'. For a start, our understanding of what this means and how such training can be effectively provided is limited. This thus gives rise to every researcher's favourite opportunity to call for more research. However, over and above more research, it calls for greater introspection among academics as to whether the institutional system we are reproducing for ourselves and the daily lives we lead as academics are indeed exemplary of the kind of 'whole person' we are keen to hoist on business students.

Introspection and enhanced awareness are the first step to becoming whole persons ourselves. This may involve the recognition that the intellectual activity that defines the academic's profession has its inherent risks for developing whole-person awareness. The spiritual teacher Eckhardt Tolle argues that many of our personal and social problems are based on an over-active identification with the thoughts in our minds, separating us from the realisation of our deeper, spiritual selves and giving rise to a narcissistic, egoic quest for material reward and recognition.

> The undercurrent of constant unease started long before the rise of Western industrial civilisation, of course, but in Western civilisation ... it manifests in an unprecedentedly acute form. It was already there at the time of Jesus, and it was there 600 years before that at the time of Buddha, and long before that. Why are you always anxious? Jesus asked his disciples. 'Can anxious thought add a single day to your life?' And the Buddha taught that the root of suffering is to be found in our constant wanting and craving (Tolle, 2005: 63).

Reflecting on the world's great spiritual traditions (note that I am not invoking institutionalised religion) is probably an unlikely place to end an academic's perspective on corporate responsibility. Yet as I pointed out at the outset, writing on the role of academics, as an academic, is necessarily a personal exercise. From my experience (and paraphrasing Ghandi) conducting research and teaching about the positive changes we want to see in the world, with a focus on the role of business in making such changes, is underpinned by the personal changes we are willing and able to make. I, for one, have important choices to make in this regard. My sense is that such choices are relevant for academia in general, as well. Only if we are willing to commit to this journey towards 'whole personhood' as academics can we hope to convincingly assist business people to do the same. Hence the world's great spiritual traditions are, after all, probably a good place to start for academics and others to reconsider our priorities and what it means to make a difference in our workplaces and in our lives.

References

Avery, C., 2006. 'The Difference Between CSR and Human Rights'. Corporate Citizenship Briefing 89 (August/September 2006)

Barkhuysen, B. and Rossouw, G.J., 2000. Business Ethics as Academic Field in Africa: Its Current Status. *Business Ethics: A European Review* 9(4):229–235.

Bourdieu, P. and Wacquant, L.J.D., 1992. *An Invitation to Reflexive Sociology*. Chicago: The University of Chicago Press.

Christian Aid, 2004. *Behind the Mask: The Real Face of Corporate Social Responsibility*. London: Christian Aid.

Freire, P., 1976. *Education, the Practice of Freedom*. London: Writers and Readers Cooperative.

Friedman, M., 1970. The Social Responsibility of Business Is to Increase its Profits, *New York Times Magazine*, 13 September.

Ghoshal, S., 2005. Bad Management Theories are Destroying Good Management Practices. *Academy of Management Learning & Education* 4(1): 75–91.

Habermas, J., 1997. The Public Sphere. In R.E. Goodin and P. Pettit, (ed.), *Contemporary Political Philosophy*. Oxford: Blackwell.

Hamann, R., 2007. Is Corporate Citizenship Making a Difference? *Journal of Corporate Citizenship* 28: 15–29.

Hamann, R., 2008. Introducing Corporate Citizenship. In R. Hamann, S. Woolman and C. Sprague, (ed.), *The Business of Sustainable Development in Africa: Human Rights, Partnerships, and Alternative Business Model*. Pretoria: Unisa Press/Tokyo: United Nations University Press.

Hamann, R., Acutt, N. and Kapelus, P., 2003. Responsibility vs. Accountability? Interpreting the World Summit on Sustainable Development for a Synthesis Model of Corporate Citizenship. *Journal of Corporate Citizenship*, 9: 20–36.

Henderson, D., 2005. The Role of Business in the World Today. *Journal of Corporate Citizenship*, 17: 30–32.

Hoffman, A.J., 1999. Institutional Evolution and Change: Environmentalism and the U.S. Chemical Industry. *Academy of Management Journal* 42(4): 351–371.

How, A., 2003. *Critical Theory*. New York: Palgrave Macmillan.

International Finance Corporation, Sustainability, and Instituto Ethos, 2002. *The Business Case in Emerging Economies*. Washington: International Finance Corporation.

Kemp, R., Parto, S. and Gibson, R.B., 2005. Governance for Sustainable Development: Moving from Theory to Practice. *International Journal of Sustainable Development* 8(1–2): 12–30.

Kuhn, T.S., 1970. *The Structure of Scientific Revolutions*. Chicago: University of Chicago Press.

Margolis, J.D. and Walsh, J.P. , 2003. Misery Loves Companies: Rethinking Social Initiatives by Business. *Administrative Science Quarterly* 48: 268–305.

Matten, D. and Moon, J. 2004. Corporate Social Responsibility Education in Europe. *Journal of Business Ethics* 54: 323–337.

Merton, R.K., 1957. Priorities in Scientific Discovery: A Chapter in the Sociology of Science. *American Sociological Review* 22(6): 635–659.

Merton, T., 1966. *Conjectures of a Guilty Bystander*. London: Doubleday.

Popper, K.R., 2002. *Conjectures and Refutations: The Growth of Scientific Knowledge*. London: Routledge.

Porter, M.E. and Kramer, M.R., 2006. Strategy and Society: The Link Between Competitive Advantage and Corporate Social Responsibility. *Harvard Business Review* December: 1–14.

Prinsloo, P., Beukes, C. and De Jongh, D., 2006. Corporate Citizenship Education for Responsible Business Leaders. *Development Southern Africa* 23(2): 197–211.

Roberts, J., 2003. The Manufacture of Corporate Social Responsibility. *Organization* 10(2): 249–265.

Rogers, C., 1983. *Freedom to Learn*. Columbus: Bell and Howell.

Rothkop, D., 1997. In Praise of Cultural Imperialism? Effects of Globalisation on Culture. *Foreign Affairs* June 22.

Sachs, J., 2005. *The End of Poverty: How We Can Make It Happen in Our Lifetime*. London: Penguin.

Sen, A., 1999. Economics, Business Principles, and Moral Sentiments. In G. Enderle, (ed.), *International Business Ethics: Challenges and Approaches*. Notre Dame: The University of Notre Dame Press.

Swanson, D.L., 2004. The Buck Stops Here: Why Universities Must Reclaim Business Ethics Education. *Journal of Academic Ethics* 2(1): 43–61.

Tolle, E., 2005. *The Power of Now*. London: Hodder and Stoughton.

United Nations, 2007. *The Millennium Development Goals Report 2007*. New York: United Nations.

Whyte, W.F., 1989. Advancing Scientific Knowledge Through Participatory Action Research. *Sociological Forum* 4(3): 367–385.

World Business Council for Sustainable Development, 2005. *Business for Development: Business Solutions in Support of the Millennium Development Goals*. Geneva: World Business Council for Sustainable Development.

Chapter 19
The Proliferation of CSR from Two Professional Perspectives: Academic Researchers and Consultants

Karolina Windell

> *Perceiving social responsibility as building shared value rather than as damage control or as PR campaign will require dramatically different thinking in business. We are convinced, however, that CSR will become increasingly important to competitive success.*
>
> (Porter and Kramer, 2006: 92)

Abstract Despite the significant research in the field of CSR over the past few years, scarce attention has been paid to the recent popularization of CSR. Building on new-institutional arguments this chapter both contributes to a theoretical discussion about the role of actors that spread ideas about corporate behaviour as well as with empirical insights from academic researchers and consultants in the field of CSR. More specifically, the chapter explores how two groups of professionals – academic researchers and consultants – contribute to the proliferation of CSR. Three observations are made. *First*, CSR has constituted a new area of work for both consultants and academics. *Secondly*, consultants and academics contribute to the proliferation of CSR because of their status as experts. *Thirdly*, consultants and academics have created attention around CSR – albeit through different means. In conclusion, consultants and academics play prominent roles in creating CSR as a new area of expertise by drawing attention to CSR and thereby creating new opportunities for themselves as well as actors to get involved in CSR.

K. Windell (✉)
University of Uppsala, Uppsala, Sweden

S.O. Idowu, W.L. Filho (eds.), *Professionals' Perspectives of Corporate Social Responsibility*, DOI 10.1007/978-3-642-02630-0_20,

19.1 Introduction

Today, we find a multitude of actors telling corporations how and why they should include the issue social responsibility in their corporate strategies. The number of self-proclaimed experts in the field of CSR has exploded. Overall the organizations and individuals contributing to the circulation of CSR have undergone a dramatic development during the last decade. Governments, trade associations, business networks, certification and standardization organizations, non-governmental organizations (NGOs), investment banks, universities and business schools, consultancies, and law firms, among others, have aided the advancement of CSR. Several efforts have been made to raise the awareness of CSR and to encourage and pressure corporations to enhance their level of social responsibility. CSR standards, frameworks, and guidelines have been issued; reports on corporate misbehaviour have been published; rankings of socially responsible corporations have been inaugurated; research on CSR has been amplified; seminars, workshops, and conferences on CSR have been organized; and fora in which advocates and opponents could discuss the idea of CSR have been arranged. And still the list of activities in the name of CSR could be much longer.

From the beginning, researchers, practitioners, politicians, and representatives of the civil society have been searching for clarification and definitions of corporate social responsibility (cf. Carroll 1979, 1999; Garriga and Melé 2004), yet there is no standard definition. The vague and ambiguous character of CSR has led to disputes over its definition. These discussions tend to address two specific questions. How far beyond the responsibility mandated by the law should social responsibility actually stretch? How should social responsibility be implemented, measured, and evaluated? Although there are varying definitions and interpretations of the content and meaning of CSR, the popularization of the idea, broadly defined during the last decade, is impressive. CSR has, thus, become an idea on the corporate agenda.

Despite the significant rise in the number of CSR studies over the past few years, scarce attention has been paid to the actual construction and recent popularization of CSR (see Windell 2006 for more on this). Studies tend instead to contain normative claims about the value and importance of CSR and ways of making it a reality in business operations (e.g. De Bakker et al. 2005; Waddock 2004; Waddock et al. 2002). In this chapter, I make no normative claims or any attempt to develop the concept of CSR. Rather I endeavour to contribute to the discussion about how ideas about appropriate corporate behaviour are actually constructed and become popular ideas.

In organisational theory the role of actor groups carrying ideas about corporations and corporate behaviours have been attended to. Consultants, business press, and academic researchers have been highlighted as important proponents of management ideas and management knowledge (Sahlin-Andersson and Engwall 2002b). Against this backdrop, this chapter focuses on the contribution of two professional groups – academic researchers and consultants – to the proliferation and construction of CSR. Building on new-institutional arguments the chapter both attempts to contribute a theoretical discussion about the role of actors that spread ideas about corporate behaviour as well as with empirical insights from academic researchers and consultants in the field of CSR. This chapter explores the ways academic researchers and consultants contribute to the proliferation ideas on the field of CSR.[1]

19.2 Actors Proliferating Ideas About Business Behaviour

Ideas can be of various types. In its etymological sense, an 'idea' is the way something is seen; thus an idea is an image or picture of something (Czarniawska and Joerges 1996). Accordingly, ideas can be images of how management should be practiced or how corporations should be run. Thus ideas are powerful, in that they shape both corporate activities and the perceptions of corporations (cf. Sahlin-Andersson and Engwall 2002c). The circulation of ideas that prescribes the correct and most efficient way of doing business influences corporate activity on a structural level in the form of organizational structure and corporate techniques; and, on a more cognitive level, in shared beliefs and expectations about corporations.

Organizations and individuals energize ideas in translation processes by shaping and using them (Czarniawska and Joerges 1996). The concept of translation suggests that actors actively translate ideas into organizational life (cf. Czarniawska and Sevón 1996; Sahlin-Andersson 1996; Rövik 1996), and moreover, that translation is a process by which actors may strive to fulfil their own political or economic self-interests (Campbell 2004: 84).

Although proponents of new-institutional theory have been accused of being deterministic and of underplaying the role of agency, the concept of translation has opened the way for acknowledging the role of actors in institutional change – albeit by addressing actors as purposive rather than strategic (cf. Meyer 1996). In this way the new institutionalism does not neglect the role of agency, but rather addresses actions as embedded in institutional context. Put differently, a new-institutional perspective does not address the way actors rationally construct institutions in accordance with their desires; rather it addresses the way in which these desires arise.

When addressing the role of agency in institutional theory, we should be sensitive to the fact that it is actually far from being a new topic. DiMaggio (1988) dealt with the subject of agency and interests in relation to new-institutional theory in his 1988 article, in which he argued that actors or institutional entrepreneurs explain the creation of institutions. DiMaggio (1988: 3) claimed that: 'institutional theories of organizations represent an important break with rational-actor models and promising strategy for modelling and explaining instances of organizational change that are not driven by processes of interest mobilization. Yet the role of interest and

---

[1] The chapter builds on two studies. First, on interviews with academic researchers in the field of CSR, documents studies of actions taken by academic institutions in the field of CSR as well as publication frequency in academic journals on CSR. Secondly, the chapter departs from interviews with consultants and document studies in the consulting field in Sweden.

agency are somewhat obscure'. For these reasons, DiMaggio (1988: 11) argued that it is necessary that explicit attention be given to agency in order to develop explanations for the emergence and reproduction of institutionalized practices and forms. Consistent with this line of thought, Hwang and Powell (2005) argue that examining actors that purposively seek to promote their own interests and agendas by calling attention to new ideas could add a new perspective to the spread of ideas and changes of institutional environments.

Actors taking the opportunity to pursue change have, within the new-institutional tradition, been seen as institutional entrepreneurs or change agents (cf. Galaskiewicz 1991; Hwang and Powell 2005; Lawrence and Phillips 2004). The discussion about actors as institutional entrepreneurs relates to an ongoing debate in new institutionalism: the connectedness and the feedback mechanisms between agency and institutions. On one hand, it is argued that actors act purposively in accordance with their interests or desires; on the other hand, we need to recognize that these interests and desires are institutionally shaped (Friedland and Alford 1991). Hence, as Lawrence and Suddaby (2006: 13) argue: '[...] practices which might lead to institutional innovations are themselves institutionally embedded and so rely on sets of resources and skills that are specific to the field of fields in which they occur'. However, actors are not to be seen as passive adopters of ideas (Friedland and Alford 1991). Some would argue, in fact, that they have 'creative capacities' (Galaskiewicz 1991: 295).

Studies of the circulation of management ideas have primarily addressed certain actors or carriers within the business community, such as consultants, business schools, and the business press, in order to explain their flow. The concept of carriers is used to conceptualize how these actor groups transfer management ideas. Nevertheless the concept is not to be interpreted as a passive process; rather these carriers in intertwined and circular processes create, mediate, and use the ideas (Sahlin-Andersson and Engwall 2002a). The studies of carriers have demonstrated that ideas are formed and circulated in interactions among the consultants; business schools; media; and, to some extent, corporations. During the later decades management models and management knowledge have increasingly been produced and circulated (Engwall and Kipping 2003, Ernst and Kieser 2002). In the 1980s and 1990s there was an expansion of management knowledge and management ideas (Sahlin-Andersson and Engwall 2002a).Total Quality Management (TQM), Management by Objectives (MBO), Business Process Re-engineering (BPR), Just-In-Time (JIT), and scientific management, among others. This also means that the number of actors and organisations construction and dissemination management knowledge has grown.

Thus, from previous research in the organizational field, we know that actor groups such as academics as well as consultants are often part of shaping and mobilizing new ideas and trends in the business community (Sahlin-Andersson and Engwall 2002a). Recognizing this, we can establish that the expansion of CSR research and CSR consulting is part of the construction of CSR; therefore it is of interest to recognize how academic researchers and consultants have conceptualized and addressed the idea. In the following sections, the role of academic researchers and consultants in their attempts to proliferate the idea of the field of CSR is described.

19.3 The Expansion of CSR Research

As CSR continued to flourish in society during the last 15 years, academic attention increased, particularly in recent years. Although academic articles on the topic of corporate social responsibility date back to the 1950s, the bulk of the research was published during the past few years.[2] In 2006, a search for 'corporate social responsibility' in peer-reviewed journals in the database, *Business Source Premier,* identified more than 2200 separate academic articles. And new journals that specifically address these topics have been established over same period. In addition to the numerous publications on CSR in academic journals, there are abundant conference papers and Master's theses (Brytting and Egels 2004). CSR has developed into a research field in its own right with a prominent position in the management literature (De Bakker et al. 2005).

Following the academic literature on CSR is a puzzling endeavour because of the myriad definitions, meanings, and terms employed. Just as practitioners and researchers in previous times sought to clarify the meaning of the social responsibility of business, a considerable number of present researchers have been striving to classify CSR, outline CSR theories, and clarify the field of CSR research (cf. Garriga and Melé 2004; Jonker 2005). A number of research studies that address CSR draw on ideas or connect to previous research on business ethics, corporate citizenship, and sustainable management, making it difficult to distinguish among the bodies of research in any of these fields (cf. Garriga and Melé 2004).

In addition, CSR is being studied within various disciplines and from various perspectives. In particular, it is striking to note that CSR is related to widely diverse parts of the corporation, and that it addresses many types of corporate activities. Several studies examine the relationship between CSR and financial performance (Margolis and Walsh 2003; Schnietz and Epstein 2005; Waddock and Graves 1997). Another strand of the literature focuses on CSR in relation to management, including the decisions and actions associated with the implementation or organization of CSR activities and how to integrate the multitude of CSR frameworks into business operations (Leipziger 2003; Waddock 2004; Zadek 1998, 2004). A third strand of the literature addresses CSR in relation to such aspects of marketing as branding and differentiation (cf. Cerne 2003; Kotler and Lee 2005; Maignan and Ferrell 2004), and to political consumption (cf. Klein et al. 2004; Micheletti and Stolle 2004; Sen and Bhattacharya 2001). Yet other researchers have examined the spread and adoption of CSR in different geographical contexts (cf. Chambers et al. 2003; Fukukawa and Moon 2004; Maignan and Ralston 2002; Matten and Moon 2004).

---

[2]See Chap. 5 for more information.

In the past few years CSR has also found its way into European business schools. For many years business ethics has been taught at universities and in MBA courses at universities and business schools, but CSR has only recently become a subject in management courses at European universities (Matten and Moon 2005). Yet today we find CSR education or research on CSR at academic institutions all over Europe. An overview of teaching and research in the field of CSR[3] in European Business Schools shows that several business schools have education in such related areas as sustainability and environmental management, whereas two-thirds of the respondents offered CSR education at executive, MBA, and undergraduate levels.[4]

Nottingham University Business School is one example of a European university with a department devoted to CSR research. The International Centre for Corporate Social Responsibility (ICCSR), directed by Jeremy Moon, Professor of CSR, was funded initially in 2002 by British American Tobacco. Here, management education and research are being conducted within the framework of corporate social responsibility. A collaborative initiative on CSR education was also instigated in 2002 when the European Academy of Business in Society (EABIS) was formed in order to mainstream CSR into business practices and theory. EABIS was launched in an alliance of business networks, governmental organizations, and academia.

CSR has, as exemplified above, become part of extensive research. PhD workshops and PhD networks have been organized around the theme of CSR, some with the financial support of the European Commission. And, moreover, as explained previously, CSR has raised increasing interest in international academic journals. Just as the growing interest in CSR can be observed in other areas in society, the proliferation of CSR is also reflected in the increase of articles in academic journals. During the period 1996–2005, in fact, 1524 articles published in more than 45 different journals and containing the exact phrase 'corporate social responsibility' were found in the database, *Business Source Premier,* well known for academic articles on business and management (Windell, 2006). The main part of these journals published only a few articles on CSR. In 12 of the journals, however, there were more than 20 articles per journal. The main part of these journals focused on business ethics, environmental issues, or management issues.

It was not only the number of articles that grew during this period. New journals devoted to business ethics and social responsibility were also established, further increasing the number of articles. Two of the most prominent journals were established in 1997 and 1998 *European Industrial Relations Review* and *Business Ethics: A European Review.* In 2001 and 2004 two additional journals – *Brand Strategy* and *Journal of Corporate Citizenship* – were established. *Brand strategy* published 46 articles focusing on corporate social responsibility in the years 2001–2004, and the *Journal of Corporate Citizenship* published 44 articles between 2004 and 2005.

---

[3] In their study, Matten and Moon include synonyms for CSR such as Business Ethics, Corporate Citizenship, Sustainability, Corporate Environmental Management, Business and Society, Business and Governance, Business and Globalization, Stakeholder Management, Governance.

[4] The study had a 24.8% response rate from the European business schools.

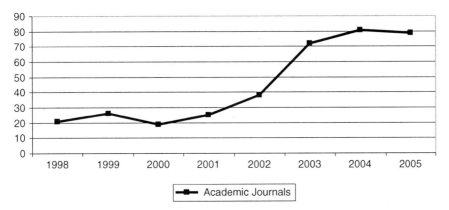

Fig. 19.1 Number of articles containing the exact phrase 'corporate social responsibility' from 1998 until 2005 in: *Academy of Management Review, Business and Society, Business and Society Review, Business Ethics Quarterly, Business Ethics: A European Review, California Management Review, European Industrial Review, Financial Management, Greener Management International, Journal of Business Ethics*
(Source: Windell, 2006)

Figure 19.1 illustrates the growth of articles on CSR in ten journals that were established before 1998 and in which more than 20 articles per journal had been published. The number of articles on corporate social responsibility escalated in 2003, with an increase of 90% over the previous year.

At the beginning of the twenty first century, academics published an increasing number of articles on CSR and a new research area emerged. Business school academics taught CSR in undergraduate, graduate, and MBA courses; they contributed to the advancement of CSR by publishing articles and by educating students who would later enter business enterprises. Moreover, over the last years we can observe that academic researchers in the field of CSR have created interface with practitioners in order to discuss questions in general about the role corporations in society and scope of corporate responsibility in particular. One area where academic researchers and practitioners come together is conferences either arranged by a university or other organizations. For example, the Humboldt University in Berlin has arranged a CSR conference since 2004. At that time it had 400 participants from science, corporations, government, and non-governmental organisations. The conference welcomed both empirical and theoretical contributions to CSR topics and, in particular, contributions that '[. . .] would inform the changes in the business community and clarify the vague meaning of CSR' were invited (Institute of Management Humboldt University 2004). Based on these assumptions, the conference in 2004 aimed at contributing to communication among researchers, politicians, corpoations, and NGOs on the consequences of increased corporate social responsibility for corporations and the overall society. Another example is the conference arranged by the organization Globe Forum. Globe Forum is a Stockholm based organization working as a matchmaker between businesses and other actors through their yearly conference. Since 2007 they have arranged an international conference on the topic of CSR and/or sustainability. The conference welcomes politicians, corporations, consultants, academic researchers, NGOs among others from all over the world. The conference has also instigated an award for the best CSR research in Sweden. At their webpage the Globe Forum states that ' the Globe Award for best CSR research should give increased knowledge about CSR issues and strengthen a business case, based on: Business-related research, Accessibility, and Business advantage' (Globe Forum, 2008). The award is distributed at a price ceremony at the conference and it provides an opportunity for researchers to market their research among practitioners.

When asking researchers active in the field of CSR – 9 researchers from Sweden, Netherlands and Norway where contacted – what they consider to be their role when it comes to proliferating ideas about corporate responsibility their common view was that they should engage in discussion and dialog with practitioners in order to drive these questions. However, the researchers also emphasized that they should above all remain critical to the subject and 'ask questions that other professionals such as consultants don't have time or interest in asking. What does this idea mean? What is driving this idea? What interests in promoting the idea does actor have?' Rather than promoting their own visions the academic researchers underline that they should remain objective, and focus on developing knowledge within the field.

Several academic researchers do however have regularly contact with practitioners in their research. Some researchers mainly have contact with practitioners when gathering data or when visiting a conference. However, some of them are regularly hired as consultants by corporations in short term projects. Moreover, the academic researchers testify that academic researchers are leaving the academia in order to work on long term basis for a consultancy or a corporation. One of the researchers argues that the impact that academic researchers have on corporation in terms of spreading ideas about CSR through their research publications is limited. However, working consultative in some corporate projects their influence is much greater.

The developments of increased CSR research, academic publications in the area of CSR as well as the interfaces among academics and practitioners indicate that CSR is carried into corporations through researchers and through students who have graduated with training in this area.

19.4 The Expansion of CSR Consulting

Consultants selling CSR services are established in several European countries, but it is the Swedish group, in the process of establishing CSR consulting, that I examine here. These consultants acknowledged ideas about the social responsibility of business and turned them into saleable services under the acronym, CSR. In Sweden CSR consulting began to emerge in the early 1990s, with the establishment of the first consultancies to address social responsibility. At this time consultants did not talk about corporate social responsibility or used the acronym CSR; rather they claimed to be working with general social concerns in businesses, business ethics, and environmental or sustainability issues.

The first consultants to explicitly acknowledge social responsibility as a new potential area of work usually belonged to the smaller consultancies, consisting of one or two people who had previously worked with environmental consulting or business ethics. During the early 1990s, corporations were indifferent to social responsibility. There were few consultants in the area, and those that did exist had a tough time finding customers and a struggle to market themselves. By the end of the 1990s, however, questions about the social responsibility of business had been raised in the aftermath of anti-globalization protests, and additional consultancies were being established. The consultants argued, however, that corporations were still unable to appreciate social responsibility consulting.

A few years later, at the beginning of the twenty first century, the number of consultants selling social responsibility services had gathered momentum. According to the consultants interviewed, their total number addressing corporate social responsibility had risen from zero in 1990 to approximately 50 in 2003. At the beginning of the 21st century, consultancies established in other areas – accounting, management, environment, or communication – began to notice CSR and broaden their area of work. During these years, people who had been working in larger environmental consultancies broke free to freelance or establish new consultancies specializing in sustainability or corporate social responsibility.

The growth of consultants was understood by the consultants themselves to be a consequence of the corporate scandals that had occurred in Sweden and other parts of the world. The Enron scandal was highlighted by the consultants as an important trigger in this debate. The overall debate in Sweden about the social responsibility of business, ethical conduct, and the role of business in society escalated during these years. In particular the corporate governance scandal in the insurance company, Skandia, centring on their bonus programs 'wealth-builder' and 'share-tracker' and the sale of Skandia Asset Management received widespread attention (Göthberg 2007).[5] Critical articles about corporate behaviour were published in the Swedish dailies; governmental representatives published reports on ethical conduct and corporate responsibility; and on 5 September 2002, the Swedish government initiated a commission to evaluate the trust for the Swedish business community and to deal with corporate governance issues (Förtroendekommittén 2004). The UN Global Compact and the Swedish governmental counterpart, *Globalt Ansvar* (Global Responsibility) were also established about this time – important initiatives that encouraged the consultants to address the social responsibility of business and to develop services in this area.

Swedish consultants did not necessarily present themselves as CSR consultants, however, because CSR was still considered to be a new label that had not yet gained a foothold. It was more common for consultants to relate CSR to other areas of the consulting field, stressing that they were, for example, management

---

[5] In 2003 the top management and corporate board of Skandia were accused of lining their pockets at the expenses of their shareholder. In 2006 two members of the top-management team were found guilty and condemned to 2 years in prison.

consultants specializing in CSR. For this reason, CSR was integrated into exist-ing consulting areas rather than being developed into an entirely new niche in the consulting field. Thus accounting consultants, management consultants, communi-cation consultants, business ethics consultants, and environmental consultants all integrated CSR in a manner that fit their existing practices. However, a few of the newly established consultancies that did not belong to any particular area of the consulting field created a new niche for themselves by relating CSR to ethical invest-ments, thereby establishing themselves as analysts in the area of ethical investment analysis.

The consultancies did not only differ in their main area of consulting, but also in their size and the geographical area of their operation. In general there were larger firms with several employees operating on a global level and smaller firms with one or two employees operating on a national level.

In the process of establishing CSR as a new area of consulting – new and saleable services had to be developed. Common types of services were developed, and con-sultants often specialized in the type of services that could be integrated into their consulting area. The services that were developed were unspecific and took dif-ferent forms in different consultancies. At the same time, they were all marketed by underlining their relationship to financial performance. CSR was marketed as one proactive management idea that would not only minimize the risks of corpora-tions being scrutinized by their stakeholders, but would also contribute to increased profitability. Making CSR into an attractive management idea meant that the con-sultants had to develop services and market these services successfully. In order to do so, they argued, they needed to convince their corporate clients about the value of CSR. During the interviews, several respondents said that the concept of CSR was looked upon with scepticism within the business community. Corporate represen-tatives and managers considered the allocation of resources to social issues to be a waste. According to the consultants, the dominating view among several managers was that 'the business of business is business'; they could not understand why they should pay attention to social issues, which were not directly related to their core business.

The consultants sought to introduce CSR to the corporate representatives in a convincing way by using arguments that linked CSR to financial performance, con-tending that economic arguments were the only effective rhetoric. As one consultant claimed:

> And then the question is raised. 'Why should corporations be socially responsible?' And there are two good arguments, although one is better than the other. First, the corporation will go bankrupt otherwise and the brand will be jeopardized. The second argument is that it is a business case and the corporation can earn cash.

This meant that moral arguments were absent, and economic arguments were promi-nent. The consultants avoided moral arguments, they said, because the corporate representatives they worked with did not listen to any arguments other than those about increased profitability.

CSR was, thus, presented as an indispensable, rational strategy, necessary for corporations in order to increase and maintain their profits and a corporate imperative for tackling increased stakeholder demands. The consultants claimed that customers, NGOs, investors, employees, governmental organizations, and the media demanded social responsibility from corporations, and that they had the power to influence corporations to a greater extent than ever before. The changing conditions in the business world were highlighted, and the consultants argued that corporations had to adjust to these changes by attending to social issues.

By using this type of argument, CSR was presented as a risk-minimizing strategy. If corporations did not implement CSR, and thus did not meet stakeholder demands, it would lead to damaged reputations and financial losses. It was put forward that CSR could be a strategy for recruiting the best employees and strengthening the corporate brand.

Initially the consultants found it difficult to find CSR work with corporations, partly, they believed because of a general lack of knowledge about corporate social responsibility and partly because of 'the dotcom crash' and the overall recession in the consulting market. However, by 2002/2003 the consultants claimed that things were slowly changing and that the demand for their services was increasing. Moreover, the market of CSR grew as the consultants succeeded in translating CSR into a management idea that addressed corporate problems – as an idea that would help corporations come to terms with new demands. Hence, the reason for corporations to address CSR was to deal with increasing pressures from corporate stakeholders. However, the consultants did not only mediate the demands advanced by other groups of actors, but also functioned as a pressure group that constructed these normative demands itself. By stressing the new pressures that were facing corporations and the need for them to increase their scope of social responsibility, they also reinforced this notion.

19.5 Discussion and Conclusions

Despite the proliferation of CSR, few attempts have been made to explain how and why the idea has spread as far as it has. Ideas of this kind, which become widespread in several settings, are regarded as superior, and as being worthwhile to imitate and adopt (cf. Czarniawska 2005). The new-institutional argument implies that ideas travel far and wide if they are universally applicable, and if they are translated in accordance with the dominating values in the local and institutional context (cf. Campbell 2004a; Czarniawska and Sevón 1996; Rövik 2002). In order to fit into different organizations, ideas must take various forms, and ideas need to be presented and packaged in a way that renders them crucial for organizational attention. The importance of rhetoric and discourse in mobilizing new ideas, innovations, or practices have been highlighted in several studies (e.g. Mueller et al. 2003; Zbaracki 1998). In other words, ideas need to be presented as simplistic and universal in order to flow and in order for the adopters to understand their relevance. In the corporate world, this means that ideas need to be presented as rational means in order to reach increased corporate profitability and success.

The consultants were – in comparison to academics – the group of professionals that most evidently drew corporate attention to CSR. They used rhetorical strategies – built on economic arguments – to translate CSR into solutions to problems related to the business world. These problems drew primarily on the ways that corporations could handle increasing demands from both stakeholders and shareholders, and how they could avoid negative publicity and an eroded brand as a consequence of not taking a social responsibility. The consultants highlighted the perspective that CSR was a business case and avoided moral arguments. In this sense CSR was presented as an idea that would help corporations to develop ethical and legitimate behaviour that was in accordance with the expectations of stakeholders and shareholders. Hence, the consultants strived to commercialise CSR in order to broaden their services into a new area of work. In this process they recognized the importance of building their arguments on economical logics.

The academic researchers are contrary to consultants not seeking to commercialize CSR. Rather they have other reasons for involving themselves in the CSR field. Researchers seek to develop new knowledge about corporate social responsibility in order to expand theories on corporate practices and business life. Their main audience is the research community rather than the practitioners; however, it is possible to argue that they have had a role in the proliferation of CSR both within and outside the academia. First, they have contributed to the proliferation within the academia by publishing an increasing number of articles on the topic – thereby drawing attention to CSR among researchers. Secondly, academics are perceived as experts valuable to practitioners. For this reason, they are hired as consultants or as lectures in order to inform practitioners on the topic. Because of the several interfaces between researchers and practitioners in the field of CSR they spread their own research results and knowledge about CSR to other actor groups.

In this chapter, the proliferation of CSR from two professionals' perspectives is described. Three observations have been made. *First*, CSR has constituted a new area of work for both consultants and academics – even though their motives for addressing CSR diverge. They have developed CSR in relation to their traditional area of work, thereby expanding their practices and area of work. The consultants expanded the area of consulting while the academics created a new field of research.

Secondly, it seems apt to argue that consultants and academics contribute to the proliferation of CSR because of their status as experts. Professionals possessing some kind of exclusive knowledge, play an important role in the organizational world by spreading legitimate management models for the appropriate organizational behaviour (c.f. DiMaggio, 1991). Academic researchers attribute the role as experts due to their perceived objectivity. They are understood as actors that develop scientific knowledge and thereby, their expertise in the area of CSR is valued as objective and trustworthy. Consultants, on the other hand, can be seen as experts because their ability to develop knowledge into practice. By converting the fluffy idea CSR into corporate actions they are believed to improve corporate performance.

Thirdly, consultants and academics have created attention around CSR – albeit through different means; academics by turning CSR into a new field of research and by engaging in dialog with practitioners, and consultants by emphasizing the economical incentives for addressing CSR. Thereby, they have presented CSR as management idea that leads to corporate progress.

In conclusion, consultants and academics have played a prominent role in the proliferation of CSR by drawing attention to CSR and thereby creating new opportunities for themselves as well as actors to get involved in CSR. It is possible to argue that professional groups such as consultants and academics can take on the role as institutional entrepreneurs by drawing attention to an idea and carrying it into new settings. However, they translate and interpret CSR differently and transport it for different reasons. The academic researchers want to contribute to new and objective knowledge in the area, whereas the consultants seek to sell new services and to change corporate practices. However, even though academic researchers emphasise the importance of their objective it can be noted that academic researchers from time to time take on the role as a consultants in order to contribute with their knowledge and have a greater impact on corporate behaviour.

Whereas this chapter has aimed to sketch the contour of the how two professional groups – academic researchers and consultants – have contributed to the proliferation of CSR further studies in the field are needed, in which key questions are: In what ways does professional expertise in the area of CSR changing the condition for, and the content of, corporate practices? And how is the expertise in the field of CSR influenced by an increased interface among academics and practitioners?

References

Brytting, T., & Egels, N. (2004). *Svensk företagsetiks forskning 1995–2001*. Göteborg: Bas.

Campbell, J. L. (2004). *Institutional Change and Globalization*. Princeton, NJ: Princeton University Press.

Campbell, J. L. (2004a). Problems of Institutional Analysis. In J. L. Campbell (Eds.), *Institutional Change and Globalization*. Princeton, NJ: Princeton University Press.

Carroll, A. B. (1979). A Three-Dimensional Conceptual Model of Corporate Social Performance. *Academy of Management Review 4*, 497–505.

Carroll, A. B. (1999). Corporate Social Responsibility: Evolution of a Definitional Construct. *Business & Society 38*(3), 268–295.

Cerne, A. (2003). *Integrating Corporate Social Responsibility with Marketing Strategies in Retailing*. Unpublished Licentiat Thesis, Lund University, Lund.

Chambers, E., Chapple, W., Moon, J., & Sullivan, M. (2003). *CSR in Asia: A Seven Country Study of CSR Website Reporting* (No. 09-2003). Nottingham: International Centre for Corporate Social Responsibility.

Czarniawska, B., & Joerges, B. (1996). Travels of Ideas. In B. Czarniawska & G. Sevón (Eds.), *Translating Organizational Change*. Berlin: Walter de Gruyter.

Czarniawska, B., & Sevón, G. (Eds.). (1996). *Translating Organizational Change*. Berlin: Walter de Gruyter.

Czarniawska, B. (2005). Fashion in Organizing. In B. Czarniawska & G. Sevón (Eds.), *Global Ideas. How Ideas, Objects and Practices Travel in the Global Economy*. Malmö: Liber & Copenhagen Business School Press.

De Bakker, F. G. A., Groenewegen, P., & Den Hond, F. (2005). A Bibliometric Analysis of 30 Years of Research and Theory on Corporate Social Responsibility and Corporate Social Performance. *Business & Society 44*(3), 283–317.

DiMaggio, P. J. (1988). Interest and Agency in Institutional Theory. In L. G. Zucker (Eds.), *Institutional Patterns and Organizations: Culture and Environment*. Cambridge, MA: Ballinger.

DiMaggio, P. J. (1991). Constructing an Organizational Field as Professional Projects: US Art Museums, 1920–1940. In W. W. Powell & P. J. DiMaggio (Eds.), *The New Institutionalism in Organizational Analysis*, Chicago, IL: University Chicago Press.

Engwall, L., & Kipping, M. (2003). *Management Consulting: Emergence and Dynamics of a Knowledge Industry*. Oxford: Oxford University Press.

Ernst, B., & Kieser, A. (2002). In the Search for Explanations for the Consultants Explosion. In K. Sahlin-Andersson & L. Engwall (Eds.), *The Expansion of Management Knowledge: Carriers, Flows and Sources*. Stanford, CA: Stanford University Press.

Friedland, R., & Alford, R. R. (1991). Bringing Society Back In: Symbols, Practices, and Institutional Contradictions. In P. J. DiMaggio & W. W. Powell (Eds.), *The New Institutionalism in Organizational Analysis* (pp. 232–266). Chicago, IL: The University of Chicago Press.

Fukukawa, K., & Moon, J. (2004). A Japanese Model of Corporate Social Responsibility? A Study of Website Reporting. *Journal of Corporate Citizenship 16*(Winter), 45–59.

Förtroendekommittén. (2004). *SOU 2004:47 Näringslivet och Förtroendet*. Finansdepartementet.

Galaskiewicz, J. (1991). Making Corporate Actors Accountable: Institution-Building in Minneapolis- St. Paul. In P. J. DiMaggio & W. W. Powell (Eds.), *The New Institutionalism in Organizational Analysis*. Chicago, IL: The University of Chicago Press.

Garriga, E., & Melé, D. (2004). Corporate Social Responsibility Theories: Mapping the Territory. *Journal of Business Ethics 53*, 51–71.

Globe Forum, (2008), Conditions for being nominated. Retrieved 11 September 2008. 11.www.gfbn.com/pages/conditions-to-be-nominated.

Göthberg, P. (2007). *Stabilitetens Dynamik – Skanidas Idéer för livet*. Uppsala: Uppsala University.

Hwang, H., & Powell, W. (2005). Institutions and Entrepreneurship. In S. Alvarez, R. Agrawal & O. Sorenson (Eds.), *Handbook of Entrepreneurial Research*: Dordrecht: Kluwer Publishers.

Institute of Management Humboldt University (2004). Call for Papers International Conference on Corporate Social Responsibility. (Vol. 2005).

Jonker, J. (2005). CSR Wonderland: Navigating Between Movement, Community and Organisation. *Journal of Corporate Citizenship 20*, 19–22

Klein, J. G., Smith, C. N., & John, A. (2004). Why We Boycott: Consumer Motivations for Boycott Participation. *Journal of Marketing 68*(3), 92–109.

Kotler, P., & Lee, N. (2005). *Corporate Social Responsibility: Doing the Most Good for Your Company and Your Cause*. Hoboken, NJ: John Wiley & Sons Inc.

Lawrence, T. B., & Phillips, N. (2004). From Moby Dick to Free Willy: Macro-Cultural Discourse and Institutional Entrepreneurship in Emerging Institutional Fields. *Organization 11*(5), 689–711.

Lawrence, T. B., & Suddaby, R. (2006). Institutions and Institutional Work. In S. R. Clegg, C. Hardy, T. B., Lawerence, & W. R. Nord (Eds.), *The Handbook of Organizational Studies*. London: Sage.

Leipziger, D. (2003). *The Corporate Responsibility Code Book*. Sheffield: Greenleaf.

Maignan, I., & Ferrell, O. C. (2004). Corporate Social Responsibility and Marketing: An Integrative Framework. *Journal of the Academy of Marketing Science 31*(1), 3–19.

Maignan, I., & Ralston, D. A. (2002). Corporate Social Responsibility in Europe and the U.S.: Insights form Businesses Self-presentations. *Journal of International Business Studies 33*(3), 497–514.

Margolis, J. D., & Walsh, J. P. (2003). Misery Loves Companies Rethinking Social Initiatives by Business. *Administrative Science Quarterly 48*, 268–305.

Matten, D., & Moon, J. (2004). *Implicit and Explicit CSR – A conceptual framework for understanding CSR in Europe* (No. 29-2004). Nottingham: International Centre on Corporate Social Responsibility.

Matten, D., & Moon, J. (2005). A Conceptual Framework for Understanding CSR.In A. Habisch, J. Jonker, M. Wegner & R. Schmidtpeter (Eds.), *Corporate Social Responsibility Across Europe*. Heidelberg: Springer Berlin.

Meyer, J. W. (1996). Otherhood: The Promulgation and Transmission of Ideas in the Modern Organizational Environment. In B. Czarniawska & G. Sevón (Eds.), *Translating Organizational Change* (pp. 241–252). Berlin: Walter de Gruyter & CO.

Micheletti, M., & Stolle, D. (2004). *Swedish Political Consumers: who they are and why they use the market as an arena for politics*. Paper presented at the Political Consumerism: Its motivations, power, and conditions in the Nordic countries and elsewhere, Oslo.

Mueller, F., Sillince, J., Harvey, C., & Howorth, C. (2003). "A Rounded Picture is What We Need": Rhetorical Strategies, Arguments, and the Negotiation of Change in a UK Hospital Trust. *Organization Studies 25*(1), 75–93.

Porter, M. E., & Kramer, M. R. (2006). "The Link between Competitive advantage and corporate social responsibility". *Harvard Business Review, Strategy & Society*. December, 78–92.

Rövik, K.-A. (1996). Deinstiuttionalization and the Logic of Fashion. In B. Czarniawska & G. Sevón (Eds.), *Translating Organizational Change*. Berlin: Walter de Gruyter & CO.

Rövik, K.-A. (2002). The Secrets of the Winners: Management Ideas that Flow. In K. Sahlin-Andersson & L. Engwall (Eds.), *The Expansion of Management Knowledge: Carriers, Flows and Sources*. Stanford: Stanford University Press.

Sahlin-Andersson, K. (1996). Imitating by Editing Success: The Construction of Organizational Fields. In B. Czarniawska & G. Sevón (Eds.), *Translating Organizational Change*. Berlin: Walter de Gruyter & CO.

Sahlin-Andersson, K., & Engwall, L. (2002a). Carriers, Flows, and Sources of Management Knowledge. In K. Sahlin-Andersson & L. Engwall (Eds.), *The Expansion of Management Knowledge: Carriers, Flows and Sources*. Stanford, CA: Stanford University Press.

Sahlin-Andersson, K., & Engwall, L. (2002b). The Dynamics of Management Knowledge Expansion. In K. Sahlin-Andersson & L. Engwall (Eds.), *The Expansion of Management Knowledge: Carriers, Flows and Sources*. Stanford, CA: Stanford University Press.

Sahlin-Andersson, K., & Engwall, L. (Eds.). (2002c). *The Expansion of Management Knowledge: Carriers, Flows and Sources*. Stanford, CA: Stanford University Press.

Schnietz, K. E., & Epstein, M. J. (2005). Exploring the Financial Value of a Reputation for Corporate Social Responsibility During a Crisis. *Corporate Reputation Review 7*(4), 327–345.

Sen, S., & Bhattacharya, C. B. (2001). Does Doing Good always Lead to Doing Better? Consumer Reaction to Corporate Social Responsibility. *Journal of Marketing Research XXXVIII*, 225–243, May.

Waddock, S. A. (2004). Creating Corporate Accountability: Foundational Principles to Make Corporate Citizenship Real. *Journal of Business Ethics 50*, 313–327.

Waddock, S. A., Bodwell, C., & Graves, S. B. (2002). Responsibility: The New Business Imperative. *Academy of Management Executive 16*, 132–148.

Waddock, S. A., & Graves, S. B. (1997). The Corporate Social Performance-Financial Performance Link. *Strategic Management Journal 18*, 303–319

Windell, K. (2006), *Corporate Social Responsibility Under Construction: Ideas, Translations and Institutional Change*. Doctoral Dissertation, Department of Business Studies, Uppsala University: Uppsala

Zadek, S. (1998). Balancing Performance, Ethics, and Accountability. *Journal of Business Ethics 17*, 1421–1441.

Zadek, S. (2004). The Path to Corporate Responsibility. *Harvard Business Review 82*, 125–132.

Zbaracki, M. J. (1998). The Rhetoric and Reality of Total Quality Management. *Administrative Science Quarterly 43*, 602–636.

Chapter 20
An Analysis of the Competence of Business School Teachers to Promote Sustainable Development in Finland

Liisa Rohweder and Anne Virtanen

> *Problems cannot be solved at the same level of awareness that created them*
>
> Albert Einstein

Abstract During the past few years, the role of business in the process of promoting sustainable development (SD) has been discussed considerably, because in order to create a sustainable world, the decisions made in corporations play an important role. Due to the evident signs of climate change during the past few years, the responsibility of businesses has risen to a totally new level. As corporations' innovative, the tendency for them to search for responsible solutions which can have a huge direct positive effect in fighting climate change increases. Business schools are central players in this process as most business students eventually end up taking executive positions in the private sector once they have graduated. From this perspective, business school teachers certainly have a key role in the process of bringing about awareness of sustainable development issues by these future managers. It is extremely important for business school teachers to understand their students' attitudes, knowledge and competence level in all sustainable development related issues. The aim of our study was to analyse business school teachers' level of knowledge, attitudes and educational practices for issues relating to sustainable development. The target group of the study was business teachers at Finnish universities of applied sciences. The study notes that, Finnish business school teachers are knowledgeable about issues relating to sustainable development. However, these teachers stress that more competence is needed in order to connect the knowledge of sustainable development toward making a choice of pedagogical and didactical methods. According to the research findings, there is a great potential to enhance the promotion of sustainable development in business life through educating professionals who have the ability to raise awareness as well as to implement the principles of sustainable development in practice. Business school teachers' level of knowledge

L. Rohweder (✉)
Haaga-Helia University of Applied Science, Helsinki, Finland

S.O. Idowu, W.L. Filho (eds.), *Professionals' Perspectives of Corporate Social Responsibility*, DOI 10.1007/978-3-642-02630-0_21,
© Springer-Verlag Berlin Heidelberg 2009

is good and their attitude is positive for sustainable development, but they lack the pedagogical tools they require to make change happen.

20.1 Introduction

Sustainable development can be seen as one of the fundamentals of any society, and failings in this respect can lead to costly consequences both in nature and human terms. During the past few years, the role of business in sustainable development has been widely discussed in the process for creating a sustainable world as the decisions made in corporations definitely play an important role. Recently, more and more corporations have also realised their role and they underline their commitment to the concept of corporate social responsibility (CSR), which can be defined as sustainable development on the organisational level. Since actors in business life have leading roles in sustainable development, their commitment to sustainability plays a key role in the whole process. Depending on the goals and methods employed, corporations can have significant impacts on the state of the natural environment as well as on the societal structures and equity in the whole world. Although the pro-activity in business life towards sustainable development is increasing, it is still relevant to ask how to run business in economically, ecologically, socially and culturally sustainable ways? Business schools are central players in this process as most business students go on to work in the private sector once they have graduated. However, the role of business schools in this respect has only recently become an issue raised in discussion (Rohweder, 2007, p. 78). From this perspective, business school teachers definitely have a key role in the process for sustainable development, and thus it is of high importance to understand their attitudes, knowledge and competence levels in sustainable development related issues and how they see their connection to CSR.

At the moment, education related to sustainable development and CSR in business schools is based on traditional economic and business life thinking (Springett, 2005, p. 148). According to Springett's research findings, business school teachers subscribe to the prevailing paradigm accepted by business life (Springett, 2005, p. 148). That is to say that according to the majority of business school teachers, ecological and social aspects of sustainable development are taken into consideration within the boundaries of what is economically rationale.

Nevertheless, the advocates for critical management theory have stressed a more value-based interpretation of sustainable development for over twenty years (see Rohweder, 2007, p. 75). In the value-based approach to sustainable development, the ecological, socio-cultural and economic pillars of sustainable development are integrated in accordance with what is considered to be just and good. In other words, business life should be founded on a completely new set of values. This change, however, will not be possible without a paradigm shift in the values and attitudes that are currently prevailing in organisational thinking.

In order to make a change happen in higher education, policy guidelines are also needed. Sustainable development has become an important issue on international, regional and national agendas concerning education policy. This is also the case in Finland, where in 2006 the Ministry of Education launched an education strategy for sustainable development, which now serves as Finland's national action plan for the United Nations Decade of Education for Sustainable Development (UN DESD).

Based on the challenges launched by the Finnish Ministry of Education and on the above reasoning of the need for change in business life, a research project was initiated to study the knowledge, competence, attitudes and practices for sustainable development among business school teachers in Finland. The research findings give valuable information for developing education for sustainable development further as the research provided knowledge of what kind of support and tools business school teachers need in order to integrate the niche of sustainable development into their teaching.

This article starts with the description of the Finnish strategy on education for sustainable development, which served as the framework for the research. Thereafter, the research process and the results of the empirical research are described. At the end, conclusions based on the outcome of the research are outlined.

20.2 Finnish Strategy on Education for Sustainable Development

In Finland, the committee on education for sustainable development set up by the Ministry of Education wrote a launching plan for the Finnish Baltic 21E Programme in 2002, and an action plan for the education sector was put together in 2006. These documents were used as starting points for the national strategy for the UN Decade of Education for Sustainable Development (DESD). The Finnish DESD policy comprises the following elements (Sustainable development in education..., 2006):

(1) The promotion of SD (including sustainable consumption and production) in education at all levels
(2) Institutional commitment at policy, steering and practical levels
(3) Ethical and integrated approach: All activities address the ecological, economic, social and cultural considerations as mutually supporting dimensions
(4) Integration: The SD outlook is included in all activities
(5) Staff development training
(6) Interdisciplinary
(7) Dissemination of information
(8) Increased networking and other cooperation
(9) Participation: empowerment of citizens
(10) Research, postgraduate and continuing education programmes
(11) The utilization of innovation.

In order to enhance the targets set by the UN and Baltic 21E programme, the Finnish Ministry of Education launched a national strategy for the UN Decade of Education for Sustainable Development as the first national DESD strategy in the whole of Europe (Sustainable development in education..., 2006). Additionally, the University Charter for Sustainable Development, the so-called Copernicus Charter, is one of the backbones of the strategy. In the Copernicus Charter over 200 European universities commit themselves to enhance SD, for example, by promoting sustainable consumer behaviour and ecological responsibility.

From the higher education perspective, the Finnish National Strategy for the UN Decade of Education for Sustainable Development states that higher education institutions should include the niche of sustainable development into value statements as well as into the vision and strategy – and operate accordingly. In other words, the idea of sustainable development should be integrated both into management systems and into curriculum and research and development work. The general aim is to empower sustainability in the society around the educational institution. Figure 20.1 illustrates the main components of the Finnish national strategy for sustainable development in higher education institutions.

Integrating the niche of sustainable development into the curriculum plays a central role in the strategy. According to the strategy, one aim of higher education is that all individuals can contribute to the process of sustainable development, which satisfies the needs of today's populations without jeopardizing the possibilities of

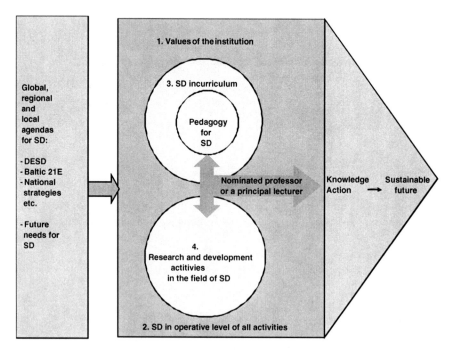

Fig. 20.1 Sustainable development in higher education institutions according to the Finnish national strategy of education (Rohweder, 2008, p. 15)

future generations to satisfy theirs. The promotion of ESD should be founded on a holistic view of development, which addresses the ecological, economic, social and cultural dimensions. It also stresses the importance of values, global ethics and the problems underlying in intra- and inter-generality. In order to achieve the afore-mentioned aims, sustainable development should be integrated as part of all courses in the curriculum. Furthermore, specific sustainable development related courses should be offered. Such courses in business education focus, for example, on CSR.

20.3 Research Objectives, Material and Methods

The aim of the research was to collect information about business school teachers' level of knowledge, attitudes and practices of education for sustainable development (ESD). The method of the research was quantitative as it was the only possibility to effectively reach all business school teachers in Finland. The research material was collected by a questionnaire that contained open claims about the themes that were central from the perspective of the Finnish National Strategy for the UN Decade of Education for Sustainable Development. The questionnaire covered the following themes:

(1) Knowledge about sustainable development in general and in the business field
(2) Attitudes towards sustainable development
(3) Teaching practices for sustainable development
(4) Development needs to promote sustainable development in business education.

The target group of the research was business teachers (lecturers and principal lecturers) at Finnish universities of applied sciences. The questionnaire was sent to all of them through an e-mail message in autumn 2006. Before sending the question-naire, it was tested by 5 higher education teachers. In order to get a comprehensive sample, all rectors of the universities of applied sciences encouraged their teachers to answer to the questionnaire by sending an e-mail to their staff.

In total, 194 lecturers from the business sector took part in the research. Concerning the respondents, 71% were male, and 29% were female. Most of the respondents belonged to the age category 40–49 years (43%). The age category 20–39 years was represented by 18 and 34% by the category 50–59 years. Five per cent of the respondents were over 60 years. The empirical data was analysed statistically, which means that distributions by background information, such as age were carried out. In addition, the necessary crosstabulations were performed.

20.4 Research Results

The research results are categorised as follows:

– Business school teachers' knowledge about sustainable development,

– Implementation of sustainable development in business education,
– Business school teachers' attitudes towards sustainable development,
– Necessary development activities in order to implement the Finnish strategy of
  education for sustainable development into practice.

20.5 Business Teachers' Knowledge About Sustainable Development

Business school teachers' level of knowledge about sustainable development in
general and from the CSR perspective is important when integrating sustainable
development into business school curricula. Fifty-seven per cent of the teachers in
the business field assume that sustainable development means, above all, taking care
of the environment, and 60% feel that sustainable development is a difficult issue
to understand in a coherent way. Most of the respondents think that sustainable
development is a viewpoint to see and understand different kinds of things; it is a
worldview (Fig. 20.2).

Over half of the business teachers think that they know the meaning of the
ecological, social, cultural, and economic dimensions of sustainability in business
studies. The competence to teach economic sustainability is on a slightly higher
level compared to the other dimensions. The contents of cultural and social aspects

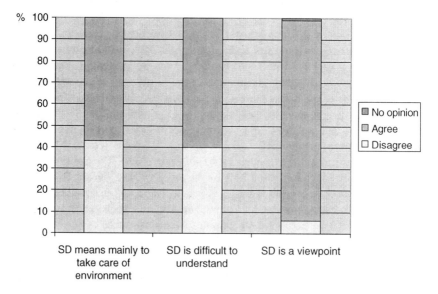

Fig. 20.2 Business teachers' opinions about sustainable development

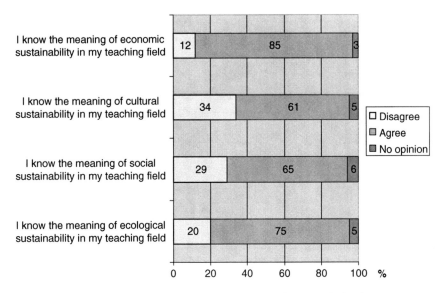

Fig. 20.3 Business teachers' opinions about the dimensions of sustainable development

are less known. Only two-thirds are aware of the meaning of these dimensions in the business field (Fig. 20.3).

20.6 Business Teachers' Attitudes Towards Sustainable Development

Attitudes towards education for sustainable development seem to be very positive among business teachers. Almost all of the respondents (94%) agree with the statement that sustainable development should be included in business studies. In addition, almost everyone (97%) feels that sustainable development is an important issue (Fig. 20.4). In other words, generally the motivation towards sustainable development, and also to teach it, is very positive among the business educators. In short, there is strong potential to enhance the role of sustainable development in business education in Finnish universities of applied sciences.

In addition to knowledge, dealing with attitudes and values are important when constructing a competence base for sustainability. Value clarification is understood as one part of higher education among teachers in the business sector, as almost all respondents agree with the statement concerning the importance of value clarification in higher education. Almost everyone agrees that although sustainable development is value-laden, it should be included in teaching in the business field (Fig. 20.5).

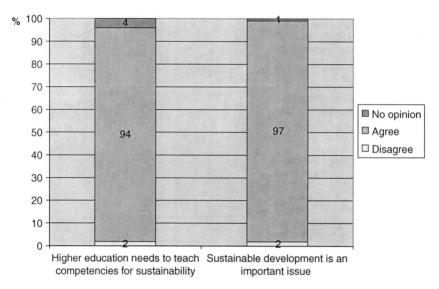

Fig. 20.4 Business teachers' attitudes towards sustainable development

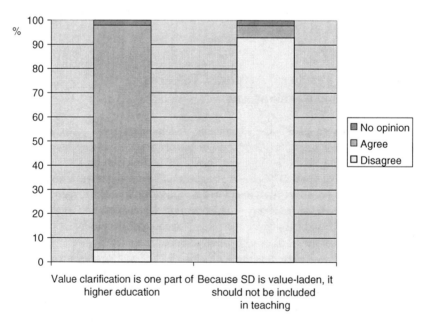

Fig. 20.5 Business teachers' attitudes towards education for sustainable development

20.7 Business Teachers' Educational Practices for Sustainable Development

Most of the respondents perceive that one aim of the curriculum is to take sustainable development into account as integrated with regard to field-specific themes. Nonetheless, 41% of the business educators perceive that sustainable development is lectured in specific study courses on sustainable development (Fig. 20.6). One explanation for these results is that integrating the niche of sustainable development is one aim of the whole curriculum. In addition, specific courses of sustainable development, such as CSR or environmental management systems, are taught in business education. At the moment, the integration of sustainable development into education is realized not only in the curriculum, but also in practice, because 59% of business educators integrate sustainable development related issues in specific study courses (Fig. 20.6).

Economic sustainability is the most commonly treated dimension of sustainable development in business education. As much as 69% of the respondents deal with the issues of economic sustainability in their teaching (Fig. 20.7). Likewise, the dimensions of ecological and social sustainable development are rather commonly discussed issues; 58% of the respondents cover them in their teaching. Cultural sustainability is the least treated dimension in business education, although almost half of the respondents (48%) still deal with cultural sustainability issues in their teaching (Fig. 20.7).

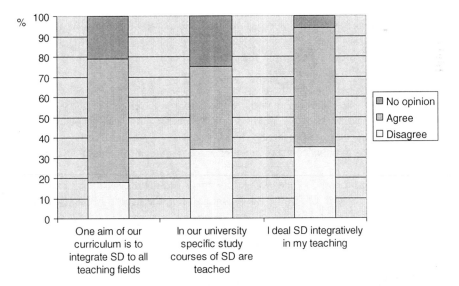

Fig. 20.6 Business teachers' practices for sustainable development

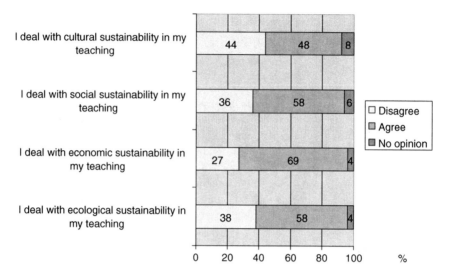

Fig. 20.7 Business teachers' practices to handle the dimensions of sustainable development

20.8 Development Needs to Promote Sustainable Development in Business Education

According to the results, the need to develop educational material of sustainable development exists; yet 53% of business teachers feel that it is difficult to integrate sustainable development into their own teaching field. Only 39% of business teachers agree with the statement that it is possible to get enough relevant knowledge concerning sustainable development issues, and 51% feel that there is not enough teaching and learning material on sustainable development (Fig. 20.8). In conclusion, it can be said that field specific teaching and learning material concerning sustainable development should be produced. In addition, pedagogical and didactic methods to enhance the competences for sustainability among students are needed.

Almost all of the respondents (95%) think that sustainable development will have a growing role in work life in the future. In addition, the need for experts to work in accordance with the principles of sustainable development is growing, according to the respondents. Ten per cent of business teachers feel that the need for sustainable development experts will decrease in the future, while 73% disagree with the statement (Fig. 20.9). One explanation for the decreasing need of experts of sustainable development is that sustainable development should be integrated into business education as such and everyone, not only experts of sustainable development, should acquire the principles of sustainability.

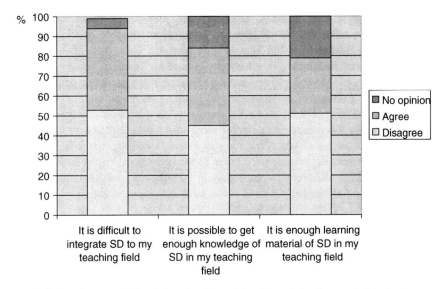

Fig. 20.8 Development needs of educational material and knowledge for sustainable development

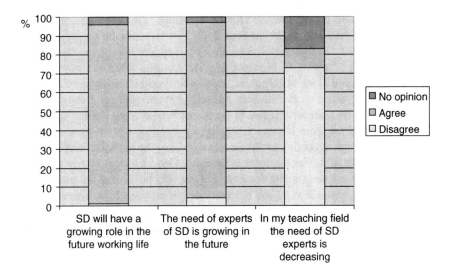

Fig. 20.9 Business teachers' opinions about the role of sustainable development in the future

20.9 Conclusions

The conducted research gave fruitful knowledge about the possibilities and challenges to integrate the niche of sustainability into business education. According to the research results, business teachers have knowledge about sustainable development. In other words, teachers are aware of sustainable development, in particular, at a general level but also in their teaching field. Nevertheless, more competence about sustainable development is needed. Teachers stress that more competence is needed in order to connect the knowledge of sustainable development toward making a choice of pedagogical and teaching methods, and, in particular, for everyday teaching. For instance, the questions concerning cultural and social sustainability are the issues that demand more discussion and new competences among business teachers. According to other research results, it is a fact that the definition of sustainable development given in the Brundtland report is not easy to operationalise. Difficulties appear, especially in the integration of the environmental, socio-cultural and economic pillars of sustainable development (see e.g., Lindroos and Cantell, 2007, p. 90).

The research was conducted in 2006, which is the same year when the World Bank expert team led by Sir Nicholas Stern published a highly regarded report on climate change (Stern, 2006). According to Stern's report, the evidence shows that ignoring climate change will eventually damage economic growth. In case actions are not implemented in the upcoming decades, there will be risks of major disruption to economic and social activities later in this century and the next, on a scale similar to those associated with the economic depression of the first half of the ****20th century (Stern, 2006). Hence, Stern explained one of the key sustainable development related issues, climate change, by using "the language" of business representatives. Ever since, there has been lively discussion in the media about corporate responsibility in fighting climate change. Business school teachers closely follow the trends going on in business life. At the time when the questionnaire was sent, the discussion about corporate responsibility had already started. This fact might have had an effect on the teachers' attitudes. On the other hand, the discussion about the role of the economic sector in the question of climate change has continued ever since. Thus, there is great potential to enhance the promotion of CSR in business life through educating professionals who have the ability to implement the principles of sustainable development in practice. One important reason for this is that attitudes towards sustainable development are very positive at the moment and also the knowledge base is at a good level among business teachers. This is a significant result, because in general value clarification is defined as one critical element of education for sustainable development (Tilbury and Ross, 2006).

References

Lindroos, P. and Cantell, M., 2007. Education for Sustainable Development in a Global Perspective. In: Kaivola, T. and Melén-Paaso, M. (eds.), Education for Global Responsibility – Finnish Perspectives, 85–96. Publications of the Ministry of Education 2007: 31. Helsinki University Press, Helsinki.

Rohweder, L., 2007. Education for Sustainable Development in Business Schools. In: Kaivola, T. and Rohweder, L. (eds.), Towards Sustainable Development in Higher Education – Reflections, 74–80. Publications of the Ministry of Education 2007:6. Helsinki University Press, Helsinki.

Rohweder, L., 2008. Strategies and Concepts of Education for Sustainable Development. In: Rohweder, L. and Virtanen, A. (eds.), Learning for a Sustainable Future. Innovative Solutions from the Baltic Sea Region, 11–16. The Baltic University Press, Uppsala.

Springett, D., 2005. Education for Sustainability in the Business Studies Curriculum. A Call for a Critical Agenda. Business Strategy and the Environment 14:3, 146–159.

Stern, N., 2006. http://www.hm-treasury.gov.uk/independent_reviews/stern_review_economics_climate_change/stern_review_report.cfm (20 November 2008).

Sustainable Development in Education; Implementing of Baltic 21E Programme and Finnish strategy for the Decade of Education for Sustainable Development (2005–2014), 2006. Reports of the Ministry of Education, Finland, 2006: 6. http://www.minedu.fi/julkaisut/index.html (21 October 2007).

Tilbury, D. and Ross, K., 2006. Living Change: Documenting Good Practice in Education for Sustainability in NSW. Madquarie University, Sydney & Nature Conservation Council, NSW.

Chapter 21
Corporate Social Responsibility and Human Resource Management: A Strategic-Balanced Model

Ananda Das Gupta

Value-based management is a good recipe for long-term success of a corporate. Living on principles and values is a must for every corporate manager.

M. B. ARhreya

Abstract Corporate social responsibility (CSR) and responsible capitalism pose a number of challenges for HRM and leadership in organisations. The HRM paradigm is based on a rational strategic management framework which is consistent with traditional economic analysis. This paradigm is limited in circumstances where organisations seek to behave responsibly with regard to a range of internal and external stakeholders and seek to take a longer term perspective when dealing with issues relating to CSR.

Corporate sustainability and corporate governance collectively are shaping organisational identities and are therefore increasingly integrated into the business strategy of successful corporations. Consequently, the field of responsible business strategy and practice is becoming one of the most dynamic and challenging subjects corporate leaders are facing today and possibly one of the most important ones which need to be addressed in shaping the future of our world.

21.1 Introduction

During the last 20 years human resource management (HRM) has become a common way of managing people. Such an approach involves Human Resource professionals partnering with other managers so that people are used in the most effective way. More recently there have been calls for HRM to demonstrate that it adds value to the business.

A. Das Gupta (✉)
Indian Institute of Plantation Management, Bangalore, India

S.O. Idowu, W.L. Filho (eds.), *Professionals' Perspectives of Corporate Social Responsibility*, DOI 10.1007/978-3-642-02630-0_22,
© Springer-Verlag Berlin Heidelberg 2009

Corporate social responsibility and responsible capitalism pose a number of challenges for HRM and for leadership in organisations. The HRM paradigm is based on a rational strategic management framework which is consistent with traditional economic analysis. This paradigm is limited in circumstances where organisations seek to behave responsibly with regard to a range of internal and external stakeholders and seek to take a longer term perspective.

One of the dimensions of corporate citizenship is an ethical work climate that includes values, traditions, and pressures exerted in the work environment to make legal and ethical decisions. An ethical climate involves formal values and compliance requirements as well as an understanding of how interpersonal relationships affect the informal interpretation of ethics.

There has been a long history of philosophical debate as to the complex nature of values/ethics as well as the validity of business or its purpose in society. Therefore it is often argued that one should find a way to lead one's business-life in harmony with one's inner life. Thus with this 'connectivity' between the subjective and objective perspectives, business is not to be regarded as something evil, unethical or tainted. Business should be considered to be sacred, depending upon the spirit in which it is set up and carried out. All is a matter of attitude and approach, which is based on three major attributes: (1) Formulating attitude of business (2) Humanization of and (3) Interiorization of management.

It becomes imperative, therefore that the fresh thinking is done so as to underline the role of Man in contrast to mere emphasis on the wage earner. Technology makes things possible but it is Man who makes it happen. Man is an integrated creature of the Divine Craftsman.

Understanding the nature of human values may be so intimately associated with what might otherwise be considered to be distinct concepts that they cannot be effectively separated from some perspectives:

(a) Economic value: The concept of the value of a thing is central to traditional economic value theory for which value is the so-called exchange or market value of a commodity. Economists distinguish between value in this sense and the value of individuals or societies, which in welfare economics mean much the same as preferences or tastes. Such values may then be realized by the appropriate allocation of resources.

(b) Value assessments and imputations: Value assessments are assertions to the effect that some action taken, will or would favourably affect the life of someone. Value imputations are assertions to the effect that someone or some group has, holds, or subscribes to some value (e.g. achievement, work, altruism, comfort, equality, thrift, friendship), or that some such thing is one of his values. The word value then means different things in these two contexts. Assessed values then become measures of the capacities of various kinds of entities, including persons, to confer benefits, whereas imputed values are measures of tendencies of persons to promote certain ends, for certain reasons.

(c) Instrumental and intrinsic values: A distinction may also be made between instrumental values, which are the means to something else, and intrinsic values, which are those desired for themselves (such as goodness, truth, and beauty).

(d) Attitudes and opinions: Many surveys of the 'values' held by people do not find it useful to distinguish between attitudes or opinions held by people and the values that they hold. A survey of values then becomes a survey of attitudes and opinions. Presumably some attitudes may be considered as relating to values, but the distinction is then difficult to establish in that context. It is difficult to identify 'values' from such survey data.

Human development can be seen as the process of giving more effective expression to human values. Many of the advocated approaches to human development are quite explicit concerning the values in terms of which they are conceived or which they are desired to enhance. The more sophisticated approaches to policy-making and management are quite deliberate in their efforts to identify the values on which any action is to be grounded.

21.2 The Attitude to Life

The attitude to life has become as immature as that to death. Millions of dollars are spent on efforts to maintain youthfulness, whether through cosmetics, cosmetic surgery or attempts to reverse the ageing process. Every other value is sacrificed to save lives in industrialized societies, whilst allowing others to die elsewhere. Individuals in industrialized societies are prosecuted for life-endangering neglect. But these same societies fail to apply the same standards in their policies towards other societies. Reproduction is tacitly encouraged without any provision for the resulting population growth or for the effects on the environment. Society evokes problems to provide solutions for its own irresponsibility – a control mechanism for the immature lacking the insight for a healthy relationship to cycles.

The challenge of the times would seem to involve a call for personal transformation through which social and conceptual frameworks can be viewed anew. Willingness to sacrifice inherited perspectives is an indication of the dimension of the challenge-most dramatically illustrated by willingness to risk death. However physical death is not the issue, and may easily be a simplistic, deluded impulse lending itself to manipulation. Destruction of frameworks valued by others is equally suspect. Such dramatics provide rewards within the very frameworks whose nature the individual needs to question, but by which he or she may need to choose to be constrained.

Values are deeply held beliefs, the fundamental building blocks of a workplace culture reflecting a view about 'what is good.' In a law firm, they can include integrity, superior performance, putting the client first, making a big profit, and so forth, but it is important to note that there is no real right or wrong in values.

There are two visions of the new approach of management: First is a new vision of business based on an evolutionary spiritual humanism. Second is the possibility of business becoming an experimental workshop for a creative synthesis of ethics and management? This second possibility, if it becomes a reality, can provide the insights, learning, experience and the capabilities for a creative synthesis of East and West in Business.

21.3 Trend Setting

To succeed in today's competitive market requires a high professional competence as well as a continual improvement of that competence. Equally important is co-operation among professionals, often of a great variety. Success also requires communication and co-operation with customers and with the community. Communication and co-operation require social and cultural competence. Cultural competence is shared knowledge and hence communal knowledge. Cultural or communal knowledge bridge the gap between individuals and between professions.

The whole set of values needed for management can be summed up in the words of dharma is the code of right conduct. In these days when corporate governance is emerging as a significant factor, we find that Indian management can emerge successfully in the market place if it is able to draw on its route for good corporate governance, which is available in our culture and tradition. But then the question may arise, how many of us are aware of scriptures, Upanishads, culture and so on. Though one may not be consciously aware, one learns about basic principles from childhood, from parents and from religion.

Spiritual identity of the character is essential for the buildup of a new paradigm characterizing integrity, truthfulness, caring, compassion, honesty and supportive attitude.

21.4 Degree of Interest

There is a private or personal interest. Often this is a financial interest, but it could also be another sort of interest, say, to provide a special advantage to a spouse or child. Taken by themselves, there is nothing wrong with pursuing private or personal interests; for instance, changing jobs for more pay or helping your daughter improve her golf stroke.

Secondly, the problem comes when this private interest comes into conflict with the second feature of the definition, an 'official duty' quite literally the duty you have because you have an office or act in an official capacity. As a professional you take on certain official responsibilities, by which you acquire obligations to clients, employers, or others. These obligations are supposed to trump private or personal interests.

Third, conflicts of interest interfere with professional responsibilities in a specific way, namely, by interfering with objective professional judgment. A major reason why clients and employers value professionals is that, they expect professionals to be objective and independent. Factors, like private and personal interests, that either interfere or appear likely to interfere with objectivity are then a matter of legitimate concern to those who rely on professionals – be they clients, employers, professional colleagues, or the general public. So it is also important to avoid apparent and potential as well as actual conflicts of interest. An apparent conflict of interest is one, which a reasonable person would think that the professional judgment is likely to be compromised. A potential conflict of interest involves a situation that may develop into an actual conflict of interest.

21.5 Human Factor

The human Resource (HR) function has gradually shifted its focus, from a narrow maintenance reactive role, to a much wider canvas, integrating HR strategy with corporate strategy empowering employees, restructuring the organization and so on.

The creative contributions (Hofstede, 1973) in a globally cooperative situation, would encompass the range of sub-systems from planning the numbers, types and skills of HR, ensuring their availability, placing in the right job, promoting and nurturing their mental health and helping them develop their special talents and skills.

In this process, new investments are needed to ignite knowledge movement in the country. We must invest in training, re-training and continuous learning immediately, observed Ganguly (1998), otherwise, we will be left behind. This massive investment is focused on re-profiting through on-job training continuous learning of the skills and competencies of managers and employees.

More recently, learning organizations (Senge, 1990) and team–building concept have emerged to serve as the basis for competitive advantage and for motivating employee for their commitment and contribution, necessary for organizational excellence in fast changing business scenario. Many large organizations are undertaking major restructuring to achieve a better 'fit' and sensitivity to external demands (Genus, 1998). A 'new' model of organization has emerged and knowledge about organizational design as a response to environmental challenges has got further refined in the 1990s. Some of the key features of this new model of the organization are that they are networked, flat, flexible and global. Table 21.1 summarizes the shift that has occurred of organizations and which led to the emergence of HRM in response to the demands and exigencies of the new organization.

Table 21.1 A comparative model

Old model	New model
Individual position/job as basic unit of organization	Team as a basic unit
Relations with environment handled by specialists	Densely networked with environment
Vertical flows of information	Horizontal and vertical flows of information
Tall (many layers of management)	Flat (few layers of management)
Emphasis on structures	Emphasis on process
Career paths upwards/linear	Career paths flexile/lateral
Standardized evaluation and reward systems	Customized evaluation and reward system
Ethnocentric	International
Single strong culture with strong expectations of behaviour	Diversity of viewpoints and behaviour

21.6 The Changes

Conventional personnel management appears to be a part of an old model of organization or of a more mechanistic organization, which is more bureaucratic in nature having lesser flexibility higher amount of centralization and high formalization level i.e. adherence to rules and regulation. Human Resource Management (HRM) on the other hand, is compatible with the new model of organization and has emerged to align with the organic design of the organizations, having cross-functional and cross-hierarchical teams, decentralized and flexible with low formalization level and a wider span of control. Interestingly, Guest (1987) has drawn a beautiful line between personnel management and HRM (Table 21.2).

Table 21.2 Stereo types of personnel management and HRM

Dimensions	Personnel management	HRM
Time and planning perspective	Short-term, adhoc	Long-term, pro-active
Psychological contract	Compliance	Commitment
Control systems	External control	Self-control
Employee-relations perspective	Pluralist, collective low-trust	Individual, developed
Preferred structures/systems	Bureaucratic	Organic developed
Roles	Formal, defined roles	Flexible roles
Evaluation – criteria	Cost – minimization	Maximum utilization (human asset accounting)

With all these new changes taking place in the realm of HR, we need to develop a 'Strong' work culture within the organization to provide a wider base for a holistic development.

21.7 Work Culture Manifestation

Based on the principles of management theory, the four factors are identified here to develop work culture in an organization:

Vision: Vision in not a mere long-term objective but a company's perspective. It indicates the legacy it would like to pass on to its succeeding generation of leaders; it is a statement which inspires its employees with a dream, goal and generates pride in them. They key question the organization should ask itself is: *What do we want to be known for?*

Basically, it has two key dimensions:

- To try and prove that an organization, when deeply committed to be values, is best equipped to lead society to a better life.
- To strengthen organization's base through the effective utilization of men and materials.

Mission: While a vision denotes one a broad general picture, a mission hones it to focus and concentrate on a particular area.

Values: According to ethical concepts applied in management, values indicate the relationship one has with others. The suggestion in the Upanishads, saha nau bhunaktu (let us all share together), implies co-operation, harmonization, combined benefits for oneself, collaborators and society, trust, and a pro-active desire for others' success.

Strategy: There are two aspects of strategy; internal and external. Internal strategy should involve employees by generating a feeling of ownership and belongingness towards the organization which naturally generates quality and excellence; Along with, innovation and growth are essential factors and must be sustained by focusing on the *sukshma* aspect (Micro –aspect, for that matter). Continuous growth can be achieved by each units and person trying to beat their previous performance. Growth does not only mean profit and turnover, but mainly a transformation Swami (1996).

Now obviously, the question arises: How to implement the four key factors, namely Vision, Mission, Values and Strategy, conductive to the enhancement of Work-Culture Development in an organization?

The techniques which is basically holistic in nature have a SEWA (Self-mastery, Empathy for workers, Worker directedness and Achievement in performance) approach in its application, is called Action By Objective (ABO) (Das Gupta, 1995) that is discussed here to provide a broad-based understanding of an 'enlightened' organization having developed the Work-Culture within the organizational milieu fully well.

We can still recollect the comments made by Warren Anderson, chairman of Union Carbide, soon after the Bhopal gas tragedy of December 2, 1984, where 6000 perished and other 200,000 injured. He said he would spend the rest of his life attempting to correct the sufferings his company had caused and trying to make amends 1 year later he reversed his earlier 'emotional reaction' saying that he had 'overreacted' and was now prepared to lead the company in its legal battle against paying damages and representations.

21.8 The Ethical Underlines

This unethical culture is part of the tenets of free market capitalism which spread its tentacles all over the world in search of cheap extraction and labour, lucrative markets and eternal financial growth. This new economics in search of never-ending growth is far removed from the ethical concerns expressed throughout history by key economic thinkers, from Adam Smith to Karl Marx and Jon Maynard Keynes. An economics devoid of equity, ecology and ethics is a most dangerous academic myth. It is important to remember that the author of Theory of Moral Sentiments. For both Adam Smith and Marx, the foundation of economic thinking was based on more fundamental ethical questions and deep-rooted humanism.

This ethical underpinning of economics is what is lacking in the increasingly mechanical and mathematical theorisation of monetarism and neo-liberal theories of 'growth' measured in terms of GDP and 'competitiveness' but never in terms of the ecological and social costs of that 'growth'. The bandwagon of sustainable 'economic growth' is based on the myth that there can be eternal growth if we leave everything in the 'invisible' hands of the market'. However, such and assumption fails to acknowledge that the economy is an 'open subsystem, which is finite, no-growing and materially closed'. Unless we consider the depletion of natural resources, the cost of pollution, human rights violation informal work in households particularly by women, social tension and a growing sense of physical and emotional insecurity, the present parameters of economic growth can be dangerously misleading. An economic paradigm that talks about accumulation and consumption signifies the greed of the few rather than the need of everyone.

In any engagement or dialogue with corporations, it is important to remember that corporations are very clear about their agenda: they are very clear about how they want to go about their trade as well as their public policy agenda. This is not the case with activist groups, consumer organisations and human rights groups. They are not clear about what they want and how they should achieve it. This is because of the multiple perspectives and interests that inform the action groups. As a result, corporations often co-opt language, people and programmes to give the impression that they care. Most of them don't. That is what happened with the campaign against the Enron Power projects near Mumbai. In the beginning Enron adopted a confrontationist approach to local activist groups, but when they found themselves cornered, they changed their strategy. They decided not only to co-opt language; they also co-opted erstwhile activists with good job offers, and local NGOs with funds. The language, style and format of Enron's public relations magazine resembled that of NGOs. They called it Dialogue and one of the firsts issues had a screaming headline: 'Struggle ends and dialogue begins'. Enron widely publicised its 'income generation' activities by distributing a few sewing machines to women and its ecological sensitivity by planting a few saplings. By changing their strategy, buy using buzz phrases such as community empowerment and ecological sensitivity, the company actually changed the rules of the game in their favour, without changing their flawed basic philosophy and operational strategies.

21.9 Some Cases from India

21.9.1 The Experiment of ACCORD

The experiment of ACCORD in the Nilgirs in South India and the formation of successful co-operative movement by tribals to plant, pluck, pack, and brand and market tea is an inspiriting example of a viable alternative. The *adivasi Munneta Sanghatana* (trade union of tribal farmers and workers) promoted by ACCORD over a period of 10 years not only managed to form and run the tea co-operatives by also succeeded in making market intervention by changing the rules of pricing. In collaboration with the students' solidarity group, the tea co-operative purchased its own plantation with substantial increase in their bargaining power.

The initiative of *Navsarjan, a dalit* action group in Gujarat, to introduce social security packages to thousands of its members through a people-friendly insurance scheme, is another laudable alternative effort.

21.9.2 *The* Kutch Mahila Vikas Sangh *and SEWA*

The Kutch Mahila Vikas Sangh and SEWA in Gujarat have proved the market potential. All over the world there are new initiatives and experiments. However, the force of the big corporations and their advertising war is so severe that all the small initiatives become invisible in the brand-marketing blitz. Hence there is a need to document such innovative experiences and alternatives and to build mutually enabling relationships between them.

When we think of corporate angles, we live in a time when cataclysmic revolutions, promising egalitarian utopias, have been discredited. But the urge to ensure a basic livelihood for all remains strong and it is not omitted to passionately dedicated social activist on the fringes of society. It is obvious to some people in mainstream of economic activity that the long-term sustainability o their business depends on the health of the environment and society at large. And thus it is unacceptable that millions of people continue to live in economic and ecological wastelands. For then 'order' would, eventually, have to be enforced by armed militias.

Therefore, any large corporations are finding odd business sense in being more socially accountable. This is quite different from corporate philanthropy, which means giving large donations to community projects, the arts and humanitarian charities. Corporate social responsibility is about modifying, or even re-making the ethical basis on which corporations conduct their business. At the same time, most such corporations are also fostering a form of globalisation that threatens to drive millions of people deeper into poverty.

21.10 The Integrative Approach

CSR, corporate sustainability and corporate governance collectively are shaping the identity of organisations and are therefore increasingly integrated into the business strategy of successful corporations. Consequently, the field of responsible business strategy and practice is becoming one of the most dynamic and challenging subjects corporate leaders are facing today and possibly one of the most important ones for shaping the future of our world.

The corporate sector is today facing a five-point crisis:

- Crisis of leadership
- Crisis of mobility

- Crisis of focusing
- Crisis of empowerment and
- Crisis of vision

Therefore, in order to come out of the crises, the main emphasis should now be given on defining the role of organization:

Setting the goals both particular and general (particularity means the objectives of various departments/units which will ultimately culminate into the general goal and general goal means the main aim for achievement by the organization)

Pointing-out the focus: The gap between the mission and the general goal and finding-out various solutions to bridge the gap:

There should, thus be a method of self-control and the way of fixing target with reference to one's own strength and weaknesses to execute the programme. It comprises the sequential conduct of the following functions:

- Reviewing and renovating strategies
- Providing a job-improvement plan
- Using present and potential performance review in a systematic way and
- Strengthening the ability and enriching the skills of the human resource through effective training and development.

The objectives should be handed down with no spirit of authoritarianism, but the process should essentially be participating. As a tool for self-appraisal and self-development, it moves towards self-reliance – the way towards becoming independent step-by-step) which is having four components:

- Self-confidence
- Better-understanding
- Team spirit and
- Excellence of work

This again, in turn, as per systems approach, serves as 'feed-back elements' in a process of 'taking form society' and 'giving to society'.

21.11 Individual Achievement

Putting focus on the treatment programme which involves all the people of the organization regarding how the goal can be achieved or the gap can be bridged through Self-Developed Teams (SDTs) in various units as against the western HR strategy model, which ultimately stresses on individual achievement rather than group achievement – a crucial factor that has been underlined in the SDT model. SDT model encompasses autonomy and creative joy that motivate people more than anything else by producing better results.

Further, there should be a focus on team-building purposes for which shared-vision building, systematic thinking, building 'mental models', empowering people and inspiring commitment, enabling better and positive results are to be established and augmented through 'designing learning process' and the consciousness approach.

Next, periodic review of the training programmes should consist of:

Reaction of participants i.e., their response towards the programme and beyond that Learning i.e., participants' intellectual assimilation of the concepts, ideas and principle of the training programme behaviour changes i.e., whether the training caused people to alter their behaviour on-the-job Impact of organizational effectiveness i.e., whether the modified behaviour caused positive results and Subjective and objective criteria i.e., subjective criteria call for opinion of participants and objective criteria relate to effects of training by measuring specific outcome.

Finally, the model results into three immediate goal achievement factors, namely

- Direction setting
- Resolution of conflicts
- Team spirit

These three factors culminate into ultimate goal achievement i.e., the elf-reliance of halo from which the following four result – oriented factors are being diffused:

- Knowledge based performance
- Value-based management
- Development-forward excellence and
- Shared goals

> A spiritualized society would treat in its sociology the individual, from the saint to the criminal, not as units of social problem to be passed through some skillfully devised machinery and either flattened into the social mould or crushed out of it, but as souls suffering and entangled in a net and to be rescued, souls growing and to be encouraged to grow ... The aim of its economics would be not to create a huge engine of production, whether of the competitive or the co-operative kind, but to give to men – not only to some but to all men each in his highest possible measure – the joy of work according to their own nature and free leisure to grow inwardly, as well as a simply rich and beautiful life for all. And that work would be to find the divine Self in the individual and the collectivity and to realise spiritually, mentally, vitally, materially its greatest, largest, richest and deepest possibilities in the inner life of all and their outer action and nature (Sri Aurobindo 2003: The Human Cycles, pp. 241–242).

21.12 Epilogue

In these days when corporate governance is emerging as a significant factor, we find that Indian management can emerge successfully in the market place if it is able to draw on its route for good corporate governance, which are available in our culture and tradition. But then the question may arise, how many of us are aware of scriptures, culture and so on. Though one may not be consciously be aware, one learns about basic principles from their childhood, from our parents and from our religion. All religions have highlighted the need for being truthful and kind and helpful.

It is generally accepted that businesses are doing far more than ever before in guarding against ethical compromises, recognising their social and environmental responsibilities, creating enhanced governance transparency and becoming more accountable to their stakeholders.

However today, despite the progress achieved, corporate responsibility and sustainability is primarily about a handful of companies that have made corporate sustainability their business philosophy, some following the principles of their founders established centuries ago, others in response to crises that threatened their survival and a few simply because they recognised the long-term value of doing so.

There are also many companies that have adopted in name only corporate responsibility strategies either because they feel obliged to follow their peers or because they see some marketing related benefits. In these cases responsible behaviour may be skin deep but... it could grow deeper.

For the large companies that have adopted CSR we can distinguish a number of common objectives:

- increased transparency and improved governance aimed at rebuilding public trust and investor confidence;
- delivering wider societal value including support for health and human rights improvements, and environmental protection;
- contributing to regional development and global partnerships for sustainable development;
- addressing in a balanced way the concerns of their key stakeholders.

These objectives express company expectations/wishes for the future development of their Corporate Responsibility and Sustainability programmes but do not always reflect current practices.

21.13 Summing Up

Loe's (1996) findings indicate that as employees perceive an improvement in the ethical climate of their organization, their commitment to the achievement of high quality standards also increases. They become more willing to personally support the quality initiatives of their management. Individuals within the company who are committed to producing higher quality goods and services can be described as feeling strongly about improving overall quality. These employees often discuss quality-related issues with others both inside and outside of the organization and gain a sense of personal accomplishment from providing quality goods and services. These stakeholders exhibit effort beyond what is either expected or required in order to supply quality products in their particular job and area of responsibility. On the other hand, those employees who are not committed to providing such quality can be described as those who work only for the pay, take longer breaks, and are anxious to leave everyday whether or not the work is completed.

One approach to developing corporate citizenship within an organization may be derived from the guidelines the Federal Sentencing Commission established in 1991.The Federal Sentencing Guidelines for Organizations (FSGO) have a significant impact on U.S. business- approach to compliance and ethics issues. Since 1991, federal judges have been allowed to impose stiff monetary penalties for white-collar crimes in cases. However, organizations that establish compliance programs may have fines mitigated if they are convicted of certain misdemeanors and felonies. Thus, the legal system is promoting value-driven corporate citizenship as a useful framework to prevent corporate misconduct.

An effective compliance program includes (Swenson 1995) (1) establishing compliance standards and procedures (e.g., codes of ethics and policies), (2) appointing a high-level executive with overall responsibility to oversee compliance, (3) exercising due care not to delegate substantial discretionary authority to employees with a past history of illegal or unethical behavior, (4) disseminating standards of conduct and policies regarding those standards, (5) having a monitoring and auditing system in place to detect criminal conduct (e.g., anonymous hotlines), (6) enforcing the standards consistently, and (7) responding appropriately to offenses and modification of the program. With such programs in place, organizations can promote higher levels of corporate citizenship. Loe's (1996) study implemented such a program and found its impact improved the ethical climate in the organization and, as suggested in this present research, in turn, promoted good corporate citizenship.

Maignan's (1997) study emphasized the role of corporate values in establishing corporate citizenship: The existence of a positive association between a humanistic culture and corporate citizenship is highlighted. In a humanistic culture, employees are encouraged to further the well-being of their coworkers and to ensure that their own decisions do not negatively affect the activities of other organizational members (Cooke and Hartmann 1989; Kilman and Saxton 1983; Xenikoo and Furnham 1996). Our results suggest that the values that foster harmony in the workplace also encourage organizational members to systematically facilitate the relationships between the business and its stakeholder groups.

Globalization along with changed norms of production, labour and environment with conditions of best practice has influenced behavior of businesses across the world. The success of the acceptance of these norms has been outside the letter of law and the adoption has often influenced state to adopt better/improved or at least changed role for itself. The norms of resettlement and rehabilitation as dictated by the Indian state are by law adopted by joint venture companies involved in extractive industries yet many other activities are also undertaken as corporate social responsibility, which are neither detailed nor dictated by law. Growth of civil society organizations has also led to increasing democratization in the marginalized and impoverished communities creating local responses to the grant meta-narratives. Yet nation state needs to evolve a new role for itself in this fast changing world.

A stable nation providing good governance is thus basic requirement for developing countries in their attempt to safe guard rights and interests of their poor and marginalized.

Yet, the business are wary of investing time and resources in proactively dealing with pressure groups, media, and local people for social or community development as they often lack familiarity and the skills to do so. Indian business has been actively involved in corporate philanthropy since the early 1900s. The charitable outlook of Indian businesses is progressively undergoing change under some external and internal influences. The increase in the momentum of corporate social responsibility has created new routes or avenues via which issues of corporate social responsibility are put to practice.

21.14 The Way Forward

Through some processes of human development, providing access to more subtle modes of awareness, new value insights emerge. In such cases there may be a very intimate relationship between the state of awareness and comprehension of the value. Emerging awareness of certain states may even lead to the articulation of more subtle understanding of commonly identified values. Certain modes of awareness can be understood as the embodiment of specific values or configurations of values.

Perhaps of most importance is the manner in which certain processes of human development integrate together previously disparate insights. Values can easily decay into empty, 'bloodless' categories unless they are sustained by appropriate levels of awareness. Human development may thus build a subtle connecting pattern between values. Such integration provides a new foundation from which action may be undertaken in a sustainable manner.

Again it is ironic that there is less and less in modern society that people are prepared to die for, or to allow others to die for. Whole societies can now be held to ransom for a single known hostage. Millions can be spent to maintain a comatose, brain-damaged patient on life-support for decades. Euthanasia is illegal, no matter what the desire of the person concerned. Exposure to risk is progressively designed out of society, to be replaced by vicarious experiences of risk through videos or with the protection of required safety devices. The paradox is that unknown numbers are however sacrificed through carcinogenic products, abortion, structural violence, massacres, gang murders, cult rituals, 'snuff' movies and associated perversions, or a failure of food and medical supplies.

References

Cooke R. A., and Hartmann, J. L. (1989): "Interpreting the Cultural Styles Measured by the OCI." in Organizational Culture Inventory Leader's Guide. Plymouth, MI: Human Synergistics, pp. 23–48.

Das Gupta, A. (1995): "Economic Management and Ethics: The Vedantic Answer," Indian Journal of Public Administration, New Delhi, July–Sep. 1995, pp. 45–53.

Ganguly, A. (1998): "The Road Ahead," Excellence in the 21st Century: Challenges and Strategies AIMA, New Delhi., pp 67–87.

Genus, A. (1998): The Management of Change: Perspective and Practices. London: International Thomson Business Press

Guest, D. (1987): "Human Resource Management and Industrial Relations," Journal of Management Studies, 24(5). pp. 503–521

Hofstede, H. G. (1973): "Frustrations of Personnel Managers," Management International Review 13 (4–5), pp. 127–143.

Kilman, R. H., and Saxton, M. J. (1983): The Kilman-Saxton Culture-Gap Survey. Pittsburgh, PA: Organizational Design Consultants.

Loe, T. W. (1996): "The Role of Ethical Climate in Developing Trust, Market Orientation, and Commitment to Quality," unpublished dissertation, The University of Memphis.

Maignan, I. (1997): "Antecedents and Benefits of Corporate Citizenship: A Comparison of U.S. and French Businesses," unpublished dissertation, The University of Memphis.

Richard, C. (1995): "Welcome and Conference Overview," in Corporate Crime in America: Strengthening the Good Citizen Corporation. Washington, DC: United States Sentencing Commission, pp. 3–6.

Senge, P. (1990): The Fifth Discipline: The Art & Practice of The Learning Organization. New York: Doubleday-Currency.

Sri, A. (2003): The Human Cycles. Pondicherry, Tamil Nadu, India: Aurobindo Ashram, pp. 241–242.

Swami, S. (1996): Indian Wisdom for Management, AMA, Ahmedabad, India.

Swenson, W. (1995): "The Organizational Guidelines Carrot and Stick Philosophy and Their Focus on Effective Compliance," in Corporate Crime in America: Strengthening the A Good Citizen Corporation, Washington, DC: United States Sentencing Commission, pp. 17–26.

Xenikoo, A. and Furnham, A. (1996): "A Correlational and Factor Analytic Study of Four Questionnaire Measures of Organizational Culture." Human Relations 49(3), pp. 349–371.

Chapter 22
Corporate Social Responsibility in the 21st Century: Some Thoughts

Walter Leal Filho

Abstract This short chapter draws some lessons taken from the papers presented in this book and presents some thoughts on future developments and trends.

22.1 Introduction

> There is one and only one social responsibility of business – to use its resources and engage in activities designed to increase its profits so long as it stays within the rules of the game, which is to say, engage in open and free competition, without deception or fraud (Friedman in Turner 2006, p. 7).

The business sector is governed by many well established rules, which have survived for centuries Pride et al. (2008). As far as CSR is concerned, since it is an emerging field the rules are still being established; not just in one particular country but worldwide, despite a wealth of experiences which have been documented to date (Idowu and Filho 2009) this field is still an emerging one.

There is a wide range of perspectives on CSR and the challenge posed by this book, was to search, identify and document some professional perspectives, we hope; has been met. At the same time, many interesting features have been identified along the way.

One aspect which has become conspicuous from the wide body of information and experiences gathered in this book is the large diversity in the means and roles of different entities to fulfill their CSR requirements and realize their CSR visions. This has happened as a result of the fact that different entities perceive CSR differently to the extent that professionals are expected to ensure that the ethical aspects of what they do in their professional callings are considered, that corporations should encourage the engagement of their employees with their local communities and that

W.L. Filho (✉)
Hamburg University of Applied Sciences, Hamburg, Germany

S.O. Idowu, W.L. Filho (eds.), *Professionals' Perspectives of Corporate Social Responsibility*, DOI 10.1007/978-3-642-02630-0_23,
© Springer-Verlag Berlin Heidelberg 2009

all their operational dealings on behalf of the company abide with both national and international laws.

The issues raised in the professionals' perspectives of CSR mean more than the above noted examples and this book has touched on some examples of what is happening on the ground and what can be achieved with the concept of CSR embedded in operational practices.

22.2 Some Lessons Learned

Perhaps the first lesson that can be learned from this book is the pressing need to work towards a stronger engagement of some of the stakeholders/professionals who are directly involved with CSR at a company level: for example accountants and corporate' secretaries.

These groups are engaged with CSR on a day to day basis and their work is central to efforts towards ensuring the success and effectiveness of CSR at company level. In addition, other professionals such as lawyers need to be involved since regulations are inevitably important to efforts towards implementing initiatives on CSR.

A further, related lesson relates to the need for a greater engagement by Management (here one is referring to companies' senior executives and board members) of enterprises as a whole and company directors in particular. Without a strong and unambiguous commitment 'from the top' (Kaliski, 2001a; b) efforts towards implementing CSR at the company level are unlikely to fully succeed.

Another matter worthy of taking into account is the issue of marketing of initiatives on CSR, a relevant issue which should not be overlooked since CSR can be a powerful tool in societal marketing. A further lesson which also deserves attention is the need to actively engage bankers and other professionals in the banking sector since the relationship between Banks and the environment have not always been perfect; especially during the current global financial crisis. Therefore, the need to undertake a thorough assessment in the sector and to continuously monitor progress ought to be a priority for all governments; not just in the first world but everywhere.

From a sectoral perspective, this book has also illustrated that in an industrial context, for example; in the manufacturing sector, in the estate management business and tourism business, there are means and ways to incorporate CSR dimensions as part of companies' operations. The democratic gains which may be obtained from CSR in local administrations, a matter largely overlooked in the past, are also significant.

The experiences presented in this book show that even though CSR is well developed in some professional contexts, others are lagging dangerously behind be it in respect of regulatory initiatives or in the level of emphasis given to the CSR debate.

This may suggest that the value of CSR as a tool to gain and upkeep competitiveness is still not very clear to a lot of people including some professionals.

Of special interest is also the close links between CSR and education and research and the experiences documented in this book provides the evidence that much can be gained by having CSR in university programmes (both at graduate and undergraduate levels) be it in respect of teaching, research or both.

22.3 Some Thoughts and Future Trends

Perhaps one of the main items which give the opportunity for further achievements in the field is the realisation that we need to further explore and translate the language of CSR to the various audiences. CSR means different things to people working in different sectors and professional settings. In addition, there are some key questions which need to be critically answered in the future, if we are to move forward the cause of CSR:

(a) What is the purpose of CSR? It is a means to promote environmental and social concerns or simply a means to improve the balance sheet?
(b) What is the attitude of a given corporation to CSR? Is this regarded as a hype which will fade away sooner rather than later, or a part of the long-term corporate strategy?
(c) How sustainable is CSR? Is this meant to be pursued for a short time and be phased out at times of unfavourable share prices or is it embedded into a company's structure?

An element which will therefore pay a stronger role in the future is in relation to the fact that a common understanding and a common perception of the concepts of CSR is important. More efforts in this direction are therefore greatly needed.

In general, CSR is characterized by a multiplicity of organisations, guidelines and thinking, which on the one hand follow the same line (e.g. promoting CSR) but sometimes overlap (e.g. promoting CSR and achieving sustainable development goals) or are contradictory at times (e.g. reducing costs and maximizing profits). The integration of these goals is important if long-term plans are to be implemented in practice.

Moreover, there seems to be little doubt in relation to the fact that the 'business case' (i.e. why companies should embed CSR) needs to be made and the role of CSR in a company's sustainability efforts ought to be more prominently emphasised.

In conclusion, prospects for the future of CSR are bright, but there is a perceived need to address current disparities so that those issues which could act as impediments to future developments could be collectively addressed and the barriers which they pose may be removed.

References

Idowu, S. O., Filho, W. L. (Eds.) (2009) Global Practices of Global Corporate Responsibility. Springer, Berlin.

Kaliski, B. (Ed.). (2001a) Social Responsibility and Organizational Ethics. Encyclopedia of Business and Finance (2nd ed., Vol. 1). Macmillan, New York.

Kaliski, B. (Ed.). (2001b) Ethics in Management. Encyclopedia of Business and Finance (2nd ed., Vol. 1). Macmillan, New York.

Pride, W. M., Hughes, R. J., Kapoor, J. R. (2008). Business (9th ed.). Houghton Mifflin Company, Boston, MA.

Turner, R. J. (2006) Corporate Social Responsibility: Should disclosure of social considerations be mandatory? Submission to the Parliamentary Joint Committee on Corporations and Financial Services Inquiry. Retrieved 10 April 2009, from http://www.aph.gov.au/senate/committee/corporations_ctte/corporate_responsibility/submissions/sub05.pdf

About the Editors

Samuel O. Idowu is a senior lecturer in Accounting at the city campus of
London Metropolitan Business School, London Metropolitan University where
he was course organizer for Accounting Joint degrees and currently the
Course Leader/Personal Academic Adviser (PAA) for students taking Accounting
Major/Minor and Accounting Joint degrees. He is a fellow member of the Institute
of Chartered Secretaries and Administrators, a fellow of the Royal Society of Arts, a
Liveryman of the Worshipful Company of Chartered Secretaries & Administrators
and a named freeman of the City of London. Samuel has published about thirty-
three articles in both professional and academic journals and contributed chapters in
edited books. Samuel has been in academia for 21 years winning one of the Highly
Commended Awards of Emerald Literati Network Awards for Excellence in 2008.
He has examined for the following professional bodies: the Chartered Institute of
Bankers (CIB) and the Chartered Institute of Marketing (CIM) and has marked
examination papers for the Association of Chartered Certified Accountants (ACCA).
His teaching career started in November 1987 at Merton College, Morden Surrey; he
was a Lecturer/Senior Lecturer at North East Surrey College of Technology (Nescot)
for 13 years where he was the Course Leader for BA (Hons) Business Studies,
ACCA and CIMA courses. He has also held visiting lectureship posts at Croydon
College and Kingston University. He was a senior lecturer at London Guildhall
University prior to its merger with the University of North London; when London
Metropolitan University was created in August 2002. He is currently an external
examiner at the University of Sunderland, University of Ulster, Belfast, Northern
Ireland and Anglia Ruskin University, Chelmsford. He is also a Trustee/Treasurer –
Age *Concern*, Hackney in East London and he is on the Editorial Advisory Board of
the Management of Environmental Quality Journal. He has been researching in the
field of CSR since 1983 and has attended and presented papers at several national
and international conferences and workshops on CSR.

Walter Leal Filho is a Professor. Walter Leal Filho has a Ph.D. and a DSc
in environmental technology, plus a honorary doctorate (DL) in environmental
information. He is the Head of the Research and Transfer Centre 'Applications
of Life Sciences' at the Hamburg University of Applied Sciences, where he is
in charge of a number of European projects. He has authored, co-authored or

edited over 40 books on the subjects of environment, technology and innovation and has in excess of 130 published papers to his credit. Prof. Walter Leal Filho teaches environmental management at many European universities. He is also the editor of the Journal 'Management of Environmental Quality' and founding editor of the 'International Journal of Sustainability in Higher Education' and 'Environment and Sustainable Development'. He is a member of the editorial board of 'Biomedical and Environmental Sciences', 'Environmental Awareness', and 'Sustainable Development and World Ecology'. His work on CSR has primarily focused on the institutional aspects and tools for benchmarking within industry.

About the Contributors

Marin Amina is professor in occupational issues at the University of Sonora, Mexico. She holds a doctoral degree in cleaner production and pollution prevention and she is participating in sustainability projects in Maquiladora industries.

Zavala Andrea is professor in sustainability issues at the University of Sonora, Mexico. She has a Masters degree in cleaner production and pollution prevention. She is the coordinator for the 'Toward a Sustainable University: ISO 14001' project at the same institution.

Dr. Konstantinos G. Aravosis is a Lecturer on Investment Analysis at the National Technical University of Athens, Greece. Moreover, he is the President of the Hellenic Solid Waste Management Association and Member of the Environmental Committee of the Technical Chamber of Greece and the corresponding Committee of the Federation of Greek Industries. His research interests include Environmental Management and Economics, as well as Investment Assessment and Analysis. He has published many papers relevant to these subjects, in books and International Journals.

Jean Bowcott is the Director of Operations of Novotel and Mercure Hotels for Central and Greater London for the ACCOR Hospitality Group.

Timothy T. Campbell, Ph.D. is head of the Corporate Social Responsibility group at Hull University Business School (UK) and has lectured, researched and consulted globally. Previously, Tim enjoyed a number of years of marketing and business development experience in industry.

José-Rodrigo Córdoba, Ph.D. is currently the Director of the MSc in Business Information Systems at Royal Holloway (University of London. UK). He has worked as a project manager and consultant for a variety of organisations in his home country (Colombia) as well as in the UK and South Africa.

Dr. Sallyanne Decker obtained her Ph.D. at London Guildhall University and is a senior lecturer at London Metropolitan Business School. Sally Anne has published a number of papers in academic journals and has also attended and presented papers at several national and international conferences.

Konstantinos I. Evangelinos is a Lecturer in Environmental Management in the Department of Environment, University of the Aegean. His research interests include Environmental Management Systems, Corporate Social Responsibility in SMEs, sustainability reporting, social capital in organizations and corporations and sustainability is Higher Education Institutions.

Dr. Ananda Das Gupta has been engaged in teaching, research and training for the last 20 years and is now the Head, Human Resource Development, at the Indian Institute of Plantation Management, a premier sectoral management school, having been promoted by Government of India in Bangalore, India. He has published research books on management from England, Oxford and Cambridge and guest edited two International journals under the famous banner of Emerald Publishing Group, England. His areas of specializations are Leadership, Strategic Human Resource Management, Corporate Social Responsibility, Organizational Development etc. He has delivered lectures in several places in India including the Department of Management Studies, Indian Institute of Technology, Madras, Indian Institute of Management, Bangalore, S.P. Jain Institute of Management and Research, Mumbai etc. He is also associated with BITS-Pilani as a Research Advisor.

Dr. Royston Gustavson lectures in the School of Management, Marketing, and International Business, The Australian National University, in business ethics, corporate sustainability, and corporate strategy. His primary area of research is corporate governance, especially the role of governance in ethics and sustainability. He has an MBA with Distinction from the Melbourne Business School, a Ph.D. from The University of Melbourne, is a Fellow of the Australian Institute of Company Directors, and an Associate Fellow of the Australian Institute of Management.

Ralph Hamann is senior researcher at the University of Cape Town Environmental Evaluation Unit (EEU), an independent, self-funded research, training, and consulting unit. He is also an Extraordinary Associate Professor at the Sustainability Institute at Stellenbosch University. With a Ph.D. from the University of East Anglia (UK), he has worked with and consulted to a range of public and private sector organisations and has working experience in Africa, Europe, and Asia. He is on the editorial board of *Environment: Linking Science and Policy for Sustainable Development* and he has guest edited two special journal editions on CSR related issues, both of which were the result of international research conferences he organised.

Elizabeth Hogan is currently a Senior Research Associate at David Gardiner and Associates in Washington DC, a consultancy for climate change and corporate sustainability. Prior to joining the firm she worked with the International Fund for Animal Welfare (IFAW) where she collaborated with members of the fishing industry in New England on conversions to whale-safe fishing gear, and also with the Camara de Industrias of Costa Rica to assist Central American businesses in the transition toward more sustainable business operations, specifically emissions management and water use. Elizabeth has a degree in Foreign Service from Georgetown University and a dual Master of Science in Natural Resources and Master of Science in Sustainable Development from the University for Peace in Costa Rica and American University in Washington, DC.

Dr. Esquer Javier holds a doctoral degree from the University of Massachusetts, Lowell in the field of Cleaner Production and Pollution Prevention. He is a professor in sustainability issues at the University of Sonora, Mexico. His recent work aims at promoting Environmental Management Systems.

Prof. Dr. Zerrin Toprak Karaman is a Lecturer at the Department of Public Administration in the Faculty of Economics and Administrative Sciences at Dokuz Eylul University (DEU). She graduated from the Department of Public Administration in the Faculty of Economics and Commercial Sciences at Ege University in 1977. She began to work as an assistant at the Department of Public Administration in the Faculty of Economics at Ege University in 1978. She was granted the titles of Doctor (1986), Associated Professor (1990) and Professor (1996) in the Section of Urbanization and Environmental Problems at the Department of Public Administration at Dokuz Eylul University. Currently, she is the Head of the Department of Public Administration at DEU and the founding director (2005) of the Center for Strategic Planning, Governance and Research in Izmir (IZISYOM). With the title of the representative of DEU, she was appointed as the Member (2006, 2009) of the Development Council of Izmir Development Agency. Since 1986, she has served as a scientific member of several commissions such as Local Authorities, Regional Development and Environment and Urbanization in the Development Plan studies. She has worked actively as a local and national strategist in the activities of Local Agenda 21, an international democracy project, practice at Izmir Metropolitan Municipality (Local Agenda 21 in Izmir) since 1996. As a member of the Executive and Facilitative Board of Local Agenda 21 in Izmir, she worked voluntarily as a director and researcher in social-development-oriented research and projects. As a result of her studies on social issues, she was appointed to the Membership of the Higher Board of Women Entrepreneurs of the Union of Chambers and Commodity Exchange of Turkey from the Youth Association for Habitat. She has published books on Local Authorities, Urban Administration and Policy, and Environmental Management and Policy. She has published several papers in national and international journals, including several on local politics, environmental problems, the Romani people in Izmir, the migration of retired European citizens in Antalya and their participation in public life, and the agreements of the Congress of Local and Regional Authorities of the Council of Europe; and scientific and personal awards from various institutions and organizations. She continues her projects on Council Preparatory Study as a 'moderator' in the activities of the Commission for 'Consciousness of Being a City-Dweller, Culture and Education' of 2009 with the Turkish Urbanization Council.

Dr. Berna Kirkulak is an Assistant Professor at the Accounting and Finance Department at Dokuz Eylul University, Izmir in Turkey. Her current research interests are: corporate finance, capital markets, and real estate investment. Berna was awarded her Ph.D. in 2005 from Hokkaido University in Japan. She received a fellowship in 2000 from the Dutch Ministry of Education (NUFFIC), received another fellowship from the Japanese Ministry of Education (MONBUSHO) in 2001, was awarded a research grant from the Turkish Scientific and Technical Research Institution (TUBITAK) in 2005. Recently, she was given a grant by the Ministry of Education in the People's Republic of China to conduct her post-doctoral research at Southeast University in China.

Dr. Adam Lindgreen is Professor of Strategic Marketing at Hull University Business School. Dr. Lindgreen received his Ph.D. from Cranfield University. He has published in *Business Horizons, Industrial Marketing Management, Journal of Advertising, Journal of Business Ethics, Journal of Business and Industrial Marketing, Journal of Marketing Management, Journal of Product and Innovation Management, Journal of the Academy of Marketing Science*, and *Psychology & Marketing*, among others. His most recent books include *Managing Market Relationships, Memorable Consumer Experiences, The Crisis of Food Brands*, and *The New Cultures of Food*. His research interests include business and industrial marketing, consumer behavior, experiential marketing, relationship and value management, and corporate social responsibility. He serves on the board of many journals.

Dr. Céline Louche is Assistant Professor at Vlerick Leuven Gent Management School. She teaches and researches into the area of Corporate Social Responsibility (CSR). In her work, she explores the way processes of change take place. A major research interest is the construction of the CSR field with a special focus on SRI and stakeholders processes. She also worked 5 years as a Sustainability Analyst for SRI at the Dutch Sustainability Research institute.

Dr. Diana Luck is a Senior Lecturer in Marketing Communications at London Metropolitan University. She is a thorough bred of the services industry. Her career started in the hotel and tourism industry. She then moved into project management and marketing. She also worked in telecommunications and in consulting services. Since 2001, Diana's research interests and consultancy work have focused on CRM and CSR.

Dr. Velázquez Luis is an internationally recognized professor/researcher in sustainability issues. He is the founder and Director of the Sustainable Development Group at the University of Sonora. He holds a doctoral degree in the major of Cleaner Production and Pollution Prevention from the University of Massachusetts, Lowell, USA.

François Maon currently is undertaking Ph.D. studies at Université catholique de Louvain, examining strategies for implementation and stakeholder dialogue development. He has conducted research in Belgium, France, the Netherlands, and the

USA Mr. Maon has presented several papers at international marketing and business society conferences in Europe and the United States and has articles forthcoming in *Academy of Management: Best Papers Proceedings 2008*, *Journal of Business Ethics*, and *Supply Chain Management*.

Ioannis E. Nikolaou is a Lecturer in Corporate Environmental Performance and Environmental Management Systems at the Department of Environmental Engineering, Democretous University of Thrace. His research interests include Environmental Accounting, Corporate Sustainability, Environmental Performance Indicators and Environmental Management Systems.

Dr. Munguía Nora holds a doctoral degree from the University of Massachusetts Lowell in the field of Cleaner Production and Pollution Prevention. She is professor/researcher in sustainability issues at the University of Sonora, Mexico. Her most recent work involves cleaner production and pollution prevention in Sonoran industries.

Olatoye Ojo, Ph.D., is a Senior Lecturer in Estate Management at Obafemi Awolowo University, Ile-Ife, Nigeria. He also currently serves as Chairman, Project Implementation Committee of the University and by virtue of this position, belongs to some other committees of the University. He is a Fellow of The Nigerian Institution of Estate Surveyors and Valuers and a Registered Estate Surveyor and Valuer by Estate Surveyors and Valuers Registration Board of Nigeria. Before entering academia, he was the Managing Partner of Olatoye Ojo & Co – a real estate consulting outfit with head office at Ibadan and branches in major cities of Nigeria. He has served as – Pioneer Chairman. He currently serves as Chairman/Editor-In-Chief of The Estate Surveyor and Valuer (the Institution's professional journal); moderator of professional examinations of The Nigerian Institution of Estate Surveyors and Valuers and External Examiner, Federal University of Technology, Minna. He has also served as Member, Education and Joint CPD Committees of The Estate Surveyors and Valuers Registration Board of Nigeria. Olatoye Ojo has published several articles in reputable national and international journals in the areas of housing, housing finance, property development and management and investment analysis. He has attended many national and international conferences and has presented papers at such fora.

Nikolaos A. Panayiotou is a Lecturer in the School of Mechanical Engineering in NTU Athens, Section of Industrial Management and Operational Research. He has experience in BPR projects both in the public and the private sector. His academic interests are Business Process Reengineering, Business Process Improvement, Performance Measurement and IT-enabling technology.

Patricia Park is Professor of Law at Southampton Solent University. She specialises in energy/environmental/maritime law. She is Head of the Law Research Centre and also teaches at the KU at Leuven, and Luneburg University. She has published and given conference papers on CSR and teaches CSR & the Ethical Company on the MBA, MAIB, and the LLM.

Dr. Liisa Rohweder is a principal lecturer for sustainable development and corporate social responsibility at Haaga-Helia University of Applied Sciences in Finland. She has published several articles and books on education for Sustainable Development (SD) and on responsible business and has experience in leading EU-funded international development projects. She works in a close cooperation with the Finnish Ministry of Education, the Finnish Ministry of Environment and the Finnish Business and Society network. Dr. Rohweder holds several commissions of trust, such as a vice chairman of the board of trustees of WWF Finland (2007–2010), chairman of the board of Finnish Association for Environmental Managment (2004–2006), representative of Rectors' of Finnish Universities of Applied Sceinces in the Finnish National Commission on Sustainable Development (2008–2012). Before her academic career she worked for 10 years in the oil and chemical industry as an energy market researcher and as a manager of the international logistic department for petrochemical shipping.

Dr. Dyann Ross is a Senior Lecturer at the Centre for Social Research, Edith Cowan University, Perth, Western Australia.

Christopher Sale is a Chartered Public Finance Accountant and the Subject Group Leader for Finance and Financial Services at London Metropolitan Business School. Chris has been in academia for a number of years and worked previously as an Accountant for a Government Department.

Konstantinos Saridakis is a business consultant in a large multinational professional services firm in Greece. He holds a degree in Mechanical Engineering from the National Technical University of Athens (NTUA) and a Master of Science (MSc) degree with distinction in Engineering Business Management from the University of Warwick, UK. He has gained significant experience with his participation in various projects both in the public and private sectors, while during the last few years he has been actively involved in the field of Corporate Social Responsibility.

Antonis Skouloudis is a researcher at the Centre for Environmental Policy and Strategic Environmental Management (E.E.P.P.D.), Department of Environment, University of the Aegean. He holds a ptychion in Economic Sciences (National and Capodistrian University of Athens) and a MSc in Environmental Policy and Management (University of the Aegean). His research interests include corporate social responsibility, non-financial reporting, triple-bottom-line performance and ethical entrepreneurship.

Dr. Valérie Swaen is Assistant Professor of Marketing at the Université catholique de Louvain and also the IESEG School of Management. Her Ph.D. thesis examined consumer perceptions and reactions to corporate citizenship activities in terms of consumer trust, commitment, and loyalty. She has published papers in *Journal of Business Ethics, Recherche et Applications en Marketing, Revue Française du Marketing*, and *Corporate Reputation Review*, among other journals.

Carol A. Tilt is a Professor of Accounting and Head of Research at Flinders University where she has worked for 15 years, and is a Fellow of CPA Australia. She has a Ph.D. in environmental reporting and her research interests include social and environmental reporting, accounting theory and NGOs. She has a number of publications in international journals including *Accounting Auditing and Accountability Journal, Critical Perspectives on Accounting, Accounting Forum* and the *British Accounting Review*. She also regularly reviews for these and other journals. Carol teaches both financial accounting and management accounting, as well as in the areas of accounting theory, ethics, corporate governance and research methods. She has supervised a number of Ph.D. projects in areas of philanthropy, business ethics and social reporting.

Dr. Anne Virtanen is a principal lecturer for sustainable development at Bioeconomy Education and Research Centre, Hamk University of Applied Sciences. She teaches on the degree programme of sustainable development and she is involved with several national and international research and development projects in the field of sustainable development. She has been a coordinator of the national project in which the competences for sustainable development degree programme were defined. She was a coordinator of the Baltic Sea Sustainable Development network between 2005and 2006. Dr. Virtanen was nominated as a project manager of the national project in which an evaluation and development data bank for education for sustainable development and global responsibility was developed. Dr. Virtanen has worked on the research projects for Ecological Modernisation of Urban Regions and Private Actors in the Public Realm funded by the Academy of Finland. In addition, she has worked in several environmental impact assessment projects, and concentrated especially on the evaluation of social impacts.

Karolina Windell holds a Ph.D. from the Department of Business studies, Uppsala University. Her primary research interest concerns the spread and construction of new ideas about management, more specifically her research focuses on the emergence of the idea CSR, which is a topic dealt with in her thesis as well as in other publications. In addition, she has been studying the relationship between media and other organizations and how this influences news production. She has been teaching undergraduates in market strategy, management, and CSR.

Subject Index

The letters 'f' and 't' following the locators refer to figures and tables respectively.